ELVIS

BY ALBERT GOLDMAN

Also by Albert Goldman

The Mine and the Mint:
  Sources for the writings of Thomas DeQuincey

Wagner on Music and Drama
  (co-editor with Everett Sprinchorn)

Freakshow: The Rocksoulbluesjazzsickjewblackhumorsexpoppsych
  Gig and Other Scenes from the Counter-Culture

Ladies and Gentlemen—LENNY BRUCE!!

Carnival in Rio

Disco

Grass Roots: Marijuana in America Today

ELVIS

BY ALBERT GOLDMAN

McGRAW-HILL BOOK COMPANY

New York   St. Louis   San Francisco
Hamburg   Mexico   Toronto
A KEVIN EGGERS BOOK

LIBRARY OF CONGRESS CATALOGING IN PUBLICATION DATA

Goldman, Albert Harry, 1927–
Elvis.
    1. Presley, Elvis, 1935–1977. 2. Singers—
United States—Biography. I. Title.
ML420.P96G66   784.5′4′00924 [B]   81–8130
ISBN 0–07–023657–7   AACR2

Book design by Roberta Rezk.

For Barry Berkman,
a faithful friend through many trials

Contents

viii

Acknowledgments

IN A WORK entailing so many sources and informants as this biography, it is virtually impossible to acknowledge every contribution. Certain individuals and organizations were so helpful, however, that they deserve especial thanks. John A. Whisler, of the Memphis–Shelby County Public Library, made available the unpublished manuscript of his exhaustive bibliography of writings about Elvis Presley. Philip W. McMullin, president, Institute of Family Research, contributed his organization's genealogical research into the Pressley Family. Dirk Vellenga of *De Stem,* Breda, Holland, provided all the information about Colonel Parker's Dutch origin. James K. Caughley furnished in addition to his oral testimony excerpts from his diary and the unpublished manuscript of his recollections of Elvis. The contributions of the following individuals lie for the most part in the area designated by the rubric following each group of names.

Richard E. Davis, Lamar and Nora Fike, Alan Fortas, Dave Hebler, Charlie Hodge, Jerry Schilling, Gene Smith, Red and Pat West, Sonny and Judy West (the Guys and the Wives); Betty McCann, Billie Wardlow Mooneyham, Dixie Locke Emmons, Debra Paget, Natalie Wood, Joan Blackman, Anita Wood Brewer, Gloria Mowel Stratton, Heidi Heissen Busley, Frances Forbes, Connie Stevens, Barbara Leigh, Linda Thompson, Ginger Alden (Elvis's women friends); Mary Jane Lyon, Floyd Presley, Vester Presley, Christine Roberts, Truitt Smith, Doshia Steele (the Presleys and the Smiths); James and Eula Dell Ausborn, Ernest Bowen (WELO); Mrs. Billie Boyd, Trellis Leeman Burch, the Reverend W. Frank Smith (Tupelo); Coach Rube Boyce, Buzzy Forbes, Mrs. Jeanette Fruchter, Farley Guy, Bernard and Guy Lansky, Mrs. William Morris (Memphis, early years); Cecil and James Blackwood, Jake Hess, Joe Mascheo, J. D. Sumner, Charles Wolf (gospel); Warden

Steve Hargett, Tom Gregory, Charles Marx, Larry Phillips (Parchman); Maurice Hulbert, B. B. King, Robert Thomas, Rufus Thomas (WDIA); Tillman Franks, David Houston, Horace Logan, John Prime *(Louisiana Hayride);* Ray Brown, Jack Clement, Frankie Connors, D. J. Fontana, Bill Justis, Stanley Kesler, Wink Martindale, Scotty Moore, Robert, Helen and Sonny Neal, Jim Stewart (Sun years); Eddy Arnold, Whitey Ford, Bitsy Mott, Father Rohling, Carl Sedlmeyer, Jr., Jimmy Rogers Snow (Colonel Parker's early career); Jean Aberbach, Chet Atkins, Mae Boren Axton, Freddy Bienstock, Bo Diddley, Al Dvorin, Bones Howe, George Johnstone, Gordon Stoker, Ben Wiseman (early recording and stage career); Pandro Berman, Marcia Borie, Bill Campbell, Raphael Campos, Jack Cummings, Bill Dakota, Richard Egan, Frank Faylen, Virginia Grant, Katherine Hereford, Carolyn Jones, Hal Kanter, Jerry Katzman, Nancy Sinatra Lambert, Marilyn Mason, Mary Ann Mobley, Gene Nelson, Willy Nichols, Jeremy Slate, Deborah Walley (Hollywood); Eddie Fadal, Sgt. William H. Norwood, Rex and Elisabeth Mansfield, Walter Schweinsmann (Army); Sister Loyola Fox, Currie Grant, Milan LeFevre, Sister M. Adrian Mully, Mike Stone (Priscilla); Chris Bearde, Bill Bellew, Steve Binder, Bob Finkel, Tom Sarnoff (Singer Special); Emilio Muscelli, Joe Guercio, Dr. Elias Ghanem, Nick Naff, Terry Riesner, Dr. Max Shapiro, Sol Schwartz, Alex Shoofey (Las Vegas); John Corcoran, Ed Parker, Kang Ree, Bill Wallace (karate); Jack Adams, Flo and Gloria Demeno, Gill Gilleland, Ed Hookstratten, Mary Jenkins, Jackie Kahane, Harry Levitch, Dr. David Meyer, Bill Morris, Dee Presley, Billy and David Stanley, Charlie Thompson, Sam Thompson, Dr. Spencer Thornton (final years); Sid Bernstein; Paul Klein (programming chief, NBC); Rocco Laginestra (formerly president, RCA Victor); Blanchard E. Tual (Colonel Parker as manager); Prof. Carole Berkin, Jerry Carrigan, Prof. Charles W. Crawford, Shelby Foote, Joe Lewis, Doc Pomus, Gloria Stavers (general background); Paul Dougher, Paul Dowling, Nick Hunter, John Lumsdaine, Sylvia Chase, Susan Braudy (films, records, tapes, transcripts); Stanley Stasiowski (IRS); Anne Pitrone (editorial assistant); Harry Hall (researcher); Barbara Hohol (typist); Joe Schoenfeld (cicerone); Rene Lachicotte (factotum).

Finally, I wish to thank Kevin Eggers, who first conceived this project; Lamar Fike, who was my guide to the Presley circle and who conducted a number of valuable interviews; Milton Glaser, who designed the spiritual portrait of the young Elvis on the dust jacket; Edgar J. Scherick, who bought the movie rights; and most of all Gladys Justin Carr, who was not only my forbearing and helpful editor but on occasion my savior.

Fame, after all, is no more than the quintessence
of all the misunderstandings collecting round a new name.

Rilke on Rodin

Prologue:
The Royal American

THOUGH democracy is ostensibly the opposite of monarchy, the mass culture that is American democracy has betrayed in every age a deep atavistic yearning for royalty. From the days of "King" Andrew Jackson to those of the "Kingfish," Huey Long; from the era of the Robber Barons to the age of the movie "kings" and "queens"; from the first black demagogues, Marcus Garvey and Father Divine, to the "Prophet," Elijah Muhammad; from the earliest Mafia chieftains to the bowing, kneeling and hand-kissing of *The Godfather;* from the regal F.D.R. to the "Imperial Presidency" of John F. Kennedy to the Great Pretender, Richard Nixon (who ordered the White House security staff costumed in the Graustarkian uniforms of European palace guards), Americans have fulfilled their craving for royalty and the trappings of royalty in so many ways that the impulse to set up kings and worship them must be reckoned one of the basic features of the national character. In this long history of infatuation with self-anointed but indubitably powerful and charismatic sovereigns, no figure looms larger than Elvis Aron Presley.

Elvis received his title, King of Rock 'n' Roll, as early, as naturally as any hereditary monarch. For many years, however, he comported himself less like a king than a prince: one of those

1

spoiled Arab princelings who throw around their money and recruit
their harems in Hollywood or St. Tropez, until the sad day comes when
they are summoned home to assume their duties as chief of the tribe.
It was not until the decade of the seventies that Elvis finally laid claim
to his royal prerogatives, the tardiness of his coronation being balanced
by the extravagance of the ceremony. Once the King felt the crown
upon his brow, he could not have enough of the perquisites of royalty,
each new claim to princely prerogative or assertion of kingly privilege
leading immediately to an even more audacious feat of self-aggrandize-
ment. As King Elvis contrived his costumes and elaborated his rituals,
as he enlarged his court and extended his largesse, as he viewed himself
even more fixedly as a man with a vast if ill-defined mission, his people
responded by according him more and more of the honor and glory
owing to a king. The immense crowds that gathered everywhere he appeared, the fanatical devotion, amounting to worship, with which he
was adored, the mad passion to make contact with the royal body—a
mania he sought to gratify by tossing sweat-stained scarves to the people—
make it obvious that his regal posturings were as much a fulfillment of
his public's deepest longings as they were expressions of his own megalo-
mania.

An American king, Elvis saw his empire extend around the globe,
until it comprised even the remotest regions, the most exotic peoples.
In fact, he inspired even greater enthusiasm and awe in other countries
than he did at home because foreigners did not recognize any faults in
his title, any limits to his vaunted powers or any rival claimants to his
throne. Consequently, the exalted status which Elvis enjoyed the world
around varied only as local customs vary in the treatment of such an
extraordinary being. If the English celebrated him with racy pop journalism, as they do their own royal family, the Germans feted him by founding
learned journals and publishing *Festschriften* packed with historical minu-
tiae. If the Russians denounced him as a symbol of the corrupt and
corrupting culture of the West, the oriental nations acclaimed him as
the ideal figure of that American civilization they were so eager to emulate
and assimilate. Not since the great days of Charlie Chaplin has any
solo performer attained such universal popularity. At the time of his
death in 1977, Elvis Presley's was the second most commonly reproduced
image in the world. The first was Mickey Mouse.

Implicit in the image of the King was always the suggestion of the
Messiah. Though Elvis was wont to say, "There is but one King," even
the fact that he felt obliged to make the disclaimer is revealing. It illus-

trates, once again, the profound harmony that existed between Elvis's deepest, most gratifying self-image—in this case as a divinely appointed Messenger, Master or Chosen One—and the yearnings of his public: those millions of faith-starved souls perpetually in search of a cult or a charismatic figure who can gratify their yearning for spiritual enlargement and fulfillment. Ironically, Elvis was just such a person himself. His own original disciple, he was the first to identify his sudden and over-whelming success as a product of divine, not merely mortal favor. Having recognized himself as one of those awesome beings who appear only once in a millennium to give a wholly new inspiration to their civilization, it was only a matter of time until he began to allow this illumination to show forth in his public manner and dress. Indeed, nothing is more apparent in Elvis's final phase than the religious aura in which he sought to cloak himself, straining after even the most extravagant effects, up to and including transfiguration.

In this climactic period, he chose as his entrance theme the apocalyptic opening bars of Richard Strauss's *Also Sprach Zarathustra,* a music that invested the King's appearance with an air of sublimity, as of the arrival of the Superman. Striding onstage in a vast coliseum holding as many as eighty thousand souls, he would stand for a moment, caught in the intersecting beams of the great Zeppelin searchlights, allowing the masses to drink in the majesty of his appearance. Clad always in white, studded and gauded with flashing jewels and metals, he gleamed as if lit from within by some preternatural radiance.

The famous costume, which commenced its evolution as little more than a stunning male negligee, had been elaborated through countless subsequent designs into a regalia. The originally abstract decorative patterns had come to focus in boldly totemic images: an orange and black tiger, a gold and blue peacock, a Mayan stone calendar, an Aztec pyramid, a triadic rainbow—every costume the King wore was fraught with meaning for his devotees. Finally, on the occasion of his greatest appearance, on the Satellite Show—the televised performance destined for an audience equivalent to half the population of the entire world—Elvis demanded and received the full regalia. From that time forth, he wore a high Napoleonic collar; a short but voluminous Elizabethan cape; a broad, massively buckled gladiator's belt; and on his chest stood rampant a crimson, gold and azure eagle. Behold His Royal and Imperial American Highness!

The private life of the Rock King conformed as closely to the royal model as did his public presence. Around his throne flocked all the familiar types found in every court: fawning lackeys, fearless bodyguards, jealous minions, feeble-minded fools, earnest petitioners, impoverished kinsmen, grasping tradesmen and even grieving mothers, bringing their sick children to be healed by the King's touch. King Elvis had his bustling majordomo, his privileged jester, his court musicians, his conscience-soothing confessor, his minister of the exchequer, his household physician and his royal goldsmith, who traveled everywhere with the King, carrying boxes of costly baubles which his master would distribute to favorites or to strangers, according to his whim. Needless to say, the King had countless concubines: poor but beautiful girls of compliant temper, dazzled by his princely glamour and munificence. Also, in every period, there was one woman, the declared mistress, as she would have been called at the court of Louis XIV, who was recognized as the special favorite and treated with appropriate respect. Above all, the Rock King, like many a famous monarch, had a sinister chief minister, a scheming grand vizier, well armed with palace spies and an infallible sense of the King's weaknesses, who spent his life enriching himself at the King's expense, while manipulating his master like a puppet.

To comprehend the phenomenon that was Elvis Presley, therefore, one must be prepared to take the concept of kingship not only literally but extravagantly, to its furthest possible reach. One must bring to bear upon this bizarre but representative American not only the knowledge of kings and courts found in Saint-Simon's memoirs of the Sun King but the more primitive notions of solar deities found in Frazer's *The Golden Bough.* One must be prepared to recognize in the life-style of a southern hillbilly showbiz celebrity those archaic customs of the seventeenth-century French court, the *couchée* and the *levée,* for even such trivial and quotidian acts as getting in or out of bed became highly formularized rituals at the court of the Rock King. Indeed, it would be no exaggeration to say that, as with his most ancient and primitive prototypes, the life of King Elvis consisted of nothing but ritualized routine. The clearest evidence of this condition is the fact that on those exceedingly rare occasions when Elvis did something spontaneous, he threw his entire entourage into a panic. Kings are cardinal figures, upon whom their worlds turn; they must not behave erratically.

Elvis compared himself frequently with the president of the United States. He declared that if he so desired he could himself be the president. Considering the sort of person that Elvis became in later life, this is a startling idea. Yet, nothing that has happened in recent times militates against the notion of a famous entertainer becoming the leader of the American people. It did not require the election of Ronald Reagan to demonstrate that at this point in their history, Americans feel most fulfilled by leaders who are, or at least resemble, movie stars. Authority in our society has devolved upon players. Why not, then, in a future time, instead of movie stars, rock stars? No less an expert than Richard Nixon assured Elvis that he had the power over people's imaginations that would enable him to obtain high office.

In truth, Elvis aspired to an office higher than that occupied by any president. He viewed himself as one who ruled the world by virtue of a unique power conferred directly and exclusively upon him by the Most High. Like Baron Corvo, Elvis Presley fancied himself a kind of glamorous pope: a prince, a potentate, a pontiff; a figure of costly robes and cumbersome ceremonies; a human icon carried about on the shoulders of lesser beings and set up in public places to shed his spiritual effulgence upon the faithful, before being restored to his throne in that strange palace that is more a sanctuary than a seat of power, more the shrine of a cult than the capital of a kingdom.

If the idea of kingship defines Elvis in his glory, it is no less apt for characterizing Elvis in his fatal decline. In his last years, the Rock King became the Fisher King. Unmanned by a mysterious wound, presiding over a shadowy court that flitted all about the country, King Elvis seemed fit only to rule a wasteland, the perfect emblem for the midseventies. The more debilitated Elvis became, the more he craved the refuge of his palace. At every opportunity, he would fly back to Graceland and shut himself up inside it for weeks, sometimes months. Though great numbers of the faithful besieged the gates and were even conducted like pilgrims about the grounds, the mansion itself presented a forbidding appearance, its windows sealed, its doors guarded. Indeed, if there were any place in America to which the word could be applied, one would have declared that Graceland was taboo.

The first step in revealing Elvis Presley is to violate that taboo. Though his house is still barred to the public, still sending forth almost palpable waves of resistance, the best way to commence the account of the most enigmatic of all our popular kings, the most obscured and distorted by the power of myth, is to break the spell that hovers over his seat and track him to his innermost retreat.

So let us imagine ourselves back in the final years of the King's reign, in possession of the supreme privilege of the royal entrée. Let us pass through the Music Gate and ascend the winding driveway to the top of the wooded knoll on which stands the famous house, more legendary than any house in America save the White House. Being forearmed with the knowledge of true Elfans, we will choose the date of our visitation in accordance with the royal calendar. It was a long-established rule, reflected in all his business arrangements, that the King must lie at home upon Christmas. When we approach the mansion, the month will be January and the time will be night, the only proper time to visit the court of the Rock King.

Chapter 1

The King's Palace, the King's Pleasure

THOUGH the holidays are long past, Graceland looks still like a picture on a Christmas card. The classic colonial façade, with its towering white columns and pilasters, is aglow with jewel lights, rose, amethyst and emerald. The templelike pediment is outlined in pale blue fire. This same eerie electric aura runs like St. Elmo's fire along the eaves, zigzags up and down the gables and shimmies down the drainpipes to the ground. Here it pales beside the brilliance of a rank of Christmas trees that have been transformed into cones of ruby, topaz, carnelian and aquamarine incandescence.

Prominently displayed on the front lawn is an elaborate crèche. The stable is a full-scale adobe house strewn with straw. Life-sized are the figures of Joseph and Mary, the kneeling shepherds and Magi, the lambs and ewes, as well as the winged annunciatory angel hovering over the roof beam. Real, too, is the cradle in which the infant Jesus sleeps.

When you step through the ten-foot oak door and enter the house, you stop and stare in amazement. Having just come from the contemplation of the tenderest scene in the Holy Bible, imagine the shock of finding yourself in a *whorehouse!* Yet there is no other way to describe the drawing room of Graceland except to say that

it appears to have been lifted from some turn-of-the-century bordello
down in the French Quarter of New Orleans. Lulu White or the Countess
Willie Piazza might have contrived this plushy parlor for the entertainment of Gyp the Blood. The room is a gaudy mélange of red velour
and gilded tassels, Louis XV furniture and porcelain bric-a-brac, all informed by the kind of taste that delights in a ceramic temple d'amour
housing a miniature Venus de Milo with an electrically simulated water-
fall cascading over her naked shoulders.

Looking a little closer, you realize that the old madams of the French
Quarter would have been horrified at the quality of the hangings and
furniture at Graceland. They decorated their sporting houses with magnificent pieces crafted in Europe, upholstered them in the finest reps and
damasks, laid costly Persian carpets on their floors and hung imposing
oil paintings on their walls. Though it cost a lot of money to fill up
Graceland with the things that appealed to Elvis Presley, nothing in
the house is worth a dime.

Take that fake fireplace that blocks with its companion bookcases
(filled with phony leather bindings) the two big windows that should
offer a commanding view of the front lawn. This hokey facsimile looks
like it was bought at the auction of some bankrupt road company of
East Lynne. Or consider the Louis Quinze furniture strewn about the
parlor. Every piece is elaborately carved and gilded, escutcheoned and
cabrioleted; but it's not only fake (Louis XV's upholsterers didn't go
in for sectional sofas), it's that dreadful fake antique that Italian gangsters
dote on: garish, preposterous, uncomfortable and cheating wherever it
can, as in the substitution of velour for velvet. Or look at the real fireplace
of white marble that stands against the back wall of the room, obviously
innocent of use. It, too, has been flanked not with bookcases but with
a great spread of smoked-glass mirror threaded with gold seams. The
whole ensemble is crowned with an electric clock inside a three-foot
sunburst that looks like someone took an ostrich egg and smashed it
against the glass.

The entrance to the adjoining music room is flanked by two tall,
narrow windows adorned with painted peacocks. Marvelously campy
as are these bits of stained glass, they can't hold a candle to the bizarre
chamber they frame. In this mad room, King Elvis's obsession with
royal red reaches an intensity that makes you gag. Not so much a room
as a crimson cocoon, every inch of it swathed in red satin drapes, portieres,
valences and braided ropes. As weird as anything in Edgar Allan Poe,
the effect is that of stepping into the auricle of an immense heart. At

the center of this king-sized valentine is the crowning touch: a concert grand piano that appears to have been dipped in liquid gold.

The entrance to the next room is blocked by a tall folding screen covered with mirrored glass. Screens and other masking devices abound at Graceland because Gladys and Vernon, Elvis's parents, imbued him with the old hillybilly superstition: Never close up windows or doors. Through this folding looking glass lies one of Elvis's favorite spots, the trophy room. A pop archeologist would find the excavation of this site a satisfying occupation. No part of Graceland was subject to more visions and revisions.

Originally, this room was a patio adjoining the dressing rooms for the outdoor pool. On hot Nilotic nights, Elvis and the Guys (known to the media as the "Memphis Mafia") would sit here cutting the ripe red hearts out of iced watermelons and vying to see who could eat the most. As they consumed this sweet satisfying pap, they would spit the pits out on the ground as Sweetpea, Gladys's Pomeranian, pranced about in the black hail. In the late sixties, Elvis decided to build a forty-foot room over the patio to house his slot car racecourse.

On a huge raised platform, a figure-eight track was laid out, in whose grooves could be fitted expensive scale-model replicas of Ferraris, Maseratis, Lotuses and Porsches. By means of an electric drive system, you could race these little cars around the tracks and up and down inclines at great speeds, which Elvis sought constantly to increase by means of continual improvements in the cars' motors. Manipulating the pistol-grip controls, you could make the cars skid, spin out and crash. It was a grand if costly game, and the Guys enjoyed it enormously.

Like all of Elvis's toys, the slot cars soon lost their charms. One day the track was banished to the attic, where it was stored alongside cartons of old teddy bears, discarded guitars and gilt lamps from the house on Audubon Avenue. Elvis never allowed anything to be cast out of Graceland except human beings. Once an object, no matter how trivial, came into his possession, it remained with him for the rest of his life.

Commencing in the Royal Period, the slot car room became the trophy room. Elvis pushed back the end wall twenty feet to make a chamber fit for a pharaoh's tomb. Then he filled it with gold. He ranked his fifty-three gold records along one wall. Against the opposite wall, he piled up a great heap of gold loving cups, gold statuettes and gold tablets, like the offerings before a shrine. The effect is less that of a trophy case than of the display case of a trophy manufacturer.

The showcase effect is even more pronounced in the center of the room, which is occupied by a set of old-fashioned department store counters, under whose glass tops or stuffed inside storage drawers and cupboards lie an immense profusion of plaques, medals, certificates and scrapbooks received from professional organizations, charities and fan clubs. Like any true sovereign, King Elvis never forgets that all his wealth and power are derived from his subjects. No matter what they offer him, whether it be a huge stuffed animal or a little crocheted doily, he not only keeps the gift but puts it on display.

The oddest feature of the trophy room is the soda fountain that stands in one corner, one of two at Graceland, the other one being downstairs in the poolroom. Soda fountains and jukeboxes are symbolic objects for fifties rock heroes, no more to be wondered at than the old binnacle in the den of a steamship captain or the pair of crossed sabers on the wall of a retired general. What is disconcerting about this domestic altar is its formica meanness. Yet it would be out of character for Elvis to own a handsome old green marble counter with mottled glass lamps and quaint seltzer pulls because Elvis detests everything antique with the heartfelt disgust of a real forward-looking American of his generation. Like so many of his kind, he gloats over the spectacle of the wrecking ball bashing down the walls of historic Memphis. In fact, he likes to get into the driver's seat of a bulldozer and smash down old buildings himself. As he says: "When I wuz growin' up in Tupelo, I lived with enough fuckin' antiques to do me for a lifetime." That is why everything about the King must be spanking new, from his Louis XV furniture to his late model Seeburg jukebox—so drab compared to a dazzling peacock Wurlitzer.

On the left-hand side of the entrance hall is the dining room. In the center of the crimson carpet is a large quadrangle of black marble tiles on which is set the table: an eight-foot oval of mirrored glass on an ebonized and fluted wooden pedestal. Round the table in great state stand ten tall, ladder-backed Louis XIV chairs with tufted velour seats. They appear to have been drawn up for King Elvis and the Nine Worthies. (When Elvis dines with the Guys, he often jokes about Jesus breaking bread with his disciples. They respond by singing the old hymn, "What a Friend We Have in Jesus," substituting "Elvis" for "Jesus.") Above the table hangs a brass Louis XIV chandelier with two tiers of scrolled candlearms fitted with glass lusters. At each corner of the room, like bumpers on a game board, are tall diagonal bric-a-brac cabinets or chrome-plated étagères crammed with statuettes, vases, jars, boxes, plaques, goblets, ewers, compotes, porringers, shells, cloches, etc., *viz:*

ceramic statuette of a grey poodle
ceramic statuette of a nude girl with perched bird
pair of Portuguese glazed pottery drug jars
five specimens of butterflies in plastic cases
artificial floral bouquet under a glass cloche
two glass bowls with bouquet of black and white feathers
model of 1932 antique radio
ceramic statuette of a trumpeting elephant

Wherever Elvis goes in his travels, he indulges his middle-aged woman's passion for knicknacks, curios and chatzkahs. A domestic appraiser once remarked that Elvis appeared to have furnished Graceland largely from roadside stands.

A familiar feature of a number of the world's greatest palaces is a room decorated in an exotic style, inspired, perhaps, by the culture of one of the ruler's most remote or colorful provinces. Graceland possesses such a room; indeed, of all the public rooms in the mansion, it is the King's favorite. The den is an addition to the original building, created by enlarging and enclosing a back porch that ran along the entire real wall. The room looks like Elvis scooped up the setting for one of his Hawaiian movies and brought it home inside a sixty-foot walnut hope chest. You reach the den by going through the kitchen, which is all white formica, walnut paneling and Kitchen-Aid stainless steel, with a couple of oddly feminine touches, like the calico carpeting and the hanging lampshades painted with fruits and vegetables. Entering the den, the first thing that strikes you is a towering statue of the god Tiki, confronting the visitor with outstretched arms holding an empty bowl. Obviously not an ashtray nor an hors d'oeuvre tray nor a place to drop your calling card, this empty basin is a puzzler. In any case, the statue serves to proclaim the room's provenance.

The style of the den could be characterized as Polynesian Primitive or Ugh! The decorator divided its sixty-foot length with another of those hinged screens that one finds all over Graceland. This one is composed of huge panels of stressed, stained pine perforated in long spermatazoid scrolls cut in the wood with a chain saw. On the side of the screen opposite that dominated by the figure of Tiki is a seating area focused upon an early-model Advent video projector.

Here, as Elvis watches his favorite football teams or boxing matches with the Guys, he enjoys the full flavor of the Polynesian Primitive. The huge sofa and the pair of oversized armchairs are carved out of the same dark coarse pine as the room divider and upholstered with thick, dark artificial fur. As the chairs have huge pawlike armrests, the impression created by this curious suite is rather like the Three Bears watching TV. This animalistic sofa is also Elvis's favorite downstairs dining spot. Like so many boy-men, he dislikes the formality of table service. Whenever possible, he has his meals served to him here on the cocktail table, a huge slab of boldly grained wood cut out of the crotch of a cypress tree and surfaced with what appears to be about a quarter-inch layer of lustrous polyurethane.

The most impressive feature of the den is the wall behind the TV, which is straight out of the lobby of a Waikiki Beach resort hotel. Constructed of layers of rough-cut fieldstone, it has been arranged artfully like a natural cataract and equipped with pipes and a pumping system so that a constant stream of soothing water flows down over the jutting rocks, catching as it falls the colors cast by the lamps concealed in the ceiling. What more perfect object of contemplation could be imagined for a man who is perpetually stoned?

As was often the case with palaces when they were inhabited by kings and not just exhibited as monuments, the grandeur of the principal building at Graceland conceals the meanness of the dependents' quarters. Though you often read awestruck descriptions of Graceland's imposing façade, you never see a word about the trailers and mobile homes up on the hill behind the house, where reside Elvis's poor hillbilly relations and caretakers. These number Aunt Nashville and her husband, Earl Pritchett; Elvis's cousin, Billy Smith, and his attractive wife, Jo; and Elvis's nurse, Tish Henley, and her husband, Tommy, a deputy sheriff. These folk comprise just a fraction of the extensive staff of Graceland. In addition to the people who live on the grounds, Elvis always keeps a couple of his men domiciled in the mansion. A garage adjoining the dining room has been converted into a full-scale apartment in which have lived first Marty Lacker, the foreman, and his family; then, Sonny West, the chief bodyguard, and his family. Charlie Hodge, the most symbiotically attached of Elvis's men, has lived continuously by his master's side since they were discharged from the army in 1960. Charlie has an apartment, well adapted to his gnomelike character, down in the basement. Graceland's housekeeper, Aunt Delta Mae—a big, bossy, iron-haired woman, often heard shouting, "Lord, I can't do a thing with these damned niggers!"—lives in what had been formerly Gladys's and Vernon's room at the back of the ground floor, which she shares now with her mother, Minnie Mae.

To this cadre must be added all the people who work at Graceland but live elsewhere. Elvis's father and his second wife, Dee, and her three boys by her first marriage live at the back of the property on an adjacent street in an attractive house with a gambrel roof. The gatekeepers, led by Vernon's brother, Vester, number enough men to mount a twenty-four-hour guard seven days a week at the Music Gate. Other members of the staff include the valets, Gee Gee Gambill and "Hamburger James" Caughley; the four or five black maids or cooks; the yardmen, who attend to the horses in the stable and the cars and other motor vehicles in the garage, as well as performing the various chores demanded by the thirteen and a half acre estate; and the office staff, which works behind the mansion in what was once the smokehouse. Finally, one must add all the rest of the Guys, who, whether they make their homes in Memphis, like Red West, Joe Esposito and Larry Geller, or in some other city, like Lamar Fike in Nashville or Jerry Schilling in Los Angeles, are often on the property. Altogether, Graceland embraces an enormous extended family in the classic southern plantation tradition.

Southern, too, is the mood of Graceland: that slumberous, monotonous, somnambulistic atmosphere in which people pad noiselessly about performing long-accustomed tasks while engaging in endless small talk and gossip. It is Elvis himself who sounds the low *Om* that is the keynote of this drowsy domestic symphony. The moment he returns from an engagement, he retreats to his upstairs apartment and remains there for long periods, virtually incommunicado.

The King's bedchamber is the most bizarre room in the hillbilly palace. The walls are padded and tufted with button-studded strips of black artificial suede. The crimson carpet covers not only the floor but rises at the foot of the bed like a red wave, atop which rides an enormous color TV set. Confronting the bed are two big windows that overlook the front lawn. Sealed with the same black upholstery that covers the walls, they are crowned with gold valences and hung with floor-length crimson drapes, producing a somberly surrealistic image, like a painting by Magritte. The space between the windows is filled with a mirror, which reflects the bed.

What a bed! An immense slab, nine by nine, a double king size, it has a mortuary headboard of black quilted Naugahide, with a built-in plastic back angle and retractable armrests of speckled metal, like the skeletons of those padded "husbands" beloved of suburban matrons. To one side is an easel supporting a large photograph of Elvis's mother; on the other a sepia-toned portrait of Jesus Christ. Back in the corners of the room crouch big round seats covered with white fake fur like enormous bunnies.

As in a funeral parlor, the light in this inner sanctum is always dim, supplied by cove lamps that illuminate the ceiling but produce below only a murky subaqueous gloaming. The air is chilled, the temperature being driven down during the hot Memphis summer by powerful refrigeration units that groan night and day to keep the King from sweating. The odor of the room is sometimes fetid, the stink of a Bowery flophouse full of dirty old men incontinent of their urine and feces. The most grotesque object in this Cave of Morphia, this black and crimson womb, this padded cell, is the King.

Propped up like a big fat woman recovering from some operation on her reproductive organs, Elvis bears a startling resemblance to the picture of his mother which he contemplates so fixedly for hours at a time. His crown of blue-black hair, showing lots of grey at the roots, reflects his mother's hair. His creaseless moon-shaped face matches her expressionless facial mask. The greatest similarity is in the bee-stung eyes, especially the dusky tint of the skin about the eyes, as if both of them wore the identical shade of mascara.

Elvis's immense bulk is owing entirely to the eating habits that he developed as a child under his mother's loving care. He gorges himself with food at every time of day or night. Concealed in his clothes closet is a full-sized refrigerator kept stocked with snacks for those abrupt and unpredictable attacks of the "munchies" that beset speed freaks. Sometimes he seeks to curb the ill effects of his between-meal noshing by stocking his box entirely with yogurt. This tactic avails him nothing, because after lapping up a couple of containers of sweet, luridly colored pap, instead of feeling his appetite sated, he experiences the deep arousal of true hunger. Then, nothing can stop his compulsive gobbling, until he has emptied twenty or thirty of the waxy boxes. Or, suppose he confines himself to healthful fruit: some fine ripe honeydew melons. Drawn like a great bear to the honey in the heart of the melon, he'll cut into and scoop out the oozing pulp in a trice, not stopping until he has put away six or eight of the massive fruits. Or if his sweet tooth is really aching, he will ring up his valet, Hamburger James, at three in the morning and send him out to buy at some all-night market a hundred dollars worth of popsicles. As the rest of the world is brewing coffee and frying eggs, James will be toting up to his master's lair a huge bowl of Eskimo Pies, Fudgesicles, Dreamsicles and Nutty Buddys. Next afternoon, the bowl will be back in the kitchen full of dry, stained sticks.

What Elvis craves most of all are those warm, home-cooked rural southern meals that his mother used to lay on the table. To assure himself that he can enjoy this kind of mess whenever he pleases, he staffs the kitchen at Graceland around the clock. The clock is, in fact, the first thing in Elvis's mind when he awakes from his erratic slumbers and casts his first addled look at the TV, which is never turned off but always turned down to the point of near inaudibility, a generator of soothing white noise. Ringing up the kitchen, he will demand the time of day. "Four o'clock, Boss," sings out the day cook, Mary Jenkins. Elvis, as besotted as Falstaff behind the arras, rejoins: "In the morning or the afternoon?"

Actually, he has no need of a telephone to order his meals. He could ring a bell and achieve the same result because he eats precisely the same meal every day. His favorite feed consists of a pound of Dixie Cotton bacon, fried to a crisp; a quadruple order of mashed potatoes, brimming with "thickenin' gravy"; a large portion of sauerkraut; a dish of crowder peas; and a stack of sliced tomatoes. Piling the sauerkraut and peas atop the potatoes, he stirs these soft foods into a thick viscous paste. Then spooning up this mush with one hand, with the other he grasps the solid foods, eating always with his bare fingers. Though he seizes his bacon strips or pork chops without utensils, he seeks to keep his fingers as clean as possible, holding his pinky erect in the air, like Chaucer's dainty Prioress, who "no wet her fingers in her sauce deep." When the King drinks from his cup, he will twist it around so that his lips touch the rim above the handle, a part never soiled by contact with another person's lips. Should you make the mistake of trying to taste something from Elvis's dish, he will sputter with rage and slap your hand away. Touching anything on the Rock King's plate constitutes as shocking a breach of etiquette at Graceland as it would at Versailles if a courtier were to have snatched one of the Sun King's ortolons from under his long Bourbon nose.

Elvis, when he eats, pays no more attention to his food than would a child. Chattering, laughing and toying with his food, distracted one moment by the TV, the next by the phone, he piddles and paddles in his plate until the meal grows cold and has to be removed and replaced by another warm meal. In this manner, he contrives to eat a sizable portion of two or even three meals at a time. This distracted but compulsive eating is the sole cause of the mysterious, much debated "disease" that blew him up at the end of his life to his final weight: 255 pounds.

Once he has filled his belly, it's time for the King to lie back again and recreate his soul. Gazing up at the ceiling, covered with squares of avocado-gold Naugahide, while steeped in the mindless euphoria of opiates, Elvis must often have felt he was staring into the cloud with the golden lining. His condition suggests those lines from Shakespeare adopted by T. S. Eliot as the epigraph for "Gerontian":

> Thou hast nor youth nor age
> But as it were an after dinner sleep
> Dreaming of both.

Elvis is never alone during his long retreats. He has never been alone for more than a few moments in his entire life. Now, especially, is it necessary that he be companioned twenty-four hours a day lest he die from an overdose or one of those queer accidents that are always befalling drug addicts. The King's gentlemen of the bedchamber must perform many services. The first and foremost is the ritual of the injection.

Unlike most drug addicts, Elvis never takes a shot in the mainline. He associates intravenous injections with the despised character of the "junkie," a type he would like to see rounded up en masse and committed to lifelong imprisonment in concentration camps. So all his liquid drugs are administered intramuscularly by skin popping. Years of being stuck four or five times a day have made Elvis's flesh resemble a pincushion. If a tiny drop of dye had been injected with every shot he has received, he would now resemble the Tattooed Lady in the circus. When it's time for his Dilaudid or Demerol or speed, the chamberlain must go up and down the back of the body or behind the legs or even into the armpits or between the toes to find a bit of skin that has not been punctured.

Once the injection has been administered, the King has to be watched carefully to make sure that he doesn't gag on his own saliva or strangle on a bit of food. Times without number his men have saved his life by thrusting their hands down his gullet and pulling out a half-masticated cheeseburger or a deadly peach pit. When Elvis has to urinate or move his bowels, he must be carried to the bathroom. If only one man is on duty, he will use a fireman's lift. Otherwise, the King will be too feeble to negotiate the distance and too unsteady to risk standing over the toilet, where he could easily fall down and brain himself. Carrying him to the bathroom is no problem: All the King's men are powerful churls. The difficulty resides in knowing when he has to relieve himself. When he sinks deeply into his hibernation, barely breaking consciousness twice in twenty-four hours, he voids unwittingly like an infant or a senile old man. At one point, he fouled himself so often that thick towels were pinned around his buttocks like great man-sized diapers.

Another danger lies in the fact that the King craves company that will not merely guard but participate in his strange subliminal existence. Like all junkies, he likes to feel that everyone is sharing in his sin so that the burden of guilt may be borne more lightly. Consequently, he has taken in his later years to employing young men who have the same longing to get high and stay high for weeks at a time. Actually, it makes life much easier for Elvis's male nurses if they're always stoned, for otherwise the boredom of the duty would be intolerable. Elvis does talk to his men from time to time, but it is such a mumbling, dopey and inconsequent soliloquy that nothing could be more annoying than being compelled to listen to this gibberish. Yet there is no avoiding Elvis's blithering because, like the Ancient Mariner, he lays hold on his listener by the arm, thus preventing his escape, while with his free hand he conducts his monologue as if it were music, slurring and stumbling, with eyes tight shut, often falling into the stammer that plagued him as a youth. At such times his frustration becomes so acute from his inability to free his tongue that the attendant is forced to slap his master's face smartly. Then the King continues his incoherent discourse, groping for the lost threads of thought, until, finally, he runs down to a long head-drooping, slack-jawed pause and blissfully nods out.

Another distraction offered to the body servants is occasional permission to invite to the King's bedchamber young women as dates. Elvis cannot bear to be seen in his ruinous condition, but he enjoys spending long hours in his large, well-appointed bathroom, where he has a comfortable reading chair. As he holds before his uncertain gaze a book of religious teachings or some science fiction novel, he sometimes detects through the door sounds that can only be construed one way. The guard has taken his young woman to bed, Elvis's bed, and is enjoying her now while his master waits patiently for the summons to return to his freshly warmed mattress grave.

When the King craves entertainment, he has a number of ways of

enjoying himself in his deep drug trances. Above his bed are suspended
a couple of color TV sets, rigged as they might be for a man suffering
from total paralysis. Elvis, who is suffering only from partial paralysis,
finds this overhead position unsatisfactory. Generally, he trains his waver-
ing attention on the mammoth screen at the foot of his bed. On its
surface he watches through droopy-lidded eyes and with many lapses
of consciousness all his favorite films on videotapes. He may enjoy the
Great Fights of the Century or brood over the Kennedy assassination
footage or imagine himself Clint Eastwood in *Dirty Harry* or feel a little
trickle of purely mental lust ogling his Danish porno films, which show
buxom wenches being fucked by horses, donkeys and boars. Best of all
he loves to laugh at the antics of Monty Python and his merry men.
The grotesquerie, the goofy put-ons, the physical extravagance, just the
sheer childish nonsensicalness of these films appeal enormously to Elvis's
sense of humor, his deepest but least recognized trait of mind.

It must not be thought that during his weeks and sometimes months
of withdrawal from the world that the King has no awareness of the
life about him. He can tune into any room or examine the fans at the
Music Gate by means of remote-controlled cameras that are planted
all over Graceland and feed back to a monitor beside Elvis's bed. It is
a common experience in this strange house to be in the midst of a conversation and notice suddenly that the camera on the ceiling has panned
around and is focused directly on your face. The King is watching!

If Elvis is in a sentimental mood, he will call, like Old King Cole,
for his fiddlers. His favorite record is a series of recitations by the aging
Charles Boyer set against a background of Hollywood strings. Elvis is
especially fond of Boyer's rendition of "Where Does Love Go?" As
the easy-listening violins play an effortless waltz, threaded with the reedy
sound of the Parisian squeezebox, the soft, husky voice of the famous
actor asks, with many thoughtful pauses and inquisitive intonations:

> *Eef the hart ees the place whaar lahve comes from,*
> *Than whaare does lahve go whan eet dies?*
> *Back een the hart whar eet came from,*
> *Ohr tarn eento tears in thee eyes?*

After a couple of verses filled with such poignant reflections, a chorus
of fresh maidens' voices bursts out of the quadraphonic speakers. On
astro-strings the music soars into that stratosphere that sorts so well
with transcontinental flights and those other flights inspired by drugs.
Thus high on silken wings, gazing into a golden haze, sustained gently

at every point on his body, as if floating in a big black tub, with ears and soul full of romantic sentiments and soaring violins, must we picture the King of Rock 'n' Roll taking his royal ease.

The only thing that can rouse Elvis from his deep drug potations is the need to go back on the road. Never at any time in the later years did King and court assemble at Graceland except on the eve of a tour. After all the years, Elvis's veterans have changed in appearance nearly as much as their bloated boss. Red West, Elvis's oldest companion, once as delicate-featured as a girl, is now a haggard, goat-faced man who looks mean even when he's sound asleep. Sonny West has become a huge, shaggy mountain man, handsome with broad cheekbones and dark eyes, but running to flesh. Lamar Fike, from being a bird-eyed fat boy with a gleaming Tony Curtis haircut, has ballooned into an immense Sidney Greenstreet type, with a sarcastic and saturnine expression affixed to his face. Approaching the awesome and alarming weight of four hundred pounds, he will soon have to undergo a dangerous, life-shortening operation that will cut enough centimeters out of his gut to rush his food through his body before it can turn to fat. Only Joe Esposito, the crew chief, looks about the same as he did when he joined the outfit. "Diamond Joe" still affects the look of a sharp, flashy "Italian gangster." Only he's gotten terribly uptight. Sometimes, he breaks out in fever blisters all over his swarthy, jowly face from the sheer stress of his job, which has shifted from being road manager to acting as Elvis's chief keeper. It's an incredibly demanding existence, symbolized by the beeper Joe wears now on his belt, as if he were a medical doctor or an emergency repairman.

Getting Elvis back into his harness after he has spent two or three weeks lost in the "dark backward and abysm" of opiates is a difficult and exasperating labor. On the eve of a tour, the star's intimates resemble Dr. Frankenstein's laboratory assistants struggling to animate the recumbent monster. Short of a jolt of heaven-sent electricity, nothing can restore the King to life. That is why Elvis, like his prototype, Buck Rogers— who never went anywhere in either his rocketship or his earth-borer without the bald, gnomish Dr. Huer—would not think of venturing forth into the wilds of Rapid City, North Dakota, or Eugene, Oregon, without having at his side his white-haired, low-keyed, methodically proficient personal physician, Dr. George Nichopolous.

Even when he has been revived by the doctor's medicines and hauled to his feet like a fallen statue by his mistress, Linda Thompson, and his feeble old father, Vernon, Elvis is hardly in a condition to do two

weeks of one-night stands or make up for all the shows he has blown
at Las Vegas. Imagine how he feels on such nights when he drags himself
to the glaring, bulb-studded mirror in his bathroom, where he examines
himself with the practiced eye of a great star and a supreme narcissist.
Always there was a part of him that was like those famous female models
who, when they study themselves in a glass, see not the ravishing image
that beguiles the world but a mass of glaring faults that grow worse
every year with age. Elvis always hated his "chicken" neck (disguised
generally with a high collar) and his "gantlin' " legs, which he was forced
to expose in all those dumb beach movies. Even as a poor lad working
in a factory he had found the money to mask the gap between his front
teeth with a cap (which is the reason no photograph taken before his
twentieth year shows him smiling). He suffers always from the sense
that he is too short, which is why in every item of footwear he owns,
from a boot to a bedroom slipper, there is a half-inch lift. Even his
fabled hair troubles him because, like his father's great healthy crop, it
has turned almost completely grey. Recently, he has had a discreet face-
lift. Now all these problems appear so trivial in comparison to the hideous
image he presents in the mirror.

He could be the Pillsbury Doughboy, so fat and puffy and pillow-
stuffed does he appear. From the rear, he doesn't look so bad: He still
has narrow "quarters" and flaring shoulders. When he faces front, or
worse, turns in profile, the effect is appalling. He looks exactly like one
of those barrel-shaped good ole buddies who spend their lives riding
high above an eighteen-wheeler—the kind who say with comic wistful-
ness: "Been a long time since ah could look down an' see mah pecker!"
So huge has Elvis grown that none of his famous costumes will fit
him. More than a score of these splendid garments hang in his wardrobe room, all of them decorated with beads from Czechoslovakia and
semiprecious stones from Brazil, outfits that cost ten thousand dollars apiece—and none of them will zip shut over his mountainous
belly!

As costume after costume is fetched forth by the frowning flunkies,
there is bound to come a moment when the notorious Presley temper
flares. Suddenly, Elvis "flashes"—and a costly gold Piaget embellished
with fire opals explodes against the bathroom wall. Instantly, poor old
Vernon is down on his creaky knees, trying to retrieve the pieces. Elvis
sneers at the shattered watch and rumbles, "Let it go, Daddy—it's jes'
money!"

Now Linda is trimming Elvis's forelock because he wouldn't see the hairdresser who came every day for a week. She's also trying to jolly her sullen lover into a better humor with her usual little quips and coquetries when he flinches or she slips, something goes amiss, and with a roar of rage Elvis seizes his lock and confirms his worst fears—she has cut off far too much! Joe Esposito has to come rushing to the rescue, inspecting the damage and calming Elvis and explaining exactly how they'll make it good when they get to Las Vegas—if only they can get there! All evening Joe has been running upstairs and downstairs, phoning out to Memphis Aero to change the flight time and trying to ease Elvis forward without appearing to push because, at the slightest sign of coercion, Elvis will throw another temper tantrum and the whole party will be further delayed.

Meanwhile, downstairs, all the Guys are lobbed out in the den watching a midnight movie. They drove down from the nearby Howard Johnson's motel in their rented cars at eight o'clock; now, it's one in the morning and still no sign of Elvis. Finally, a phone rings in the kitchen. The word comes from on high. "Boss is ready!" Instantly, the Guys shoot out of their chairs and rush to the vestibule to receive their King, their gold insignia, a lightning bolt crowned with the letters TCB ("Takin' Care o' Biz") glittering on their chests. As they stare at Elvis descending the long, steep staircase, they are astonished at his latest traveling costume.

He's wearing a red terry-cloth robe with a monk's hood from which protrude the bottoms of his black nylon pajamas and his patent leather boots. His head is enveloped completely in the cowl, save for the face and eyes, which are screened by tinted aviator glasses with the initials EP worked across the bridge. Two bulges on either hip show that he's packing his pearl-handled Patton .45s. (Inside his left boot is a two-shot Derringer.) Like some ancient bellman, he's carrying in his hand a large makeup kit, shaped like a tiny chest of drawers, in which he keeps his money, his credit cards and his drugs.

No sooner does he reach the bottommost step than he turns wordlessly to enter his grandmother's room. The old lady is a strange, weird-looking creature: a tall skinny scarecrow with a wizened little face always covered up with sunglasses, the senile bride of the Murnau Nosferatu. She will be lying back in her Lazy Boy chair watching TV or be bent over her organ, which sends low churchy vibes through the house late at night. "Ah gotta go to work, Dodger!" sings out Elvis, as he kneels ponderously beside the old woman and pats her on the back. "If you need anythin', you jes call me at the hotel. Ah'll call you every day, so don't worry about nuthin'." Minnie Mae smiles blindly and says, "You take care now, sonny boy. Dontcha work yeseff into a sickness." Then, as he kisses her on the forehead, she reaches a long emaciated arm around his neck and returns his embrace.

Back again in the vestibule, Elvis shouts as if he were still in army bivouac, "Move it! Let's go!" Joe echoes the order, "Hit it! Let's roll!" Instantly, the front door flies open. Sonny, riding shotgun in the limo, ducks out and opens the car's rear door. Elvis marches straight down the hall; then, just as he's about to step across the threshold, he breaks his stride for a second to reach down and snatch something off the hall table. Always when he leaves home, he makes that last nervous grab for a book, a walking stick, a long, silvery police flashlight. Then he's out the door, down the steps and into the limo.

What a limo! It's the biggest Mercedes made, a huge six-door stretch-out in midnight blue, dubbed by its makers *Der Grosse Pullman.* Curtained all round for privacy and equipped with a bar, TV and radiophone, it's the last word in four-wheel luxury. As Elvis and Linda settle back on the thick red cushions, covering themselves with a fox fur rug, Red drives down the curving road to the Music Gate. A gaggle of fans sets up a shout in the cold night air as the big car pauses at the highway, then turns sharply right to disappear into the night. No sooner does it clear the gate than the long line of cars parked along the wall of the estate suddenly springs to life. These are fans who have been sitting out here in the chill for hours just to enjoy the pleasure of following Elvis to the airport. Now they take off in pursuit. This impromptu motorcade has been anticipated, like every other detail of Elvis's carefully guarded life. A second, smaller Mercedes has now caught up with *Der Grosse Pullman* to act as a buffer between Elvis and his followers.

During the ten minutes it takes to reach the airport, Linda tries to make conversation while Elvis sulks. On the other side of the glass partition that divides the passenger from the driver's compartment, Sonny is on the phone calling the airport tower and informing it that Elvis is approaching. As soon as the tower gets the word, it flashes the news to the security guards at the private gate and to the crew of the *Lisa Marie* out on the strip. When Captain Elwood Davis receives the message, he reaches up to his serried instrument panel and flips a switch marked "Logo." Eighty feet behind him, two bright floodlights suddenly illuminate the towering tail of the airplane. Like a great white sail it stands out against the night sky emblazoned with the gold lightning bolt crowned with TCB and topped off with an American flag.

Elvis likes to boast that he is the only entertainer ever to own for his personal use a four-engine jet airliner. He acquired the big plane to mark his fortieth birthday, his original intention being to fly about the world in an exact replica of *Air Force One*. When he discovered that the cheapest Boeing 707 on the market was $888,000 and that customizing it to suit his tastes would bring the cost up to a million and a half dollars, he yielded to reality to the extent of purchasing a plane that was fifteen feet shorter: a Convair 880 that had carried ninety-six passengers when it was owned by Delta Airlines. When you run your eye along the great white hull of the royal coach, you're reminded instantly of *Air Force One* because the plane bears the same broad red and blue band from nose to tail. Elvis was chagrined by the fact that he could not have the glittering silver hull of the presidential plane. He compensated for this and other such frustrations by fashioning the interior far more luxuriously than would any head of state, save perhaps an oil sheik.

What Elvis demanded for his travels was a flying hotel suite. The forward cabin is a very plushy, oddly effeminate club room, furnished with two long curving bench sofas covered with fat cushions of crushed velour, one aquamarine, the other chocolate brown. The plush aqua carpet catches the light from the arched ceiling, which is padded with canary yellow vinyl. Along both sides of the cabin run continuous bands of short drapes, like café curtains, made of fabric dyed like bull's-eyes of blue, orange and brown stained glass. The club room contains also some card tables, leather lounge chairs, TV monitors and a fifteen-thousand-dollar quadraphonic sound system.

Behind this room is the dining-conference room, which is furnished with six huge leather spaceman chairs ranged along either side of a surfboard-shaped Danish modern table with a green leather surface and a teak rim. Meals served on this spiffy board are framed with silverware bearing Elvis's personal monogram. The room also boasts a communications center, including a skyphone that can be used to make calls anywhere in the world.

The most important compartment is, of course, the bedroom. Elvis insisted that it be located at the rear of the fuselage so that he could embark or disembark without having to show himself to the people in the main cabin. This demand conflicted with his other imperative: that the room be very quiet, the quietest spot in any plane being forward, not aft of the engines. As for decor, Elvis wanted an airborne version of his bed-and-bath suite at Graceland. Like the Boy in the Bubble, he had come to feel that he could not survive outside his artificially contrived personal environment.

The bedroom of the *Lisa Marie* is decorated entirely in shades of restful blue: royal blue for the carpeting, which runs up to the windowsills; pale blue for the huge velvet bedspread; royal blue again for the suede headboard. At one end of the bed is the TV monitor, ready to display the antics of the Monty Python troupe. Just beyond the TV installation is the dressing room, with its large plate-glass mirror bordered with theatrical lightbulbs. Finally, there is the bathroom, which gathers together in a final flourish the whole *esthétique de Elvis*.

Picture a plastic bathroom counter in a shade of brilliant lapis lazuli with a canary yellow sink. Atop the sink is an ornately patterned, gold-plated nozzle and faucet fixture, whose handles are real lapis, à la Sherle Wagner. *Voilà!* With this assemblage of precious metal, semiprecious stone and cheap plastic, combined ostentatiously but unimaginatively into the sort of private fixture dear to the heart of a Palm Springs matron (or a rich old queen), you have the epitome of the King's taste.

The moment Elvis arrives beside the plane, the crew goes into action. The baggage has been loaded long since, the flight plan brought up to date. The moment the cabin is sealed, the firing sequence is initiated. One engine after another is ignited and brought up to full power to test its airworthiness. Then, when all the engines have been checked out, the fifth jet engine, the auxiliary power unit (employed in place of those massive trucks the airlines use), is switched off and raised on steel cables into the forward baggage compartment. All buttoned up and ready for flight, the copilot calls the tower: "This is eight-eighty Echo Pappa waiting for taxi and take-off instructions." "Eight-eighty Echo Pappa," replies the tower, "you're cleared for runway eighteen left. Taxi and go into position and hold." After idling at the end of the runway, while a dozen or more French-built Federal Express jets go aloft, the *Lisa Marie* is cleared for take-off, thunders down the runway and lifts into the air.

The big plane soars majestically across the country carrying the King lobbed out in his queen-sized bed with all his men in the forward cabin playing hearts or watching in-flight movies or eating cheeseburgers prepared in the galley's microwave ovens. As the King voyages high above his demesnes, the air controllers send greetings to the great man. At the end of each dry, professionally phrased message, indicating which controller has received the plane on his radar screen, there is always a final enthusiastic personal message for this plane: "Give 'em hell, Echo Pappa! . . . Wish I were with you, eight-eighty! . . . Tell Elvis we love 'im! Now, I'm gonna hand you off to Denver Center on one-oh-eight point seven. Have a good evening!" All across America, the invisible voices from the ground hail the King as he advances on his royal progress.

Chapter 2

The View from
the Imperial Suite

THE *Lisa Marie* lands just before dawn at Las Vegas and taxis to the Hughes Air Terminal, a private facility immune to gawkers. The Hilton International has been alerted by skyphone and advised of the ETA. The moment the plane comes to a stop, it is surrounded by black limousines and a stake-bed truck for the luggage. Everyone leaves the plane before Elvis, who is the last to board and the last to disembark. Finally, he comes down the stairs, gripping the rail firmly, looking like the Mad Monk or the ruler of one of those remote and exotic kingdoms who is given every year his weight in gold. No sooner does the door slam shut on Elvis's limousine than the machine lurches forward and starts racing for the hotel as if it were an ambulance. When it nears the immense building, standing on the valley bottom like a rocket city straining for release, the car makes a sharp turn to avoid the main entrance and pulls up at a freight-loading area in the back. The King enters the hotel near the kitchen, and after threading a maze of industrial passageways, reaches the service elevator that will carry him up thirty floors to the penthouse.

Entering the Imperial Suite at dawn, Elvis and his party could behold one of the greatest sights of Las Vegas. The designer of this lavish and dramatically situated apartment arranged it for just such trumpet-blowing moments. As you enter, you pass through three successive foyers, which open wider, wider, wider, until suddenly you're standing at the top of a couple of very broad stairs that lead down into an enormous sunken living room, extending from side to side about sixty feet. Directly opposite you is a wall of glass through which you gaze due east at the mountains, flaring at this hour with spectacular colors. Instinctively, you walk across the room, open wide the French windows and step out onto the roof of the hotel, the highest point in the entire valley. Into your nostrils flows the crisp clear desert air, as you glut yourself on the flaming colors in the sky.

Nothing like this ever happened when Elvis Presley arrived at dawn atop the International Hotel. Had anyone been so bold as to open the drapes that hung along the wall to allow the morning light and air into the room, he would have been fired on the spot. Like Count Dracula retreating to his coffin, Elvis entered his apartment intent not on the vital signs of light and warmth but demanding the darkness and the chill of a tomb.

You may be sure he found it, for he never arrived at any hotel without having had his rooms prepared for him by an advance party that would have included one of his valets. In Las Vegas this team arrives from Elvis's home in Los Angeles with a truckload of stage costumes and other paraphernalia promptly on the stroke of noon the afternoon preceding Elvis's appearance. This is the earliest moment they can gain admission to the suite, which has been occupied up to that hour by the star of the preceding show or some other bigwig. Now with the help of the hotel staff, they come off the service elevator, past the uniformed security man who sits always at a table outside the Imperial Suite, checking every visitor's identification. Elvis's men have already received their plastic I.D. badges bearing their pictures, numbers and party designation.

They come with an immense load of luggage: no less than fifty-two pieces. The most conspicuous items are the "rollers," black fibreboard cases on little wheels that open up like old-fashioned steamer trunks, providing hanging space for costumes on one side and six drawers for folding wear on the other side. Seven of these rollers will be taken downstairs later in the day to Elvis's dressing room, where the costumes will be hung up and the other gear set out. Now, the task is to prepare Elvis's bedroom and bathroom according to the master plan, which is set out in three notebooks carried by one of the assistant valets.

The master bedroom has a king-sized bed on a dais. At its left foot on a swiveling pedestal is the TV set. To this instrument the men immediately attach a videotape unit so that Elvis can enjoy his favorite bits of sex and violence. Next, they remove from specially constructed boxes Elvis's religious library: two hundred and fifty volumes dealing primarily with the occult. His favorites, like *The Impersonal Life* or *The Autobiography of a Yogi*, he carries by the dozens so that he can lay them like tracts on prospective proselytes. Next to his bed are laid his closest companions, the Bible and the *Physician's Desk Reference* (to drugs). He will also want the latest issues of *The Watchtower* and the publications of the Self-Realization Fellowship, along with the current numbers of all the karate magazines: *Black Belt, Fighting Stars, Inside Kung-Fu.*

Once the books have been arranged, the next item of importance is the hi-fi system and Elvis's record collection. His taste in music has never altered in twenty years. He's still listening to the Golden Gate Quartet, the Harmonizing Four and all those rich, black, burbling barreltones: Billy Eckstine, Roy Hamilton, Arthur Prysock and Brook Benton. Nowadays, though, he is drifting back to the country music that he first heard as a child. That is why the valets set the radio dial to the local country station.

Next, the Exercycle must be brought up from the storage room and set up in the bedroom. The humidifiers and air purifiers must be installed to guard against "Vegas throat." The little refrigerator stocked with Mountain Valley spring water. A bowl of fruit is placed within reach. The last touch is the proper positioning of Elvis's trophy from the Junior Chamber of Commerce as one of the Ten Outstanding Young Men in America. Elvis is very proud of this award and when he gazes at it, he sometimes recollects his embarrassed, almost strangled little speech of acknowledgement: "I, I, I'd like you folks to know that I was the hero of the comic book. I saw movies and I was the hero of the movie. So every dream I ever dreamed has come true a hundred times."

The next job is stocking Elvis's bathroom. It is the subject of one entire notebook. Among the more revealing items are the great variety of powerful laxatives and Fleet enemas. Like all junkies, Elvis suffers from a paralyzed colon. Opiates immobilize the striate muscles that produce defecation. The abnormally large doses of laxatives that he must take to rouse his numbed gut force his body to the opposite extreme. Sometimes, he loses control of his bowels completely. Many a morning, it is necessary to strip the bed before the housekeeper arrives, lest the

gossip spread through the hotel that "Elvis Presley shits in his bed."
Hamburger James is always bustling out of the Imperial Suite with some
unspeakable object in his hand. If it isn't a load of king-sized sheets
stained with urine or feces, it's a bath towel wrapped around a cache
of spent plastic syringes. James is a sly fellow. He has learned to take
an elevator to a floor far from the penthouse, where, espying an unat-
tended trash truck, he can dump his incriminating bundle and then make
off again without anybody being the wiser.

The packing lists call for at least two hair dryers; a dozen professional
beautician's brushes with black plastic handles and white plastic bristles
and two dozen combs. There is also Prell Shampoo for Dyed Hair and
a hair spray called Presto. Elvis's other toiletries are nothing special.
He brushes his teeth a couple of times a day with Colgate. He sprays
himself with Brut. If he wants a close shave, he uses a Wilkinson straight
razor; otherwise, he employs an electric razor.

One item need not be stocked in quantity: soap. Elvis's brand is
Neutragena but he rarely bathes. Lamar says Elvis takes a "whore's
bath"—a quick negligent wipe of the armpits and the crotch. He may
not even do that much. Priscilla was so disgusted by Elvis's lack of
personal cleanliness that when she renovated their last house on Monovale
Road, she had his shower stall rigged with three spray nozzles: one
for the head, one for the torso and one for the lower extremities. It
was a good idea, but Elvis objected. Taking showers was dangerous.
How many times had he slipped and fallen!

Once the bedroom and bathroom have been prepared, the crew goes
to work on the wardrobe closets. They unpack Elvis's street clothes,
never worn in the street, of course, but carried for those times when
he has to get out of bed and face strangers. Since he saw *Superfly*, he's
been dressing like a black pimp. From his old friends, Lansky Brothers,
he has bought a dozen frock coats and vests, jivey planter's hats and
cravats, in a whole rainbow of colors, all cut from the crushed velvet
that has become his favorite fabric.

Never a man to take less than the most, Elvis buys two pairs of
pants with every suit, as if he feared he might wear one out, and matching
shirts by the dozen. His boots are San Remos or Verdis, all patent leather
in white, black or blue, size 11D, with dancer's soles and heels (crisscross
black rubber threads). Under the boots he wears calf-length socks in
matching colors. Elvis is five feet, eleven inches tall, but with a half-
inch lift and an inch or inch-and-a-half heel, he appears to be well over
six feet.

The two items he gives away from the stage—his flamboyantly colored scarves and his flashy rings—he carries by the gross. Originally the scarves were authentic items of wardrobe. Then, Elvis realized that it was foolish to throw anything of value to the fans. So he ordered a load of gaudy rags from a little tailor in Vegas, which he distributes now with princely gestures. The rings that people are always fighting to get he buys from Schwartz and Ableser, a jewelry shop in Beverly Hills where Elvis likes to hang out. He buys a lot of cheap junk, such as Tiger's Eyes, that flash in the stage lights like real gems. The fans assume that the rings must be valuable because Elvis is wearing them. Actually, they're just the tawdry prizes that come with this particular box of Cracker Jack.

Elvis's real jewelry is in his makeup kit. The moment he arrives in the suite, he hands this treasure chest to his valet, who places it on the right-hand side of the bed, within easy reach. The case is arranged in the same strict order that characterizes everything in Elvis's periphery. The top drawer contains his various pills, tablets, spansules and pulvules. There are round white Quaaludes stamped "Rorer 714"; shiny "Black Beauty" Biphetamines; garnet-colored Placidyls in round 100- or 200-milligram capsules and elongated 500-milligram spansules; flesh-pink Demerols; heart-shaped Dexedrines; and deadly little tablets of Dilaudid in innocent ice-cream colors—green, gold, lavender and yellow—each with the number of milligrams stamped on it, ranging from one to four. Each cylindrical plastic vial containing these drugs bears a label reading: "Caution: A federal law prohibits the transfer of this drug to any patient other than the patient for whom it was prescribed." The names on these labels (unbeknownst to them) are Lamar Fike, Red West, Sonny West, James Caughley and Lisa Marie Presley. Elvis's syringes and injectable drugs are carried in a smaller, auxiliary case.

The second drawer is filled with jewelry, including his diamond horseshoe ring, his diamond-studded wedding band and his kenpo karate ring, a fat red ruby. Also in this compartment is his wallet, which is usually empty. Another wallet contains his driver's license, credit cards and union cards. The prize item in this drawer is the gold-and-blue enamel shield that Elvis received when he was appointed by Richard Nixon an agent of the Bureau of Narcotics and Dangerous Drugs. There it lies just below all those illegally prescribed pills.

The next drawer holds a spare tooth cap, a tube of Blistex (for cold sores), a nail file and a button of eye shadow. The bottom drawer may contain as many as four expensive watches of various designs.

The moment Elvis reaches his bedroom, he divests himself of his robe, takes off the two .45s he is carrying in holsters and places them on the table beside his pillow. Then, he sits down and allows the valet to remove his boots and extract the two-shot over-and-under Derringer. Next, he takes a handful of sleeping pills and washes them down with a long swig of mineral water straight from the bottle. The moment Elvis seems comfortably disposed in bed, Hamburger James wheels in the cart on which he has been keeping warm the King's cheeseburgers. Placing a towel for a tablecloth across the bedspread, James serves the meal. The cheeseburgers are done to a hard, friable texture. Elvis is disposed to choke on his food and often has to be whacked on the back. By the time he has finished eating, he should be ready to nod out. Tonight, the disruption in his routine produced by the trip excites his habitual insomnia. It is Linda's job to soothe and coax and smooth him down until he submits to sleep.

As Elvis lies against the pillow with his left arm thrown across his eyes, Linda sits at the edge of the bed reading in a low soft voice from Kahlil Gibran's *The Prophet*. Elvis's favorite passages are those that deal with love and marriage:

> *Then Amitra spoke again and said, And what of Marriage, master?*
> *And he answered saying:*
> *You were born together, and together you shall be forevermore.*
> *But let there be spaces in your togetherness,*
> *And let the winds of heaven dance between you.*
> *Love one another but make not a bond of love.*
> *Sing and dance together and be joyous, but let each one*
>   *of you be alone.*

As Linda reads, she casts glances at Elvis from time to time. She's hoping she'll see some sign that he's growing drowsy. At one point, he's so still, she pauses, looking at him carefully and almost holding her breath. Suddenly, he starts awake and says in a querulous little boy's voice, "Mommy, I have to go to the bathroom!" "All right," says Linda, in a soothing maternal tone, "Mommy will take you." Then, she half holds and half hauls Elvis as he labors to disengage himself from the sheets. Linda is a big strong girl, like a female athlete. She gets one of Elvis's arms over her shoulder and walks him step by shuffling step to the bathroom. Then she supports him as he urinates into the toilet.

Now they are back in the bedroom and Linda is opening the Bible to read to Elvis his favorite passage, Corinthians: I, 13. When they first met, she had these verses inscribed on a plaque which he could keep next to his bed. Elvis's Bible is well worn and heavily underscored. She finds the chapter quickly and commences reading the famous words: "Though I speak with the tongues of men and of angels, and have not charity, I am become as sounding brass or a tinkling cymbal." Elvis lies back with a blissful expression on his face, like a child hearing his favorite bedtime story. He has every word memorized and may even mumble in unison with her at times. Especially he enjoys the last part, commencing: "When I was a child, I spake as a child: but when I became a man, I put away childish things."

"Mommy," Elvis whines as soon as the reading concludes, "I need more of my sleeping medications." Linda is growing a little exasperated at this point. This refusal to sleep, this demand for more pills, it's the pattern that always precedes one of Elvis's bad spells, which conclude invariably with an overdose and a big panic. She's been with him enough years to know the dangers of giving in to his sick demands. So when he says to her in that sad little boy voice, "I need more sleeping medication—I'm awake," she replies firmly, "Honey, you are *not* awake. You're asleep. Just close your eyes and you'll go right to sleep." He's very cranky tonight. "No!" he insists. "I'm wide awake now! I need some more sleeping medication."

This is always the way they carry on because ostensibly Linda controls the pills, and he loves to wheedle them out of her. She is not about to give in because she can see that he is deliberately hanging onto the edge of consciousness and could easily fall asleep if he would just let go. She denies him again and again; he protests, whines, pleads, and even stirs as if to reach for the bottle himself. Finally, she can bear it no more. An anger, a deep resentment that she hardly knew she harbored, suddenly forces itself out through her lips.

Standing upright and staring down at him reproachfully, she says: "Do you want to die that badly? Why put yourself through this torture? Why don't you take one of those guns there and blow out your brains? Just do it quickly and don't make the people who love you suffer by watching you kill yourself inch by inch." It's an astounding statement. Nobody ever talks to Elvis like that. Even she never talks to him like that. The words just popped out of her mouth as if someone else were saying them through her.

For a moment, he stares at her in astonishment. Then he starts to giggle and gurgle like a baby. Half closing his eyes, he snickers and murmurs in baby-talk, "Okay, Mommy. Aw'll go sleepy." Amazed to see him back down for once, she returns to her soothing mother voice and murmurs: "Just lie there and close your eyes, Baby Buntin'—and hush!"

At about the same time that Elvis is losing consciousness, twenty-six stories below him Colonel Parker is waking up and preparing for a busy day. The Colonel has a year-round suite of three rooms at the end of a wing on the fourth floor; one of his many perks from the hotel. As you walk down the corridor, the first sign you see of the Colonel's presence is two huge replicas of Nipper, the RCA dog, mounting guard. Then, the walls exchange their normal appearance for that of a board fence around a construction site. They are heavily placarded and postered all over with pictures of Elvis—the spoor of the Abominable Snowman. When you enter the Colonel's private quarters, you are assailed by a barrage of the same visual static. The rooms resemble a junk shop. They are crammed with chatzkahs, bric-a-brac, curios, mementos and gimmicks from floor to ceiling. There are statues of elephants, huge teddy bears, trick store items and relics of old promotion campaigns. On a shelf near the door is an ancient promotion kit for *Tickle Me:* a packet of twenty-five chicken feathers in all sizes and colors ranging from pinfeathers to turkey quills, and a furry purple caterpillar with silvery cut-glass eyes and a lolling red tongue. When you stroke it with your finger, it curls up or wriggles or turns somersaults.

The walls are covered with photographs of the Colonel and Elvis. There is the famous early shot of the Colonel seated in his shirtsleeves at a typewriter with the young Elvis curling his lip: Colonel is batting out a snappy press release by the hunt and hit method. Next to it is the standard Hollywood picture of the famous pair, seated side by side in directors chairs, puffing happily on long cigars. Next to that is one of the shots used years ago on a Christmas card: Elvis gotten up in a cute little suit on one side of a towering tree and on the other side a rotund Santa, none other than Kris Kringle Parker. The Colonel's favorite pictures of himself show him in full military uniform: either as a slender young man in the Smokey the Bear hat, crumpled cotton khakis and leather "leggins" of an American soldier between the great wars or in jowly middle age wearing the elaborately swathed, sashed, and tasseled uniform of a Southern colonel in the Civil War.

Looking about these eccentrically decorated rooms, which the Colonel has redecorated at the hotel's expense every time he has a run of bad luck at the tables, you discern great stashes of loot tucked away under every counter and in every corner. Cases of fine wine, boxes of Cuban cigars, cartons of slab bacon from Early's Honey Stand in Franklin, Tennessee, crates of Mountain Valley water, which Colonel calls his "Arkansas champagne." The apartment resembles an eccentric millionaire's fallout shelter. Everywhere you look, you see the things that businesses give their best customers as gifts and favors: heavy crystal ashtrays, elaborate carving sets, silver gilt goblets, executive clocks, numerous RCA appliances in the latest models—radios, phonographs, color TVs. There is so much plunder piled up in these rooms that you make your way through them with difficulty.

The Colonel is a man who believes in mixing business with pleasure; in fact, business is his pleasure. On a morning like this, he may have invited to breakfast a couple of men from the hotel's publicity department. They will be served a prodigious meal: the finest fruits, all out of season and every piece perfectly ripe (once the Colonel had a young man fired from the kitchen staff because he sent up some bananas that weren't fit to eat); costly rib eye steaks topped with fried eggs; imported cheeses; country ham and bacon; hot biscuits and coffee cake. A waiter will stand at the table all through the meal lifting the silver covers on the dishes and piling up the plates. Colonel will drink cup after cup of scalding hot coffee that would make another man scream with pain. If the old man is in a good mood, he may even take a flaming match and lower it down his throat. Then, he lights up one of his immense Montecristo's and sucks in the joy of perfect contentment. When the meal has concluded, at least half the expensive food will be carted back to the kitchen as garbage. The Colonel, like Elvis, is a heroic consumer, a great waster and squanderer, an exemplar of that age now past when every successful, self-made American felt a deep and satisfying compulsion to piss it all away.

At nine o'clock sharp, the Colonel's orderly will report for duty. He's always some immaculately dressed young robot who is loaned to the Colonel by the hotel as a go-fer. One of the world's greatest freeloaders, the Colonel is not content just with meals, rooms, offices, transportation and lavish gifts, he's also very keen on getting his pounds of flesh. For years a whole succession of attractive young men from RCA, MGM and the William Morris Agency have toiled as the Colonel's lackeys.

The Colonel is a master of busywork; all day long he piles up lists of urgent chores that require the attention of many men to perform. It is vital to the Colonel's *amour propre* that he always be rapping out commands, shouting, "*Mister* Diskin!" or "*Mister* Parkhill," like Charles Laughton in *Mutiny on the Bounty.* Then he sends them off on some damn fool task. In fact, one of his favorite expressions after he delivers an order is, "That's a command!" You always expect his men to reply, "Aye, aye, sir!" and swing a smart salute.

Once the orderly has reported for duty, the Colonel is ready to hold his first meeting of the day with his staff. The Colonel can never have enough of meetings, those invaluable occasions when he can lecture his men or think out loud or reminisce about the good old days in the carnival. Meetings are the Colonel's way of holding court, and he has his retinue, no less faithful and obedient than Elvis's Guys. Tom Diskin, who started out with the Colonel way back in the days before Elvis, is still on deck. Diskin is a very intelligent man, a fact belied by a life spent echoing every statement by his boss, "That's right, Colonel!" Mr. Diskin has both gained and lost a lot through his years of faithful service. He's been very liberally paid—the Colonel believes in binding his men to him with hoops of gold; on the other hand, the Colonel has driven Diskin so hard over the years that his nerves have cost him a good portion of his stomach.

George Parkhill is another of the Colonel's veterans. Parkhill is a big man, over six feet tall and scaling about two hundred forty pounds. A sharp dresser, adorned always in fancy jewelry and wearing Bally shoes, he gives the impression of having come from people with money. At one time he was a VP at RCA; then the Colonel took him on and has kept him ever since, although the two have had some bad fallings-out produced by Parkhill's intolerance for the Colonel's unending bullshit. Like other members of this group, Parkhill has a florid complexion.

The Colonel's secretary, Jim O'Brien, like George Parkhill, has never married. Very devoted to his master and very efficient in his job, he has been with the Colonel since the late fifties. Colonel picked him up from Jean Aberbach of Hill and Range, another man who always prefers men to women as secretaries. The only woman who has ever been a member of the Colonel's entourage is Lou Ann Miller, who was originally a secretary for the hotel's former general manager, Alex Shoofey. Miss Miller is a tall, attractive spinster in her midthirties, always neatly dressed in skirts and blouses with a minimum of jewelry, somewhat perfunctory in manner but very solicitous of the Colonel's needs. She's the type of woman who identifies completely with her boss. The Colonel gives her plenty to do: virtually round-the-clock demands. Rest assured, however, that there has never been anything improper about their relationship. Colonel Parker is a man who has never been known to look at any woman save his wife, Marie.

Colonel's staff has completed much of its work by the time Elvis opens. In fact, with Elvis's semiannual appearances in Las Vegas reduced to two weeks from the customary four, demand for tickets to his shows has reached such a pitch that one wonders just how important it is that Colonel Parker and a half-dozen aides labor day in, day out, preparing tacky ads, vulgar radio pitches and corny souvenirs to turn on the fans.

Once the Colonel's staff has helped itself to coffee and settled down at the long table, Colonel will start issuing orders. "George, have you got the album covers ready? If you don't, why don't you call Mel Ilberman and if Mel hasn't got 'em, call Pat Kellegher and if he hasn't got 'em, find out what's happenin'!" As Parkhill starts to answer, objecting, "Well, I don't know . . ." Colonel cuts him off with a curt, "I don't wanna hear 'don't know'—find out now!" Fixing his hard blue eyes next on Tom Diskin, the old man asks: "Now, Mr. Diskin, when's Mr. Rocco comin' in?" (Colonel has never learned how to pronounce the name of RCA Victor's president, Rocco Laginestra.) "Make sure now that Mr. Rocco is taken care of." Between each sharply worded command, the Colonel takes a puff on his big dark cigar and a draught of coffee. Really, there's nothing much to do: The ritual of business far exceeds its substance.

Finally, he figures he's discharged his obligation to appear busy. "O.K., that's enough!" he barks. "Now, everybody, let's go to the office. We'll work there for a while, and then we'll go on from there. Now, let's go!" With that, he claps his hands loudly, like a kindergarten teacher demanding attention, and storms out the door of the suite to his office across the hall. There he sinks down at once at a desk and places a call to his home in Palm Springs. Getting his wife on the line, he engages in a little homey banter. "How are you honey? How you doin'? Cats O.K.? Everythin' is fine here. I'll be home on Friday. I'm bringing some fresh catfish. We'll have a fry downstairs." The Colonel is always careful not to inquire too carefully about his wife's health because she'll tell him how she feels—*bad!* The Guys call her "the most miserable woman on earth." Her favorite expression is "I hate it!" She is ailing but not yet invalid. Once in a while she still gets herself together to visit her husband in Vegas. She may even play a little 21, but if she loses, she's liable to throw the cards in the dealer's face.

Once the obligatory morning call to the house has been made, the Colonel will declare, "I think we better go down to my casino office." That's the signal to commence the day's gambling. Arriving at the back of the casino, cigar smoke pouring from his mouth, walking very fast with his cane in hand, looking neither to left nor right, the Colonel, you'd swear, is heading for an important appointment. God forbid anyone obstructs his progress or dares to touch him on the arm! The old man will go berserk with rage and raise his cane threateningly. After a short stop at the casino manager's office to exchange pleasantries, the Colonel will say, apropos of nothing, "Well, okay, I'm goin' out to my other office"; then he will make his way through the jungle of slot machines on his way to the wheel. He may toss some money into the slots as he proceeds; if he hits, one of his men will stop to collect the silver. Once the Colonel reaches the table and greets the dealer, he completely shuts out the rest of the world. It makes no difference whether he is playing on a cold table or surrounded by a crowd of people: He is alone with his obsession. "Red'll be my color today. Gimme a stack o' red!" he snaps at the croupier, who is wearing a white styrofoam boater with a red ribbon around the crown stamped in gilt letters, "ELVIS." Obediently, the man slides an enormous stack of chips across the board.

As Colonel Parker starts his morning play, in a little room near the entrance to the showroom, the hotel's maitre d' is poring over his huge pasteboard seating charts. Emilio is a nice, plump, smiling, middle-aged Italian, who talks as if he had a mouth full of marbles. At this time of day he does not wear his frilly blue jabot shirt or his custom-tailored tuxedo or his costly studs and cuff links. He is attired in a dark English blazer and looks quite scholarly with his half-glasses sliding down his nose. As the switchboard operators in the adjoining office receive frantic calls for tickets for the severely rationed performances, Emilio ponders deeply the problem of accommodating such a demand. Elvis's appearances at the hotel are regarded by the maitre d' as the greatest and most challenging moments of his career. At the same time, he is exercised by the thought of how much money these two weeks will put in his pocket and those of his men, all of whom are sworn to pool their gratuities and then receive shares that are calculated carefully in terms of rank, seniority and various other considerations. Though no one but Emilio will ever know precisely how much money is entailed in such operations, a little basic arithmetic produces some startling results. If one computes the tips for one night, figuring two thousand couples, with the average tip twenty dollars—ten dollars to the captain who seats them and ten dollars to the waiter who serves them—the bottom line is twenty thousand dollars. As hundreds of people will pay anything to obtain admission to the shows and as everyone wants seats as close to the stage as possible, it may be assumed that considerably more than the minimum gratuity will be received: say, thirty thousand dollars a night for fourteen nights straight or over a half million dollars in tips. As all this money is in cash, in small bills, it's clear that Emilio is looking at a very good thing through his half-glasses.

As the maitre d' wrestles with the problem of the giant 747 that has just landed with a couple hundred wealthy Japanese or the question of where to put Cary Grant or what to do about the fire marshal, who keeps threatening to enforce the legal seating limit, Hamburger James is at the mail desk in the lobby collecting all the letters that have arrived addressed to Elvis or members of his group. Sorting through the lot swiftly, he divides the fan mail, which will be returned to the office at Graceland, from the personal mail. The latter he divides again between that destined for the Guys and Elvis's personal mail, which is given to Joe. Joe decides what letters should be given to Elvis just as he decides what reviews Elvis should read, what callers Elvis should receive and what news of the group Elvis should hear.

James takes the elevator to the thirtieth floor, where he receives from the security guard the key to the front door. Letting himself into the hushed apartment, he walks across the living room and opens the drapes slightly, allowing a subdued light to enter the room. Next, he turns on the big color TV that faces the sofa, being careful to keep the volume very low. There must no more be jarring sounds than there are garish lights. Finally, he goes to the gilt-trimmed white bar, where he takes a champagne glass and fills it with eighteen brightly colored vitamin pills, including A, B12, C, D and E.

At that moment, he hears the bell at the service entrance, whose ring signals the arrival of room service with Elvis's breakfast, ordered always the preceding night. Entering the big bare kitchen, James opens the door and helps the waiter roll the cart down the two steps into the sunken living room and across the carpeted floor to the wrought iron, glass-topped coffee table where Elvis takes his meals. Lifting the covers to make sure the order has been filled precisely and verifying that the flame is burning inside the warming oven, James signs the check and tips the waiter.

Now he goes back to the bar, where there is a direct line to Elvis's room and presses the button. After a long pause, Linda's voice comes on the line. "Tell E," says James, "that his breakfast is here." Then he hangs up and moves quickly toward the coffee table. Taking a cloth from the cart, he covers the table; then, he sets it with silverware, Saltines,

butter patties, sliced tomatoes, a bottle of Mountain Valley water and
the glass full of vitamins.

Elvis emerges from his bedroom looking very groggy and wobbly.
He braces himself against the wall for a moment; then, he steers a cautious
course across the living room to the sofa. His hair is down in his face.
He wears blue pajamas under a dark blue bathrobe. His boots are unzip-
pered and in his hand is a gleaming .45, which he plants beside his
plate. As James prepares to serve the meal, Elvis picks up the glass
full of vitamins and downs it at a gulp. He prides himself on his ability
to swallow any number of pills at once. Then he takes the bottle of
mineral water and drains it.

James serves the meal noiselessly. No speech is permitted before the
second cup of coffee. He pours the first cup, steaming hot and extra
strong. Then he places before his master his invariable order for breakfast:
a six-egg Spanish omelet, twenty strips of crackling crisp bacon, an order
of hash browned potatoes and a pitcher of fresh-squeezed orange juice.
Elvis's first question is: "Where are the Guys?"

"Joe went out to the airport to git Lisa. Sonny is talkin' to the security
dudes. Ole Red is laid up in his bed."

"Tell him to get his ass up here," growls Elvis, who is not to be
trifled with when he awakens.

As James bustles across to the phone at the bar, Linda appears in
her negligee. She's bright and cheery in the "morning." Giving Elvis a
kiss on the forehead, she settles down at his side on the sofa.

Linda and Elvis have had some strange experiences here. One of
the best remembered is the night in February 1974, when, after the
first show, they came back to the penthouse to relax and watch television.
Linda went into her bathroom and was sitting on the commode when,
suddenly, she heard an explosion and saw, simultaneously, a hole appear
in the roll of toilet paper next to her knee and a mirror on the other
side of the bathroom explode into shards of glass. Pulling herself together
and rushing out into the living room, along with several of the Guys,
she discovered Elvis lolling on the sofa facing the common wall with
the bathroom holding in his hand a still-smoking Savage .22 pistol. He
had taken a shot at a light fixture, missed his aim and put the bullet
clear through the wall and nearly into Linda's leg.

Elvis often relieves his boredom or vents his anger by picking up
the gun that always lies near his hand and either pointing it at the
cause of his displeasure or firing it. That is why his valets check his
weapons constantly to make sure the first chamber is empty. If they

had not taken this precaution, certain people now living would be dead and Elvis Presley would be alive but behind bars. Elvis's favorite target is any television set that offends him with a malfunction or a bad program. Once Elvis fired into a TV and the bullet ricocheted and hit Dr. Nick above the heart. Just a spent bullet. Nothing to be alarmed about. That is also Elvis's attitude when somebody questions the wisdom of his firing the pistol into the ceiling of the penthouse. "If this is really the penthouse," he drawls, "there ain't nuthin' above us that *could* get hurt!" How's that for logic? The one funny part about this bit is the way the Guys cover for their boss by buying all the TVs he blows out, saying that Elvis has taken such a liking to the set that he can't bear to leave without it. You can always judge what Elvis's mood has been on a tour by counting the number of mechanical corpses being schlepped off the plane at Memphis.

About three in the afternoon, Elvis goes downstairs to rehearse with the orchestra. He hates to rehearse. He hates to even be here in Vegas. In fact, there is no part of Elvis's career that he still enjoys. He has done it all so many times in so many places to so many ga-ga audiences that the whole business fills him with disgust. People whisper that he's suffering from a serious illness. They're right! It's called terminal boredom.

When he arrives onstage, the cyclorama is up, exposing the brick walls and pipes behind the stage. The electricians are up on tall ladders adjusting the lights. The carpenters are assembling the platforms for the orchestra. Elvis makes the rounds, greeting the principals: the conductor, Joe Guercio; the drummer, Ronnie Tutt; the lead guitarist, James Burton; and J. D. Sumner of the Stamps Quartet.

Guercio is a nervous, fast-talking dude who wears tinted aviator glasses and gives off an aura of breathless showbiz ring-a-ding-ding. A mediocre musician, he left the highly competitive New York studio world to labor at Las Vegas. Eager to please, he's very deferential toward any star. As Elvis's show never changes from one year to the next, there isn't much to discuss. Maybe the conductor has come up with some little gimmick to give the show a slight air of originality, like doing the *2001* theme in the disco version popularized by Deodato. Elvis winces at the word "disco," as if Guercio had said "tampon." Still, Elvis has spent a lifetime listening to half-assed ideas like this and trying to make them work. He agrees to give the new version a try. Guercio, delighted to have had an idea accepted, turns around eagerly to the band and goes into the new ta-ta-tum, ta-ta-tum *2001*. Elvis listens, casting mocking glances at Red, as if to say, "Ain't this a crock!" The whole thing is ridiculous; but when it's over, he agrees to try it that night.

Now they start going through the other tunes. They play the arrangements by heart, and Elvis blows out the lyrics in half voice, sitting on a stool with his mineral water beside him in a silver ice bucket. From time to time he interpolates dirty lyrics. He laughs at every little goof and goofs on himself, mocking his own style of singing. When they get to the big production number, which is the only good thing that Elvis has added to the show in years, a medley called "American Trilogy," Lamar and the hotel's lighting man come out on the stage and explain that they're going to throw some projections onto a screen that will drop in behind Elvis during the piece. Unfortunately, they can't demonstrate the effect just now because the projector operator hasn't arrived; but if it doesn't work out, they can always cut it. Again, Elvis is instinctively suspicious but he agrees. It's his day to be big about things. He mustn't get the engagement off on the wrong foot. Suddenly, in the middle of the next number, he bolts from the stage, with a couple of the Guys taking off with him. He's not sick or upset. He just figures he's had enough of this crap. It's time to get back upstairs and get a taste of his favorite honey.

While the rehearsal has been proceeding on the stage, beneath the stage that diligent mole, Hamburger James, has been burrowing into cabinets, closets and wardrobe drawers, unpacking, with the aid of an assistant, the seven rollers that he has brought down from the Imperial Suite. The star's dressing room at the International is on the same lavish scale as are all the accommodations in this gargantuan establishment. Not a room but a suite, this subterranean flat comprises a large lounge, equipped with a bar and furnished for either relaxing between shows or holding those informal receptions for VIPs after the show which allow both the famous entertainer and his famous guests a moment of exclusive communion. Off the lounge is the dressing room proper, equipped with all the customary facilities and two bathrooms. Adjacent to the dressing room is a tiring room, with a bed for those who crave rest and a piano for those who wish to warm up before the performance, as Elvis did in his more vigorous days, gathering the vocal quartet around him to sing gospel songs before going onstage.

As Hamburger James removes each costume from its case, he examines it carefully for tears or stains or stuck zippers, which require the application of his ever-ready graphite squirter. At the same time that he is rubbing scuff marks off white boots with a rubber eraser, on the subterranean shopping mall, Linda is trying on a white kid frontier suit with fabulous fringes at Suzie Cream Cheese. A floor above the mall, in the hotel's lobby and in the casino and the maze of public rooms that spread from the Keno parlor in all directions, like a major New York subway station, everywhere you look, you see Elvis posters, Elvis banners, Elvis, Elvis, Elvis. Silver-sequined guitars, giant pink teddy bears, yellow hound dogs, white boaters with red ribbons emblazoned "Elvis": As the Guys say, "You can't take a crap without looking up and seeing Elvis." The Colonel has converted the entire hotel into a giant snow job.

There will be but one show tonight: a dinner show that commences at eight with the meal and then offers an hour and a half of entertainment, commencing at ten. Admission is by invitation only, which means the house will be composed almost entirely of friends and well-wishers, most of them invited by Colonel Parker. The real grind does not start until tomorrow. Elvis has one night to work into the harness. At this point in his career, there is always the distinct possibility that he will not go the distance.

When Elvis gets back upstairs, he is greeted by Priscilla and little Lisa, who runs gleefully into her father's outstretched arms. The child lives with her divorced mother in an apartment at the Marina del Rey in Los Angeles, but she often sees her father either on the West Coast or in Memphis. Nothing pleases her more than spending time with Daddy because he spoils her outrageously. Elvis and Priscilla hold diametrically opposed views on child-rearing. She is a great believer in discipline and character-building. He feels that the primary value of success lies in being able to do exactly as you please and granting the same privilege to those you love. Lisa is being reared, therefore, in a totally schizophrenic manner, subject one moment to firmly enforced rules and order, released the next to run wild and imitate all the bad examples set by her father. Priscilla has balanced on a tightrope for years, trying on the one hand to preserve an atmosphere of good-humored cooperation between herself and Elvis, while, on the other hand, attempting to maintain some control over her daughter when she visits her father.

Priscilla looks much more beautiful now that she has gotten away from Elvis. Freed from the obligation to dress, make up and wear her hair in the vulgar styles that Elvis demanded, Priscilla has reverted to her natural appearance as an exquisite and tremulously feminine little creature accoutered in the latest and most sophisticated fashions. In this respect as in every other she stands in total contrast to Linda, who is not especially beautiful but who has a much bigger, bolder and more stagy appearance and the exhibitionistic personality of a real southern belle.

Elvis puts on an air of affectionate familiarity with Priscilla in public, but he makes her terribly nervous and apprehensive, as well he might, after years of alternating threats of physical violence with abject pleas for her return. Sometimes when he's really stoned, he'll dial up her number and when she answers, he'll just sit there speechless holding the receiver in his hand. Though Elvis hasn't loved Priscilla in years, he can never recover from the mortal wound his pride received when he learned that she had taken a lover.

It pleases him, however, to think that Priscilla and Lisa will be in the audience when he walks out on stage. Whatever his faults as a human being, he is still the King when he stands before his public. That is the way he likes everyone to see him and think of him. So he insists always that on opening nights Lisa be flown to Las Vegas, even if it's necessary that she go back home the very next morning, so that she will see her famous daddy in all his glory.

By 6:30, the faithful Hamburger James is back downstairs, preparing himself for the big event of the day: dressing his master for the stage. Since James has been gone, there have been many deliveries and visits to Elvis's dressing room by porters, maids and bellmen. A big red banner emblazoned with gold letters has been stretched across one wall of the lounge, shouting: "Welcome Back to a Wonderful Stay." Huge wreaths of red roses stand about, as for a funeral, bearing cards from Conrad and Barron Hilton, Rocco Laginestra and other big shots. More interesting are the cards from the staff: the greetings from waiters in the showroom, maids who clean the penthouse, casino managers and pit bosses, all of whom look to Elvis to boost their income dramatically by his appearances.

James has seen all these tributes so many times before, he pays them scant regard. His concern is first the bar, which he is pleased to see has been freshly stocked for visiting VIPs and equipped with a hot plate on which James will prepare the tea with honey that Elvis drinks to prepare his throat before he goes on stage. James fills up the humidifiers with water and switches them on. Checks to see that there are towels in the bathroom—not that Elvis will take a shower but he must be rubbed dry when he comes offstage drenched in sweat.

By the time James has everything in readiness, he hears the familiar voice of Colonel Parker, who is entering the suite with Tom Diskin.

James bustles out and pours the two men cups of coffee at the bar. Colonel quizzes James about Elvis and receives vague answers. James is in awe of the Colonel, a man he assumes to have nearly divine powers; but the valet is not one of the Colonel's snitches, like Joe Esposito or Charlie Hodge. By the time the Colonel has poured the cup of hot coffee down his asbestos throat, there is a racket in the hall signifying the arrival of Elvis.

The King's progress from one suite on the roof of the hotel to another suite in its basement is one of the most ritualistic performances of his ceremonial day. Though no one will see Elvis come downstairs but the hotel staff, he dresses always for the occasion as if he were going out on a date. In fact, it's the only time in the day when he does dress properly, with a jacket and a scarf and all his fancy jewelry. As he prepares himself to sally forth, all the Guys gather in the main foyer of the suite, chattering nervously in anticipation of the moment when Elvis will appear. Then, suddenly, he is among them, perfectly dressed and groomed and smelling of Brut.

Striding vigorously, as if determined to go somewhere in a hurry and set something straight, Elvis comes out of his wing with nary a sunshaded glance to left or right. Instantly, all the Guys close about him, like Secret Service agents guarding the president. The service door to the Imperial Suite swings open. The security man on duty presses down on the transmitting button of his walkie-talkie and reports to his control center: "Fourteen is in progress. He has just taken Elevator Nine and . . ." The freight elevator is operated by another uniformed guard, who twists his key and closes the door. As the car drops to the second floor, all the Guys start chatting Elvis up like football players at a pep rally. They joke, they jolly, they pour on the good vibes. One thing they never do—touch him. Elvis stands in their midst, clad in black, masked by his shades, his hair perfectly styled and locked in place, looking as if he had been quick frozen.

When the elevator door opens on the bare concrete, fluorescent-smeared service corridors of the second floor, the hotel's main floor, another security guard is standing by to report Elvis's arrival at his station. It is about a three-minute walk through the maze of passages that lead eventually to the dressing room. In the old days, Elvis used to charge along these corridors with the same momentum with which he left the penthouse. Then, as the drugs took hold of him, his pace slackened, his step faltered. Finally, his equilibrium got so bad that somebody got the bright idea of providing Elvis with a golf cart to drive through the passageways. Now, without a moment's hesitation, Elvis hops inside the machine, which is ready to roll, and looking straight ahead, as if it were the most natural thing in the world, he starts driving through the hallways at the back of the hotel, surrounded by jogging henchmen and uniformed guards, past steaming kitchens and rattling pantries, past a big plate-glass window that lets in upon the employee's cafeteria, where, in response to the cheers of the workers, he raises his hand mechanically, like any ruler waving from any open car to his people.

When Elvis reaches the hydraulic elevator that communicates between the showroom stage and the dressing rooms directly below, the two guards accompanying him report his position again to central control. It is the static-ridden voice of the guard's walkie-talkie that the alert ears of Hamburger James catch now, as he darts into the hall to take up his station.

As Elvis walks into the lounge, he gives the makeup case he has been carrying to James and greets the Colonel and Diskin. "Step into my office, son," says the Colonel, gesturing toward the inner room. Colonel always closets himself with Elvis before a show. He will have some little item to report: what celebrities will be in the house or who wants to have his picture taken with Elvis. Actually, all the Colonel is interested in doing is giving his property the once-over. The old man lives in constant fear now that Elvis will collapse or cop out or do something erratic onstage that will cause a scandal. Elvis knows he's being examined. Like any junkie, he's a practiced actor, adroit at deceiving the squares and making them believe that he's straight. He doesn't wear those sunglasses night and day for nothing. After a very brief exchange, during which Colonel does all the talking, the old man leaves. Now James enters the room with an assistant to commence the ritual of dressing the King.

All Elvis has to do to prepare himself for the stage is to remove his street clothes and don a jump suit. You would think one assistant could handle the job. In fact, it requires the efforts of many men to prepare Elvis for exhibition. As soon as the King has stripped down to his thin white dancing briefs, no different really from a pair of women's panties, and sits down on his chair—an act that flexes as many tubes of flesh about his midriff as has the Michelin Man—he asks nervously: "Where's Elias?" Though he is traveling with his personal physician, whose black medical bag is stuffed with goodies, Elvis likes to maintain a close working relationship with his local doctor. Dr. Elias Ghanem arrives so punctually after his presence is inquired after that he appears to have been summoned up like a genie. He even looks a little like

Sabu, with his swarthy skin and dark eyes and boyish features. He and Elvis closet themselves briefly in the bathroom, where the doctor gives Elvis his preshow injection; then, the door opens and Elvis resumes dressing, as the doctor ducks out of the dressing room.

As Elvis sprawls in his chair with outstretched legs, waiting to feel the effect of the shot he has just received, Hamburger James busies himself about his master's knees. First, the valet takes a couple of huge Band-Aids and sticks them on the kneecaps; then, he slips over Elvis's feet and draws up his legs those elastic bandages that athletes wear on their joints. The purpose of all these dressings is to cushion the shock in case Elvis is inspired to go down on one knee in one of his Al Jolson salutes to the house. When you weigh over two hundred pounds, falling on one knee can be a shocking, even a shattering, experience. Next, James takes Elvis's hands, one at a time, with their long, thin, spatulate fingers, and wraps about the fingers ordinary-sized Band-Aids that will protect Elvis's skin from the fingernails of the women who clutch at him. The bandages will also prevent his rings from sliding off; they are not sized for his hands because he intends to give them away.

Once the protective padding has been affixed, it's time to cope with the natural padding, the huge belly that makes Elvis look as though he has swallowed a watermelon. As Elvis gets to his feet, aided by James's assistant, the valet wraps his master in a white corset. They don't call it a corset: The word is "brace." It's a surgical-looking garment that gathers the flesh in front and secures it from behind with a web of laces. Naturally, it is not a good thing for a singer to be laced into a gut sling that will restrict his breathing, especially when he's short of breath from other causes, as is Elvis. These days, however, nobody ever judges or even thinks of Elvis Presley as a singer. The sole criterion for his performances is his physical appearance, measured entirely by his weight. A good performance is one, for which you'd have to go back several years, in which he appears slender and youthful; a bad appearance is one in which he looks and acts so obese and dopey that everyone is embarrassed.

Now, laced into his corset, Elvis is shown the few costumes that still fit. He chooses for this evening an outfit embroidered with the crowned head of King Tutankhamen. Next, they have to get him into it. While James hunkers at his master's feet, ready to slip the leg over his foot, James's assistant offers his shoulder for support. Elvis chicken-legs his way into the garment and stands free for a moment while James runs the zipper up to the sternum. Once the massive, ten-thousand-dollar, solid gold gladiator's belt is fastened around the waist, another device for hiding the star's girth, the costuming is complete.

Charlie Hodge arrives now to give Elvis's hair the final touches. When the famous coif, so well trained that with one shake of the head it falls into place, has been arranged and secured with hair spray, James pops up to give Elvis a farewell squirt of Brut. Finally, the last gentleman of the dressing chamber, Joe Esposito, appears to make his token contribution to Elvis's dress. Joe takes one of the brightly colored scarves that James is holding and arranges the cloth carefully about Elvis's neck. Meantime, James has folded neatly the dozen scarves that Elvis will cast into the audience that night in a climactic ceremony suggestive of the distribution of the eucharist. Elvis will proceed from one side of the stage to the other shadowed by little Charlie, who will deftly loop each scarf about Elvis's neck, where it will lie for a couple of seconds receiving the charismatic charge of the King's body. Then, like a perfunctory old priest, Elvis will snatch off the scarf in a reflexive and self-absorbed manner, all the time singing into a hand mike, and throw the orange or golden cloth into the sea of outstretched arms and hands.

The overhead P.A. announces now that the comedian is in the final five minutes of his routine. James takes the lavishly decorated cape from the wardrobe and secures it at the back of Elvis's high Napoleonic collar. "How do I look?" asks Elvis, staring into the mirror, as if he were addressing his other self. As his men chorus, "Great, Boss!" he turns abruptly toward the door, signaling that the investment is complete.

As Elvis is ushered to the wings at stage left by Red and Sonny, who show the way with red flashlights, he is beginning to feel the clarifying effect of his last injection. It will take him a couple of numbers before he hits his stride, but by the time the show is underway, he will feel a furnace burning inside his body and the sweat will start to pour out of him. Even so, he has abused his body so badly for so many years that no matter what the drug or the dose he takes, he can no longer recover his natural manic energy.

His stage movements these days are sluggish and constrained, his speech is often slurred, his once-remarkable memory fails him and his voice is very uneven. So often does he crack on the high notes that measures have been taken to disguise his failures. The back-up singers are miked so that when Elvis reaches for a high note and misses, one of the men behind him will hit the note and in the resulting mix, controlled by the sound technician, the audience will not be able to detect that the ringing note they hear did not come from Elvis, standing there with his mouth open and his arms flung dramatically apart.

On this night, everything goes wrong from the start. As the orchestra takes off into the new version of the *2001* theme, Elvis suddenly realizes that he doesn't know exactly where to make his entrance. Elvis always makes a no-bullshit entrance, walking right on without an introduction and collaring the mike like a man who means business. Usually, all he has to do is start across the stage and there is an ovation. Tonight, when he steps out on the boards, he realizes that his timing is off. He isn't getting the sort of hand he should receive. As he goes into his opening numbers, he is bugged by the thought that nothing is working out properly. The ensembles are ragged, his voice is rough, the stage monitors aren't loud enough so that he can really hear himself. Though he keeps on smiling and singing, a terrible rage is starting to seethe inside his breast.

Usually, the high point of the show is "American Trilogy." This flag-waver symbolizes everything that Elvis has become in his maturity. The number starts off with a wistful performance of "Dixie," Elvis singing lone and bluesy, with a drummer-boy snare in the background. On the words, "I was born early one frosty morn," his voice rises keenly because the line reminds him of his own birth one bitterly cold morning back in Mississippi. He sings it now as if that time were a thousand years ago and he a grieving exile from his homeland. Then, the music slides into "The Battle Hymn of the Republic," the drums beating strongly and the brass taking stentorian snorts into the deeps or cresting high on silver foam, as the massed voices behind Elvis create the impression of a great host advancing. Suddenly, though, the mood shifts again; and at this moment, the last great moment of his musical career, he would sing in a voice of deep poignancy a few lines from an old black spiritual titled "All My Trials." Achieving a sudden, hushed intimacy with his vast audience, he would croon as a mother to her child, "Now, hush little darlin', don't you cry. You know your daddy's bound to die." That line sent chills down many a listener's back. It was one of those unconscious prophecies that great performers sometimes make from the stage. For one instant it would raise the level of this crass and blowsy show to where Elvis should have always stood, with the men and women of soul. Soon, though, the "Battle Hymn" would return, the noise and theatrics would mount up to a great rabble-rousing climax and that one little spark of beauty and sincerity would be lost in the tawdry blaze of a showroom spectacular.

This night is cursed from beginning to end. Instead of the show reaching its full emotional climax with "American Trilogy," the whole performance collapses during this number into a complete fiasco. Just as Elvis is getting into his wistful, nostalgic recollection of "Dixie," down from the overhead, with an audible whirring of machinery, comes a round projection screen. Elvis spins around to greet the portent and exclaims with the hand mike close to his lips: "What's that! The moon comin' down?" Then as the slides start to flash on the orb, they prove to be horribly embarrassing pictures for a southerner: shots of slaves being auctioned on the block and cruel overseers walking about with whips. As the "Battle Hymn" commences, the Lincoln Monument appears on the screen, followed by stagy movie footage of the Civil War. "Good night!" exclaims Elvis. "Maybe I oughta get a pointer and . . . 'Next, class, we have . . .' " Finally, somebody orders the screen hauled up again, and the number ends to confused applause and laughter.

By the time Elvis comes offstage, he is ready to kill. Brushing past everyone in the wings and charging down the stairs to the dressing room, he sends a string of curses sailing after him that alarms the Guys. No one can calm him, no one can console him. Only the timely appearance of Dr. Nichopolous, bringing balm for the star's wounds, can soothe the raging Elvis. That night there is no party, no receiving of congratulations from celebrity guests, no hanging out with the Guys. Elvis goes back to his room to sulk and brood and vow that never again will he play "this fuck'n Vegas!"

About six in the morning, aroused by a subtle, unconscious prompting, Linda awakes and rolls over in bed to check on Elvis. Instantly, she realizes that something is wrong. His breath is coming with unnatural slowness and with long, rasping, rattling noises that make him sound like a man who is drowning. Putting her hand on his face, she is shocked to feel that it is ice cold. Switching on the bed lamp, she sees immediately that he is unwell because his skin, always pale, has now an ashen, deadly hue.

"Elvis! Honey! Wake up!" she urges, eager to assure herself that this is nothing serious. Elvis replies only with another of his long, gagging breaths, which seem to come only with great effort and at long intervals. "Elvis!" she snaps with alarm. *"Wake up!"* He makes no response at all. Now, she steels herself to do something that she detests but which she knows she must do. She slaps Elvis's face smartly with her open hand. He just lies there as if she had never touched him.

Now, Linda is terrified. She picks up the phone and dials Joe's room. Joe comes on the wire groggy and thick-voiced. The instant he gets the message, his voice changes. "Hold on," he barks. "I'm calling Nick, and I'll be up there myself in a minute."

Joe and the doctor arrive at practically the same moment. Dr. Nicho-polous is wearing an undershirt and slacks. In his hand is a black medical bag. He takes one look at Elvis and asks Linda to leave the room. Then, he and Joe go to work.

"Well, Marcus Welby," cracks Joe, "why don't you give him a shot? What are you waiting for?"

Nick, who has been holding Elvis's pulse and is now listening to his heart with a stethoscope, looks up with an expression of melancholy resignation imprinted on his face. "Sometimes it's not as easy as you think," he sighs. "Here, help me get him into that chair."

Chapter 3

Redneck Roots

THE TENNESSEE hills are not designated as such on any map. The phrase is a local appellation used by the folk of several counties in the northeast corner of Mississippi for the subsiding southwestern margin of the Appalachians. Forming a strong natural barrier to the flow of people from east to west, these mountains captured many migrant settlers, who found in isolated valleys or upland meadows the promise of security, privacy and sustenance enough to maintain life. So detached from the world did these people become that eventually they appeared like survivors from a much earlier age. A race of Rip Van Winkles, when they awoke in the twentieth century they discovered that the world had long since forgotten their folkways, which derived from the seventeenth century. Mountain men, hillbillies, they constituted a distinctive breed of southern yeomanry, closely related to their cousins in the hills of the Carolinas. In Mississippi, especially, they were an odd lot because they represented the state's least characteristic area, a spur of piedmont stuck in the flank of a region of rolling black prairies or table-flat delta lands or hot coastal plains taking the sluggish wash of the Gulf of Mexico.

To the northerner cooped up in his immense cities and prey to strange fancies about the "real America," people like these hill folk are synonymous with the great modern dream of "roots." They are imagined as holding fast to their turf like European peasants, who in some instances have occupied the same spot of ground for nine hundred years. As for the hillbillies, nothing could be further from the truth. A more deracinated and restless race could not be imagined. Though some of them maintained the same regional ambit through a number of generations, typically they moved every year. Migrant farm laborers or share-croppers, with no real stake in the soil, they were seekers after better situations. As there are rarely any better situations for people incapable of standing still and improving their own lot, the hill folk wandered endlessly without ever finding anyplace where they could strike roots and settle down permanently.

Just as the hillbillies had no real awareness of the present, they had no grasp on the past. As Lord Raglan demonstrated in a classic argument, history is almost entirely a function of literacy. Given a population that cannot read or write, history becomes myth. Though the folk may live like fossils of a distant past, they have no recollection of that past, even when it bears on their nearest blood relations. When an interviewer in 1956 told Vernon Presley that he bore an old English name, he replied with honest surprise: "I never heard tell of any of my kinfolk coming over from anywhere." Then, reflecting further, he allowed: "I guess it must have been a long way back. We just seem always to have been here. And it's the same with Gladys's family, the Smiths."

Elvis Presley, a lot better educated than his nearly illiterate father, never had the vaguest idea of who his people were until just before he died. Then, he received from a genealogical research organization in Salt Lake City an elaborate family tree, which traced the Presleys back nine generations to the "emigrant," the first man of the line who came to America. He proved, not surprisingly, to be an Anglo-Irishman, named David Pressley.[1] Nothing is really known of this man or his son, Andrew Pressley, Senior, except that they landed, apparently, at New Bern, North Carolina, in the 1740s and were soon granted extensive tracts of probably quite worthless lands along the Rocky River, then the boundary between the Carolinas. It is not until we reach the third generation of the family in this country that we get a little flash of individual identity around the figure of Andrew Pressley, Junior.

---

[1] Because Elvis's ancestors were illiterate, there was no settled spelling for their name, but the traditional spelling, "Pressley," conveys the correct pronunciation, whereas "Presley" leads to the common error of pronouncing the name "Prezley."

Assuming that Andrew wasn't lying when he turned up in front of a pension board many years after the Revolutionary War and claimed to have served two hitches as a "summer soldier"; assuming further that on his second hitch this blacksmith from Rowan County, North Carolina, remained with the other 150 militiamen in his battalion, who were stationed in the center of the front rank at the Battle of Eutah Springs, South Carolina, the last major engagement of the War of Independence fought in the South: assuming all this and accepting his sworn testimony that "he received several [musket] balls through his garments," it would follow that Andrew Pressley, Junior, was a minor American hero. For of one thing we can be sure: His volunteer unit fought with great bravery on that hot morning in the year 1781.

After skirmishing up a dirt road through a piney wood near the Santee River, the militiamen burst onto an eight-acre farm clearing and saw drawn up before them, ready for battle, two thousand Redcoats. Instead of hugging the cover of the woods, the militia made straight for the British. "It was with equal astonishment," wrote an eyewitness after the battle, "that both sides contemplated these men steadily and without faltering, advance with shouts and exhortations into the hottest of the enemy fire, unaffected by the continual fall of their comrades around them." The militia were overwhelmed eventually by a British bayonet charge; but they had won the first honors of the day, which concluded with the English retreating on Charleston, from which they never again emerged until the war's end.

When the skimpy documents of those early times allow us next a glimpse of Elvis's ancestors, we discover not a patriot or hero but a coward, deserter and a bigamist. In 1861, Dunnan Pressley, Junior, married Martha Jane Wesson at Fulton, Mississippi, the seat of Itawamba County. This district in the northeast corner of the state had been opened to settlement in 1832 by a treaty with the Indians, the Chickasaw Cession. Dunnan was drawn to the region, most likely, as were many other veterans of the Mexican war, by the search for cheap land. In those days, the going price for an acre of richly timbered soil was twenty-five cents. To a poor settler, children were another vital resource. Dunnan produced two children with his new wife in quick succession: Rosalinda and Rosella. The latter, born in 1862, was Elvis Presley's great-grandmother.

Just a couple of months before Gettysburg, in 1863, Dunnan returned to the wars, enlisting in Ham's Regiment of Mississippi Cavalry. No longer the naive young Tennessee volunteer he has been in the Mexican War, Dunnan was intent this time on fraud. Obtaining the rank of corporal and a three-hundred-dollar bounty for his horse, he no sooner joined his unit than he was listed on its rolls as a deserter. Then, a couple of months later, he joined and deserted Davenport's Battalion in precisely the same manner, taking the bounty and then taking French leave. Now, having twice deserted the cause for which he had sworn to fight, he rounded off the job of shucking his responsibilities by abandoning his wife and infant daughters.

The manner of Dunnan's departure was preserved for over a century in the memories of his descendants. His granddaughter, Mrs. Robie Stacy, recalled in 1977: "My mother told me that when she and her sister were just little babies, their grandparents had taken them to church one Sunday and when they came back, their father, Dunnan, was gone. He went back to his other wife and child."

Dunnan drifted west in his declining years through Arkansas to Missouri, where he died in 1900, petitioning to the end for an increase of his soldier's pension because of incapacitation owing to: "irsepulas and rheamtism weak eyes and dafness in the right ear and gravil or disease of the kidness." Meantime, his abandoned daughter, Rosella, grew to be a very strange and mysterious woman. Commencing at the age of nineteen and continuing over a period of twenty-eight years, she bore at least nine illegitimate children. Never once did she identify her lover or make any claim on him—or them.

Rosella supported her brood by working as a wandering farmhand. Her life can be viewed as a sustained act of protest against her mother's fate. Instead of marrying and risking the pain and humiliation of abandonment, she never married. Yet she did not relinquish the primary role of woman in her world; indeed, she sustained it more fully than many and entirely through her own resources. She found her compensation, however, in never having to share her children's love with any man, even to the slight extent of permitting her children to imagine their absent and unknown father. On this last point, she was firm as a rock: "I can't remember anyone ever talking about who our father was," recalls Mrs. Doshia Steele, one of the surviving daughters of Rosella, in 1980 a tiny little woman of ninety-three, who lives to this day not far from her mother's last home on the old McDaniel Farm near Fulton. "It was a big mystery when we were children. My mother just didn't talk about it."

Like the Pressleys, Gladys's family, the Smiths, originated in the Carolinas and moved westward over a span of several generations. Elvis's great-great-grandfather, John Smith, is listed in the census of Atlanta in 1850. In 1874, his son, Obe Smith, married a widow from Alabama, Ann Mansel, and established the family in northeastern Mississippi in the area of Saltillo, just north of Tupelo. The second-born of this union was Robert Lee Smith, Elvis's grandfather. "Bob" Lee's marriage to Octavia Lavinia "Doll" Mansell was perhaps the most significant alliance in Elvis's genealogy, for there is strong reason to believe that husband and wife were first cousins, a potentially dangerous mating combination. Genetics may explain why the children of Bob Lee's brothers and sisters turned out well, whereas Bob and Doll produced children who exhibited an abnormally high incidence of addiction to drugs and alcohol, emotional disorders and premature death. Particularly was this true of the male side of the family.

Consider Gladys Smith's three brothers: Tracy was born deaf and dumb; Travis died in his thirties; Johnny died at the age of forty-six (as did Gladys). Both Travis and Johnny were heavy drinkers and danger- ously violent when drunk, given to brandishing knives and guns. This same pattern is just as clearly marked in the next generation. Four men carried the name Smith in this group: Junior and Gene, the children of Lavelle Smith; and Bobby and Billy, the sons of Travis Smith. The oldest boy in each of these families came to an early and violent death: Junior died of a convulsion before he was thirty, after a life darkened by homicidal madness; Bobby committed suicide a few years later by swallowing arsenic. Finally one comes to Elvis, whom we see now as possibly the victim of a fatal hereditary disposition.

No emotional blight affected Bob Smith; he was a merry man, and his daughter, Gladys, resembled in youth her frolicsome father. Though Gladys sank deep into depression in later years, her basic disposition was always fun-loving, even a little manic, like that of her famous son. "She laughed and joked all the time. Jolly—just as jolly as could be," recalls Gladys's cousin, Mrs. Mary Lyons, who knew Gladys in her teens. "She wanted everybody to be happy, everybody to be enjoying themselves. Dancing—she was always skipping around trying to dance. When she was in the house, she'd be apunching one of us in the ribs." All of this sounds exactly like Elvis.

When Gladys was nineteen or twenty, her father, who had already gone blind, began to fail. The family decided to change its survival strat- egy. In the past, they had been sharecroppers and migrant workers. "If a place didn't suit," recollects Truitt Smith, another cousin, "they'd move on. Generally, it didn't suit." Now, they decided to take advantage of the development of the garment industry at Tupelo, which had become during the early thirties one of the model towns of the "New South," that melding of the agricultural and the industrial so strongly supported by the New Deal.

The Smiths took a house in East Tupelo so that the unmarried girls in the family would have easy access to work. Gladys obtained employment at the Tupelo Garment Company, working twelve hours a day, five or six days a week. It was piecework, stitching shirts together at a sewing machine. An efficient operator could earn thirteen dollars a week, which was considerably more than the wages of an agricultural laborer.

East Tupelo in the early thirties consisted of a score of dingy white frame bungalows arranged on a grid of muddy rock roads where the old Saltillo Road leads north off the highway from Birmingham to Tupelo. Situated where the last foothill melts into the plain, the hamlet looks out across a broad and swampy bottom, threaded by the Mud River and crossed by the highway levee, to the city of Tupelo, with which at the time it had no affiliation.

East Tupelo was full of Pressleys: so many, in fact, that at one time twenty-six children at the local school bore the name. Jessie Pressley, Elvis's grandfather, had come first, followed by his brothers, Noah and Calhoun. Jessie had quit school at eleven to go to work. In 1913, at the age of seventeen, he married Minnie Mae Hood, a tall, homely girl from a solid local family. At first, they farmed for shares some land in Clay Community, just west of Fulton. It was here that their two boys, Vester and Vernon, were born. When the owner of their farm sold the land after the war, the Pressleys moved to East Tupelo. Now the family was enlarged by the birth of three daughters: Delta Mae, Gladys Earlene and Nashville Lorene. By this time, Minnie Mae had come to hate her young husband.

Jessie was actually a very likable fellow; his problem was that, like his famous grandson, he was not the sort of man who should have married. His younger brother, Calhoun, once offered a good characterization of Jessie:

> For most of his life Jessie drifted from one job to another all over Mississippi, Kentucky, Missouri. He was a sharecropper in the summer and a lumberjack in the winter. Jessie worked hard and played hard. He was an honest man, but he enjoyed drinking whiskey and was often involved in drunken bar brawls. As a result, Jessie spent many a night sobering up in jail.
>
> He was a slim, handsome man about six feet tall with black

hair. I reckon Elvis inherited his looks from Jessie. He was also a dapper dresser. Clothes were one of the most important things in his life. We used to call him "the lawyer" because he dressed so smart. He loved fine clothes. His favorite suit was a tailor-made brown one with pearl buttons. He saved up for months until he had enough money to buy it—twenty-four dollars. He paraded around town like a peacock, with his head in the air and a cane in his hand. Owning expensive clothes was his only ambition in life. He hated poverty and he didn't want people to know he was poor. He felt that if he wore a tailor-made suit, people would look up to him.

Calhoun Pressley makes it appear that Jessie's penchant for fine clothes and drink were just idiosyncrasies that affected him alone. In fact, they caused his family great suffering. The family sometimes went without food because Jessie had squandered on drink the money they needed to subsist. When he went far afield in search of work, months would elapse without any word from him or any remittance. The effect this waywardness had on his children is not hard to imagine. Vester and Vernon received virtually no education. At the age of forty, Vernon could barely sign his name.

When Gladys met Vernon, she was already a woman: twenty years of age, making a good living and very much in command of her life. She was attractive, almost pretty, with dark hair parted at the side and pulled tight around her head, and large dark eyes under strong brows with a shadowy tint to the surrounding skin. This distinctive dark coloring Gladys got from her mother, Doll, who had a dusky complexion. Vernon, on the other hand, was very blond, with the distinctive features of the Presley men: the long muscular neck, the bony hard face, the keen little eyes—the Grant Wood American Gothic look. Just a typical country younker at sixteen, Vernon must have fallen at once under the sway of Gladys, who was not only older but a much stronger personality. Gladys was a worker; Vernon was a shirker. Gladys was an ebullient extrovert; Vernon was always uptight and distrustful. Most important, Gladys possessed some intelligence and imagination; whereas Vernon was always a dullard and a donkey, a boy destined to spend a lifetime trying to become a man.

Their marriage, everyone agrees, was a love match. It was also, most likely, a somewhat impulsive act. "We should have been in school, but we eloped," Gladys told a reporter in 1956. "We didn't elope very far,"

added Vernon. "We just went down the road to Verona and got married."
In fact, they were not married in Verona, which is five miles south of
Tupelo in Lee County, but in Pontotoc, which is twenty miles west of
Tupelo in Pontotoc County, the area in which Gladys was born. Embarrassed, evidently by the disparity in their ages, they falsified the figures
on the marriage license. She claimed to be nineteen, though she was
twenty-one; he added five years to his age, claiming to be twenty-two.
Having achieved what they regarded as a proper balance of ages, they
became man and wife on June 17, 1933.

Vernon and Gladys moved in at first with the Jessie Pressleys. Vernon
was working for a well-known dairy farmer and cattle and hog broker
named Orville S. Bean. Bean made a business of loaning money to people
to build their own houses, the houses becoming his property until he
had received his principal and interest through monthly rent payments.
When Gladys became pregnant in the spring of 1934, Vernon took a
$180 loan from Bean and, with the aid of his father and brother, built
a two-room cabin on a lot owned by his father next door to the Presley
house on North Saltillo Road. This is the famous "birthplace" and an
eloquent example of the transfiguring power of the Presley Myth.

The house which attracts as many as a million visitors a year bears
today a totally different aspect than it did when Elvis Presley was born.
The local ladies who are the keepers of this shrine were horrified by
the shanty's original appearance and took great pains to transform it
into the cute little doll house which it should have been according to
the Myth. They painted the bare grey boards gleaming white. They papered the rough wooden walls with primrose-patterned wallpaper. They
hung dimity curtains at the windows. They filled the cramped interior
with a clutter of objects which the Presleys never had the money to
purchase: a sewing machine, a baby's high chair, solid pieces of furniture
and electric appliances, such as a fan and a radio. Then, they hung a
swing on the tiny front porch and landscaped the grounds. When they
were finished with their foolish labors, they had effected the typical substitution of fantasy for history that is the essence of Elvis Presley's story.

Chapter 4

The Little Family

LONG BEFORE Gladys came to term, she became convinced that she was carrying twins. So strong was her belief that she and Vernon chose names for the unborn children, whom she was likewise sure would both be boys. The boys' first names were taken from the male side of the family: "Jessie" was chosen in honor of Vernon's father; "Elvis" was a tribute to Vernon, being his middle name. The twins' middle names were selected with great care to make them rhyme both to the ear and the eye, thus proclaiming Gladys's ultimate intuition: that these babies would be not merely fraternal but *identical* twins.

To attain the mirror effect she was seeking, she distorted the spelling of the twins' names, either deliberately or inadvertently through ignorance: "Elvis Aron" was spelled with a single "a" and "Jessie Garon" with an "o" instead of the customary "i." Further signs of ingenuity are the equivalent number of syllables in each name and the balance struck by matching one Old Testament name, Jessie or Aron, with one ancient English name, Elvis or Garon. The final twist in the name knot attached the boys to their father by giving them all one name that rhymed: viz., Aron, Garon, Vernon. It was not, however, the connection with the father but the link with the other twin that was paramount. Gladys wanted

61

to assure that throughout his entire future life Elvis Aron, for example, could never hear, speak or read his own name, without hearing in his mind its faint chiming echo—Jessie Garon.

All these loving refinements in the selection and adjustment of names for identical twins who exist only in the imagination of an expectant mother attest to an extraordinarily high degree of prenatal fantasy. Though events were to confirm Gladys's prediction to a surprising degree, they could just as well have turned out otherwise. By anticipating the future not only so vividly but so extravagantly and with such complete disregard for probability, Gladys declared herself a woman impatient with reality and prone to paint over the ordinary face of things with fantastical forms and colors reflecting her own hopes and fears. This turn of mind was highly characteristic of all three members of the little family.

Elvis, for example, got the idea in later years, when he was absorbed in the study of the occult, that he might be a divinely appointed Master, Messenger or Messiah, put on earth to perform some momentous mission. Nothing could dissuade him from this belief and everything that he observed about himself, whether it were a little crease on his palm in the shape of a cross or a fancied likeness between his face and the image in a religious painting, confirmed him in his conviction that he was the "One." Significantly, it was in the circumstances of his birth that he found the strongest confirmation of his divine calling.

Vernon confided to Elvis that he had known the exact moment of his son's conception because at that instant he had blacked out. Though there were other, more rational, ways of interpreting this momentary loss of consciousness, Elvis insisted on seeing it in terms of his grand obsession. It was a clear sign, he argued, that at the critical moment, his father's body had become the vehicle for a higher being. Thus, like the heroes of mythology, Elvis came to believe that the man he called "Daddy" was no more his father than was Joseph the father of Jesus. Further confirmation of this weird notion was the story Vernon told of going out into the backyard on the night of the birth and being astonished to see the heavens ringed around with a blue light. This recollection thrilled Elvis because blue was a color he had long identified with himself and to which he attributed supernatural significance.

As these few examples suggest, the Presleys are not sober witnesses to their own history. Time and again they twisted the anticipation or recollection of events into the gratifying forms of wish fulfillment. This is the first reason why the Presley Myth is so unsound as biography.

The second, more important, reason is the eagerness with which people everywhere translate the quirky squiggle of real happenings into the smooth, regular patterns of mythology. Myth, after all, is what we believe naturally. History is what we must painfully learn and struggle to remember. The conflict of myth and history is particularly evident in the story of Elvis's birth.

According to the Myth, Elvis Presley was the first born of identical twins (the mythic hero is always the first child), the second twin being dead upon birth. It is highly characteristic of the mentality of Elvis Presley's millions of fans and numerous hagiographers that none of them ever thought to verify this story by seeking out the appropriate records. Not until 1980 was the truth about Elvis's birth revealed, when Mrs. Sara Potter, the daughter of the attending physician, Dr. William Robert Hunt, discovered an entry in her father's record books that set the matter in a true light.

Dr. Hunt was an old-time country physician who maintained an office over Riley's Jewelry Store on Tupelo's Main Street. By the time he retired in the fifties, he had supervised the birth of 1,854 babies. This figure is significant because it suggests the doctor's penchant for careful bookkeeping. For every year of his practice, going back to his first year, 1913, the doctor kept a "baby book" in which he entered the circumstances of each "labor case." Thanks to the baby book for 1935, we know now the basic facts of Elvis's birth, facts of which Elvis himself remained ignorant throughout his life, he having been one of the first of those millions who have been deceived by Gladys's and Vernon's curious propensity for making unaccountable alterations in their family history.

On the night of January 7–8, a bitterly cold night in northern Mississippi, Dr. Hunt attended Gladys Presley at home. Most likely, he was seeing her for the first time. He noted in his book that at 4:00 A.M. Mrs. Presley was delivered of a stillborn son. Then, at 4:35, she had a second delivery, another son, who survived. On the birth certificate, he spelled the surviving baby's name "Evis Aaron," which is undoubtedly the way it was pronounced. He noted that the father was a white, eighteen-year-old laborer. In his baby book, he recorded that the family was unable to pay the fifteen-dollar fee, but that he collected the money eventually from "welfare." Thus was born the King.

According to the Presley Myth, Gladys's prediction was fulfilled: The two boys to whom she gave birth were identical twins. As will soon be obvious, this idea had enormous importance in Elvis's life. Yet, can it be regarded as a fact? Elvis claimed that he bore the sign of an identical twin visibly on his body in the form of an odd webbing which stretched between the second and third toes of his right foot. Needless to say, such an anomaly indicates nothing about twinship, the idea being simply an old Negro superstition. Actually, there is no evidence whatsoever that Elvis's twin was an identical sibling. The random odds are three to one against such an occurrence, and the only way of determining the fact in infancy is through laboratory tests.

These rational considerations were, of course, very remote from the mental world of the Presleys. Once Gladys's hunch that she was carrying twins was confirmed by the event, it would have taken a lot more than scientific argument to persuade her that she was mistaken in her insistence that the twins were identical. The conviction that preceded the birth persisted after the birth to give rise to many other unfounded ideas. Gladys was not simply ignorant: She was highly superstitious, a hillbilly Cassandra, given to prophetic dreams and weird intuitions, quick to identify chance happenings as signs and omens—all traits of mind which she imparted to her son. What were the mental constructions that she built upon the death of the twin?

We know that she grieved profoundly for Jessie Garon. He was laid out in a tiny coffin in the living room and buried in an unmarked grave in nearby Princeville Cemetery. His death cast a deep shadow over the birth of Elvis, who, psychologically speaking, was born under a bad sign. The birth, which had been anticipated as a welcome access of life, double life at that, produced in fact a double death: Not only did Jessie Garon perish but Gladys was informed by the doctor—or concluded herself—that she could never again bear children. Perhaps this is why her grief for the lost twin proved to be an affliction without a term. Soon, she had transformed the dead infant into a spooky presence about the house.

One of the first things that Elvis Presley learned at his mother's knee was that he had a dead brother identical to him in every respect. He heard his mother talk about this brother constantly, invoking him by name, just as if Jessie Garon had once enjoyed the life that Elvis was leading now. His mother told him that the personality of the dead twin was transferred to the living twin, thus planting in his mind the notion of metempsychosis, which blossomed years later in the conviction that he was a reembodied Master who had lived in ancient times. She also taught him that Jessie Garon was an angel up in heaven with whom Elvis could commune through prayer. Often mother and son went to the cemetery to visit the dead Jessie's grave. At the age of four or five, Elvis began to hear his brother's voice, enjoining him to do good deeds and lead a good life. In fine, as Elvis grew up, he had beside him always a phantom double, a secret sharer, a veritable *Doppelgänger*. This spirit brother is one of the most important characters in the life of Elvis Presley, for from adolescence onward, Elvis exhibited with increasing clarity all the signs of a split personality. His behavior patterned itself into two sharply opposed selves, which embodied two radically different fantasy systems, one inspired by an extravagant notion of goodness, the other by a no less exaggerated idea of evil. Every feature of Elvis's subsequent life and career bears the unmistakable stamp of this dichotomy.

As a child Elvis aspired to be a saint on earth. At the age of nine, for example, he received the baptism of the spirit, a sacrament of the Pentecostal church. This occasion filled him so with the spirit of Christian charity that he took his only possessions, a handful of comic books, and gave them away to the neighbor children. Subsequently, his parents bought him a tricycle, a costly gift for people so poor. Elvis gave the tricycle away not once but several times, until finally his parents were compelled to allow the gift to stand. Nothing was more basic to Elvis Presley, therefore, than a passionate desire to be good and do good. One can see this impulse asserting itself with increasing urgency all through his life up to the very end. On the other hand, this yearning to be a living saint was countered by an equally powerful compulsion which drove him in the opposite direction and made him often a diabolic figure: not just a man who does wrong but who seduces others into the path of sin and relishes their fall. This Bad Elvis also gained in power as the years passed and often threatened dire deeds, which were averted often only at the last moment by the intervention of other people or by the awakening of Elvis's better self.

Two years after Elvis was born, Gladys witnessed the lingering death of her mother from tuberculosis. Doll was laid to rest beside her husband in an unmarked grave in the pastoral cemetery beside the little frame church at Springhill, not far from Saltillo. Gladys, once so cheerful and ebullient, so eager to dance and make others dance, was being clouded over by repeated sorrows. First, the death of her father, then the death of Jessie Garon, now the death of her mother: one misfortune piled atop the other. One worse thing was shortly to befall her and complete the revolution in her personality. She was to see her handsome young husband, the sole support of herself and Elvis, taken off to prison.

No one at this late date recalls distinctly the details of the crime.

Vernon, Travis Smith (Gladys's twenty-three-year-old brother) and a certain Lether Gable were charged with forging a check on Orville S. Bean. Evidently, it was a check made out to Vernon by his employer for a small sum: say, eighteen dollars. Vernon and his friends conceived the crazy notion of altering the figure on the check so that it read, say, twenty-eight dollars. Nobody can explain why these young men acted in this manner or how they hoped to escape detection. All that can be recollected is that the sum was very small.

An accusation was lodged, and the evidence was laid before a grand jury. On November 17, 1937, the *Tupelo Journal* reported that "three men, Travis Smith, Luther [*sic*] Gable and Vernon Pressley [were] indicted for forgery and placed under bonds of $500." Initially, all three entered pleas of not guilty. Then, in the time between the indictment and the trial, intensive efforts were made by the families of the young men to persuade Orville Bean to withdraw his charges. Noah Presley, who was a close friend of Bean, offered twice the amount of the money that had been stolen. Bean proved vindictive. He was determined to prosecute the men to the limits of the law. The offense was a felony. Despite the smallness of the sum, the penalty was severe.

When the circuit court met for its May session, the case of the three young men appeared on the docket. Their choice was to stand trial, with conviction virtually assured and a harsh sentence in prospect, or to change their plea to guilty and throw themselves on the mercy of the court. The final disposition of the case appears in the minutes for the ninth day of the sitting, May 25, 1938, when, in a brief interruption of the proceedings, the presiding judge, Thomas J. Johnston, announced the sentences for all those cases that had been concluded. Under docket number 9756, "State *vs.* Travis Smith, Lether Gable and Vernon Presley," the following notice appears:

"Plea of not guilty entered on a former day this day withdrawn and Defendants at this time issue a plea of guilty to a charge of forgery; upon such plea it is ORDERED AND ADJUDGED by the Court that the defendants for their said offense be and each is hereby sentenced to serve a term of three (3) years in the State penitentiary, and they are hereby remanded to the custody of the sheriff for safekeeping in the county jail until called for by the proper officer or agent for transportation and delivery to said institution."

"Said institution" meant only one thing: *Parchman.* A dread name. A name that cries the blues. An American concentration camp pitched in the heart of the Mississippi Delta. Parchman meant laboring from sunup to sundown six days a week under the searing Delta sun. Parchman meant the "long lines": rows of men in blue-and-white striped pajamas, laboring along the cotton furrows or in the chain gangs beside the highways under the shotgun of a trustee mounted on a horse. Parchman meant that if a man did not deliver his two hundred pounds of cotton a day, or if he were guilty of some other offense, he would be disciplined with "Black Annie," an eight-foot leather belt that was laid across the prisoner's back under the stern eye of the warden.

When the sheriff's van drove Vernon Presley and his mates down the legendary Highway 61 in the first week of June 1938, the cotton couldn't have been more than six inches high. Cotton was the soul of the Delta and the real reason for Parchman. Cotton demanded the kind and quantity of labor once supplied by African slave gangs. When the slaves were freed, some shrewd old men in Jackson decided to replace them with prisoners. Thus Parchman became one of the greatest plantations in the South: twenty thousand acres in extent, at some points thirty-five miles across. One half of the land was planted in cotton; one half in corn, cane and all the garden crops necessary for the sustenance of two thousand inmates. Almost totally self-sufficient, the prison colony was farmed under the supervision of a local planter at a handsome profit for nearly half a century.

Eighty percent of Parchman's population was black, which meant eight of the ten camps were black. First offenders were supposed to be kept apart from hardened criminals, but this ideal could not always be realized. Just four years before Vernon's incarceration, as the result of an extensive reform of the penal statute, a medical staff had been added to the prison, which hitherto had had none. There was also a recreation officer and a camp musician—none other than the famous blues singer, Bukka White. His crime? Murder. Place of arrest? A recording studio in Chicago. In May 1939, White was recorded at Parchman by Alan Lomax. His song had a certain grim appropriateness: It was titled "Sic 'Em Dogs on Down."

How long Vernon served is open to question. The last five months of his three-year sentence were commuted by the governor, probably for good behavior. His official date of discharge was January 4, 1941. No sooner did he plead guilty than Orville Bean turned mother and child out of their house. They moved next door with Vernon's parents, and Gladys went to work as a seamstress and laundress. By the time Vernon was released, the whole economy of the country was being transformed by the war boom. Vernon told the compiler of a "fanzine" in

1956 that he spent the war years working in a defense plant in Memphis, returning home only on weekends. (As a felon he was draft-exempt.) His prolonged absence had a profound effect on Elvis's development.

Nearly always alone with his mother from the age of thirty months to eleven years, Elvis became a classic mama's boy. Neighbors and relatives of the Presleys recall distinctly the details of Gladys's behavior with Elvis: how she "worshipped" the child; how she never let him out of her sight; how she escorted him to school and back every day; how she would panic and start shouting if she couldn't find him; how she forbade him to go swimming or do anything that might possibly endanger him; how she would attack any child with whom Elvis got into a fight.

The most suggestive feature of the relationship of mother and son is their extreme physical intimacy. Elvis slept in the same bed with Gladys until he was at the threshold of puberty. His most characteristic gesture of affection for his mother was petting her, particularly on a lump of flesh that rose at the base of her neck atop the spine. His nickname for his mother was also suggestive of years of childish petting and patting: He called Gladys, "Satnin'." This name, like all the affectionate terms in which mother and son conversed, was a treasured relic of Elvis's baby prattle. Other such words were "sooties" for "footies" and "Butch" for "milch." So elaborate and private did this affectional language grow that in later years strangers watching Elvis "petting on" his mother and communing with her in baby talk got the impression that mother and son "spoke the secret language of some weird religious cult."

Constantly in his mother's company, Elvis was no less constantly urged to open his mind and reveal to his mother all his thoughts and feelings. So accustomed did Elvis grow to sharing his inner life with his mother, so dependent did he become on her judgment and advice, that in later years he thought nothing of waking her up in the middle of the night if he had some problem on his mind which kept him awake. There can be no question that the extraordinary introversion that characterizes Elvis throughout his adult life, his extreme reluctance to confide in anyone or reveal his inner thoughts, is explainable by the fact that he believed there was only one person in the world who could understand and guide him. When he lost his mother, he closed up like a clam.

Another way in which the bonds between mother and son were strengthened was through the pampering and coddling which characterized the relationship. Though the Presleys were desperately poor when Elvis was a child, money was found to buy him expensive gifts, like a bicycle or a guitar. Elvis was stuffed with scarce food and even provided with silver table utensils, like a little prince. He was a lonely little prince, however. One of the most important features of his upbringing was the fact that he was kept apart from his relatives, from the local children and from the world in general. In effect, he was reared to be a recluse.

Though too little evidence of Gladys's character has been preserved to allow one to speak with confidence of her inner being, there were many reasons for her to prolong and intensify her relationship with Elvis far beyond what is normal for mother and child. The principal reason was that she had no other person to love. Her mother and father were dead; toward her sisters and brothers she displayed an ambivalent attitude. Indeed, so detached did Gladys become from her kin that people said in later years that she had been reared as an orphan. Vernon had proven himself an ineffectual boy-man rather than a capable husband and father. At the critical moment in the marriage, he had made a foolish and fateful error, which shifted the entire responsibility for caring for Elvis onto Gladys's shoulders. So Gladys concentrated all her love on her son.

Vernon's habitual absences did not serve to make his presence at home any more welcome. Quite the contrary: Vernon had a highly disturbing effect on Elvis. In later years, Vernon recalled that every time he did something against which Elvis had been warned by Gladys, the child would exhibit the most extreme anxiety. "When we went swimming," Vernon chuckled, "Elvis would have fits if he saw me dive. He was so afraid something would happen to me." Fires were commonplace among the wooden shanties of East Tupelo. Gladys recounted Elvis's behavior when he saw his father running in and out of a house trying to save the furniture: "Elvis was so sure his daddy was going to get hurt that he screamed and cried. I had to hold him to keep him from running in after Vernon. So I said sharp, 'Elvis, you just stop that. He's all right. Your daddy knows what he's doing.' He quieted right down." (You can bet he did when he heard his mother's masterful voice.) These stories show the child's keen fear of death and his terror at the prospect of his father's death, an eventuality that had been given an especial reality by Vernon's imprisonment and long absences.

Elvis's apprehensiveness about Vernon is mirrored by Vernon's fears for Elvis. The story most frequently repeated among Presley intimates concerns the night that Vernon awoke from a nightmare convinced that his own house was afire. Without a moment's hesitation, he scooped up Elvis and tried to throw him out the window. You couldn't find a clearer projection of how many an adoring father feels unconsciously about the intrusive presence of his infant son. After all, before Elvis came along, the immature Vernon was Gladys's baby.

According to the Myth, the Presleys were a deeply religious family. They attended a little country church, where they sang often as a trio: mother, father and tiny son. It was a church of the First Assembly of God, a fundamentalist church, a Pentecostal church; hence, a church of the most earthy and impassioned religious expression, where Negro hymn singing alternated with outbursts of speaking in tongues and dancing in the spirit. Here, Elvis first imbibed the deep soul of the South. Here, he witnessed revival meetings that implanted forever in his mind the image of that charismatic stage figure, the itinerant preacher: part minister, part entertainer; part saint, part demoniac. Here, more than anywhere, Elvis was shaped by the profound forces that eventually burst out again on the vast stage of the Rock Age. So teaches the Myth.

Imagine, having heard this gospel for a quarter of a century, how it must feel to pick up a phone one day in New York City and call a number in Verona, Mississippi, which is answered by a youthful-sounding voice: that of the Reverend W. Frank Smith, who became minister of the First Assembly of God Church in East Tupelo in the year 1944. Reverend Smith, being a real preacher and not the figment of some rock writer's imagination, is quite astounded at the reputation of his church and its service, as well as by the reputed behavior of those once-familiar members of his congregation, the Vernon Presleys. He remembers them and that time quite clearly. Indeed, his life having had a firm consistency, leading him today in much the same paths as when he took up his ministry, he recollects that early time with ease. To sum up his testimony, he scorns the Myth as a lie. He contradicts it down to the finest detail. He cannot imagine how such preposterous notions were ever believed by anyone.

The legendary church was not some country tabernacle, with peaked roof, tiny steeple and tall pointy windows. It was simply a one-story house, no different in kind from any other in that community of four-room bungalows. The congregation comprised about twenty-five members. The service began at eleven and lasted for an hour. The congregation, standing in its places and clapping time, would sing such familiar hymns as "Fly Away" or "I'll Be at the Roll Call Up Yonder." These hymns would be accompanied by the piano, and Reverend Smith made it a practice to bring his guitar and strum along with the singing.

The services were always decorous. Though the members were free to shout "Amen!" or "Praise God!" there was no speaking in tongues or overtly emotional behavior. Reverend Smith preached always the message of Jesus. He might grow heated in his tone, but he does not consider himself a demonstrative preacher. He would remain close to his pulpit and employ only the conventional gestures of emphasis. Traveling evangelists would appear sometimes at the church, but they were never of the extravagant, spellbinding variety. Nothing they did could be characterized as dancing or "cutting up." Once a month, there would be a testimony service. Several members of the congregation would get up and make little avowals. A member might say: "Well, I wanna thank the Lord for savin' *me*. And bringin' *me* to the church."

Reverend Smith does not recollect that the Presleys ever distinguished themselves in any way by their singing, either individually or by performing as a family trio. There were people in the congregation who sang solos, but Vernon and Gladys were not among them. Vernon's cousin, Sayles Pressley, was the principal singer. He had organized an amateur gospel quartet and sometimes led the congregation in its hymn singing. The minister recollects teaching Elvis a few guitar runs and noticing that the boy had an instruction book for his instrument. Music was not among the worldly delights banned by the Assembly of God; nonetheless, the church was highly puritanical. The members were forbidden to go to movies or dances, to drink alcohol or smoke tobacco.

During my conversations with the Reverend Smith, he asserted repeatedly that he did not see any source for Elvis's singing or performing style in the practices of the little church in East Tupelo, though he did believe that later, in Memphis, Elvis came under influences, including gospel performers, who might have decisively affected his imagination. But the Elvis Presley known to fame was not shaped in a country church.

Elvis's real inspiration came from the first from the radio. In the forties, powerful transmitters in Nashville and Memphis began to beam all sorts of music into the area of Tupelo. As soon as Elvis obtained access to a receiver, his musical education commenced. The first product of this education was a prize-winning performance, which the boy gave at the age of eleven, singing a song he had learned off the air.

The occasion on which Elvis Presley first got up on a public stage and sang a tune was Children's Day at the annual Mississippi-Alabama Fair and Dairy Show. The song he chose embodied, most likely, his deepest emotions: It was the Red Foley hit, "Old Shep," a very old-fashioned, highly sentimental ballad in which the singer recalls with keen nostalgia a dead pet dog. The melancholy reverie that is the substance of this song strikes one at first as an incongruous theme for an eleven-year-old boy; but when one reflects on Elvis's upbringing, with the ghost of Jessie always at his side, the selection and his success in rendering it makes perfect sense. That day he won second prize. First prize was awarded to six-year-old Becky Harris, who sang a sexy, bluesy number called "Sentimental Journey" that would have been far more appropriate than "Old Shep" to the Elvis Presley known to fame.

In 1946, the Presleys moved into Tupelo and Vernon got a job driving a truck for the wholesale grocery firm of L. P. McCarty. Though Elvis is always associated with Tupelo, he lived in the city less than three years. According to the Myth, these years were spent in a horrid black slum, known by the pungently Dickensian name of Shakerag. Though the ordeal of living in a black slum is something every true fan is supposed to grieve over, at the same time—by the paradox of *felix culpa,* the fortunate fall—this descent to the depths is regarded as the source of Elvis's extraordinary mastery of the black musical idiom, to say nothing of all the jivey dance steps he cut. As always, the Myth is mistaken. Elvis did live in a slum, but it was not the notorious black slum in the northwest quarter of the city; it was on the east side of town, on Commerce Street, where the shopping mall stands today. The family did not remain long at this address; they moved several times, their next house being in Mobile Alley, a narrow lane that ran at right angles to the railroad tracks near the fairgrounds. Finally, they wound up in the northeast quarter, near the slaughterhouse, on North Green Street. All of these neighborhoods were white; all were poor and ugly. They were no worse, however, than living in a two-room shack in East Tupelo. At the time, Vernon was earning $22.50 a week, which was doubtless a lot more than he ever received from the tight-fisted Orville Bean.

No sooner had Elvis won a prize singing a country song than he met a real-life country musician, Tupelo's only native entertainer, Mississippi Slim. Slim (whose real name was Carvel Lee Ausborn) had a kid brother, James, who was in the same class as Elvis at Milham Junior High. In the company of this brother, Elvis began to visit the local radio station, WELO, which was virtually across the street from the house in Mobile Alley. Every Saturday morning Mississippi Slim would broadcast in front of a tiny audience. Watching performers working in radio studios became from this time forth an important feature of Elvis's life. As the radio studio was no different from the recording studio, Elvis was already familiarizing himself as a twelve- or thirteen-year-old boy with what was soon to become one of his two major theaters of creative expression.

Otherwise, Elvis was a classic autodidact. He never studied music. He never sat in with other musicians. His access to clubs and jamming joints was nil. His strange fantasylike approach to performing owed a lot to mere ignorance and inexperience. Apart from his early and rather superficial acquaintance with Mississippi Slim, one would be hard put to name even one other secular musician with whom the young Elvis Presley was acquainted until he had actually begun recording and performing professionally.

In September 1948, the Presleys packed up their few belongings in a decrepit 1937 Plymouth and took off for Memphis. Elvis said in later years that they were broke and that Vernon was hoping to find a job in the big city. The move—made abruptly after the school year had commenced and surrounded subsequently with a cloud of secrecy—suggests some fresh misfortune was about to descend upon the family, which they averted by flight.

The automobile in which they made their escape had a very stiff and balky accelerator. Its operation was generally assigned to Elvis so that his father could concentrate on the driving. So we must picture the little family on that fateful day, proceeding up Route 78, the morning sun behind them, driving through rolling country, the highway festooned fantastically for miles with great growths of kudzu weeds, with little blond Elvis, dressed in overalls, giving the old heap the gas, while Vernon steers and applies the brake and Gladys sits surrounded with her little pile of worldly goods, staring glumly out the window.

Chapter 5

Portrait of the Artist as a Young Punk

IN THE customary accounts of Elvis Presley's life, the journey of the little family to Memphis always ends with an ominous roll on the kettle drums. Expelled from the bucolic world of Tupelo, these poor innocents are depicted as being swallowed up in the hell of the big city. Even worse, they are glimpsed being sucked down to the bottommost ring of the inferno—the public housing projects. *The projects!* Just the naked word is enough to summon up fearful images: sinister asphalt playgrounds, looming concrete monoliths, steel elevator doors that close like traps on their prey. Like so much else in the legend of Elvis, this impression is totally false.

The Lauderdale Courts is a drab little pile of red brick buildings constructed during the New Deal and reflecting in its austere but idealistic design the influence of the New Towns in England. The "big" building is but three stories high and bent in a sprung C configuration. The Presleys resided on the first floor at the right hand side of the main entrance in apartment 328. Across a broad front lawn, edged with neatly trimmed shrubs and shaded with trees, were the other buildings: a pair of two-story structures and a row of garden apartments with good-sized gardens. The basic image in Elvis's day was of an island of sensible but severe-looking suburban housing set in a sea of decaying gingerbread tenements.

Far from being a bad deal, the Courts were the Presleys' lucky strike. They moved in May 1, 1949, after having spent a wretched winter in a roach-infested old house, where they had to cook on a hot plate in their single room and share a common bathroom. For this slum lodging, they were charged the same rent, $35 a month, which they paid now to the Memphis Housing Authority for a two-bedroom flat with all the modern facilities. Yet the Presleys never had a good word for the Courts. Their biggest complaint was the requirement that every tenant declare his income. Rent was pegged to salary according to the formula: one month's rent equals one week's salary. Vernon had gotten a job on the loading platform of United Paint, not many blocks distant, which paid, with the customary four hours overtime, $38.50 a week. Now, twice a year, he had to go to his boss and get him to write the Housing Authority, telling it exactly how much he was earning. If you earned more than three thousand dollars a year, you had to move. Vernon bitched about that one for the rest of his life. He would sit up in the hillbilly palace at Graceland, surrounded by every luxury, shaking his head gravely and sighing, "They just wouldn't let you get ahead."

Vernon's real problem was that he had a wife who rarely worked, a son too young to work and a mother who had no intentions of seeking her first job at the age of fifty-four. Minnie Mae had moved in with Vernon as soon as he got his new apartment. She had been divorced by Jessie in 1947, after thirty-four years of marriage. Vernon said always that his father had deserted his mother, but the truth was precisely the opposite.

A tacit policy consigned to this particular housing unit all the war widows and divorced or abandoned mothers. These women, knowing nothing of relief checks, had to be the men. They worked long hours for low pay in sewing factories, cafeterias and hospitals. Their children worked, too. Consequently, there was no rowdiness, no dissipation, no crime. The apartments were kept immaculately clean because every so often a keen-eyed lady would appear unannounced at your door to peer inside your stove or cast an appraising glance at the hardwood floors, which had to be kept gleaming. Public assistance southern style, the Lauderdale Courts were a far cry from the welfare jungle of the North.

By the time the Presleys moved into their new home, Elvis had nearly completed the ninth grade at L. C. Humes High School on Manassas Street, about a twenty-minute walk from the project past the loading platform where Vernon labored with a painter's cap on his head. Gladys continued her practice of walking Elvis to and from school, but the first day the boy was so alarmed by his new environment that he ducked out of the building and ran all the way home. Humes was a lot larger than the schools to which Elvis was accustomed. A big red brick building with "gothic" trim, it was dedicated to turning out "commercial" and "vocational" graduates. Most of the 1,600 kids majored in drafting, home economics or secretarial skills. Of all the dumb activities in this dumb working-class school about the dumbest was shop: Elvis Presley's major.

Every day, like a prisoner in some old-fashioned penitentiary, Elvis would arrive in a workshop full of obsolescent power tools and don a long dark apron. Then, he would go to a storeroom presided over by a student trustee and ask for his "project." Out would come a carving board or a salad bowl or some other infantile object upon which he was expected to labor for the next hour. As he stood at his bench sanding or planing or polishing, along would come the shop teacher, Mr. Widdop. Like any other shop teacher, he's a dour old dude with a couple of clip-on pencils on the bib of his apron or in the breast pocket of his work coat. As he inspects Elvis's project, he lays an angle on it to make sure that it's "square" or a level to make sure it's "true." Then, he takes out a hard, sharp carpenter's pencil and scores lines in the wood, indicating where more work remains to be done. Poor Elvis looks down on the surface and realizes what hard labor it will be just to sand off those damn pencil marks. As the shop teacher accompanies his desecration of the project with brusque comments, Elvis keeps murmuring like a depressed but obedient darkie, "Yessir, yessir!"

For the rest, we haven't the slightest idea what Elvis did at Humes until his last two years. He appears to have entered the school like a drop of water disappearing into the ocean or a lump of lead sinking to its bottom. Painfully shy and totally self-effacing, he was one of those kids who are always found head down in the back row of the classroom. His social invisibility was paralleled by his academic mediocrity. Early and late, in grade school at Tupelo and in high school at Memphis, he was your classic C student. Though sometimes he did a little better in his favorite subject, English, or brought home bad grades, which were caused, most likely, by too much after-school work, he was best characterized by the word mediocre.

Gladys did not permit Elvis to play out of her sight until he was fifteen. Even then, his whole world outside of school and church was confined to a circle of a few blocks. Yet, because these blocks were in the heart of the city, they were rich in recreational facilities. In the immediate vicinity were a swimming pool, a movie house, a record store hangout, several ice cream parlors, Ellis Auditorium (Memphis's largest hall), an Odd Fellows' lodge with a poolroom and St. Mary's Church, which had dances for kids, as well as a U.S.O., where the local girls could dance with servicemen under strict chaperonage. After school, the boys played football, sometimes challenging the "culleds," who lived across the way near St. Joseph's Hospital.

The greatest fun all year came in June when the Cotton Carnival filled Main Street with fancy floats and pretty girls all dolled up as for Mardi Gras. Along historic Front Street, where the cotton factors had their offices overlooking the steep cobblestoned embankment leading down to the Mississippi dockside, a great red-and-white carnival would erect its midway and set up its mechanical rides. The carnival was always one of Elvis's favorite recreations, especially those booths where you can win a teddy bear by toppling wooden bottles with a well-aimed baseball.

When Elvis was fifteen, he started going steady. The girl was a skinny little tomboy named Betty McMann, who lived on the third floor. Though the pair spent a lot of time together for a year, they couldn't afford anything more expensive than a Dutch treat on Saturday afternoon at the Suzore Number Two, a narrow little rerun house with wooden seats and faded prints of horror films, where you could see two features and a string of serials for fifteen cents. Betty would have much preferred to go dancing at St. Mary's. She worked hard many an afternoon in her living room trying to teach the embarrassed and awkward Elvis how to do the two-step. The lessons were not successful. Indeed, it is one of the ironies of Elvis's life that, famous as a figure of chorybantic ecstasy, he was never able to dance with a girl. Elvis was one of those people who can dance only by themselves.

In the evenings, when the weather was warm, Elvis would come out on the front stoop after supper and entertain the neighbors by singing and playing his guitar. Everyone enjoyed his performances and encouraged him to sing, but he was so shy that he would never commence his performance until it grew dark. (At parties, he would insist that all the lights be extinguished.) Once he was satisfied that he was invisible, he would chord the instrument softly and sing sentimental country songs, one of his favorites being the Eddy Arnold tune, "Won't You Tell Me Molly Darling?" Some nights, he changed the girl's name to "Billie," a gesture designed to please his second girlfriend, thirteen-year-old Billie Wardlow.

A big-boned country lass, tall, pretty, vivacious, with a thick rural accent learned in Mississippi, Billie inspired Elvis to offer her such amusing gifts as a box of chocolate-covered cherries and a skinny gold bracelet with a pendent heart. Unlike Betty McMann, who wanted to go dancing but settled for the movies, Billie Wardlow would not accept less than the best. She insisted on going to the U.S.O. and cavorting with the servicemen. This soon ended her relationship with Elvis, who, never having had to share anything, was the least likely boy on earth to share his girl's attentions with another boy. When the moment of parting came, Elvis got big tears in his eyes. "Billie," he cried, "I was gonna ask you to marry me!" Then, looking at her hard, he added, "If you ever tell anybody I cried over you, I'll never talk to you again!" On that note, the brief romance ended.

Elvis was now sixteen. Never again during his school years did he become involved with a girl. Instead, he became involved in a profound emotional crisis that transformed him from a silly little country boy running around in a plaid shirt and farmer jeans to the "weird kid with the sideburns"—and the adolescent hero of an age of adolescents.

The onset of Elvis's emotional crisis was signaled by the appearance of recurrent nightmares. These dreams were so powerful that they resembled states of absolute possession or even the condition of being spellbound. Night after night, as Elvis lay sleeping on the sofa in the living room, he would imagine that he was being attacked by a mob of angry men. They would circle him ominously as he hurled at them defiant challenges. Then a violent struggle would commence. Elvis would cry out in his sleep and lay about him fiercely. Sometimes, he would leap out of bed and whirl the bedclothes about his head, under the impression that he was swinging a heavy chain. Or he would be wakened violently by an agonizing jolt of pain as he smashed his fist into a wall or tore off a toenail kicking against the sheet. If he did not awaken, he might rise from bed in a cold sweat, with eyes open but glazed, and make for the nearest door or window.

Once when he came to consciousness, he found himself standing out in the hall of the building, naked except for his Jockey briefs. Evidently, he had fled his attackers by slipping out the door of his apartment and mounting the stairs toward the third floor, where both Betty and Billie lived. Aghast at finding himself exposed in public, he was about to run for shelter when he was stopped cold by the sound of people entering the building downstairs. With a flash of horror, he realized that he was caught. Listening desperately to the voices, he recognized one of them as that of a girl who lived on the second floor. Scampering up to the third floor on bare feet, he was able to avoid humiliation by cowering there on the landing while the girl kissed her date goodnight.

Any ordinary family of that day who observed their child exhibiting such startling symptoms would have taken him straight to a doctor. The Presleys were not an ordinary family: They were hillbillies, on familiar terms with the weird. They associated Elvis's behavior with his father's nightmares and decided that this was an hereditary affliction, something that simply had to be borne.

The primary image presented by Elvis's nightmares is the familiar paranoid delusion of the one against the many. This image may have been born of fantasy or it may have been inspired by reality, for at the time that Elvis began to suffer these nightmares—the critical period of his sixteenth year—he was involved at school in scenes of persecution that were not much different from those that flashed on his mind while asleep. Though it is impossible to say which came first, the dream or the reality, the issue is not of any ultimate importance because Elvis's persecution was as much a product of his strange personality as were his dreams.

The cause of Elvis's troubles at school was, significantly, the first unmistakable expression of his genius. On a summer's day in the year 1951, Elvis Presley decided to crown himself with the world's most celebrated hairstyle. This momentous decision was arrived at only after years of earnest experimentation. Elvis recognized early, apparently, that his strength lay in his hair: his dirty blond, baby-fine locks. Billie Wardlow remembers going downstairs once after school to visit with Gladys and discovering that Elvis's mother had given him a kinky, curly permanent. Another time, Billie screamed with shock when Elvis appeared in a Mohawk, a single strip of hair running down the center of the skull. Now, all these experiments were about to conclude in the making of a masterpiece.

Like an artist rendering deliberately and confidently a finished sketch, Elvis went not to a barbershop but to a local beautyshop and ordered the astonished operator to fashion his hair into a classic Duck's Ass. He had already allowed his sideburns to grow down his pimply, Clearasil-daubed cheeks as far as his ear lobes. He also sought at this historic moment to raise a mustache because the ultimate purpose of all these efforts was simply to make him look older. Informed by the beautician that his hair grew "every which way," Elvis bought his first little round tin of Royal Crown Pomade, a really potent grease used by the local

Negroes to fix their conks. Elvis applied so much of this gook to his hair that it turned several shades darker and acquired such a lustrous sheen that it appeared glazed.

Next, he required a change of clothes. Over to Beale Street he goes, not many blocks distant, heading for the store patronized by the local black pimps and players: Lansky Brothers. Bernie Lansky is out in front of the shop, as usual, hustling the trade. A jive-talking Jew of a type familiar in every black ghetto, Lansky smiles and makes his pitch: "Hey, man, what you need today?" Elvis drifts around the tables, piled high under glaring fluorescent lights with gabardine slacks and shirts in brilliant hues. He picks out a pair of shiny black pants with a colored inset along the seam, lime green or lemon yellow. (His trademark pink-and-black combinations date from his twentieth year.) The pants are pegged at the ankles, ballooned at the knees, pleated at the waist, which rises in a four-inch band to just under the bottommost rib. A skinny suede belt is threaded through the dropped loops and the buckle whipped around to ride above the left hip. A loud "gab" shirt with a rolled "Mr. B" (Billy Eckstine) collar worn turned up, and the metamorphosis is complete. Elvis is proto-Punk.

This act of self-creation marks the true beginning of Elvis Presley's career as a pop culture hero. Though he's still years away from rock music and the Sun Studio, he's already very close to the classic Presley image. The image precedes the talent, as it was destined likewise to outlive the talent, becoming an imperishable pop eidolon.

Elvis's image derives directly from the style that was popular after World War II in the working-class neighborhoods of New York. Thousands of young men dressed and looked and carried themselves much like Elvis Presley when he was still in bib overalls. The real question about the Presley look is not where did it come from but how could a little cracker boy in the slums of Memphis get hip to it? A good clue is provided by the name which Elvis gave to his legendary hairstyle. Instead of calling it, as everyone else did, a Duck's Ass, Duck's Tail, Duck's Wings or D.A., Elvis referred to his famous comb as the "Tony Curtis Cut."

In 1949, Tony Curtis made his second appearance on the screen in *City Across the River,* the movie version of Irving Shulman's *The Amboy Dukes,* a pop novel about a Jewish youth gang in Brooklyn. Assuming that Elvis saw this film, it was bound to make a deep impression on him. Set in a slum no different essentially from Elvis's scabrous neighborhood, its characters lower-class vocational high school boys with parents

similar to Vernon and Gladys, the film turns on the accidental murder
by the boys of their shop teacher. The character portrayed by Tony
Curtis—who wears a gleaming, flawlessly shaped D.A. with a teasing
forelock—is a charming and slightly girlish sort of "bubie" boy, who
is good with his fists but very sweet, and speaks in a singsong pattern
that sounds like baby talk. If ever a film was designed to speak to a
young man's condition and temperament, this was the picture for Elvis
Presley.

When Elvis turned up at Humes in the fall of 1951 looking like
Tony Curtis, he discovered a great truth: Private dreams carried into
public places can turn into terrifying, humiliating nightmares. The tough
working-class kids turned on Elvis as if he had been Tiny Tim. They
baited, mocked and jeered him. They said he looked "like a squirrel
jes' come down outta the trees." Soon it was open season on squirrels.

No matter how much the kids tortured him, Elvis refused to relinquish
his strange image. This refusal to back down and conform has been
glorified for a quarter century as the defiant act of a rock rebel. One
of the cardinal features of the mythic Elvis is the idea that he was a
guy who wouldn't let the world push him around. Not troubling anyone
else, just enjoying his own dream, he would never provoke a fight; but
if someone put him down, even if they looked at him the wrong way,
you dig?, he would turn into a real ass-kicking redneck mother! This
idea is enshrined elaborately, for instance, in the classic hagiography
of rock saints, *Rock Dreams,* a volume of imaginary portraits of rock
stars and their milieus by the Belgian artist Guy Peellaert.

Turning to the page that evokes the high-school Elvis, we gaze upon
a handsome and serene young man with a weight-lifter's torso, leaning
casually against a lamppost in downtown Memphis with the dreamy
expression of Lord Byron leaning against a broken column. Behind the
saint lurks an obscenely fat and ugly biker, clad in leather jacket and
military cap, holding in one ham-hock hand a can of beer. He is staring
with a derisive grin at the back of Elvis's head, which we know is coiffed
in a ravishing D.A. The dramatic implications of the encounter are spelled
out in the legend, composed by the British pop critic, Nik Cohn (the
man who wrote the story on which *Saturday Night Fever* was based):
"Outside the poolhall, standing in the sun, I was minding my own business
and combing my hair, when along came a carhop [*sic*] and called me
dirty names. First the length of my hair, then the cut of my clothes,
and then the way I curled my lip. He stared into my eyes and spat on
my blue suede shoes. Right there on the pavement, with one foot in

the gutter, I cut him all to pieces." There you have the mythical Elvis Presley, king of the streets.

Now, let us lay beside this devotional picture a candid shot of the real sixteen-year-old Elvis at Humes. The source this time is *Elvis— What Happened?* and the speaker is Elvis's lifelong friend and companion, Red West. Red is a senior at the time, a tough, aggressive, football-playing poor boy, whose ribs are visibly deformed from rickets, a disease produced by not having enough money or enough brains to eat right. Red walks into the boys' room and discovers that he has stumbled upon a squirrel-hunting party.

> The place was full of smoke; you could hardly see in front of you for all the smoke. But I could see far enough to notice that old "E" was in a whole heap of trouble again. About four or five guys had him in there, and they were holding him and pushing him up against the wall and then grabbing him from behind. They were yelling and laughing and wising off at him and his hair. They decided that they were gonna cut his hair.
>
> I knew the guys who were hassling Elvis. They were on the football squad. When I saw Elvis's face, it just triggered something inside me. I mean, they weren't really bad guys; they weren't gonna kill him or anything but there was a look of real fear on his face. He was looking like a frightened little animal. I just couldn't stand seeing it. When you're very poor, you tend to let everyone look after their own troubles; but that face of Elvis—I can see it to this day. I saw that face like that many times later. It always had the same effect on me. Just churned up something inside me. It's a child's face and it asks for help.
>
> "Now look," I said to this bunch: "this ain't gonna do anyone any good. There ain't no need for this. If he likes his hair that way, well, no sense in hassling him. Now, if you cut his hair, you're gonna have to cut my hair, too; and that's gonna develop into something else."

Red was Mister Bad Ass. The other boys backed off.

This scene shows that Elvis's famed rebellion was nothing of the kind. Elvis didn't set out consciously to break any rules or violate any taboos or provoke either his peers or his superiors. He was inspired by a movie to make himself over into an image that he found esthetically and imaginatively fulfilling. Obviously, he was not prepared to fight for his right to maintain his pose. His fearful and supplicating attitude is

conveyed very well in Red West's description. It is exactly the attitude
of a kid who has been attacked in a manner that he did not anticipate and cannot repel. His only emotion is fear; his only thought to
escape.

If Elvis is not a figure of youthful rebellion, an ass-kicking redneck
spoiling to take on the world, what are we to make of his stubbornly
defiant behavior? Assuming that he was too naive to anticipate what
would happen to him when he turned up at school looking like a freak,
why didn't he wise up and protect himself from further persecution by
wearing his hair like all the other boys with their crew cuts and flattops?
Why did he continue to behave like a homosexual who struts in drag
down some mean street knowing full well that his provocative appearance
invites abuse and injury?

If you ask the homosexual why he takes such risks, he is liable to
reply by turning the question around and demanding to know why his
appearance should make other men react so violently. This turn of mind
was also highly characteristic of Elvis Presley. When he became famous
doing an act that was denounced by virtually every adult that witnessed
it as a male burlesque show, Elvis denied heatedly that there was anything
improper in his performance. What was wrong, he kept asking, with
all these crazy old types who said he was dirty?

One could dismiss such professions of innocence as hypocritical lies,
the phony excuses of a performer who knows exactly in what his appeal
consists but is too smart ever to admit the truth. When you examine
Elvis's life in detail, however, you find countless instances of contradictory
behavior that appear to spring out of a personality that was unconsciously
dichotomous. He's like the character of the rich drunk in Chaplin's
City Lights whose behavior at night is in total contradiction to the way
he acts during the day.

What happened to Elvis when he adopted his famous image was a
second birth, whose pangs were those violent and painful nightmares.
Out of this birth emerged a second, hitherto repressed personality, which
stood in total contradiction to the cute little mama's boy who was the
furthest thing in the world from a street punk. The model this new
personality was formed upon was that nightmare figure of the fifties—
the juvenile delinquent.

At first, this new bad-assed Elvis is little more than a shell: a haircomb
and a costume inhabited by a shy, self-doubting, self-effacing kid. Eventually, though, this shell begins to fill with the man it proclaims. *Sartor
resartus.* Clothes make the man. Five years later, Elvis has become the

tough punk that he set out unconsciously to emulate as a boy. He's pretty good with his fists, and he's already started pulling guns on people. The first gun he pulls, on a marine in Memphis, is, significantly, a starter's pistol that fires nothing but blanks. By the end of his life, Elvis will own every deadly weapon in the modern small arms arsenal and will be a seventh-degree black belt in karate. His last film project will star him as a karate instructor who is really an undercover narc. When the film writer asked Elvis for his ideas about the character, Elvis snarled: "I want to be the baddest motherfucker there is!" It takes time to grow a second self, but the start of this process is visible from the moment Elvis adopts his famous look.

It must not be thought that once the Bad Elvis started to emerge the Good Elvis began to recede. Quite the contrary: Both characters developed apace, alternating, like the faces on a turning coin. Thus, at the very moment when Elvis was carefully modeling himself upon the image of the slick, sinister, big-city hoodlum, he was also struggling determinedly to become a football hero and was joining the R.O.T.C., whose neat military uniform he wore with great pleasure. Even more mind-boggling was his announcement that his ultimate ambition was to become a Tennessee State Highway Patrolman. Cops and crooks, good guys and bad guys: Elvis would play both these parts all the rest of his life and always in full costume.

Between the extremes of Elvis the Good and Elvis the Bad there now began to emerge the amorphous figure of Elvis the entertainer. Until his last year in high school, Elvis reserved his playing and singing for his neighbors at the Courts. Having mustered the courage to brave the bullies in the school, he now found the strength to overcome the even greater threat posed by an audience of strangers. The credit for luring him into the open goes to his homeroom teacher, Miss Elsie Scrivener.

"I never knew Elvis could sing," recollected Miss Scrivener in later years, "until someone in my class said Elvis should bring his guitar to our homeroom picnic. Elvis did bring his guitar, and while everybody else was running around doing what young people do, Elvis sat quietly by himself playing and singing to the few who gathered around him. Slowly, other students began to come to him. There was something about his plaintive singing which drew them like a magnet." When Miss Scrivener was put in charge of the annual variety show, she asked Elvis to appear—along with thirty other kids. The arrangement was simple: Each youngster would perform a single piece. The one who received the most applause would then be declared the winner and perform an encore as his reward.

The night of the show, there was an unaccustomed air of tension backstage at Humes. Some of the kids were really eager to win and be acclaimed. As they went out onstage to sing their songs or play their pieces, they pushed themselves to the limits. It was precisely the sort of highly competitive situation that Elvis had been shying away from through all his years in this school. Tonight, however, he was standing on much surer ground than he had ever felt in the classroom or the shop or on the playing field. He knew his game. He appeared onstage wearing a solid red shirt, which he had borrowed for the occasion. He chose as his song the same piece with which he had won seven years before at the Tupelo fairgrounds: "Old Shep."

When he got into this familiar tearjerker, using his "plaintive" voice, he projected the pathos of the boy grieving over his dead dog so perfectly that even some of the teachers broke down and cried. The kids were amazed at how well Elvis sang. They gave him a tremendous hand. When they got through clapping and shouting, there wasn't much doubt about who would be declared the winner. Even then, Elvis could not believe that he had won. Miss Scrivener had to practically push him back onstage, urging, "It's you, Elvis! Go on out there and sing another song!" When he came off, he was walking on air. "I'll never forget the look on his face," the teacher exclaims when she recalls the moment. "They really liked me, Miss Scrivener," Elvis gasped. "They really liked me!"

Chapter 6

Quartette

Elvis's sixteenth year was his most decisive. This is the reason, most likely, why all the rest of his life he remained so much like a sixteen-year-old boy. He dreaded nothing more than a disturbance of the ideal pattern that he established at this time. Basic to the pattern was the perfect positioning of his polar twins. Elvis the Bad acquired the classic punk look and began his evolution toward that Snarling Darling who would become eventually the greatest hero of rock 'n' roll. Elvis the Good moved off at this time in precisely the opposite direction. He elected to become a lay priest, a gospel singer, a dancer before the Lord.

Elvis's discovery of the world of gospel took place one night in this same year at Ellis Auditorium, where he went to attend an all-night sing. This was a very odd thing for a teenager to do, but it must always be borne in mind that Elvis Presley was a very odd teenager. The show he witnessed had a profound effect upon him. Chances are it was the first real show he had ever seen. As a sing is one of those parochial institutions endemic to the South, it is necessary before we go any further to describe in some detail the scene that would have greeted the naive and impressionable youngster.

For days before the event, he would have been hearing the ballyhoo for the sing on the radio. The phrase "all-night" must have been especially titillating for a kid who went to bed normally at ten o'clock. Actually, this traditional epithet was just typical American hyperbole. The shows were four-hour concerts, beginning at eight and concluding at midnight: not all night by any means but a very late hour for God-fearing folk. The audience would have numbered several thousand people. Such entertainments were very popular at the time in Memphis, which, in the early fifties, had become the national headquarters for white gospel. As for the composition of the crowd, we have a neat characterization of them from the mouth of Elvis's favorite gospel singer, Jake Hess: "There's church people that don't go to movies; they go to sings for entertainment. There's people that don't go to church; the sing is their church. Then, there's John Q. Public: the people that just like male quartet." Even Zarathustra couldn't say it better.

The bill for the sing would have numbered five quartets. So stereotyped was gospel at this time in the form of the vocal foursome that the commonest designation for the music was "quartet," spelled often "quartette," in conformity with that characteristic southern predilection for the archaic. In truth, there was nothing venerable about quartette but the hokey spelling of its name. A more crassly commercial type of entertainment could hardly be imagined. For years the presiding spirits of the gospel world had been shrewd businessmen, like the founder of the quartet idiom, James D. Vaughan, and his successor, Virgil Oliver "V.O." Stamps, publishers of religious music who used gospel quartets as traveling salesmen, assigning them territories, equipping them with touring cars and paying them a percentage on all the songbooks which they sold at sings, singing conventions or through their local broadcasts, which were generally sponsored by flour companies.

It was in this manner that the most famous of all gospel quartets, the Blackwood Brothers, weathered the Depression and matured their skills until they achieved widespread popularity in the early fifties. The Blackwoods—James, Doyle, Roy and R.W.—were the sons of a sharecropper in Chocktaw County, Mississippi. While singing on the radio in Jacksonville, Mississippi, they were discovered by V. O. Stamps, who recruited them for his singing sales organization and consigned them for the next ten years to the blizzards and heat waves of Shenandoah, Iowa. Now, in 1951, they are local celebrities in Memphis, heard every day at noon on the radio and the hosts for the monthly sings at the Auditorium.

The Blackwoods' closest rivals are a much more flamboyant group that soon became Elvis's favorites: Hovie Lister and the Statesmen, whose lead singer is the great Jake Hess. The other quartets might have included the Sunshine Boys, from Florida, whose bass is J. D. Sumner (who in later years led Elvis's backup quartet); the Speer Family, from Atlanta (who appear on Elvis's first RCA records); the Stamps Quartet from Dallas; or the original Jordanaires (not the pop group that accompanied Elvis but a group of young Missourians who were the greatest white exponents of the traditional Negro spiritual style). In the treasured next-to-closing spot would appear the hometown favorites, the Blackwood Brothers.

The staging for these performances is of the simplest: the act curtain is closed when one enters the house, and a bit of scenery representing a stone balustrade or some equally unlikely object has been erected along the curtain line. A couple of old-fashioned standing mikes, such as you would see in a broadcasting studio, are stuck up in the middle of the stage, their cables running conspicuously across the floor. A grand piano, "the only appropriate accompanying instrument," according to V. O. Stamps, is parked on a steel dolly to the right of the mikes.

Though the stage setting might be called minimal or austere, you certainly wouldn't apply those words to the costumes or the style of the performers. "Lurid," "garish" or "Nigrah" would be more appropriate terms for the five performers who come charging out onstage this night, without benefit of introduction, wound up to the intensity of a black flash act. In fact, judging by their costumes, the Statesmen could have just finished a highly successful appearance with the annual Gospel Train show at the Apollo Theater in Harlem. They're wearing heavily draped double-breasted suits, redolent of zoot suits, made of raw silk and dyed in a spectacular color of solid red, glinting with iridescent sparklers. Their hair, which if combed straight forward would fall below their chins, is soaked with pillow-staining VO5 and teased up into Chinese pompadours that are impossibly high. As their beefy piano player, MC and honcho, Hovie Lister, squats hastily on the revolving stool and starts thumping out a fast um-chick, um-chick rhythm, this jive-assed quartet divides like a pack of smartly smacked pool balls, and, each pair seizing a mike, they streak off into one of their patented flag-wavers, "It Will All Be Over," an insanely cheery and eupeptic paean to death.

"It will all be over . . . the journey here will end . . . a new day will begin . . . we'll join the choir of angels singing out the victory song"—racing along at breakneck speed, the quartet suddenly falls silent as the bass, the towering "Big Chief" Weatherington, an organ-pipe of a man, goes into a growling ostinato, a locomotive wheel of sound, repeating with nimble tongue endlessly: "Just-a-little-while, just-a-little-while, just-a-little-while." When he's established his hypnotic drone, the other voices come charging in on top of the wheel:

> *Just a little while to stay here.*
> *Just a little while to wait,*
> *Just a little while to labor,*
> *In the path that's always straight.*

Meantime, the audience—they're a little slow, after all, this is the first number—has finally gotten over its shock at this musical Blitzkrieg and is shouting its approval. Now Big Chief and the other voices go into a fast antiphon, like banging a ball up against a wall:

> BASS: *And we will shout!*
> TRIO: *Hallelujah!*
> BASS: *And we will sing!*
> TRIO: *Hallelujah!*

Now they've got the audience on the ropes. It's time to "turn them out," give them the coup de grace. Suddenly, the individual voices, entering one after another at progressively higher pitches, pile up into a spectacular vocal pyramid, like circus tumblers.

> *Just a little while!* . . .
> *Just a little while!* . . .
> *Just a little while!* . . .

Then the bass does a vocal nose dive down in the hurricane cellar, producing a chord that spans three octaves. But they're still not through! Just when the crowd is tensing to acclaim them with shouts and applause, they take off again, after this false cadence, and start a series of upward transpositions. Now each time they sing a verse, they step off from a higher position on the scale. Up once they go; up again they go; the third time, they're way up in the attic and the tempo is quickening when suddenly—would you believe this?—the high tenor takes off in a Nigrah shouting style that brings down the house. They're singing, "Sweeping through the pearly gates," and going like Ben Hur, and this dude is echoing back the phrases from on high in falsetto, like some big old mammy in a Sanctified church. Before the audience can recover, the quartet goes into a riff straight out of the book of some old swing band, repeats it a few times in perfect harmony; then, with a startling chord pulled out of their mouths like bubble gum, they suddenly pop and stop!

As the applause dies down, old Hovie gets up and collars a mike and thanks the folks right hearty in that cornpone accent they so love to hear. Pausing for a second, as if to take thought, he offers a little confession:

"While the boys was singin' that song, mah mind turned to a favorite subject of every man, woman, boy and girl—*love!*" There's an audible gasp from the house: "He can't be meanin' . . . ah mean to say . . . wha's that he? . . ." No, it's O.K.! He means the *other* kinda love! "Love is a great word," ole Hovie intones like a preacher. Then gettin' up into that Pentecostal pulpit tone, he gives it to all those doubting Thomases, right between the eyes: "God-gave-his-only-begotten-son-and-his-only-begotten-son-gave-his-life-on-Calv'ry!"

There! That should hold 'em. Now he just rounds it off nice: "That was a love that supersedes all love that man has ever known. [How 'bout that "supersedes"? There's some language for ya! Right outta the good book!] It's love that give me the joy an' the heppiness in mah heart. And it's the LOVE! [pause] that makes me free tahnight! *Listen!*"

Now, the "boys" go into "It's Wonderful to Know He Is Mine." This is one of Jake Hess's show-forth tunes. Everybody knows Jake: He's that little dude there with the eyes that keep poppin' open like a baby doll's (Jake says he does that for the people in the back rows) and the little hands that work like puppeteers' fingers. Hell! He looks like a cute little puppet himself with that big nutcracker mouth on him. What a voice! So clear, so clean, so sh-har-ply ar-tic-u-la-ted. He sounds like he's vocalizing the syllabification in the spelling book. Now, he's going into his specialty: the recitation. "When Ai-eh yam disc-cour-raged": He's really punchin' out those syllables now. Funny, if he were anyone else, you'd say he sounded like one of those high-pitched faggots— you know the kind that talk so affected with a clothespin on their nose? "Or Ai yam fi-illed with glooooom." Oh, boy, he can really color a note: shade it real dark. "Gaw-od se-ends his a-ngel to-oo see-eek in ma-ah roo-oom." He's really got everybody transfixed with this thing he does with the words. Singers say he got it from Billy Eckstine.

Though Jake's an eccentric, he's no clown. He's the greatest stylist in the business. When the Quartet gets into one of their I-love-you-Jesus vocal valentines, Jake sings with such refinement of tone and dynamics, such startling attacks and swooning melismas, that he virtually reduces the whole house to tears.

Somewhere in that house is Elvis Presley, who is soaking all this up like his mother's thickenin' gravy. When the day comes for him to record "Hi want you, Hi need you, Hi luh-huh-huh-huv yew-hew!" he will reveal what these sings taught him. When he records gospel, he will simply steal the Statesmen's arrangements.

Christian sentiment, Christian joy, the hand-clappin', foot-stompin' enthusiasm of that ole-time religion, these are the staples of a gospel sing; but shoutin' and weepin' aren't the only sources of entertainment. Gospel shows produce a lot of laughs. Those who know the Lord and love the Lord and dwell with the Lord are comfortable in the Lord's presence. They can take their ease in Zion and laugh their ass off! That's J. D. Sumner's job: to get the people laughin'. Ole J.D., he come out walkin' with his Sunshine Boys: they all be wearin' black shoes and he got on red! Then, he starts talkin' to the people in that cold-cellar voice of his, tellin' them how it feels to be a new boy in town.

"We're stayin' over here at a *ho*-tel, and that girl they got runnin' the elevator—she must be new to the job. I come to get on the elevator this mornin', an' she jus' threw that thing in high gear and we went all the way to the bottom! We hit with a thud an' I let out a groan! She turned around to me and said, 'What's the matter? Did I stop too quick for you?' I said, 'Oh, no! I always wear mah britches down around mah ankles!' "

It doesn't take much to make these folks laugh. If they don't laugh enough to please J.D., he's got this other thing he's famous for doing. It's called the Gooney Bird. J.D.'s a big tall man, as dignified as a cigar store Indian. When he wants a laugh, however, he'll suddenly throw his arms up in the air with his coattails in his hands and go to jumpin' and hoppin' around the stage like a big crazy buzzard flittin' around a dead varmint on the highway.

When intermission comes, the folks have a chance to get a cold Coke and buy the new songbooks and the glossy eight-by-tens of the quartets, which they can get autographed after the show. As the admission is only a quarter for kids and fifty cents for adults, the musicians must hustle for every extra buck. If they've got a little record company, as do the Blackwoods, they'll have somebody out in the lobby selling their big heavy 78s. LPs are kinda newfangled for this crowd.

The Blackwoods, who are local celebrities, get a tremendous hand when they walk out onstage dressed all in white. They're much more conservative than the Statesmen; in fact, for years they wore nothing but black. They stick pretty closely to the more traditional, black-influenced gospel tunes in those tight seesaw rhythms that lurch rather than rock. Their lead singer, the little WASPY-looking James Blackwood, is no match for Jake Hess, but the group is a very tightly meshed, neatly efficient machine for grinding out the old favorites. When they want to get hot, they have a piano player who goes into a flat-out boogie-woogie (which if his skin were black would be called barrelhouse and be a shame before God!). The bass singer runs scales on these boogie numbers using his vocal chords as if they were a string bass. The fact is that some of their hits, like "Peace in the Valley," were written by black composers, but no matter how much of the black style these white boys take, it always comes out sounding as Caucasian as the Klan.

It isn't hard to imagine the effect of this show on the young Elvis Presley. He would have been dazzled by the costumes, hairstyles, jivey stage antics and virtuoso singing. He would have been astonished to see how the stuffy old music of the church could be transformed into such thrilling entertainment. He might even have felt that strange stirring that passes through a man when he catches his first glimpse of the world where he is destined to spend his life. Though Elvis never became a conventional gospel singer, he did bring the gospel flavor and tone to every sort of music he sang.

When the Blackwoods moved to Memphis in 1950, they chose as their church the First Assembly of God. Their baritone, R.W., enrolled his younger brother, Cecil, in the same Sunday school class as Elvis. Therefore, in addition to seeing the Blackwoods every month at the Auditorium and watching them broadcast from the Hotel Peabody, he also saw this famous group perform many times in his church and soon became friendly with the younger brother in the weekly scripture class. These personal associations are important because Elvis was such a shy boy that if he had not been so encouraged he might not have been able to step over the line that divides the fan from the star. As it was, he soon found himself backstage at the Auditorium talking to the first professional musicians he had met since his childhood acquaintance with Mississippi Slim in Tupelo.

The first gospel star to befriend the weird-looking kid with the sideburns was J. D. Sumner. J.D. recalls Elvis coming around so often and asking so many questions that he made a nuisance of himself. He also made himself such an accustomed presence that the first time he failed to appear, J.D. noticed his absence. Next time they met, the singer asked his most devoted fan what had kept him from the show. Elvis confessed that he couldn't raise the fifty cents for the ticket. After that, J.D. sneaked the boy in through the stage door, until Elvis got a job at the shows selling Cokes from an ice chest slung over his shoulder.

Once Elvis had discovered white gospel, it would have been natural for him to open his ears to black gospel, which was also broadcast every day on the radio in Memphis, a city renowned for its "shouting" churches. Black gospel exhibited a totally different character than white gospel. Instead of being a holy vaudeville full of straw-hat tunes, soft-shoe rhythms and J-E-L-L-O harmonies, black gospel was the bedrock of soul, "the forge and the flame" of black song. What's more, at this moment in its history it was undergoing the final degree of secularization that would make it soon the most vital component of the new R & B, which would become in turn the foundation for the new rock 'n' roll.

By turning his attention now to such immensely influential musicians as the Soul Stirrers (a quintet whose leader, R. H. Harris, was the model for Sam Cooke and Bobby "Blue" Bland); the Harmonizing Four (whose legendary bass, Jimmy Jones, Elvis discovered years later parking cars in North Carolina); the Swan Silvertones (perhaps the greatest of all black quartets); and such solo voices as Clara Ward (the model for Aretha Franklin) and Sister Rosetta Tharpe (a major influence on Dinah Washington and Little Richard), Elvis was not only cutting into the mainline of black vocal music but was doing so just at the moment when this whole buried world was about to burst onto the stage of national consciousness. Gospel soon inspired a wide range of pop music, extending from the "Sanctified" Ray Charles (whose big 1955 hit, "I Gotta Woman," was just a pop lyric pasted over "My Jesus Is All the World to Me") to the appearance of the greatest of all R & B quartets, the Drifters, whose inspired lead singer, Clyde McPhatter, was originally a gospel singer, to the endless proliferation of do-wop groups ("do wop" is derived from the familiar gospel chant, "do Lord"), this juvenile fad being simply the reductio ad adolescence of a cappella gospel quartet.

When Elvis got out of high school in 1953, he wasn't thinking, as his yearbook pictured him, of "doing a bit of picking and singing" in a country and western club: His sights were trained on another goal entirely. He wanted to be a professional gospel singer. What's more, he almost reached this goal. Having befriended at church the son of the minister, Jimmy Hamill, and developed a good relationship with his Sunday school classmate, Cecil Blackwood, Elvis was hovering around a newly formed gospel quartet called the Songfellows. At first, he was just hanger-on, a guy who would go along for the ride whenever the group got a gig. Then, one night when they were all in the car, one of the boys started praising Elvis, saying: "Why, he can imitate anyone—Jake Hess, Frank Sinatra, Dean Martin. . . ." From that time forth, Elvis was often invited to sing with the group.

His first job working as a single was at the Eagle's Nest, in a motel, swimming pool and nightclub complex on the outskirts of town. The customary entertainment in this room was western swing music, the band of the moment being the Johnny Long Orchestra. Elvis performed in the lulls between the band's performances. He came onstage, as he does in *Jailhouse Rock,* trying to get the attention of a roomful of chattering men and women sitting at tables covered with red-checked cloths. Instead of singing a country and western tune, however, he would open his mouth and start belting out the current hits of Dean Martin! Can you dig it? "When the moon hits your eye like a big pizza pie—*that's amore!*" Twang, twang! Of all offbeat images of Elvis Presley, this little snapshot has got to be the most bizarre.

With nothing to encourage his dreams of a singing career except an occasional spot at the Eagle's Nest, where nobody listened to him, the eighteen-year-old Elvis Presley had little going for him. It was one of the dreariest periods of his life. Most of his waking hours were spent working on an assembly line. His uncles, Travis and Johnny, had been employed for years at Precision Tool, on McLemore and Kansas. When Elvis and Gene Smith finished with their schooling, the older men got the boys jobs at the factory. Precision Tool manufactured 90- and 101-millimeter shells for the army. Elvis's job was to insert three rods and twelve screws into the shell casing. He and Gene were the fastest men on the line. They worked from 7:00 in the morning till 3:30 in the afternoon. The pay was good for beginners: $1.65 an hour or sixty-six dollars a week. That was considerably more than Vernon Presley was earning after working for five years at United Paint. The only problem Elvis had on the job was caused by his long hair. The older men threatened to crop his head and Gene's. The boys offered at first to fight it out; then they thought better of it and went to the barber for a light trim.

In this same winter just before his nineteenth birthday, Elvis got a new job, which paid less money but pleased him much more: driving a truck for Crown Electric. Elvis had always been crazy about cars and other motor vehicles. No sooner did he get a driver's license at seventeen than he got his picture in the paper changing a tire in the citywide Road-E-O. (He came in second, "losing first place," as the school principal announced at assembly, "by a sideburn.") It wasn't just machines that excited him, it was the romance of being a truck driver.

With Elvis contributing his wages to the family, the fortunes of the Presleys finally began to mend. They had been forced to leave the Courts the previous winter because with Gladys working part-time as a nurse's aide and Elvis doing a variety of odd jobs, including a couple of punishing months working a full-time shift after school at MARL Metal, a kitchen furniture manufacturer (Elvis's job application raised a lot of laughs because at seventeen he claimed no less than five dependents), the Presleys' combined income inched up over the maximum allowed by the Housing Authority. They moved first to an apartment on Cypress Street, which was unsatisfactory. Then they moved again, to an old gingerbread frame house on Alabama Street, whose front porch faced their former building at the Courts. The house was divided into a duplex. The Presleys occupied the ground floor, with Gladys and Vernon sleeping in the only bedroom, Minnie Mae bunking on a cot in the dining room, and Elvis crashing on the sofa in the living room. The upstairs flat had been rented by the house's owner, Mr. Dubrovner, the orthodox Jewish ritual slaughterer, to Rabbi Alfred Fruchter, the orthodox rabbi of a nearby *shul*.

The young rabbi and his wife, Jeanette, became friendly with the Presleys and were often useful to them in small ways. Mrs. Fruchter remembers loaning Gladys small sums of money. She recalls how charming it was to see Elvis come home on Friday and give his paycheck to his mother. The Fruchters were also good people to have as neighbors because they possessed two important devices that the Presleys lacked: a telephone and a phonograph. On a weekend, while Vernon and Elvis would stand out in the street washing the green 1942 Lincoln Zephyr coupe—which Vernon had bought for fifty dollars and given to Elvis for his eighteenth birthday—Rabbi Fruchter would entertain himself by playing records of those great, operatically-voiced cantors, Shlomo Kussevitsky and Moyshe Oysher. In all the digging around for the roots of the Presley sound, no one has ever considered the possibility that he was influenced by Jewish cantorial singing.

In February 1954, Elvis met Dixie Locke, the first girl with whom he ever got involved in a serious relationship. Dixie was just a kid at the time: a fifteen-year-old high school sophomore. She had gone one night with a couple of other girls to a high-school hangout called the Rainbow Rollerdome. At some point in the evening, she spotted an odd-looking boy whom she often saw at church. It was she who approached Elvis. He was not in a condition to approach anyone because he had put on a pair of roller skates without learning how to skate and was clinging anxiously to the safety rail. As always he was spectacularly costumed. He had on a pink suit with a bolero jacket and a black stripe down the pants leg—a car hop's outfit. When Dixie introduced herself, Elvis engaged her in an intense conversation that continued as he got her out of the roller rink and into his car and over to Kay's Drive-In on Crump Boulevard.

Elvis poured out his whole story to Dixie. He told her that he came from desperately poor people: that his father was incapacitated for work with back trouble, that his mother was also ill, that he himself was unemployed and that even the old car he was driving was borrowed. It wasn't until he had brought Dixie to the door of her house in South Memphis that Elvis finally confessed that he had been fibbing, admitting that both he and his father had jobs and that the car was his own. Dixie assumed later that Elvis had been testing her: seeking to determine whether she would accept him at the very lowest figure. She may well have been right: Elvis was obsessed all his life with the thought that women wanted to "use" him. On the other hand, it may have been that he simply wanted pity and used the infantile device of feigned afflictions to make sure that he got the full measure of sympathy from this responsive young girl.

Dixie was not disposed to take the meeting as anything out of the ordinary, but to Elvis it represented a great new dawn of love and affection. Though neither he nor Dixie lived in homes that had telephones, he discovered that she could be reached through an aunt who had a phone and lived next door. Arranging for a date that very weekend, Elvis showed up at the Locke house wearing another of his bizarre costumes. With his long greasy hair and sideburns and pimply complexion all contributing to the highly negative impression he made on Dixie's father, a laborer at the Railway Express terminal, and her mother, both of whom were reluctant to allow their daughter to go off for the evening with such an obvious weirdo, Elvis came close to a humiliating rejection. Yet, by dint of numerous "Yes, sirs" and "No, ma'ams," those mechanical gestures of politeness that served Elvis so well throughout his life, the parents were brought around and the couple released to spend the rest of the evening in another prolonged talk.

Elvis, never the one to dillydally when he knew what he wanted, soon set the relationship on a routine course that would last until he started going out of town to work. Every weekend, he would bring home his paycheck and give it to his mother or father, who would give him back fifty cents or a dollar for his weekend date. If there was enough money to put gas in the car, he would drive to South Memphis, pick up Dixie and take her to the Suzore, where they would see a cheap double feature. After the show, they would go to Charlie's, a dim little shop across the street, where an ancient man sold snacks and phonograph records. Elvis would get a Pepsi and Dixie a NuGrape soda; then they would adjourn to a booth, where Elvis would listen with a spellbound expression on his face to recordings by black blues singers. His favorite record was "Tomorrow Night" by Lonnie Johnson. When Dixie's curfew came at eleven o'clock, Elvis would drive her home or put her on the bus. The only variations in the routine were the nights when they went to Riverside Park, the little patch of green overlooking the Mississippi from the bluff in front of Front Street, where they could sit on a bench under the Confederate monuments and neck—until they were rousted by the searchlight on a patrol car—or the nights when they went out to a teen hangout near McKellar Lake, where most kids danced to the juke box but Dixie and Elvis didn't because Elvis couldn't. They also went to a lot of all-night sings, Dixie sharing in Elvis's tremendous enthusiasm for the music and especially for Jake Hess. Dixie cannot remember Elvis ever voicing his ambition to become a professional singer.

Dixie soon became acquainted with the other members of the Presley family. She found the atmosphere of the home depressing and disconcerting. Instead of the strong father to whom she was accustomed, she discovered in the Presley household a total inversion of the natural order. The child was the head of the house, the mother came second and the father was in the place occupied normally by the son. The mother viewed their social position as that of people at the very bottom of the barrel. Dixie now understood why Elvis would talk about her typical working-class family as if they were "uptown." The other feature of the Presley family that impressed Dixie was their extreme reluctance to make friends or even visit other people. Again, Dixie attributed this reclusiveness to Gladys, who she realized wanted nothing better than to take Elvis and retreat to a desert island.

In the summer of 1954, Elvis's dream of joining the Songfellows finally became a reality owing to a horrible disaster that shocked the city of Memphis. The Blackwood Brothers had become extremely successful by this time, largely because of a recording contract with RCA, which produced an immediate hit, "The Man Upstairs." In June 1954, they had won first place on the *Arthur Godfrey Talent Scout Show,* which greatly increased the demand for their appearances all over the country. To squeeze their bookings closer together, they had started traveling by light airplanes, which they bought instead of chartered. Their baritone,

R.W., got interested in flying and qualified as a pilot. Then, on the night of June 30, 1954, just before the quartet was about to perform at Clanton, Alabama, R.W. took off in the group's two-engine Beechcraft, with the bass singer, Bill Lyles, and a local lad, to test the conditions for their departure later that night. When he tried to land on the short dirt strip, he crashed. The plane burst into flames and all three men were killed.

On July 2, the dead men were given a huge public funeral. Services were held at the Auditorium and Frank Clement, the governor of Tennessee, pronounced the eulogy. The Statesmen and the Speer Family sang. Thousands of grief-stricken people attended the ceremonies and watched the funeral cortege move solemnly through the streets of Memphis. Elvis was deeply affected by the disaster and spent a whole night sitting on a park bench with Dixie grieving.

James Blackwood announced that he would never sing again. Gradually, as he overcame his sorrow, he determined to re-form the group and continue his career. J. D. Sumner was hired to replace the dead bass singer. Then, a replacement was sought for R.W. Finally, it was decided that the most appropriate substitute would be his brother, Cecil.

Not two weeks after the crash, Cecil turned up one day at Elvis's house with important news. He announced that he was leaving the Songfellows for the Blackwoods. Now there would be an opening in the junior quartet. Elvis could have his long-sought chance to become a professional gospel singer.

Elvis listened to Cecil with obvious astonishment. Then his expression changed to one of chagrin. "I can't do it!" he snapped. "Why not?" demanded Cecil. Elvis paused for a moment. Then, looking Cecil hard in the eye, expecting perhaps a rebuke, he repeated, "I can't do it." This time he added the surprising explanation, "I done signed a contract to sing the blues."

Chapter 7

Hoot 'n' Holler

THE BLUES that Elvis was about to record was not
the country blues nor the city blues nor even the Memphis blues:
It was rhythm and blues, the sound of the postwar black ghetto.
In the year 1954, R & B was starting to spill out of the ghetto,
but it still wasn't the kind of song with which most white singers
were familiar. Nonetheless, the nineteen-year-old Elvis Presley
showed himself highly knowledgeable regarding this and a number
of other black styles, both current and past, secular and religious.
How did Elvis learn to sing black?

The customary answer, that Elvis grew up with "all that" around
him in Mississippi, is no longer tenable. As for the notion that
the adolescent Elvis spent a lot of time hanging around the blues
joints on Beale Street, all one has to do to test that idea is imagine
how Gladys would react to such a pasttime. Why, every weekend
people got killed down on Beale (though the bodies were always
rushed to some other part of town, a practice that inspired the
local proverb: "You never find a dead nigger on Beale!"). No, it
is unthinkable that the boy who spent his weekends with a little
high school girl going to the movies and listening to records at
Charlie's would slip into the darkest and most dangerous part of
the ghetto to hear somebody sing the blues. In fact, the real source
of Elvis's precocious knowledge of the blues was exactly the same

as that from which he had drawn his original inspiration as a little country singer: the radio.

Just one month after Elvis's arrival in town, in October 1948, the South's first black-oriented radio station went on the air at Memphis. A feeble little 250-watter at seventy-two kilocycles, it was just a shout at the bottom of the dial. No radio station in history, however, has ever exerted a greater impact on musical taste. A whole school of subsequently famous performers grew up listening to the station. What they got out of the experience was certainly as valuable as any Ph.D. ever granted in Afro-American Studies. Not only did they obtain unlimited "exposure" to both the secular and sacred music of black people, they also received a marvelous education in black humor and language through the raps and bits of their professors, who were the South's first "personality jocks." As if all this weren't enough, a couple of these professors subsequently became famous practitioners of the arts they taught. They became, in fact, some of the biggest names in the last phase of urban blues and soul music. As nothing of substance has ever been published on the "Mother Station of the Negroes," let us tune in now on the story of how the blues were reborn at Memphis.

The establishment of the South's first black radio station was purely a case of do or die. In 1948, WDIA was a hapless little country music outlet teetering on the verge of bankruptcy. Faced with the decision whether to give up and get out or do something new and risky, the white owners of the station, Bert Ferguson and John R. Pepper, decided it was better to go black than go broke.

Now the owners were faced with the problem of finding the proper staff. Black announcers and DJs from the North could have been brought down to Memphis, but how would they go over with the people down on the plantations? What's more, if you got some uppity nigger from the North, he might say something on the air that would make a stink. The best thing would be to find a good local man who could handle the job.

The first announcer recruited proved to be a perfect choice. Professor Nat D. Williams, known subsequently to generations of black Memphians as "Nat Dee," was a history teacher at Booker T. Washington High School. Though some feared he might be too highbrow for the common folk, the Professor's late-afternoon "drive-time" show, *Tan Town Jamboree,* became extremely popular because it featured all the latest R & B hits.

The next black jock to be hired had a showbiz background and was hip to the style of Negro DJ's in the North. In the age of re-bop, rhyming slang and jumped-up music, the idea was to talk fast-fast-fast, a verbal Blitzkrieg that blew the listener's mind. Listening to his new jock streak down the track one day, Mr. Ferguson said, "Maurice, you talk so fast, you oughta have a name that means speed. From now on, you're gonna be 'Hot Rod' Hulbert." A few weeks later, Hot Rod Hulbert was racing through a station break when his tongue slipped and he identified himself as "Hard Rod Hulbert." That got him a lot of attention.

Soon Hulbert was working a three-a-day schedule at the badly under-manned station. Each show went on the air at a different hour, was aimed at a different audience and demanded a different mood and rap. Hulbert complied by dividing himself into three different Rods. At eight in the morning, following Nat Dee's sunrise show, *Tan Town Coffee Club,* which was mostly R & B, "Maurice Hulbert, Jr." would go on the air with his gospel show, *Tan Town Jubilee.* As the driving beat and raucous shouting of the Five Blind Boys, the Dixie Hummingbirds and the Mighty, Mighty Clouds of Joy blared over the air, Hulbert would come on like a black preacher up in the pulpit. Between his pitches for hair-straightener and Dixie Peach Complexion Creme, he would read passages from the Bible in a deep, inspiring scripture voice. He went over so well with this act that he was invited to play Jesus in the annual Christmas drama at the Auditorium.

At ten o'clock in the morning, Hulbert would shift masks to do a program aimed at the housewives, maids and laundresses: *Sweet Talkin' Time.* Now, he was "Maurice the Mood Man": smooth, sexy, intimate. Reaching down into his deepest, richest, most vibrato-throbbing voice, he would talk to the girls in valentines:

> *You bring sunshine into my life,*
> *You make me forget the toil and strife.*
> *You take out of me the years*
> *I've struggled through with so much sorrow and tears!*
> *It was difficult to resist because—pause!*
> *You—pause!—were—pause!—temptation!*

With the last word, he'd drop the needle into a slick white rendition of "Temptation," that classic erotic romantic ballad with its jungle-drum beguine break.

At three o'clock in the afternoon, "Hot Rod Hulbert" made his first appearance of the day, talking like a chattering hipster teletype, going a mile a minute as the way-out MC of the *Sepia Swing Club.* This show was all up!-up!-up! Jokes and jive and patter picked up off the street. One day doing a fast blitzy commercial for E-Z Credit Layaway, his tongue, as he recalls, "got stuck in my eye teeth so bad I couldn't see." As the words of the commercial came tumbling out as a series of nonsense syllables, Hulbert snapped to the fact that he had invented a tongue twister. He wrote it all out—O-ble-doo-ba-blah-blah-blah-doo-*lay-a-way*—and discovered there were nineteen syllables in all. That gave him an inspiration: For nineteen days before Christmas he taught his radio listeners one new syllable a day, until they could riddle off the whole long preposterous bit, like a scat-singing jazz vocalist. So many people mastered the trick that everywhere you went in black Memphis, you heard the silly syllables.

We have no way of knowing how much of WDIA's programming Elvis Presley absorbed in the five years between his arrival in Memphis and his first efforts as a professional singer. We do have Elvis's testimony that he listened to the station constantly. What is more, no sooner did he become famous than he offered to lend his support to the station. There are a number of photographs of Elvis at WDIA's annual Goodwill Revue in December 1956. Apparently, the racial taboos of Memphis forbade Elvis's appearance on the show, but he was on hand to lend his support to the cause. There is also a picture from this time of Elvis shaking hands with WDIA's most famous disc jockey, Riley B. King, better known as B.B. King.

King was not long off the plantation when he arrived in West Memphis, Arkansas, where there was a local station, KWEM, that split its broadcast schedule between white country music and black blues. The presiding presences on the black segments were Sonny Boy Williamson, King's idol, and Chester Burnett, soon to become famous in Chicago as Howlin' Wolf. When Riley King heard there was a new black station in Memphis, he took a bus to the downtown Greyhound terminal and then walked three miles out to Union Avenue, reaching number 2074 in a pouring rain. King went on the air that very day and soon was a regular on a show called *Pay Day*. Eventually, he got a sponsor, a tonic called Pepticon. His show's theme was a blues jingle:

> *Pepticon sure is good,*
> *Pepticon sure is good,*
> *Get it anywhere in your neighborhood.*

By the time the young singer had worked up to a staff job on the *Heebie Jeebie Show,* he had expanded his name to read "Beale Street Blues-Boy."

Programming all the best R & B music, the stuff with the most soul, King spun the first records of Lloyd Price and Fats Domino, as well as those of established stars like Louis Jordan and Dinah Washington. If he found a side that appealed to him by a white singer, like Frank Sinatra, Bing Crosby or Frankie Laine, he would toss it into the pot. Though WDIA programmed very little white music, there were always some songs, like Johnny Ray's bizarre hit, "Cry," that appealed to the black audience.

By 1951, B. B. King had built a reputation as a club act and recording star. He was getting so many out-of-town bookings that he had to give up his radio job. His replacement was another black entertainer destined to become nationally known: Rufus Thomas. A husky, bald-headed, rubber-legged clown of a man, Thomas had joined the Rabbit's Foot Minstrels way back in 1935. Over the years he had amassed a great deal of showbiz experience. As the MC of the weekly amateur night at the Palace Theater on Beale, Thomas was still active on the stage, though he made his living stoking the boilers at the Memphis Luggage Factory. His style as a DJ was superfly. To open his midnight show, *Hoot and Holler,* he would shout:

> *I'm young and loose and full of juice!*
> *I got the goose so what's the use?*
> *We're bright and gay but we ain't got a dollar!*
> *Rufus is here—so let's hoot ' n' holler!*

By 1954, WDIA was making so much money with its black programming policy that the whole operation was refinanced and put on a big-time footing. From a feeble little 250-watter, the station was switched overnight to a mighty 50,000-watt transmitter that reached out for hundreds of miles to gather into its net the huge black population of the entire tristate area: Tennessee, Mississippi and Arkansas. Now, when you picked up an advertising, media marketing or music biz trade paper, you saw ads that laid it right on the line. "America's Only 50,000-Watt NEGRO Station Covers the Golden Market of 1,237,686 Negroes— nearly 10% of America's Total Negro Population." Can you imagine the heat a statement like that engendered in the loins of any red-blooded American space buyer? Hey! It was heavy! Inevitably, it inspired the owners of other Memphis stations to wonder whether there might be some way, some trick of media miscegenation, that might allow them to cut a slice of this rich black devil's food cake. You couldn't sell the culleds unless you spoke their language, of course. But what if you found some good ole boy with a crazy line of jive like the nigger pusenality jocks that could towahk that same shit! Hey! You'd have yeseff sumpin', wouldncha, son? Well, that's 'zactly how Brother Dewey Phillips got his shot.

Dewey Phillips! What a natural-born freak! You think city people are wild? You think all that off-the-wall jive comes from the Harlem ghetto? No, mah boy, they's many a crazy, likah drinkin', pill poppin' countrah boy that kin get hissef jes' as racked-up 'n' ragged as the craziest coon they ever treed on Beale Street. It's a damn shame that we just can't take the paper on this page and stamp it in a pressing plant like one of those little old pressed-paper records to let you hear this good ole boy do his stuff. No tricks of typography, no Tom Wolfe razzamatazz on the top buttons of the typewriter—#*¢%&*!!!—will ever simulate the sound that this nut made over the late-night, deep-South radio circa 19 and 54.

Just picture yourself cruising around Memphis in the premidnight hours, with your car radio tuned to WHBQ, which broadcasts from the mezzanine of the Old Chiska Hotel (Chickasaw, the Indians of the Memphis bluffs) down on Main Street. You've just heard Howlin' Wolf practically masticate the mike with his big chops as he rasped, "*Bay—bee, wheredya spen' las' night?*" Suddenly, the announcer's mike switches on, and another Arkansas voice, nearly as harsh and contorted, a white cracker voice that sounds like its owner is just recovering from having his face pushed through a windshield, comes on the air spewing words like a Stengun. "Dat-wuz-de-Wolf!" gushes the voice. "Now, it's ole Phillips, playin' da *Red, Hot 'n' Blues,* comin' threw HBQew in *Ho*-tel Chisko, on the magazine flowh. We cumin' atchoo cutahsey People's Fernitcher Company, 310 South Main, where ya jes pay a little down an' pay for it while ya wearin' it out—or when they ketch up with ya! Ha! Thass more like it! It's awright! Nervous? Gitten' a divorce? It's OK. Jes' tell 'em Phillips sentcha! Now, anybody wannah buy a fur-lined mousetrap? No! Well, got one here by Sister Rosetta Tharpe—'Strange Thing's Are Happenin' Every Day!' " At that instant, out of the speaker blasts the red-hot trumpet voice of the inspired sister shouting biblical phrases in thrilling, flawlessly phrased jazz licks, echoed ritualistically by the stoic mezzo of Marie Knight, as the air waves crepitate with the rockin', rollickin' boogie-woogie beat of the lady herself, playing lime-tart acoustic guitar, like Scrapper Blackwell with Leroy Carr on a rompin' an' ravin' night in Naptown.

Dewey Phillips, that classic cornpone speed freak, was soon to play an important part in the unfolding of Elvis's fame as the first DJ ever to broadcast an Elvis Presley record. The maker of that record was also named Phillips, though there was no family relationship between the men. Sam Phillips, the proprietor of Sun Records, was Memphis's foremost independent record producer. Not your typical indie operator—a Jewish hustler from Big Town—Phillips was an earnest, cat-faced country boy from the Bible Belt, born and reared near the same little city that had produced W. C. Handy, Florence, Alabama. Instead of getting into the music business by running a record store or a nightclub in the ghetto, Phillips began his career in radio. His first job was spinning white gospel and country music discs at a station in nearby Muscle Shoals. Perhaps the most important difference between Phillips and other R & B producers was that he made to every record he cut a very tangible and absolutely indispensable contribution: Phillips was the recording engineer.

The creator of the "Sun Sound" learned the craft of recording music in the late forties while working as a station engineer at WERC in Memphis. One of his regular assignments was taping for subsequent broadcast over the CBS network the bands that played at the Skyway Room atop the Hotel Peabody. In 1950, Phillips decided to supplement his salary by establishing a professional recording service. The studio he constructed, largely with his own hands, has been restored recently as a landmark by Gray Line Tours. Located about a mile from Elvis's old home in the Lauderdale Courts, 706 Union Avenue is a narrow, deep, one-story building that looks about right for a neighborhood hardware store or painting supply shop. The façade is two tall display windows flanking a narrow door. Inside is a very small reception area that was once narrowed even more by desks on either side: one for Phillips and the other for his receptionist, secretary and woman-of-all-work, Marion Keisker.

Passing through another doorway into the main portion of the building, you find yourself in a good sized, thirty-by-eighteen-foot recording studio lined with white acoustic tile. Patterned after the typical radio station of the time, the room's only peculiarity was a dog-leg wall designed to break up the sound waves and improve the chamber's acoustics. Phillips used a maximum of eight Shure, RCA and Electrovoice mikes positioned on upright stands or hanging from booms. No baffles were employed and according to Phillips's technical assistant, Jack Clement, the principal source of the much-admired Sun Sound was simply leakage from one instrument into its neighbor's mike.

The back wall of the studio has a raised horizontal window behind which is the control booth. Here Phillips installed an RCA radio-style console with five input channels controlled by rotary "pots" or knobs. On either side of the console stood the Presto lathes for cutting custom discs: one for microgroove, the other for 78s. At the back of the booth were the tape recorders: two big bulky Ampex 350s. The famous "slap-back" echo, the hallmark of Sun Records, was not produced by an echo chamber. A second mike was run from the soloist to a second tape recorder and this recording was overdubbed on the primary recording with a split-second delay. No other overdubbing was done. The recording procedure consisted simply of striking a balance between the mikes and then capturing the whole performance in a single take.

Memphis Recording Service advertised, "We Record Anything—Anywhere—Anytime." In practice, "anything" reduced to an endless series of weddings, funerals, conferences and public addresses. Phillips would cart his portable gear out to the job and take down the words of ceremony or business for nine dollars per LP side. If you came into the studio, you could make a 78 RPM record for just four dollars.

No sooner did Phillips complete his studio than he began to get some business of an entirely different kind. Independents in other parts of the country, Chess in Chicago and Modern in Los Angeles, for example, were very interested in obtaining recordings of unknown but promising performers in the Memphis area. The arrangement was that Phillips would engage the musicians and pay the cost of the session; then, if the results were what the out-of-town company was seeking, it would lease the master from Phillips and pay him so many cents per side sold. In this manner, the obscure radio engineer found himself making the first recordings of subsequently famous artists like B. B. King, Howlin' Wolf and Bobby "Blue" Bland. Not only did Phillips's recordings pass muster as viable commercial products: A couple of them astonished every-one by climbing to the very top of the R & B charts.

"Rocket 88," a honking, hard-driving paean to the life-style symbol-ized by the new rocket-tailed Oldsmobile 88, was put together by the then totally unknown Ike Turner, who was working as a DJ on a station in Jackson, Mississippi. Issued by Chess with the name of the singer, Jackie Brenston, on the label, the record not only rocketed to the Number One position but remained on the charts for seventeen weeks. Another side, called "Booted," featuring a mediocre singer named Roscoe Gordon, repeated the success of "Rocket 88" by reaching first place and hanging on the charts for thirteen weeks. These successes were enough to convince Sam Phillips that instead of just functioning as an engineer, he should become an independent record producer. Thus was born Sun Records, its logo a crowing red rooster standing on a fence haloed by a bright yellow rising sun.

Sun issued its first record on March 1, 1952. A screeching duet for alto saxes, it went nowhere. Several subsequent releases fared just as badly; eventually the whole first year of operation had to be written off as a loss. Though Phillips was working with first-rate black talent, such as the famous pioneer of the electric harmonica, Little Walter— soon to become one of the greatest stars of the Chicago blues style— Sun couldn't produce a hit.

In addition to the problems of making successful records, Phillips and his partners faced some steep business hurdles. Breaking into the record business has never been easy, while making out in the hucklebuck world of R & B had long challenged the resourcefulness of even the greatest hustlers. Hits were the name of the game. Without them, no indie could survive. One way to get a hit was to come up with a new gimmick. This is exactly what Rufus Thomas supplied when, almost a year to the day after the company's first release, he came into the office with a hot new idea.

Thomas had written an answer to a record that was rapidly climbing the charts: Willa Mae Thornton's "Hound Dog." Answer records were an old device in the R & B game: a great way to catch a free ride on the coattails of somebody else's hit. His answer, "Bearcat," was fine so far as the words went: Rufus threw Willa Mae's putdown of shiftless men right back in her teeth. The problem was they were stuck for a tune, always the item in shortest supply in the music business and especially hard to come by at Sun, which had no house composers or arrangers and was far away from the teeming brains in the Brill Building. As speed was vital if they were to cash in on a current hit, someone suggested that they rip off the original tune. Sam Phillips agreed. The record was cut the same day and rushed into production. It hit the charts and started to climb. On the strength of its success, Phillips landed a series of distribution deals in key markets. Then, the funk hit the fan.

"Hound Dog," written by Jerry Leiber and Mike Stoller with Johnny Otis, had been issued by Peacock Records of Houston, which was operated by a very tough and belligerent black dude named Don Robey, who was notorious for traveling around town with a couple of pistol-packing bodyguards. Robey sued Phillips for violation of his copyright and BMI refused to license the "new" song. A judge ruled in Robey's favor, but when the two producers started thrashing out their problems, they decided it was better to let the rip-off remain on the market making money they could share than simply to kill the record. Phillips wound up paying two cents per side to Robey and all court costs.

Having scored with one gimmick, it was time to look for another. One day Phillips received a promising demonstration record from Nashville. It was a black vocal group singing a song titled "Just Walkin' in the Rain," written by their lead singer, Johnny Bragg. The group's name, the Prisonaires, was explained by the fact that they were all serving time in the state penitentiary at Nashville. Working out a fast deal with the prison officials, Phillips obtained the services of this vocal chain gang. They arrived under heavy guard to give their "command" performance. Strange to say, the record leaped to Number Ten on the country music charts and was covered immediately by a number of pop singers, including the still unknown Johnny Ray. Subsequently, the Prisonaires recorded a song of praise for Tennessee's music-loving Governor, Frank Clement ("Well, what about Frank Clement? He's a mighty, mighty man o' god!"), and won their release from the slammer. The Prisonaires scored their hit in April 1953. After that Sun did not have another hit until Elvis Presley broke through in the summer of 1954.

Elvis turned up at 706 Union Avenue for the first time on a Saturday afternoon in the fall of 1953. According to the Myth he came to cut a record as a birthday present for his mother. As his mother's birthday was long past and the Presleys had no phonograph, this story can be discounted as an early attempt to exploit Elvis's relationship with Gladys. Elvis himself stated that he had no expectations of a singing career at this time but was simply curious to hear how he sounded on record. The two tunes he cut that day were oldies by the Ink Spots, and it's indicative of Elvis's mimetic approach to recording that he sought to copy both the high, sweet tenor of Bill Kenney in the chorus and the deep resonant bass of Hoppy Jones in the talking bridge. Elvis described his guitar playing as sounding like "somebody beating on a bucket lid."

Though Elvis's performance was gauche, his voice triggered a strong association in the mind of Marion Keisker, who was alone that day at the studio. She recalled Sam Phillips saying repeatedly, "If I could find a white boy who could sing like a nigger, I could make a million dollars." Keisker wrote down Elvis's name and Rabbi Fruchter's phone number. Beside them she noted: "Good ballad singer. Hold."

Elvis got his big chance at Sun about nine months later when Phillips, eager to cut a new song but needing a high, soulful voice, gave in to Keisker's urgings and agreed to try "the kid with the sideburns." Elvis came panting into the studio, having run virtually the whole way from Alabama Street. After trying repeatedly to copy the demo record, he faced finally a disappointed and exasperated Sam Phillips, who demanded, "Well, what *can* you sing?" Elvis started pulling tunes out of the air, ranging through every style but with the emphasis falling on his hero, Dean Martin. When the audition ended, Elvis hadn't sold Phillips. The producer said Elvis needed "a lot of work." Elvis said that he would like "to get me a band."

As it happened, Phillips had a western swing band on tap called Doug Poindexter's Starlite Wranglers. The guitarist, Winfield Scott Moore, was an ambitious young fellow, fresh out of the service, recently married, working at his brother's cleaning plant but eager to make a career in the music business. Phillips put Elvis together with Scotty Moore and with his neighbor on Belz Street, Bill Black, an older musician, a burly clown who played string bass. As the three men began to work together, they discovered a common ground in their sense of time. As Black remarked in later years, "Rhythm was what Elvis went by."

Just before Phillips recorded Elvis Presley in the summer of 1954, he appears to have changed his recording strategy. He began to swing away from black artists and concentrate on white country singers. His real goal remained, however, finding a way to combine the feel of black music with the audience appeal that could be generated in the pop market only by a white singer.

Chapter 8

Solar Flair

ON THE EVENING of July 6, 1954, the nineteen-year-old Elvis Presley arrived at 706 Union Avenue for his first professional recording session. After a day on which the temperature had reached 102 degrees, the tightly sealed, white-tiled studio was sweltering. At nightfall, a mist blanketed the city. Perhaps this soggy atmosphere accounts for the quality of Elvis's initial effort, a corny country ballad titled "I Love You Because."

On the first take, Elvis employs a specious tenor that slides from note to note with greasy insinuation, while the electric guitar runs tremolos up and down the strings, like wiggling water bugs. When Elvis reaches the talking bridge, his voice becomes expressionless, his sentiments unbelievable. Hollowly, he recites: "Ah love you . . . Ah love you, baby . . . because . . ."—*because it says so in this dumb song!*

In a later take, he *whistles* the introduction and omits the embarrassing recitation. This time, though, the tempo drags so badly that the song hovers on the verge of collapse. Sam Phillips could not have been feeling optimistic when he switched on the studio monitor and told the boys to take a break.

Before the session Phillips had suggested to Elvis that he do one of the songs of Arthur "Big Boy" Crudup (pronounced

Croodup), a pioneer of the Mississippi-Chicago electric blues style. They had talked over all the Crudup numbers that Elvis knew—"Cool Disposition," "Rock Me Mama," "Hey Mama," "Everything's All Right"— and settled on "That's All Right Mama," Elvis's especial favorite. Now, during the break, the fidgety Elvis started goofing on this tune, trying to raise a laugh.

"Elvis just started clowning," recollects Scotty Moore. "I joined in as soon as I found out what key we were in. Then, the control room doors opened. Sam was in there doin' somethin', and he came out and said: 'What are y' all doin'?' Elvis said, 'I don' know—just goofin' off!' Sam said, 'Well, that sounds pretty good. Back up and see if you can figure out what you're doin', and let's put it on tape.' So we kinda talked it over and figured out a little bit what we were doin'. We ran it again, and of course, Sam is listenin'. 'Bout the third or fourth time through, we just cut it—and that was that! It was basically a rhythm record. It wasn't any great thing. It wasn't Sam tellin' him what to do. Elvis was joking around, just doing what come naturally, what he felt."

The record so modestly described by one of its makers was, in fact, a remarkable feat of breathing in one cultural atmosphere and breathing out another. When you play the Presley side immediately after hearing the Crudup cut, you can hardly believe that both singers are doing the same tune. The difference is as great as that between Mick Jagger and Aretha Franklin singing "I Can't Get No Satisfaction"; in fact, the difference is rather the same, the later version in each case being what might be called the eroticization of the original.

Crudup's old recording summons up the atmosphere of the South Chicago blues bars during the days of go-man-go jump jazz. The tempo is fast, the rhythm is tense, the vocal delivery is as hard and straight as a hard, black bowling ball rolling down a polished alley. Elvis's performance, by contrast, suggests a farm boy lying up in a fragrant hayloft daydreaming of what he'd like to do with that little mama who is giving him such a runaround. The rhythm is relaxed and rural, the guitar chimes like a bell, the atmosphere is vernal—a hillbilly *Frühlingstimmen!* There is intensity, though, in the singing. Pitching his voice way up high, in a range that suggests ecstasy, Elvis phrases the lines so that they stretch and yearn and writhe like a boogaloo; then, when he reaches the refrain, "That's all right, mama, that's all right with me," he teases and taunts and releases the tension he has been building in a cadence that drifts down with sensuous little swells and diminuendos like a dancer boogeyin' down. The total effect can be summed up in one word—*sexy!*

Sam Phillips skillfully seconded this inspired interpretation by enhancing the high ecstatic voice with a subtle aura of quavering echo. It's worth noting that this was the first time Phillips ever employed this effect in recording a white singer. It was a stroke of genius—perhaps the most brilliant inspiration of this famous producer's career. Indeed, when you weigh the forces that contributed to Elvis Presley's breakthrough, Phillips's claim to importance appears completely justified. Not only did he give Elvis the right steer in directing him away from lugubrious ballads to the currently fashionable R & B material, but he attached to his new star's raw and untrained voice the electronic prosthesis that masked his vocal faults while it transformed—or should we say transfigured?—his vocal quality into the now legendary Presley sound.

The balance of this first session was spent in finding a song that would work as the B side of the Crudup tune. The solution that was arrived at entailed another transmogrification of a traditional style. Impelled by some profound and instinctive principle of cultural compensation, these southern boys and their bossman decided to make the flip side of their bid for fame a take-off from the other side of the southern racial barrier (or the other end of the state of Tennessee), a classic white-trash bluegrass song: Bill Monroe's "Blue Moon Over Kentucky."

Just as in the Crudup song Elvis stretched and writhed, as if under the spell of spring fever, so in this country classic, at the points where Monroe is snapping off his phrases like rattraps or shooting up abruptly into a yodeler's falsetto, Elvis is caressing the open-vowelled rhymes—"on a moonlight *naiiiight,* stars were shinin' *braiiiight,*" in rising and falling glissandos, like a Neapolitan tenor. (No wonder he came to have such an admiration for Mario Lanza!)

Having flourished his leek so triumphantly with the Crudup song, it was natural that Elvis should let out his mind a little further on this follow-up recording. If "That's All Right Mama" enjoys the honor of having been Elvis's breakthrough, his first great moment in the ring, "Blue Moon" enjoys the distinction of being the first side on which Elvis opens up his bag of tricks. The first and greatest trick is what has aptly been called Elvis's "vocal orchestration." This is the knack of using the voice to suggest all the instruments and effects that are lacking in the threadbare world of folk music. As a young man who had heard a vast amount of music but who had no greater musical resources than his vocal chords, his rhythm guitar and his tiny two-piece, semipro "band," Elvis Presley found himself in the familiar position of the musically inspired, musically initiated, but musically deprived all over the world. His solution to his problem was the classic solution, the solution that occurs instinctually to every musical primitive—he made himself into a one-man band.

Now what do bands do when they open up a tune? They set the mood, establish the rhythm and build up the listener's expectations by playing an introduction. What happens in these introductions? Well, the band sets a riff, a simple rhythmic phrase bitten off from the first notes of the melody; then they play a flashy cadence and cut the mother loose! Which is just what the nineteen-year-old Elvis Presley did that hot night in the studio at Memphis with "Blue Moon." As Scotty and Bill and Elvis himself laid the rhythm, a Western swing rhythm, Elvis vocalized a riff built on the phrase, "Blue moon . . . Blue moon"; then, when he came to the cadence, he improvised a lick that will go down in history as the quintessential Presley get-off. Down the scale he tumbled in vigorous syncopation, singing, "you're Go-nah BRING-ah me BACK mah BAB-y to-NIGHT" while the reverb gave his voice a bizarre fun house echo. Only then, did he raise his voice to the "singing" level and deliver the song.

These naive artifices of the young Elvis Presley show him functioning as an instinctive composer. He's starting to apply all the things he learned during his curious apprenticeship to the gospel stage. Syllabifying the words—"you're go-nah bring-ah"—was, of course, the hallmark of Jake Hess's vocal style. Actually, it is an ancient practice that goes back to the very origins of American syncopated music in the ragtime era around the turn of the century. The classic example is that minstrellike song (parodied by T. S. Eliot in "Sweeney Agonistes"), "Under the Bamboo Tree," which is phrased: "If you like-ah me like I like-ah you," etc. Far from being an expression of the way-out new world of rock 'n' roll, this gimmick was hoary with eld. So were, if the truth be told, most of Elvis's characteristic mannerisms, including not only his favorite vocal tricks but his dance steps, catch phrases and stage postures. Remember that Elvis studied showbiz in the oldest schools in the nation: the all-night sing and the black southern radio. His notion of what was hip was almost quaint.

Being "out" is sometimes better than being "in." Especially is this the case when you're destined to become the embodiment of a culture as profoundly regressive—in all senses of the word—as was rock 'n' roll. The motto of this music was never better articulated than in that song of the sixties that ran: "Gonna buy me a time machine and go to the turn of the century. Everything's happening at the turn of the century." Rock from the beginning was a throwback to an earlier and more naive kind of music than the commercial jazz or the Broadway show tunes that had dominated American consciousness during the thirties and forties. Year by year, step by step, rock delved back into the past until finally it created the climate for a full-scale revival of ragtime, the thing that was "happenin' at the turn of the century." So Elvis Presley's naive mimickry of the styles and sounds of preceding genera- tions—the introductory riffs of the swing bands, the hubba-hubba rhythm vocalizing of the twenties, the cornball glottal stroke—stood him in good stead when it came time to reverse the course of American musi- cal history and start driving with eyes firmly fixed on the rearview mirror.

The jazzing up of the country style coupled with the rusticating of the R & B idiom, itself derived from black rural roots, established a new genre in American music called rockabilly. No sooner had Elvis shaped the basic mold than into it poured the talents of a whole school of hitherto unknown performers, commencing with Carl Perkins, Johnny Cash, Jerry Lee Lewis and Roy Orbison (all Sun artists), and going on to include Buddy Holly, the Everly Brothers and the early Beatles; for as John Lennon remarked, "Before Elvis there was nothing."

To think of a nineteen- or twenty-year-old boy producing this sort of effect with his very first efforts as a professional is to recognize that the young Elvis was a pop genius. As Kant says, genius exists to allow nature to give new rules to art, its distinctive hallmark being originality. To comprehend the originality of an Elvis Presley, however, you have to recognize first that it derives in great degree from an apparently oppo- site principle: the instinct of mimickry.

The secret of Elvis's art lay not in an act of substantive creation but in a recasting of one traditional style in terms of another. To make such a transposition, you have to be stylistically sophisticated. You have to see all the familiar styles lying before you like so many spots of color on a painter's palette. Such sophistication would have taken many years to develop in the premedia world of popular music. Once, however, every American child started growing up with unlimited access to every kind of music provided by radio, any boy with a good ear and the neces- sary talent could get hip fast.

Elvis Presley was from his earliest years a marvelous mimic. This gift was fundamental to both his great success and his great failure as an artist. It enabled him on the one hand not only to pick up on the going thing but to do all sorts of tricks with the currently popular styles, including the basic trick of transmuting one style into its opposite. On the other hand, Elvis's mimetic aptitude exposed him to the temptation to turn into a commercial copycat.

During his Sun years, he used his talent to create a music that was essentially playful and parodistic. In approaching pop song in this spirit, he established the basic esthetic for rock 'n' roll. Rock is not, as is always said, simply an amalgam of blues, country, pop, etc. This is to define it by its sources and substances instead of its soul. The music's essence lies in its attitude. That attitude first comes to expression in Elvis, then in Little Richard and then in the Beatles, to name the greatest performers in the tradition. All of these singers are at bottom parodists. They assume the identity provided by a particular style; then, working behind this mask, they achieve the exhilarating freedom of the ventriloquist talking through his zany dummy. Inevitably, they tend toward falsetto and caricature. They may even wind up becoming parodies of themselves, as did Elvis, Little Richard and John Lennon. What's more, the degree of sophistication, allusion, and fantasy in their work may vary greatly from the purely instinctive sass of Little Richard to the much more calculated "styling" of Elvis to the sometimes brilliantly resourceful travesties of John Lennon, which shade into the bizarre but compelling juxtapositions of surrealism. The important thing is to recognize that the root of rock is in the put-on and the take-off, the characteristic fusion of enthusiasm and mockery that was almost universal in the pop culture of the fifties: a slant on things that you find as much in *Mad* or the routines of Sid Caesar or the comic pornography of Terry Southern as you do in the funny songs of Leiber and Stoller or the funny singing of Elvis Presley.

On one of the rejected takes of "Blue Moon" that has surfaced in recent years, you can hear Sam Phillips exclaiming through the studio monitor: "Hell, that's different! That's a pop song now, Little Vi! That's *good*!" How good it was became apparent on the following Saturday night, when Sam Phillips took a demo of his new record over to Dewey Phillips at WHBQ. Dewey had premiered other Sun releases; he was always willing to give the local product a spin. Elvis's record posed a problem, however, because Dewey programmed nothing but black singers. As he and Sam Phillips were discussing this difficulty, Dewey got the idea of calling in another, younger, DJ, who was preparing his morning broadcast. This was Wink Martindale, later well known as a quiz show MC. Martindale offers a good description of what happened on this famous night.

"Dewey called me in after Sam brought the record down to get my opinion. He played it for me. I thought the guy was black. Sam said, 'No, he's not black. He's white. He drives a truck for Crown Electric.' Then, he told the story of how Elvis had come in to make a record for his mother's birthday and so forth. He told me, 'We've been working for a year and a half to get something commercial.' Dewey had some hesitancy about playing the record because he played nothing but race music. Finally, around nine-fifteen or nine-thirty, he put it on the air. The results were incredible.

"You have to understand that Dewey always took a lot of requests and even talked to people on the air. This was before TV, and every kid in Memphis was listening to him. This night the switchboard lit up like a Christmas tree. Dewey would play 'Blue Moon Over Kentucky,' then turn it over and play 'That's All Right Mama.' It was just those two sides for the rest of the evening. Finally, Dewey said to Sam, 'Get that guy down here!' Sam got in touch with Elvis's mom."

Gladys Presley recalled in 1956 that Elvis "fixed the radio that night and told us to leave it on that station. Then he went to the movies. I guess he was just too nervous to listen." When Phillips reached Gladys, Dewey Phillips got on the line and yelled, "You just get that cottonpickin' son of yours over here to the station. I want him on the air." Gladys was thrilled. "I ran over and I hugged Vernon and I suppose I cried a little bit. Then we both went looking for Elvis."

Elvis had retreated with a friend to the dark security of the Suzore 2. When he spied his mother going down the aisle searching for him, he whispered: "Mama, what's happening?" "Plenty, son," said Gladys, "but it's all good." Then Gladys and Vernon took the boys over to the radio station on the mezzanine of the Chiska Hotel. When Elvis came into the studio, Dewey Phillips barked: "Sit down. I'm gone interview you." "Mr. Phillips," trembled Elvis, "I don't know nuthin' 'bout bein' interviewed." "Just don't say nuthin' dirty," snapped Phillips.

Many years later Phillips told a writer: "I asked him where he went to high school. He said, 'Humes.' I wanted to get that out because a lot of people listening had thought he was colored. Finally, I said, 'All right, Elvis, thank you very much.' 'Aren't you gone interview me?' he asked. 'I already have,' I said. 'The mike's been open the whole time.' He broke out in a cold sweat."

The next month produced a flurry of developments in Elvis's catapulting career. Five thousand orders for the record were booked in the first week after it was played on the air. Officially released on July 19, by the end of the month it was Number Three on Memphis's country and western chart. Immediately a swarm of people approached Elvis to seek some financial advantage from the newly fledged performer. Sam Phillips advised Elvis to sign a ten percent deal with Scotty Moore as booking agent to discourage the sharks. Phillips also had the good idea of calling a local disc jockey named Bob Neal, who was promoting a country show at the Overton Park Shell, to ask if there was a spot on the program for Elvis. Neal asked what it would cost him. Phillips said Elvis would work for free just for the publicity. Neal countered that they better get him in the union and pay scale, which was virtually nothing. Phillips then got together with Joe Cuoghi, who owned Popular Tunes, a record store on Poplar Avenue, and they split the cost of an ad in the paper showing a cut of Elvis's head and advertising his appearance as if he were the star of the show and the headliner, Slim Whitman, were just an added attraction.

On the night of July 30, 1954, Elvis Presley made his real debut as a public performer. The Shell in Overton Park is a small acoustic mirror placed on a shallow but broad stage at the bottom of an amphitheater cut into a hillside and furnished with long benches. Elvis had his turn at the commencement of the program. Walking onstage with Scotty Moore and Bill Black, he waited till Scotty had plugged in and then kicked off with "That's All Right Mama," giving the tune everything he had. No sooner did he start singing, than he began to hear a lot of shouting and screeching from the audience. Too obsessed with going over big to worry what was causing the noise, he kept on singing and banging his guitar till he got through the tune. Then, after the applause, he launched into "Blue Moon." Again, there was a lot of unexplained noise from the crowd. When Elvis finished this time, he discovered that he had stopped the show cold. The audience was demanding an encore. As Elvis huddled with the band, he demanded: "What's makin' 'em holler so much?" "It was your leg, man!" Scotty and Bill told him, laughing. "It was the way you were shakin' your left leg. That's what got 'em screamin'."

Chapter 9

The Hillbilly Cat

THE BIGGEST payoff Elvis received from his first hit was a shot at the most prestigious country music show in America: *Grand Ole Opry.* As with everything else in the career of Elvis Presley, this overnight hop to the top of the country jamboree circuit was an unprecedented short circuit of the usual laborious course which commenced typically on some little hillbilly station out in the sticks, then worked up to one of the popular regional shows, like the *Wheeling Jamboree* or the *Louisiana Hayride,* until, finally, the aspiring star reached the oldest and most successful program of them all, broadcast from the capital of country music, Nashville. What an audition for the *Opry* offered was a chance to become an *Opry* regular: one of the more than a hundred performers who appeared at least twenty times a year, receiving in addition to a fee of about forty dollars the right to use the name of the *Opry* in all their publicity and to be booked by the *Opry*'s Artist Service Bureau on the tours that played to millions of people every year.

Though the *Opry* represented the summit of aspiration for any true country act, it was a highly unsuitable showcase for Elvis Presley. During the course of its thirty-year history, the *Opry* had become a bastion of conservatism. Its audience was comprised of old people and kids, with nary a teenager in attendance. The program had a deliberately old-fashioned barn dance atmosphere that relied heavily on nostalgia for the good ole days. Only one black man had ever been a regular, and there was a strict taboo against the use of drums on the *Opry* stage. Booking Elvis Presley with his long hair, lurid clothes and rhythm and blues style into this house was like throwing him into the lion's den.

September 25, 1954, the date of Elvis's first and only performance on the show, was selected by Sam Phillips because it coincided with the release of Elvis's second record: "I Don't Care if the Sun Don't Shine" coupled with "Good Rockin' Tonight." On the morning of that memorable day, Elvis, Scotty, Bill, Sam Phillips and Marion Keisker piled into two cars and drove the two hundred miles from Memphis to Nashville, stopping finally in the alley behind the famous old Ryman Auditorium. A relic of the religious revivals of the late nineteenth century, the Ryman is a forbidding-looking brick and stone Romanesque structure suggesting a cross between a church and a prison. The fan-shaped interior is filled with steeply-raked curved wooden benches dimly lit by bullet-shaped painted-glass windows. Elvis, who had imagined the pantheon of country pops as a more resplendent place, spent the afternoon wandering around the quaint old building exclaiming: "You mean this is what I've been dreaming about all these years!"

Jim Denny, the truculent manager of the *Opry*, refused to allow Elvis to plug his new record. He insisted that the young singer perform the two songs that had already been successful. He also raised hell because Elvis hadn't brought his "full band"! The show divided then, as now, into half-hour segments, each one presided over by one of the reigning stars. Elvis was assigned to the portion MC'ed by the current hero of country music, Hank Snow. The feisty little Snow would soon learn to know Elvis only too well; at this time, he had never heard of him. When the time came to make the introduction, he snapped: "What's your name?" "Elvis Presley, sir," came the answer. "No," Snow snorted, "I mean what name do you sing under?"

Chet Atkins, destined soon to become the organizer of Elvis's recording sessions at Nashville, caught his first glimpse of the new star that night. He was shocked by Elvis's appearance. "I couldn't get over that eye shadow he was wearing," recalls Atkins with a sly smile. "It was like seein' a couple of guys kissin' in Key West." Atkins remembers Elvis going over well with the audience. Unfortunately, he provoked the ire of the choleric Denny, who voiced his disgust bluntly. As soon as the show was over, Denny told Elvis: "We don't do that nigger music around here. If I were you, I'd go back to driving a truck."

All the way home to Memphis, he cried hot tears. Monday morning, he was right back where Denny said he should be: driving a truck for Crown Electric.

The disaster at Nashville was soon offset by a solid success on the *Opry*'s rival show, the *Louisiana Hayride*. In fact, Elvis could have begun his radio career with triumph instead of defeat if it hadn't been for Sam Phillip's failure of judgment in booking him on the *Opry*. The *Hayride* was the logical choice for Elvis because in its short six-year history it had proven itself just as open and receptive to new talent as the *Opry* had been closed and scornful toward novelty. The great Hank Williams had gotten his start on the *Hayride*, as had Webb Pierce, Slim Whitman, Jim Reeves, Faron Young and so many others that the show had been tagged "The Cradle of the Stars."

The *Hayride* was presented in the massive Shreveport Municipal Auditorium, which has a seating capacity of about 3500. The set for the broadcasts was a big painted drop depicting a barn and silo set against a country landscape and overhung by a huge spreading tree whose leaves were glued on a hanging border. On the front of the barn was painted in bold letters, "LOUISIANA HAYRIDE" and the call letters of the station that produced the show, KWKH. The format for the three-hour show was a succession of fifteen-minute sequences, each one featuring one of the regular performers on the show.

It was early in the program when the announcer, Frank Page, introduced Elvis. "Just a few weeks ago," he said, "a young man from Memphis, Tennessee, recorded a song on the Sun label; and, in just a matter of weeks, that record has skyrocketed right up the charts. It's really doing well all over the country. He's only nineteen years old. And he's a singer who's forging a new style. *Elvis Presley!* Let's give him a hand! [Applause] Elvis, are you geared up with your band to let us hear your songs?" Elvis was not only geared up but wired up. His voice, so high, so rural, so charged with nervous tension, raced along as he replied: "I'd like to say how happy we are to appear on the *Louisiana Hayride*. And we're gonna do a song for you—[to Page] you got anything else to say? We're gonna do a song for you we got on Sun Records that goes like this. . . ." Then, Elvis and his boys were off and running, shouting and strumming "That's All Right Mama."

So warm was their reception that Elvis and the Blue Moon Boys— as they were starting to call themselves—were invited back the following week and offered a one-year contract. The agreement stipulated that they would work a forty-eight-week session, with weekends off at the discretion of the management. Remuneration was "scale": eighteen dollars for the leader and twelve dollars for the sidemen. In other words, Elvis and his two men were expected to drive four hundred miles down from Memphis and four hundred miles back every weekend to spend the most valuable night of the week working on the *Hayride* for a grand total of fifty-four dollars!

The real compensation lay in the fact that Elvis would soon become a familiar name in the "territories"—Texas, Louisiana, Arkansas—where everyone listened to the *Hayride*. He would be able to pick up a lot of bookings in the area and also participate in the package shows that were constantly put together by various promoters who drew on the pool of talent that had been assembled by the *Hayride*. Eventually, Elvis would work every small town in the region, becoming especially popular in Texas, where he played a five-day tour at least once a month, opening, say, in Wichita Falls and playing one-nighters in Bryan, Conroe, Austin and Gonzales; or opening in Shreveport and moving west to Paris, San Marcos, Austin and Nacogdoches. It was no accident, therefore, that Elvis Presley's first fame was in this part of the country and that his first fan club was organized in Dallas.

Radio was the real foundation of Elvis's success. Radio put him before a large listening public at a time when he had only a few records. Radio broadcast these records far beyond the limited advertising and distribution powers of Sun Records. Radio inspired local bookers to engage Elvis. Radio even spread Elvis's story by affording him a chance in every town he played to get on a local DJ show and give an interview. As we shall see soon, though Elvis came to fame in the age of television, it was always radio that did the basic work of spreading the Presley gospel.

All through the fall and winter of 1954–55, Elvis continued to record at Sun. It is unfortunate that we cannot accompany him through these legendary sessions, but there is no way to reconstruct his progress in detail. As so many of the songs display the same devices of performance, however, we are justified in taking them as a whole and discussing them as a consistent body of work. As such, they stand in marked contrast to the recordings Elvis made even in his first year with RCA. Indeed, it is widely felt today that the Sun records represent the best of Elvis Presley and that the moment he shifted to Victor, the quality of his work became markedly commercial. What then distinguishes the Sun records and makes them superior?

The first thing one has to say is that they are not all superior. The slow ballads, like "I Love You Because," "Harbor Lights," "Blue Moon," etc., are distinctly inferior not only to the rhythm tunes but to the ballads that Elvis recorded as early as 1957. The poise, the vocal control, even the quality of voice demanded by ballad singing were obviously resources that Elvis did not command at the commencement of his career. What we are talking about when we say that the Sun records are his best are only the rhythm songs.

What makes these performances so interesting is their extreme eccentricity. They are extremely playful, witty and inventive. Every tune is cast in a different mold, which usually has nothing to do with the original. Each song sets running through Elvis's mind a stream of musical associations that constitute a kind of fantasia inspired by the song. The basic appeal is, therefore, to the musical imagination. To characterize these performances in terms of mere energy or rhythm or any ethno-musical quality is wrong. The performances are densely detailed, quirky with oddity, sometimes downright funny. The reason they don't wear thin, as do Elvis's later and more famous recordings, is the same reason why jazz recordings hold the attention through dozens of playings: The performances are highly spontaneous and have the not easily exhausted suggestiveness of brilliant sketchwork. Essentially, they are play: the play of high spirits that sends ideas shooting in every direction like sparks. They might even be considered the comic flip side to the even denser and more suggestive blues fantasias of that other brilliant young recording genius, Robert Johnson.

The clue to the esthetic of all these sunny sides is in the false start that Elvis makes on "Milkcow Boogie." He commences this song by singing in the style of an old country bluesman, mimicking the tintype vocal quality, phrasing and tempo. Then, after a few bars, he breaks off abruptly and exclaims: "Hold it, fellas! That don't *move* me. Let's get real, real gone for a change!" Then, they take off again, doing a green-apple quickstep that transforms the tune into a headlong rhythm song. Elvis rides the vocal line like a bucking bronco, improvising freely as he dashes along. What he is saying, in effect, is that the time has come to jazz up the old blues. Yet, the truth is that twenty years before he made this recording, jazz musicians were performing the same trick with tunes that they would play in conventional style and then swing. Twenty or thirty years before swing, the trick would have been to rag the tune. Back around the turn of the century, as Jelly Roll Morton demonstrated on a classic Library of Congress recording, New Orleans musicians turned a French Quadrille into "Tiger Rag." In fine, what Elvis is doing in his Sun records is repeating instinctively that process

of making music new by recharging its rhythm in a way that has characterized every stylistic revolution in the history of twentieth-century pops.
This instinctive compliance with the deepest pattern in our popular musical culture gives the Sun sides an archetypal quality.

As to the distinction between the Sun records and those Elvis made
in his first years for RCA, the distinguishing difference is not vocal or
technical or emotional: It is mental. Elvis is much more creative at the
commencement of his career. He is much more lighthearted. He's having
fun and coming up with an endless stream of amusing ideas. Instead
of laboring to copy a hit by Little Richard or masticating a piece of
musical bubblegum, he's sending up a lot of old or old-fashioned tunes
that don't deserve to be treated seriously. This prevailing tone of high-
spirited mockery explains also why he fails so completely with the ballads.
Not only does he lack the poise and control they demand; he doesn't
genuinely sympathize with them. He has to put on an act when he
mouths these trashy complaints. It's hard to be a great crooner at the
age of nineteen.

In November 1954, Elvis got a call from the promoter who had
booked him on the Overton Shell show, Robert Neal Hobgood. Bob
Neal was one of the best-known public personalities in Memphis and
its environs. Broadcasting from the local country station, WMPS, he
was on the air twice a day with two very popular shows. In the early,
early bright, from five to eight A.M., he entertained the folks from two
hundred miles around with hillbilly records, cornball jokes and ukelele
solos on the *Bob Neal Farm Show.* At noon, he was back on the air
for an hour with the *High Noon Roundup,* a show divided into fifteen-
minute segments, including one that featured the Blackwood Brothers.
There was a studio audience for this show. Seated among that little
audience was often the young Elvis Presley, who during his lunch break
would bop over to the station in the basement of the Peabody Hotel.
In the afternoons and evenings, Neal would do what he called his "promotions." These were little country music shows which he staged within
a hundred-mile radius of Memphis. The routine was invariable. In the
late afternoon, Neal, his wife, Helen, and the oldest of his five children,
Sonny, would take off in their Lincoln and drive down to, say, Hernando,
Mississippi or Eldorado, Arkansas. There, at the local schoolhouse, they
would meet two or three second- or third-string acts from *Grand Ole
Opry,* who were eager to work any date just to gain the experience
and exposure. Helen would sell tickets at the door: fifty cents for children,
one dollar for adults. Sonny would hawk glossy souvenir pictures of

the "stars." Bob Neal would be the show's MC, warming up the house with the same corny patter and ukelele playing he did on the air. After the show was over, Neal would give the school its cut for the use of the auditorium, divide the rest of the take between himself and the other performers, then dive gratefully into the back seat of his car to get some sleep in anticipation of his show early the following morning.

As if this were not enough hustling for one man, Neal also ran a record store that bore his name on Main Street, next door to the Warner Theater, and operated a management agency at 160 Union Avenue called Memphis Promotions. It was while wearing his manager's hat that Neal called Elvis. Neal had been impressed recently by the young singer's success on the *Louisiana Hayride*. Now he wanted to know whether he was correct in assuming that Sam Phillips had Elvis tied up in the neat little business package. When he asked Elvis whether he had a manager, the answer was no. This was not quite accurate, of course, but Elvis was not going to pass up the chance to get a real professional manager just because he had a little deal going with Scotty. Elvis and Neal came to an agreement immediately and Scotty made no objections to the arrangement.

The deal was quite conventional. Bob Neal was to undertake all the duties of a personal manager: pushing records, booking dates, handling business arrangements. In return, he was to receive fifteen percent commission. He suggested also that the boys take twenty percent off the top and set it aside as a promotion fund. D. J. Fontana, the drummer Elvis had picked up on the *Hayride,* would continue receiving his hundred dollars a week in salary and Elvis, Scotty and Bill would divide the balance according to their usual split: fifty percent to Elvis; twenty-five percent each to Scotty and Bill. The term of the contract was one year. It was at this time, in November 1954, that Elvis finally quit his job at Crown Electric.

When Neal started calling up DJs to promote Elvis's records, he found that his new client did not fit the bill. The country jocks said that Elvis sounded like a blues act. The R & B jocks said that Elvis sounded too country for their shows. Gradually, Neal realized that Elvis's records would not sell his talent. Elvis's personal appearances would have to create the demand for the records.

These appearances now became more frequent. Neal had the schoolhouse circuit down pat. He could book a lot of locations just on the strength of his own name. He could advertise the shows on his radio programs. He had a lot of acts who would open the shows for fifty dollars. Soon business was humming. In the period of a year, Elvis and the Blue Moon Boys played close to two hundred dates.

Once Elvis got busy on the road, he had to buy a car. Naturally, nothing but a Cadillac would do. Though he could only afford a second-hand machine (financed through Bob Neal), the day he got his first "Cad" Elvis felt that he had attained one of the great goals of his life. He sat up half the night gazing at the car from his hotel window.

Sad to say, on a run down to Texarkana not long afterward the rear of the car caught fire and the treasured vehicle had to be abandoned. With the insurance, Elvis went out and got another Cadillac. He had it painted pink and black, which now became his personal colors. Next, he bought his parents a pink and white Ford. By this point, the boy was launched on a career of car buying that probably has no equal in the annals of our car-crazy country.

What sort of show did Elvis put on in these early days? It was a country show, of course. It was also a corny show because both Elvis and Bill Black regarded themselves as comedians. Black, a big burly man with a big bull fiddle, did all the bits that were standard for entertainers who played "dog-house" bass. He twirled and slapped the instrument with all his might. He straddled and rode it around the stage as he played. He mugged and clowned, fighting hard some nights to break down the audience's resistance to Elvis's strange garb and no less strange style of performing. As the boys had to do forty-five minutes onstage, they couldn't confine themselves to their records. They ran the charts, doing all the current hits. The only thing that remained constant from one show to another was Elvis's determination to get to the audience and drive it wild.

In the country districts, deep in the Bible Belt, Elvis would work himself to the point of exhaustion, trying to get a rise from the house. When he had completed his frenzied performance, the staid farm folk would applaud politely and then come up to the stage to chat with the man whom they heard on the radio every morning between milking and breakfast, Bob Neal. They would talk to the DJ as if he were a preacher and ask him about his family as if he were a friend. They had no eyes for that wild spark, Elvis Presley. When the shows hit the bigger towns, however, the reaction would be entirely different. It was one night at Little Rock that Bob Neal saw an audience react so extravagantly to Elvis that it set his mind running on the stories he had read years before about the bobby-soxers swooning over Frank Sinatra.

Many nights on the way home, Elvis would sit beside Helen Neal and ask her earnestly: "Do you think I'll make it?" He wasn't talking about his singing career. From the jump, Elvis wanted to be a movie star. Mrs. Neal remembers Elvis's ideal as being someone like Clark Gable. Sonny Neal, three years Elvis's junior but a lot closer to him than his mother, recollects Elvis's hero accurately. Elvis aspired to be the second Rudolph Valentino. He fancied himself as a Latin lover. That was the real meaning of the famous sideburns. That was also the reason why at this time Elvis posed for beefcake shots, stripped to the waist with his hair tousled and his face set in a sullen, sultry leer. He even began to tell people that he had an Italian ancestor on his mother's side of the family.

This surprising identification with the film idol of the silent era, a man who was dead before Elvis was born, is the first unmistakable sign that Elvis had discovered the essence of his appeal and was starting to cultivate a corresponding image. It is also a sign of prescience, for nothing better defines Elvis's future role than the formula: teen Valentino. If you add to the basic image of the sultry Latin lover the further garnishings of an erotic style of music and dance, the tango for the twenties, rock 'n' roll for the fifties, the parallel is perfect. Soon Elvis would even have crow-black hair.

Elvis's sexual appeal brought a lot of girls around to the parking lot. Mrs. Neal used to pull her son and Elvis into the car right after the shows. Actually, she had no cause for alarm. Elvis behaved in a very puritanical manner. Sonny recalls: "Elvis was really a prude. Girls lost their appeal for him when they were easy to get. He always said that he wanted to marry a virgin." Though Elvis was uptight about girls, he was often threatened by tough teenagers who resented the way he excited their girls. It was largely to counter these threats that Elvis began taking along Red West, who would drive the car and act as body-guard, just for the fun of getting out of town.

Once Elvis began to make some money, he bought the two things he most desired: a new pink Cadillac and a little house for the family. A big new car and a private home were every American's birthright in the fifties, like forty acres and a mule in an earlier era. The pink Cadillac was Elvis's personal symbol of success. He sang a song titled "Pink Cadillac" on his show, and when he recorded "Baby, Let's Play House," he put a pink Cadillac into the lyrics. (No one, incidentally, has asked why he made this change. The reason is that in the original version by Arthur "Hardrock" Gunter, the lyrics ran: "You may go to college, You may go to school, You may get religion." References to religion were out of the question at Sun Records, whose proprietor regarded himself as something of a preacher. Phillips must have told Elvis to invent something new to replace the offensive line; Elvis inserted what he took to be the supreme symbol of hipness: a pink Cad.)

Most young boys fresh out of the slums would have behaved exactly as did Elvis Presley in buying a flashy car. How many, one wonders, would have taken their first real money and put it into a house? Here we see the other side of Elvis, the side that always contrasted so strongly with the flamboyant clothes and the punk attitude: the profound attachment to the notion of home and the longing to have a home of which he could be proud. This first house was a little brick bungalow stuck out on the pavement running along Lamar Avenue near the Airways Theater. The house still stands, somewhat disguised by an addition to its front, serving now as a day nursery. Walking through the four rooms of the original building, you feel like you're in a doll's house. The Presleys had no more space here than in their apartment at the Courts, but the house symbolized a great change in the family's fortunes and status. Now the one-time indigents were tax-paying property holders. They had fulfilled the ideal of the Memphis Housing Authority: "From slums to public housing to private ownership."

No sooner did the fortunes of the family improve than Vernon Presley quit his job at the paint factory. Ostensibly, he was going to look for another job that wouldn't put such a strain on his bad back, but he never found that new job. The Neals were very friendly with the Presley family at this point; they tried constantly to find work for Vernon. Soon, however, they realized that no matter what the job, Vernon was sure to quit after just a day or two. One day when Bob Neal was talking to Elvis, he was astonished to hear the youngster say that he was eager to succeed because his folks were getting too old to work. At the time, Vernon was not yet forty! The point of the remark is not that Elvis exaggerated his parents' age, but that Vernon exaggerated his disabilities so that he would not be expected to work any longer. As matters turned out, Vernon Presley never did have to go back to work. He retired, in effect, at thirty-eight.

In February 1955, Bob Neal booked Elvis and the Blue Moon Boys on a ten-day tour of the Southwest with a number of well-established country acts, all traveling under the supervision of the show's headliner, Hank Snow. The association which commenced at this time with Hank Snow Enterprises was destined to continue until Elvis broke away to headline his own show. Far more important is the fact that through his work on the Hank Snow tours Elvis first came into close contact with the booker of these tours: Colonel Thomas Andrew Parker.

Chapter 10

The Flying Dutchman

COLONEL TOM PARKER is not a man about whom the world has ever harbored any doubts. Brash, flamboyant, out-front, the Colonel has always declared himself for just what he is: an old-time carny. The ideal portrait of the Colonel would pose him on the bally platform of a freak show, thrusting his elephant-head cane aggressively against a lurid, grotesque poster of Elvis, the Two-Headed Boy (a papier-mâché dummy), while bellowing through a mouth stopped intermittently with an enormous cigar: "This monstrous mistake of Mother Nature was born just as live as you and I. That's right, folks, born *alive!*"

The last great embodiment of that classic style of American show business epitomized by P. T. Barnum and his famous motto— "There's a sucker born every minute"—Colonel Parker is a figure that not only lives but looms inside the imagination. *Bigger than life!*—as he might ballyhoo himself—he seems to have stepped out of the gaslit, tanbark past or sprung from the rich, spermy soil of American folklore. Nothing could be more American than Tom Parker, unless it were the man with whom the Colonel is invariably identified, W. C. Fields.

Perhaps it is this mythic aura that makes so many people regard the Colonel as a lovable old rogue. Or perhaps his charm lies in the fact that he has always been so blatant about his tricks and impostures. Instead of trying to cover up his origins in the flimflam world of the carnival, the Colonel has always gloried in his past, boasting, like Barnum, of his chicanery. Writers have filled up whole chapters with tales of the Colonel's cunning. Millions of people have chuckled over such stories as how he sold foot-long hotdogs with no meat in the middle; how he painted sparrows yellow and sold them for canaries; how he put an electric hot plate under his dancing chickens, making them high step to "Turkey in the Straw"; or how he strewed manure over the exits from his tent show so that he could rent ponies to suckers who were afraid to step in the shit.

Reading over these endless accounts of shams and shucks, shifts and slights, shticks and scams, you recognize in the Colonel at last a primitive and elemental character, the hero of many folk cultures from the ancient Greeks to the nineteenth-century Yankees—the *trickster*. As for his literary archetype: How about something coarse and Germanic, like *Till Eulenspiegel and His Merry Pranks?* To really grasp the essence of the Colonel, however, you must descend even below the level of the mythic and folkloric to the primordial plane of the animal kingdom. Beneath his identity as the flashy carny, the merry prankster or the dissembling trickster, the Colonel possesses a totemic identity as the elephant man. The elephant is his personal symbol and fetish.

When you enter his office, for example, you discover before his desk two stools positioned to receive visitors. Each stool is supported on upholstered elephant legs terminating in big round feet with enormous toenails. As you gaze around the room, you see many statues and figurines of elephants carved in ivory, alabaster, marble and hardwoods. The Colonel's cane, never far from his side, is topped with an elephant's head. The elephant is, of course, a symbol of fortune. With his trunk down, he represents bad luck; with the trunk raised, good luck. All the Colonel's elephants hold their trunks arched aloft in triumph.

The elephant also figures largely in the Colonel's history. There is the story, for instance, about the time the Colonel was stranded in a town without enough money to pay his hotel bill. What does he do? What do characters in folktales do? They go out and find their totem animal, who soon rescues them from their predicament. This is precisely what the Colonel did. He found an elephant—such heroes always know how to summon their magic beasts—and strapped upon its massive back an old-fashioned icebox. Then he solicited ads and samples from local food merchants and paraded the beast through town bedecked with the stores' names and displaying their wares in the big wooden box. When the promotion was complete, Colonel had the money to pay his bill and enough food to sustain him for days to come.

Using the elephant as an attention-getting device has always been standard operating procedure for Colonel Parker. Back in the days when he was managing Eddy Arnold, the Colonel would arrive at the annual convention of the country music DJs at the Andrew Jackson Hotel in Nashville leading an elephant. Hobbling the beast outside the hotel entrance, the Colonel would drape its sides with an immense cloth reading "Never Forget Eddy Arnold." Even when the days of such promotions were far behind him, Colonel never lost his attachment to that legendary creature, the pachyderm. During the filming of *Follow That Dream* at Crystal River, Florida, in the sixties, Colonel insisted on visiting an ancient elephant he had known in his carnival days. The old elephant man could not rest content until he had fed the animal, which gave signs of remembering him: wagging its huge head and shuffling its ponderous feet in their shackles.

Yes, the Colonel and the elephant have a great deal in common. The elephant's vast bulk symbolizes the Colonel's gross corporeality. The elephant's thick hide represents the Colonel's imperviousness to pain or shame. The elephant's reputation for wisdom and mnemonic power correlates with the Colonel's sagacity and nostalgia. Even the elephant's longevity, its air of eld, is highly appropriate to the Colonel, who, even when he was a relatively young man, referred to himself always as the "ole Colonel." Nor should it ever be forgotten that when enraged the elephant is a very dangerous animal, especially the rogue elephant, the elephant that has left the herd to roam abroad, terrorizing the countryside. Yet, it's also highly characteristic of Colonel Parker, a classic wise guy, that he should poke fun at his own cherished totem. Once somebody asked the Colonel, "What's all this stuff about elephants never forgetting?" Glancing keenly over his cigar, the Colonel snapped: "What do they have to remember?"

Just about everything that constitutes Colonel Parker's identity and modus operandi can be associated with the carnival. The particular carnival for which the Colonel worked was, appropriately enough, the greatest in the world. The Royal American Shows was the brain spawn of the King of the Carnies, the late Carl Sedlmeyer. Orphaned as a child in Nebraska, Sedlmeyer struck out on his own as a teenager and wound up with a job in a touring carnival. Graduating from freak show operator to carnival boss in 1921, Sedlmayer went to work to make his show the best and most up-to-date on the road, voicing his goal in one gruff phrase: "I want everything *massive*—bigger'n everybody!"

Sedlmeyer revolutionized the carnival business by carting out to the most remote rural districts the fabulous new thrill rides that were found hitherto only in the innovative amusement parks of the metropolitan East. Touring with huge roller coasters, airplane spins, loop-the-loops, and Dodge-em cars, the Carny King pitched Luna Park every night in the hinterlands of western Canada or the American Midwest. Perceiving that "lights draw people like bugs to a window," he decreed that every ride must be outlined in garish neon. His competitors snickered at the thought of all that fragile glass tubing being shattered in the rough and tumble of travel by rail. Sedlmeyer solved the problem by adding to his train a wagon that housed a self-contained neon tube factory.

The atmosphere in which the Colonel grew to maturity was not, therefore, the stale air of some sleazy little tent show. Colonel Parker started in the big time. Rallying every spring at Tampa (where Parker had his home for sixteen years), over a thousand people would board the bright red-and-white pullmans of the Royal American's private train. Seventy cars, including many double-length flatcars, were required to haul this steel and canvas city, with its knocked-down rides, tractors, trucks, cranes, shops and motor-generators, with enough juice to light up a city of fifty thousand.

The Shows' itinerary was designed to carry it from coast to coast in concert with the annual fairs held in Canada and the United States. (Sedlmeyer contrived the title of his carnival so that it would have one word, "Royal," that appealed to Canadians and another word, "American," that would draw his own countrymen.) The opening date was always the Memphis Cotton Carnival in May. (Elvis Presley, a typical carnival sucker, never missed an appearance of the Royal American. Colonel Parker had left the carnival, however, by the time the teenage Elvis began to throw baseballs at wooden bottles.) From Memphis the mighty train would roll north and west to St. Louis and then further north to Davenport, Iowa, for the Shriners Jubilee. Crossing the Canadian border, it would play the Red River Exhibition at Winnipeg and the regional fairs at Brandon, Calgary, Edmonton, Saskatoon, Regina and Port Arthur–Fort William. At the height of summer, the red-and-white cars would be rolling through the Midwest, heading for the Wisconsin State Fair at Milwaukee, the Minnesota State Fair at Minneapolis–St. Paul, the Mid-America Fair at Topeka and all the other state fairs in Kansas, Oklahoma, Arkansas and Louisiana. By the time the carnival had reached the Gulf Coast, it would be November and time to head back to Tampa for a quiet winter of repairing the equipment and repainting the rig.

Picture now the Royal American Shows as it looked in the thirties when Tom Parker was a young man. Arriving in town at a railroad siding, the carnival would form up in a parade and march through the city with its band blaring and all its performers in full costume. Arriving at the fairgrounds, the first job would be laying out the midway to the length of a mile and a half. Lining it would be countless booths and stands, wagons and tents manned by pitchmen, "sticks" (shills), barkers, showgirls, ticket sellers and chow slingers. Though the major attraction was the rides, the carnival offered all the traditional tent shows.

There was the Hawaiian Revue tent, with its grass-skirted, bra-topped dancers, ukelele plinking, aloha-shirted musicians and spectacular, near-naked fire-eaters. The White Revue tent offered a typical vaudeville show, full of hoofers, singers, novelty acts and a pit band. The Colored Revue tent was Negro vaudeville, which meant you could find everything from an old-time blues star down on her luck or a couple of clownish comics like Butter 'n' Beans to a brilliant jazz performer. The Illusion Show tent focused on spooky apparitions and truncated ladies. The Freak Show tent featured a dude who swallowed a glowing neon tube. The Midget Show was a big doll house, with all the midgets seated in their little chairs waiting to be introduced by the "head of the house," a testy, mean-faced little fellow with slicked-down hair, bow tie and Buster Brown shoes, who gave his spiel in a high-pitched voice without ever once losing the look of a chronic headache victim. The last and most exciting of these side shows was the Motordome: a nightmarish wooden funnel around which motorcycles roared until their riders were spinning at an angle of ninety degrees to the perpendicular.

Where was the young Tom Parker in this vast and complicated entertainment, which, as we know, is also a very tight, exclusive and hierarchical society? Accounts differ: Some place Parker in a "grab joint," dishing out cotton candy and red caramel apples; others put him in charge of the "pie car" or company commissary, a rather responsible job for a young man. All we know for sure is that after his marriage the Colonel and his wife were a fixture in the carnival for many years. Chances are that having joined the show when he was in his early twenties and having remained with it for nearly a decade, Tom Parker worked at a number of jobs that took him through the whole labyrinthine operation and gave him a marvelous grass-roots education in show business.

More important than what the Colonel did in the carnival is what the carnival did for the Colonel. Some of its lessons are obvious. The

Colonel's whole notion of publicity, for one thing, comes straight out of the circus-carnival tradition of ballyhoo and bunkum. When the Colonel first started managing Elvis, he gave the new star of rock 'n' roll the whole carny treatment: elephants and midgets, banners and posters. Parker would get into the ticket booth to hustle like a pitchman or stand out in the lobby holding a fistful of programs on high like a hawker. Even in later years, after Elvis had earned hundreds of millions of dollars and become a household word the world over, every time he opened at Las Vegas, the Colonel would set to work like some hard-pressed front man papering the town before the arrival of the show. He would expend prodigious amounts of time, energy and money lining the highways with billboards, covering the placard sites with quarter sheets, transforming the hotel lobby into a forest of banners and posters. The radio would blare spot announcements every half hour and the newspapers were full of ads for the show. All this ballyhoo for a performer who had sold out the entire engagement weeks before he arrived in the city.

Ballyhoo, however, was the least of the lessons the Colonel learned in the carnival. Far more important was the education he received in manipulating the public. Most people don't realize that when Barnum made his famous remark, he was using the word "sucker" in its professional sense, as the term employed in the circus-carnival world for "customer." So basic is the notion of deception—of hokum, bunko, and bamboozle—to this world that no other concept of the customer exists but that of the *mark*. All the classic yarns of the carnival turn on acts of deception that enable the carny to fleece the sucker by exciting his desires and imposing on his credulity, while offering him nothing truly commensurate with either his expectations or the price he pays for the show. This is the philosophy that Colonel Parker imbibed in his youth and subsequently applied to his management of Elvis Presley.

The most important gift the Colonel developed in his carny days was his remarkable capacity for not only outwitting and getting over the sucker but for reading his mind. An interesting recollection by one of the Colonel's oldest associates has Tom Parker in his early years operating a "mit camp" or palm-reading booth. This sort of activity was forbidden in the Royal American, but it might have been something the Colonel did out of season. Even if the story is false in fact, it is true poetically, for Colonel Parker is a man of extraordinary psychic gifts. He is, for example, an accomplished hypnotist. Often during the years when the Presley organization was condemned to the tedious routine of making movies, Colonel would combine his love of practical jokes with his powers of mind control to produce scenes of irresistible humor.

During the shooting of *Kid Galahad,* for instance, the Colonel hypnotized Elvis's bodyguard, Sonny West, and instructed him to walk up
to the film's director, Phil Karlson, and tell him that the movie stank,
the acting was horrible, the direction disgusting and the whole production
a terrible waste of time and money. As soon as the next break came,
big, burly Sonny walked up to the director and launched into this outrageously insulting speech. The director's jaw dropped open in shock and
remained hanging there while the Colonel drank in the scene, chuckling
deep inside his mountainous belly without betraying his feelings on his
face. Finally, Karlson screamed: "Who is this man? Get him off the
set!" When the joke was explained to him, the director expressed astonishment that Sonny could have performed the prank at such length without
ever once cracking a smile. "He was under hypnosis," explained the
Colonel; "he couldn't have done it any other way." Turning to Sonny,
the director demanded: "Is this true?" "Yes, sir, it is," avowed Sonny,
who could never imagine how he performed all the strange and embarrassing feats he accomplished under the Colonel's direction.

The Colonel's powers as a psychic were not limited to hypnosis.
He has suffered for years from a ruptured disc in his spine, which is
why he always uses a cane. Yet he would never submit to an operation,
preferring to control the sometimes excruciating pain by means of his
special mental powers. The Colonel also claims to possess the evil eye.
He would often recount to the Guys the story of the boardinghouse
lady who hounded him so fiercely that he was compelled finally to do
something to which he was profoundly averse. He put a hex on the
woman and soon she came to disaster. When the old Colonel, sitting
backstage like Tecumseh, leaning on his cane, would tell that tale, Lamar
Fike recalls feeling chills running up and down his spine.

Depending on whether you view such capacities as evidence of possession of occult powers or simply as psychological acuity coupled with
prodigious willpower, the fact is that the Colonel is a man with an
enormous capacity for controlling other men or for hoodwinking them
in ways that make them play into his hands. Like any great con man,
the Colonel sees everyone as a mark and instinctively prepares to rip
him off. Sometimes he gets his way by bluffing; sometimes by playing
on the sucker's hopes and fears; sometimes by bullying. Whatever the
means, the goal is invariably the same: The Colonel must always get
the better of the other man.

Though Colonel has made as much of his chicanery as Jack Benny did of his miserliness or W. C. Fields of his detestation of children, nobody apparently has ever regarded the Colonel with distrust. Quite the contrary: When you talk to the Colonel's business associates, they invariably assure you that the Colonel is the soul of honor, a man whose word is his bond. Indeed, in some instances the Colonel's word has been his bond. The William Morris Agency, for example, represented Elvis throughout his entire career, and its president, Abe Lastfogel, is one of the Colonel's closest associates; yet the agency never had a formal representation agreement with Elvis Presley. In fact, if you believe the story that has been circulated in show business for the past quarter century and is credited even by Elvis's agents at William Morris, Colonel Parker never had a contract with Elvis Presley. All their multimillion-dollar deals were made supposedly on the strength of a handshake. What greater faith could a manager inspire?

Trading on his word, while developing relationships of total trust, has enabled the Colonel to dispense with a great many of the accustomed appurtenances of business. Though for the past quarter of a century the ole Colonel has swum like a sea lion through an ocean of money, he has contrived to do so without leaving many more traces than a swimmer in the sea. Though his signature appears on certain contracts, and he has owned a couple of companies, he never incorporated officially until 1974. He rarely writes a check, has never owned a credit card and insists on paying for everything in cash. Though he is a big man in a business that is thoroughly internationalized, the Colonel has never owned a passport. Why doesn't he have a passport? According to the Colonel, he could not provide the necessary proof of birth because he was a foundling.

Avoidance of overseas travel—or is it just avoidance of Immigration and Naturalization?—is paralleled in the Colonel's life-style with avoidance of legal proceedings. Though the Colonel is a highly combative man who has spent many years in a business that generates a lot of litigation, he has contrived never to be in the position of suing or being sued in person. In this manner, he has gone through a long life without ever once appearing in court.

One other peculiarity of the Colonel's is worth noting in this connection. He enjoys a reputation as one of the Internal Revenue Service's very best customers. Where other men go to great lengths to avoid paying taxes, the Colonel is so eager to pay his tax bill and so careless of opportunities to dodge behind shelters that it is said he *overpays* the tax man.

When you add up all these eccentricities, they compose themselves into a pattern that is not altogether unfamiliar. They constitute the low profile of a man who is eager to have the minimum possible contact with the authorities. By always making nice with IRS, avoiding the courts, authorizing no credit investigations and not subjecting oneself to the scrutiny of the immigration officials, a man may pass a long life in this country without ever being required to divulge exactly who he is. Yet, why should any man of Colonel Parker's wealth, power, probity and fame wish to pursue such a strange course?

As far as the Colonel's personal reputation is concerned, it is no less excellent than his reputation as a businessman. He appears to be a faithful husband, married to the same woman now for fifty years: the former Mrs. Marie Ross, née Mott. The Colonel has no children of his own but was always helpful to his wife's son, Bobby Ross, a Tampa public relations man who died of multiple sclerosis in 1977. Though extremely demanding of his employees, Parker has always been exceedingly generous toward them in money matters and retained the loyalty of his key men for as long as twenty-five years. Virtually unique in his profession for having limited himself to a single client, Colonel Parker has always been willing to offer advice and professional counsel to acts and fellow managers from whom he has no expectation of gain. Tommy Sands, for one, profited greatly for many years from the Colonel's discreet advice, as did Ricky Nelson. Though the Colonel is far from being a religious man, he has always made liberal donations to the Roman Catholic church near his official residence at Madison, Tennessee, and acted as a friend to the local priest and nuns.

Neither a drinker nor a doper, Colonel Parker appears to have, apart from work, only two passions. One is eating, which he has done on such a scale that he now tips the scales at three hundred pounds. Over the years, his oval face has melted like a lump of butter into a waffle stack of double chins. His protuberant belly and breasts give him the profile of Buddha in a loud Aloha shirt. His other passion is gambling.

Colonel Parker is a prodigious gambler at roulette and craps. In Las Vegas, where he maintains an apartment year round, he is considered one of the highest rollers in the history of the resort. He averages about ten months a year in the city and an hour a day in the casinos. He does all his gambling in public, though Vegas has opulent private accommodations for high rollers. At roulette, the Colonel likes to make the maximum wager: ten thousand dollars. As a good croupier will make the wheel spin every two minutes, it is possible to lose three hundred thousand dollars an hour. The Colonel's losses are reported to have sometimes exceeded a million dollars in a single month.

Gambling on this scale can be interpreted in many ways. Professional gamblers describe the Colonel as a "dumper"; that is, a man who plays without system or restraint, thus, in effect, throwing his money away. As earning this money has been the whole purpose and pride of the Colonel's life, we are faced here with the familiar paradox of the man whose pleasures invert his normal personality, presenting him in a totally unsuspected character. What could be more perverse than the spectacle of the Colonel, so shrewd, so manipulative, so masterful, submitting himself haplessly to games of chance that entail the minimum amount of skill and maximum amount of luck? No wonder he surrounds himself with so many trunk-up elephants! He has need of them. Actually, these talismans appear to do him no good. No one can ever recall his making a great score. Testing his luck every day, he finds it as uniformly bad at the gaming table as it is good at the bargaining table. The choice of the roulette wheel as his principal diversion is particularly ironic because it summons up the image of a perpendicular wheel of chance that you always find at carnivals. By playing at roulette, the old carny transforms himself into his opposite, the sucker.

Doubtless there is an element of addiction in the Colonel's dedication to gambling. One hears that he cannot keep the wheel out of his mind even when he is far from the casino. Sometimes, he will call from his home in Palm Springs and lay bets by phone. Also, he employs his great power in Las Vegas to increase the hazards of his play. On at least one occasion, he has insisted that the wheel be charged with *two* balls. There is an image to ponder: the man who plays with two balls!

No one doubts the Colonel's capacity to sustain his huge gambling losses, though some have questioned the propriety of incurring such losses in the same hotel with which he had to negotiate on behalf of his client. On the other hand, you don't hear those stories about Colonel Parker and Elvis Presley being owned by the Mob that you hear about so many entertainers in Vegas. Whatever the Colonel's problem, assuming that he has one, it would not appear to be the result of any criminal activity. More than one investigator has checked out the Colonel's record with the law. The finding has invariably been the same: "The man is clean."

Having considered other possible reasons why the Colonel would want to maintain a very low profile vis à vis the government, one comes at last to the possibility that there could be something buried in his past that he does not want to come to light. The Colonel was forty-seven years old when he first became famous through his association with Elvis Presley. It could well be that when the Colonel realized the magnitude of his lucky strike, he made a decision to inter his past and cover his traces permanently.

This view of the matter gains a lot of support when you investigate the Colonel at firsthand. The first name that a knowledgeable journalist crosses off his list of prospective sources is that of the subject himself. The Colonel's routine with would-be interviewers is notorious. He never turns down a request for an interview. What would be the fun in that? Rather, he grins like the shark eyeing the mark and replies graciously, "I'd be delighted to give you an interview. Do you want the short or the long version? The price of the short is twenty-five thousand dollars; the long is one hundred thousand dollars." That takes care of the inquiring reporter.

How about the Colonel's men: those long-term colleagues who have spent as many as twenty-five years by the Colonel's side? The answer is obvious. They are not going to tell you anything that the Colonel hasn't authorized. So a good many more names are scratched off the list. Now, we turn to the ex-employees, generally men who occupied minor positions as glorified go-fers. There are a number of them working still in Hollywood, New York or Las Vegas. When you tell them that you're interested in their experiences with Colonel Parker, they turn to stone. If they're frank, they'll tell you that it might be worth their current job if they talked freely about their former boss. The Man has big ears and long arms. He's regarded as vindictive. He inspires fear and rules by fear.

Or, perhaps, you do find some ex-errand boy or old carnival grifter who doesn't feel vulnerable. What can you learn from such a man? Just the usual little comic anecdotes that have been rehearsed countless times. How the Colonel bluffed this dude or conned that sucker or how he likes his eggs and sausages in the morning. So you give up on the go-fers and go to the couple of major clients that the Colonel represented before his long stint with Elvis. There's Hank Snow, for one, still wearing his fancy western duds and sporting the kind of phony-looking toupee that suggested the word "rug." When you pronounce the name "Tom Parker" in Hank Snow's hearing, he sputters with rage: "I won't say anything for the man or against the man!" Wham! That ends that interview. So you turn to the other surviving star with whom Parker enjoyed a long relationship: Eddy Arnold.

Arnold receives you in a little off-the-highway office on the outskirts of Nashville. The sign on the door reads Logan County Utility Company. Ruggedly handsome still at sixty-two, smiling genially as he parks his feet on his desk as if it were the pot-bellied stove in the country store, the Tennessee Plowboy appears quite willing to kick back and run the story of his years with the man he calls Tom Parker because when Arnold met the Colonel, he hadn't yet assumed his famous title.

Arnold reaches down into the inexhaustible bag of stories about how the Colonel wheeled and dealed so that his client got paid up front or how he cut into the concession operations: all the usual small-time hustles and tricks that are the Colonel's stock in trade. Finally, growing impatient with this palaver, you pop the key question: "If the relationship was so happy, why did you fire Parker?" Arnold smiles and waves his hand in dismissal of the issue. "It was simply a matter of temperament. Tom is a very flamboyant man. I'm a very conservative man." With that fatuous remark, the interview concludes.

Once you've had enough of the freeze-out, the clam-up, the what-he-eats-for-breakfast and how-he-chisels-his-buck routines, you are free to draw certain conclusions about Colonel Tom Parker. The first and most important finding is that though Parker has spent many years disporting himself inside one of the world's most intently ogled fishbowls, he has managed to deflect any serious attention aimed at himself. Now you see me, now you don't! That's his style. Clearly, he had been very careful to confine his activities to the smallest possible circle of colleagues and coworkers, maintaining these relationships unaltered for a lifetime. Most significantly, he has made it clear to everyone who ever worked for him that the price of talking about him would be a lot higher than anything they might be paid. In a word: The Colonel is impervious to investigation.

Once you abandon the effort to investigate the Colonel directly, there is nothing left to do but review once again the old press reports that are every writer's point of departure. The Parker file, you soon discover, consists for the most part of the same old stories and bits of information (or misinformation) endlessly hashed and rehashed. Much of this material has an apocryphal air and some of the stories—like the familiar yarns about the Colonel and the patent medicine Hadacol—are demonstrably false. What is most remarkable is not the hearsay character of the accounts but the sheer paucity of personal information. One would think he were reading about some legendary showman in the early nineteenth century rather than a living man with offices in Los Angeles and Las Vegas.

How Elvis Presley's life was kept secret for so many years is no mystery at all: Elvis was the Howard Hughes of show business, living always behind thick walls of stone and flesh, a virtual recluse from the age of twenty-three. Colonel Parker, on the other hand, is a man who has been constantly visible for thirty-five years and whose work throughout that entire period has entailed continual contacts with the press. How he remained so undisclosed for all this time is quite another story. The ole Colonel turns out to be the best illusionist in the history of the stage. The man without a shadow. The man without a past.

As the Colonel grew a lot more visible after the time he met Elvis, in 1955, the best way to review his history is to trace it backward from that point, observing where the solid road of fact becomes the stumbling path of legend and pure speculation. For the nine years from 1953 back to 1944, Parker managed Eddy Arnold. This was a relationship that anticipated in several respects the Colonel's career with Elvis. As with Elvis, so with Arnold—it was a case of taking a young, virtually unknown singer and developing his career until he reached stardom. Arnold had appeared on *Grand Ole Opry* and had cut a few records for RCA when Parker took him in hand, just as Elvis had performed on the *Louisiana Hayride* and cut his handful of sides for Sun when the Colonel hooked him. With Arnold, a far less original and exciting talent, the climb was slower than with Elvis but the results were eventually quite impressive. The Tennessee Plowboy recorded many hits, starred on his own radio show, led his own touring company and eventually obtained a two-picture contract in Hollywood. Parker's attitude toward these pictures was prophetic of how he would manage Elvis's movie career. He told his client: "The pictures will be lean on artistic quality, but they will be acceptable as movies." Those words could stand as the motto of Elvis's entire film oeuvre.

Though Eddy Arnold was not a star of the first magnitude, he prospered greatly under the management of Tom Parker. What's more, just as he did later with Elvis, Tom Parker devoted himself body and soul, night and day, to his only client. As Arnold himself has said: "When Tom's your manager, he's all you. He lives and breathes his artist. I once said to him when he was managing me, 'Tom, why don't you get yourself a hobby?' He looked me straight in the eye and said, 'You're my hobby.' " Why, then, did Arnold dismiss Parker?

Various stories are told at Nashville. According to one account, Arnold had developed deep suspicions concerning Parker. One day, while they were working at Las Vegas, Arnold walked into Parker's room and saw his manager snatch a piece of paper off the table and conceal it guiltily. Arnold demanded to see the paper. Parker refused to disclose what he was holding. The men got into a violent argument, virtually coming to blows. Not much later, Parker, resting in the garden of his home in Madison, Tennessee, received a telegram from Eddy Arnold. It read: "Your services no longer required. From receipt of this wire consider yourself dismissed."

Prior to his stint as Arnold's manager, the Colonel represented an old-fashioned pop singer in his declining years: Gene Austin, once universally familiar for his recording of "My Blue Heaven." Austin was one of the first generation of twentieth-century American pop singers, along with Henry Burr and Vernon Dalhart, voices known to the current generation only through the time-machine evocations of Tiny Tim. By the time Parker tied in with Austin, only old-timers would pay to hear such a hopelessly dated entertainer. When the war came along, imposing severe restrictions on travel and heavy taxes on entertainment, Austin and Parker gave up the ship.

The title "Colonel," which so well befits Tom Parker, is honorary, of course, having been bestowed on him first in 1948 by the governor of Louisiana, Jimmy Davis, himself a former country singer. The Colonel did have some actual experience of military life when he served in 1930 and 1931 in America's tiny peacetime army. He was stationed at Fort Barrancas, in the mouth of Pensacola Harbor, and at the legendary Schofield Barracks in Hawaii (which explains, most likely, why Elvis Presley, who so rarely gave benefit performances, did two free shows in Honolulu, both for the benefit of the military.) Nothing is more characteristic of the Colonel's personal manner than his identification with the style of an old-time regular army officer. He speaks habitually in military jargon, orders his men about with a commander's brusqueness, signs his field orders "The Colonel," and even enjoys using his title to solicit salutes from unsuspecting servicemen. Indeed, if you didn't know better, you would swear that Tom Parker was in fact Colonel Thomas Andrew Parker, U. S. Army, Retired.

When the United States entered World War II, Tom Parker filled out the obligatory questionnaire from the Selective Service Bureau. When the draft board in Tampa received the form, it learned that the registrant was born at Huntington, West Virginia on June 26, 1909;[1] that he was

---

[1] No record of this birth exists in the files at Huntington nor was a recent investigation of Parker's origins by the local paper, the *Herald-Despatch,* able to turn up a trace of the Parker family.

married with one child; and that his employer was Gene Austin of Hollywood, California. A couple of weeks later, Tom Parker was classified 3A: "registrant deferred by reason of extreme hardship to dependents." In January 1944, with the war in its most critical phase and the reserves of military manpower nearly exhausted, Tom Parker was reclassified 1A. Two months later, after a preinduction physical, his classification was altered to 4F. The Colonel was out of the war.

Prior to the war, Tom Parker was the dogcatcher of Tampa. It is said that he took the job in 1940, after failing to make a go of a pony ride at the Florida State Fairgrounds. Parker was motivated to become the "field agent" for the Hillsborough Humane Society, according to a Tampa newspaper article, by two considerations: 1) his fondness for animals; 2) a rent-free apartment located above the animal shelter. As we shall see, this job, so odd-looking at first glance, was actually an echo of the Colonel's childhood. Perhaps that is why he threw himself into it with such zeal. Not long after he set to work, he got his picture in the paper performing a canine rescue mission. At thirty-two, he's already very hefty; he's going bald and covering the blemish with a natty hat, one of those shiny-visored garrison caps worn in the old days by bus drivers and filling station attendants. The picture shows the back of the Colonel's old coupe which he has adapted to his new work by lettering the trunk with the word "Ambulance." The action of the carefully posed shot consists of Parker raising the trunk door on an animal cage, while his wife Marie, smartly dressed and coiffed, looking a little like a magician's assistant, prepares to stash inside the cage the cute little puppy in her arms.

Not content just to notify the papers of his latest exploits removing stranded cats from trees or rounding up vicious strays, Tom Parker dressed himself at Christmas as Santa Claus and gave away puppies as presents to children. As if all this were not enough, he also renovated the dilapidated animal shelter and established the city's first pet cemetery.

It is when one tries to follow the Colonel's history back before the year 1940 that the trail begins to disappear. We know that he worked in the Royal American Shows in this period, but though the founder's son, Carl Sedlmayr, Jr., is still living, he is very reluctant to talk about Tom Parker. Another source who proved singularly unhelpful for this period was the Colonel's brother-in-law, Bitsy Mott, a one-time shortstop for the Brooklyn Dodgers and the Philadelphia Phillies. After one of those intolerably long and vague conversations that are the favorite pastime of good ole boys, Mott summarized his impressions of a lifetime acquaintanceship with the Colonel in a phrase that could serve as a motto for the whole enquiry: "That man's a mystery."

When you trace back everything that has ever appeared in print about the Colonel's early years, you find that it all originates in a unique interview with the Colonel conducted by an Associated Press reporter in 1956 and published in January 1957, on the first anniversary of the Colonel's takeover of Elvis's career. As this is the one and only time when Colonel Parker has ever pronounced publicly on his birth and upbringing, it's worth reading the original lines:

> Parker was born 47 years ago in West Virginia, where his parents happened to be touring with a carnival. Mom and Dad died before Tom reached the fifth grade, so he wound up with his uncle's traveling show, the Great Parker Pony Circus.
>
> At 17, young Tom struck out on his own with a pony and monkey act. Most of his stands were on the cherry soda circuit, an affectionate title given a business arrangement where a soft drink company pays the act about $3 a day to accept its bottle tops as the price of admission.
>
> Parker soon traded in his pony for a typewriter and became press agent for a series of carnivals, circuses, and showboats. He developed first name friendships with Tom Mix and Wallace Beery, both carnival men before the movies found them.
>
> In 1932, while wintering with a carnival in Tampa, he met, wooed and wed his wife, Marie, who now helps with the bookkeeping.[2]

It seems astonishing that at this late date nothing more is known of Colonel Parker's origins than these few statements; yet they constitute the entire substance of what passes as biographical accounts of the Colonel's early years, the paucity of the information being disguised by padding and recasting and the enlargements produced by speculation, association and sheer fantasy. Actually, when you examine these skimpy little paragraphs in a skeptical frame of mind, what they resemble most are those potted "bios" that were cooked up in the good old days by Hollywood publicity departments to invest with glamour or pathos the otherwise drab or disreputable life of some newly discovered star. I'm sure it has occurred to more than one showbiz professional that this

---

[2] The wedding must have taken place in another state or in another year because the Florida Office of Vital Statistics has no record of this marriage in its files for the year 1932.

bio is no less fictional than those produced by the Hollywood flacks.

Having traced Colonel Parker's history back to its beginnings, we have wound up in the dark; and that is where we would remain, if Tom Parker had his way. However, in the late sixties, a new clue to the Parker mystery appeared in a very eccentic booklet titled *The Hillbilly Cat*. Written by a Dutch fan, Hans Langbroek, this book belongs to a genre of writing that focuses on such esoterica as recordings rumored to have been made but never released and bits of film that may once have existed but can no longer be found. Written hippie-style—"you know, yesterday, when i got home i did not feel like much at all"— and suffering from a very inadequate command of English, the book would not normally inspire much interest except as a curiosity. However, when the author comes to the subject of Colonel Parker, he makes a number of statements that are so bizarre that they stop the reader in his tracks. A quick check reveals that some of these remarks are simply false: for example, the assertion that Parker managed Tom Mix and brought him to London in 1947, where he rode his horse through the lobby of the Savoy Plaza. This amusing anecdote is undermined by the fact that Tom Mix died in the year 1940. What is one to make, however, of the statement that Tom Parker was born not in the United States but in Holland, at Breda, and that his real name is "Andre van Kuyk"?

"Preposterous!" you say. I would say so, too, but for the fact that the author is Dutch, which suggests, in turn, that he might have access to sources of information unknown to Americans. With that thought in mind, I made inquiries in Holland and—lo and behold!—a couple of really astonishing articles arrived by mail from a newspaper in Breda, *De Stem (The Voice)*. These articles, by a reporter named Dirk Vellenga, assert that Tom Parker is actually the long-lost son of a local family whose name is van Kuijk and whose surviving members include several sisters and a brother, to say nothing of the Colonel's boyhood friends. (Longevity appears to be a common trait amongst these folk.) The family has a lot of evidence with which to back up its claims. One of the prime proofs is the astounding resemblance between the surviving van Kuijks and Tom Parker. They also have some pictures of Parker as he appeared when he left home, pictures that are very hard to associate with the Colonel's current image. The best way to test the family's claim is to consider carefully the story the Dutch reporter collected from their lips.

Thomas Andrew Parker, according to this account, was born on the date he always cites, June 26, 1909; but his place of birth was not

Huntington, West Virginia: It was the old Catholic city of Breda in the Brabant region of southern Holland. The Colonel's father, Adam van Kuijk, was originally a country man, born and bred in the village of Raamsdonksveer, on the River Maas. A soldier for many years, he was renowned for his ability to manage horses. At the age of thirty-four, the elder van Kuijk married Marie Ponsie, a woman of French ancestry, whose family peddled at a small carnival that moved from town to town on a barge in the Low Country. The pair had nine children, of whom Tom Parker—whose full name is Andreas Cornelis van Kuijk— is the fifth. The father is remembered as a harsh and tyrannical man; the mother as a very pious Catholic. One of her daughters became a nun.

Van Kuijk the elder operated a livery stable in an ancient quarter of the city, now demolished, called the Vlaszak. The father's principal customer or employer was a well-known warehousing and freight forwarding company, Van Gend en Loos. The social position of the family was by no means a lowly one. The father enjoyed the privilege of voting, and his relations included shipping men and small merchants. The upper crust of Breda society consisted then of military officers, whose position was paramount because the city had been for centuries a fortress town under the aegis of the Dutch royal family. As the van Kuijks lived very close to a military barracks, one of Andreas's earliest and most abiding impressions must have been of the handsomely uniformed army officers to whom the townsfolk deferred to as superior beings. It is interesting to note that the van Kuijks lived above their stable, just as the Colonel lived years later above the animal shelter at Tampa. One is also struck by the fact that the Colonel's mother bore the same name as the Colonel's wife, Marie, who is the Colonel's senior by eight to ten years.

Tom Parker's nickname as a boy was "Dries." A number of his childhood friends remember Dries quite well. The picture composed by their recollections is that of a very gay, audacious and headstrong lad, given to jokes and stunts, fond of animals of every kind and wild about circuses and fairs. Indeed, the whole personality of the mature Tom Parker is quite apparent in these tales of his childhood. One of his favorite games was to play circus with the horses entrusted to his care and even allow the animals to run free. The elder Parker was enraged by this behavior, which threatened his job, and punished the boy severely. Dries was not the sort of lad that discipline could check. Soon he was back performing some other prank, equally outrageous.

Even as a boy, Parker showed himself highly resourceful at getting what he wanted. He showed a playmate how to get into the soccer games for free by picking up some bit of lumber and carrying it through the gates, as if they were employees of the groundskeeper. Once, when they were caught and barred from the stadium, Dries went home, got the shovel from the coal scuttle and then dug a hole under the fence for himself and his buddy.

The young Dries van Kuijk was also very clever at making money to buy sweets and other treats. It is recollected that he never ran an errand without being paid. He even got into the ballyhoo business as a boy, driving a wagon decorated with billboards around town to advertise a circus. The circus was an obsession with the boy; he used every device conceivable to get tickets not only for himself but for his little sisters. Once, hearing that a circus was playing at a nearby town, he ran away from school so that he could see the show.

As even repeated whippings would not make a scholar out of Dries van Kuijk, he was apprenticed early to a barber. When a customer wanted a shave, Dries was supposed to apply the soap; then, after the shave, remove the residues of lather. He didn't last long on the job because every time he heard music in the street, he would run out of the shop, leaving the customer in his chair with soap still on his face.

As Dries grew older, his escapades became more daring. Once he stole a bike from a delivery boy and rode to the inland port of Oosterhout, where his Uncle Willem was a barge captain. When Dries was sixteen, his father died. His uncle, Johannes Ponsie, a ship captain of Rotterdam, was appointed guardian of the children. Dries went to live with him, but on his sister Adriane's birthday, September 15, 1927, came back to Breda. That night he seemed in especially high spirits, rushing about serving the company and singing songs which he had composed himself. Shortly after his departure, his trunk was delivered to the family's house. Inside were found his clothes, his birthday presents and even his official papers. Dries had slipped away from Holland.

He arrived in America at the age of eighteen and found lodging with a Dutch family, who corresponded with his family in Holland. No sooner had he learned enough English to get about than he slipped away again and traveled all over the United States riding the rods of freight trains. After a year's adventuring, he returned to Holland on the evening of his mother's birthday, bringing gifts for the whole family. How he must have relished their astonishment at his startling and triumphant reappearance!

Once Dries van Kuijk got a taste of life in America, it was just a matter of time till he took off again. Uncle Johannes saw clearly how matters stood and told the family: "Nobody can hold that boy down. When he wants to go, he'll go." In the summer of 1929, Dries van Kuijk left Holland for his second trip to America. Apparently, he attached himself to a rich family on the boat, claiming that he was an orphan whose family lived in the States. He had told the Dutch family with whom he stayed the first time that he was eager to enlist in the American army. Now he put this plan into effect. He arranged that five dollars a month be deducted from his pay (which was twenty-six dollars a month) and sent to his mother. The first check arrived in January 1930, which establishes the date for the start of his military service; his period of enlistment would have been two years.

During these two years, Dries corresponded extensively with his family and friends in Holland. He sent home pictures of himself in uniform and in civilian clothes. His life appeared to be moving smoothly and satisfactorily in the new path he had chosen. It was noted that instead of signing his letters "Andre," he was now using the mysterious name, "Tom Parker." Otherwise, nothing occurred that could explain what happened next. All the family knows is that in January, 1932, the letters and the money orders stopped arriving—and *nobody ever again heard a word from Dries van Kuijk.*

For thirty years the van Kuijk family speculated on what had become of its missing member. At the end of World War II, the family began to fancy that Dries might turn up among the millions of American soldiers in Europe. Every week, Tom Parker's mother lit a candle for him in the Catholic church at Eindhoven, where she had moved to live with one of her daughters. When the mother died in 1958, she had no idea that her long lost son was a famous figure in America, the prosperous manager of the world's most successful entertainer.

It was not until 1961 that the van Kuijk family discovered what had happened to the boy who had left home thirty-two years before. One of Dries's sisters saw a picture of Elvis Presley and Colonel Tom Parker in a ladies' magazine, *Rosita.* She recognized Dries immediately because of the strong resemblance he bore to another of her brothers. The family took its story to the magazine, which published an article that became, in turn, the source for the statements in the little book by Hans Langbroek. One of Parker's brothers, Ad van Kuijk, actually went to the United States and met the Colonel and Elvis in Hollywood. When he returned to Holland, he refused to discuss the meeting. Other members of the family wrote to the Colonel but never received answers. Among their speculations was the notion that their brother was concealing his identity because he had something shady in his past: Perhaps he had entered the United States illegally or had deserted from the American army. After Elvis's death, efforts to reach the Colonel were redoubled. The only thing that anyone received by way of reply was a small American flag.

This account is supported by a number of witnesses; but when you settle down to ponder it, you begin to have your doubts. Could it not be simply a case of that familiar phenomenon: the obscure claiming kinship with the great, the rich, the famous? What, after all, are the grounds for the identification? An old photograph that looks nothing like the man we know. A couple of old letters signed "Tom Parker." A brother who goes to see his famous relative and returns with nothing to say. It's hardly evidence that would stand up in a court of law—or in that equally strict court of judgment which should be run by anyone presuming to the title of biographer. The only man, one concludes, who could resolve the issue is Colonel Parker—and he ain't talkin'! Or so I thought until that morning in January 1980, when, suddenly, the oracle spoke.

I was sitting in my office going over the story for the hundredth time with Lamar Fike. As usual, we were getting nowhere. Lamar, who had traveled extensively with the Colonel in the old days, did not see the man as remote and unapproachable. He was accustomed to calling up the Colonel and getting straight answers. It was natural, therefore, that when the discussion reached its customary impasse, he should say, "Why don't I call the Colonel and pop the question?" I stared at him with, I'm sure, the deepest skepticism imprinted on my face. Then, I replied, "Why not?"

When Lamar got the Colonel on the wire, he set the old boy up nicely. Speaking in the tone of the young disciple, which is so gratifying to the old master, he commenced by saying, "Colonel, you always told me, 'If there's somethin' you want to know from me, don't sit around stewin'—just ask!' " From Hollywood the voice of the aged man was heard in New York saying, "That's right, Lamar. What is it?" "Well, Colonel," says Lamar, as if this were the damnedest thing he'd ever heard tell of, "there's a book come out that says that your real name is Dries van Kuijk and you were born in Breda, Holland." There was a slight pause at the other end of the line and a perceptible change of tone. "Oh, yeah," answered the voice, obviously caught off balance and struggling to regain its composure. "That's appeared in about fifteen different places. That's as old . . . that's been out since I came out of the army fifty years ago. Hell, that's no news!"

Lamar was so flabbergasted by this unexpected rejoinder that he protested: "But Colonel, I've known you for over twenty years—why didn't you tell me that you were a Dutchman?" The Colonel, always fast on the comeback, snapped: "You never asked me."

Chapter 11

Under
New Management

THE MAN who brought Tom Parker and Elvis Presley together was Oscar Davis, one of the pioneers of country show business. Davis's was a world of county fairs, livestock shows, rodeos, firemen's carnivals, circuses, fiddling contests, jamborees, tent shows and promotional tours on behalf of patent medicines, flours, chows and tobacco products. In contrast to Tom Parker, who talked out of the side of his mouth and looked like a huckster, Oscar Davis aspired to the image of the tycoon. Small, dapper, with wavy iron-grey hair, he wore always a four-hundred-dollar suit with his shoes polished, his nails buffed. His most famous promotion was the public wedding of country music's greatest hero, Hank Williams.

Seeking a way to mend the fortunes of the alcoholic and morphine-addicted Williams, Davis hit on the idea of making the famous entertainer's second marriage a well-promoted spectacle. Twice in one day he filled to capacity New Orleans's 14,000-seat Municipal Auditorium—once for the rehearsal and once for the ceremony—with people who paid from seventy-five cents to $1.50 to see the emaciated, balding, skull-faced singer, costumed in fancy western duds, take as his bride a diminutive, pretty, fresh-faced girl caparisoned in lace and tulle. The wedding grossed $30,000, plus a mountain of gifts which Davis wheedled out of the local merchants. The ceremony was, to be sure, an imposture because Williams had married already in secret to avert interference by his enraged first wife. The promotion, however, was a triumph.

Having earned and lost millions in the course of a long and billowy career, Davis found himself in difficult straits when Hank Williams was delivered to his last concert, on New Year's Day, 1954, stone cold dead in the back seat of his car. Davis had no choice but to hire out to other promoters as a front man: one of those ballyhoo artists who blow into a town a week before the show and start bombarding the airwaves with cannon-voiced announcers thundering: "COMING TO TOWN! THE BIG SHOW! DON'T MISS IT!" It was, in fact, while spending a day at WMPS in Memphis in October 1954, preparing his "spots" for an upcoming Red Foley show, that Davis discovered Elvis Presley. Always on the lookout for fresh talent, the keen little promoter asked Bob Neal if he would play some records by this new kid about whom there was so much talk. Neal not only spun the discs but offered to take Davis out to the Eagle's Nest, where Elvis was working with Scotty and Bill. Davis found Elvis "sensational." Next time he sat down to cut up touches with his old crony, Tom Parker, he told him about this amazing boy in Memphis, who was driving all the women crazy.

Next time Colonel Parker got to Memphis, he arranged to meet Elvis, Bob Neal and Sam Phillips in a little restaurant across the street from the Auditorium. Nothing notable happened at the meeting. The Colonel had never seen nor heard Elvis perform. All he could say was: "Oscar tells me you're sensational. I'm going to see if I can book you on one of my shows." It was all over in a couple of minutes. The earth did not tremble. Contact, however, had been established.

Early in 1955, Colonel Parker decided to get a firsthand report on Elvis Presley. He summoned to his home at Madison, Tennessee, just north of Nashville, Hank Snow's son, Jimmy Rodgers Snow. The young Snow had grown up in the country music business and was himself a competent performer who was beginning to appear on his father's tours. The Colonel told Snow that he was sending him to Lubbock, Texas, where he would work a one-nighter at the Cotton Club with a young singer who was getting very hot. What the Colonel wanted was a complete rundown on Elvis on and off the stage.

Jimmy Snow had seen everyone in the country music business, but he had never seen anyone like Elvis Presley. " 'Elvis the Pelvis,' " he writes in *I Cannot Go Back,* "as he was already being called, sauntered on stage in black pants with pink stripes down the legs, topped off by a black jacket and pink shirt with collar turned up to catch the ends of his hair. Guitar hanging from his neck, curls dangling over his forehead, eyebrows arching over lidded eyes, he grinned seductively at the girls in the front rows. Leaning forward with feet apart and clutching the mike, he warmed up with a slow ballad, then jumped into what the crowd came to see. Hips grinding and shaking, legs jerking and snapping, arms flailing the guitar to a fast drum beat, he drove the females into hysterics." These "females," it should be borne in mind, were not kids. Country music appealed to an adult public. It was mature women, not little girls that Elvis was turning on in the early days.

When Snow came back to Madison with an enthusiastic report on the new singer, the Colonel lost no time in booking him on a ten-day tour of the Southwest in February. Meantime, Parker went to Shreveport for three weeks to make a study of the possibility of establishing an artist management bureau for the *Louisiana Hayride*. It was during this period that he got his first eyeful of Elvis onstage. The Colonel was recovering from a heart attack at this time; the sight of Elvis must have given him a charge of vitality. The next time Parker booked Presley, it was for a big two-week tour in May.

The sexual excitement of Elvis's female listeners had already at this very early point in his career shaped his act into its distinctive form. Whatever his original intentions may have been when he first became an entertainer, he had learned by now that his strongest drawing card was his raw sex appeal. Consequently, instead of carrying on like a wild young boy who doesn't know his own attractiveness, Elvis had begun to study how to increase his seductiveness. Bob Lumen, a seasoned country singer, recollects the shocking effect of Elvis's opening, which by now was as deliberately provocative as that of an old-time jungle show.

"This cat came out in red pants and a green coat and a pink shirt and socks, and he had this sneer on his face. He stood behind the mike for five minutes, I'll bet, before he made a move. Then he hit his guitar a lick, and he broke two strings. I'd been playing ten years, and I hadn't broken a *total* of two strings. So there he was, these two strings dangling, and he hadn't done anything yet, and these high school girls were screaming and fainting and running to the stage. Then he started to move his hips, like he had this thing for his guitar. That was Elvis Presley playing Kilgore, Texas. He made chills run up my back, man!"

This good description conveys the essence of Elvis's act at the moment before his great breakthrough. The note he strikes is one of erotic challenge. You can see him standing there with his legs spraddled, his lip curled in the famous snarl, green eye shadow giving his pale, poached face a ghoulish hue, as he stares menacingly at the girls with his broken-stringed guitar lying in his hands like the child murdered unwittingly by Frankenstein's monster. By this point Elvis has joined the rogues gallery of violent, crazy, sadistic teen heroes of the fifties, alongside Marlon Brando in his black leather jacket and visored military cap, leading his motorcycle gang into Our Town; or the psychopathic Vic Morrow, switchblade in hand, stalking Glenn Ford in the high-school classroom; or, closest of all, Michael Landon, watching the girl gymnast flex her body sensuously on the parallel bars, then, at the sound of a clangorous schoolbell, exploding before your eyes into the hideously hairy shape of a teenage werewolf.

Elvis's genius lay in combining the movie myth of the menacing teenager with rock 'n' roll music so as to create a whole new performance idiom appropriate to that wild new form of entertainment, the rock concert. Out of his threatening poses, frenzied gyrations and spontaneous psychodrama sprang the whole tradition of hard rock. Overnight, the basic image for a hot young singer became a crazy looking boy with a guitar in his hand cutting up all over a stage. So profound and pervasive is this image today that we can't imagine a rock singer under any other aspect. Consequently, you could say that Elvis's influence as a stage performer far surpassed his effect as a recording star because even though his musical idiom soon went out of style, every real rock act that followed him for the next twenty-five years derived directly from his stage rhetoric.

It's amusing to observe how quaint or even archaic are the resources which Elvis rediscovered for his highly innovative stage style. Those broken, hanging strings that awed Bob Lumen, for example, were invented a century before Elvis Presley   by Niccolò Paganini. The demonic violin virtuoso of the Romantic Age, also famous for his long hair, pale mask-like face and aura of diabolic evil, would play madly on his fiddle until suddenly, twang!, a string would break and hang haplessly from his instrument. A signal to stop, to cool it, to get things back under control, the broken string worked on Paganini only as a challenge driving him on to even greater and more awesome feats of virtuosity. No sooner had he demonstrated that he could outplay the greatest violinist with only three strings to his instrument then twang!, he had suddenly broken another string! Now the challenge is even greater, the transpositions and fingerings more fantastic, as he fights to do with only two strings what other men can barely achieve with four. Then, twang!, my God!— he's broken yet another string! Now he's down to the G string, the thickest string, the string upon which he can perform like the devil himself, because, according to the legend, all his other strings rotted away during the years when he was confined to a damp dungeon for unspeakable crimes. Ah, the classics!

Once again we see that it was Elvis Presley's function to recapture the past every time he took a step into the future, his talent lying precisely in his capacity to revive in the arid atmosphere of the Age of Ike the flamboyance and extravagance of the long-submerged romantic spirit. Nor should it be thought that Elvis's tricks were confined to matters of song or stage technique. He was also very crafty about his sex appeal.

Though it is holy writ that Elvis was the natural man instinctively vying with and defeating the uptight Goliaths of fifties philistinism, and though many a long rap has been laid down about how this simple— but heavily hormoned!—country boy overthrew with one mighty shot from his pelvic sling the enemies of a free, open, untrammeled sexuality, when you talk to those behind the scenes, you get a very different picture of the Simon Bolivar of the crotch. Consider the testimony of another young country singer of that day, David Houston, a friend of Elvis's from Shreveport, who traveled with him extensively in this period. According to Houston, here is how the natural man would prepare himself to go onstage: "He would take the cardboard cylinder out of a roll of toilet paper and put a string in one end of it. Then, he'd tie that string around his waist. The other end, with the cardboard roller, would hang down outside his drawers, so as when he got onstage and reared back with that guitar in his hand, it would look to the girls up front like he had one helluva thing there inside his pants."

Having discovered that he could drive the girls wild with his onstage performance, the shy, reticent, easily embarrassed Elvis began now to extend his stage image into his private life. If he drove the girls crazy, he was no less crazy about the girls. Everyone who knew him at the time recalls how obsessive was Elvis's pursuit of women. Every week when he came down to Shreveport, he would put up at the Al-Ida Motel, which was on the rough side of town in Bossier (Cajun = Boshur) City. One of the hottest tonk strips in the South, Bossier City was the "service center" for nearby Barksdale Air Force Base. "After dark," wrote Erskine Caldwell, "when the rainbow-colored, plastic-encased, rocket-shaped neon lights burst into all their crazy-crystal glory, Bossier City is a dazzling three-mile strip of booze, girls and ear-jarring nightlife." Though Elvis still didn't smoke or drink, he had become a night-prowling cat, who must have been thrilled down to the bottom of his penny-loafers by the antics he saw in this little sin city.

Elvis chased every girl he met. He never stopped cruising. He arranged his dates in shifts so that as one girl was leaving his room another one would be arriving. Sometimes he would have three or four girls in his room at once. If a girl proved coy, Elvis might resort to force to overcome her resistance. One girl threatened to sue him for rape, David Houston recalls. When her mother showed up at the hotel, Elvis had a long talk with her alone in the room. Afterwards, Elvis confided to Houston: "I think I could make the mother, too."

Persistent rumors in Shreveport suggest that Elvis may have gotten a girl pregnant during this reckless time. There's no way of verifying or disproving this tale. The woman is supposed to have had the baby, a girl, and subsequently married a man who had money and doesn't want any unpleasant memories being stirred up after all these years.

Elvis's first big tour with Hank Snow commenced on May 1, 1955, at New Orleans and then zigzagged through Louisiana, Alabama and northern Florida—classic redneck country—in a series of one-night stands. Elvis hit hard in every town along the route. He appeared on the first half of the program along with acts like Jimmy Rodgers Snow, the Davis Sisters and the Wilburn Brothers, all lightweight performers. The second half of the show offered the bigger names, commencing with the Carter family and building up through Slim Whitman to the boss himself, Hank Snow. All through the tour, the performers on the first half of the bill kept complaining to Snow that they couldn't follow Elvis's act; so Snow put Elvis in the next-to-intermission spot.

It was in this slot that Elvis appeared on May 13 at the Gator Bowl at Jacksonville, Florida, before an audience of 14,000 people. Few of these folk had ever heard of Elvis Presley because they lived outside the range of the *Hayride* broadcasts. Elvis appeared onstage that night wearing a pink suit with a lacy pink see-through shirt that resembled a woman's blouse. In the course of his brief turn, he used every trick he knew to turn on the girls. As he bowed off, he shouted "Thank you, ladies and gentlemen!" Then, lowering his voice and breathing heavily into the mike, he leered, "Girls—I'll see you backstage!" It was meant to be a gag. Some gag! In a flash, about half the audience leaped to its feet and started running toward the dugout that led down into the locker room where the performers dressed.

Elvis stayed one step ahead of the mob, receiving some good downfield blocking from the police. Gladys and Vernon, seated in the stands, watched the flight and pursuit in horror. When Elvis ducked into the dugout, he appeared to be safe in his hole; but someone failed to close the door and about a hundred girls came screaming into the locker room. They attacked Elvis head-on and started tearing off his clothes. He climbed out of reach atop a shower stall. The police finally cleared the room, save for one scraggly little girl who was found hiding behind a partition. As she slunk out, one of the boys noticed an odd-looking hump in her dress. Kicking at it, the dude dislodged what proved to be one of Elvis's shoes. When it was finally judged safe for Elvis to leave that night, he walked out in the parking area and found his pink Cadillac had been scarified from end to end with girls' names either scrawled on the finish with lipstick or scratched into the paint with pins and rings.

This startling outburst of violence, which terrified Elvis's parents, shocked his fellow troupers and brought down denunciations on his head from the local authorities, thrilled Colonel Parker to the core of his old carny man's heart. What appalled and disgusted straight people made the hustler's palm itch with greed. Elvis, the Colonel saw in a flash, was sucker bait. He could be jounced and dangled in front of millions of girls across the country who would pay anything for a chance to get close enough to ogle him and scream at him and reach out their hands in hysterical fits trying to touch him. Elvis had to be handled right, of course, like any freak attraction, or the whole thing could get out of hand and result in some terrible disaster. He would also have to be paced properly or his fad would burn out quickly. It would take a lot of shrewdness to exploit this kid to the limits he suggested. The Colonel knew that he was the man for the job. From the moment of the first Presley riot, Elvis was, in the Colonel's mind, already his "boy."

Staking out Elvis Presley as his next mark and getting the boy safely into the net were, however, two very different things. Though none of the obstructions in the Colonel's path were formidable in themselves, in their aggregate they constituted a veritable obstacle course. The first and most fundamental job was to con Elvis and his family into believing that they would be much better off under the direction of Colonel Parker than they were with Bob Neal. This problem was made all the more difficult by the close familial ties which had developed between the Presleys and the Neals. Mrs. Presley often spent the evenings when Elvis was on the road visiting with Helen Neal, the two mothers sharing their concerns over their young sons, who were often out at work or play together. Then, assuming the Colonel could put away the Presleys, there were the problems presented by the professional people who had contracts with Elvis. Neal was the most obvious but not necessarily the most important of these businessmen. Sam Phillips was really a bigger problem because he controlled Elvis's future in both the recording and music publishing businesses. The Colonel was convinced that nothing could be done for Elvis's career in these areas until he was sprung from the grasp of Phillips and put into the hands of one of the major companies, which had the publicity and distribution apparatus to make Elvis's records big hits. Finally, there was the contract with the *Louisiana Hayride,* which the Colonel regarded as a sin and an outrage. Not only did the program pay virtually nothing for Elvis's services; it kept him running in and out of Shreveport all year long, when he should have been free to travel for weeks on end in any direction his career took him. Here was another hold that would have to be broken at the earliest opportunity.

Of all the problems facing the Colonel at this moment, none was more basic than the job of ingratiating himself with Elvis and convincing the boy that his future lay in allowing the Colonel to manage all his affairs. The first order of business, therefore, was gulling Elvis. Needless to say, this was not hard to accomplish. Elvis was just a naive young kid infatuated with his first taste of fame and indifferent to everything that did not feed his hungry ego. The first trick was to flatter the kid outrageously, tell him that he was much too good for these dumb little country shows. That he should have his own show. That he should be on TV. That he should record for RCA. Then, tell him what they all want to hear: "You should be in pictures." At the same time the Colonel was basting Elvis with butter and bullshit, he did not neglect to stuff his mouth with bread. Elvis's price was $250 a night for himself and the band. The Colonel would negotiate with Bob Neal to keep the price low and prove to Elvis that his manager wasn't very successful at earning him money. Then, when the Colonel got Elvis out on the road, the old boy would start slipping brand new hundred dollar bills in the kid's pocket or taking him shopping in the pimp clothing stores he loved. Soon Elvis was making more in "bonuses" than he was in fees. He was also calling Colonel Parker by a new nickname: "the Admiral."

Vernon Presley, who was both stupid and greedy, was no problem at all. The Colonel made a swift conquest of this spineless creature. The real problem was Gladys. The Colonel, with his shrewd eye for people, knew only too well how vital it was to his success that he get the mother's approval for his takeover. So concerned was the Colonel about making the proper impression on Gladys that he adopted an elaborate stratagem to put her away.

One of the Colonel's old cronies was the rube comic Whitey Ford, well known as "the Duke of Paducah." In the summer of 1955, Ford received a call from the Colonel that commenced, as did all the Colonel's scams, as an innocent bit of business. As a sideline to his showbiz career, Ford ran a sausage and egg farm; the Colonel asked Ford that day to bring over "a mess of sausage and a couple dozen eggs." When Ford made the delivery, he found his friend in a ruminative mood. Taking out a couple of records with yellow labels, the Colonel said: "I want you to hear a young singer I'm thinkin' o' managin'. I want your opinion of him." Ford was impressed by the freshness and vitality of the voice. He gave the records his enthusiastic endorsement. Then, the Colonel broke out his pictures of Elvis. Ford took one look at the boy and exclaimed, "If I had me a lad like that, I'd hop on the first plane to Hollywood." That was just what the Colonel wanted to hear. Now he leveled with Ford.

He told him that he was arranging a tour that would feature Elvis and Hank Snow's son, Jimmy Rodgers Snow, and the Carter Family. He wanted to place the Duke of Paducah on the bill. In exchange he wanted a favor. Actually, two favors. First, he wanted the Duke to keep an eye on these young boys and make sure they didn't do anything disgraceful. More important was another matter. When the tour hit Little Rock, its last date, Elvis's mother and father would be on hand. The Colonel wanted to meet the mother, but he was afraid that she might not react to him and his proposition in the right way. So what the Colonel wanted Ford to do was to go in first and soften up the mother. Ford was a nice, gentle, well-spoken man, a man with a reputation for God-fearing behavior. He would make a good impression on Mrs. Presley. When he had gotten into conversation with her, he could tell her all the good things about Colonel Parker—like how much money he would make for Elvis. Then, when the Duke had gotten the mother in the right mood, the Colonel would step in and take over.

When the tour reached its next-to-last stop, Monroe, Louisiana, the Colonel appeared. He had a meeting with Elvis; then, after the show he told the Duke of Paducah: "You're riding with me." As they rolled up the highway toward Little Rock, the Colonel gave the Duke his final instructions. "Here's the plan," he said, employing his customary military lingo. "When we get to Little Rock, I'm gonna stay outta sight. You will have a dressing room with Elvis. Elvis is gonna bring his mother and father in there. Then, Elvis is gonna say, 'Now, Mama, the Duke here has been with Parker for a long time. He knows him from A to

Z. He'll tell you anything you wanna know about him.' That's your cue to soft soap the old lady."

That night everything went like clockwork. Gladys and Vernon appeared in the dressing room after the show. Elvis introduced them to the Duke and then beat it out the door. He didn't go far, however; he laid his ear to the keyhole and listened carefully to the ensuing conversation. The Duke took his time and brought the conversation around to the point slowly. He was a real country man, like the Presleys, a man who inspired confidence and friendship. More than once during the conversation, he described himself as a Christian. Once he had established the proper rapport, he came quietly but firmly to the point. "Mizz Presley," he said in his thickest rural accent, "ahve known Colonel a long time. Ah seen what he done for Eddy Arnol'. Ah know his methods and how he works. There's nobody else like him aroun'. He'll definitely make Elvis a star. He'll make Elvis so much money, he'll never be able to spend it. That may sound to you like an exaggerated statement, but you'll find out that ah'm right."

Gladys was skeptical. Also a little distrustful. She asked embarrassing questions, like: "What church does Colonel Parker belong to?" That was a pisser! Colonel Parker had never been in a church in his life, unless it were to set up a bingo game. Somehow the issue was skirted. Finally, Gladys fell back on her last line of resistance. She acknowledged that the Colonel might be good for Elvis, but she didn't see any way that the arrangement could be made because Elvis "done already signed with Mr. Neal and Mr. Phillips an' the radio station down there in Shreveport." The old Duke chuckled richly when he heard these fears. "Mizz Presley," he said, "let me tell you sumthin'. Time the Colonel get through with all these people not only will Elvis be free, but them folk will be braggin' 'cause they onct worked with Elvis Presley." At that moment, Elvis opened the door and walked in, saying: "Mama, I want you to meet the Admiral—Mr. Parker!"

That night as the Colonel and the Duke drove toward Nashville, the old carny was feeling both relieved and concerned. He told Ford that though this was an important obstacle out of the way, there were still a lot of other problems before him. The biggest of these was Elvis's manager, Bob Neal. Neal, as the Colonel knew, was a man who had spread himself too thin. He had made so many commitments that he couldn't commit himself heart and soul to any one thing. That was his great weakness. Colonel Parker, on the other hand, was a manager who made it a point never to have more than one client, to whom he dedicated himself night and day. In the long run, therefore, the Colonel had more to offer Elvis than did Bob Neal. Still, what would happen if Neal refused to give Elvis up?

The solution proved to be simple. The Colonel went to Neal and told him that there was a good chance that RCA and Hill and Range would put up a big sum of money to purchase Elvis's recording and publishing contracts. This was a matter over which Neal had no authority whatsoever; yet, in exchange for his goodwill, the Colonel was willing to give Neal a percentage of the commission the Colonel would earn if he closed the deal. That put Neal in the Colonel's pocket. Neal informed the Colonel that offers for the contract were constantly coming through the office and the price was constantly rising. Sam Phillips had offered the contract originally to Owen Bradley at Decca for $5,000; Bradley had turned it down. Randy Wood of Dot Records was offered the contract subsequently for $7,500; he, too, turned it down. Then, the great Mitch Miller, the A & R genius of Columbia, called to ask the price; Neal relayed a demand from Phillips for $20,000. Miller rang off in a huff. The Colonel snorted when he heard these prices. He told the astonished Neal that the proper price for the contract was $50,000. That's what they should be shooting for. Fifty big ones!

Though every account of the translation of Elvis from small-time to big-time assigns all the credit for the advancement to Tom Parker, this is not just. It was Hank Snow, RCA's top country artist, who first brought Elvis Presley to the attention of Victor's man in Nashville, Steve Sholes. Snow also alerted his publishers, Hill and Range, to Elvis (as did Ernest Tubb), thereby initiating a relationship that was far more influential in the development of Elvis's singing and recording career than was his association with RCA. Though Hill and Range is not a household word, like Victor, this young company was then the most resourceful and innovative organization in the business. Its proprietors, Julian and Joachim (Jean) Aberbach, were highly sophisticated Viennese Jews who got into music publishing in Berlin back in the days of cabaret and "Goodnight Sweetheart." Though the most unlikely men in the world to become hillbilly music magnates, they saw the opportunity presented by the hitherto largely ignored field of country (Hill) and western (Range) and made a fortune.

Hank Snow was not being altruistic in promoting Elvis. He hoped to profit. He and Parker were equal partners in a tour-packaging agency called Hank Snow Attractions. They had taken under contract already a number of performers and were looking for fresh talent. Snow assumed that eventually he and Parker would manage Elvis jointly. This intention is reflected clearly in the very first contract Parker signed with Elvis on August 15, 1955.

According to the Presley Myth, Elvis and the Colonel never had anything more binding between them than a handshake. A relationship of twenty-two years that grossed over a hundred million dollars—all on a handshake! It is astonishing how universally this preposterous story is believed. What a great tribute to the Colonel that he could con the toughest suckers in the world into believing this audacious lie! In truth, the handshake story is not only false but repeatedly false; for on top of his first contract, Colonel Parker piled one after another, until, eventually, the articulation of his business relationship with Elvis Presley came to resemble a nest of jackstraws. All of these personally authored and sometimes legally ambiguous instruments betray the practiced hand of the hustler. Let us consider for a moment the initial contract. First, the document:

A G R E E M E N T

SPECIAL AGREEMENT between ELVIS PRESLEY, known as artist, his guardians, Mr. and/or Mrs. Presley, and his manager, MR. BOB NEAL, of Memphis, Tennessee, hereinafter referred to as the Party of the First Part, and COL. THOMAS A. PARKER and/or HANK SNOW ATTRACTIONS of Madison, Tennessee, hereinafter known as the Party of the Second Part, this date, August 15, 1955.

COL. PARKER is to act as special adviser to ELVIS PRESLEY and BOB NEAL for the period of one year and two one-year options for the sum of two thousand, five hundred dollars ($2,500.00) per year, payable in five payments of five hundred dollars ($500.00) each, to negotiate and assist in any way possible the build-up of ELVIS PRESLEY as an artist. Col. Parker will be reimbursed for any out-of-pocket expenses for travelling, promotion, advertising as approved by ELVIS PRESLEY and his manager.

As a special concession to Col. Parker, ELVIS PRESLEY is to play 100 personal appearances within one year for the special sum of $200.00 (Two hundred dollars) including his musicians.

In the event that negotiations come to a complete standstill and ELVIS PRESLEY and his manager and associates decide to free-lance, it is understood that Col. Parker will be reimbursed for the time and expenses involved in trying to negotiate the association of these parties and that he will have first call on a number of cities, as follows, at the special rate of one hundred, seventy-five dollars ($175.00) per day for the first appearance and two hundred fifty dollars ($250.00) for the second appearance and three hundred fifty dollars ($350.00). San Antonio, El Paso, Phoenix, Tucson, Albuquerque, Oklahoma City, Denver, Wichita Falls, Wichita, New Orleans, Mobile, Jacksonville, Pensacola, Tampa, Miami, Orlando, Charleston, Greenville, Spartanburg, Asheville, Knoxville, Roanoke, Richmond, Norfolk, Washington, D.C., Philadelphia, Newark, New York, Pittsburgh, Chicago, Omaha, Milwaukee, Minneapolis, St. Paul, Des Moines, Los Angeles, Amarillo, Lubbock, Houston, Galveston, Corpus Christi, Las Vegas, Reno, Cleveland, Dayton, Akron, and Columbus.

Col. Parker is to negotiate all renewals on existing contracts.

This agreement is fraught with conflicts of interest. Though Parker is now, in effect, one of Elvis's agents, he stipulates also for an enormous number of concert dates played in distant cities at reduced rates. He is, therefore, both the artist's agent and employer. What's more, we observe that Parker signs on behalf of Hank Snow Attractions, clearly committing himself to a joint arrangement with Hank Snow to promote and employ Elvis. Precisely how Parker aced Snow out his share of Elvis Presley has never been revealed. We do know that Snow threatened to take the Colonel to court, and, as we've seen, the mere mention of Parker's name even today makes the choleric Snow boil with rage. Clearly, the first person who got a screwing from Colonel Parker once he had cut into Elvis Presley was Hank Snow.

How did the Colonel propose to "build up" Elvis? A rare and revealing close-up of the Colonel's hustling is provided by Arnold Shaw, then the general manager of a New York publishing house, who paid a visit to Parker at Madison in August 1955, just at the moment when the Colonel was starting his new campaign. Devious, sly, always playing with an ace up his sleeve, the Colonel broached the subject of Presley with Shaw by playing a couple of the Sun recordings. Shaw was not impressed especially by the singing, but he was struck by the "animal sex appeal" exuded by the eight by ten glossies that the Colonel produced next. "In Georgia and Florida the girls are tearing off his clothes," the

Colonel told Shaw, "but he's unknown north of the Mason-Dixon Line." Then, giving his mark an appraising stare, the Colonel came to the point. "You're a big man up North," he smiled, employing his half-flattering, half-mocking put-on style. "Let me see you get his records played in the Big City." "What's your interest, Colonel?" asked Shaw. The Colonel's answer was astonishingly frank. "This kid is now managed by Bob Neal of Memphis," he replied. "But I'll have him when Neal's contract finishes in less than a year."

When Shaw returned to New York, he was carrying two copies of each of Elvis's Sun releases. The first person to whom he gave the records was one of the most influential DJs of that day: Bill Randle, the successor to Alan Freed in Cleveland and a weekend jock in New York. Randle decided the records were too crude for his New York show, but when he played the two sides in Cleveland, one of the great strongholds of the new rock music, he got precisely the same reaction that Dewey Phillips had triggered a year before at Memphis. The Colonel's ploy had worked. Elvis was breaking now above the Mason-Dixon Line. Meantime, Colonel Parker was busy working on the project that he had neglected to mention to Shaw: negotiating the sale of Elvis's record contract to RCA. Getting the records on the air in the North had been vital to the success of this campaign.

Why did Sam Phillips want to sell the Presley contract? Phillips himself has said many times that he was strapped for cash and that he had no idea how successful Elvis would become. Why was he so lacking in vision? The answer is simple. Elvis was not selling great numbers of records for Sun. Though he was sensational on a stage, he was not a big item in the record stores. "That's All Right Mama" backed by "Blue Moon Over Kentucky" sold twenty thousand copies; the next record sold about five thousand. At that rate, it's no wonder that Phillips decided to cash in his chips and put his money into his next star, Carl Perkins. The exchange worked brilliantly at first; by the time Elvis got his first record out on RCA, Perkins's "Blue Suede Shoes" was the Number Two side in the United States. After that, the balance tipped dramatically toward Elvis, and Phillips must have been deeply chagrined.

Elvis's feeble sales record also explains why the negotiations with RCA took so many months to gel. Steve Sholes was eager to buy, but he had to persuade the corporate executives that this virtually unknown singer was worth more money than anybody had ever paid for a new performer in the history of the record business. All through the summer of 1955 Sholes kept telling Parker, "Give me some ammunition so that

I can make headway in New York." Finally, the Colonel got the break
he was seeking. In July, "Baby, Let's Play House" became the first
Elvis Presley record to appear on a national chart; it rose to Number
Ten on the country and western list and remained a chart record during
the entire period of the final negotiations.

A full step beyond the earlier Sun records and the bridge to "Heartbreak Hotel," "Baby, Let's Play House" exemplifies Elvis at the peak
of his early style. The original recording by "Hardrock" Gunter
is a grimy little blues sung in an ambling back-beat style that goes
nowhere. Elvis's version is electrifying. His voice bursts out of the loudspeaker with a searing cry; his fast staccato passages crepitate eerily,
thanks to the echo effect; and when he settles into the final ride-out,
riffing on the syllables of "bababababy [hiccup] bababababy [hiccup],"
he sounds like a Hawaiian war chant. The fantasia on the blues which
had produced such witty and amusing effects on the early Sun sides is
now beginning to generate a bizarre honky-tonk atmosphere that will
soon permeate American popular music and form the exciting but grotesque backdrop for the Rock Age.

November 21, 1955, was the date on which the prolonged negotiations
for the purchase of Elvis Presley's recording and publishing contracts
were finally concluded. On that date a whole sheaf of legal agreements
was signed, sworn and filed away in New York, Memphis and Madison,
Tennessee. Colonel Parker updated his original agreement with Elvis
in a new instrument which designated him as "sole and exclusive Advisor
and Personal representative." Parker also signed an agreement with Bob
Neal that committed both of Elvis's agents to pool their percentages
(fifteen percent for Neal, twenty-five for Parker) and divide the sums
equally, until Neal's contract elapsed on March 15, 1956. The other
agreements were those which the Colonel had negotiated between Elvis
and the various recording and publishing interests who were now to
become such vital factors in the young star's career. These agreements
have never been accurately reported.

It is said always that RCA paid $40,000 to purchase the contract
from Sun, whereas the truth is that only $25,000 was paid by RCA
and the other $15,000 was paid by Hill and Range. It is also said that
Elvis received a bonus of $5,000, whereas, in fact, the $5,000 was all
money that was owed Elvis by Phillips in unpaid royalties. In all these
distortions and exaggerations one detects the hand of the Colonel, who
controlled the publicity for the event and who was seeking, as always,
to astound.

The value of the recording contract purchased by RCA needs no comment. Not only did the firm obtain the right to make new records, but it acquired all the old records on Sun, as well as all the unissued material that was in Phillips's archives, including a number of songs that had never been issued but which would now be used to pad out Elvis's first albums. The value of the publishing rights, for which Hill and Range paid nearly as much as RCA did for the recording rights, is another matter entirely. To grasp what was entailed in this deal and the profound effect it had upon the future career of Elvis Presley, it is necessary to have a clear conception of the modus operandi of the music publishing business at that time.

Unlike publishers in the past, who had made most of their money from the sale of sheet music, publishers in the fifties derived their principal income from the rights associated with the sale and commercial usage of phonograph records. One great source of income was the so-called mechanical rights in a song, which meant then the flat fee of one cent per side for each record sold by the manufacturer. The other principal source of revenue was the broadcast rights, a fee computed by a elaborate actuarial formula that reflects the amount of play the song receives over the air.

As there is an intimate connection between the commercial success of a song and the fame of the singer who records it, Hill and Range had adopted the stratagem of establishing for famous singers independent publishing companies that would obtain the rights to all the songs recorded by the singers so that they received not just the royalties paid performers by record companies but a large portion of the publishing royalties. The arrangement was one of reciprocal benefit to all involved: The songwriters would be eager to have their songs published by Presley Music (BMI) or Gladys Music (ASCAP) because in this manner they would be assured of having their songs recorded by Elvis. They would be so glad, in fact, that they would voluntarily surrender one-third of their own royalties and even allow Elvis Presley to affix his name to the song as one of its cowriters. On the other hand, Elvis could be counted on, once the system was operating properly, to confine himself exclusively to recording songs to which he held the publishing rights because on these songs he earned far more money than he would if he recorded a rival publisher's material. Finally, Hill and Range would profit handsomely because they would receive as compensation for operating these new companies fifty percent of all their income. This large sum was rationalized as being fair compensation for the task of securing the songs, doing the paperwork and running the enterprise on sound business principles. It's worth noting that in the years ahead, Hill and Range, which had been founded only eleven years before it acquired Elvis Presley, grew to become the largest independent music publishing house in the world.

Bringing all this down to the level not of dollars but of cents—music publishing counts its multimillion-dollar revenues in pennies—we can imagine ourselves receiving, as Elvis must have received, the primer explanation of why it pays the performer to play the publishing game. In the midfifties the standard royalty paid by the record companies to performers was five percent of ninety percent of the retail price of a record (with step clauses that increase the rate for sales above a quarter, a half, three-quarters of a million records sold). As a 45-RPM record sold then for eighty-nine cents, the per-record royalty was approximately four cents. If the performer had a fifty-fifty copublishing deal, he received in addition to this four cents half of the two-cent mechanical fee (one cent for each side) and half of the broadcast fee, perhaps another penny. Now, instead of four cents, he has six cents. Putting it all together, the performer nearly doubles his income. That's what Professor Parker must have hammered into his young pupil's head, using a cigar for a ferrule.

With the money starting to come in on a greater scale than ever before and his credit reaching the sky, Elvis sold his little bungalow on Lamar and bought a new, more comfortable house on Getwell Road, in the vicinity of the Kennedy Veteran's Hospital. Instead of being set right out on the edge of the road, like the old house, this new dwelling had a large yard and was situated in a better neighborhood. It was at this time, too, that Elvis fulfilled a long-standing wish by purchasing for Gladys a pink and white Crown Victoria Cadillac that would match his own pink Cad. Gladys no longer drove a car, but the sentiment is what counts.

Elvis himself received a very valuable gift at this time: nothing less than his first great hit—"Heartbreak Hotel." It's ironic in view of the elaborate arrangements that had just been concluded to secure for Elvis precisely such valuable new songs that this now-legendary composition should have been offered to him by a couple of obscure writers who had never set foot inside the Brill Building and were far beyond the purview of the talent scouts at Hill and Range. Indeed, the story of the song's composition is interesting both for the light it throws on the mental processes of songwriters and for the way it anticipates instinctively, as it were, the method by which Elvis was to acquire not only new songs but the styles in which to perform these songs.

The tale begins in Gainesville, Florida, where Tommy Durden, an obscure band musician and songwriter, is conning the front page of the *Miami Herald,* before turning to the racing page. Splashed across the front page is the picture of a corpse with a headline that shouts: "Do you know this man?" The accompanying story explains that the man committed suicide after destroying every identifying mark on his clothing. A note he left contained only one scrawled line: "I walk a lonely street."

Durden was strangely excited by this incident, especially by the phrase, "I walk a lonely street." The line was associated in his mind with his favorite kind of music, the blues. Getting in his car, he drove to the house of Mae Axton, a publicist who had befriended Elvis on his appearances in Jacksonville, near Gainesville. This busy lady was, in addition to being a schoolteacher, publicity writer and "personality" on local radio and TV, a songwriter. One of her ambitions was to write Elvis Presley's first big hit. When her friend and writing partner, Tommy Durden, walked in that day with the paper and showed her the story, she agreed at once that they should try to turn it into a song—for Elvis.

Sitting down at the piano and starting to improvise blues licks, Durden concentrated on the phrase that had suggested the song. Mae Axton, who was struck more by the thought of the man's family seeing the picture and recognizing him with broken hearts, suggested that they arrange the lyric so that at the end of the "lonely street" there be a "heartbreak hotel." With those two themes to guide them, the partners plunged into the composition, only to be interrupted by the arrival of yet another of Mae Axton's writing partners, Glen Reeves, a local singer and entertainer in Jacksonville. When Axton explained to Reeves that she and Durden were writing a song for Elvis Presley titled "Heartbreak Hotel" and would welcome his help, Reeves said that the title was "the silliest thing I've ever heard." He refused to have anything to do with the project. Leaving to run some errands in the neighborhood, Reeves returned an hour later to find the song completed and recorded by Durden on Axton's tape recorder.

Now Axton went after Reeves again because she knew that her friend could do a perfect imitation of Elvis Presley's "shaky" style, and she anticipated that if she could demonstrate the song in Elvis's own style, he would be more likely to accept it. Reeves agreed to the request and in a few minutes, working from the chord symbols and the handwritten word sheet, he had shouted and shuddered the blues into the little mike of the home recording machine. To show her appreciation, Axton asked Reeves if he would like to have his name on the song and a share of the writers' earnings. For the second time that afternoon, Reeves refused to have anything to do with this "silly" song.

At this point, Mae Axton took off for Nashville, where the annual DJ convention was in progress, to sell her new song. The moment Elvis heard the tape, his eyes lit up and he exclaimed, "Hot dog, Mae! Play it again!" Once Mae Axton saw that Elvis was taken by the song, she made him a proposition he couldn't refuse. Having heard at the hotel that RCA was about to buy Elvis's contract, Axton told Elvis that if he would agree to make "Heartbreak Hotel" his first record for Victor, she would make him the third writer and let him have a third of the song's royalties. The rest we know.

What isn't known but is really far more important and interesting is the fact that Elvis copied closely the style on the demo record of Glen Reeves. So close was the resemblance that, as Tommy Durden remarked: "I was convinced when I heard the record that Elvis was even breathing in the same places that Glen did on the dub." This curious circular relationship between the demo singer, who is struggling to copy the style of Elvis Presley, and Elvis Presley, who is copying the style of the demo singer, is one that will occupy us soon, when we come to the discussion of Elvis's system of recording, a method that sprang up spontaneously the moment even such naive, semipro songwriters as Tommy Durden and Mae Axton began to pitch songs at Elvis Presley. Even at this very early time in his career, Elvis was more than a singer: he was—with the "shaky" voice that Sam Phillips had given him—an *image*.

Chapter 12

The Nation's Only Atomic-Powered Singer

JITTERY" is the word for Elvis at his first recording RCA session, held at Nashville on January 11, 1956, three days after he turned twenty-one. First, he paced all over the studio while the musicians were setting up.[1] Then, to break the tension, he did something that was to become the preparatory ritual for all his subsequent sessions: He sat down at the piano and, summoning the backup singers around him, launched into "I'm Bound for the Kingdom," followed by "I'll Tell It Wherever I Go." There is an amusing yet deeply revealing quality to this spontaneous outburst. At first glance, it must have seemed so incongruous. Here's this freaky-looking sex-teaser cranking up to record a jivey, salty black ghetto ditty in which he impersonates a cat whose only use for women is "Money, honey!"—and how does he get in the groove? He sings hymns! Yet, at the same time, in this schizzy behavior one recognizes the essential Elvis Presley, the boy who wanted to be a gospel singer and who has finally fulfilled this ambition in

---

[1] Steve Sholes decided to beef up Elvis's skimpy accompaniment with a vocal trio and a couple of additional rhythm players. Ben and Brock Speer of the Speer Family were hired to sing lead tenor and baritone; Gordon Stoker of the Jordanaires was engaged to sing first tenor. The band was enlarged to include Floyd Cramer on piano and Chet Atkins, Sholes's right-hand man, on rhythm guitar.

the most bizarre manner by getting together at a Methodist radio station with some of the same gospel singers he once admired at the all-night sings to record rhythm and blues songs derived from gospel music but fitted now with lyrics that most people regard as "common," "low-down," or just plain "dirty."

The first tune cut that morning was the Ray Charles hit, "I Got a Woman" (renamed for Elvis's juvenile public "I Got a Sweetie"). No sooner did Elvis go into the song than producer and engineer were startled to see their new star start bouncing around in the studio as if he were onstage. Elvis was off mike more often than he was on. Sholes stopped the session and told Elvis that he would have to stand in one spot or they would never get an acceptable take. Elvis, always eager to please, replied meekly, "Yes, Mr. Sholes." When they got the next take, however, it was obvious that a lot of the rhythmic verve had drained out of the performance. "Please, Mr. Sholes," Elvis begged, "don't make me stand still. If I can't move, I can't sing!" Sholes told the engineer's assistant to rig two more mikes on either side of the one Elvis was using. Now, he would be picked up whether he bopped to the east or bopped to the west. No sooner was this problem solved than another surfaced. Elvis held his guitar so high and hit it so hard that the sound interfered with the voice recording. How were they to solve this problem? Someone came up with the idea of giving Elvis a soft, felt ukelele pick. With this feathery instrument, he could play hard and not make a din.

As soon as the session got cooking, Elvis removed his white buck shoes. Instantly, the small studio was filled with a funky odor. "Ah'm sorry about the stink, guys," Elvis apologized, "but ah been out on the road and ah ain't taken a bath in three days." This was typical of Elvis both early and late. His doting mother hadn't given him any guilts about dirt and body odor. Though he was constantly grooming his gleaming hair, he was always, as Gordon Stoker puts it, "semi-dirty."

The harder Elvis worked, the more he reminded the musicians of an athlete playing a big game. At one point the pick flew out of his hand, but Elvis kept whacking the strings with his bare fingers until his hand began to bleed. "Why didn't you stop?" asked the astonished Steve Sholes. "Ah didn't wanna break it up, it was goin' so good," smiled Elvis, like an injured halfback reporting to his coach on the bench. Later in the session, Elvis hit the floor in a kneedrop that split the seat of his pants. He was always destroying his clothes. In fact, the reason he wore the oversized jackets that are now the hallmark of the punk style is not because he thought they looked better that way but because they gave him more elbow room.

"What the hell was that all about?" the reaction in other parts of the country was swift and clear. CBS, a national network, nay, a national institution!, had just committed the unpardonable sin of filling the American living room with the obscene antics and barbaric yawps of a leering, sneering juvenile delinquent. It was like the opening shot of the Civil War. Suddenly, *Stage Show* was the second Sumter. Next morning, the program's producers were flooded with wires, calls and letters denouncing the show and threatening reprisals.

When the Nielsen ratings came in, they showed that Como had taken 34.6% of the viewers compared with a lousy 18.4% for *Stage Show*. These initial ratings were prophetic of what happened on all of Elvis's subsequent appearances on this faltering program. Though "Heartbreak Hotel" soon reached the Number One position on the pop charts, Como beat Presley, hands down.

The most important result of the Dorsey shows was an offer from Hal Wallis, the famous movie producer, to give Elvis a screen test. Both Elvis and the Colonel were agreed that the goal of all their efforts should be a career in films. "Singers come and go," said Elvis, "but if you're a good actor, you can last a long time." The fact is that Elvis lacked any real commitment to rock music. He didn't even want to remain a singer indefinitely. In Elvis's eyes nothing was greater than being a movie star. That was what he had always wanted and if he could get it through singing—great! But, if you had to sustain your star status by continuing to sing, then you hadn't really made it into the big time: the class of the Rudolph Valentinos, and James Deans. That was the sort of star Elvis had always aspired to be. So the opportunity to have a career in movies was for Elvis the beginning of a dream come true.

The screen test was set for April 1 at Paramount Studios. A veteran character actor, Frank Faylen, who had a few days free from Wallis's current production, *Gunfight at the O.K. Corral,* was asked to play opposite Elvis in a scene from Wallis's next picture, *The Rainmaker.* Stills of the session show Elvis dressed in rough-out clothes acting in a broadly macho style, chomping on a cigar, poking his finger in Faylen's belly and carrying on like a rough young stud. Faylen remembers that Elvis acted much too nice at first; the old actor had to urge the kid to get tough. Wallis, who had been impressed by Elvis in the first place because of his obvious sex appeal, was delighted by the test. "I felt the same thrill," he remembers, "I experienced when I first saw Errol Flynn on the screen. Elvis, in a very different, modern way, had exactly the same power, virility, and sexual drive. The camera caressed him."

The deal, which was the realization of Elvis's wildest hopes, was for seven years and three pictures, at a starting salary of $100,000 and increasing by increments of $50,000 in the two succeeding films. Wallis's most recent discovery before Elvis had been the comedy team of Dean Martin and Jerry Lewis; they had started at $50,000 a picture and worked up to $75,000. Clearly, Colonel Parker had done a good job of bargaining for the first picture. But by committing Elvis to a long-term agreement at fixed prices the Colonel made a big mistake. It wouldn't be long until everyone in the Presley circle was saying, "We don't make any real money on the pictures we do for Mr. Wallis."

Having no suitable picture in which to cast Elvis, Wallis decided to create for his new star a skillfully customized vehicle. He commissioned an original screenplay from Hal Kanter, who had fashioned for Wallis the adaptation of Tennessee Williams's *The Rose Tattoo,* that had won two Academy Awards the preceding year. While this project was in preparation, Wallis received an offer from Twentieth Century-Fox to stick Elvis into a picture it was preparing to shoot, titled *The Reno Brothers.* What Wallis received for the loan of his new acquisition, whose value was rising every week, is not known; but chances are the fee went a long way toward defraying the $100,000 promised Elvis for his first picture.

While the wheels were beginning to turn in Hollywood, they were spinning off their axles on the rock 'n' roll road. The summer of 1956 marks the dizzy apogee of Elvis Presley's career as a rock star. During these hot months, his life became a blur of one-night stands, broken only by quick dashes to radio, TV, film and recording studios. Typical of the fast pace was the thirteen-day stretch from June 22 to July 4. Elvis gave sixteen regular performances in half a dozen cities, flew up to New York to rehearse for a network TV show, came back again two days later to do the show, remained for another day to record two of his greatest hits, then wound up on the night of the Fourth headlining a big charity benefit at Memphis.

The run began with a three-day weekend at the Paramount Theater at Atlanta, where Elvis did four shows a day between screenings of *Fury at Gunsight Pass.* The bill was an all-country package (in Tom Parker's mind Elvis was still a C & W act, not a rock 'n' roller), featuring the Carter Family and two baggy-pants rube comics from *Grand Ole Opry:* Rod Brasfield and Papa Sype. The great moment of every show occurred toward the end, when Elvis made a spectacular entrance riding up from the bottom of the orchestra pit in an old-fashioned band car.

Stepping off the elevator into the lurid glare of a colored follow spot, he would shout the first phrases of "Heartbreak Hotel"—and bring down the house! Then, he'd drive straight into the current Little Richard hit, "Long, Tall Sally," doing some of his fast jive moves. For a change of pace, he would next sing "I Was the One," giving it that under-the-echoing-overpass plangency that was so popular at the time. Having cooled the mood with this exercise in acne-spotted self-pity, he would reach back now to his Sun days for "Baby, Let's Play House." Finally, the set would reach its emotional peak with Elvis's first great R & B ballad: "Hi want yew, Hi need you, Hi luh-huh-huh-huv yew-hew!" Working in a blue spot and giving the song the full gospel treatment, he would fall on his knees begging and pleading and sometimes wind up lying face down with his head in the footlight trough.

After this outburst, it was time to drive the kids out of their kugels with three solid rockers in a row: "I Got a Sweetie," "Blue Suede Shoes" and the song that would become soon Elvis's trademark, "Hound Dog." Bowing and waving and saluting the crowd, he would stand in sweaty exultation for a moment. Then, the stage lights would dim, the curtains would part and the screen would flash forth the coming attractions.

The next stop was Savannah. Elvis traveled whenever possible by road, using two of his fleet of four Cadillacs (each a different color) to carry himself, his band and his two cousins, Gene and Junior Smith. The Smith boys were referred to by the other performers as "the hillbilly creeps." Junior, the older of the two, looked exactly like what he was: a psychopathic killer. A skinny, craggily handsome young man, he resembled closely the actor Jack Elam. Always grimacing, glaring and flashing forth from his disturbingly expressive face signs of his essential craziness, Junior disquieted a lot of people. They would have been terrified if they had known his real story.

Drafted during the Korean war, Junior had been sent to the front. The pressures of battle coupled with the tactics of the Koreans, which included the use of civilians as human booby traps, snapped his mind. One day, when a Korean family approached him with hands outstretched, he lowered his BAR and blew them all away. For this act of madness, he received a medical discharge. Now, the killer had been assigned a lifesaving mission.

Elvis's lifelong disposition toward nightmares and sleepwalking had been violently aggravated by the enormous emotional pressures of his big breakthrough. Gladys had become highly alarmed at the thought that some night in a strange city, all alone in a hotel room, Elvis would rise from bed to nip out a window or walk blindly, as he did once as a kid, into the middle of a highway. To guard her son from inadvertent self-destruction, she attached the Smith brothers to Elvis's side, with their most important duty being to sleep every night in the same room, or, preferably, in the same bed, with the somnambulist.

The *Elvis Presley Show* was preceded always by Oscar Davis, who launched the spot announcements over the airwaves and inserted the standard little ad in the paper, showing the picture of Elvis that appears on his first album, singing ecstatically with eyes shut and mouth wide open, slugged with the line Colonel had coined for his boy—"The Nation's First Atomic-Powered Singer." Colonel Parker himself was often away from the tour during this busy summer, negotiating new deals all over the country and getting signatures on his two-foot long contract, bordered with snapshots of the star and spelling out in the most minute detail how many inches of newsprint the concert promoter must provide, how many cops he must hire and how many yards before the gate must be cleared so that Colonel's souvenir hawkers would not have to compete with the local hucksters.

Elvis and his boys reached Savannah after driving all night from Atlanta. That night Elvis did two shows, one at seven and the other at nine-thirty, each time packing the 3,500-seat auditorium, mostly with screaming girls. The behavior of the girls was described the following day in the *Savannah Evening Press:* "They hung over rails with glassy eyes and pawed wildly at the air. Those near the stage held out their hands and screamed for Presley to kiss them. One held up a baby to be kissed. One swooned a genuine swoon. Cpl. C. C. Dickerson of the city police said he took a 13-year-old girl to St. Joseph's Hospital in a state of hysteria. It was frightening. Women have discovered burlesque— and they love it! He used the guitar the way Sally Rand used to use a bubble." There were some men in the audience. The reporter character- ized them as "strangely silent. They had a subdued, even frightened look about them—sort of green around the gills." After the show the reporter found Elvis in his dressing room with a towel wrapped around his neck, looking like "a boxer who had gone fifteen rounds." Asked how he felt after his ordeal, Elvis replied: "A show really wears me out, but if I get to 'em, that's what counts."

The next night the show played in Charlotte, North Carolina, in the big, domed Coliseum. The day before Elvis's appearance, the *Charlotte Observer* reprinted a piece by TV critic John Crosby of the *New York*

Herald Tribune that denounced Elvis as obscene. Such attacks were commonplace at the time. Elvis was assailed all through his first big year by a chorus of newspaper writers, pulpit preachers, high-school teachers, police officials and local politicians. These folk were not only genuinely shocked by Elvis's antics but quick to identify him as a symptom of the dread problem of juvenile delinquency. Not content just to attack Elvis verbally, some of his assailants demanded that action be taken either to curb Elvis's performances or to run him out of town. It was not just the sting of a damning article that Elvis was feeling the day he gave an interview to a reporter from the local paper: It was the fear that his newly won success might suddenly go up in smoke.

The reporter met Elvis and Junior Smith in a luncheonette near the hotel where they were staying. As the boys ate up a mess of barbecue, the reporter jotted down his impressions of Elvis. His "knees bounced while he sat," noted the writer. "His hand drummed a tattoo on the table top. His eyes, under his long lashes, darted from booth to booth, firing rapid winks at the girls who stared at him. 'Hi ya, Baby!' he breathed at one girl. She flopped back in her booth, looking like she'd been poleaxed." When the waitress brought Elvis coffee, he "reached down and fingered the lace on her slip. 'Aren't you the one?' she asked. He replied, 'I'm the one, Baby!' "

Once Elvis had filled his belly, he replied at length to the TV critic of the *Tribune.* "This John Crosby guy," he began, "who does he think he is? He says I'm obscene. Nasty. What does he know? Did you see the show [the second *Milton Berle Show,* June 5]? This Debra Paget was on it. She wore a tight thing with feathers on the behind where they wiggle most. Sex! Man, she bumped and pooshed out all over the place. I'm like Little Boy Blue. Yet, who do they say is obscene? Me! It's because I made more money than Debra. Forty thousand dollars a week! Them critics don't like to see nobody win doing any kind of music they don't know nuthin' about. The colored folk been singing it and playing it just the way I'm doin' now, man, for more years than I know. Nobody paid it no mind till I goosed it up."

The reporter asked the inevitable question about how long Elvis figured rock would last. Elvis replied that he didn't know but it didn't matter. "When it's gone, I'll switch to something else," he remarked confidently. "I like to sing ballads the way Eddie Fisher does and the way Perry Como does, but the way I'm singing now is what makes the money. Would you change if you was me?" With that parting shot, Elvis got up, paid his check and sauntered down the block with Junior until they reached a poolroom. The reporter left the star chalking his cue.

That night, he continued, "Presley burst onstage staggering and flailing like a moth caught in a beam of light." It took the efforts of twenty cops to keep the crowd from hurtling onto the stage. When the reporter cornered a fan and asked her what she thought of Elvis, she had the answer at the tip of her tongue. "He's a doll," she teased, "and I love to play with dolls."

Most of the young fans were content to dream about playing with Elvis. The mature women who came to the concerts were not content with dreams. They wanted action. On this night, for example, when Elvis got back to his hotel room he heard a knock. Without thinking, one of the Smith boys opened the door. In charged a highly-wrought woman, who seized Elvis and hurled him onto the bed. In the ensuing scuffle it took all three boys to subdue the woman and push her out of the room. Elvis loved football, but these female tackles! Hey, son, they wuz somethin' else.

Wednesday night Elvis was in Augusta, Georgia, facing a sellout crowd of six thousand at the Bell Auditorium. When the local press caught him backstage after the show and started quizzing him earnestly about his musical accomplishments, Elvis told them that he didn't know a sharp from a flat. "In my kind of music," he joked, "you just get out there and go crazy." The interview had to be broken off abruptly because Elvis was heading out that same night for Charleston, South Carolina.

His Charleston show was held in a dilapidated ballpark, the stage a flatbed truck parked on the pitcher's mound. The performance went off without incident. What happened afterward made the wire services. Elvis was sitting in his Cad, preparing to leave for the railroad station. Suddenly, a lady reporter came rushing up to him and seized him by the sleeve. "I've got to make a deadline!" she cried. Looking down at the woman's brightly painted fingernails, Elvis leaned over and bit her on the finger. She screamed and shouted, "What's the big idea?" "I was only trying to be friendly, like a little puppy dog," Elvis replied teasingly. "Well," said the woman, "that's the first time anybody ever bit me out of friendship." Elvis had the answer to that one, too. "Lady," he drawled, "if you wanna get ahead in this business, you gotta be different."

Friday morning Elvis arrived in New York for a script rehearsal of the *Tonight Show*, with Steve Allen, Imogene Coca and Andy Griffith.

Allen had launched his new Sunday-night program the preceding week. His competition was *Talk of the Town,* the long-established Ed Sullivan show on CBS. Obviously, Allen could not afford to have the kind of stink on his program that had occurred after the *Milton Berle Show.* On the other hand, Elvis was a hot new attraction, not the sort of act you'd want to cancel. The solution was to defuse the bombshell with humor. Elvis would be presented in a comic skit and do his solo in a funny setting. The audience would be invited to laugh its indignation away.

Elvis's appearance on the Steve Allen show was the most ridiculous performance of his life. It symbolized just as clearly as the famous from-the-waist-up appearance six months later on the rival Ed Sullivan hour the incapacity of television to either accept Elvis Presley or leave him alone. Allen and his gag writers had come up with two shticks for Elvis. He was to play in a skit that was a parody of hillbilly radio shows, like the *Louisiana Hayride;* and he was to sing, dressed like a concert violinist in tie and tails, his new song, "Hound Dog," to a real basset hound. Neither device produced any real laughs and both gimmicks prevented Elvis from giving the public what it wanted. The fans were furious at the way their hero had been treated. Next day they picketed the studio with signs reading, "We Want the Real Elvis."

The Steve Allen show played Sunday night. Monday morning, Elvis was back at work, this time at the RCA studios on East 24th Street. In the course of one long day's work, he produced two of his biggest hits: "Hound Dog"[1] and "Don't Be Cruel." Unlike "Heartbreak Hotel," which was composed with Elvis exclusively in mind, "Don't Be Cruel" was written by a man who had never heard of Presley. Otis Blackwell—once described by Jerry Lee Lewis (for whom the writer composed "Great Balls of Fire") as "a little colored fellow in a derby hat"—was out on the street scuffling to survive when he got his big break with this song.

Blackwell had started out in the music business as a singer who worked the round robins (going from one joint to another in the same night) in Brooklyn. By 1953, he was writing the jivey, jumpy R & B tunes typical of the day. On Christmas Eve, 1955, he was hanging out in front of the Brill Building, rock 'n' roll's Tin Pan Alley, on Broadway

[1] Elvis picked up "Hound Dog" from Freddy Bell and the Bellhops during an engagement in April at Las Vegas. Bell did the song with different lyrics from those on the sheet music, including the line, "You ain't never caught a rabbit." Hence the difference between Elvis's vocal and the original recording by Willa Mae "Big Mama" Thornton.

at Forty-ninth Street, when a hustler happened along and asked the down-in-the-mouth composer if he had any songs for sale. Blackwell pulled out a sheaf of compositions and was promptly ushered into the office of Moe Gale, one of the great wheeler-dealers of the game. Gale bought six songs for twenty-five dollars a shot. One of the six was "Don't Be Cruel."

Six months elapsed between the time the song was sold and Elvis Presley's recording session. During that time two important developments occurred: 1) Blackwell was conned into giving up half his royalties to Presley and allowing the singer to put his byline on the song; 2) Blackwell made up a demonstration record in which he sang his song in his own highly distinctive style, accompanying himself on the piano while beating a cardboard box in place of a drum.

"Don't Be Cruel" was Elvis's favorite among his early songs. It was also vitally important to his career because it established a new pattern for a Presley song. Hitherto, Elvis had been identified primarily with either C & W or R & B material. Now, he got a taste of the contemporary pop rock idiom. The song was a flirty, teasy, put-on of a lover's complaint. It had a catchy jinglelike simplicity that made it as contagious as a new slang word. In a word, it was slick.

The combination of Presley and pop proved sensational. The song not only became the Number One tune in the country but remained in that spot for nine weeks, not disappearing from the charts until clocking a total run of twenty-seven weeks—both incredible records. Significantly, the only Presley record to do better was another Blackwell tune, "I'm All Shook Up," which also stayed on top of the heap for nine weeks but remained on the charts for *thirty weeks*. Guided by these stupendous hits, Elvis quickly found his real groove. Henceforth, he and his publishers were always looking for tunes that conformed with the Blackwell formula.

"Don't Be Cruel" was released—in one of the greatest all-time marketing mistakes—as the B side of "Hound Dog." "Hound Dog," profiting from the heavy play automatically accorded the A side, rose swiftly to the top of the charts and remained there for a month. Then, the record flipped over and "Don't Be Cruel" followed "Hound Dog" as the Number One side. As in the parallel case of the Beatles' "Penny Lane" (A) and "Strawberry Fields Forever" (B), the decision to put both potential hits on the same disc resulted in a great bargain for the fans and a great loss of money for the singer and the record company. Elvis raised hell about this decision, but the simple fact was that RCA was just pumping out the product as it came to hand without any thoughts of stretching it. Nobody at Victor knew anything about the new world of rock. As far as they were concerned, Elvis was just a flash in the pan. The idea was to exploit him to the limit now that he was hot.

On the evening of July 4, Elvis played a charity benefit at Memphis. The place was Russwood Stadium, a now-demolished baseball field in the downtown area, once the home of the Memphis Chicks. The crowd was the biggest Elvis had ever faced: fourteen thousand people, stretching back from the red-white-and-blue bedecked bandstand on the third base line through the infield, the outfield and up into the bleachers. The program, which began at eight, was one of those interminable affairs, crowded with amateurs and semipros, which provincial cities generate out of their own resources. The MC was Dewey Phillips, juiced to the gills. For nearly three hours before Elvis appeared, ole Dewey kept bringing them on with a big hand: the orchestras of Bob Morris and Aaron Bluestein, the Admiral's Band of Navy Memphis, a barbershop quartet called the Confederates, Charlotte Morgan's dancing Dixie Dolls and one Helen Putnam, founder of Fat Girls Anonymous, who dedicated a song to Elvis—"A Good Man Is Hard to Find." Finally, just before eleven, when the hot, restless, uncomfortably seated crowd—which had been teased into squealing twenty-nine times by the mention of Elvis's name—had had its patience stretched even further than Colonel Parker would have dared to try it, Dewey bawled into the mike, "Here he is!"

Nobody needed to be told who "he" was. Instantly, the vast crowd erupted in shrieks, shouts and tumultuous applause. Elvis bopped out onstage under the glaring arc lights wearing a shiny black double-breasted raw silk suit and a red tie. Pacing back and forth along the stage apron, waving to the crowd and then bending down to shout greetings to his family in the first row, he finally came to rest long enough for Dewey to make the presentation of a scroll commemorating Elvis's contribution to the program. Then, mindful of the fans who had complained about his disguised and muted appearance on the Steve Allen show, Elvis collared the mike and barked: "I'm gonna show you what the *real* Elvis is like tonight!" With that he went into his usual act, ranging from "Heartbreak Hotel" to "Blue Suede Shoes" and including a couple of his early Sun numbers, such as "That's All Right Mama" and "Mystery Train." After he had worked himself into a sweat and the audience into a frenzy, he grabbed the mike one more time. With his blond hair falling in his face and his voice like a mush-mouthed Jimmy Stewart, he made a vow that was a prophecy of his whole future life. "Ah just wanta tell y'awl not to worry," he drawled. "Them people in New Yahk an' Hollywood are not gone change me *none!*" As rebel yells split the night skies like skyrockets, Elvis was into "Hound Dog" shouting: "They said you was high-classed—but that wuz just a lie!" Then, he threw his hand up in a farewell salute and left the stage, disappearing in a phalanx of police who hustled him out of the stadium.

Chapter 13

The Early Days
of Sexually Inspired
Mass Hysteria

SUPPOSE you're a shrewd operator like Colonel Tom
Parker, and you've lucked into the hottest new attraction in show
business. Now, how do you go about making your star look like
a star? Do you go out and find a bunch of other young dudes
who are nearly as talented and put them all together in a great
big flying circus with your man in the lead plane? Hell, no! Are
you kidding? That's thinking like a chump. The trick is to go the
other way entirely. That's right! Don't let another of those crazy
rock 'n' rollers come within a mile of your boy. Don't let anybody
who has a scrap of talent step on the same stage. Go out and
shark up a lot of lames and lops, clowns and clods, who'll screw
up so bad they'll make your kid look like Caruso. That's how you
showcase a star!

So when Colonel Parker took Elvis under his exclusive management in March 1956, he called up a booker named Al Dvorin in
Chicago, a guy from whom he used to buy midgets back in the
days of Eddy Arnold, and he started ordering up every half-assed,
two-bit, washed-up or wet-nosed vaudeville act still shuffling around
the old circuits. Soon the Colonel had Elvis surrounded with a
bizarre carnival of tap dancers, acrobats, magicians, comedy jug-
glers, Irish tenors, xylophone players, nightclub comics, chanteuses

and DJ MCs. The most amusing touch was the band. Now, here's Elvis Presley, the hottest boy in the music business. Shouldn't he have a great fifteen-piece show band recruited out of the studios of Memphis and Nashville: guys who can really cut the mustard? Forget it! The Colonel hires a club date sextet called the Flaim Brothers, who are an economy version of the Lawrence Welk band—accordion and all. They like to play tunes like "Every Little Breeze Seems to Whisper Louise." Nice straw-hat, skating-rink, Polish Falcon music. Also, the band is a little small at six pieces. You can get away with that stuff in the South. Up North, especially in the larger houses, the union demands much bigger bands. In Chicago, for example, where Elvis played a sports arena, the Colonel discovered that the house contract called for twenty-two musicians, including violins!

Well, Colonel paid them their scale; only he wouldn't come up with a nickel for extra parts. So all night long the extra musicians had to sit there faking! The horn players put their instruments to their lips, the fiddle players ran their bows across the strings—but no music sounded forth because the players were staring at empty music racks. Colonel told Al Dvorin, who looks like the Great Gildersleeve (and was once a band leader), to get up in front of the orchestra and conduct with the tip of his lighted cigar. Ha! That showed 'em! Colonel even did a little conducting himself. Gathering all his men backstage, he shouted, "Now, what do we say?" Then, waving his arms in time, he joined the swelling chorus of voices chanting: "One, two, three—*fuck 'em!*"

The Elvis Presley Show may have been funnier than the *Gong Show*, but only the Colonel was laughing. Here's what happens on one of these occasions. In the afternoon, the audience is like that for *Captain Kangaroo:* vast numbers of eight- and nine-year-old girls popping bubble gum. In the evening, the average age is thirteen and the proportion of females may run as high as ninety percent. Now, in those days, nice little girls, especially in the South, did not go to public performances dressed like the cast of *Grease.* It would have been unthinkable for any properly brought up child to appear at a theater or auditorium wearing pedal pushers or short shorts or jeans and a T-shirt. All that *Schlumperei* had to wait for the slovenly sixties. These junior misses wear long billowing skirts over crinolines or tight sheaths and chemises (cocktail dresses) over even tighter girdles and nylons. They curl and spray their short hair. They apply pancake, lipstick, liner and nail polish. They bedeck themselves with earrings, bangles, and charm bracelets (including always the gold calendar leaf with their birthstone). They jiggle on heels. Some of them are even wearing white gloves. If they are going steady, they wear their boyfriends' rings on chains around their necks. The other appurtenance with which they come equipped is a Brownie camera with a flash attachment. Elvis never walked onstage during those years without being irradiated by a barrage of flashbulbs.

So we have two or three or five thousand steamy, screechy, jittery, jabbery little girls jammed into some decaying movie palace or Masonic temple in Augusta, Richmond, or Savannah. For weeks, they've been waiting to see their god, Elvis Presley. Now, they've nestled down with a vast rustling of petticoats and a vast exhalation of baby powder, deodorant, and cologne in this crummy old theater. The house lights dim, the band strikes up and out in front of the brightly lit curtain steps a local DJ, some flattop nitwit with a bow tie, who's shouting "If anybody leaves their seats the show will be stopped!" Finally, the curtains part, but instead of the long-sought Elvis, there's this little girl, not much older than themselves, banging away on this xylophone and trying to sing. Well, girls: What are we gonna do about it? That's right! Everybody scream and boo and hiss! Or, better, start chanting rhythmically: "WE WANT ELVIS! . . . WE WANT ELVIS!"

Finally, the poor little girl with the mallets in her hands runs off into the wings crying. As the next act goes out to take her place, Colonel Parker—the old hypocrite!—comes to comfort the child. "They wouldn't listen to me! . . . They wouldn't give me a chance!" The poor child is crying her eyes out. Colonel is very kind and understanding. He comforts her. He dries her tears. He tells her, "That's show business. You have to learn to take it. You're gettin' paid." Meantime, the old Irish tenor is getting clobbered by the same hysterical screaming mob. Only this old dude is a veteran of many years on the stage. The moment he sees the game is up with "Mother Macree," he signals for "Donegal." He starts clapping his hands and yelling at the girls to join him. Pretty soon he's got them working as his rhythm section. He survives for a couple of tunes and runs for his life.

Wave after wave they come, the showbiz kamikazes, doomed to die in the face of an audience that has now been driven half mad by sheer frustration. The comic can't tell a single joke. He can't even make himself heard! Finally, he starts to work in dumb show and do pantomime. The acrobatic dancers have trouble hearing the pit band, there is such a roar and shriek of protest when they hit the stage. Finally, when the massacre is complete, the house lights go up and the audience scrambles out of its seats for what proves to be a very long intermission.

This is the Colonel's big moment, his star turn. Standing out in the lobby with a stingy brim hat on his head, a big cigar jammed into the corner of his mouth, holding aloft with one hand a sheaf of glossy photos while with the other he makes a constant jingle in the pockets of his change apron, Colonel is back on the midway hawking worthless trinkets for outrageous prices. He gets a buck for these "autographed" eight by tens of Elvis. It's a moody, bluesy, low-down Elvis in the picture, with his fist buried in one chubby cheek and his Novocain lip turned down in a sullen—or is it a sulky?—pout. You can also buy an Elvis Presley songbook, with a lot of songs he never sang, and a souvenir program, which proves you actually saw him. It's the Presley paraphernalia industry in its infancy.

When the girls get back in their seats after intermission, they're a giant mass of fidgets. The reappearance of the MC, wearing a sports jacket and white bucks, is greeted with hysterical screams. The girls feel that finally they are about to have their wish fulfilled. Their long wait is over. Elvis is about to appear. Imagine what they do when the MC shouts: "America's foremost gospel quartet—the Jordanaires!" Gospel quartet! Jordanaires! Screeeeeeeeeeam! What a blast of baffled rage, what a temper tantrum, greets the four neat young men dressed in plaid blazers as they come bouncing out onstage to go into "Let the Good Times Roll." Thank God, they have a hit record at this moment, "Sugaree," which finally grabs the audience. Then, they do a fast-stepping "Down by the Riverside"—and run for their lives!

By now the Colonel's scheme has produced its intended effect. The show has teased and tortured its highly vulnerable audience until just the name, *Elvis Presley,* will bring down the house. That is what happens when the MC bawls: "Ladies and Gentlemen: the man for whom you've all been waiting—ELVIS PRESLEY!!!" At that instant five thousand shrill female voices come in on cue. The screeching reaches the intensity of a jet engine. When Elvis comes striding out onstage with his butchy walk, the screams suddenly escalate. They switch to hyperspace. Now, you may as well be stone deaf for all the music you'll hear. From this point on, you're gazing through a dense wall of acoustic steam.

The Elvis of '56 wore traffic signal colors—a bright green or a bright red sports jacket over navy blue slacks, with red socks, white bucks (with blue soles) and sometimes a *cummerbund!* He dressed his guitar in a tan, hand-tooled leather case with his full name carved conspicuously on a diagonal across the skin. Elvis loved to tease his audience. The moment he reached center stage, he would collar the mike, bend it down like a tango dancer's partner, spread his legs as if for a shootout and then shout, "Welll . . ." Just as every girl in the audience leaned forward in anticipation of ecstasy, Elvis would stop suddenly, laugh at the kids for having been taken in, then rear back to start again with another "Welll . . ." This childish game would continue until he released the band to go into "Heartbreak Hotel."

The moment Elvis appeared, dozens of girls would bolt from their seats and run down the aisles to the orchestra pit, where they would snap their hero's picture. There must be a million fading snapshots of Elvis Presley taken in 1956 alone. What did the girls see that drove them out of their minds? It sure as hell wasn't the All-American Boy. Elvis looked nothing like the stock young movie star of the day: all those crisp-cut, white-buck, dumb schmucks with names like Tab and Rock and Bob, names that rhyme today with faggot. Elvis was the flip side of this clean-cut conventional male image. His fish-belly white complexion, so different from the "healthy tan" of the beach boys; his brooding Latin eyes, heavily shaded with mascara; the broad fleshly contours of his face, with the Greek nose and the thick, twisted lips; the long greasy hair, thrown forward into his face by his jerking motions—God! what a freak the boy must have looked to those little girls peering at him through their camera finders. And what a turn-on! Typical comments were: "I like him because he looks so mean"; "He's fascinating—like a snake"; "I hear he peddles dope"; "He's been in and out of jail"; "He's gonna die of cancer in six months." Oh, those teenyboppers wailing for their demon lover!

Like the gospel acts from whom he learned his trade, Elvis's style onstage was busy, busy, busy! From the moment he hit the boards until he ducked off twenty minutes later, he never stopped moving. Elvis's famous "gyrations" came from the same source as his vocal tricks plus a few things he picked up at local dances. Though Elvis was not a dancer and had to lash his body to make it move, he understood instinctively that his kind of music demanded action. This recognition set him apart from all the other white performers of his day and the character of his moves distinguished him just as strongly from all the contemporary black acts.

John Lennon once remarked that every rock act he had ever seen fell far short of the mental image of the performer he had formed listening to his records. Even the great Little Richard, for example, presented an awkward and constrained image onstage, half standing, half crouching at the keyboard of a piano, looking as though he had caught his hands in the instrument's teeth or was receiving some Coppelia-like charge from the keyboard without which he might collapse like a rag doll. As for the famous do-wop groups of the day, some of them moved skillfully, but they were all choreographed by the same man, Honi Coles (formerly of Coles and Atkins), which made them blur together in a slick, jivey idiom that did not convey the raunchy quality of rock music. In Elvis's moves, as in his original recordings, he exhibited a kind of genius: a capacity to project the substance of the music through the attitudes of the body that reinforced his singing and made him a total performer, his own best medium.

Lacking any training or natural flair for dancing, Elvis was forced like John Travolta in *Saturday Night Fever* to confine himself to the few steps he could cut. He would stand with his spraddled legs squarely before the mike shaking both limbs at once, as his band used to say, "wearing out his britches from inside." Suddenly, he would throw down his left hand, which would start fluttering like a hummingbird's wing. As a pained, ecstatic expression of possession crossed his face, his legs would start flailing like rubber hoses. Then, one-two! one-two!, he would snap his legs like scissors, the knees knocking, as in the Camel Walk, one foot coming to rest on toepoint. Next day the newspapers would report that Elvis did "bumps and grinds."

The suggestion of the burlesque dancer was especially strong when he would get down to the slow ball-and-sock-it conclusion of "I Got a Sweetie." Turning in profile, while grabbing his mike stand for support, he would shoot out his legs in a series of hot shots that were the pimp-walkin' daddy's equivalent of a bump. The difference was that where the stripper or the black jive dancer, like James Brown, works to make such moves smooth and sensuous, Elvis projected an idea of sex that was animalistic and violent, like a stamping stallion. His erotic pantomime suggested not so much the coitus of the burlesque dancer or the masturbation of the go-go girl as the aggressive and brutal motions of rape.

Though Elvis wasn't a stripper, he was a terrible tease. He played with his little-girl audience the way a little girl plays with her dolly. "I love you . . . I hate you . . . I kiss you . . . I kill you!"—this was the subliminal monologue he conducted through his onstage movements and gestures. The great externalizing device for his erotic charade was the standing microphone. Elvis was your classic mike mauler. The moment he came on, he would seize the mike by the neck and bend it down like the female partner in an apache dance. He would haul it all over the stage. Shake it violently. Straddle it. Force it down, down,

down, until it was parallel with the ground. Finally, he would abandon it to throw himself down, taking care to fall just short of those frantic fingers reaching out desperately to touch him, just inches from those contorted, tear-stained faces crying, "Please! . . . Please!"

No matter how much they begged and pleaded, it did them no good. Oh, he might run one finger deliberately across his forehead and then flick it on the audience's faces, sending the colored drops of sweat flying over the footlights. That was the origin of the sweat-stained scarves he flung into the house in his last years. Or, perhaps, he did impulsively extend himself and kiss one girl on the forehead. As she screamed and fell over backwards, he was up on his feet again, whirling away from the stage apron, dancing out of reach of all the thousands of other girls who suddenly realized—"He kissed her!" Screeeeeeeeam!!!

In the gospel tradition, the goal of the performer is not only to work the audience up to a feverish pitch of excitement but to keep pushing until they have been driven over the edge of self-control and out of their minds. At this point, the higher powers are supposed to intervene. What about Elvis and his little girls? Did they experience states of transcendental ecstasy and illumination? Or were they possessed by the infernal powers and driven to commit sins of the flesh?

Neither reaction was ever reported. The weaker sort screamed and cried and finally were reduced by their tantrums to the hapless state of infants who have wet their pants. The bolder sort were transformed into raging maenads bent on violence and destruction. They didn't just want to tear off their Orpheus's clothes. They wanted to tear him to pieces. The Greeks had a word for it: *"Sparagamos"*—the rending to bits of the sacrificial victim. That sounds extravagant, but the fact is that on several occasions Elvis Presley came very close to being killed by his adoring fans.

As early as 1956, Elvis had developed his famous escape technique for getting out of the theater alive. As he got into his last number, "Hound Dog," he would drag the mike further and further to the side of the stage. Finally, on the last note of the song, he would dive into the wings and race for the car standing beside the stage door.

As the audience threw its last fit, the MC would intone: "Elvis has left the building." Denied even a single encore, the fans were always left clamoring for more.

Chapter 14

Going Commercial

THE EPOCH-MAKING success of "Heartbreak Hotel" should have inspired a series of sequels that would have enabled Elvis to project his private psychodrama in a number of extravagantly emotional songs, precisely as his black counterpart, Little Richard, was doing at this moment with his even wilder and more frenzied persona. Sad to say, nothing of the sort happened. Elvis could never get the material that matched his act. Neither a songwriter like Little Richard, nor a singer who was permitted to work with songwriters to produce the special vehicles his unique image demanded, Elvis was condemned from the start to fit himself to whatever material he was given.[1] So while Little Richard went on during the next two years etching the most powerful and indelible profile in the history of hard rock, Elvis went on patching together a crazy quilt of musical odds and ends—old songs, new songs, black songs, white songs, good songs, bad songs—that failed to

[1] Colonel Parker, who started isolating Elvis the moment he became his manager, made it a strict rule that no writer ever be allowed to get near the singer. For this reason many of Elvis's most important writers, such as Otis Blackwell and Doc Pomus, never met their famous client. What Colonel feared was that Elvis would say he liked a song to a writer who had not agreed to surrender the coveted one-third of his royalties. Then it would be impossible to make the writer kick back because he had his hook in Elvis's mouth.

add up artistically just as surely as it added up commercially to the greatest score in the history of the music business.

One of the reasons for this haphazard eclecticism was the long delay on the part of Elvis's new masters in the Brill Building in plotting his future course and in securing for him a steady supply of original songs. During most of Elvis's greatest year, 1956, he was obliged to adopt the same recording strategy as that employed by all the established white pop stars: the notorious practice of "covering" current R & B hits. Covering a record means recording the original material anew. The practice was common at the beginning of the rock fad because the good records were coming out on the independent labels with relatively unknown performers. They were thus highly inviting to famous singers recording for major companies because the big names could displace the unknowns and the big labels could advertise and distribute their product much more successfully. Though Elvis didn't as a rule indulge in the worst form of this practice, which was to jump on a new record the moment it surfaced and steal the whole arrangement, which was not then protected by copyright law, he did copy virtually note for note a great many songs introduced by major black performers.

Setting aside the moral issues involved in such a blatant rip-off, one comes to the real issue: Why was the most original and creative white singer in America suddenly reduced to the practices of the outdated white pop singers? No satisfactory explanation of this behavior has ever been offered; but it's likely that Elvis suffered at this time from both the temptations presented by effortless success and by the difficulty of imposing a new vision onto material that was itself so new and powerful that he could not imagine any way of improving it. At Sun Elvis had recast originals by mediocre R & B men like Arthur Crudup, Junior Parker and Roy Brown. Now he was up against all the greatest performers in the style, commencing with Ray Charles and Little Richard and going on to Joe Turner, Fats Domino, Lloyd Price, Willa Mae Thornton and Clyde McPhatter. Though it is often said that Elvis sang black music better than any of his white contemporaries, does anyone really believe that he sang it better than the greatest black artists? Without the enabling charge of contempt Elvis felt for the old-timers or mediocrities he sent up at Sun, he could not work his magic. You can't one-up something that is hipper than you are. So instead of inflecting his mimicry into parody, he now settled for just the mimicry, taking as his basic model Little Richard, whom he despised as a "screamer" but whose style he appropriated for use not only on his covers of Little Richard's tunes but on those of other singers as well. It is at this moment, therefore, that Elvis Presley first becomes what it is usually assumed he was from the start: "a white boy who could sing like a nigger."

The decisive moment in Elvis's recording career came in September 1956, when Hill and Range finally got its new Presley assembly line running. At this point two very important things happened: 1) Elvis began to receive a steady stream of music custom-crafted to his image; 2) his image was modulated so that he became less the hard rocker and more the masticator of black-flavored bubble gum. For the old shlock-meisters in the Brill Building had finally figured out how to deal with the rock 'n' roll fad. After years of diluting and cleaning up R & B for the white teen market, they finally recognized that real R & B wasn't the most appropriate source for white rock because it reflected the raunchy life of the ghetto instead of the cars, Cokes and pajama parties of white kiddieland. At this point there commences the movement from rock to shlock that would lead in a few years to the era of Fabian and Frankie Avalon. Though Elvis Presley was vastly superior to these travesties, he is the pivotal figure in the movement away from R & B and toward the cutesey, teensy tunes epitomized by "Teddy Bear."

The manager of the new Presley tune and toy factory was a genial Swiss named Freddy Bienstock, a nephew of the publishers, Jean and Julian Aberbach. Bienstock's principal responsibility was collecting material for Elvis to record. If Elvis were making a picture with six scenes in which he sang a song, Bienstock would circulate among his six "contract writers" (typically words-and-music teams whose royalty earnings were credited against a weekly stipend paid by Hill and Range), a description of each of the scenes, with the understanding that the writers were free to submit material for every spot. Soon Swiss Freddy would be winging his way toward Hollywood with thirty-six musical chocolate bars.

RCA had no recording facilities on the West Coast at this time, and Elvis could not tolerate the atmosphere of the huge studio sound stages: so the sessions were held at the best independent studio in town, Radio Recorders, on Santa Monica Boulevard near Hollywood High. The engineer for all the Presley sessions down through the years was a big, affable man named Thorn Nogar. His assistant was Bones Howe, known today as an independent record producer. Nogar and Howe were astonished at the way Elvis Presley made records.

In those days studio time was doled out to musicians like nights at Mt. Palomar are allotted to astronomers. Recording sessions rarely exceeded three hours, and the goal was to cut four sides an hour. When Elvis came to town, RCA threw the rule book out the window. The studio might be booked solid for as much as a month. The musical instruments, mikes, baffles and other gear would be put in place and there they would remain until the work was completed. When Elvis was in the mood, he was a fast worker: Once he cut *fifteen sides* in a single mammoth session. If he were not in the mood, however, he might abort the session in an hour. "It's not happening," he'd say—and split!

Another source of astonishment was the way Elvis turned a session into a party. He liked to stay "loose as a goose"; so he would arrive with not just his band but his boys. They would rib each other and clown around in the studio. Then Elvis would seat himself at the piano, which he played by chording in one of two keys, and spend an hour singing hymns. As the all-night sessions wore on, the young men would get hungry. Immense quantities of junk food would be brought in and consumed: fifty or sixty hamburgers, mountains of greasy French fries, gallons of Pepsi Cola. When Elvis left a studio, it looked like it had been the scene of a sixth-grade picnic.

Elvis short-circuited all the customary preparations for recording. Instead of spending weeks closeted with writers, arrangers and producers, selecting songs, preparing scorings and rehearsing the new material, he would walk in cold and record everything at first sight. No performer since Fats Waller had ever displayed such a breezy attitude in the face of phonographic immortality. Elvis had absolute confidence in his powers. He could spot a hit at a glance. Memorize a song after hearing it only twice. After forty takes, he would tell the engineer to go back to number seventeen because that one had worked the best.

Though Elvis was a highly spontaneous performer onstage, who led his band a merry chase (Bill Black used to quip: "We're the only band in the business that takes its cues off the singer's ass!"), once he settled down to hone a hit, he became as compulsively repetitive as the most meticulous diamond polisher on 47th Street. He would lavish as many as *sixty* takes on a single song. His exhausting efforts to attain precisely the effect he was seeking were not determined, as might be supposed, by the struggle to achieve technical perfection. Far from it! Elvis would never hesitate to release a flawed performance if it had the right feel. He was seeking not to gratify the musician's ear but to tickle the teen fan's fancy. Commercial to the core, Elvis was the kind of singer dear to the heart of the music business. For him to sing a song was to sell a song. His G clef was a dollar sign.

Steve Sholes, a middle-aged man who had spent his entire life in the record business, soon realized that Elvis knew more about teen taste than any producer in the game. He confined himself to acting at these sessions as a benign and acquiescent father figure. Eventually, he was to spend the long nights sound asleep on a sofa in the lounge. Hal Wallis, on the other hand, would spend entire nights observing the sessions with fascination. He pronounced Elvis a "genius."

The real secret of Elvis's method lay not so much in his genius as in that interesting professional device, the demonstration record. When Freddy Bienstock collected his songs in New York, he would hear them first in the time-honored manner: played on the piano and sung by one of the writers. After he had selected the most promising pieces, he would arrange to have them recorded as demos. Ostensibly, the demo was just a device for conveying the music to performers, like Elvis, who couldn't read notation. Actually, these recordings were selling devices, designed carefully to make the song appealing to the singer at whom they were aimed.

Making demos for Elvis Presley swiftly became a highly developed art. The canny writers who got a shot at the greatest hit-maker in the business did not neglect to study their customer. They analyzed his style, his tastes, his favorite keys and rhythms and even his preference in titles. If one member of the writing team were a singer of professional caliber, he would do the singing. Otis Blackwell, for example, had a highly distinctive way of voicing and phrasing his songs. Elvis copied this delivery note for note on "Don't Be Cruel." As Blackwell recalls: "After he came out with 'Don't Be Cruel,' and I heard how close it was to the demo record I had done, I made sure I did all the demos for my songs. I didn't mind that he copied the demos so closely: I figured making good demos was a surer way of getting him to record my stuff." If neither of the writers were a man who could put a song across, one of several singers would be employed who were especially adept at mimicking Elvis (precisely the approach adopted by Mae Axton when she got Tommy Durden to demonstrate "Heartbreak Hotel" in Elvis's "shaky" voice).[2] Elvis's standard instrumentation would be employed to give the records the Presley sound. Eventually, the demos became so important

[2] In addition to Otis Blackwell, who demonstrated other writers' songs as well as his own, the singers on the Presley demos included such subsequently familiar performers as Brian Hyland ("Itsy Bitsy Teenie Weenie Yellow Polka Dot Bikini"), David Hill ("Two Brothers"), P. J. Proby ("Niki Hoeky"), Mort Shuman (later a big star in France), Dorsey Burnette (another Memphis rockabilly), Glen Campbell and Leon Russell.

that they were recorded under the supervision of the young Phil Spector, who was brought to New York by one of Elvis's writing teams, Leiber and Stoller. When the demo was finished, it resembled a costly custom-tailored suit. All the song required to exhibit its perfect fit was to be tried on.

The first step in a Presley recording session was invariably the audition of the demos. Like every feature of Elvis's life, this procedure quickly hardened into a ritual. First, Freddy Bienstock would go into the control booth with his stack of discs. Removing from its tan sleeve a shiny, oddly smelling, ten-inch seventy-eight RPM acetate, he would lay the record on the turntable, lower the tone arm and send the music blaring into the studio. There Elvis would stand, surrounded by his musicians, poised to make the decision on which the fate of the teen world might turn for the next six months.

Elvis's responses to the auditions were as curt and decisive as the gesticulations of a Roman emperor judging a gladiatorial combat. If the song did not appeal to him, he would make a slashing sign across his throat, signaling, "Cut!" If the song attracted him, he would rotate the palm of his hand above his head, signifying, "Take it from the top!" Once Elvis had made a selection, the audition would stop and the recording process would begin.

If Elvis liked the arrangement on the demo, he would order his men to copy it note for note. If he objected to the arrangement, he and his players would concoct a "head" (unwritten) arrangement. The only parts lacking on the demo were the vocal echoes: These colorless vocables, like the styrofoam chips employed in packing a valuable object, were manufactured swiftly by the Jordanaires, who were typically facile studio musicians.

As nothing matters on an Elvis Presley record but the star, most listeners instinctively tune out the mediocre playing and singing of Elvis's accompanists. Elvis should have tuned them out himself and replaced them with players at least as good as those on the demos. Making any change, however, even the slightest, in his customary dispositions was something that was unthinkable for Elvis at any time in his life. So his original backing remained on his records until, ironically, it was the accompanists who quit Elvis. (The first defections occurred in the summer of 1957 when Scotty and Bill quit in protest against the fact that they were still being paid $150 a week [$250 on the road] while Elvis was making millions.)

Though Elvis constantly improved as a singer in his early years, developing a voice as "phonogenic" as Caruso's, he just as consistently declined as a creative force in music. Clearly, he was the victim of his own success. Instead of struggling as he had to do at Sun to come up with an original version of each tune he recorded, he could now turn out dozens of records by simply copying his best demos, giving the songs the little idiosyncratic touches that teased the teenyboppers to ecstasy. As his music deteriorated into a series of simple-minded formulas, as his demos got consistently better, as his fans became habituated to acclaiming every new record as if it were a revelation, Elvis found himself rolling toward the pinnacle of success in a rocking chair. Never has anyone ever been so richly rewarded for doing so little.

The only thing that could have saved Elvis's soul at this point would have been to refuse, as did the Beatles, to take the easy, obvious way to success. Such thoughts never crossed the mind of the young Elvis Presley. He assumed his success was only momentary so why shouldn't he cash in on it in every way he could? He had no higher values than those represented by chart positions, gold records and gross sales. Elvis was, in short, the classic commercial artist.

Among the first songs he cut on the West Coast were the pieces intended for *The Reno Brothers* (later retitled *Love Me Tender*). This stock western, set at the end of the Civil War, was planned originally as a straight drama. When Elvis was added to the cast, Fox decided to capitalize on the great commercial opportunity presented by his first appearance by interpolating four tunes. Just the year before, Mitch Miller had scored an enormous hit with an authentic Civil War song, "The Yellow Rose of Texas." Now, music researchers everywhere were feverishly turning over old songbooks looking for more of the same kind of material. One of the most popular songs of the Civil War was "Aura Lea," a sentimental salute to a golden girl couched in that idiom preserved still in fraternity house drinking songs and high school anthems. Simple and mellifluous, wistful and haunting, this period piece was perfect for the picture. The only problem was the verses—"Aura Lea! Aura Lea! Maid of golden hair!"—which were too quaint and literary for all those gum-chewing pubes in tight toreador pants. So for the limpid English of the original was substituted "Love me tender," which sounds like a TV commercial with a talking steak.

Listening to Elvis's recording of the song today, one is astonished at how badly he sings it. His voice is husky and lacking in resonance; his delivery at the slow, demanding tempo is uncertain in pitch. He still has great difficulty in a ballad making himself sound sincere. One imagines with what wistful beauty Bing Crosby would have voiced this pretty period piece. Needless to say, Elvis's vocal inadequacies made not the slightest difference to his doting fans. Before the record could be shipped to the stores, RCA booked 856,327 orders. In those days when you "shipped gold," it wasn't fool's gold.

The primary reason for this tidal wave of demand was the extraordinary preview that the song received in the course of Elvis's first appearance on Ed Sullivan's *The Talk of the Town*. This performance is one of the great pseudoevents of entertainment history. Not only has its importance been grossly exaggerated, but the facts have been remodeled by the fantasies that shaped the Presley Myth. According to the widely publicized legend, Sullivan was so scandalized by Elvis when he first appeared on the tube that he was moved to say, "I wouldn't touch him with a ten-foot pole!" Then, when Elvis appeared on the rival Steve Allen show, raising its ratings, Sullivan was compelled to eat some very expensive crow. Even in the act of surrendering to Elvis, however, Sullivan is said to have expressed his distaste for "The Boy Who Dared to Rock" by ordering his cameramen to shoot Elvis only from the waist up. As Elvis performed in this truncated manner, Sullivan stood in the wings fuming and murmuring audibly, "Sonovabitch! Sonovabitch!"

This famous tale is about ninety percent fiction. Sullivan knew nothing and cared nothing about Elvis Presley when he was first approached by William Morris to put the young rock star on his program. What made Sullivan explode with rage at the suggestion was an infuriating experience he had had the year before with Bo Diddley. When Sullivan heard Diddley's big hit, "Bo Diddley," at rehearsal, he had reacted in much the same spirit as those people who were outraged by Andy Warhol's Brillo boxes. To an impresario's ears, the song was a bad joke: just the same stupid phrase repeated over and over again with the singer's name comprising the bulk of the lyrics, like a soap jingle. Determined to have Diddley sing some "real" music, Sullivan told Diddley to do Tennessee Ernie Ford's new hit, "Sixteen Tons." Diddley could not believe that he had been forbidden to plug his hit record—the whole purpose of his appearance on the show. He assumed instead that he was being given the rare opportunity to perform *two* songs.

That night he led off with "Bo Diddley" and then went into "Sixteen Tons." Sullivan exploded with rage. He cut Diddley off in the middle of the tune. Then, cornering the singer backstage, he ranted: "You're the first colored boy who ever crossed me up on a song!" When Diddley received his check for seven hundred dollars, he was ordered to endorse it and hand it back. After such a fiasco, it's easy to imagine how Sullivan felt about having another of these rock 'n' roll weirdos on his program.

Eventually, of course, Sullivan did have to come to terms with Elvis. Instead of paying the $5,000 that had been asked originally, he was forced to ante up $50,000. Fearful that next time the price might go even higher, he made a deal to have Elvis on the show three times in the next six months. The first show was a remote from Hollywood on September 9. Elvis was not shot from the waist up on this program: That famous incident—which has come to symbolize more than anything else the moral tone of the fifties—occurred on the last show. And it had nothing to do with morality. It was, in fact, the very opposite of censorship, being a deliberate tease intended to suggest that there was a lot more going on "down there" than in truth there was. Likewise, it is ridiculous to imagine Sullivan standing in the wings during the first show fuming with moral indignation because actually he was on vacation at the time and the show's host was Charles Laughton.

So much for the fictions—what of the facts? The most important fact is that the program provided an occasion for the whole nation to tune in on the phenomenon about which it had been hearing for the past nine months. Elvis's fame and his position as the greatest showbiz sensation of the day had now been firmly established. It was Elvis who made this program famous, not the program Elvis. As a show, it was nothing that anyone would want to see again. Elvis was never comfortable on TV—what rock act has ever been shown to good effect on this medium, saving the Monkees? Rock and TV are the ideal illustration of Marshall McLuhan's dictums about the incompatibility of hot performers and cool media. What's more, Elvis had gotten so much flak about his TV performances in the past that he must have felt morally obliged to ride this rocket to fame with a very tight rein.

Whatever the reasons for his poor showing, he talked, looked and performed like an amateur on a local talent show. He developed such a case of fidgets during "Love Me Tender" that he appeared like a little boy desperate to go to the bathroom but too embarrassed to ask the way.

This amateurish performance was witnessed by 82.6 percent of the viewing audience or an incredible fifty-four million souls, one-third of a nation. (The record stood on the Sullivan show until 1964, when it was broken by the Beatles.) On the strength of the appearance and the subsequent flood of orders for the new song, RCA tossed out seven new 45s on the market and Fox retitled *The Reno Brothers Love Me Tender,* increasing its customary order for three hundred prints to five hundred and fifty.

If TV was not the secret of Elvis's overnight fame, what was? Clearly the number of people he reached in live performances was relatively small. The amount of attention he received in the national press was far less than a comparable phenomenon would receive today. What's more, the tone of all the articles was either ambivalent or antagonistic. Elvis's phonograph records were crucial to his success, but the public had first to discover these records. Almost invariably this crucial discovery was made through radio.

Radio, the medium that Marshall McLuhan likened to the "tribal drum," was the great evangelizing voice not only for Elvis Presley but for rock in general. Significantly, the first rock hero—the man who named the music, established the rock concert, made the first rock movies and reached the widest audience with the sound he dubbed "The Big Beat"—was a disc jockey: Alan Freed. The Pied Piper of Rock and the other 1,700 DJs of the fifties dictated the cultural climate for seventeen million teenagers. As these kids got up in the morning or came home from school, as they rode in cars or lay on the beach with their portables, as they did their homework in the evening or snuggled in their beds at night with the lights out and their minds open in the most suggestible condition, the DJs enjoyed an incomparable opportunity to mold the imagination of an entire generation. Some of these men achieved a tremendous hold on their young audiences and were transformed in the kids' fancies into surrogate fathers: a point well made in the otherwise over-idealized but beguiling film about Alan Freed, *American Hot Wax.* Television, by contrast, meant very little to the teens because until the advent of shows like *American Bandstand* (not broadcast nationally until the summer of 1957), television programming was aimed exclusively at adults and children.

By the end of 1956, Elvis Presley was being universally acclaimed as the King of Rock 'n' Roll. The boy who began the year as an obscure country singer broadcasting from a hillbilly station at Shreveport, the regional entertainer who spent his life out on the highway rushing from one schoolhouse or community center to another in the Deep South, the Sun recording artist whose greatest achievement was landing a side on the country and western charts was now, less than twelve months later, an American hero. Nobody in the history of show business has ever made it so big so fast.

Even the Beatles, who broke all of Elvis's early records eventually, seem like shleppers when you compare their hard, steady pull to the top with Elvis's breathtaking ascent. Instead of characterizing Elvis's triumph in conventional metaphors—the long, billowy road, the steep ladder, the tightly closed door—you are obliged to seek images that suggest speed, violence and, above all, the sheer inadvertence of the man who walks into a room filled with volatile gases, lights a match— and is blown through the ceiling! Clearly, if you want to understand the phenomenon of Elvis Presley or how he "did it," you have to start with the powerfully explosive vapors and not with the puny little match.

The vapors are, of course, the frenzied atmosphere of youth culture in the fifties. From the start of the decade down to the advent of Elvis, history's first generation of culturally autonomous teenagers had been working itself up to a climactic outburst. As the endlessly incited energies of this rebellious generation charged the national atmosphere, they furnished a classic demonstration of William Blake's great vision in *The Marriage of Heaven and Hell* of the schizophrenic character of any true revolution, which will appear to those whose authority is threatened like a monstrous fire-breathing dragon risen from the deeps, whereas to those who welcome the new order, it will seem as sweet as a harpist by a pastoral stream. As the new generation seethed and heaved like the proverbial sea before the storm, the adult world struggled to anticipate the shape of things to come.

All the famous youth movies of the fifties can be interpreted as images of terrified anticipation. First, the teenagers appear in *The Wild One* (1953) as Nazi Huns, riding across the steppes of Sonoma on their snarling mechanical ponies led by that grim-visaged Attila, Marlon Brando. Then, they are seen as vicious, sneering slum bums, mugging an idealistic young teacher in *Blackboard Jungle* (1955), whose theme song is "Rock Around the Clock." Finally, the ultimate image of the teenager—as a weird and hideous monster, a Grendel assailing the split-level mead hall—is snapped into focus in *I Was a Teenage Werewolf* (1958). Thus was youth viewed by adults in that day; more importantly, thus did youth regard itself: as a new perhaps monstrous race.

When youth culture swung into the traditional path of a great song and dance mania—instead of a mass outbreak of juvenile delinquency— the guardians of the fifties should have breathed a sigh of relief. Rock, though of an unprecedented coarseness, vulgarity and violence, conformed fundamentally with historically sanctioned patterns of adolescent behavior. That's what men like Alan Freed—the type of older man who identifies with the kids, the Timothy Leary of his time—kept telling the country. The fifties, obsessed with its "menaces"—the Commie menace, the Pachuco menace, the Black menace, the Beat menace, the Hipster menace, the Teenage menace, the menace presented by everything that did not conform to the constricting canons of "normalcy" in that most abnormal age—had no ears to hear. Rock, a relatively harmless and innocent enthusiasm, was condemned as obscene, insurrectionary, criminal and "racious." This relentless opposition assured its success.

Rock swiftly became what anthropologists call a "peripheral cult": a rite of the excluded and powerless, who exhibit symptoms of possession by alien demons (whose presence is manifested by the appearance of foreign words in their mouths, words like "man," "cat," "baby," "rock"). To exorcise the demons and restore the "sick" to their normal selves, the cult contrives through the use of inciting music and dance to arouse its members to a state of ecstasy. In this open condition, they can be freed of their demons through the ministrations of a charismatic shaman, who possesses the remarkable gift of taking the evil spirits into his own body and soul, where he either defeats them in combat or placates them by sweet offerings.

If this analogy appears farfetched, reflect again on the paramount image of the whole era—the spectacle of thousands of young girls screaming out their lungs while they exhibit first one, then another stereotyped posture of frenzy, like the illustrative plates in Charcot's books on hysteria. How do these hapless agonies differ from the frenzies of black charwomen hurling themselves into the cathartic service of some ghetto storefront church? The truth is that rock ministered to its young devotees and relieved them of distresses that were no less real than those of oppressed minorities for being the products of prosperity.

All cults develop eventually a profound yearning for a great leader or hero or messiah who will embody the ethos of the group in a totally fulfilling and redemptory image. So great was the craving for such a hero in the rock cult that its frantic devotees acclaimed some of the most preposterously amateurish or mawkish performers ever seen on the American stage. Though today it seems hard to believe, when Bill Haley landed in England for the first time in 1956, there were riots at the docks. Riots for a moon-faced, spit-curled clod like Bill Haley! Critics and showbiz professionals of that day were driven to the limits of exasperation by the spectacle of such crude and inept performers attaining unprecedented popularity. What the old pros were slow to recognize was that the kids cared nothing for professional skills and talents; what they demanded were projections of themselves. The identification between the rock public and the rock star was the most blatant ever witnessed. The moment a performer opened his mouth at a rock concert, he found himself drowned out by an enormous echo, as every kid in the house sang the same song in the same voice. As Mel Brooks makes his archetypal rock star, Fabiola, explain: "They're doin' the singin'—I jes' got the mouth!"

The obvious mediocrity of the first white rock stars could not be tolerated for long, however. Inevitably, the kids, brought up on slick professional showbiz and Hollywood movies, began to yearn for a rock star who was handsome, talented and dynamic. The ideal rock star had to meet a very elaborate set of specifications that had been established by the complex course of youth culture during the preceding years. Obviously, he had to be very young, unlike the Benny Goodmans or even the Frank Sinatras of the previous generation; for rock was not, like swing, a style that aspired to sophisticated adulthood, but a frankly regressive music fixated on the moods of early adolescence. Instead of looking clean and wholesome, like the Hollywood youth idols, the rock star had to exhibit a totally different ideal of beauty—hoody and dangerous, mysterious and demonic—because one of his basic functions was to scare the hell out of the parents and teachers who were persecuting his "people." At the same time that he presented the image of a motorcycle hoodlum or a Brooklyn hitter, he had to appear to the gaze of the initiated as a sensitive and vulnerable soul, like the first great teen saint and martyr, Jimmy Dean. Finally, it was vital—because the music was steeped to the lips in the sounds and lingo of the black ghetto and best performed with the corresponding black body English—that the new hero be a cultural mulatto: a "white nigger." In fine, what rock 'n' roll demanded was a handsome young stud who looked dangerous but was really a pussycat who could sing and swing his ass like a jiveass black bluesman.

Chapter 15

The New Jimmy Dean

THE GIFT of perfect timing that accounts so largely for Elvis's success in the nascent world of rock 'n' roll did not desert him when he arrived in Hollywood to make his film debut. Far from it! In the film capital, he found an opportunity awaiting him just as great as anything he had encountered in the music business. Only the year before, Hollywood's most brilliant young star, the fascinating Jimmy Dean, had died on the highway in his white Porsche Speedster. His demise opened up a gap in the Hollywood pantheon that could easily have become a niche for Elvis Presley.

Indeed, from the beginning of the decade down to the moment of Elvis's advent, there had been a clear line of development in pictures that made the youth star and the film about modern youth one of Hollywood's most promising new genres. Marlon Brando had established this idiom with *The Wild One,* a cinematic treatment of a real incident in which a gang of bikers took control of a small town and terrorized the citizenry until the arrival of the state police. That film had projected a mutely intense, almost enigmatic image of the youth hero as a young man of feeling, a sort of Byron of the motorbike, posing, musing and communing with his counter-wiping beloved, while his good-natured but potentially dangerous gang parties it up in a whirl of hipster slang, street-gang high jinks and progressive jazz. Morally, the picture said that the failure of the parental generation to act with firmness and authority was responsible for the damage the delinquent kids were inflicting on society. Dramatically, the film projected the incapacitating anguish that is the most characteristic response of American parents when confronted with their children's misdeeds and defiant nonconformity.

The next film to take up the theme was *Blackboard Jungle,* which substituted for the jivey, inadvertently destructive but basically goodnatured kids of Brando's motorcycle gang a really threatening and ugly group of slum school punks who are prepared to use criminal tactics in their assault on the social authority represented by the school's teachers. Again the anguish of the parental generation—coupled this time with its idealistic belief in the goodness of youth and its eagerness to educate young people—is projected vividly by Glenn Ford, who finally succeeds in detaching the good kids from the leadership of the bad kids, thus resolving the dilemma of juvenile delinquency by removing the rotten apples from the barrel.

By 1956, when the best film in this tradition, *Rebel Without a Cause,* appeared, the debate over rebellious and delinquent youth had gone beyond the old beliefs in discipline or the segregation of good and evil. This film was the classic statement of enlightened popular opinion in that day, which held that the disturbed behavior of kids was the product of the psychological and moral flaws of their parents. In this picture, the implicit ideal is a strong father, a mother who is supportive instead of domineering, and a set of moral principles that is not cancelled the moment some danger impends that can be averted by lying or covering up the truth. Without such parents and principles, the film argues, youth is condemned to the role that James Dean so brilliantly realized: the kid who would be good if only he were given the chance to be good by an ugly world that comprises, on the one hand, his cowardly and role-reversed parents, and, on the other, the violent and self-destructive kids who kill each other playing chicken with their hot rods. Never before or since in American movies has any actor so resourcefully and so beautifully portrayed the type of modern middle-class youth, with all his charm and sensitivity and moral confusion, his pain and rage and bafflement, his curiously sexless yearning for love and his highly romantic capacity for friendship, all leading up to one of those remarkably lyrical and dreamlike catastrophes that were the great ideal of a theater and cinema inspired by the poetic melodrama of Tennessee Williams.

Whatever value one assigns to these films and actors, the point is that when Elvis Presley arrived in Hollywood he had a marvelous opportunity to step into a vigorously welling stream of cinematic energy, a genre and a tradition already well established, which could have offered him opportunities to play parts that were suitable to his age, appearance and public and that would have satisfied his ambition to become a good actor and to count for something more than a box office attraction. He was intensely aware of the opportunity created by the death of Jimmy Dean—at this time Elvis's favorite actor—and was nearly frantic with the desire to jump into Dean's shoes. The very first article on Elvis in *Photoplay,* written by a reporter who interviewed Elvis on the first day of shooting for *Love Me Tender,* represents the rock star discussing earnestly with his producer, the young and much-admired David Weisbart (who had produced *Rebel*), the possibility of starring in a projected *Jimmy Dean Story.* Elvis is quoted as saying, "I could do it easy. I want to play that more than anything else."

In another interview, Weisbart made an extended comparison between Elvis and Jimmy Dean. Pointing out the differences in the two young stars' temperaments—Elvis he found gregarious, Dean a loner; Elvis an enthusiast, Dean a calculating professional—Weisbart concluded by explaining just where he thought Elvis's strength lay and how he could be expected to succeed without either the training or the experience in acting that Jimmy Dean had gained from Lee Strasberg and the New York theater world. "Elvis's great charm," argued the producer, "lies in his immaturity; but he is still a shrewd kid, with all of Jimmy's knowledge and ability to use charm. . . . Acting skill will probably ruin him because his greatest asset is his natural ability. That is what Jimmy appeared to have, and that is what made him a great actor." If ever prophecy were perfectly phrased and absolutely fulfilled, it was this astounding prediction by the late David Weisbart, which sums up Elvis's entire film career, twenty-nine feature-length pictures in twelve years, in a couple of astute sentences.

Elvis, as Weisbart saw clearly after working with him in *Love Me Tender,* was a natural. This one word says it all. He produced instinctually effects of "charm" that real actors attained through art. If his career were managed so as to preserve this innocent and natural appeal, he might score the same kind of success as a Jimmy Dean. Tamper with the magic, however, try to make the kid an "actor," and you would reduce him to a condition that was valueless. Many people will scoff at this notion, but how much does it differ from the facts of Elvis's singing career? Everyone who has examined Elvis's recording history has come to the same conclusion: that his first records were his best, though, paradoxically, he became infinitely more artful as he gained experience. As Elvis was just a boy with virtually no professional experience when he first stepped into the recording studio, what is one to conclude but that the subtle amalgam of common styles and individual talent that he had brought to focus instinctively was worth more than all he learned and developed in a lifetime of prodigious musical activity and success.

The condition of being a natural is a highly precarious one that is not likely to survive long unless it is carefully guarded. Had David Weisbart gone on to make the *Jimmy Dean Story* with Elvis Presley, it's quite possible that Elvis's career might have been given an entirely different direction in Hollywood. As it turned out, however, Elvis went from *Love Me Tender,* in which, as we shall see, he offers what is far and away his most appealing film performance, to film after film in which he became a stock figure until, step by step, he was reduced to one of the ugliest and most repulsive presences on the American screen. It was a long and deadly fall, a decline so drastic that no performer less mindlessly adored by his public could possibly have survived it.

Once Colonel Parker had tossed Elvis into the first picture that came along, heedless of whether or not the part suited him or whether he would receive the proper direction or whether he should be fortified with acting lessons, all the rest was up to Elvis. It was a simple case of sink or swim. Elvis turned on his charm at the first cast party and started wooing his fellow actors, appealing to their sympathy for the greenhorn, while they marveled that anyone so successful could act so humble. In adopting this sucking up to the stars approach, Elvis revealed how totally dissimilar he was from his idol, Jimmy Dean. When Elia Kazan called Dean out of his dressing room on the set of *East of Eden* to introduce the other, well-established players, Dean had gone from one actor to another, sticking his mid-finger up and snarling, "Fuck you! . . . Fuck you! . . . Fuck you!" Jimmy Dean had no intention of being coopted by a Hollywood he despised. Elvis Presley just wanted to be accepted.

Elvis took a lot of crap from the other actors on his first film: jokes about his blue suede shoes—which he gave away to the crew; jokes about the neck-brace posture he adopted to avoid spoiling the erectness of his collar when he turned his head; jokes about his mascara and his accent and his eagerness to please, which extended to putting on a show for the visitors to the set during breaks in the shooting or after lunch in the commissary.

Lunch was the one moment of the day to which the other actors on this dumb picture looked forward because they had a standing invitation to join Elvis and the Colonel in a special dining room. The ole Colonel liked playing host to the young players. He was like that kind of mother who seeks to make friends for her shy darling (while keeping a sharp eye on him) by inviting his classmates every day to lunch in a tearoom near the school. Elvis's classmates were repulsed by the Colonel. Richard Egan was grossed out by the old man's habit of wearing his undershirt as his only shirt. Bill Campbell got angry when the Colonel tried to pin a big pink button on his jacket reading "I Love Elvis." "Parker," he snapped, "what in hell do you think you're doing? I'm trying to make a name for myself in this business and you want me walking around like a guy wearing a sandwich board!" "We don't generally give away these big buttons," jived the Colonel. "You'll be sorry you didn't take it some day."

Still, lunch with Colonel meant that you could eat steak every day—while Elvis ate mashed potatoes, gravy and burnt bacon. One afternoon, when they had all settled in their places and were eagerly awaiting the sirloins, they noticed the Colonel was missing. "Oh," says Elvis, "he went over to the office to do something. He'll be back." Finally, at the end of the meal, the Colonel appears. He's red-faced and angry. "What's up?" everybody choruses. The Colonel isn't loath to say. "Those goddamned people!" he bursts out, glad to have a chance to blow off steam. "They called me up there and asked how much they'd have to pay to get Elvis for this picture they're planning. They said it was for one of those extravaganzas where they use a lot of people from the musical end of the business. All Elvis had to do was sing two songs which they had all orchestrated and set to go. 'He doesn't have to do much work: Just fly in, make the session and go home.' 'Well, sir,' I said, 'that'll cost you seventy-five thousand dollars.' Jesus! They went crazy! So after they huddled and whispered and argued over the money, I got fed up with their game. I said: 'I'll tell you what I'll do. You got a pair o' dice?' They said, 'What do ya wan' 'em for?' I said, 'Well, I'll roll you for him. Double or nothing!' An ya know something? They wouldn't do it! So I walked out on them. To hell with 'em!"

While the Colonel was recounting this bizarre business meeting, which, after all, concerned Elvis closely—even presenting him with the startling image of being diced over in just the way the old southern planters used to gamble for prize slaves—Elvis went right on eating his meal, as if nothing of consequence were transpiring in his presence. Bill Campbell marveled over this indifference, especially to the constant wheeling and dealing for great sums of money that went on continually around Elvis. As Campbell saw it, Elvis had simply resigned himself to being a "property." "He was absolutely aware of the fact that he was not his own individual, that he belonged to a bunch of people—not just Colonel Parker. It went far beyond that!" Indeed, it did!

After the day's shooting, Elvis would go to the screening room and watch the rushes until perhaps seven. Then, he would duck into Bill Campbell's Thunderbird, shoot out the back gate onto Olympic Street— to avoid the crowds of fans hanging around the main gate—and dash back to his hotel, the Knickerbocker, off Hollywood on Ivar. Here, on the eleventh floor, he shared a suite with his country bumpkin cousins, Gene and Junior Smith. Though Elvis was now living smack in the heart of that wonderland which he had been reading about for years in the pages of *Photoplay* and *Silver Screen,* he never had any time to explore Hollywood. After he had eaten his supper in his room, talked to his mother on the phone and studied his lines for the next day's shooting, it would be time to turn out the light and fall into a troubled sleep. On the weekends, the best fun he could find was an amusement strip in Long Beach, where he could limber up his arm throwing baseballs at wooden bottles or go flying on the thrill rides. That would have been the extent of Elvis's amusements in Hollywood, if at this moment he had not run into the only man whom he would ever befriend in the movie colony: Nick Adams.

Actually, you didn't run into Nick Adams; he ran into you like a fast-talking, brightly smiling, exhaustingly aggressive door-to-door salesman for baby pictures or white leatherette Bibles. Though Adams was only a couple years older than Elvis and a relative newcomer to Hollywood himself, he had already earned a well-deserved reputation as the biggest pain-in-the-ass in town—the sort of guy who, when you saw him coming, dictated an immediate change of course and acceleration in the opposite direction. What Adams was forever selling was himself: a property which, to hear him tell it, was nothing less than sensational— "the greatest little actor to hit this town in years." In fact, he had very little going for him either in terms of looks or talent or professional experience. He was just another poor kid from the sticks who had grown up dreaming of the silver screen.

Born Nicholas Adamshock, son of a Lithuanian coal miner in Nanti-coke, Pennsylvania, Adams had come out of the same grinding poverty in which Elvis had grown up. After serving a hitch in the Coast Guard, he took off for the Heavenly City with two hundred dollars in his pockets and an extraordinary determination to make something of himself. Scuffling to survive, he worked as a filling station attendant, a short-order cook and once obtained a free room by offering to care for an old lady's cats. Not having money to buy food, Adams ate the good liver which the lady provided for the animals and fed the beasts on scraps from garbage cans. The story of how Adams got his first part in the movies sums up his character perfectly. Slipping onto the set of *Mister Roberts,* he jumped in front of the famous director, John Ford, and went into a lousy impersonation of Jimmy Cagney. "Throw him out!" bawled Ford; but then, when the kid kept popping up again and again on the set, Ford finally surrendered and gave Adams a three-line part to shut him up. Adams made those three lines stand out like a major speech. But it's doubtful he would have gotten much further at this time if it hadn't been for his knack of cutting into difficult, withdrawn stars, the first of whom was Jimmy Dean.

Adams ingratiated himself with Dean precisely as he was to do a year later with Elvis Presley. He offered himself to the shy, emotionally contorted and rebellious Dean as a friend, a guide, a boon companion, a homosexual lover—whatever role or service Dean required. Dean ridiculed Adams publicly, but he did get him a bit part in *Rebel Without a Cause.* Getting tight with Jimmy Dean meant also becoming friendly with the whole circle of young actors and actresses who hung out with Dean at the Villa Capri and Googie's, the all-night hash joint next door to Schwabb's. Adams was soon on close terms with Jack Simmons, Dean's mousy, bespectacled roommate; Natalie Wood and Sal Mineo, teenagers who were still attending school three hours a day on the studio lot; Rafael Campos, the Dominican actor familiar from his role as the Puerto Rican kid in *Blackboard Jungle;* Russ Tamblyn, another screen hoodlum, married at the time to Venetia Stevenson; and Dennis Hopper, with whom Adams was sharing a house when he met Elvis. All of these friends of Jimmy Dean were introduced to Elvis by Adams, who saw Elvis, whom he contrived to meet almost the day he stepped off the train in Los Angeles, as a substitute for the late Jimmy Dean.

Meeting all these famous young actors must have convinced Elvis he had really arrived in the movie business. What would have pleased him a lot more was making some progress in his hapless efforts to woo his leading lady, the sizzling Debra Paget. Elvis—later so canny about revealing his romantic attachments—wore his heart on his sleeve una - shamedly at this time. He even violated his strict rule of addressing every- one as "Miss" or "Mister" by referring to Debra as "Debbie." When a reporter asked Elvis if he had any favorite female stars, he replied: "I love 'em all, but I've got one special gal—and she's the only gal for me. But she keeps me 64,000 miles away." "Who could that be?" blurted the reporter, hot for the big scoop. With a boyish grin, Elvis sighed— "Debbie!" An hour later, the reporter caught up with Debra Paget, who was having lunch. "What's this about cold-shouldering Elvis?" he asked. "Oh, that!" she exclaimed, going into the nervous laugh with which she follows every statement. "I'll admit," she continued, "that my impres- sion of Elvis, before I met him, was the same as many others who don't know him. I figured he must be some kind of moron. Now, I think the best way to describe his work is to say it's inspired." Still, she didn't deny that there were lot of miles still separating them, even though they played man and wife in the film.

Elvis, for his part, could never understand why he wasn't making more ground with Debbie. Every night, he would pour out his heart to his only trusted confidante, his mother, seeking some solution to his problem in her wisdom. Gladys told her friends in Memphis that never had she heard Elvis go on so before about any girl. Between the pressures of appearing before the camera every day and the frustration of pining for the distant and inaccessible Debbie every night, Elvis's wire-strung soul began to jangle. Gene Smith recalls that Elvis walked in his sleep every night. One night Gene caught Elvis going out the window of their suite on the eleventh floor.

Awakening the somnambulist was a risky business. If you shook him, or even touched him lightly, he was likely to gather you into his dream and punch you out as his nearest assailant. Gene Smith solved this problem by employing a special hands-off technique. The trick was to switch on the lights and then, in a low soothing voice, call out—"El- vis?" At that moment, the dreamer would suddenly snap out of his trance and demand earnestly, "What was I doin' this time?" As soon as he heard his latest caper, he would burst out laughing. Though every- one around him was deeply concerned by his obvious propensity toward self-destruction, Elvis took the matter very lightly. He always said that he would live forever. The truth is that if he hadn't been so carefully guarded, he might have followed his hero, Jimmy Dean, to an early grave.

Why was Debra Paget so resistant to Elvis—a handsome, famous, prosperous, well-mannered and universally adored young star? True, she was a couple of years older than he at an age when every year counts. Also, having been reared in show business and having appeared in pictures since her fourteenth year, she was more sophisticated than the young rock star. Then, there was the fact that Debra was Jewish. For a young man as devoutly Christian as Elvis, this might pose a problem; yet, as we shall see, Elvis was always drawn to Jewish people and even, on occasion, expressed the wish that he might himself be one of the "chosen people." So even the barrier of religion would not have posed an insuperable obstacle to a serious relationship, and it was precisely such a relationship that Elvis had in mind when he began courting "Debbie."

As for Debra Paget, everyone in Hollywood agreed that she was a very nice girl. She lived with her mother, father and sisters in a very theatrical house in Beverly Hills that was celebrated for its menagerie, which included a chimpanzee (Elvis acquired one himself eventually), an orange gibbon, a macaw and numerous other tropical birds and fishes. Elvis became familiar with the house and family when he asked Debra Paget for a date, and she astounded him by replying that she had never gone out on a date, but that he was welcome to come and visit her at her home. Virtually any man would have been titillated by this reply; but for Elvis Presley, it was an incredible turn-on. It was nothing less than the sudden, unexpected realization of his most fervid longing: to find a perfectly beautiful, lusciously erotic girl, who was, at the same time, a very proper and well-bred virgin.

Once Elvis began visiting his beloved's home, he realized that the dominant personality in the family was Debra's mother, who had been in the theater and still used her stage name, Marguerite Gibson, or as she was known to everyone, Maggie. In finding the family firmly under the rule of mother, Elvis was once again discovering a condition that fulfilled his natural inclinations. How startled he must have been when soon it became apparent that this mother was nothing like the kind of mother he had always known. Maggie was brassy. She drove around town in a jewel-studded Cadillac. She used very salty language. Some people said her stage experience had been primarily in burlesque. In fact, she was your classic Jewish stage mother: the female equivalent of Colonel Parker. Not only did she control Debra, like a puppet at her fingertips, but she managed her in the formal business sense. Like the Colonel, she lived and breathed her "artist."

Maggie had groomed Debra very carefully for her career. She had brought her up to be a movie star in the classic forties mold: a second Jane Russell, one of those smolderingly erotic beauties whose slightly flawed facial lines were eclipsed by their bustlines, which were always dramatized for the movie viewer by their plunging necklines. Having done a certain amount of, shall we say, "exotic dancing," Maggie had taught her shy, soft-spoken giggling daughter the same arts. In fact, once, at Las Vegas, where some bigwig like Bob Hope was putting on a benefit, Debra performed a routine that was so vulgar that even the hardened showbiz types who were running the show were outraged. Nobody blamed Debra, of course; everybody recognized her for what she was: a puppet in her mother's hands, the kind of girl who could exist all day on a single glass of water because her mother had forbidden her to drink and gain the few ounces the water would add to her body weight. What pissed the show people off was the way the old girl made sweet, innocent Debra camp it up like some cheap hooker.

It would be wrong to suppose, however, that Maggie crushed a blossoming romance between Elvis and Debra. True, the old lady didn't dig this pimple-faced kid worth a damn. She had very different ideas about the sort of man who should get her carefully treasured daughter. It was Debra herself who turned thumbs down on Elvis. Even today— now the wife of a wealthy Texas oilman and the mistress of five homes— Debra Paget retains a slightly patronizing air when she talks about Elvis. "He was a very sweet, very simple kind of person," she recalls. "He just liked to get on his motorcycle and go off into the night." Then, she laughs in a low throaty voice. Reflecting on the experience, she confides: "I never told anyone before, but Elvis asked me to marry him after the film. He called long distance from Texas. My family didn't go for the idea." Elvis, as we shall see, proposed to several women in this period of his life. That he made the offer to Debra after the film is interesting in view of an incident that occurred before the picture was completed.

One night while he was visiting Debra at her home, Elvis raised again the issue of their having a proper date. She told him that she never dated because she devoted herself entirely to her career. Then, she said that he would have to excuse her this night because she had a pressing business appointment. Elvis got aboard his bike and rode off into the night. Only he didn't go far. In fact, he doubled back quietly and kept watch on the house, suspicious of what a business appointment late in the evening might signify. Sure enough, not long after he took up his post, he saw a Chevrolet sedan pull up with a couple of very straight-looking dudes inside it, dressed in conservative business suits. One of them went to the door, rang the bell, passed inside; then, shortly afterwards, he came out escorting Debra, who was beautifully dressed. They all got into the car and drove away. Elvis memorized the license number and the next day made some inquiries. He was astonished when he learned that the car and its crew were the possessions of no less a person than Howard Hughes.

At the same time that Elvis was courting Debra Paget, he was introduced by Nick Adams to Natalie Wood. The actress was at this time an eighteen-year-old girl living with her working-class parents in Sherman Oaks. In taking up with Natalie Wood, Elvis was swinging to the opposite extreme from Debra Paget. If Debra Paget was the sizzling Jane Russell type, Natalie Wood was everyone's cute little pansy-eyed daughter, now a pixiesh teenager in pedal pushers and babushka, riding around Beverly Hills perched on the back of a motorbike. Actually, Natalie Wood was just as dedicated to her career as Debra Paget; both girls had studied in different grades at the same studio school. (In the Mother's Room, Maggie Gibson always managed to say something so shocking that Natalie's mother had to fight to keep herself from fainting dead away.) At eighteen, Natalie Wood was a veteran of fourteen years in pictures. She was an instinctively independent and mature young woman who resented being treated as a carefully chaperoned child. When she got involved with the Jimmy Dean crowd, she found just the world she had been unconsciously seeking. "They were the gods," she recalls. "I just wanted to be exactly like them. What we used to talk about was how unhappy we were. Whoever was the unhappiest, whoever came closest to suicide the night before, he was the winner."

Now this young woman, full of the heady lore of Stanislavski, bongo drums, Porsches and existentialism, eager to be free and independent, identified with Hollywood's handful of New Wave actors, comes face to face with Elvis Presley—her antithesis. Naturally, she's fascinated. Elvis is "wonderful looking—such a sensuous mouth"; he's "tremendously sweet"; but the most intriguing, almost startling, thing about him is that he's "terribly conventional"! "He was the first person of my age group I had ever met who said to me: 'How come you're wearing makeup? Why do you want to go to New York? Why do you want to be on your own? Why don't you want to stay home and be a sweet little girl? It's nice to stay home.' " Elvis was so square, he was fascinating. "We'd go to P. C. Brown's and have a hot fudge sundae. We'd go to

Hamburger Hamlet and have a burger and a Coke. He didn't drink. He didn't swear. He didn't even smoke! It was like having the date that I never ever had in high school. I thought it was really wild!"

The other thing that was remarkable about Elvis was the fact that he was genuinely religious. "I hadn't been around anyone who was religious," explains Natalie. "He felt he had been given this gift, this talent, by God. He didn't take it for granted. He thought it was something that he had to protect. He had to be nice to people, otherwise, God would take it all away."

Before Elvis went back to Memphis, he and Natalie discussed the possibility that she might come and visit him in his new home on Audubon Avenue. "His parents called my parents and asked if I could be their house guest. I would be very fully chaperoned and Nick Adams would be there. My parents were quite strict. Normally, they would have said, 'No.' But they liked him so much . . . they thought he was such a religious boy and his parents sounded so nice over the phone that they decided they would let me go." So it came about that on October 31, three days after Elvis's second appearance on the Sullivan show, Natalie Wood, dressed in a black sweater and black pedal pushers and toting three stuffed tigers, arrived at Memphis, where she was greeted by Nick Adams and Elvis and escorted through a crowd of fans and autograph hunters to a $12,000 custom-fitted white Lincoln Continental, which Elvis piloted home.

When Natalie saw the hundreds of fans besieging the little spruce-green tract house, served by souvenir peddlers, hot dog and popcorn vendors, she was shocked and horrified. She came from a world where all the biggest celebrities lived, but she had never witnessed anything like this carnival atmosphere around a film star's home. When Elvis tried to pull into the driveway, the fans blocked his path. Nonchalantly, he leaned out the window and said: "As soon as I pull the car into the garage, we'll all come back out here and talk to you all." "Don't forget now, you promised!" chorused the fans. If Natalie figured this was just a line to get into the house she soon learned differently. No sooner had they parked the car than Elvis marched them out to the low iron fence, embellished with metal musical notes, where they chatted with the fans for half an hour and Natalie had to field endless questions about whether she was having a romance with Nick or planning to marry Elvis.

A few hours later, having had supper and met Mr. and Mrs. Presley (Natalie found Gladys "very laid back"), the three young stars took off into the glamorous Memphis night—after first signing more auto-graphs at the gate. Elvis drove around town, stopping a couple of times so that Nick could hop out of the car and buy ice cream cones. At 11:30, the big white car pulled up in front of the Chicksa Hotel on Main Street; Elvis ushered his guests up to the mezzanine, where Dewey Phillips was laying his crazy rap on the city. An off-the-wall interview followed, with much playing of Elvis records and goofy laughter. When the show went off the air at midnight, Elvis and his party descended to the street, where they found a crowd of one thousand people assembled outside the hotel. In front of the crowd were numerous flashbulb-popping photographers and newspaper reporters, asking questions not much brighter than those the fans popped.

Five or six hours having passed since supper, Elvis was now hungry. Regaining his car with considerable effort, he started driving out Union Street followed by a motorcade of about fifteen automobiles. Arriving at one of his favorite joints, the Gridiron, he ushered his party inside the cheap interior, fired up the juke box and settled down for a solid breakfast of tough-fried eggs and burnt bacon. By 1:30 in the morning, the party was back at Audubon Avenue, where the crowd still numbered two hundred souls. Once again Elvis had to negotiate to get inside his driveway. Once again, all three young celebs had to oblige with answers and autographs till two in the morning.

Throughout the following week, the same routine was followed day in, day out, with the only variations being movies in place of Dewey Phillips and spins on Elvis's Harley Davidson bike in the afternoon instead of tours in the big white car. Natalie was accustomed to riding on the back of a bike from her days with Jimmy Dean. What she could never accept was the long tail of cars that followed Elvis everywhere he rode. The drivers of the foremost cars sometimes pulled abreast of the bike and conducted neighborly conversations with the local hero.

Just as bizarre was the fishbowl atmosphere of the house. One after-noon, while Elvis was playing Ski Pool with Nick Adams in the den, five teenage girls, standing on tiptoe, witnessed the whole game from an open window. The rule was that any fan was welcome to wander around on the property so long as he was not disruptive. If he made too much noise, he was asked to leave. When Natalie asked Elvis why he put up with this outrageous violation of privacy, he said that he owed his success to the fans and that it was his duty to tolerate their behavior and fulfill their requests for appearances and autographs every day.

On that responsible note the visit ended, and Natalie Wood, accompanied by Nick Adams, emplaned for L.A., that peaceful place.

Love Me Tender opened on November 15, 1956, at that ancient citadel of youth culture, the New York Paramount. Long before daybreak, hundreds of kids from the five boroughs came bubbling up out of the subway entrances of Times Square to form a queue around the theater, which had erected on its marquee a thirty-foot colored cutout of Elvis playing his guitar. When the first kids to see the show were quizzed about their reactions, they objected vehemently to the fact that the movie was not a rock 'n' roll picture, did not deliver the real Elvis and made the horrible mistake of killing off their new hero in the last reel—an error that the Hollywood hacks tried to rectify by summoning up the ghost of the dead Elvis in the last frames to sing a spooky reprise of the theme in Wraithe-Vision.

Though all of these criticisms were valid, they don't alter the fact that in his first film Elvis makes his most appealing screen appearance. This movie is a monument to Elvis the Good: a young, innocent, healthy, clean-looking blond, with an irresistible smile and cuddly teddy-bear quality that makes him the ideal playmate for every thirteen-year-old girl who ever lived. David Weisbart said: "Elvis was the character, even to the sideburns, the minute he stepped off the plane." It's true: This accidentally adopted role suited Elvis better than any part he was ever to play in his subsequent career of twenty-eight starring roles.

His first appearance sets the tone for everything that is to follow. By this point in the picture a lot of stock action has gone by—a train robbery, a chase, a big welcome-home scene. Then, finally, the camera catches its first sight ever of Elvis Presley. He's dressed in shirt-sleeves, rough trousers and peasant boots and he's plowing behind a team of mules: the archetypal southern farm image. You glimpse him first from a distance, as he's being called to the house to welcome home his brothers. As the camera zooms in for the close-up, Elvis breaks into a big smile, a lovely, sweet, unself-conscious smile that radiates its warmth across the screen. At this moment, teenage audiences all over America burst into uncontrollable screams. If anything in the history of pop culture could be called an epiphany, this moment is it—Elvis Presley dawning upon the movie consciousness of America.

To review the picture properly, you would need an instrument not yet developed but likely to come some day soon, as our culture evolves ever more in the direction of the tactile, the gustatory, the olfactory, the universe of the infant. This instrument, something like the infrared camera, will respond not to the visual outline of the object but to its *vibes.* Point the instrument at *Love Me Tender,* and you observe in scene after scene a characteristic pattern. There will be Debra Paget, seething with repressed sexuality like a severely contained but unmistakable nymphomaniac: her finely shaped breasts always protruding, her voice low but hot, her face that of an elegant cat in heat. Richard Egan produces a contrasting signal: He is a man of steel with a face carved of the same cold, unyielding material. Everyone else is dead, inert, a prop brought in and set up for the shooting. The only fluently live creature in this curious cast is Elvis, who at every moment is giving off waves of sentient feeling: one moment tender and affectionate; the next, troubled and hurt; the next, furious and violent, a being composed entirely of feelings that surface as naturally as notes from a singer's mouth.

The only false notes he strikes are in his livelier songs, where he slips into the body rhetoric that made him famous but which is utterly anachronistic in this archaic and rustic time frame. When he sings "Love Me Tender," addressing it to Mildred Dunnock, playing his mother seated in a rocking chair, the love and tenderness that beams from him is delicious. How apt that in his first picture, he sings a love song to his mother! It reminds one of the only real anecdote still told in Hollywood about this film. Elvis was supposed to pull a gun and brandish it, while his mother said, "Put down that gun!" In the first take, the moment the mother gave the command, Elvis instinctively complied, saying, "Yes, ma'am."

It is revealing of the mental set of the more sophisticated reviewers of this charming performance that not one of them had a good word to say for the picture. In fact, *Love Me Tender* inspired the most famous put-down that Elvis Presley ever received. It appeared in *Time* as a neat little column of print resting on a picture of Elvis standing beside his mule's hindquarters. It read:

Is it a sausage? It is certainly smooth and damp-looking, but who ever heard of a 172-lb. sausage 6 ft. tall? Is it a Walt Disney goldfish? It has the same sort of big, soft, beautiful eyes and long, curly lashes, but who ever heard of a goldfish with sideburns? Is it a corpse? The face just hangs there, limp and white with its little drop-seat mouth, rather like Lord Byron in the wax museum.

But suddenly the figure comes to life. The lips part, the eyes half close, the clutched guitar begins to undulate back and forth in an uncomfortably suggestive manner. And wham! The mid-section of the body jolts forward to bump and grind and beat out a low-down rhythm that takes pace from boogie and hillbilly, rock 'n' roll and something known only to Elvis and his pelvis. As the belly dance gets wilder, a peculiar sound emerges. A rusty foghorn? A voice? Or merely a noise produced, like the voice of a cricket, by the violent stridulation of the legs? Words occasionally can be made out, like raisins in cornmeal mush. "Goan . . . git . . . luhhv . . ." And then all at once everything stops, and a big, trembly tender half smile, half sneer smears slowly across the Cinemascope screen. The message that millions of U.S. teen-age girls love to receive has just been delivered.

Thus spake *Time*.

Chapter 16

Starring Vehicles

PUTTING rock 'n' roll on the big screen of the Holly-wood exploitation movie proved almost as difficult a task as putting it on the little screen of the network variety show. The moviemakers' problem was not one of the incompatibility of art and medium: their difficulty was entirely one of talent and tradition. No major director ever addressed himself to the task of translating the rock world to the screen; on the other hand, those hacks who did under-take this job were preprogrammed to an extraordinary degree by the long history of movies about jitterbugs and swing bands com-piled in the late thirties and early forties.

From the first rock movie (Sam Katzman's quickie, *Rock Around the Clock,* starring Bill Haley and Alan Freed) to the last, the basic effect was simply *déjà vu.* Rock came across as swing in crinolines. Not only had you seen the story a hundred times before, with its preposterous dialogue peppered with archaic jazz slang and vintage handclasps, but you had witnessed, it not performed, all the suppos-edly original dance steps, been startled by the purportedly "barbaric" sounds and enjoyed countless times the ritual triumph of youth over age, hot over cool and inspiration over constipation.

Part of this time-loop effect can be blamed on rock itself, which in its early years was often little more than a gag reflex regurgitating the high-school enthusiasms of the Swing Age, commencing with the Lindy and the Boogie-Woogie and going on to the cult of the jalopy, the jukebox, the screaming, swooning bobby-soxer, the anguished young singing star, et cetera, et cetera. The real problem with these pictures, however, was not simply the repetitiveness of pop culture: It was the fact that the filmmakers were middle-aged men who were so confident they knew what was happening in the youth culture that they never bothered to give their subject a thought or even a look.

The one exception to this repetition compulsion was Hal Wallis, whom we have seen sitting in on Elvis's recording sessions, getting a firsthand impression of the real thing. Now that it was time to launch Elvis in his first starring vehicle, Wallis ordered the writer and director of the film to go down to Memphis to meet the star on his home turf and see the new hero do his stuff. Elvis was about to take leave of the *Louisiana Hayride* in a grand farewell performance that would bring his whole phenomenon into vivid focus.[1] Unfortunately, by this time the writer had completed his screenplay. The suggestion proved valuable all the same, for something of Elvis's inspiration did penetrate Hal Kanter, which is the reason why his film, *Loving You,* is the most full-blooded rendering we possess of the early Elvis.

No damned Yankee, Kanter had grown up in Savannah and retained his capacity to speak in flawless dialect of "crocus sacks" and "flying Jennys." He trained a shrewdly appreciative eye on Elvis Presley and his milieu. Picked up by Elvis himself, driving an orchid-colored Fleetwood, Kanter was carried out to the house on Audubon. Giving it a fast once-over, he was particularly amused by Elvis's bedroom, which was papered in a yellow sheet covered with blue and orange flowers, and embellished with ceramic minstrels on plaques. The twin beds were cozied up with fancy quilted coverlets and adorned with blue stuffed poodles.

No sooner had the menfolk settled down in the den than Elvis raised a question about the script. Wallis had expressly forbidden Kanter to bring with him a copy of his screenplay for fear that Colonel Parker or Elvis himself might raise objections to the story before the shooting had commenced. As it turned out, Elvis was interested in just one rather obscure point. "Mr. Kanter," he said thoughtfully, "is it the kind of

[1] In April 1956, after eighty-four appearances, Elvis ceased broadcasting on the *Hayride.* As his contract did not terminate until September of that year, Colonel Parker bought him out for ten thousand dollars in cash and a commitment to play a farewell concert at some future date.

interviews. Then, the warm-up acts, all exact replicas of Elvis Presley, doing his songs with his gestures and dressed in his clothes. Finally, the apocalyptic moment when the star appeared in a hall that was crepitating with the heat lightning of thousands of popping flashbulbs. At that instant an immense scream was heard, which rose and fell without ceasing throughout the entire time that Elvis was onstage, so loud a noise that you couldn't hear enough of the music even to know for a certainty what song Elvis was singing. Hal Kanter, an old pro, was highly impressed. He determined to put this milieu on the screen. "If I came to scoff," he reflects today, "I went away a prophet."

After the Christmas holidays, when it came time to start work on the new picture, Elvis invited his family to join him in Hollywood. For Vernon and Gladys, this was a startling suggestion. In all their lives, they had never gone further than the 104 miles from Tupelo to Memphis. Now, they were expected to cross the entire continent. Like their son, they sought company for the journey. During the alterations to their house, they had made friends with the building contractor who had built their swimming pool. He was named Carl Nichols. His wife, Willy, became a special favorite of Gladys, who rarely made friends. Willy Nichols recollects Gladys as being a very different person from the mater dolorosa that one sees in all the family photographs. "Everybody played up the sadness," says Mrs. Nichols, "photographing her when she was real sick or when Elvis was drafted. She was happy. She liked to eat and cut up. She loved to ride around and see everything."

The happiest moment in Gladys's life, Willy Nichols believes, was the night they all agreed to go out together to Hollywood. "She called us up one night," Mrs. Nichols remembers, "and she was in the best mood you've ever seen. She was laughing and she said, 'Willy, we're goin' to California!' " When the Nicholses arrived at the Presley house, Gladys was beside herself with joy. She told Willy, "You're the truest person I ever met." Then she presented her friend with a little brass bracelet that had a locket containing Elvis's picture, a piece of jewelry that Elvis had originally given to his mother. As the evening wore on, Gladys's hilarity became so extreme that Vernon was moved finally to tell her she had better quiet down. She was becoming hysterical.

No sooner did the preparations for the trip commence than Gladys began to display a side to her personality that no one had ever before divined. The simple soul who always wore "dusters" and spent her life preparing crowder peas and thickenin' gravy suddenly became the well-

groomed mother of a movie star. She went to Lowenstein's Department
Store and with the aid of a "costume coordinator" bought an entire
wardrobe of very attractive clothes. She paid a great deal of attention
to her hair, having it styled every day. She began to anticipate all the
things they would do when the reached movieland. She told Willy that
as soon as they got there, they would buy French poodles, the old-fashioned movie stars' favorite pets. They bought them, too, Willy naming
hers Pierre and Gladys dubbing her dog Duke after her favorite movie
star, John Wayne. Gladys also lectured Vernon on how to behave during
the trip, telling her husband, who was very tight with a buck: "We
have to tip big. We're expected to do it and we're in a position to afford
it." Gladys showed so much savoir faire about this Hollywood trip that
Willy began to wonder whether her friend had not once been screenstruck,
just like her son.

The two middle-aged couples spent four days riding across the country
on America's dying railroads. They would sit in their compartments,
laughing and telling stories. Gladys had been feeling quite ill after Christmas; in fact, in January, she had entered the hospital for two weeks to
receive a thorough checkup. Now on the train she had trouble sleeping,
but she was determined to enjoy herself. When Gladys was in a good
mood, she would sing in a deep vibrant voice that reminded Willy of
Elvis's voice, especially after it deepened and darkened in later years.
One day Gladys said, "I can't understand all this fuss over Elvis. I
think I have a better voice than he does." Then, she broke into "Heartbreak Hotel." Mrs. Nichols was astonished at how well Gladys brought
off the song with its difficult leaps. Indeed she could never stop marveling
over how similar were mother and son. Their faces showed a marked
resemblance. They both mumbled when they talked. They were both
brooders and loners. What's more, they were both destined to early
deaths, a fact of which Gladys appeared to have foreknowledge.

One day she told Willy Nichols that she did not expect Elvis to
live beyond the age of thirty-five. She was fearful that he would be killed
by a lunatic or by a jealous lover. She was appalled at the crazy ideas
and emotions that were revealed in the fan mail that came pouring into
the house, so much fan mail that even at this early date the Presleys
had to hire a professional secretary to answer it. Most of all, though,
Gladys feared that Elvis would be killed by his own life-style: his lack
of sleep and headlong rushing from one activity to another. She always
saw the boy burning himself out. As for herself, she was convinced
that she would soon be dead. She was resigned to dying. She warned

Willy to say nothing of the matter to Elvis. This trip to Hollywood was Gladys's last—and only—fling.

Willy also obtained some insight into the relationship of Gladys and Vernon. She observed that Gladys was the master in the house and a very jealous master at that. Vernon was a handsome man at forty: tall, well-proportioned with a great head of wavy hair, just beginning to turn grey. He liked to wear flashy clothes, just like his son, and drive around in luxurious automobiles. Gladys noticed that Vernon often spent a great deal of time out at the fence in front of the house talking to the pretty young women who hung around waiting to see Elvis. On more than one occasion, she cautioned her husband. If Gladys got upset, Elvis would always assume that his father had done something wrong. He'd get Vernon out in the car and demand: "What have you done to her now?" Poor Vernon. He was always on the defensive with these two allied against him.

When the Presleys and the Nicholses arrived in Hollywood, they received a royal welcome. Elvis quartered them in the Knickerbocker Hotel, where he was staying, and brought them out to the lot every day to watch the shooting. Willy Nichols found the routine of moviemaking boring. Gladys appeared very pleased to meet the actors and especially Mr. Wallis. Hal Kanter could appreciate the pride of a southern mother in her little boy. He arranged to give the Presleys a marvelous souvenir. In the scene at the end of the picture in which Elvis performs in a theater, Kanter seated the Presleys and the Nicholses among the film extras and flashed their pictures on the screen. After Gladys died, Elvis refused ever again to see *Loving You.*

On the weekends, when Elvis wasn't working, he would take his family and their friends sightseeing. He would show them the homes of the stars. Two places excited him particularly: Red Skelton's house, which he admired for its ostentatious decor, and Debra Paget's house, which he now contemplated with nostalgia. The Presleys and the Nicholses also met Elvis's latest actress friend, the beautiful Joan Blackman, who at eighteen had just begun working in pictures.

She had met Elvis on the Paramount lot, while walking in the company of some other girls, distinguished not just by her looks but by the fact that she was wearing red pants. Elvis came cruising along in the hot rod which he drives in *Loving You.* Taking one good look at the shapely brunette in the red pants, he shouted—"Hey, you, c'mere!" That started what turned out to be a typical Presley affair. He introduced his new girlfriend at once to his mother. Then, they all went to the movies. It was the premier of *The Ten Commandments,* a picture after Elvis's own heart. He became so excited during the showing that he started narrating every scene for his guests, as if the film were in a foreign language. As he went over the biblical scenes, he would throw in a lot of technical details he had picked up recently about filming. Gladys kept trying to hush him to avoid being embarrassed, but Elvis continued to lecture heedlessly throughout the entire movie, as was always his wont when a picture turned him on.

Joan Blackman concluded that Elvis was not naive about women, just scared. She was a virgin and Elvis was quite content to leave her that way. She interpreted his timidity as anxiety that something nasty would get back to Gladys. Actually, Elvis was always loath to have sex with any woman he respected. What's more, at this particular moment, he was probably still upset by the first paternity suit ever to be brought against him, by a girl who had filed an affidavit in Ohio. In any event, the hot but adolescent affair with Joan Blackman was soon over. Eventually, the pair were reunited in a couple of movies, but there was no further romance. Years later, the actress ran into Elvis backstage at Las Vegas. He looked at her, obviously stoned, and said: "You had your chance." That became a standard line with Elvis.

The Presleys and the Nicholses left Hollywood after a one-month stay. Elvis followed hard on their heels, returning to Memphis in mid-March. When he got back, he learned from his family that they had just found a beautiful new house. Elvis had been insisting for months that they leave their home on Audubon because it afforded so little privacy and produced so much tension with the neighbors, who resented bitterly the carnivallike atmosphere created by the fans. In fact, at one point the neighbors had banded together and brought a public nuisance suit against Elvis. The magistrate did not find in their favor. He said the behavior of the fans was not Elvis's responsibility and that otherwise he was a good householder. In fact, the judge remarked, with some asperity, Elvis Presley's house was the only one on the street that had been paid for in full. Nonetheless, it was time to move, if for no other reason than the fact that Elvis was now a wealthy man and a movie star who should have the sort of home that befitted his impressive status. It was with the intention of fulfilling Elvis's dreams that the former tenants of the Lauderdale Courts set out on their house-hunting expedition. It was typical of their hapless approach to any sort of business that they entrusted this serious and costly undertaking to the first person who came along.

Virginia Grant was a young and inexperienced real estate agent in 1957, one of those gushy southern ladies whose mouths go a mile a minute but never manage to keep up with the frothing volatility of their exuberant temperaments. One day in February, Mrs. Grant was waiting for a client at Lowenstein's East, a suburban branch of Memphis's leading department store, when she spied standing at the curb a "gorgeous pink Cadillac." Naturally, she had to see who was sitting inside the Cad. When she recognized Gladys Presley, the young woman summoned up her courage and knocked on the window of the car. "Hello," she said, "aren't you Elvis Presley's mother?" "Why, yes," the lady said, "how did you recognize me?" "From pictures in newspapers and magazines," came the flattering reply. That was all it took to get the conversation going. The real estate agent was too wise to identify herself as such at first; but, when Gladys asked her if she worked, her profession emerged naturally. Once the ice was broken, Gladys informed the keen young agent that the Presleys were in the market for a big house with some land not far from town. One month later, Virginia Grant was driving the Presleys around Memphis, looking at houses. It was after they had rejected a property because it was too small that suddenly the young woman thought of Graceland.

A typical southern suburban mansion, built about 1910 of pink Tennessee fieldstone and adorned with an imposing white-columned portico, the house was owned by Mrs. Ruth Brown Moore, whose deceased husband had named it after his wife's aunt. Long unoccupied, it was badly in need of repairs, having become over the years a white elephant. The only use that anyone had found for the place was to house the Sunday school of the Graceland Christian Church. On the other hand, the fabric was sound, the grounds extensive and the district, Whitehaven, was at this point the fastest growing upper-middle-class neighborhood in Memphis.

On the morning of March 19, Virginia Grant meets the Presleys again at the house. This time, Elvis is present. Mrs. Grant is so stunned by his appearance that she almost blacks out. Elvis, for his part, acts as if nothing of consequence is taking place. He walks through the rooms, giving them a very casual once-over. Then, discovering a piano in the drawing room, he sits down and starts to chord out a tune. Having gotten this bit out of his system, he gets up and continues his breezy survey of the house, remarking that the place "sure needs a lot of work." As he proceeds, he starts coming up with ideas for decorating: colors, contrasts, types of furniture. Finally, he voices his goal: "It will be a lot nicer than Red Skelton's house when I get it like I want it." With that bit of heavy name-dropping to indicate the league in which Elvis Presley bats, he reaches for the tentative agreement and without deigning to even glance at its stipulations, he scrawls his signature across the bottom. Hell! Didn't he sign all his contracts that way? Never did him any harm, did it?

No sooner does the word of Elvis's purchase appear in the papers than Mrs. Grant is faced with her next challenge: The Presleys had offered their house on Audubon as part payment on Graceland. Mrs. Moore's representatives had allowed Elvis $55,000 for the property, which he had bought for $40,000, but which he had improved considerably with the den and the pool. Elvis had agreed to add ten thousand dollars in cash and take a note for $37,000 at three or four percent interest with Equitable Life to make up the balance of the total price of $102,500. At the last minute, however, a bubble gum company came up with a much heavier offer for the house on Audubon, which it wanted to demolish, chop up in pieces the size of matchbooks and give away as a premium: for every five packs of bubble gum a free piece of Elvis Presley's house. The idea delighted Elvis, who pronounced it a "cute little gimmick." It made Vernon rigid with greed. Nothing could be done until the deal had been cleared with the Colonel, who had extensive dealings with franchise and souvenir companies. Imagine everyone's disappointment when it turned out that they couldn't close with the offer because Elvis already had a deal with another bubble gum company!

The truth was that by this point in his career, Elvis had a deal with every sort of company that could profit by his endorsement. In August 1956, Colonel Parker had signed an elaborate contract that was aimed at spinning off from the basic product—Elvis—a half-hundred satellite products, ranging from lipsticks to phonographs, from jeans to fountain pens. He had assigned the rights to merchandise the name and image of Elvis Presley to Special Projects, Inc., the corporate label of a very sharp merchandiser named Hank Saperstein, who also held the rights to the Lone Ranger, Wyatt Earp, Lassie, and Ding Dong School. This deal put the Colonel in hawker's heaven. Now, instead of having just a souvenir program, a songbook and a couple of glossy pictures to sell, the Colonel could preside over a whole store filled with Presley paraphernalia.

In the clothing department of the store, a young girl could purchase an entire Elvis Presley outfit: jeans (black twill with emerald green stitching) with Elvis's signature stamped on a leather pocket patch; an Elvis

Presley Ivy League button-down shirt; canvas shoes with tops and linings stamped with a drawing of Elvis and his guitar; and Elvis Presley rock 'n' roll bobby-sox to wear with the shoes—or without shoes at the next sock hop ball. In the novelty department, the young lady could buy an Elvis Presley wallet or a statuette of Elvis or a charm bracelet, selling for just one dollar, whose charms included a tiny framed picture of Elvis, a guitar, a hound dog and a cracked heart, symbolizing "Heartbreak Hotel." At the cosmetic counter, she had her choice of a variety of lipsticks in shades like "Tutti Frutti Red" or "Hound Dog Orange." In the music department, she would discover in addition to Elvis's records two new portable RCA phonographs covered in blue denim (to suggest "Blue Suede Shoes") and embossed on the lid with Elvis's signature in gold. On a special stand at the door, she would find the most inspired product of all: a portrait of Elvis in phosphorescent ink that would glow in the dark. Just the thing for the Elvis idolator who lies abed at night listening to his records and dreaming of one day meeting and even kissing him.

Saperstein knew his business. In just six months from the starting date of his franchise operations, he reported gross sales of twenty-six million dollars. Elvis's cut ranged between four and eleven percent of the wholesale price: say, three-quarters of a million dollars. Colonel Parker, who coveted above all else Elvis's merchandising income, took a fifty percent commission.

Elvis's third film, *Jailhouse Rock,* is far and away the most interesting picture he ever made and the most penetrating treatment ever accorded the murky world of rock 'n' roll. Unlike *Loving You,* which weaves a sophisticated comedy, sustained by professional players, around an Elvis who is not required to do much more than what he always did on stage, *Jailhouse Rock* focuses exclusively on Elvis, taking him step by step through the archetypal life of a rock 'n' roll star. Instead of offering a conventional plot, with intrigues, discoveries, reversals and bold dramatic climaxes, this taut, acerbic black-and-white picture (*Loving You* is in candy color) has the air of an exposé or an anatomy of a world concealed from the public. Though the picture never makes any big splashes, it absorbs the viewer and offers something interesting at every carefully scripted moment. It also has the gall to present Elvis Presley as an obnoxious young punk and a shallow, egotistical Hollywood show-off. Elvis detested the picture and never had a good word for it. It was too close to the truth.

The success of *Jailhouse Rock* owed nothing to the circumstances under which it was conceived, produced, played or timed. The film was the product of the same Hollywood B-movie machine that ground out all those horrible pictures that soon made Elvis Presley the biggest putz in the history of filmmaking. In fact, this picture was less carefully nurtured than many other Elvis movies because it was conceived strictly as a one-shot, low-budget gamble aimed at cashing in on a passing fad. The producer, Pandro Berman, stood at the time at the mid-point of a thirty-year career that comprised no less than eighty films, including all the Fred Astaire classics. He regarded Elvis then, as he does today, with scant respect. "Let's say, he had a lot of personality; he was not an actor," remarks the brusque, businesslike Berman, who is totally devoid of cant. "The important thing is: We got a break. Instead of going out and hiring a guy like Irving Berlin or Jerry Kern and paying a fortune for music, these punks from hillbilly Tennessee wrote the music, and we paid twenty cents for it." (The "punks" in question were, of course, the "legendary" Leiber and Stoller.)

Money was the only consideration in the making of this picture, as it was in all of Elvis's movies. As they say in the business, the money was "duplexed": There was all the money you *saved* by making the whole film depend on the star's appeal; then, there was all the money you might *earn* if the picture caught on with the rock-hungry youth audience. Even so, Pandro Berman, if left to his own devices, would never have thought of making a movie with Elvis Presley. He was engrossed at the time with more important things, like his production of *The Brothers Karamazov.* It was Berman's wife (and sometime assistant producer), Katherine Hereford, who came up with the idea of building a movie around Elvis. She had seen him in *Love Me Tender,* and, like millions of others, she had observed: "When you saw his face come up on the screen, it said something."

The deal for the picture was made by MGM's boss, Benny Thau, negotiating with Abe Lastfogel, the president of William Morris, who was the mouthpiece for Colonel Parker. At first glance, the terms appeared to be a triumph for the Presley interests: a quarter of a million dollars in salary against fifty percent of net profits plus all the publishing rights to the songs—all this for a young star who had only one picture in circulation. The other end of the deal was not something you would read about in press releases or movie chitchat columns; yet, it was no less, perhaps much more, important. MGM, which had no proprietary interest in Presley, was determined to make this movie on a shoestring.

The entire budget, apart from Elvis's salary, was $400,000: probably the smallest sum of money ever allocated to a Presley picture. Such a budget normally guaranteed that the product would be Grade Z schlock.

Colonel Parker couldn't have cared less about the quality of the movie. When Berman asked the Colonel if he should send the script to Elvis, the Colonel said no. "Do you want to read it?" persisted the surprised producer. Again, the Colonel said no. Suspecting a trap, Berman insisted: "What *do* you want?" The Colonel, no less surprised, replied: "I don't want nothin', except to get all the music I want in the picture and have it done by my boys." Even if the movie profits were small, the Colonel would reap his profits from the record sales and publishing royalties. No wonder he was so indifferent to the picture's quality. As for Elvis, he could always console himself with a fleet of new Cadillacs.

Holding down the budget meant in practical terms that none but the most mediocre supporting players would be employed, that the sets would be the cheapest back-lot interiors, that there would be no production numbers and that the shooting schedule would be the tightest humanly possible. Here the key man was the director. Berman knew from the first who he would use on this film; in fact, this director was to work with Elvis again so it's good we get his professional profile from his boss. As Pandro Berman saw him: "Richard Thorpe was the fastest director on earth. He never looked at a script. He never tried to butt into the story. He never interfered with casting. He was just the most efficient shooter you could buy. Any time you wanted a picture shot on a budget and a schedule that was very tight, you got Richard."

Born under so many bad signs, *Jailhouse Rock* was saved from its natural fate by one man and one man only: its writer, Guy Prosper. Already a respected scenarist and later a writer who was nominated a number of times for awards in connection with such successful films as *Birdman of Alcatraz* and *The Spy Who Came in from the Cold,* Prosper was not the sort of man who would normally be called on to crank out this kind of film. Both Berman and Hereford were apprehensive that he would decline the job; but they played their hand right, promising Prosper that if he helped the studio with this little project, he could expect something much better the next time around.

Virtually every screenwriter who ever did a Presley picture made some use of the Presley Myth: What sets Prosper and his screenplay apart from all the others is his debunker's attitude toward the Myth. Instead of treating it sympathetically in the Hollywood tradition of glamourizing the star as an innocent kid with an unwitting genius for turning people on, Prosper inverts the convention and makes the Myth into a rock 'n' roll version of *What Makes Sammy Run?* His rock star is a once-innocent but always hot-tempered and violent kid who has been embittered and wised up by a stretch in prison. A cruel, ego-tripping punk, he's interested less in fame than he is in money and power. Being basically a prick—or sometimes a bitch—he is a character with some dramatic definition instead of being the juvenile jellyfish that Elvis was normally condemned to play.

Looking at the film today, it reads almost like a deadpan but caustic documentary on the early days of the rock and record business. Instead of showing the hero as a charismatic figure flailing around in front of madly enthusiastic audiences, the whole picture takes place behind the scenes, in the then unfamiliar world of the recording studio, the TV studio, the offices of larcenous record producers and shyster attorneys. The heroine, a good-natured, attractive but essentially maternal girl, is introduced as being an "exploitation girl" for a record company. How's that for an "inside" characterization? Instead of the characters talking about the thrills of performing or how much they love the fans, the conversations are normally confined to commercial strategies and money: Elvis is even made to pronounce the phrase "capital gains" (which in his mush-mouthed accent is irresistibly funny). In short, this pioneering account of the Big Rock Candy Mountain is much closer to the truth than any picture about rock ever made subsequently, the scammy, squalid and often tragic history of the music having never once made a dent in the simpleminded adolescent infatuation on which the whole Rock Age rests.

The picture, which is informed throughout by a very sarcastic sense of humor, opens up with a shot that is a parody of Elvis's first appearance on the screen in *Love Me Tender*. Instead of showing this son of the soil plowing behind a mule team with reins around his neck, you see Elvis, sporting his famous smile, riding a grotesque-looking excavating machine like a mechanical camel. He's a working stiff, as always; and, as soon became the convention in all his films, he's pretty quick with his fists. On payday, he's drinking it up with the boys in a bar when one dude makes some very ungentlemanly remarks about an aging slattern and the honorable young Elvis punches him in the mouth. In the ensuing brawl, Elvis inadvertently kills his adversary. Like the hero of any old blues, he goes straight to prison. Here he is caged with a marvelous character: a barrel-shaped good ole boy named Hunk Houghton, who is an ex-country music singer and the boss of all the prison rackets.

Elvis is dumb and slow; Hunk is hip and fast. He works earnestly at giving the kid the game. He also demonstrates his singing prowess, offering to teach Elvis a few guitar chords. Elvis responds by outsinging Hunk, which earns him a spot on a corny little TV show which is broadcast from the prison to prove how jolly life is in the joint.

When a load of fan mail arrives at the prison for Elvis, Hunk suddenly snaps to the fact that the kid might be a property. Concealing the mail from Elvis, he cons him into signing a fifty-fifty partnership deal. Naturally, there would be those in the audience who would associate this scene with the way they imagined the fat ole Colonel got Elvis's name on the dotted line.

Even in prison Elvis's temper is not dampened; he gets into a free-for-all in the mess hall that leads up to one of the kinkiest scenes in any rock movie: a stripped-to-the-waist, wrists-tied-to-the-rail flogging that must have brought some very troubled memories back to haunt Vernon Presley. Eventually, however, the kid is cut loose to make his way in the world doing the corny country songs and licks that he has learned from his music teacher, Hunk. Big-hearted Hunk even gives the kid the name of a cabaret and its owner in some distant city, implying that all Elvis has to do is walk in the door, say, "Hunk sent me," and he'll be given a job.

Now we get some of that classic guitar-man imagery that springs right out of the soul of rock, but which quickly fades from the genre Presley picture. Elvis is shown a room in a SLEAZY HOTEL; he goes to a cheap JOINT (which has neon champagne glasses on its façade); he meets the classic bald-headed, cigar-smoking, geriatric NIGHTCLUB OWNER; he discovers that the only job he can get is as BUSBOY! Ah, it's a good, solid shaming he takes here; and, with his temper, you know he ain't gonna take it but *so* long! There's one worse thing that can happen to him, however: He can jump onstage without permission, crank up his guitar, sing his song, and then BOMB! In fact, he can do even worse: All the while he's singing in a very soulful voice, some middle-aged jackass sitting at ringside with a cute young chick can be telling stories (traveling salesmen jokes, doubtless) and braying with LAUGHTER right through Elvis's song. Well, sir, that leads to the kicker: the moment when the kid comes leaping off the stage like a cougar and SMASHES HIS GUITAR to smithereens right on the jackass's table. Now, that's what you call good early punk and it's a pity that Elvis, the proto-Punk, never got to do it again.

No sooner does Elvis go charging out of the club than this girl he met at the bar, this "exploitation girl" for Geneva Records, which has a big star named Mickey Alba (Frank Sinatra, Perry Como, Vic Damone, etc.), comes running out after him. As they go driving off in her convertible, she tells him that he wasn't very good. When he won't listen to her, she urges him to make a custom recording and hear how he actually sounds to the public. Here, of course, we're tracking right into the famous Sun studio; and in the sequence that follows, one wonders whether Elvis, who was in charge of the music in this picture, might not have reproduced pretty accurately what happened at the famous first session in 1954. His new girl brings him a backup band that consists of Scotty Moore, Bill Black and D. J. Fontana plus Mike Stoller on piano.

The first time he sings his song, "Treat Me Nice," it's very similar to those sentimental things he did first at Sun. Then, after he hears the playback, he decides to jump up the tune just as he jumped up "That's All Right Mama." Like many features of this highly realistic movie, this sequence hovers on the border between a fiction that is based on reality and a reality that is like something out of fiction. In any case, the session ends with a new style being born. Now it's just a question, so Elvis thinks, of getting the record produced.

Elvis has yet to learn the truth about the record business. When he plays his demo for a coolly indifferent producer at Geneva, he's told that they aren't interested. As he's leaving, though, the producer suggests that the demo be left with him overnight so that he can play it "over the wire for J. R. in New York." Inevitably, the whole concept is pirated. Elvis discovers in the booth of a record store that the tune he was on the verge of bringing out on another label is already Mickey Alba's latest hit on Geneva. "He stole my style, my—everything!" cries Elvis, the boy who in real life stole so much from so many singers.

The movie Elvis rallies quickly and decides to take the game into his own hands. Forming a partnership with his record lady, he goes into business for himself. Next time you see him in the studio, he's Elvis Presley for sure: doing a typical Leiber and Stoller tune and making with the motions, just as Elvis always did while cutting his records.

At this point in the story, the relations between Elvis and his partner have become rather sticky. She's in love with him, of course. But he's so self-absorbed, he hardly knows she exists. He insists, when asked, that their relationship is based strictly on money. What confuses her is the inconsistency of his behavior. One night she takes him out to suburbia to see her folks. They're typical of college-town eggheads. When they learn that Elvis is in the music business, they start to gabble about progressive jazz. This drives the movie Elvis just as crazy as it would the real-life Elvis, who hated jazz because he couldn't understand it.

When Elvis and the girl hit the street, she scolds him for his attitude. He silences her with a very brutal kiss. When she angrily demands: "What made you think I'd fall for a cheap move like that?" he replies, "That was no cheap move—that was (smirk) the beast in me." Again, proto-Punk, but, alas, as so often happened when Elvis tried to act tough and "hoody" on the screen, he muffs the line, which has to be delivered with a rather complex amalgam of scoffing, sneering and swaggering.

Success follows now that Elvis has taken everything into his own hands. He ties in with a creepy lawyer, who manages the business. He talks percentages and volume sales. He's just about to make his first big appearance on TV, when out of nowhere comes old Hunk, fresh out of the can after doing an eighteen-year stretch. Hunk demands a shot at the tube; the kid warns him that he's hopelessly out of date. Hunk's number is cut by the producer, but Elvis stars in the most brilliant song and dance routine to be found in any Presley picture: the "Jailhouse Rock" number.

This famous bit of footage was just an afterthought by the producers of the film. It wasn't part of the original scenario or budget but when Alex Romero, the dance director, came up with the idea of choreographing the title song, another $25,000 was found for the sequence. Presley purists put down this number as too slick and chorus-boysy. Actually, it was the one time in Elvis's entire career when somebody with a bit of skill and authority got the kid to move as if he knew where he was going. The jivey strutting style he adopts is perfectly in keeping with his natural body language; the only difference is that instead of faking all his moves with the force of a football lineman hurling himself down a row of staggered car tires, Elvis makes his moves with definition and style.

The worst feature of the picture is its melodramatic ending. Hunk, a schlub but still a man, grows enraged at the way Elvis abuses his long-suffering exploitation girl. He socks the kid in the jaw and then— God forbid!—in the throat. Elvis loses his voice and there is much pother about whether he will ever sing again. When he strikes up "Loving You," you're supposed to be overwhelmed with joy, but if you're a music buff, you note with disgust that Leiber and Stoller have failed, as usual, to write a good ballad: The song sounds like a saloon version of "Love Me Tender."

The other criticism of the film is that Elvis walks through it like a storeroom dummy instead of an actor. The sweetness he projects in his first picture and the sullen self-involved anger he exudes in his second picture are followed here by what became his standard screen role: the smug, stupid, embarrassingly self-conscious screen rooster. It's too bad the bait didn't take because Elvis never again got to appear in any picture that offered him such marvelous opportunities to confront himself.

Chapter 17

Boy-Man

W HEN ELVIS got back to Memphis in the summer of 1957, he found Graceland completely renovated. The walls were pure white with cornices of gold-leafed dentilation. The floors were covered with thick white shag carpeting. The windows were hung with floor-to-ceiling drapes, red for the winter, blue for the summer, opened and closed by concealed motors. The furniture was oversized and custom built: huge slabs of foam rubber upholstered in nubby fabrics. Smoked-glass mirrors covered whole walls and glass-topped tables added to the feeling of lightness and glitter in the once dark and decrepit rooms of the old mansion.

Elvis exulted in the appearance of his rock palace. He was also amused by the homey country touches that his parents had added to the grand design. The original Beverly Hillbillies, Gladys and Vernon had installed behind the neoclassic, Victorian eclectic house such humble rural structures as a chicken coop and a hog pen. Vernon, who had claimed that he was no longer able to work, labored for hours stuffing sausages in his big garden, where he grew purple hull and crowder peas, cabbages and tomatoes, pole beans and peppers, "Eyetalian" squash and eggplant. Around the grounds strutted a couple of screaming peacocks that would enrage everyone when they jumped up on the hood of a gleaming Cadillac or Lincoln to scratch at their reflections in the windshield. In the afternoon, the folks would go out for a drive. Gladys would take her tin of Garret snuff, her snuff-dipping stick and a Maxwell House coffee can for a spittoon. Vernon would take a chaw of good tobacco, Bull of the Woods or Day's Work. Then, they'd get into a brilliantly hued Fleetwood and take off for a little run over to the Nichols's place or out the road, where they could buy ripe watermelons.

Elvis, for his part, threw himself into all those pleasures that appealed most to his adolescent heart. Indeed, you could say that his primary goal once he became famous was to turn back the clock to that time when he was a wretched little cipher at Humes and relive those bad old days so as to experience them the second time around in precisely the opposite manner. Instead of being a pariah, he was now the richest, handsomest, most popular kid in the school.

Instead of appearing at the Rainbow Rollerdome teetering self-consciously on a pair of skates he couldn't manage, praying for some young girl from church to recognize him, Elvis would rent the whole damn place after midnight, when normally it shut down, and throw a wild skating party for at least forty kids that would last till dawn. Everything would be laid on in a style that would thrill any teenager's heart. The electric organ would play Elvis's favorite skating tunes. The chili dogs and Hoagies would be on the house. When you went to the skate-renting counter and gave the man your size, he would offer the skates for free. Presiding over the entire entertainment would be your gracious and charming host, the boy with the most, Elvis! Yeah!

The appearance of this palace of pleasure? On the outside, it rather resembled a rambling one-story brick church, with high arched windows and gothic parapets. Inside, it was a typical high-school gym: a Quonset-arched ceiling supported by exposed steel trusses; suspended from the ceiling, a couple of big gas heaters with whirling fans and shiny, galvanized tin exhaust pipes; a vast wooden floor marked off in circles and quadrangles; a pipe railing protecting the spectator seats; bare walls adorned with a number of large reproductions of religious paintings, such as the Crucifixion; some swags of red-white-and-blue bunting hanging from the rafters; and there, in the middle, suspended from a crossbeam, a big electric sign, ribbed with neon, flashing imperatively: "Couples."

Not content with just throwing the party, Elvis would dictate every move on the floor. Inspired to fulfill his most cherished fantasies, he invented a novel game called War. Oh, it was hell on wheels! Just the preparations for the event would scare off many of the guests. First, a large supply of pads and protective bandages would be handed about, as if in preparation for a nice lethal game of ice hockey. Then, the first-aid team would take up its position at the side of the arena, busying itself with opening boxes of Band-Aids and uncorking various flasks and bottles of antiseptics, anesthetics and restoratives. Next, sides would be chosen, with perhaps eight men to a team. Girls were not allowed to play as a rule, though an exception was made for one extraordinarily tough tomboy named Linda Mulinex. Linda was Miss Hell on Wheels.

The object of the game was to floor the members of the opposite team by any means possible. Basically, it was a free-for-all on skates. The two teams would line up at opposite ends of the rink, with Junior Smith, who acted as referee, standing in the middle of the floor. Junior would glare right and left—making psychotic grimaces—to assure himself that everybody was ready. Then, he would blow a shrill blast on a whistle, straining so hard that he would double over from the waist. Instantly, the two ranks of players would come charging down on each other, wooden wheels slamming against the wooden deck, bodies going into bends and crouches, with elbows thrust out in postures of attack or defense.

Sonny West recalls vividly the first time he played War. He was introduced to Elvis by Red West, Sonny's cousin, who identified the big boy in the flattop as "fresh meat." The next thing he remembers is skating full tilt at this Linda Mulinex. "Hell!" thinks Sonny, a 190-pound football player, "I don't wanna hit no girl!" Veering off to one side, he tries to skate past her. Linda comes right at Sonny, spinning in a dizzying cartwheel. Instinctively, Sonny throws out a muscular arm and knocks her to the floor. Next thing he knows, Linda has recovered and is hard on his tail. Before he can make his clumsy feet execute a turn, she comes up behind him and gives him a sharp chop with her forearm right behind his knee. Sonny drops as if shot.

Scrambling to his feet gamely, he's about to get under way again, when he feels another hatchetlike chop behind his knee. Again, he takes a header. After he's been cut down a few more times, Sonny scrambles for the safety of the sidelines. There, he hangs to the wall, panting hard and looking ruefully at the busted-out knees of his new Levis. Instantly, Elvis is beside him, demanding, "What are ya doin'?" Sonny waves toward Linda and gasps, "I'm stayin' away from *her!*" "Then you're not playin'?!" raps Elvis. "I *can't* play!" cries Sonny. "Every time I get ready to hit someone, I find myself on my butt! You keep that damn girl away from me, an' I'll git out there." Elvis gave the necessary orders and got Linda off Sonny's ass. That did not end the big boy's problems, however. Before the night was over, he had had his cheek split open and been knocked cold by a shot to the head from a pair of skates. Each time he was laid out, the first-aid team rushed to his rescue. Sonny was impressed at how efficient they were: They even had sophisticated "butterfly" bandages to close the cut on his cheek instead of using a needle and thread.

Though War was violent and dangerous, the game that frightened Sonny the most was the Whip. Once he was so unlucky as to wind up at the tail end of a giant whip that numbered thirty skaters. As they raced around the rink, the speed of their motions went up and up. On a fast turn at the end of a line of thirty people, a skater could be doing thirty miles an hour! It was on one of these racecourse turns that Sonny suddenly lost his grip and went flying off at a tangent like a man shot from a cannon. He hit the guard rails at the side of the floor and went flying over them to land in the wooden seats. He was lucky that night to get out with his life.

Did Elvis expose himself to similar risks on the floor? His participation in these violent skating games, as in the equally dangerous games of football he loved to play, appears to have been something less than absolute. Though he threw himself into the game for all he was worth, there was an understanding among the players that Elvis was not to be damaged. If someone got into the game who didn't understand the unspoken rule or who had the temerity to go after Elvis deliberately, Red and Sonny would soon improve this fool's knowledge of the sport. Once one of the skating instructors got the dumb idea of impressing his girlfriend by dumping Elvis. Red and Sonny soon settled his hash. While Red skated into the hapless pro from one side, Sonny struck the showoff such a blow that he flew clean through a hole in the guardrail and smashed himself to bits against the seat barricade. When a player's injuries were too grave for the first-aid team, it was customary to summon an ambulance and cart him off to the hospital.

When the roller rink no longer appealed to him, there were always other and even more dangerous recreations. One of these was motorcycle racing. Elvis would have the Shelby County police shut down a stretch of Highway 51 late at night. Then, he and one of the other boys would crank up their big Harley-Davidsons to enjoy some sport. As everyone knows who's ever ridden with one of these massive hogs between his legs, there's something deeply thrilling about the experience of being astraddle a really mighty bike. If you run the monster up to those speeds, in excess of 100 m.p.h., which it's capable of attaining, the thrill becomes even keener. What Elvis most enjoyed was putting the final cherry on top of this elaborate sundae of nocturnal speed and danger. As he and Lamar Fike would roar down the empty highway, they would pull up beside each other, adjust their positions and then reach out—to touch hands at 120 m.p.h. A Michelangelesque moment!

Was all this just good clean fun? No, of course not. It was the kind of crazy, compulsive behavior that characterized everything Elvis Presley did. Not only was Elvis intent on rewinding the dreary spools of his dismal high-school career to relive the past in triumph: He was just as determined to live down the reputation of being a sissy, which he had incurred when he was under his mother's thumb. Elvis was bent on demonstrating to his little world—and later, to the whole world!—that he was a macho man. He would take all the risks, including the risks nobody has to take. He would play with the big bad boys and beat them at their own games. He would experience what southerners have always been best at experiencing: the ecstasy of self-destruction. They call it "Going to Jesus."

Elvis's other amusements in Memphis were of a more pacific, if not of a more conventional character. He had always enjoyed the movies. Now that he was a movie star, he enjoyed them even more. Only, he felt that he should enjoy movies in the manner that best suited him. Why should he experience the inconveniences of viewing films in public theaters? Why should he have to incur the cost of building a movie theater on his property at Graceland? There was another solution readily available to him. He could lease a neighborhood movie house for the hours when he most wanted to see the latest pictures. This sensible decision soon gave rise to a remarkable practice: nothing less than the King's first full-blown courtly ritual.

Like everything Elvis did for fun, the movies would invariably begin after midnight. Their venue would change, depending on circumstances, but the typical site was the Memphian: a small, 1940-ish Art Deco house located in the area of Ovington Square, about a ten-minute drive from Graceland. During the day, one of Elvis's boys would have called the man who booked the first-run pictures for the big downtown houses. Elvis had his pick of all the pictures scheduled for release in Memphis within the next six weeks. His tastes could be summed up in one word—action. He had no use for love stories, musicals or straight dramas. He wasn't keen on westerns either. His real joy was who-done-its, terror movies and certain kinds of comedy. To make sure that he would not be disappointed by the selection, at least three or four feature films would be on hand when he arrived at the theater.

Elvis displayed an attitude compounded of magnanimity and exhibitionism at his private screenings. He didn't mind if as many as a hundred fans or other members of the hoi polloi shared the picture with him, provided they knew their place and showed him the proper respect. This crowd of commoners would gather at the front of the theater long before Elvis's arrival, tipped off by the members of the young King's entourage. Elvis would enter invariably through the stage door and take his favorite seat in the empty theater, about twelve rows back in the center. No one was permitted to sit in front of or beside him except his date, who was always seated to his left. On his right, a small table was placed on which were arranged his little Hav-a-Tampa cigars, his Pepsi, his chewing gum and, later in the evening, his food, which was brought in from all-night hamburger stands and pizza parlors. Once the King had been enthroned, the front doors of the theater would be thrown open and his guests would enter, taking their seats at the back of the house.

During the hours from midnight to dawn, the regular staff of the theater would be on duty. You could go back to the snack stand and get your fill of hot buttered popcorn. You could give an order to a gofer who would run out to bring back pizzas and cheeseburgers. If you wanted to go to the men's room while Elvis was inside, you had to wait until the King had completed his toilet. Elvis never went to the john without his henchmen, who stood guard at the door until he was ready to return to his seat. In this as in every other feature of the evening, he enjoyed absolute control.

If the film did not interest him, he would shout at the projectionist to turn it off and go on to the next offering. If, on the other hand, the movie interested him greatly, he might order it rerun. Once he saw *Dr. Strangelove* three times running, from about 1:00 in the morning till 5:30; then he had the last reel repeated about three times more, explaining that Peter Sellers was such a subtle actor you could not understand exactly what he was doing in just a few viewings. If the movie were interesting but it slowed down for a love scene, Elvis would do a little spontaneous editing, demanding that the unexciting scene be omitted and the projectionist get on to the next good part. Sometimes, so much footage was omitted that the party had to break up early because the supply of film on hand had been exhausted.

Elvis enjoyed the acting of heavies: his favorites numbered Marlon Brando, George C. Scott, Clint Eastwood and even Frank Sinatra in a serious role. He wasn't impressed by women on the screen, and he virtually never looked at one of his own films. On the very rare occasions when he would screen one of his own pictures, everyone would be barred from the theater but Elvis and his closest associates. Generally speaking, he found his own pictures very hard to take. "Who's that fast-talkin' southern sonovabitch up there?" he would challenge, looking at himself. In later years, he would examine his image with horror, exclaiming, "Too fat! Too fat!"

The only quiet, private pleasure that Elvis enjoyed was the poignant experience of nostalgia. Though revisiting the scenes of one's childhood is a satisfaction sought generally by the middle-aged or elderly, from the age of twenty-one on Elvis Presley was often engrossed in contemplating his humble origins. Taking along a trusted confidant, he would drive slowly and thoughtfully around the Lauderdale Courts, past Humes High, through Overton Park, recalling aloud the experiences and emotions he associated with these places. Sometimes, he would drive down to Tupelo and show his friends where he had grown up, stressing the extreme poverty of his childhood and brooding deeply over the most dilapidated sections of the town. To avoid attracting attention, especially in Memphis where the appearance of one of his cars was certain to summon up a spontaneous escort, he would put a disguising cap on his head and go out for his reminiscent cruise in a panel truck that was used to haul garbage off the property at Graceland. Driving along in low gear, sometimes late at night, once again a truck driver with a little cap on his head, Elvis would get deep and bluesy contemplating his awesome translation from a slum project to a palace.

Elvis always stressed the vital fact that he had made his money while he was still young and able to enjoy it. The attainment of wealth in middle age was a goal he scorned. Happiness, in his view, was a condition possible only in youth. No matter what you had when you were older, it would be vitiated by the very fact that you were older. Age was the enemy of joy. The real goal of life was never to succumb to age. One of the reasons Elvis would spend so much time examining his face in mirrors was to see if he could discern the first faint traces of the aging process.

If he discovered a line forming in his skin, he would quickly apply facial creams or lotions designed to restore the skin to its babylike natural smoothness. If he detected some slight loss of hair from his comb, he would shout in anguish. Sometimes he made minuscule marks on his scalp with his eyebrow pencil, taking care each day not to wash these little dots away. They marked his hairline and their purpose was to enable him to measure any recession of this vital line, this lifeline. As for grey hair, he knew that would come early because premature greying was characteristic of the Presleys. Fortunately, it posed no problems once he had begun to dye his hair. In his thirties, Elvis's hair was thickly streaked with grey. To paraphrase the ad, "Only his hairdresser knew." He also began to dye his eyebrows and even his eyelashes. No hair was too small or inconspicuous to escape his careful scrutiny. If the enemy of life were age, a man had to confront his foe with the vigilance of a soldier posted on a dangerous frontier.

The only other danger that Elvis faced were the cranks whom Gladys dreaded so much. The first serious threat from one of these crazies surfaced one morning in August, when word came up from the gate that an FBI man had arrived who wanted to speak with Elvis. Elvis and the boys met the agent in the living room. He showed his identification and then popped open an attaché case. Reaching inside, he confronted them with a letter which he held between the second knuckles of each index finger. "I want you to look at this carefully," he said. "This is a death threat from somebody upstate. We already know the town where it was postmarked. What I want you to tell me is do you recognize anything about this letter?" Elvis looked at the letter closely and read it slowly aloud. "No matter how you try to get away from us, we will kill you by gun or by bomb. Either from another car or a person or an airplane." Elvis was shocked. "Is this for real?" he asked the agent. "You have to treat it as if it were," the man replied. "Do you carry a weapon?" Elvis replied, "No, but I think I'll start." That marked the beginning of a practice that eventually developed into a mania.

After the FBI man left, Elvis and the boys sat down to breakfast. "I don't understand this," said Elvis. "Why would someone want to kill me?" Lamar replied: "Hey, man, maybe somebody's so pissed off at what you've become that he just wants to cut you down out of envy." "Well," says Elvis, "they're not gonna get me without a battle." The boys looked at each other mutely. Then Elvis exclaimed: "This is ridiculous! Let's go see some movies or something!"

Lamar was all for seeing movies that afternoon. "All right," the big fat boy said, "let's go!" Elvis hesitated for a moment; then he said with studied casualness, "Go outside and crank the car—I'll be with you in a minute." Lamar made a face: half smirking, half quaking. "This is like one of those Al Capone movies," he complained. "You want me to go out and crank the car. If it blows up, I'm the one that goes!"

By the time they got out of the last movie, it must have been nearly eleven o'clock in the evening. Elvis had his whole gang with him that night: George Klein, Gene Smith, Cliff Gleaves and Lamar. As always, they had parked the car in an alley behind the theater. "Lamar, go crank it up," says Elvis. Lamar went through the ritual, opening the hood, getting under the car, doing the whole checkout, while Elvis explained to the other guys what he feared. Finally, Lamar jumped in the driver's seat, hit the ignition and jumped out like a madman. The car hummed smoothly. At that point, all the boys piled aboard and took off for Graceland, with Elvis at the wheel.

As they drove home through the night, a rainstorm came down on the car, dampening the mood of hilarity. Approaching the gate at Graceland, they were just about to start up the driveway when suddenly, out of the darkness, stepped a strange man. He signaled to Elvis to open his window. Lamar was frantic. "Elvis, go on through, don't stop, don't open no window, this may be it!" Elvis said, "I gotta find out what this guy wants." With that he rolled down the window and the man stuck his head in the car. His approach was so sudden and direct that Elvis whipped out his gun and Lamar backed him up instantly with another gun which they had stashed in the car. Holding two pistols just inches from the man's face, they demanded virtually in the same breath: "What do you want?" The man stared at them in astonishment for a moment. Then, he gasped: "I want an autograph for my daughter."[1]

The most curious feature of Elvis's life-style in this early period is his pattern of relations with women. Almost any other boy, given the opportunities that Elvis was granted, would have behaved more wickedly. Nothing wipes out moral restraints and psychological inhibitions faster than enormous wealth, popularity and power. Though everyone who derives his success from public endorsement, from rock stars to ministers of the gospel, recognizes the necessity to be wary of public disgrace, the greater the powers a man achieves, the greater the possibilities for dissembling his sins. Elvis Presley at the height of his glory could have indulged himself in the most outrageous manner if he had so desired. The curious thing is that once he became famous, Elvis behaved as if he didn't dare to step over the line of conventional morality.

---

[1] The FBI apprehended the writer of the threatening letter, who turned out to be an emotionally disturbed young woman. In striking anticipation of John Lennon's murderer, she had threatened first to commit suicide. Instead, she committed herself to a mental institution.

In this connection, it is illuminating to see what Elvis made of his sexual opportunities once he had become a movie star. Hollywood and Las Vegas offered him endless possibilities for gratification. In a couple of years he might have compiled a record of conquests that would have put Casanova in the shade. Instead, what did he do? First, he dedicated himself to a couple of self-involved stars, who regarded him as either a foolish bumpkin or the ideal Coke date. Then, having extended the field of his conquests to Las Vegas, where *everybody* gets laid, Elvis fell into the pattern of inviting the more appealing girls to Memphis and Mama— not precisely the behavior of a rake. Finally, having had his first little fling with the starlets and the show girls, he gave up the whole enterprise as a bad show and retreated to the pleasures of his home town.

Most of these pleasures had nothing to do with sex. If Freud hadn't destroyed the notion that there is some time in life when we have not yet discovered sexual pleasure, one might be tempted to describe Elvis's adventures in Memphis as "presexual." They were certainly highly immature. His most gratifying relationship with the members of the opposite sex was a very cozy foursome he established between himself and three fourteen-year-old girls who were ardent fans. These girls accompanied him to the movies, the amusement park and roller rink. They joined him in warm weather for evenings around the swimming pool. They would grieve when he left for a tour or a film production. They would rejoice when he returned and their accustomed life with him resumed. They spent the last days with him before he entered the service and visited him in Texas before he left for Germany. Not until Elvis had returned from the service and invited Priscilla Beaulieu to live with him at Graceland did the trio Elvis called "the old gang" break up. Because they spent so much time with Elvis and because their relationship was of a sort that was clearly an ideal fulfillment for Elvis, it is important to see how the first rock star related to the first circle of groupies.

Gloria Mowel was the first of the three girls to meet Elvis and the one who introduced to Elvis the other two: Heidi Heissen and Frances Forbes. Gloria's father worked for an Oldsmobile agency that operated a garage the Presleys patronized. One day when this kind father saw Elvis's car in the garage, he got the idea of trying to wangle an invitation for his daughter to meet the hero of Memphis. When Vernon Presley came in to pick up the car, Mr. Mowel told the star's father about his teenage girl, who was such a dedicated Elvis fan. Vernon agreed to arrange a visit.

On that great day, whose date Gloria can never forget—October

11, 1956—she rang the bell at 1034 Audubon Avenue. Instead of being ushered into the presence by a maid, Gloria was suddenly confronted by Elvis himself. Entering the house, she recognized "Ruby Baby," a recent hit by Billy Ward and His Dominoes (whom Elvis loved), playing loudly on the phonograph in the den. Elvis offered her a Pepsi and they started a conversation—which continued on and off for the next five years. Elvis, Gloria soon perceived, was both very emotional and very lonely. He was drawn to girls, but he didn't trust them because he couldn't be sure whether they were crazy about him or just his public image. Though Elvis was always the center of attention wherever there was a crowd, a position he demanded and sometimes connived to obtain, when he was alone with Gloria or the other girls, he seemed better pleased. In such intimate meetings, he was very low-keyed, quiet, playful and apt to chatter endlessly about the most trivial things.

Once Elvis found a person or a thing he liked, it became an obsession with him. As soon as Gloria had won Elvis's confidence, she was always invited to the house. She would accompany Elvis on his usual round of amusements, but she also spent a lot of time with him at the house, either out in the back, where he would shoot his BB gun, or in his bedroom, where they would sometimes engage in furious pillow fights with feathers flying everywhere. Elvis loved to roughhouse with his teen-age girls. They loved it, too—until he went "too far." As Gloria recalls: "We'd tickle, fight, laugh, mess around; but all you'd have to say is, 'Stop!', and he'd roll over and quit. It would never be mentioned again that night. But next time, it would be the same thing exactly. You'd fight with him, kid around and scuffle. The next thing, he'd get serious and you'd just push him away. I think that if he really pushed, I would have done it. But he had a saying he told me once: 'I'll never break a virgin. There's too many prostitutes walking around.' "

Though all three of these girls were going to junior high, their nights with Elvis generally ran till three or four in the morning, his usual hours. Making the rounds with Elvis, they might drop in on Dewey Phillips's show and then drive out Poplar Avenue to Joe Cuoghi's record store, Popular Tunes, where they'd sit around after closing, playing all the new sides. Then, Elvis would want to go home and eat a big meal, or, if it were warm, find some place that had cold watermelons and bring them back so that they could cut out their sweet red hearts and enjoy the southern farmer's late-night treat.

The best times were those nights when after tumbling in and out of the pool for a couple of hours, they would go upstairs with Elvis to have a real teenage pajama party. Elvis had a dressing room at the top of the stairs with a long mirror. The girls would bustle around Elvis, blowing his hair dry. He would say to Gloria and Heidi: "Frances was jealous tonight because I was throwing you in the pool." The girls would giggle and continue grooming their mutual "lover." When they had finished restoring Elvis to perfect condition, he might turn the tables and start lecturing them on how to apply their makeup. Elvis wanted them to wear heavy eye shadow and sophisticated, sexy makeup. He might even take the eyeliner and apply it himself. When everyone was looking pretty, they would troupe down the hall to Elvis's bedroom.

Elvis's favorite color at the time was dark blue, a drastic change from the pink and black he had favored a couple of years earlier. His bedroom had white walls, but the drapes and the spread over the enormous bed were blue with white leather piping. Behind the bed was a big smoked-glass mirror. Elvis and the three girls would all sit on the bed, yoga style, with him in the middle. He'd tickle one of the girls and make her toss and giggle. Then, he'd kiss her. Turning to another one, he'd say, "Gloria is jealous 'cause I kissed Frances" or "Frances is jealous 'cause I kissed Heidi." After they had tired of this play, Elvis would turn out the light. Then, he would lie down on the bed with an arm around a girl on each side and the third girl lying across his feet.

Nothing would be said during this blissful teenage *Liebestod*. The ecstasy was of that intensely quiet and motionless character that suggests the bliss of the fetus floating in the amniotic fluid. "You never wanted it to end," murmurs Gloria, when she thinks back on that experience today. "When you were in that room, you wanted to shut out the whole world for the rest of your life."

When the hour got very late, Elvis would sit up and kiss each of the girls in turn, saying: "I love you and I'll see you tomorrow. Now, get Lamar to take you home." The girls would come marching down the stairs to find Lamar dozing upright on the sofa. The fat boy's job was to sit up and wait for them. When he'd look at his watch and discover it was four A.M., he often panicked. What would the girls' parents say? Would he have to take the tongue-lashing that was directed at Elvis? Actually, nothing ever happened. Elvis had a great gift for disarming parents and persuading them that though their fourteen-year-old daughters spent a lot of time in his bedroom, nothing improper was going on. Perhaps he drew strength and conviction from the fact that these pajama parties were so innocent.

What Elvis found in the company of his three fourteen-year-old by a line of people waiting for a table. "Oh, lord! This is unbelievable!" the fat boy burst out. "How often do you get a chance to go out with someone like Elvis Presley?" The more Lamar tried to beat Anita down, the more stubborn she became. Finally, she said, "Tell him to call me again," and hung up the phone. Now, there was nothing for Lamar to do but acknowledge that the invitation of which every young woman in America dreamed had just been rejected.

Actually, Anita started crying the moment she got off the phone. She was convinced that Elvis would never call her again. She had lost her great opportunity. It was true, of course, that she was not an Elvis Presley fan. She had never bought one of his records nor gone to see him in person or on the screen. The only time she had seen him, in fact, was once when her mother called her into the living room and pointed at the TV set, saying, "Look at this boy from Memphis. Isn't he cute?" Still, you didn't have to be an Elvis Presley fan to know who Elvis was or what it meant to be asked out by him, especially if you were a girl trying to make a career of singing. Anita's principled behavior paid off, however; it made an impression on Elvis, who was always measuring people by the way they reacted to him, tempting them to grab and then despising them when they took. Two weeks later, he told Lamar to call Anita again. Meantime, George Klein had spoken with the young woman and made it clear that Elvis watched her show and was very taken with her appearance.

Her first date was a perfect introduction to the glamorous world of Elvis Presley. A huge black Cadillac limousine pulled up at Anita's door. The hulking Lamar, wearing a dark suit like a chauffeur, bustled out and escorted Anita to the car. When she sat down at some distance from Elvis, she got an instant flash of annoyance from the handsome star. The principal object of the evening was to cruise by the Strand Theater on Main Street, where the staff was erecting a cutout of Elvis above the marquee in preparation for the opening of *Loving You*. Back and forth the limousine crawled, as Elvis and his boys appraised the display. Then came the most impressive move of the night. As Anita recalls: "After a while we headed back out toward Whitehaven. Elvis called Chenault's, his favorite restaurant, on the car phone and asked them to have the private dining room ready in fifteen minutes." Sounds pretty heavy, doesn't it? The luxurious limousine, the car phone—whoever heard of such a thing in Memphis? Hey, this was the big time! The results of all this pomp and circumstance were not what might be anticipated. "When we got to Chenault's," continues Anita, "my ham-

burger and Elvis's special—a cheeseburger with bacon instead of hamburger meat—and all the trimmings—were already fixed and waiting
for us." At least they got what they ordered.

Once Elvis began to court Anita, he pressed his suit very hard. Just
two nights later, she was picked up again and taken to a special midnight
showing of *Loving You* that was restricted to Elvis, his family and friends.
Anita made a good impression on everyone. Three nights later, Elvis
picked her up again, this time in his white Lincoln, to "carry" her to
Graceland for supper.

The meal, which had been cooked by Mrs. Presley, was served by
a black maid. The menu? It was that traditional southern home cooking
that Elvis prized above any food in the world: sauerkraut and wieners,
blackeyed peas, tomatoes, potatoes and a huge coconut cake that Mrs.
Presley had baked herself. The only uncomfortable part of the evening
occurred when Elvis invited Anita upstairs to see his quarters. She was
very impressed by the smoked-glass mirror covering an entire wall behind
the enormous bed and the way the thick navy blue carpet ran into the
bathroom. No sooner had he shown her the bathroom, though, than
he started to get fresh with her. "I think he was fixin' to test me out,"
is the way Anita sees it now. "Boy! He got testy real quick! I was nervous.
I didn't know what to expect. I had heard so much back then about
him. I stood my ground and said, 'I think it's time for me to go home.'
That was about it."

Though Elvis had picked up his date, it was Lamar's job to take
her home. Lamar was not happy about the way the evening was ending.
He identified totally with Elvis: A rejection for his boss was a rejection
for Lamar. "Look," he stalled, "is there any way you can keep yourself
around here?" "No," insisted Anita, "I'll be going." Poor Lamar. He
was struck dumb. Always so loquacious when it didn't matter, now
the best he could offer was a hapless, "My God!" As Anita marched
out the front door, clutching the pink and black stuffed poodle that
Elvis had given her, the big fat boy with the gleaming D.A. opened
the door of the car and then slid behind the wheel to make his delivery.

Once again, standing her ground did Anita Wood no harm with
Elvis Presley. Elvis was accustomed to dividing women into good girls
and the other kind. Eventually, he would get to the point where, when
he first met a girl, he would say: "Are you a good girl?" If the answer
were, "Yes," that would be the end of his play. With Anita, Elvis felt
that he knew where he stood. There would be no crossing the line.
They could kiss and pet and carry on all they pleased, but the thing

itself would never happen. Not unless he married her. So, in all essential respects, Elvis's relationship with Anita was no different from his relationship with the Three Musketeers, Gloria, Heidi and Frances. In both cases there was a lot of playing around, but there was no boogeyin'. As Anita says, "I'd been taught that there were some things that you just save for marriage. I don't care what the situation is. Still, he knew that I loved him. He didn't have to worry about me. I think there were plenty that were always available. I saw evidences of it everywhere. I think he respected me."

Though Anita was not pressured to submit to Elvis sexually, she was forbidden on pain of instant banishment ever to reveal to anyone, even her closest friends, the character of her relationship with Elvis. No matter how much time they spent together or how long they were involved or how seriously they discussed marriage and having children, Anita was not permitted even to say that she was Elvis's steady girl. "Colonel Parker was the one he blamed for everything," says Anita. "Colonel Parker, he said, would not let us get married. For the sake of his career, we could not publicly admit that we liked one another or were going together. I always had to say that we were just friends because otherwise the publicity would hurt his image. He had to be free so that all the girls, the fans, could love him."

Though Anita could not assert that she was Elvis's steady girl, the relationship was common knowledge. When Elvis left in late August to tour the Pacific Northwest, he gave his "Little Beadie Eyes" a diamond ring garnished with sapphires. He kissed her publicly at the train station at Memphis, and the press published pictures both of the kiss and the ring on Anita's finger. Matters appeared to be taking their course.

At this moment Anita won yet another contest: *The Hollywood Star Hunt.* The semifinals took place at a movie house in New Orleans. Anita took along her entire family. As she stood in the backstage gloom behind a giant screen hearing the muffled voices of Jayne Mansfield and Tony Randall in *Will Success Spoil Rock Hunter?,* she offered up a little prayer. It was the same prayer that she always uttered before she stepped onstage: "Dear God, let me do my best and let me make the best of whatever happens." Then she strutted out under the glaring lights in a gleaming white bathing suit. After a quick change, she was back onstage in an evening gown singing in a husky, bluesy voice, "Walkin' After Midnight." She was declared the winner. What was even better, one of the judges offered to fly Anita to Hollywood immediately for a screen test. When Elvis called her that night from Spokane, he seemed as delighted as she was about the victory. "I told you all along you'd win, honey," he said. "It's wonderful. I'm so glad. My little girl's gonna be a movie star." A week later, they were reunited in Hollywood.

Elvis put Anita up at the Knickerbocker and showed her around town, just as he had done for his parents. When the night of his big concert at the Pan-Pacific Auditorium arrived, however, he did not invite Anita to the concert or the party afterwards in his hotel suite, a celebration to which all his friends in Hollywood had been invited. The absence of Anita Wood was noticed the next day by the gossip columnists. Undoubtedly, it was another instance of the policy Elvis had adopted—at the Colonel's behest—of holding himself apart from Anita on public occasions.

In any case, Anita had her own career to think about. Her screen test had been successful, and she had been signed to appear in two pictures, the first of which was titled *Girl in the Woods*. At this point, however, a sudden cloud appeared, which cast a pall over Anita's rosy prospects. The production company began to have financial troubles. Anita found herself unsure of what would happen next. It was a critical moment for her, a moment at which she needed support and counsel. Elvis could have provided the support and the Colonel the counsel; instead, matters took a very different and disappointing course.

Though Elvis had at first greeted Anita's success with enthusiasm, he now appeared to have cooled to the idea. Instead of sustaining her through this crisis in her career, he pleaded with her to give up the fight and come back to Memphis, where he was idle and wanting her. "Come home, Little," he would urge. "Just come home right now!" Anita, alone, confused, anxious, out of her depth, finally decided to give up and take comfort in her lover.

When she got back to Memphis, however, she found Elvis no more ready for marriage than he had ever been. Soon, Anita was back at work, picking up the pieces of her shattered career.

Chapter 18

The Last Days of Elvis the Pelvis

LATE in August 1957, Elvis and his entourage took off on what proved to be his last concert tour until the seventies. A three-week sweep of the Pacific Northwest, reaching up into Canada, this tour corresponded to a similar string of one-nighters that Elvis had played in the spring, commencing at Chicago and working up through the Northeastern states and over the border to Toronto, Montreal and Ottawa. The territory in each case was familiar to the Colonel from his days with the Royal American. The style of the tour was also reminiscent of the carnival. Elvis played nothing but football and soccer stadiums, using a flatbed trailer as a stage. His entrance was classic. Gotten up in a ten-thousand-dollar thread-of-gold and rhinestone tuxedo, which Colonel Parker had ordered from Nudie of Hollywood, Elvis would make the complete circle of the arena seated on the back of a white Cadillac convertible, waving at the crowd as if he were a circus star.

The ole Colonel was back in his element, traveling from town to town, in private pullman just as he had in his carnival days. He indulged himself in a frenzy of ballyhoo and contemplated the crowds with satisfaction. They were not impressive by modern standards. Ten thousand people was the largest audience Elvis drew;

the gross receipts for twenty shows were a mere $375,000. Alan Freed had taken in $300,000 the year before during twelve days at the New York Paramount without a superstar like Elvis. Freed, however, enjoyed the advantage of drawing on the greatest concentration of rock 'n' roll fans in the country; whereas Elvis Presley was never allowed to play New York at the height of his fame, being condemned instead to tour most of the time out in the sticks.

This observation raises the vital issue of the Colonel's basic ability as a manager. It is quite likely, for example, that even in 1957 Elvis had the same capacity to draw gigantic crowds that the Beatles evinced just eight years later. Nothing happened between 1957 and 1965 to make it easier to go from the little stadium to the big stadium; in fact, during those years rock 'n' roll lost its original power and lay dormant awaiting the revival produced by the "British Invasion." If the Colonel had been the genius of management that he appears in the Presley Myth, he would have seen and seized the fantastic opportunity that presented itself at this supreme moment. Instead of hustling Elvis through the provinces, Colonel should have steered his great attraction through all the major population centers of America and Europe, just as Barnum did with General Tom Thumb and later Jenny Lind. Instead of earning $25,000 for a show, Parker might have anticipated Sid Bernstein's mighty score at Shea Stadium in 1965, when 55,000 fans paid $385,000 to see a single performance by the Fab Four. Colonel Tom Parker was no Barnum. He was not even a Bernstein. He was just a canny, cautious, tight-assed old tent-show man who was so busy thinking of all the nickels and dimes he could collect with his corny pictures and programs that he never had the time or the mind (or did he just lack the *nerve?*) to go for the big score. It was not until other, more audacious men had blazed the way that Colonel Parker finally got into the biggest time and toured the aging Elvis through the super-bowl circuit in the seventies.

The Pacific Northwest tour ran smoothly until it reached Vancouver; then, all hell broke loose. The arrangement that night was the standard setup: the flatbed parked down near the goalposts and protected by a portable iron fence, which was guarded by a detachment of Canadian Mounties. The first half of the program passed without incident. The MC, an ex-vaudeville juggler named Howard Hardin, an old friend of the Colonel, told a couple of corny jokes, tossed a few objects in the air and then brought on the acts, which included: the Burns Twins and Evelyn, a tap trio; Joe Termini, a comedy violinist; Wells and the Four

Fays, a fast acrobatic team; Paul Desmond, an impressionist; and the Jordanaires, working the closing slot before intermission.

When Scotty, Bill and J. D. came out on the trailer to set up their instruments after the intermission, there was a noticeable swelling and heaving in the crowd on both sides of the field. When Elvis appeared, the crowd screamed so violently that it seemed they could not contain themselves. They couldn't. After the second number, both sides of the stadium were suddenly transformed into human waterfalls. Thousands of kids leaped out of their seats and came pouring onto the field so that they could get a close-up view of Elvis.

Now the Mounties were driven back to the iron fence, where they formed a thin red line. Elvis was getting a kick out of the fans' reactions. He began to tease and taunt the kids, sitting on the very edge of the stage with the mike bent down nearly parallel with the ground, making all sorts of inciting signs. For half a dozen numbers, he kept up this childish game, while the Mounties struggled ever more valiantly to hold back the surging mob. Finally, as Elvis leaped into a wild fast rocker, the crowd could take no more. Giving a tremendous shout, they came vaulting over the barricade.

Some kids were impaled on the iron and began to scream in agony. Others locked in hand-to-hand combat with the cops. Elvis yanked the mike off the stand and began to retreat, singing all the while. Suddenly, the Colonel screamed: "Get your ass off the stage!" Two guys reached out and grabbed Elvis, one under each armpit. They picked him up bodily and threw him into a car. Scotty Moore remembers running for his life with his guitar clutched in his hand. The crowd mounted the stage and began seizing everything in sight: music, equipment, chairs, stands. It was a good old-fashioned ass-kicking rock 'n' roll riot.

Next day the local press complained loudly, adding ruefully that not only had Elvis provoked the riot but he had also outdrawn the Canadian Exposition and was now somewhere south of the border, running like a bandit with all those Canadian dollars. The Colonel read the newspaper accounts aloud for the boys with great relish. Yes, sir! They had left town just like a scammy little carnival on the run.

When Elvis hit Hollywood in the last week in October for a pair of concerts at the Pan-Pacific Auditorium, he was all charged up and dying to show the movie people what he could do on a stage. He had played their game through three pictures; now they would play his! This moment was actually the pinnacle of his entire career. His album of songs from *Loving You* was Number One on the album chart. "Teddy

Bear" was still among the top ten on the singles chart. The *Peace in the Valley* EP (extended play) was the top record in that genre. The title song from *Jailhouse Rock* had just been released and would be by November 1 the Number One record in the country. On top of all that, the premier of *Jailhouse Rock* was scheduled for the week before Elvis's two concerts. No performer in the history of the business had ever had a greater concentration of hits and scores at a single moment in his career. Nor had anyone ever remotely approached this kind of success at the age of twenty-two. Elvis was on top of the world.

The old Colonel knew that this was a golden opportunity to demonstrate to the Hollywood brass just what his famous boy could produce in terms of both performance and box office. The Pan-Pacific was a big old exposition building with an interior shaped like an enormous Quonset hut. The seating consisted of temporary bleachers; the stage was built on nine-foot risers draped with blue velour. The capacity of the house was precisely 9,200 admissions. The Colonel decided to sell 9,200 tickets. He gave strict orders that there was to be no "paper": not one free ticket, even for the most important members of the press. By exacting every last dime from the dates, he contrived to gross $56,000 for two nights' work.

Elvis's first concert at the Pan-Pacific was the most notorious performance of his career. He had provoked scandal and complaints of obscenity many times before. He had had police cameras focused on him and outraged parents, teachers, clergymen and journalists denounce him aplenty. These things had always occurred, however, in provincial areas, where, presumably, the people were very square. L.A. was another story. Los Angeles, while not enjoying the reputation for tolerance that San Francisco has earned, was nonetheless one of the most sophisticated towns in America when it came to entertainment. When the Colonel stood in Elvis's dressing room on opening night and urged his boy to give "one helluva show," Elvis had no fears of censorship. Not in L.A. In fact, he probably wouldn't have had any trouble if it were not for the very special audience he had drawn.

Stacked up on the bleachers of the old hall that night were not nine thousand adults but nine thousand kids. Ninety percent of these kids were girls. The average age of these girls was thirteen. They were the hard-core Elvis fans: the ones who ran out and grabbed the first tickets that went on sale, which was the reason they had tickets when thousands of other people who wanted to see the show were turned away at the box office. These junior high girls had sat for nearly an hour in a state bordering on desperation as they viewed the idiotic antics of Colonel Parker's Time Loop Variety Circuit. Then, they had been turned out for an intermission so that the Colonel's hawkers could cut into the kids with an endless variety of souvenirs and chatzkahs. Now, at last, they were back on their hard board seats waiting with nearly hysterical tension for the appearance of their god.

When Elvis swaggered onstage that night, he got a blast of screams that nearly knocked him flat. He was a juicy piece of beefcake, all right, wearing the gold tux jacket with its rhinestone lapels over black trousers. (He had destroyed the gold trousers by leaping off the stage onto a cinder track in Seattle.) He was wearing one of his George Raft gangster black shirts with a gold four-in-hand tie. By now he had eschewed his trademark guitar so as not to spoil his new Hollywood look. When he slashed into his first number, "Heartbreak Hotel," the deafening wave of screams commenced again. It never stopped for the next forty minutes. As the girls screamed and cried and tore their hair and beat on each other in a frenzy; as they shouted and hollered and moaned in ecstasy; as they spoke, sang, cried aloud the words of each song in unison with Elvis—or even, according to some reports, lost control of their natural functions and reduced themselves to the condition of hapless infants who have to be "changed"—Elvis met every fresh outburst of mania with ever more extravagant gestures and grimaces, leg movements and hip swayings, knee-drops and flat-out falls on the stage.

After all these years in the "live," he had dredged up out of his memory of all the movies he had imbibed in his adolescence and all the gospel shows he had witnessed back home in Memphis an extraordinary vocabulary of stage antics and mannerisms. He loved above all else to impersonate the jive-ass nigger pimp, who snaps his elbows into his waist as he flings his long fingers out from bent wrists and then with a head tilted provocatively awry and a killing look in his eye, runs those tight elbows up his sides in a pants-hitching gesture that says, "Ahm ready for *any*thing, bitch!"

To the naive young girls, highly charged but highly repressed, these gestures were experienced as heavy turn-ons. They also were noted grimly by a number of local reporters. Yet, what really provoked the scandal that erupted the next day was none of this behavior but a purely spontaneous outburst of high spirits with which Elvis concluded the show.

Colonel Parker insisted always that when Elvis performed onstage, he should have parked conspicuously beside him the symbol of the company that sold his records. So on this, as on countless other nights, sharing the spotlight with Elvis was Nipper: the familiar RCA Boston Bull, with his head cocked cutely listening to "His Master's Voice." It had become Elvis's custom to reach out from time to time and give Nipper a friendly pat on the head. After all, the poor thing sat there so patiently all night. How could you ignore him completely? Especially during his last number, "Hound Dog," Elvis was likely to make play with Nipper. On this night in Hollywood, however, carried away by the audience's frenzy and by his own desire to give the greatest and most uninhibited performance of his career, Elvis suddenly abandoned all restraint. Throwing his arms around the huge dog, he flung himself with it on the floor and rolled over and over toward the stage apron. The girls went out of their minds at the sight of Elvis embracing this big, cute, lovable dog, almost as yummy as a teddy bear. They screamed their approval, as Elvis leaped to his feet and rushed offstage and into the waiting limousine. Some evil-minded adults, however, left the theater with the idea that Elvis had capped an obscene performance by pretending to bugger the dog!

When word was received at the headquarters of the Los Angeles Police Department that Elvis Presley was buggering a huge dog onstage as part of his show at the Pan-Pacific Auditorium, you can imagine the officers' reactions. They determined to do their duty. They called up Colonel Parker and warned him that Presley had better clean up his act and tone it down or face possible charges. Then, borrowing a leaf from the well-publicized procedures of the Jacksonville, Florida, authorities, the police arranged to have three sixteen-millimeter motion picture cameras set up in the auditorium for the second show to provide ocular evidence of the "act," in case it was deemed advisable to press obscenity charges.

When Elvis sat down to breakfast the afternoon following the first concert, he found the Colonel at the table, immersed, as always, in the morning papers. He made a point of reading aloud to Elvis a column in the *Mirror-News,* written by the entertainment editor, which read the riot act to Elvis. Commencing with its first word, "Sexhibitionist," and running on for more than a dozen paragraphs, the article assailed Elvis bitterly for giving an obscene performance aimed at exciting the "libidos" of "little girls." The writer was not content to castigate Elvis for doing "bumps and grinds" or "contrived sensual gestures" or producing music that was "a lascivious steaming brew": He went on to compare him with an "ancient Caesar" and the concert to "one of those screeching uninhibited party rallies which the Nazis used to hold for Hitler." It was a pretty startling review for a boy who prided himself on being so religious and so pious toward his mama.

When the Colonel concluded his reading, Elvis burst out in that rage that was always smoldering beneath the surface of his carefully contrived cool: "Those muthafuckahs! Ah never been obscene in mah life! Ahm 'bout sick o' this shit! Ah tell ya one damn thing—ahm gonna do one helluva show tonight! Ahm not gonna let 'em put me up agin a wall!"

When Elvis stepped out onstage that night, he found sitting at his feet a galaxy of young stars: Carol Channing, Rick Nelson, Russ Tamblyn, Venetia Stevenson, Sammy Davis, Jr., Nick Adams, Vince Edwards, Tony Franciosa, Rita Moreno, Debbie Minardos, Tommy Sands, and a number of others whose names mean nothing today. This was Raphael Campos's party. He had collected money from everyone who wanted to see the show and secured from Colonel Parker the entire first two rows of seats. In other parts of the hall were many other movie bigshots, including Hall Wallis and Abe Lastfogel. Colonel Parker, who had cornered the (battered secondhand Japanese) binocular concession, got his big thrill of the evening when he rented a pair of glasses to the famous producer and closed his hand around the big man's cash.

After Elvis had sung his first tune, he pointed to the cameras aimed at him and quipped: "I wonder if they're gonna release this in theaters?" Then, he continued in a more earnest vein: "I'm sorry this came up, but we're not gonna let it stop us from puttin' on the best show we can for you people. If they think it's obscene, that's their problem, not mine!" With that, he winked at the camera and put his hands around his head to form a halo. "I'm gonna be an angel tonight!" he cried. Then, as the house roared its approval, he went into his next song. Despite his defiant rhetoric, he did tone down his show, which met, nonetheless, with hysterical applause.

When Elvis got back to his dressing room, he found awaiting him a reporter from the British music journal, *Melody Maker.* "I made over a million dollars this year," Elvis crowed, "but I'm no musician at all. I can't play the guitar, and I never wrote a song in my life. Yet I get my name on songs, and I collect a third interest of *all* the songs I sing." Flashing a wry grin, he added: "There doesn't seem any point in my studying music." Having delivered these lines, which could have come from the script of *Jailhouse Rock,* he went off to the party that was awaiting him at the Beverly Wilshire.

Though Elvis was now a big man in American show business, he still partied like an adolescent kid. No drinking was permitted in his presence, no drugs—God forbid!—and, as far as eating was concerned, sandwiches and chocolate cake furnished forth the victory banquet. With a room full of movie stars, what would you suppose the entertainment to be? Believe it or not, those who were disposed to be entertaining took turns imitating famous movie stars. Sammy Davis, Jr., got behind a desk at one end of the room and arose as the good Dr. Jekyll. Then, he ducked back down, and came up as the evil Mr. Hyde. Nick Adams did his amateurish takes on Cary Grant, Bogart and Brando. Vince Edwards offered Clark Gable. Billy Murphy, of *G.I. Joe* and *Sands of Iwo Jima,* also did Gable. Chump-change movie stars doing real movie stars. The mediocrity is the message.

Actually, the only real excitement felt on the occasion was that which thrilled through the fifteen-and-a-half-year-old Ricky Nelson. Ricky had recently done an Elvis Presley imitation on the *Ozzie and Harriet Show.* Instantly, he had received a bag full of fan mail and a contract from Imperial Records. Now, he was about to go out on the road and play his first big dates. Having achieved overnight fame by imitating Elvis, Ricky was a little self-conscious about showing up at Elvis's party. Marcia Borie, the maternalistic editor of *Photoplay,* had to sit with Ricky for about half an hour at the pharmacy in the lobby of the hotel while he soothed his nerves by slurping down a thick chocolate malted. Finally, he said: "You know Elvis—you go first!" With that they proceeded to the Presidential Suite, the disciple quaking at the thought of encountering the master face to face.

When they stepped into the foyer, Elvis spotted them immediately. "He rushed through the crowd like Andrew Jackson at the Battle of New Orleans," recalls Borie, "pushing everyone aside. He took Ricky in his arms and lifted him. Ricky was about five feet ten—not a little boy! "You're Ricky Nelson," Elvis cried. "I've seen you. Did David come, too? Mom and Daddy here?" Ricky was so nervous, he jumped up to get a Coke. Borie said to Elvis, "Ricky's in awe of you and now he's starting off on his first tour. If you could give him a few tips, it might make a world of difference to him." Elvis took Ricky by the shoulder and led him into another room and shut the door. When Borie talked to Ricky later, he said that Elvis had filled him up with dos and don'ts. He was enormously helpful. The funny thing was that Elvis was in awe of Ricky because he had watched him so many times on his dinky little TV at home. All that night, the two of them never took their eyes off each other." What's more, when Marcia Borie went out on the road shortly thereafter with Ricky, she saw him get virtually the same response from thousands of screaming fans as Elvis had produced at the Pan-Pacific.

Ricky Nelson was, of course, just the first of a legion of Elvis imitators, many of whom would enjoy highly successful careers for a few years. Nothing demonstrates more clearly than this phenomenon how much the success of such simple performers as rock stars depends on the tastes of their audiences rather than upon the performers' own skills. Once some innovative entertainer has cut the die, any number of copies can be stamped out, as long as the public's tastes remain fixed. Let the tastes change even a little, however, and virtually all the imitators blow away. This, in brief, is the history of rock in the fifties.

King Creole, Elvis's last movie before entering the army, is generally regarded as his most successful performance as an actor. Based on Harold Robbins's *A Stone for Danny Fisher,* the film was transposed from Chicago to New Orleans to allow Elvis to get down closer to his roots and do his songs in the honky-tonks of the French Quarter. Actually, the picture brings Elvis around very close to the point where he entered the movie world with his viewing of Tony Curtis in *City Across the River.* Allowing for the difference between tough neighborhoods in the North and South, the type of character, the basic milieu, the conflict of whether to fall in with the J.D.s and gangsters or stand free as a good guy, all these things make the picture a kind of confirmation of Elvis's first intuitive divination of his role as a movie star. His performance is quite believable, for once, but not especially exciting. As always he moves through his role with a curious sort of preoccupied and self-obsessed defensiveness that flares up easily into rage. Elvis the movie star is rather like Elvis the sleepwalker.

The gain in histrionic credibility is, unfortunately, offset by a loss of conviction in the musical numbers. They are all staged in backlot cabarets that don't ring true and with onstage performances by Elvis that offer nothing that anybody else couldn't do. Instead of the innocent charm of *Love Me Tender* or the punk violence of *Loving You* or the slick, arch choreography of *Jailhouse Rock,* we get for the first time in a Presley picture that dumb, head-on treatment of the guy with the guitar in his hand that became forever after the albatross hung by Hollywood around the neck of the once-charismatic Pelvis. Instead of grieving over the fact that Elvis was never given a great dramatic part, what should trouble Presley fans is the fact that Hollywood, by this time in its history, had lost its effortless knack of knocking out brilliant and inexpensive musicals. The notion that Elvis was an unfulfilled actor is a pipe dream. Elvis was an entertainer, a type of performer who is basically the opposite of an actor. Instead of having the gift of impersonating or at least suggesting a personality other than his own, the entertainer's gift is for making everything he does a vehicle for the exhibition and exaltation of his own personality.

On December 20, 1957, Elvis Presley received his army induction notice. This ended a period of more than a year during which both Elvis and his public had lived in constant dread of his being drafted. No period in Elvis's early life was more painful or injurious to him than the two years he spent in the service; yet, when you read the published accounts of this ordeal, you get the impression that he spent his time in uniform experiencing no more discomfort than the ordinary soldier. In fact, if you're a believer in the Elvis Myth, you will argue that the army experience was highly beneficial to Elvis because it quashed once and for all the criticism of him as a menace to American youth and earned him the respect and admiration of every real red-blooded American male.

The absurdity of this view becomes apparent the instant you stop seeing Elvis Presley as a pawn in a public relations game and start empathizing with him as a human being. For from Elvis's viewpoint, he had nothing to gain from the army and everything to lose. At the time he entered the service, he was at the very peak of his fame. With fads and fashions in pop music changing constantly, with a host of imitators and rivals springing up to steal his stuff, with fame itself such a freaky and chancy thing, what likelihood was there that he could come back two years hence and pick up exactly where he left off? There was none; and, in fact, Elvis never did regain the momentum he lost when he entered the army. So, from Elvis's point of view, his conscription was the worst sort of disaster that could have befallen him as an entertainer and a new star.

As for his personal emotions, apart from considerations of career, anyone who appreciates the extreme sensitivity and vulnerability of the young Elvis will realize with what feelings of anxiety and despair he must have regarded the prospect of giving up his friends and family to live in a barracks among total strangers, many of them men who might regard him with envy and hostility. Instead of being the master of his fate, he would now be transformed overnight into the passive victim of circumstances. Instead of protecting himself by building up layer upon layer of insulation against the world, he would be suddenly alone and naked. Instead of being able to use his talent to put a magic circle around himself, he would now have to rely entirely on his capacity for physical endurance and blind obedience. Any way he looked at the army, it had to strike him as a nightmare.

All this anyone could see by simply viewing Elvis's predicament from his perspective. What no one could have seen, if Elvis had not revealed the truth to a trusted confidant, was the ultimate horror of this nightmare: Elvis's conviction that he did not have to go into the service but had been persuaded into volunteering by the arguments or trickery of Colonel Parker. To get this story straight, we have to skip ahead six months to a time in the summer of 1958, when Elvis was undergoing his basic training at Fort Hood. True to his nature, he found on the base a man in whom he could confide as he would a parent: Master Sergeant William Norwood, now retired and living at Killeen, Texas.

As the company sergeant of Elvis's unit, Norwood was the man immediately in charge of Private Presley. An unsentimental but kindly man, married, a father, he responded instinctively to Elvis's need for sympathy and understanding. When Elvis wanted to see Anita Wood during the recruit training period, a time when no recruit is allowed off limits, Sergeant Norwood arranged for the young couple to meet in his house, which was on the base. When Gladys became gravely ill and Elvis was having trouble gaining an emergency leave, Sergeant Norwood exerted himself to solve the problem. This was the sort of man whom Elvis adopted as his protector and counselor during his months at Hood. It makes sense, therefore, that Elvis would confide in the sergeant and reveal to him what Elvis believed to be the true story of how he got into the army.

In October 1956, more than a year before Elvis received his draft notice, *Billboard* published an article datelined Fort Dix, New Jersey. Purporting to be the inside dope from the army brass, the article announced that Elvis Presley would be drafted the following December and would go into Special Services. He would receive only six weeks of basic training; then, he would be released to resume his career on behalf of the army. His hair would not be cut. He would be given a lot of dental and orthodontic work. He would be given leave to do another picture for Paramount. He would be free to continue recording and appearing on television. In short, Private Presley would get the softest deal that any man had ever received from the U.S. Army.

But at this time Elvis Presley had not even taken his preinduction physical examination and been classified 1A. Consequently, as far as the army was concerned there was no reason to assume that Elvis would ever serve in the military, much less to concern itself with what sort of deal he should be offered. What's more, even if the army had been anticipating this special case, it is unbelievable that it would have considered making him such an offer because it would be sure to provoke a storm of criticism. The true source of the report, therefore, could not have been the army. What was it?

When Elvis heard the story, he was profoundly shocked. He had approached his draft board long before and requested that they notify him confidentially and in advance when his number was about to be called. Now, he felt betrayed. Rushing to the office of the draft board in Memphis, he said, "Hey, I thought we had a deal!" The chairman of the board, Milton Bowers, assured Elvis that they did have an understanding, which the board had honored to the letter. Elvis was not in danger of being drafted and the board had just released a denial of the whole report, which certainly had not come from Memphis. When Elvis persisted in demanding an explanation, the only suggestion Bowers could offer was that some evil reporter held a grudge against the star or was just seeking to create a stir with some sensational copy.

Neither explanation is very likely. Reporters have to clear their copy through editors, and editors are prone to ask where sensational stories come from when they have no clearly attributed sources. In this case, a clue to the true source is provided in the article, where it is said that the only people who would know the date of Elvis's induction were army officials and some of his "closest business associates." Elvis Presley had only one close business associate in his entire lifetime: Colonel Thomas Andrew Parker. Could the Colonel have leaked this damaging story? Why would he do such a thing?

No sooner had Elvis received assurances from his draft board that he was not about to be called up than Colonel Parker offered his view of the matter. He told Elvis that they couldn't turn their backs on *Billboard*. He pointed out that the story was already generating an incredible barrage of attacks from veteran's organizations, congressmen and just plain citizens. This bad publicity could ruin Elvis's career, the Colonel assured his gullible protégé, if they didn't do something to counteract it. If Elvis didn't soon take a preinduction physical and clarify his status, everyone in the country would assume that he had pulled strings and found some dark way to shirk his duty. In fact, what the Colonel wanted Elvis to do was to go back to his draft board and make arrangements with them to have a private examination. As for cushy deals in Special

Services, that sort of thing would also have to be renounced. Elvis must serve his time just like any other American boy. If he did that, he would come out of the service with a wonderful image. If he did any goldbricking, it would hurt him in the long run.

Needless to say, this was very bad advice. No war was in progress in the year 1956. Though a few irate veterans may have been angered by Elvis's apparent immunity to the draft, they had no power over Elvis's career. The vast majority of his fans were horrified at the thought of Elvis going into the service and were destined to protest this development a lot more vigorously than anybody ever protested Elvis's civilian status. As for a Special Services assignment wreaking Elvis some injury, the notion is preposterous. Hundreds of entertainers, both great and small, had worked all through World War II and during the Korean War entertaining the troops and doing bond-selling and recruiting tours. No one would have regarded it as improper if Elvis had lent his talents to the army. The only man who could have seen such an act as an infringement on his rights would have been Colonel Parker, who, as we shall see, was not above demanding that even the president of the United States pay for the privilege of having Elvis entertain at the White House. As always, however, Elvis took the Colonel's cockeyed advice and requested the draft board to arrange a quiet examination, which he took in January 1957. Found fit, he was immediately classified 1A.

As to the question of why the Colonel should have urged Elvis to interrupt his career at its peak in order to join an army that was in no hurry to draft him, we find ourselves up against one of the most baffling questions posed by Colonel Parker's mysterious machinations. We do know that during this period, Elvis had come to take a very condescending and even antagonistic view of the Colonel and his activities. Elvis told one of his close friends in Texas, Eddie Fadal, that "anybody could do my booking because it ain't that much of a job, scheduling me." Elvis could have said as much to other people and the word gotten back to the Colonel, who kept Elvis surrounded always with a network of spies. It is possible that the Colonel, who had found Elvis such a simple and easy-to-manage lad, was now becoming fearful that the boy was taking off in the same direction as the character he portrayed in *Jailhouse Rock*. Could the con who runs the rackets in the big house and who the kid reduces eventually to his flunky be a disguised portrait of the Colonel and a prophecy of his future role in the Presley camp? Who knows what fears lurked in the scammy heart of the Colonel during this crazy early period when Elvis's success was growing at such an astounding rate that nobody could predict where it would go or what effects it would have on its real author. Perhaps the whole army nightmare, of which the Colonel did make extensive use to change Elvis's image, was at bottom a device to cut the King of Rock 'n' Roll down to size. If that was its purpose, it succeeded brilliantly. As John Lennon remarked when he was informed that Elvis had died—"Elvis died the day he went into the army."

Chapter 19

A Deadly Induction

WHEN ELVIS drove up before the office of the draft board on Main Street on the morning of March 24, 1958, he saw a crowd of fifty or sixty reporters and photographers gathered to witness his induction. Colonel Parker was clearly visible in their midst, holding a big cluster of red balloons stamped, "See Elvis in *King Creole.*" This was the Colonel's big day. He and the army, after close consultation, had worked out a deal. The colonel would give the newsmen a free hand so that he could benefit from their stories in launching his campaign for the New Elvis, the boy who gave up everything—fame, fortune, the glamour of stardom—to do his bit for Uncle Sam. The army would employ the same publicity to get off its back all those congressmen, columnists and veteran's organizations that had been beefing about Elvis getting a soft deal in Special Services. Both the Colonel and the army would come out winners. The only loser would be Elvis.

The result of this strategy was the greatest carnival ever staged at the induction of an American draftee. By the time Elvis and the dozen other boys who were entering the service with him had been brought to Kennedy Veterans Hospital for their medical examinations, the crowd of media representatives had swelled to two hundred, enlarged further by numerous fans and bystanders who were attracted by the rare opportunity to see the star at close range. At every step of the normally confidential examination procedure, Elvis was dogged by photographers determined to give their public the most candid view possible of the event. Elvis was photographed clothed, half-clothed and virtually naked, standing against a measuring scale stripped to his Jockey briefs. As the beam of the ophthalmoscope went into his eye and the probe of ornascope into his ear, the ubiquitous news camera followed the medical instruments. Everything was recorded save the moment when the doctor slipped the vinyl glove on his hand and shoved his finger up Elvis's ass. What a pity that this, the most eloquent and emblematic moment of the entire ritual, could not have been recorded for posterity!

In the late afternoon, Colonel Parker dragged Elvis before the movie and TV cameras to read some of the congratulatory messages that had come pouring in on this occasion. Governor Frank Clement wired: "YOU HAVE SHOWN THAT YOU ARE AN AMERICAN CITIZEN FIRST, A TENNESSEE VOLUNTEER, AND A YOUNG MAN WILLING TO SERVE HIS COUNTRY WHEN CALLED UPON TO DO SO." The Colonel urged Elvis to read some more of this malarkey into the camera. Elvis demurred. When the Colonel spurred his colt harder, he reared. Suddenly, Elvis's true feelings flashed forth: "It's me that's goin' in and what happens will be to me—not you!" Virtually no one reported the remark. When the day's work was done, there was nothing left but the time-honored act of raising the right hand, swearing the oath of allegiance and taking one step forward. At that moment—as the press never tired of repeating—Elvis Presley became US53310761.

When the Greyhound bus bearing the recruits to Fort Chaffee, Arkansas, left the hospital, the fans took off in hot pursuit. Cutting in and out of its path, like a flock of speedboats racing around a steadily advancing tug, the "Elfans," as they had started calling themselves, tracked their man all the way to his barracks on the base. When, finally, long after dark, a couple of white-helmeted M.P.s finally put a stop to the pursuit, admonishing the girls, "These barracks are for men only," one fourteen-year-old teenybopper glared at the military cops and spat out the single word—"Balls!"

If Elvis thought his media ordeal was over, he soon learned differently. His first chow hall breakfast was reported more exhaustively than any meal in history. Two dozen photographers gathered around the table to capture the star in the act of spooning up his cereal or forking in his sausage and eggs. Colonel Parker directed the shooting himself, as he did the afternoon clothing issue. The Colonel was in such high spirits that he even tried to slip a string tie, such as he was wont to wear, into Elvis's stack of uniforms. Elvis didn't enjoy the joke. "No, sir," he said, tossing the tie aside, "if I wore a string tie in here, I'd have to take the punishment, not you!" The Colonel comported himself more discreetly at the crowning event of the whole procedure, Elvis's G.I. haircut.

As the floodlights blazed and the cameras ground, a smiling civilian barber in a white smock welcomed Elvis to the chair. Switching on his electric clippers and brandishing them in the air, he ran them up the mythic sideburns. As the hair came off, he tossed it playfully in the air, letting it drift to the ground. Elvis had prepared himself for this event. Rather sheepishly he joked: "Hair today, gone tomorrow!" Now, the humming clippers were plowing up the back of the celebrated coif, shearing the hair off in disfiguring lanes. The photographers, whipped to a frenzy by this primitive rite, begged the barber to go slower. *Life* alone filed 1,200 pictures from Chaffee.

The instant the clipping was complete, a specially coached porter rushed forward with a broom and swept all the hair into a pile, which he then dumped into a bin to be taken out for immediate destruction. As the sweep-up proceeded, Colonel Parker lectured the newsmen on the enormous value of the hairs thus wantonly destroyed. Elvis was upset despite himself. He forgot to pay for the haircut with his sixty-five-cent chit. The barber called his famous customer back, thus redoubling his embarrassment. Elvis ran out of the shop and ducked into a phone booth. When the photographers sought to press their lenses against the glass, the Colonel interposed, intoning with the solemnity of a jailer, "The boy's entitled to speak to his mother without being disturbed." When Elvis got through to Graceland, he discovered that his mother had taken to her bed and was "grieving."

That word became now the motto of Gladys's declining life. The shock of having her baby snatched from her was more than she could bear. Elvis was gone and there was no saying when he would be back. When people sought to console her, she would burst out weeping, "They're not going to take care of my boy . . . he has a quick temper . . . he'll get confused!" There was no comforting her. All day, she would go about the house wringing her hands and saying, "I feel that something's happened to him."

After a few days at Chaffee, Elvis was dispatched to Fort Hood in Texas for training as a tanker. When the Colonel turned up at the head of his press corps, he was met by a very determined WAC colonel, who told him, "You will have carte blanche, as promised—but just this one day. After today, nothing!" By the end of his first week in the army, Elvis was able to call home and report, "They finally got the reporters off my back. These cocksuckers! They really got me locked up here." Private Presley had been assigned to A Company, First Medium Tank Battalion, 32nd Regiment, of the famed Hell on Wheels Division, formerly commanded by General Patton. Now his future was clear for the next few months. He would receive eight weeks of "basic"; a fourteen-day leave; another eight weeks of special training in tank warfare; two weeks of unit training; then, his unit would be shipped to Germany as replacements in the Third Armored Division, the cutting edge of the NATO armies.

Fort Hood was an open base, which meant that Elvis could receive visitors any time he was off duty. One of his first and most welcome callers was a former disc jockey, then a motion picture theater operator in Waco, Eddie Fadal. As soon as Elvis could get away on weekends, he made the Fadal home his retreat from the base. Often he would arrive with Anita Wood, who spent almost every weekend with him in Texas. Elvis would always inspect every room in the house before he settled down, explaining that he had a great fear of hidden photographers. Then he and Anita would vocalize in the den until supper, which was prepared by Fadal's wife La Nelle to conform exactly to Elvis's tastes. Elvis never ate beef, preferring the meat of the hog. His especial delight was a rich dessert, like banana cream pie or Bavarian chocolate cake. He would start with one big slice and then consume the entire pie or cake. Eddie Fadal made it a practice to drive down to Hood early every week with a freshly baked pie or cake plus the latest 45s and copies of *Box Office* and *Motion Picture*. He quickly became the second most important person in Elvis's private support system. The first was Master Sergeant Bill Norwood.

A wiry little dude with a country voice that must have reminded Elvis of his Uncle Vester, the sergeant had been a recruit instructor since before World War II. Once he had allowed Elvis to use his private phone, the sergeant found himself the recipient of many more visits, which gradually developed into a routine that included coffee in the morning and supper at night. Elvis complained constantly of homesickness and depression. One night he broke down and cried bitterly. When the tears had stopped flowing, the sergeant spoke: "When you come in my house," he advised in his dry Texas drawl, "you can let it all out.

Do whatever you want to and don't worry about anything. But when you walk out of my front door, you are now Elvis Presley. You're an actor. You're a soldier. So, by God, I want you to act! Don't let nobody know how you feel on the inside." Elvis mumbled, "Yes, sir."

The final exercise of the first eight weeks was the toughest moment of basic: a week in the field entailing fourteen-mile marches under the broiling Texas sun with seventy-pound packs. About half the men in Elvis's outfit collapsed under the strain, but Elvis made it through, even though he had the extra burden of being the assistant squad leader. Sergeant Norwood, no mean judge, was delighted with his famous pupil's performance. He told him: "Presley, you're a natural-born soldier."

When Elvis got back to Memphis on his first furlough, he looked fitter than at any other time in his life. He had dropped twelve pounds and lost a lot of the baby fat in his cheeks. His jaw was long and lean; his chin as squared off as an army corner. Many people were surprised to see him again a sun-bleached blonde. The only question about his physical condition that couldn't be answered by looking at him was, "How's your voice?" That issue was soon resolved when he took off on June 10 for Nashville for the only recording session of his army years.

The Colonel had been receiving a lot of requests from both the army and RCA to allow Elvis to perform publicly and to record. There was nothing in army regulations to prevent Elvis from making dozens of records, providing he cut them on his own time. As Elvis was the fastest hit-maker in the history of the industry, even a handful of sessions would have provided Victor with enough product to carry it comfortably through the next two years. Colonel Parker was dead set against these proposals. He told Elvis, "I want the can empty!"

Colonel's strategy was aimed both at RCA and at Elvis. Emptying the can was always the Colonel's first move before any contract negotiations. Already the Colonel was preparing to renegotiate Elvis's contract when he reemerged in 1960. On the other hand, emptying the can would mean that when Elvis got out of the service, he would be forced to resume his recording career from ground zero: a point of psychological disadvantage which, along with all the other problems he would face at that time, would make Elvis more dependent than ever on his manager. The Colonel also knew that having an empty can would compel RCA to reissue a lot of Elvis's old records. To a hustler like the Colonel, it was far more gratifying to sell the same record twice (in different wrappings) than it would be to come up with a new record. The former course could be represented as a triumph of merchandising skill—almost as good as a hot dog with no meat in the middle. Any damn fool could sell a new Elvis record. So Elvis got his orders: "You will go in there and do one night's recording. After that—nothing for the duration."

No sooner did Elvis get back to Fort Hood than the rest of the family began arriving. Lamar turned up first, driving a white Mark II Continental that made a sensation in little Killeen. The next day Vernon, Gladys and Grandma arrived in a white Fleetwood towing a trailer full of household goods. Elvis had worked a fast deal with a man who sold house trailers to obtain the use of a three-bedroom model for a couple of months. When the family checked out the trailer, they realized that it was hopelessly inadequate. A quick house hunt turned up a three-bedroom ranch house that belonged to a local politician. The politician scalped the Presleys, charging them $1,400 a month. Elvis shrugged off the cost. What did it matter as long as they were all together and comfortable? Why, the house was virtually a carbon copy of their old home on Audubon Avenue.

Despite the perfection of his living arrangements, Elvis could never persuade his mother that they were well off in Killeen. Gladys missed her home. She dreaded the day when Elvis would be shipped overseas. When Elvis would tell her that they would live overseas just as they lived here in Texas, Gladys would shake her head and say, "I jes' can't see mahself over theah in a fereign country. Ah've left nuthin' over theah, and ah'm not tryin' to find anythin'. It grieves me." Everything grieved Gladys at this time. She complained of pains in her abdomen and would get so nauseous in the morning that she couldn't stand the odor of eggs frying. She would pick quarrels with Vernon, hollering insults at him, especially her favorite epithet for her husband, "steercotted"—deballed. If Elvis were present during the fight, he would get very upset and seek to intervene. Sometimes, in the evenings, it was obvious that Gladys was drunk. Her voice would glide up into a foolish falsetto; her speech would be badly slurred. Elvis hated to see his mother drunk. He would cry out at such moments, "Momma! momma! what are you doin' to yourself!" Then he would embrace her and lead her off to bed.

Though Elvis never looked so healthy in all his life, Gladys kept harping on the dangers of military service. She was not entirely wrong. One day, after Elvis had been out firing .50 calibre machine guns, he came home complaining about the ringing in his ears. Gladys warned: "Elvis, you better be careful with your ears. You know you play by ear and you can't read music. You should be careful with your ears."

She may have reminded him also that when he was a child he had chronic ear trouble for which he was treated in the good old southern way by having urine poured in his ears.

Next morning, when Elvis turned up at Sergeant Norwood's quarters to have his customary cup of coffee, he repeated his mother's warnings. Norwood told him to take sick call and have his ears checked. When Elvis got back from the dispensary, he was carrying a note from the doctor. It said that Elvis had a perforated left eardrum. He was not to be exposed to any loud noises, especially gunfire.

Norwood puzzled over this news. He told Elvis that it posed problems. If they obeyed the doctor's orders to the letter, Elvis's training would suffer. He would attract attention. It might be said that he was goldbricking. Elvis, for his part, did not want to withdraw from any part of his training. So they decided that henceforth when they went to the firing range, Elvis would stuff his ears with cotton. When he wasn't firing the guns, he would stay far away from their concussions by going to the rear of the unit to handle ammunition. Meantime, Sergeant Norwood would work to get Elvis's classification changed from a tanker to a reconnaissance scout, a job that would keep him with the division but well away from gunfire. Despite the sergeant's efforts, Elvis remained with the tanks and their .90-mm. guns for another two months, until his unit shipped out for Europe. (In later years Elvis's hearing deteriorated markedly. When he returned to the stage in the early seventies, he complained constantly that he could not hear himself through the stage monitors. No matter how high the monitors were set, Elvis demanded that they be turned up higher. Soon he had the "hottest" stage in the business.)

During the first week in August, Gladys called her doctor in Memphis. She asked him to come down to Killeen to examine her. He replied that he had no license to practice medicine in the state of Texas. Vernon took her to a local practitioner in nearby Temple. He could not diagnose her condition. She began to turn sallow and finally yellow. Lamar grew alarmed at her appearance. He told Elvis that his mother should go back to Memphis and get proper medical attention. Elvis would not allow her to leave.

Finally, Gladys's condition grew so alarming that Elvis was forced to relinquish his mother. Reluctantly, he drove her and Vernon to Temple and put them aboard the Sante Fe. When she turned up a couple of days later at the doctor's office in Memphis, he insisted she enter Baptist Memorial Hospital for tests. He was not alarmed, but he was puzzled at this sudden jaundice in a normally healthy woman.

The most obvious cause of her condition was hepatitis, but the diagnostic specimens did not indicate the presence of infectious disease. The liver was inflamed, but it was difficult to determine why. Specialists were brought in for consultation. They argued over whether the cause might be cirrhosis of the liver or perhaps a clot that was blocking the portal vein. Meantime, the condition of their patient worsened.

Gladys's doctor was not entirely familiar with his patient nor was she entirely honest with him. Gladys Presley was a woman of very unhealthy habits and temperament. She was grossly overweight from improper diet. She never got any exercise. She drank to the point of drunkenness but never confessed this to her doctor. The most sinister ingredient in her self-destructive way of life was the consumption of diet pills. Gladys had started using these amphetamine compounds years before and increased their usage as she became increasingly dependent on them. It was said in her family that she was ashamed of her obesity and wanted to improve her appearance, especially when Elvis became famous and photographers were constantly taking her picture and printing it in magazines and newspapers. Eventually, the amphetamines were bound to have a deleterious effect on both her body and her mind. Extreme irritability of the sort which Gladys displayed in the final months of her life is a typical effect of amphetamine abuse. Being of a secretive nature, Gladys confided nothing of this history of drug use to her doctor.

As Gladys's condition worsened, Elvis tried to obtain an emergency leave from Fort Hood. Significantly, Gladys had broken down on the eve of Elvis's departure for Germany. His whole unit was on point of embarkation status. As the request was processed through the chain of command, Gladys's life began to slip away. Elvis was on the phone with the doctor every day and the reports were increasingly alarming. Finally, Elvis could no longer tolerate delay. He announced that if he didn't get his leave that day, he was going to take off for Memphis without leave. Some wires were pulled in Washington and Elvis was released.

Elvis reached his mother's side late Thursday night. She rallied when she saw him, but the doctors warned that her condition was still grave. For the next thirty-six hours Elvis and Vernon kept a vigil at the hospital, where they were joined by the family and Elvis's friends. Finally, on the second evening, Elvis was persuaded that his mother was feeling better. He left the hospital, picked up Frances, Gloria and Heidi and went to the Crosstown Theater to see Paul Newman, one of his favorite actors, in *The Hustler*. After the show they all went back to Graceland

and sat talking to a late hour. Then Elvis told Lamar to take the girls home.

At three in the morning, the phone rang. It was Vernon. "Elvis, your momma just died." Then he went on to explain how she had been "suffering for breath" and had suddenly been killed by a heart attack. Elvis was so stunned, he didn't know what to do. He had to talk to someone who could help him. Instinctively, he picked up the phone and dialed Sergeant Norwood.

The sergeant describes Elvis's tone as "livid." He was talking and crying at the same time. He told Norwood the story of the deathbed vigil, the sense of relief he had experienced when he went to the movies, then the shock of being awakened by his father telling him that his mother was dead. His long rambling monologue went on until four in the morning. At that point, Sergeant Norwood told Elvis that he should hang up so that Norwood could get in touch with Elvis's superiors and arrange for an extension of his leave.

Lamar, returning a few minutes later, saw the front door of the house standing wide open. A night wind was blowing through the trees. An eerie feeling was in the air. Without switching off the motor, he started to get out of the car, when he saw Grandma come bustling out the door. "Lamar," she snapped, "you gotta take me down to the hospital. Gladys just died." When they stepped off the elevator on Gladys's floor, Lamar was startled by a fearful sound. It was Elvis and Vernon keening, sending up the heartrending cries of hillbilly folk afflicted with grief.

"I heard this horrible wailing," Lamar recalls. "It just made my skin crawl. I had never heard anything like that in my life. I came around the corner and Elvis saw me. 'Oh, Lamar, my baby's gone!' He was hugging me and crying on my shoulder. Then, he grabbed hold of Grandma. Finally, he said, 'Come on, Lamar. Mama really wanted to see you. She's always askin' about you. She was always worried about you.' Then he grabbed hold on me and we went in her room. The body was all covered up. He started patting her stomach. 'Look here, Satnin','' he said, 'here's Lamar.' I couldn't handle it. I had to get out."

Elvis remained beside the body rocking back and forth in grief, until the hospital attendants asked him to leave. He and Lamar made their way downstairs and went out the back of the hospital into a loading area. Dawn was just breaking. At that moment a hearse drove up. Elvis seized Lamar by the arm to detain him. Lamar saw a look of hate come into Elvis's face, the jaw flexing spasmodically. They stood there waiting until the body was wheeled out with a red velvet pall over it.

When Elvis saw the body, he burst out again. "Oh, Lamar, what am I gonna do without Satnin'? Oh, Lord, they're taking her away from me!"

The doctors, puzzled by Gladys's death, requested an autopsy. Elvis didn't want to know why his mother had died; he was intent on keeping her alive in his mind. No autopsy was permitted. As in the case of Elvis's death years later, no one was ever to know precisely what killed Gladys. Instead, all the energy inspired by the occasion was lavished on preparations for a great funeral. Vernon wanted to have loudspeakers put out on the grounds of Graceland and the ceremonies turned into a huge public event. He got in touch with James Blackwood and requested that the famous gospel group sing at the funeral. Next, the casket had to be ordered. Elvis wanted the finest available. Then, arrangements had to be made at the house to lay out the body in the music room.

Later that same morning, the hearse came up the driveway bearing Gladys's body. Elvis was on the lookout. The moment he saw the big black coach driving up the hill, he shouted to Vernon: "Daddy! Momma's comin' home! Look, Momma's here!" When the huge casket, silver-finish-on-copper, had been mounted on the catafalque in the music room and the lid raised, Elvis threw himself on the body. Then, he stepped back to admire his mother. "Look at my Mommy!" he exclaimed. "She's fixed up so pretty!"

Gladys had been beautified by the undertakers. Her hair had been styled, her eyelashes brushed out. She was dressed in a costly outfit which Elvis had bought for her. "My Momma loved beautiful things—but she wouldn't wear them!" cried Elvis, who had always been exasperated by Gladys's refusal to allow him to lavish on her furs and jewels. As he stood there, consuming Gladys with his eyes, he demanded to see her feet—"her itty-bitty sooties!" The undertakers exchanged perplexed looks. Reluctantly, they obliged, raising the satin coverlet and exposing the slipper-clad feet. Instantly, Elvis clasped Gladys's feet and fondled them, pouring out a stream of unintelligible baby talk.

When Anita Wood arrived, she found Elvis sitting in front of the house wearing his favorite outfit: a frilly white tuxedo shirt, open at the neck, with tight white pants and white buck shoes with high backs and big square tongues. "Come here, Little," he commanded, "I want you to see Momma. Come on . . . she loved you." The moment they arrived beside the coffin, Elvis fell again into his baby-talk blandishments, pointing to each part of Gladys's body and exclaiming over her "itty-bitty lips" and her "itty-bitty hands" and working down finally to her "itty-bitty sooties," which he insisted that Anita examine carefully. Anita was disturbed by Elvis's bizarrely infantile behavior, but what really shook her was the moment when he whipped out his comb and began to run it carefully through Gladys's hair.

Eddie Fadal arrived at Graceland that afternoon. He was greeted by Elvis, who threw his arms around Fadal's neck and then led him straight to the casket. "Look at those hands!" Elvis exclaimed. "How those hands toiled and worked for me . . . all the things that Momma did for me. . . . Oh, those beautiful hands! . . . How they toiled, emptying bedpans in a hospital!" Elvis was clearly becoming hysterical at this point, and Fadal began to long for the presence of a doctor who might prescribe some soothing drug. No sedative was administered; instead, everything conspired to make Elvis frantic.

Word had gotten around Memphis that there was to be a great wake at Graceland and that everyone should come bringing gifts of food and drink. As dozens of women—many of them with designs on Vernon—came bustling up the driveway and into the house with shopping bags, cardboard cartons and dishes covered with silver foil, cellophane and Saran Wrap, the house began to look like the site of a church social. Half-eaten sandwiches, wet paper cups, soiled plates, crumpled paper napkins and other garbage littered the once immaculate rooms with their elegant gold cornices. Heaven knows what might have happened if at that moment the ole Colonel had not appeared, like Lee before Richmond, instantly taking command of the situation and driving back the hordes of milling women.

The Colonel saw at a glance that the fans would demolish the house if they were allowed another day of freedom on the property. He told Vernon that the funeral must be held at a funeral home. Vernon, usually so humble before the Colonel, insisted that the funeral be at Graceland. That was how country people always did their burying—from home. The Colonel was not to be dissuaded. When the director of the Memphis Funeral Home arrived that evening, he found the two men at each other's throats. Finally, the Colonel prevailed. Arrangements were made for the services to be conducted the following afternoon at the funeral parlor.

That night Elvis was completely distraught. He could not be persuaded to leave his station beside the casket. The more people who arrived at the house, the more extravagant Elvis's behavior became. Finally, he turned in exasperation to Lamar and cried: "I can't stand to see anybody else! These people are driving me crazy!" Lamar went to work at once clearing the house of guests. Vernon was furious, but he had his hands full with the Colonel. When it got late, a doctor was summoned who gave Elvis a shot to put him to sleep. He suffered violent nightmares.

Early the next morning, the body was conveyed to the Memphis Funeral Home, a massive old Spanish colonial mansion with white brick walls and a heavy tile roof that spreads its bulk under the lofty shade trees on a corner of Union and Pasadena. For four hours that morning, an endless stream of people entered the front door of the funeral parlor, filed past the silver casket in the state room and then departed through the back door of the building. When they got out into the street, they remained waiting to catch a glimpse of Elvis and his family. By the time of the funeral, about one in the afternoon, three thousand bystanders had gathered in the normally quiet and empty neighborhood.

That morning at Graceland, Elvis had come staggering downstairs, appearing at the point of collapse. He was wearing a very handsome new suit. "My Momma would have loved this suit," he exclaimed to Willy Nichols. Willy understood: It was a new suit that Gladys had never seen. At that point, Elvis went rubber-legged and a couple of people rushed up to support him. All the rest of the day, he staggered and stumbled, as if drunk with grief.

Now that Gladys was out of reach, Elvis began to fondle Vernon just as he had always done with his mother. "Oh, Daddy . . . it's a grey-haired Daddy . . . he's a Satnin' Daddy . . . he don't know how to do any better," Elvis would drool, as he patted his father fondly on the head.

As the time for the funeral approached, Elvis demanded that Gladys's doctor leave his patients and come to Graceland. He wanted the doctor to sit at his side during the ordeal ahead. When the doctor arrived, he found Elvis and Vernon taking turns rubbing salt in each other's wounds. Elvis would say to Vernon: "Well, Dad, she's not gonna be feedin' those chickens no more." Vernon would echo: "No, son, she won't be feedin' those chickens any more." The Colonel, meantime, was busy barking orders into the phone. He had arranged in just one night the route of the funeral cortege, the extensive security measures to be taken by the Memphis police and the notifications to be given to the press. Always averse to even the slightest passing reference to death, the Colonel snuffed out his sense of mortality on this occasion by indulging himself in an orgy of work.

By the time the limousine with the Presley family pulled up at the funeral home, the body had been moved to the West Chapel, a life-

sized version of those cardboard churches with celluloid windows that
are placed beneath Christmas trees. Decorated in mock-Tudor style, the
room boasts golden yellow walls pierced with fake stained-glass windows
lit from behind with garish green floodlights. Massive brown pews flank
a crimson-carpeted center aisle which leads up to an area that is called
the "stage." With its flat proscenium arch, draw curtain and backdrop
of a Palladian window filled with opaque panels, the "stage" resembles
closely a college drama club setting for *Gammer Gurton's Needle* or
Ralph Roister Doister.

While the nearly four hundred guests who could squeeze into the
chapel were taking their seats, the funeral directors were busy behind
the curtain carrying in the flowers from the state room and banking
them around the massive silver casket raised on a low plush prie-dieu.
Just before the ceremony commenced, Elvis and Vernon were ushered
behind the curtain to pay their last respects before the casket lid was
closed.

Elvis, his face swollen, his eyes red and heavy-lidded, could hardly
draw himself away from the body long enough to embrace tearfully
James Blackwood and J. D. Sumner, who had arrived just in time. Re-
minding the Blackwoods that he had come to the funeral of their brother,
Elvis choked out, "I know you understand what I'm going through."
Then Elvis, Vernon, Grandma and some relations were ushered into
the family room, which is contrived so that the family of the deceased
may have a full view of the stage without being visible to guests in the
pews. At that point, the Blackwoods and the organist disappeared behind
the fake windows, the Reverend James Hamil took his stand at the
lectern and the curtain was opened.

The prayers and the eulogy were not long in duration, but the singing
was extended far beyond what had been planned. Elvis dashed behind
the window screen repeatedly, demanding every hymn that came to mind.
The Blackwoods obliged with "I'm Redeemed," "Precious Lord Take
My Hand" and "In the Garden." The hymn that had the greatest effect,
however, was Gladys's favorite: "Precious Memories."

Singing like a solemn barbershop quartet, the Blackwoods intoned
the sentimental verses:

> *Precious memories, unseen angels*
> *Sent from nowhere to my soul.*
> *How they linger, ever near me,*
> *And the sacred past unfolds.*

Then the ringing tenor of James Blackwood blared:

> *As I tread down life's pathways,*
> *No matter what the years may hold,*
> *While I ponder, hope grows fonder.*

Finally, after a swelling statement of the refrain, J. D. Sumner reached down into his deepest, most sepulchral range to sing with flesh-creeping effect:

> *In the stillness of the midnight,*
> *Precious sacred scenes unfold.*

Vernon Presley faltered at this point and Eddie Fadal had to brace him. By the time the service had concluded, Elvis was wracked with grief.

No sooner had the curtain been drawn and the funeral workers begun to remove the casket to the hearse than Elvis commanded them to stop. He insisted that they open the lid again so that he could have one last moment with Gladys alone. The men obliged. As they stood in embarrassed silence, Elvis threw himself over the casket and mumbled incoherent words of baby talk.

Outside the funeral home, a crowd of three thousand people had gathered. A hundred and fifty uniformed officers comprised the funeral detail. Policemen were stationed at every block along the route to the cemetery and patrol cars were positioned at every major intersection.

The cortege was led by the commanding officer, Inspector Legg, in a patrol car with a flashing dome light. Following next came the long black Cadillac limousines of the funeral director, the preacher and then the funeral coach, bearing the casket and flowers. The train of family cars followed, led by Elvis's limousine. Eight motorcycle patrolmen rode up and down the line as flankers. As the cortege rolled down the tree-lined blocks of old Memphis, making for the highway, thousands of people stood along the sidewalks watching silently, the men covering their hearts with their hats.

Forest Hill Cemetery is off Highway 51, just three miles distant from Graceland. When the procession reached the cemetery gate, a sizable crowd had already assembled. Reverend Hamil got out of his car and led the way up the hill to the gravesite, followed by the pallbearers carrying the coffin. When the casket had been put upon the lowering mechanism and dropped part way into the grave, Elvis and Vernon were brought to the graveside.

The ceremony at the grave was brief. After the last prayer had been said, Elvis half leaped, half fell on the casket, crying aloud: "Oh, Satnin',

I wanna go with you! I don't want to stay here! I can't be without you!" The extravagance of his grief shocked the bystanders. Lamar reached down and seized Elvis, trying to drag him to his feet. "Get up, people are watching you," he hissed. "Get away, man, get away!" Elvis snarled. He was holding fast now to the lid of the casket as if he would never allow it to be buried. It took the combined efforts of several men to get him to relinquish his grip. At last he was led stumbling down the hill to the waiting car.

BIB OVERALLS: The first shot of the most photographed man in history. *(United Press International Photo)*

THE LITTLE FAMILY: Vernon was fresh out of prison when this shot of the family in its Sunday best was snapped in East Tupelo, about 1941. Elvis favored his father strongly as a child, but in adolescence he began increasingly to resemble his mother, a likeness that showed most strongly at his death. *(Globe Photos)*

DIONYSIUS AT 19: Elvis just after the release of his first record on Sun. The King label, one of whose records Elvis is holding, was a pioneer in recording R & B records with country singers and C & W records with R & B voices, precisely the two things that Elvis did on his first record. *(United Press International Photo)*

TEDDY BEAR: When word got around that Elvis liked to win stuffed animals at carnivals, he was inundated with padded beasts. Shown here in his girlish boudoir in 1956, he can almost be heard saying, "I don't collect 'em, but if people send 'em to me, I keep 'em." *(Globe Photos)*

THAT'S MY BOY: A classic shot used to illustrate the 1957 AP story that marked the first anniversary of the Colonel's takeover as Elvis's exclusive manager. Elvis offers his practiced lip curl while Colonel plays PR man, employing his hunt 'n' hit typing technique. The original caption offered this penetrating analysis of Elvis's character: "He's like most other twenty-one-year-old fellows," says Colonel Tom. "He has a few dates, takes care of his folks, and tries hard to live right." *(AP Newsfeatures Photo)*

HEROES OF THE SILENT MAJORITY:
The Oval Office, December 21, 1970. On the eve of his speech proclaiming drugs "America's Number One Problem," President Nixon appoints the drug-saturated Elvis Presley (just look at his eyes!) a special agent of the Bureau of Narcotics and Dangerous Drugs. *(Courtesy of National Archives and Records Service)*

THE CARY GRANT PICTURE: The twenty-year-old Dries van Kuijk as he looked on the eve of his departure for America.

THE FLYING DUTCHMAN: Andreas Cornelis van Kuijk, AKA Colonel Tom Parker, was born and reared above a livery stable in Breda, Holland. In this archive shot of the now demolished Vlaszak district, the van Kuijk house is the second from the left; the ground-floor doors of the stable are partially visible.

HOW MUCH DOES IT COST IF IT'S FREE?: Colonel Parker in the rare act of giving something away. *(Globe Photos)*

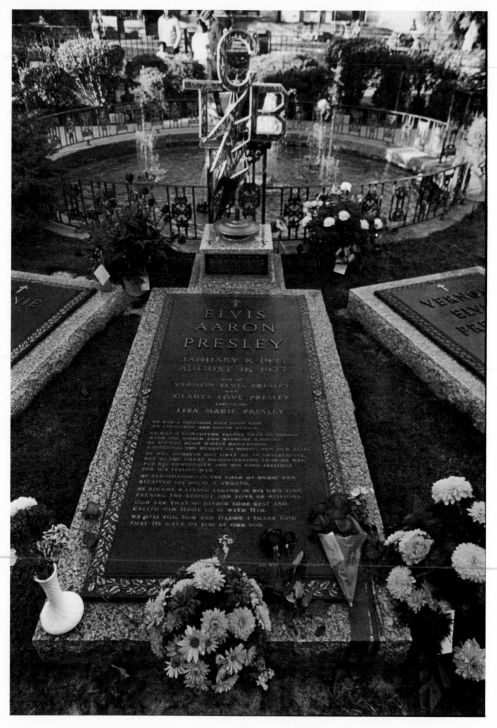

THE ROYAL TOMBS: The little family united in death in the meditation garden adjacent to the swimming pool at Graceland. The eternal light beneath the symbol of the Memphis Mafia appears to have blown out. *(James Hamilton)*

Chapter 20

A Lonely Little Boy, 5,000 Miles Away

A GREAT CHEER broke from the throats of five hundred kids the moment Elvis set foot on German soil. All that morning, October 1, 1958, they had watched the S.S. *General Randall* come creeping spectrally through the fog into its berth in Bremen. Then, as the ship was made fast and the gangplank was lowered, the kids had begun to jostle the American military police and duck through their lines. When Elvis appeared, wearing his dress uniform and toting his bulky duffel bag on his right shoulder, the kids went berserk. Elvis must have felt he was back in the States, as he smiled and waved and then boarded the troop train surrounded by an escort of shiny-helmeted M.P.s and marines in dress blues.

The train with Elvis's eight hundred-man battalion rolled south all that day and late into the night bound for Friedberg, in Hesse, about an hour's drive northeast of Frankfurt. When the men finally stepped off the coaches, around one in the morning, they registered instant disappointment. Not allowed even a glimpse of the quaint little town, with its picturesque castle, they had been deposited directly upon U.S. government property.

The weather was cold and damp. The fog was so thick you could not see ten feet in front of your face. After a night's sleep in receiving quarters, they rose early next morning to take a look at their new home. Ray Barracks consisted of nothing but long lines of austere grey-brick buildings. Back in the thirties, it had housed Hitler's S.S. troops. Now it was garrisoned by the 32nd Battalion of the American Third Armored Division. Still it looked like what it had always been: Friedberg Kaserne, the next step up from a military prison.

After a couple of days of reclaiming baggage and being issued winter clothing and combat gear, the men could see how they had fared in the military lottery. Elvis had been assigned to Headquarters Company as a jeep driver in a reconnaissance platoon. All his noncoms and officers were new. It was a case of starting all over again from scratch. Elvis, who hated change and dreaded Germany, could not have been happy. The only cheering development he could anticipate was the imminent arrival of his family.

Vernon, Grandma, Lamar and Red (who had joined the family during its last weeks at Fort Hood) were still at Graceland when Elvis left for Europe. His departure from the Army Marine Terminal in Brooklyn had been another of those pseudoevents staged by the brass with the "aid and advice" of Colonel Tom Parker. While 2500 relatives of the departing troops stood about on the heavily fenced and guarded dock, Elvis conducted a lengthy press conference. Every moment of it was recorded by movie cameras and tape machines so that it could be rebroadcast around the country in the evening and eventually released as an EP, titled *Elvis Sails*.

The Presley family had seen bits of the conference that night on TV. They had laughed heartily when Elvis explained to the American people how delighted he was to be giving up his career and leaving the country for a year and a half. "I'm glad to be going," he assured the press. "Before I was drafted, I'd been trying to arrange a European tour. Now I'll get to see Europe anyway. I'm looking forward to my first furlough in Paris. I'd like to meet Brigitte Bardot." Then, he marched bravely up the gangplank with his duffel bag on his shoulder while an army band played a ponderous medley of "You Ain't Nothin' But a Hound Dog," "I'm All Shook Up" and "Teddy Bear." If the family could have seen how that finale was produced, they would have laughed a lot harder. Elvis had walked the plank no less than eight times carrying that borrowed duffel bag.

Bad Nauheim, the town in which the Presleys settled, is an old spa that had a population, in that period, of 14,000. Its narrow cobblestoned streets wind around blocks of five-story Victorian buildings whose steeply pitched roofs are crowned with quaint towers, ornamental spires and lacy weathervanes. During the afternoons, all the cure guests engage in the great central-European pastime of the *Spaziergang,* the reflective or convivial walk, with hands clasped behind back or linked arm-in-arm, under the elms, oaks and poplars of the allées that lead to the band shell, where an orchestra of frail violins and reeds plays light-opera airs.

Though the population of this staid old place was elderly and valetude-narian, the arrival of *Der Elvis* brought an immediate influx of young people. On his very first weekend off the post, Elvis was walking in the park with Lamar when they were accosted by a German photogra-pher. He was accompanied by a cute little blonde of high school age with a provocative ass. The photographer suggested that Elvis pose with the girl. Elvis put his arm around her and faced the camera. When she looked up into his face, he stared down at her. Suddenly his sullen pout dissolved into a charming smile. She smiled back mutely. That smile opened up a whole new life for Margrit Buergin.

Up to this moment, she was one of millions of kids in dreary postwar Germany, growing up in homes with no man, a hard-pressed mother and the whole emphasis of life on learning some skill that would get the girl out of school and into the business world. At the age of sixteen, Margrit was already working a double shift: as a typist for a Frankfurt electrical goods company during the day and at night as a student at a secretarial school. Once Margrit smiled back at Elvis Presley, she was no longer a little typist: She was Cinderella.

Elvis got her number from the photographer and called her apartment. Margrit's mother could not speak English, but she ran out and got a neighbor, who delivered the stunning news that their caller was *Der Elvis!* When Margrit got home from school she was dumbstruck. She sat by the phone all that night wringing her hands, as if the next day she had to face a firing squad. Sure enough, at 10:30, the phone rang again. Like every German teenager of her generation, she had a few words of English. Through the dense emotional fog of the moment, she managed to comprehend that *Der Elvis* was asking her to go the following weekend to the movies. *Shrecklich!*

Elvis, for his part, was thinking just like any young lad eager to make a good impression. Instead of dispatching one of his minions to fetch Margrit, as he would have done in Memphis or even Hollywood, he got in a Mercedes cab driven by his new chauffeur, Joseph, and had himself driven to Frankfurt. Arriving at the tiny flat occupied by the Buergins, he endeavored to charm Frau Buergin, who was beside herself with excitement.

Frau Buergin dispatched her daughter with the notorious rock star, without a moment's compunction. She had no illusions about life. Actually, she had nothing to fear. Elvis was into his little southern gentleman bag. Instead of taking the virtually paralyzed girl to the nearest hotel and getting down, he brought her back to Bad Nauheim and introduced her to his father, his grandmother and his closest friends. Then, he began taking her out two or three times a week, giving her money for cabs and clothes and escorting her to every entertainment he could discover, from the Frankfurt zoo to a nightclub in town, called La Parisienne. Naturally, it was Margrit's first *Nachtlokal.*

Needless to say, this steady dating did not go unremarked by the local press, the national press or the international press. Overnight, Margrit Buergin, sixteen-year-old typist and after-work secretarial student, became an international figure. She was soon receiving forty letters a day. The letters came principally from other women in America and Germany. American women hysterically called Margrit a "whore" and a "tramp." The Germans used a more complicated expression that translates "plaything of the occupying American prick." For Christmas Elvis gave his "Little Puppy" a gold watch studded with diamonds.

Though Elvis had found himself a German girlfriend, he didn't for a moment consider this relationship any betrayal of his long-standing love affair with Anita Wood. In fact, he thought that his only problem with Anita was the temptation his absence offered her to date other men. To affirm his good intentions and warn her against the dangers of her situation, he did something one day that was unprecedented in his life: He wrote Anita a letter.

"I haven't dated a single girl," he assured his "Little Beadie," adding, "when I marry it will be Miss Little Wood Presley." Above all, he implored her to trust him and to "keep yourself clean and wholesome." Then, with many anxious warnings about revealing the contents of the letter to anyone, he signed himself "Yours alone and forever"—and went back to playing with his "Little Puppy."

One month after Elvis's arrival in Germany, his unit received orders to proceed to Grafenwöhr for special training. Loading their tanks aboard flatcars and boarding coaches themselves, the men of the 32nd Armored Battalion journeyed about a hundred miles southeast to a point just short of the Czech border. "Graf," as the G.I.s called it, had a well-deserved reputation as the Hellhole of Europe. It was the Nazi Fort

Hood: a vast tract of hilly, wooded country that had been cleared of people twenty years before and fitted out with gunnery ranges, antitank traps and every other device necessary to train tank crews. During the winter the weather was bitterly cold and the ground covered with snow. Most American tanks had no heaters and a jeep, such as Private Presley was driving, was about as comfortable as sitting in a big ice-cube tray.

Visiting troops at Graf were restricted to the base during their stay. The only pastimes open to enlisted men at Graf were drinking beer, shooting pool or going to the movies. Naturally, Elvis chose the last. It was one night at the post movie house that he met the second German girl to become part of his life-support system overseas: Elisabeth Stefaniak.

Elisabeth was also a product of the war and the wrenching effects it had on German society. Born in 1940, she was too young to remember her father when he went off to the Russian front to fight for his Führer. When the war ended, Elisabeth and her mother were safe, having lived always in western Germany: The problem was what had happened to her father. He was reported simply "missing." Then, one day in the early fifties, he returned from Russia—with a Russian wife. An acrimonious divorce followed, and Elisabeth's mother ended by marrying an American sergeant named Raymond McCormick. The sergeant did one tour of duty in the States; then he was returned to Germany, winding up at Graf, where he was an instructor in ammunition loading and handling.

After living in the States for several years, coming back to this dreadful outpost on the front lines of the Cold War was no joke for a young girl. Sergeant McCormick was an Archie Bunker type. He took a low view of the morals of most G.I.s. Though there were thousands of men on the base, Elisabeth, who was now eighteen years old, was not allowed to date a soldier. Nor could she get a job because, technically, she was an American citizen; the Germans preferred to hire cheaper-paid Germans. Putting it all together, you could say that Elisabeth Stefaniak's prospects were dim.

Like every other teenager in the world, Elisabeth was very curious about Elvis Presley. When she learned that he was on the post and went to the movies every night, she quizzed the manager of the movie theater about his famous guest. The manager confirmed that Elvis would slip into the movie house every night about ten minutes after the picture began; then, he would slip out again a few minutes before it ended. The trick was to get to him before he made his getaway.

A few nights later, Elisabeth, having been presented to Elvis by another G.I. at the movie house, is walking with him through the wooded
area that leads to the segregated zone where the married noncoms live
in apartment buildings. When they reach Elisabeth's apartment house,
she invites him to come up and meet her mother and her stepfather,
the sergeant. Elvis declines instantly. Still, he lingers. He prolongs the
feeble conversation. Finally, he bends down and kisses her. Then he
strides off alone into the woods, calling out as he disappears: "Come
on back to the movie and I'll be seein' ya!"

Elisabeth stumbled up the stairs to her apartment and lay awake
all night thinking of the extraordinary thing that had befallen her. The
next morning, she told the story to her mother and stepfather. Sergeant
Bunker made a face and shrugged, "Who cares?" Elisabeth's mother
was enormously excited. She, too, was an Elvis fan.

That night Elisabeth was back at the movies—and so was Elvis.
They met every night for a week. Every evening he would walk her
home, but always he refused to go upstairs and meet the family. Then,
without any invitation or announcement, Elvis came to the McCormicks'
house on Thanksgiving Day.

Once Elvis had gotten his foot not only through the door but under
the table, he started showing up at odd times of the day. He might
pop over at ten in the morning, driving his jeep, and come up for coffee
in the kitchen. Or he might come around in the evening for supper.

Once a good ole boy has filled his belly, what's he gonna do next?
You got it. He takes himself a nice long snooze. Once Elvis had made
himself at home at the McCormicks', he would stretch out on the couch
after breakfast and cop some Zs. He also took to borrowing the sergeant's
old Buick, hauled over from the States. Pretty soon Elvis was driving
Elisabeth to the movies every night.

Now, the boy has taken his girl to the movies. The night is still
young. They have the car. What are they going to do? There's only
one thing Elvis wants to do. Drive slowly around Grafenwöhr and talk
to Elisabeth. Not talk about the scout problem they were given that
day or how all their tanks have parts missing or how he got a new
heater for his jeep. No, Elvis wants to have that deep communion, that
solacing confessional hour, that he enjoyed for so many years with Gladys. A man has problems and there's no better way to get them off
his chest than to tell them to a woman, a sweet, sympathetic woman,
who will just soak them up like a sponge.

One night Elvis got so deep into his musings and his confessions that he violated one of his deepest taboos: He talked about his father. As Elisabeth listened, hardly daring to breathe, much less speak, Elvis told her that when his mother was hardly cold in her grave, his father had started running after other women. As he described the scenes he had witnessed just before they left Killeen, and even more recently at Bad Nauheim, he grew more and more upset. Finally, he pulled the car over and burst into loud racking sobs.

Elvis left Grafenwöhr just before Christmas. On the day of his departure, he came to say goodbye. He explained that he had need of a secretary back at Bad Nauheim who would lend a hand with the mail and act as interpreter in the daily business with the Germans. Elvis was offering this job to Elisabeth.

A couple of days later, Elisabeth, wearing a red coat for identification, was standing on the train platform at Bad Nauheim waiting for Elvis to pick her up in his spanking new white BMW sports car, which the press had dubbed *"Der Elviswagen."* Soon she had met Vernon, Grandma and the Guys. Everything was delightful until she realized what lay in store for her.

Elvis, as usual, was looking for unlimited service at a rock-bottom price. Elisabeth was informed that her duties would not be confined to answering letters and translating the chatter of the local merchants. She was also expected to help out Grandma with the cooking and the dishes, to aid Vernon with the shopping and to do any other odd chores that seemed inappropriate for the menfolk who sat around idle all day long. Her remuneration was the grand sum of thirty-five dollars a week. (Elvis always paid his salaried employees thirty-five dollars a week in the early years because that was the amount he received while working for Crown Electric.)

What was worse than the pay was the discipline imposed on her. Having just escaped from a man who wouldn't allow her to date the only men available, Elisabeth was startled to hear from Elvis's own lips that she must not think of dating anyone while she lived in his home. He insisted in fact, that she not even *look* at the boys who lived in the house or came there on visits. If he discovered her in this forbidden act, he would growl, *"Caught!"*

It was a blue Christmas for everyone in the Presley family that year. Red and Lamar had to squeeze Vernon to get a few dollars to buy gifts for their families at home. Elisabeth was distressed about her situation. Elvis moped around the house brooding on his dead mother. Even Grandma, normally so cheerful, couldn't get herself together to make a real Christmas dinner. Vernon and the boys went to the dining room at the post in Friedberg and had G.I. turkey.

The more depressed Elvis became, the more he complained about being in the army. He would sit on the edge of his bed and let it all out to Lamar: "It's like starting all over again," he would lament. "It's like when I was working for the Loew's State and Crown Electric. Seventy-eight dollars a month—shit! I make that in a minute!" Lamar would pour his soothing platitudes over the irate Elvis, but the monologue of complaints would only grow keener. "Here I am a singing star and a movie star and I gotta act like one o' the guys! It ain't easy bein' one o' the guys. I ain't never been one o' the guys, and I never will be one o' the guys!"

Adding to Elvis's gloom was the steady stream of letters from Anita, who was now getting upset over all the stories in papers about his relationship with Margrit. Elvis decided to write Anita and deny everything. This time he concedes that he had "seen" the German girl about whom Anita was reading; but, he insists, it had been only once when she was in the company of a photographer. As the girl didn't speak a word of English, how could they possibly have been dating? The real truth, Elvis protests, is that never in his whole life has he been so "lonesome and miserable." His only consolation is to lie in bed at nights thinking about his "Wittle Beadie," about her little eyes and little nose and little hair, which some nights he imagines brushing his cheek and getting him so hot that he starts swearing! No matter. Like General MacArthur, he vows: "I shall return." Meantime, he urges her to get Tommy Edwards's record of "Soldier Boy." From now on, he says, that will be their song. Then, he signs off with a tremulous P.S.: "No one ever reads this, OK?"

If the characters in *Grease* wrote letters, they would be exactly like these soliloquies Elvis mailed from Germany. He sees himself as a character in a wailing R & B ballad, a "lonely little boy 5,000 miles away," accused falsely of loving another girl when all he really wants is Little Wittle Beadie. Oh, it all begs to be poured into a microphone and stamped on shiny vinyl and blasted out over the airways, with a fast-talking DJ jumping in at the end to blither, " 'Lonely Little Boy' by Elvis Presley— for Anita and the gang out there in Whitehaven!" Yes, it's a very teeny Elvis that you find in these sad-assed letters from Germany: that lonely melancholy boy who spent his life dreaming of things he wanted, only to discover when he got them that they didn't make him happy.

Chapter 21

Teen Angel

GOETHESTRASSE 14, the blocky, three-story, white
stucco house into which Elvis settled after he and his boys had
been kicked out of a couple of hotels for disturbing the elderly
guests with water battles and playful acts of arson, was full of
heavy, overstuffed furniture and that fusty, dreary, old-world atmosphere that Elvis loathed. An even bigger problem than the house's
depressing atmosphere was its owner, a widow named Frau Pieper.
One of those big, hard, busty jobs straight out of *The Katzenjammer
Kids,* Frau Pieper was the human equivalent of a German tank.
She was loud, aggressive and ugly, all of which would not have
mattered a damn if she had been willing simply to rent her house
for ten times its proper value and clear out. The difficulty was
that she made it a condition of the rental that she remain living
in the house in a room next to the kitchen. She argued that she
had no other place to live and that her services were essential as
housekeeper. Like a fool, Vernon acceded to this outrageous demand
and the family was saddled for the next fifteen months with a universally detested house mother.

Once Elvis settled into the house, his life locked into a routine
that never varied. Reveille at Goethestrasse 14 would sound raucously at four-thirty in the morning, when Lamar would wake up

299

the whole neighborhood by gunning the mighty engine of the *Elviswagen*. If it had snowed the night before, as it often did, Lamar would have to lay his ponderous bulk behind the haft of a broad shovel to get the car clear of the house. When Elvis got up, everyone got up: That was an unspoken rule. Grandma and Elisabeth would go into the kitchen and prepare a breakfast designed to please only one person—but served to everyone. There were always lots of big, fat, round "cat's head" biscuits, thick gravy made from bacon drippings, hard-fried eggs and burnt bacon, jam, syrup, butter, coffee and ice-cold cling peaches out of cans. Elvis would mix the butter, syrup and jam together, spread the mixture on the split biscuits, then convert them into "soaks" by dipping them deep in his coffee. The bacon he would eat with his fingers, holding it by the fat end and nibbling on the lean. The peaches were his dessert, icing the fat in his belly and leaving a sweet taste in his mouth as he set out bitterly to drive the seventeen kilometers to the base.

As soon as the boss was out of the house, everyone would go back to bed. They would get up again at a normal hour and set to their tasks. Elisabeth and the boys would go into a glassed-in back porch that served as an office and start reading and answering the vast amounts of mail that were delivered daily by the APO. The volume of the mail, even over here in Germany, was so staggering that it would take the three of them many hours each day to reply to the most likely correspondents. Virtually everyone in the household had become adept at forging Elvis's signature so it was possible to make thousands of teenagers in Europe and America happy in the possession of an authentic letter written and signed by Elvis himself.

Vernon loved to play the hard taskmaster. Orville Bean at last! Though he paid the boys nothing, giving them at most fifty cents or a dollar a week for beer money, he didn't hesitate to chastise them if they were remiss in their duties. Even Elisabeth, who was such a sweet and obliging girl, always busy about the house from early morning to late at night, was chewed out fiercely for the slightest infractions of discipline. Once Elvis came home for lunch and found Elisabeth writing in the office. "What are you doing?" he asked. "Writing my mother a letter," she replied innocently. That afternoon, as soon as Elvis had cleared the house, Vernon came down on her like an angry Egyptian overseer. He reprimanded her severely for engaging in personal business on Presley time. Elisabeth protested that all her time was Presley time, that she had no set hours or duties and was expected to toil from before dawn to long after dark. Vernon bore down even harder at this sign of insubordination, giving her that hard, mean, nasty redneck tongue.

Apart from bossing the hands, Vernon's other duties took him often to the commissary, where he would lay in supplies of Hormel chili, Pepsi, canned Vienna sausage (Elvis pronounced it "Vaih-ennah"), peanut butter, canned crowder peas and dairy supplies. By this point, Vernon had bought himself a good solid burgherlike black Mercedes that would lend him dignity. His trips abroad often lasted much longer and produced much less yield than a time and motion analyst would allow reasonable. Like most southern men, Vernon had a knack for slippin' away that baffled the curious.

Supper was served at six. Sauerkraut and weenies were the standard fare. Sometimes there'd be steak and gravy—but only when Elvis was away on field exercises. Elvis's absences tended to encourage a very different life-style: trips to the movies and meals in German restaurants where, like renegade Jews, the boys and Elisabeth would stuff themselves with forbidden foods like Hassenpfeffer, Wienerschnitzel, Sauerbraten and red cabbage, even Wildschwein (wild boar), marinated for nine days in strong spices. Living as prisoners of a juvenile egomaniac, Elisabeth, Lamar and Red didn't often get a chance to go out and play.

In the evening, the townsfolk would gather before the house to watch the ceremony of the autograph signing. Elvis had established this ritual as a device for relieving his family of day-long disruptions by concentrating the unavoidable requests into a half hour in the early evening. All day the house would stand there blank, apparently deserted, almost spooky, with its black-green rolling shutters repelling the gazes and the lenses of the inevitable priers and gawkers. On the wooden blind that covered the French windows at the front of the house, there would be displayed a placard that gave directions to visitors. Hand-printed in defective German, it read:

Wegen vorgeschriebener Ruhe der Kurgäste is das Betreten des Grundstucks untersagt.

To preserve the prescribed rest of the medical patients traffic in this area is forbidden.

AUTOGRAMME VON 19:30   20:00
Autographs between 7:30–8:00 P.M.
   Only Please

When the magic hour arrived, Elvis would appear before the house, dressed in his army fatigues and cap, to sign the postcards, pictures and album sleeves handed to him by fans. There was never any violence or disorder during these sessions, but after a while they began to bore him. At that point, the routine was altered. Lamar or Red would come out of the house and explain that Elvis was indisposed but eager to sign their souvenirs. Then the boys would collect the stuff, bring it indoors, forge Elvis's signature upon it and return it to the patiently waiting fans.

Once this chore was out of the way, the family would gather for the balance of the evening in the parlor, which boasted a piano as well as a radio and a phonograph. Elvis might seat himself at the piano to play and sing or they might tune in a disc jockey show on the Armed Forces Network, the only station they ever listened to in Germany. Elvis's favorite record was "The Bells," Billy Ward's weird and lurid evocation of the funeral of a sweetheart.

By nine, Elvis would be hungry again. He would give Elisabeth the high sign and she would go into the kitchen to prepare his bedtime snack. Peeling several bananas, she would slice the fruit and mash it in a bowl with lots of peanut butter. Then she would spread this mulch on slices of bread, cap the sandwiches with more bread and toast them under the grill. Elvis would eat four or five of these rich concoctions. His other nighttime favorite was even more leaden. This was a fried potato sandwich. The potatoes were sliced a quarter inch thick and browned in the fat of bacon that had just been removed from the frying pan. The sandwich would consist of fried potato, burnt bacon and onions, plastered with mustard. This mess, too, would be seared under the grill.

By ten o'clock, Elvis would be climbing the stairs to his bedroom on the second floor. He would lie abed for a while, reading the latest issue of *Mad* or *Cracked,* laughing aloud at the gags. When he fell to sleep, Red and Lamar might go out to the Beck's beer bar, where they would nurse two steins for the balance of the night.

The weekends would see some lifting of the gloom that clouded the week. Elvis, freed of his duties at the post, would invite some of his army buddies to the house. One of his favorites was a clean-cut, well-bred young man named Rex Mansfield, who had been by Elvis's side since they were inducted together at Memphis. "Rextus" earned Elvis's respect in the first weeks at Hood by refusing to accept payment for taking Elvis's duty as corporal of the guard during a visit by Anita. Rex had said, "I'll expect you to do as much for me." That was always the best way to talk to Elvis, who automatically divided everyone he

met into those he could take for granted and those whom he would
have to take seriously.

A very different sort of man was Joe Esposito, a dark, stocky, second-
generation Italian from Chicago, who was a company clerk. Joe was a
hustler who had studied accounting by day and hung out with Mob
guys by night; he even boasted of having dated the daughter of Tony
"Big Tuna" Accardo, the alleged boss of the Chicago Family. Perhaps
it was from these wise guys that Joe picked up his skills as a shylock,
which he used to good effect in Germany. Lending money to G.I.s at
a hundred percent premium, Joe made an extra seven or eight thousand
dollars a year. It was in this manner that he first met Lamar, who borrowed money from Joe and then repaid him by introducing him to Elvis.

The most entertaining of Elvis's new army cronies was a little dude
from Decatur, Alabama, named Charlie Hodge. This lad grew so close
to Elvis in the years to come that he became Elvis's shadow. He was a
shrunken shadow, only five feet three. He had a big, man-sized face
on him, but his body was like a suit draped on a hanger: good fit at
the shoulders and the rest hanging over nothing. Charlie was an accomplished gospel singer and country musician, who had gone to the Stamps
Gospel School and worked for years as one of Red Foley's Smokey
Mountain Boys. Of all the men who got tight with Elvis, he was the
only one who was a professional musician and entertainer.

Evenings on the weekends would start out much as they did during
the week; but around midnight on Friday, Elvis would always get the
itch to go out and run around in the cars. He would go upstairs and
comb his hair and prepare himself carefully to leave. Then, he would
come down and give the command to move without allowing anybody
else as much as a moment to take a leak. If someone complained he
were tired or seemed reluctant to go, Elvis would whip out his quart
jar of Dexies, obtained from a pharmacist on the post, and shake out
four or five. "Take a cup of coffee with this," he would urge: "it'll get
into your bloodstream faster." Then the boys would jump pell-mell into
the cars and take off for Frankfurt.

Elvis's favorite entertainer in this big modern city was a female contor-
tionist who worked in a club that was rigged for gymnastic performances.
After watching her twist her body into astonishing knots, Elvis finally
obtained an introduction to the lady and even dated her. All the boys
chuckled in lubricious delight at the thought of what this chick could
do in the sack. The Pelvis never divulged what sort of relationship he
enjoyed with the Pretzel.

During this winter, Vernon met Dee Stanley, the wife of Master Sergeant Bill Stanley, a much-decorated veteran who had been General Patton's personal bodyguard during the invasion of Europe. The Stanleys lived with their three little boys in nearby Wiesbaden. The relationship commenced when Dee Stanley, a vivacious, high-strung little woman from Tennessee, called Elvis and invited him to supper. Elvis countered by inviting her to his hotel for coffee and then substituting his father as host. Vernon took a shine to Dee at once; soon he and the Stanleys had become a threesome. One afternoon, he got Dee into bed and the threesome became a triangle. The romance was cross-hatched by guilt, conflict and anxiety. Bill Stanley, a heavy but contrite drinker, sought to enlist Vernon's help in averting a divorce. Dee, who rendezvoused with Vernon at Graceland after flying back to the States to put her children into a home, was concerned that Elvis would block her marriage to his father. It was while matters were at their most precarious that Vernon went out shopping with Elisabeth one day and nearly killed them both.

Vernon accelerated to pass a car in front of him on the Autobahn. Just at that moment, the car he was trying to skirt moved into the passing lane to get ahead of another car. Vernon hit his brakes so hard that his machine went into a skid and struck the median. Flipping over and rolling three times, the car flew across the oncoming lanes and crashed into a tree on the far side of the highway, coming to rest upside down.

When Vernon extricated himself from the car, he stuck his head back inside and yelled: "Honey, are you all right?" Elisabeth had been struggling to get free, but she had discovered that she was paralyzed. "My back hurts—I can't move!" she cried. At that moment, some motorists stopped and pulled her free of the car. She told them to call Frau Pieper. Shortly afterward, an ambulance arrived and took Elisabeth off to a nearby hospital. Vernon chose to remain with his car, which is where Elvis found him when he came roaring up in the *Elviswagen* with Lamar.

The call to Frau Pieper had found Elvis at home. Terrified at the thought that his father might be injured, Elvis pushed his BMW up to 150 miles an hour getting to the wreck. Once he saw that his worst fears were unfounded, he grabbed Vernon and took off for home. He never suggested that they go to the hospital to learn how Elisabeth was faring. She was very lucky. X-rays disclosed that her back was not broken and that her paralysis was only a temporary condition owing to shock.

When they arrived home, they found Captain and Mrs. Beaulieu sitting up and waiting for them with grim expressions on their faces. The Captain dressed down the enlisted man. The mother scolded her daughter. There were to be no more visits with this Elvis Presley. That much was fixed, settled, beyond discussion. Priscilla was not broken-hearted. From the start she had seen the whole idea as a fantasy. What's more, she couldn't believe that Elvis would ever want to see her again. Why should he, when every girl in the world was dying to meet him? Imagine her surprise when she learned through Grant that Elvis was pressing for another meeting the following weekend. Now she would have to persuade her parents.

Captain Beaulieu was actually Priscilla's stepfather. An enlisted man in the marines in World War II, he had worked his way up from the ranks, qualifying after the war for an air force training program that had landed him a navigator's berth at the big air base at Wiesbaden. He had married Priscilla's mother several years after she was widowed. Her first husband, Priscilla's father, was a handsome naval pilot named James Wagner. While flying home in 1945 to visit his wife and five-month-old infant daughter, Lieutenant Wagner had crashed and died. Priscilla still carried a yellowed picture of him in her wallet. One of the reasons for her apparent maturity was the fact that she was the oldest child in a family that now numbered four younger brothers and her little sister, Michelle.

Currie Grant did a splendid job of reassuring the Beaulieus about Elvis's character and intentions. He explained that far from being one of those crazy showbiz types, Elvis was an exemplary young man who lived with his father and grandmother in the most respectable manner; that his little weekend parties were chaste entertainments, where the boys and girls sat around the piano singing songs or snacking on pizza and Pepsi. As for the problem of conforming with Priscilla's curfew, Elvis was so keen on avoiding any future difficulty that he had offered to provide a car and a driver expressly for this purpose. That weekend, Priscilla returned to Bad Nauheim.

Gradually, the rhythm of her visits changed from weekends only to twice a week, three times a week, eventually four times a week. It must be borne in mind that these visits were not just little runs across town. Lamar would collect her in Wiesbaden very early in the evening and drive for nearly an hour until they got to the house on Goethestrasse. Then, when the evening was over, they would have another long drive, this time at night in winter with the road often blanketed by heavy fog. Visibility was so poor sometimes that Priscilla would have to get out of the car and lead Lamar through the thick vapors. Many a night they got home long past the appointed hour.

As the frequency of Priscilla's visits increased, the venue of these little trysts also changed. Now, instead of a party around the ole pie-ano, with lots of other boys and girls present, as well as Daddy and Grandma—those watchful chaperones!—in the kitchen, the famous sex hero and his teen angel were spending the whole evening alone together in his bedroom. In a word, Elvis had contrived to transform Bad Nauheim into Memphis, Goethestrasse 14 into Graceland, and his empty, lonely evenings into deeply absorbing pajama parties.

Still, there was one important difference. Instead of cavorting or communing with a collective identity comprised of three fourteen-year-old girls, Elvis was now focusing all his attentions on just one fourteen-year-old girl. This was an unprecedented event in his life. In the past, whenever Elvis had sought to establish an intimate relationship with a girl of the age on which he was fixated, he had found it impossible to achieve any real rapport. Junior high girls were always so overwhelmed with Elvis's fame and mystique that they could never relax and accept him as their teenage boyfriend. They always kept harping on the fact that he was a star, a hero, a king! This was the ironic and exasperating price that Elvis paid for success. He had priced himself right out of the fourteen-year-old market.

Priscilla, however, was different. Even years later, Elvis was still marveling over this child's self-confidence. As he told an interviewer: "Priscilla was just a kid—more than ten years younger than me. But she wasn't like so many of the other girls. I guess most of 'em were a little overawed by me, by what I'm supposed to be. Dunno why, because I'm shy myself and do my best to make other people feel at ease. But with this chick, it was different. She didn't give the impression that in any way she was tongue-tied." In fact, as Elisabeth Stefaniak recalls: "It's like she could get away with more smart talk than the other girls. He would put them in their place real quick but not her." Priscilla's appeal was not confined to youth, beauty, innocence—important as those things were to Elvis. What made her unique was the fact that she could hold her own with the famous star, sitting up there in the bedroom talking about cars, movies and eye makeup, and even evincing at times a certain pertness, even sassiness, suggesting that she held herself nearly equal to Elvis. What a wonderful thing that must have been to him; for if she treated him as an equal, he was equal: he was free at last to regress to that age where he was most comfortable: sweet sixteen.

What did the Beaulieus make of the fact that their daughter was constantly being carried off by a fat man in an expensive Mercedes to spend the evening with a notorious sex symbol? Clearly, they were given something more reassuring than Currie Grant's Norman Rockwell portrait. As soon as Priscilla told Elvis that the lies she was forced to invent every night to explain her late arrivals at home were creating a threat to the continuation of the visits, Elvis decided to go straight to the heart of the problem. He and Vernon paid a call on the Beaulieus. What precisely they told the Captain and Mrs. Beaulieu is not known, but it must have turned on the fact that some day—once he had gotten out of the service and had reestablished his career—Elvis would want to settle down and marry and live just like any other successful young man. Though no promise of marriage was made at this early date, the thought of marriage was clearly in everyone's mind. Nor is this surprising in view of Elvis's lifelong penchant for proposing marriage at the earliest possible moment. Whatever the substance of this conversation, the facts speak for themselves. Having started off by telling her daughter, "I wouldn't send you across the street to meet Elvis Presley," Mrs. Beaulieu was now telling Priscilla that her relationship with Elvis represented a "once in a lifetime opportunity."

After a long summer at the post in Friedberg, Elvis's unit received a red alert. Captain Betts, the company commander, told the men: "Don't leave anything behind that you want to keep." Elvis took alarm immediately. "This is it!" he shouted as he entered the house that day: "They're going to ship all civilian personnel home." Lamar, fearing an immediate invasion by the Russians, cried: "I hope they send us soon! I don't wanna be here when a war starts!"

The alert turned out to be merely a test of the unit's readiness, but the 32nd Armored did ship out immediately for Wildflicken, a mountainous region near the Swiss border that was already deep under snow and ice. During the ten days the exercise lasted, the battalion lost about half its equipment. One slip on the narrow mountain roads and a tank would plunge down a two- or three-hundred-foot declivity. Elvis had put a tank heater in his jeep in anticipation of the cold. One bitter night, he turned on the heater, pulled a poncho over his head and went to sleep. In the middle of the night, he awoke gasping and choking, feeling that he was about to die. Carbon monoxide from the engine had filled the tent made by his poncho and would have killed him, if a chance breeze hadn't blown the covering off his head and revived him. Elvis staggered out of the jeep and collapsed on the ground. Lying there, he looked up at the stars and thanked God for sparing him.

When Elvis returned from the field in the fall of 1959, he found the first unmistakable signs of his reviving career. Hal Wallis had come over from Hollywood to supervise the work of a second-unit production crew, which was going to film backgrounds for Elvis's first movie when he got out of the service. Predictably, it would exploit his past two years in the army and dramatize the lighter-than-life adventures of a G.I. tanker in Germany. Elvis was not happy with the idea. Naturally, he kept his disappointment to himself and his most trusted confidants. He craved roles that were not simply thinly disguised and fantasized versions of Elvis Presley. Being a professional good guy, always eager to please, however, he couldn't level with Hal Wallis or with anyone in a position of authority. He would spend the rest of his long career in Hollywood lamenting the fact that he never got any good parts. What he never learned was that actors don't just *get* good parts: they *demand* them.

The other news at Goethestrasse was downright unpleasant: Vernon informed his son that Dee would be coming soon to live with them. Why Vernon and Dee did not marry at this time is a mystery. She had her separation agreement and was, presumably, well along in her divorce. A few more months of separate domiciles and the pair could have married and cleared the air of any questions of impropriety. By moving in with Vernon before the divorce, Dee created fresh threats of scandal. Elvis could not have approved of such an arrangement; but he was in a compromising position himself, carrying on with Priscilla up in his bedroom four nights a week. (Vernon and Dee were married at Huntsville, Alabama, on July 3, 1960. Elvis was conspicuously absent.)

The last months in Germany went by so rapidly that they are just a blur in the minds of those who lived with Elvis. When the date for departure had been set, three weeks short of the two-year term of the draft, Elvis sent the family home. On the final day, when Elvis climbed aboard the DC-7 at Frankfurt Airport, the crowd around the plane was so dense that Priscilla could not get beyond the outer fringes. Elvis had promised to wave to her when he entered the cabin—and he did wave. The crowd took the wave as intended for it and roared back a farewell that would have drowned the voice of a dozen fourteen-year-old girls. One photographer who knew the truth did contrive to capture Priscilla at the final poignant moment. The photo he snapped is one of the most touching in that immense album stamped ELVIS.

The picture is of a very young but very pretty girl, one of those young girls who bear already on their faces the unmistakable signs of a woman's beauty. The finely cut lips are parted. The hand is held up in an arrested salute. The feature that rivets the viewer's gaze is the eyes. They are beautiful eyes, nearly innocent of makeup. What is so extraordinary about them is their clouded ecstatic focus, as if they were the eyes of a seer gazing raptly into the future.

Chapter 22

About Face!

A BLIZZARD was driving over McGuire Field, near Fort Dix, New Jersey, when the DC-7 carrying Elvis and his detail began its landing approach. Terrified of flying, Elvis had anesthetized himself by swallowing a handful of sleeping pills before he took off at Frankfurt. After the refueling stop at Prestwick, Scotland, he had dropped into a deep sleep. Now, after fourteen hours in the air, he was wide awake and staring grimly out the window into a wall of glimmering white.

Down and down the plane glided, an interminable descent, punctuated by hysterical sick jokes about crashing. Elvis, tense with fear, his left leg jiggling frantically, dug his fingers into the armrests and braced his body. Suddenly, it seemed his worst fears had come true. The plane struck the ground with a violent impact and hooked sharply to the left. Just as the soldiers started shouting in terror, the ship straightened out and rolled down the tarmac. Coming in on instruments with the ceiling zero, the pilot had missed the runway.

Though Elvis's landing was bumpy, the rest of the road was as smooth as love and money could make it. The Colonel had engaged a railroad magnate's luxurious private car to spare Elvis the stress of any further flying. The forty-eight-hour journey quickly became a royal progress. Everywhere the train paused, even if it were just a whistle stop in the middle of the night, jubilant crowds appeared to salute their King's return from exile. Elvis would appear on the coach's "back porch," attired in his stunning dress blues, three stripes and a rocker on his sleeve, smiling and waving like a war hero. When the train pulled out of the station, the Colonel would start tossing photos and flyers at the crowd.

Elvis's arrival at Memphis's Union Station was tumultuous. Under heavy police escort he was conveyed to Graceland. When he stepped through the door and embraced Dodger, his happiness was complete. Nothing had changed. Everything would be as it had been before. He was still the King. If any doubts remained about his status with the public, they were wiped out in the first week.

One million orders were received for Elvis's first new record—even before he could set foot in the studio. On top of this million-dollar blank check, Elvis received the unheard-of fee of $125,000 from Frank Sinatra for a guest shot on the Timex special. Imagine receiving $125,000 (worth three times that amount today) for singing two songs! *Life,* which had pilloried Elvis in 1956, offered now to plaster his picture across its glossy cover. Colonel Parker had the gall to ask for $25,000—offering to refund the money if *Life*'s newsstand sale that week did not increase thirty-five percent. *Life* was so outraged that it cancelled Elvis's picture for the cover. Meantime, Hal Wallis was urging Elvis to leave at once for Hollywood to start work on his new picture, which was already in production. RCA was equally insistent that its greatest star do nothing before he filled up the "can."

The overwhelming demand for Elvis was not simply a product of his long absence from the scene. It was also an expression of the desperately imperiled state of his kingdom. During the years when he was in the army, rock 'n' roll had fallen on evil days. The original power of the music, derived from the great tradition of R & B, had been frittered away in the adaptation of black adult experience to white teenage innocence. In the mouths of Elvis travesties, like Frankie Avalon and Fabian, the stars of *American Bandstand,* rock had swiftly been reduced to rubbish.

At the same time that the teen twerps were taking over, the real rockers, the young men of talent, were being wiped out in an extraordinary plague of disgraces and disasters. Rock, had established all-time records for unwarranted success; now it set comparable standards for undeserved misfortune. Buddy Holly, Richie Valens and the Big Bopper perished in a plane crash. Little Richard ran up such an enormous bill with the I.R.S. that he was forced to take refuge, first in the ministry and then in Europe. Chuck Berry was indicted (later convicted and imprisoned) for a violation of the Mann Act. Jerry Lee Lewis's burgeoning career was blighted by scandal. Carl Perkins never recovered his momentum after cracking up with his band on the road to the *Ed Sullivan Show.* Eddie Cochran was killed in a cab crash in London that permanently crippled Gene Vincent.

As if all this weren't enough, in November 1959 commenced the climactic disaster—the payola scandal. The first shock was felt one after-noon that month, when Alan Freed came on the air sobbing, right in the middle of "Shimmy Shimmy Ko-Ko-Bop" by Little Anthony and the Imperials. In the voice of a dying man, he announced that as of that moment he was resigning from WABC. Swiftly, it was revealed that he had refused to sign a statement declaring that he had never taken money to plug records. Two days later, on his *Big Beat* TV show, he took his final farewell of the New York public, leaving the kids in tears and inspiring one girl to cry at the camera—"Now, they've taken away our father!"

Overnight, the atmosphere of the music business changed from the cheerful uproar of Tin Pan Alley to the eerie silence of an abandoned boom town. "No longer are the lobbies of the Brill Building thronged with businessmen, wildly ecstatic over a newly recorded song or newly released disc," wrote a trade reporter. "The crowd that used to stand in front of the Turf and Dempsey's or Hanson's Drugstore has faded away. Disc jockeys cannot be reached by phone, distributors are out of town, A & R men are suddenly vacationing, and many record company officials answer their phones in soft, whispering voices." Suddenly, the Big Beat had become the Big Stink.

At the very moment of Elvis's return, a congressional investigative committee, fresh from hearing how Charles Lincoln Van Doren had repeatedly deceived the public on the *$64,000 Question,* was now learning that RCA distributors wrote checks to DJs with the name of the record to be plugged on the check, that Morris Levy of Roulette Records held two unpaid mortgages in the name of Alan Freed and that Dick Clark, a twenty-nine-year-old DJ from Philadelphia, held an interest in thirty-three record and publishing firms which provided him with an income of $500,000 a year. Under orders from Mr. Clean over at the White House (whose closest aide, Sherman Adams, had received a vicuna coat, electric appliances and a very expensive business trip from Bernard Gold-fine, a Boston businessman) to "clean up the mess," the committee had jolted the whole country with its revelations of corruption in the music and broadcasting industries. (The industries defended themselves with more honesty than brains by asserting that one of their oldest traditions was "pay for play.") Rock 'n' roll, long the target of parental rage, the fury of the old pops establishment and the public press, was now hanging on the ropes, waiting for the knockout.

The final defeat of the old rock was produced not by its political opponents but by a hard-punching young black contender called the Twist. With the advent of Hank Ballard, Chubby Checker, the Peppermint Lounge and the Philadelphia Sound, American popular music, that part of it at least that was alive and happening, suddenly jumped into a new groove called soul. As the disillusioned white teenagers mourned the demise of their heroes, the rest of the country put an invisible hula hoop around its hips and merrily shook its ass.

Elvis Presley, that cat's whisker on the crystal of popular consciousness, was quick to pick up the S.O.S. from the sinking ship. He was just as quick to make off in the opposite direction from the wreck. His first recording session, thrown together on the spur of the moment to capitalize on the enormous excitement produced by his return, does look backward at the days of do-wop. Its only hit, a scratch single, "Stuck on You," sticks a hook reminiscent of "I'm All Shook Up" into the mouth of a black gospel drone, a contrivance just good enough to ring the Pavlovian bell and send the schlocky tune to the top of the charts. With his second session, however, at the new Studio B at Nashville, a landmark event, running all night long from the evening of April 4 to the following afternoon, Elvis revealed his new course bearings.

The two great hits that came out this session, "It's Now or Never," which sold nine million copies, and "Are You Lonesome Tonight?," which sold a mere five million, were both unabashed, middle-of-the-road, lily-white pops. Elvis vocalized these tunes, as he did almost everything in this extraordinarily eclectic session, as a crooner. His voice has a honeyed mellowness and even in some of the songs an effeminate softness and sensitivity. He caresses the phrases of the romantic tunes with a tremulous-lipped intimacy that is the vocal equivalent of bedroom eyes. These famous hits prophesied the Presley movies of the sixties. "It's Now or Never," a Caribbean version of "O Solo Mio," embellished with exotic castanets, mandolin twitters and a rhumba rhythm, summons up perfectly the atmosphere of all those tropical resort milieus in which Elvis was destined to star in the succeeding decade. Not only a symbol of the abrupt volte-face which Elvis executes at this time in his career, the song declares the direction in which he is soon to head.

The ringing high A with which this Neapolitan classic ended demonstrated another important feature of the new Elvis: His voice had finally matured. Always a singer of unusual vocal endowments for the pop market, Elvis now revealed himself in possession of an instrument with an enormous range of two and a third octaves, extending from the baritone's low G to the tenor's high B. Though he never mastered completely the knack of moving smoothly through the "channel" from the low chest tones to the high head tones, he demonstrated a great improvement upon his early records, which, as in a song like, "I Want You, I Need You, I Love You," sound sometimes like the product of two distinctly different voices: one a strong dark baritone, the other a high nasal country tenor. From this time forth, the vocal inadequacies that marred the early ballads will vanish, and Elvis Presley will take his position in the long tradition of romantic crooners, commencing with Russ Colombo and Rudy Vallee and leading down through Bing Crosby and Frank Sinatra to, on one side, the white epigones of the "Groaner" and the "Voice," Dean Martin, Perry Como *et al.,* and on the other, the "sepia" side, Billy Eckstine, Roy Hamilton, Arthur Prysock and Brook Benton—the latter four Elvis's very special favorites.

Having now aligned himself with traditional pops, an identification that was enforced further when he appeared on television with Frank Sinatra looking, in his Miami Beach tuxedo, like a candidate for the Rat Pack, Elvis retired from the stage and exchanged his identity as the King of Rock 'n' Roll for that of an old-fashioned Hollywood juvenile. One would think, reading most accounts of this astonishing about-face, that nothing was more common in show business than for enormously successful superstars to abandon at the height of their popularity the image, the medium and the act which made them rich and famous to go off in search of a fresh career. Elvis's commitment to the movies was nothing new, of course; the question is: Why, having found a way to combine a successful career in film with an even more successful career as a stage performer, TV attraction and recording artist, did he sacrifice all these mutually reinforcing activities to the one for which he was least gifted?

Clearly, he grossly overestimated the importance of being a movie star and grossly underestimated the power of rock 'n' roll to endure and revive. (Or was it a case of scorning that at which one excels and envying what is beyond one?) Whatever Elvis's motives in making this false step, they could not have carried him far if they had not been reinforced by Colonel Parker, who dictated that Elvis concentrate entirely on films to the exclusion of every other sort of activity.

The Colonel appears to have arrived at this decision after prolonged discussions, during the years when Elvis was out of the country, with his Hollywood cronies, Hal Wallis and Abe Lastfogel, president of William Morris. These three showbiz veterans worked out between them a comprehensive strategy for exploiting Elvis when he got out of the service. Their basic goal was to widen his appeal by making him over into the image of a latter-day Bing Crosby, a good-looking, charming crooner with a flair for comedy. They were inspired partly by the fear that Elvis's public was too narrow and his stance too controversial; partly by the opportunity, which was offered by his military service, to make a fresh start with a clean, wholesome image.

Colonel Parker was attracted to the plan not only because it promised to make Elvis a major movie star but because it offered a means for rigidly controlling his star's public exposure. The plan was as mechanical as clockwork. Three times a year, at Christmas, Easter and during summer vacation, Elvis would be made available to his fans. Each motion picture would spin off a soundtrack album and each album would yield a hit title song. The title song would become a vital part of the ballyhoo for the picture and inspire DJs to play other cuts from the album. All three components of the package would reinforce each other. Then, when the product had been exploited to the limit, there would be a total blackout of Elvis in all media. The fans, deprived of their hero, would start to build up fresh expectations, which would be gratified when the whole process was repeated four months later.

Everybody stood to make a lot of money from this system. Abe Lastfogel's agency would take a flat ten percent off the top for negotiating on Elvis's behalf and drumming up new customers. The Colonel would take his customary twenty-five percent of Elvis's gross income plus whatever he could hustle for himself as technical director, publicity consultant or supervisor of security. Hal Wallis, the principal but by no means the only moviemaker, would obtain an easily marketable and relatively inexpensive supply of pictures.

Elvis Presley films were budgeted generally so that fifty percent of the budget was allotted to Elvis's salary. If Elvis received seven hundred fifty thousand dollars, the total cost would be one and a half million dollars. Assuming that profitability commences when the producer has recouped twice the cost of the negative, everything over three million dollars would be gravy. A successful Presley picture earned about five million dollars, a not-so-successful film about four million dollars. As everything moved swiftly, the filmmaker could earn one to two million dollars in the space of a year. What's more, a really clever producer like Wallis could use a Presley picture in a cross-collateralization deal, a financing device that Wallis may not have invented but which he certainly pioneered.

Elvis was "bankable," which meant that you could take his commitment to make your cheap-shot, teeny-weenie-bikini beach-party movie to the bank and use it as collateral to raise the enormous sum required to make a major motion picture that could win you an Academy Award. Cross-collateralization enabled Wallis in 1964, for example, to bank the shlocky *Roustabout* into his last great picture, *Becket*. As the famous (and enormously wealthy) producer remarked in 1969, when the game was up: "The Presley pictures were made, of course, for strictly commercial reasons." Hal Wallis never had any delusions about Elvis Presley's value in motion pictures. He looked at the meat and stamped it "commercial."

There was, unfortunately, one slight drawback to this otherwise perfect scheme. It assumed that Elvis Presley was like Kickapoo Joy Juice, one of those alcohol-laced tonics that could be bottled and peddled in any manner that was most convenient. All the medicine man had to worry about was doling out the product so that each bottle had its full effect but not so great a kick as to diminish the demand for the next bottle. What those mighty minds, Tom Parker, Hal Wallis and Abe Lastfogel, lost sight of was the obvious fact that Elvis drew his extraordinary power as a star (and his immense draw at the box office) from the fact that he was the King of Rock 'n' Roll, the emotional focus of seventeen million teen minds in America alone and as many more in the rest of the world. Take him off his throne, deprive him of his essential image, remove him from living contact with his people and their world and reduce him to the level of a traditional Hollywood musical comedy star—and what did you have? Just another version of those Tads and Tabs, Rocks and Rickys, who were the dying Hollywood's notion of where kids were at in the sixties.

It can be argued that the picture pundits proved their point by grinding out twenty-five Presley films in one decade, all of which made money. But the challenge was how to make the money without destroying the property. When the picture people got through with Elvis Presley in the late sixties, he was the laughingstock of the entertainment industry.

What's more, the rockers who did not desert the sinking ship soon found that the vessel had been transformed into an immense transatlantic steamer that plied back and forth from England to America with a whole new crew of musicians to replace those who had been lost in the fifties. Soon the new "rock" was a vastly bigger and more profitable business than anything ever dreamed of in the days of rock 'n' roll. The opportunity that Elvis would not abide was seized by other performers, who eventually broke all of Elvis's records and made him seem like some old father figure lost in the mists of the past.

Elvis's first postarmy picture, *G.I. Blues,* launched the campaign on behalf of the new, "mature" Elvis Presley by producing the greatest anticlimax of his entire career. Millions of kids had waited for many months to witness the first full-length performance by Elvis since *King Creole.* Finally, the moment had come. They poured into six thousand theaters across America and what did they see? A creaky old service musical of the sort that was ground out while the movie industry marked time during World War II. The story was trivial, the characters cardboard, the music corny military call-and-response routines. The most terrible disappointment was Elvis. The famous sideburns had been shaved off. The classic D.A. shorn to regulation length and covered with a garrison cap. The bop clothes, the hoody windbreaker, the blue suede shoes—all gone! With them went Elvis's face. Instead of the Novocaine lip, the pale, poached skin, the heavy-lidded, kohl-eyed look, the Presley phiz was now as straight and square as that of Ken, the Barbie Doll.

So keen was Hal Wallis on domesticating the Hillybilly Cat and making him "family" that he undercut the movie's wheezy old plot, about a bet made by two G.I.s to see who can score first with a sexy nightclub dancer, by presenting Elvis—whom the story requires to be a lady-killer—in a Dagwood Bumsted routine with a bawling baby and, in another bit, singing with wide-eyed innocence a cutesy Bavarian folk song behind a puppet show. No mere softening of the Presley image, *G.I. Blues* turned Elvis inside-out and upside-down. It also turned him off.

Elvis didn't go down without a fight. He disliked *G.I. Blues* and put the heat on Colonel Parker, who was dickering again with Twentieth Century-Fox, to get him better parts, a serious role. Elvis's keenest wish in Hollywood was always to be given a chance to prove himself in a dramatic film in which he sang no songs and strummed no guitars and demonstrated that through sheer force of his soul and talent he could thrill a movie audience the way he thrilled a concert audience. In *Flaming*

Star, his second film after his return from the service, he got the chance he had been seeking.

Cast as the half-breed son of a white rancher and an Indian woman, Elvis returned to that legendary world of nineteenth-century America in which he had made his movie debut. He got to play tense confrontational scenes, shoot guns, suffer wounds, ride horses and explore the whole Western macho movie ethos. He certainly looked the part. He even brought off some of the early scenes, especially where he is seen guarding his Indian mother from the marauding local ranchers. As the action gets heavier and more violent, however, the artificiality of his performance becomes increasingly obvious (just as it does in *Love Me Tender*) until, eventually, Elvis and the picture collapse in a jumble of silly clichés.

This largely unconvincing and tediously plotted Western was followed by *Wild in the Country*—a picture that seems to have been compounded (by the washed-up Clifford Odets) of reminiscences of Tennessee Williams and *Peyton Place.* Elvis's part, that of a sullen, sexy, southern youth being driven to violence—though destined for final salvation—derives very clearly from *King Creole.* What makes the film interesting at moments is the appearance in it of the young Tuesday Weld, who plays a sluttish unwed mother living with her conniving father and constantly inviting the brutal advances of that smoldering young stud, Elvis. Menacing sullenness, overbearing arrogance—these are notes that Elvis could strike convincingly on the screen because they were characteristic of his true personality. The subtle balance, however, by which a good actor could sound these repellent notes and at the same time retain the audience's sympathy was something that Elvis never mastered. Either he looks and acts ugly, producing a feeling of disgust; or else he is not convincing as a heavy and you don't take him seriously.

These two pictures mark the end, for all practical purposes, of Elvis's career as a serious film actor. Neither film received the sort of notices that would have encouraged Elvis in his acting ambitions; more importantly, neither picture made much money. At this point, Colonel Parker, Hal Wallis and Abe Lastfogel could say to Elvis: "I told you so." Henceforth, Elvis was confined to lighthearted musical comedies, commencing with his most commercially successful film: *Blue Hawaii.*

Concocted by the same team of Hal Wallis and Hal Kanter that had produced Elvis's best movie, *Loving You, Blue Hawaii* demonstrates the complete lack of respect for Elvis that had now become characteristic of his Hollywood manipulators. The picture completes the job, well begun by *G.I. Blues,* of metamorphosing Elvis the Pelvis into Elvis the Putz.

Taking up the story of Elvis after he gets out of the army, the picture offers us a characterless young man with two very vivid parents: a Mai Tai-drinking pineapple planter and his kooky southern-belle wife, played with a caricatured accent by Angela Lansbury. The rebellion of that once dangerous insurrectionary, Elvis Presley, has been muted now to cranky reluctance to follow in his father's footsteps. Instead of planting pineapples, Elvis (who never learned to swim) plays at being a beach boy, displaying a disappointing physique—flat chest, skinny legs, weak arms—and no apparent familiarity with water sports. His girlfriend is the handsome but maternal Joan Blackman, to whom he relates like a college boy to his older, married sister.

The picture's only complication is provided by a sulky and sassy teenage girl, one of a party of four which Elvis is guiding about the islands. When this naughty creature throws herself at Elvis in her nighty, he turns her firmly across his knee and gives her a good parental spanking. Having proven his maturity by punishing a girl similar to his former fans, he now completes the rites of conformity by getting married. The wedding is represented in an almost hieratic ceremony in which Elvis and his bride, mounted like human effigies on a barge, are conveyed with preternatural smoothness across a lagoon to a quaint old missionary chapel. The symbolism of the once wild, exotic and rebellious Pelvis frozen into the immobility of a figure atop a wedding cake and conveyed like a glazed-eye somnambulist toward the altar was one that profoundly gratified the drive-in crowd. The picture grossed many millions.

Marco Millions would have been the most appropriate property for Elvis in the sixties. Once Elizabeth Taylor had established the benchmark of the million-dollar salary with *Cleopatra,* the Colonel could not rest until he had found a way to raise his boy's price to this mystic number. Eventually, he succeeded. In Elvis's palmiest years, his price was one million dollars against a sizable percentage of the producer's profit. By the midsixties, Elvis Presley was the highest-paid actor in Hollywood.

What wasn't revealed was the fact that Elvis had to surrender half of this money to the government in taxes. The Colonel never permitted his boy to employ any sort of tax shelter. In fact, the only advice on taxation which the Colonel offered took the form of holding up before Elvis's anxious gaze all those poor devils, like Joe Louis, who had once been big stars but, who through failure to pay their taxes, had come to grief. Elvis was glad to pay when he heard what happened to you when you tried to beat Uncle Sam.

After the great success of *Blue Hawaii,* the Hollywood moviemakers demanded that Elvis appear henceforth in pictures concocted to a fixed formula. The Presley picture soon became one of Hollywood's most stereotyped products: the entertainment world's equivalent of a franchise hamburger. Like the burger, the picture looked big and appetizing— until you got into it. Then, you realized that it was totally synthetic, devoid of any genuine satisfaction. Compounded with mechanical precision out of the same invariable ingredients, prepared with astonishing rapidity, sold for a good price but actually scrimped in the making and aimed at a totally indiscriminate public, the product got steadily worse over the years until its grand and total effect was sheer nausea.

The prime ingredients of this beefcake formula were Elvis, a famous vacation resort and a bevy of good-looking girls led by some young "sex kitten" whose career was just beginning and whose price was rock bottom. The story lines, some of which were old, like *Kid Galahad,* some new, were stupefyingly similar. Elvis was always cast as a handsome young stranger of working-class status who has just blown into town and stumbled over the most incredible looking collection of girls. His identity as a racing driver, a sailing captain, a helicopter pilot, a deep-sea diver, a boxer, an acrobat, a photographer, a roustabout, a ranch hand, gambler, etc. was simply a matter of the costume he wore. His silicone-cheeked face, his tooth-capped smile, his helmet of shiny jet-black hair ("five inches of hot-buttered yak wool": *Time*) varied no more than does the head on a display window dummy. Though Elvis spoke lines, threw punches, and did a lot of driving in these pictures, his basic identity was that of a dummy.

In the movies, Elvis always displays an "attitude." He's aloof or annoyed, impudent or sarcastic; he walks around with a chip on his shoulder. These adolescent postures are reflected by the girl, who is bitchy and standoffish, ostentatiously indifferent to his appeal. The whole first part of the picture is always devoted to their huffs and sneers, as they trade put-downs or toss curtain lines over their shoulders. What brings her around eventually is simply the fact that she is the weaker of the two: not the weaker person but the weaker sex. The attitude toward women in Presley pictures is extremely condescending. The assumption is that the only thing women have on their minds is men. If they reject a man, he need not take the rejection seriously because it is simply a sign that the woman is playing hard to get. Elvis is a cool customer who jives along, confident that he'll come up a winner in the last reel.

As the new morality of the Swinging Sixties began to soak down to the grass-roots level, the moviemakers began to insinuate first a little and then a lot of dirt into these pictures. The girls now wear bathing suits that reveal their nipples and creases; they talk in double entendres and pose provocatively. Eventually, the movies became soft-core pornography played, like an old burlesque routine, with a very dead pan. Elvis's entrance in *Tickle Me* is a classic of the genre. Carrying his saddle to the bunkhouse of a dude ranch, he stumbles (literally, with a big pratfall) over a group of yummy young things exercising in short shorts. The camera ogles their leader so that both Elvis and the audience view her from behind and between her legs.

Perhaps the most preposterous feature of all these pictures is the way their hero constantly bursts into song in the most unlikely places. The flat, banal tone, the travel brochure settings, the obvious effort to create an illusion of verisimilitude subverted completely the conventions of musical comedy. As for the quality of the music, it matched perfectly the level of the movies, both combining to plumb below the level of pop culture to what might be called pap culture.

Blue Hawaii is the best of the postarmy Presley film scores; of the worst, one is not obliged to speak, if only out of respect for the dead. Elvis's Brill Building writers, it should be borne in mind, were not accustomed to composing for dramatic situations, as were the famous songwriters of the thirties and forties, who had grown up in the New York theater. The only man who could consistently contrive something that would work in the absurd situations offered by the scripts was an obscure tune tailor named Ben Wiseman. Ever hear of Ben? No? Well, you're not alone. Nobody outside the business has ever heard of Ben Wiseman. Yet this dude composed no less than *fifty-seven* songs for Elvis Presley. Imagine: Elvis Presley, the King of Rock 'n' Roll, at the peak of his life and career—and what does he do for ten years? He devotes himself to realizing with every nuance of style and soul the immortal songs of Ben Wiseman!

In 1964 Colonel decreed that henceforth Elvis should record nothing but movie soundtrack albums. After all, there's no sense in competing with yourself! Elvis despised these songs and would often explode in the studio, crying: "What am I gonna do with this piece o' shit?" Eventually, he grew so dejected that he relinquished the last bit of control he held over his career, the supervision of his recording sessions, and bowed his neck to the same yoke borne by the paid-by-the-hour jingle-makers. He would allow the musicians to record the entire soundtrack; then, he'd go into the studio alone, put on the earphones and pour his voice like molasses over the trash that came pouring out of the "cans." Colonel Parker would take it from there.

Colonel's power increased in direct proportion to the decline in Elvis's power. Power was, in fact, the Colonel's ruling passion, not greed. Having obtained total control over Elvis Presley, it was no great trick for the Colonel to obtain extraordinary influence in all the big entertainment companies that were dependent on Elvis's enormous popularity. RCA Victor, for example, was an ailing and ill-managed company when it hired Elvis Presley. After failing to shove the "45" down the throat of the record-buying public, the company started losing ground rapidly to its competitors. Elvis stopped this retreat single-handedly and revived the company's fortunes. From 1956 to 1962, Elvis produced thirty-one of Victor's thirty-nine-million-selling singles. For ten years straight, he accounted for about twenty-five percent of the company's total business. Imagine what a man like Colonel Parker could do with this sort of leverage! He not only exploited his position to obtain extraordinary benefits for himself and his client, but he made damn sure that he would never have to share his power with any new rival.

Many students of rock music have puzzled over the fact that, having scored such an enormous success with Elvis Presley, RCA did not follow up this great coup by hiring many other rock acts. The usual explanation is that RCA, identified primarily with classical music, was just too snooty to mess around with the likes of Buddy Holly or Frankie Avalon. This is like saying that General Motors, the manufacturer of the Cadillac, resented the success of Chevrolet. The truth is that every time RCA would start to show interest in another potentially competitive act, Colonel Parker would threaten to deprive the company of Elvis Presley. As no new star could possibly compensate Victor for the loss of its greatest asset, the once-powerful record maker had to limp through not only the fifties but the *sixties* with only one other major rock act on its roster, the Jefferson Airplane.

Colonel's success in bamboozling the record executives was matched for a number of years by equal success in bulldozing the movie companies. In the midsixties the Colonel cut into the faltering MGM, negotiating a series of deals that culminated with Elvis being put on salary at the beginning of 1966 at the staggering sum of $75,000 a week. Needless to say, the more Colonel got for his boy, the more he also got for himself.

One of the most frequently repeated of all Colonel Parker stories has a fifties TV executive offering Parker the once awesome sum of

$50,000 for a single appearance. The Colonel's famous comeback is: "That'll do just fine for me, but how much are you gonna give the boy?" It's a good bet that none of the millions of people who have chuckled at this bit of con-man repartee has ever grasped its true meaning. What it confesses is that Colonel Parker always expected to receive something for himself over and above what he got as Elvis's representative. The Colonel's favorite action was "side action."

The most obvious thing he got at both Paramount and MGM was a large suite of offices, which he decorated in his inimitable manner and outfitted so that every day he could enjoy lunch in an atmosphere reminiscent of the carnival cookhouses of his youth. One large room of the office was always equipped with a big table covered in authentic old-timey oilcloth, a huge freezer-refrigerator combination, an electric range (courtesy of RCA) and an immense and continually restocked supply of the Colonel's favorite foods donated by some well-wisher. As there was never anything for the Colonel and his large staff (whose salaries were paid by MGM, RCA and William Morris) to do in the office, the Colonel drilled his "army," as he came to call them, in the arts of looking busy.

The moment the security officer announced the approach of a visitor, Colonel would sound the alarm. Instantly, the feet would come down off the desk tops, the letters to absent friends would be thrust in drawers, the phones would be raised for imaginary conversations and the men would start shuffling big stacks of quite meaningless papers. Colonel would press a button under his desk and activate a ticker-tape, which he would appear to examine with great concern, muttering like Billy Rose on a bad day, "Not good . . . not good!" When the visitor entered the office suite, he would be impressed by the extraordinary bustle of business.

The Colonel's favorite guest at lunch was Abe Lastfogel, the "Little Square Man," as he was once known, in allusion to his doll-like stature and his impeccable reputation for honesty in business dealings. One of the most powerful figures in the history of entertainment management, the president of MCA became the Colonel's most valuable ally in Hollywood. Lastfogel knew infinitely more about the picture business than did Parker, who had come to Hollywood knowing virtually nothing. Equally important was the fact that Lastfogel possessed that image of rabbinical respectability so precious to a man like the Colonel, who exuded from every pore the bad odor of the carny. With the well-connected Lastfogel initiating the deals and astutely conducting the negotiations, the Colonel was free to kibitz and direct the game from behind the scenes. The "Little Square Man," for his part, gained a lucrative account plus the pleasure of indulging his humor, which delighted in clever rogues. The price he paid was eating a lot of ham and pork.

As the years wore on and public tastes changed, Colonel didn't have to put on an act when he murmured, "Not good . . . not good!" The first sign of Elvis's diminishing popularity was the drop in his record sales. Colonel's solution was to rig the market. He got RCA to apply pressure to its distributors and dealers to preorder each new Presley record in huge quantities. When a million orders had been booked, the Colonel would signal the company to release the disc. RCA would announce that it was "shipping gold." A certificate would be granted. When the record failed to sell, the merchants would quietly exercise their right to unlimited returns. Then it would be the stores' turn to ship gold, fool's gold, back to the fools who mined it.

When the movie business began to decline, Colonel had no such simple device for maintaining the illusion upon which Elvis's fame depended. At best he was able to counter arguments that the general public had lost interest in Elvis by pointing out that Elvis had a hardcore following of two hundred fifty thousand fans who saw every Presley picture three times, thus assuring a minimum paid attendance of seven hundred fifty thousand persons.

Elvis had, as everyone knows, the most devoted fans in the history of show business. Once he cleaned up his act, he lost a lot of the kids, but he gained in their stead great numbers of middle-aged matrons and even old grannies, who murmured reflexively at every mention of his name: "He was so good to his mother." Mother's Day became, in fact, one of the major festivals of the Presley cult, marked generally by a radio promotion featuring Elvis singing hymns.

The most interesting aspect of the fans' behavior was the instinctive manner in which they indemnified themselves for the loss of the King's living—as opposed to his "canned"—presence. Like the loyal followers of an exiled ruler or holy man, the fans built in their homes shrines to the King that were remarkably similar to the shrines to the emperor once found in every Japanese house. One wall or sometimes one whole room would be converted into a domestic chapel, more or less elaborately decorated with devotional pictures, books, relics, mementoes and symbols of the cult. By playing Elvis's records and concentrating on his familiar image, a really devout fan could achieve an effect of communion with his King that was no different essentially from that of a religious person meditating on his god.

Such passive contemplation, however, was never enough for the Elvis zealots. They demanded a more vigorous and physical form of worship, which was first brought to perfection by the greatest of all the Presley organizations: Britain's Official Elvis Presley Fan Club. Once a year, this group, virtually none of whose members had ever seen Elvis in the flesh, would have a big jamboree at which many of the members would appear onstage to give their impressions of Elvis (thereby anticipating by many years the race of Elvis impersonators who sprang up when the hero died). Clearly, when the King is away, the cats will play—at being the King.

To maintain the profitability of the Presley movies in the face of declining box office receipts, ever more drastic cost cutting became necessary. The Colonel worked tirelessly to get the resort hotels and the local tourist bureaus to pick up the tab for the location shooting. Film directors were superseded by TV directors because the latter could work faster. When Hal Wallis indicated he had had enough of Elvis, the Colonel took up with Sam Katzman, "The King of the Quickies": a man with a genius for low-budget, low-mentality movies. Eventually, the shooting time for an Elvis Presley feature was reduced to seventeen days.

As Elvis saw his dream of becoming a great movie star turn into the nightmare of grinding out three horrible pictures a year, he became bitter, cynical and estranged. The aura of acrimony that envelops him in these films, which comes off him like body odor, was really the leakage of rage and self-hatred produced by the ordeal of appearing in what he called "my latest travelogue."

Chapter 23

The Fun Years

WHEN ELVIS PRESLEY returned to America after his years in the army, he was a changed man. His mother's death, his father's remarriage, his own sufferings in the service, as well as the prolonged interruption of his career and his anxiety about its revival, had eroded the great self-confidence he displayed in his early years. His first TV appearances, particularly his queer showing on *Frank Sinatra's Welcome Home Party for Elvis Presley,* testify to the change in the man that underlay the change in the image.

The first signal that something important had happened to Elvis was sexual. The Elvis who had appeared on the Dorsey, Berle and Sullivan shows, who had starred in *Loving You* and *Jailhouse Rock,* was butch. He had a chunky, clunky aura as he stood four-square before the camera and blasted out his soul with total indifference to public opinion. Even his legendary shyness, cunningly exploited in those scenes in *Loving You* in which he plays opposite the sophisti- catedly sexy Lizabeth Scott (who has a wonderful time toying with this *enfant terrible,* alternately seducing and mocking him), comes across as a kind of strength, the coiled-up power of a boy whose manner warns: "Don't get me started or you'll be sorry!"

After the army, Elvis appears very delicate and vulnerable, as

if he were recovering from major surgery. He wrings his hands as he talks. He has become extremely wary. With his preposterous Little Richard conk, his limp wrist, girlish grin and wobbly knees, which now turn out instead of in, he looks outrageously gay. When he confronts the much smaller but more masculine Sinatra, Elvis's body language flashes, "I surrender, dear."

Nor is this sudden loss of his former virility merely a deceiving appearance: It is paralleled by many more significant changes in Elvis's manner of conducting his life and career. Instead of partying with his peers, the young actors and actresses of the Jimmy Dean clique, Elvis locks himself up now in a house with six stooges and never goes out to play. Instead of falling in love with a beautiful film star, he herds hundreds of anonymous groupies through his bedroom. Instead of being basically a sympathetic character with some ugly traits, he becomes an arrogant punk who closely resembles the character he portrayed in *Jailhouse Rock*. As for his career, he abandons all control over it and submits himself completely to the machinations of Colonel Parker and his cronies in Hollywood. All these changes attest to a profound metamorphosis in the character of Elvis Presley. Though they first become manifest when he is discharged from the service, we must search for their source in that deadly wound Elvis suffered when his mother died.

Gladys was as much the source of Elvis's self-confidence as she was the cause of his extreme dependency. She was also his only confidante and his moral governor. Once Gladys died, Elvis found himself desperately alone and naked. His first instinct was to retreat from the world and wall himself round with people who were devoted to him, body and soul. His second impulse was to drown his sorrows in an endless round of parties and games that would keep him perpetually distracted from his real state of mind. His ultimate resolution was the most fateful: It was to sever the link between his past and present by totally inverting the relations between his life and his image. Instead of being an innocent and naive kid who impersonated publicly a wild and orgiastic figure, Elvis would now play in public the All-American Boy, while off camera he indulged himself in an endless debauch of sex and drugs.

The inception of Elvis's new life-style was a two-week furlough that he took in the summer of 1959 in Paris with several of his boys. Settling down at the posh Hotel Prince de Galles, he swiftly discovered an old-time nightclub on the Champs Elysées called the Lido, which had a chorus line bearing the legendary title, The Bluebelle Girls; in other words, the descendants of those turn-of-the-century chorus girls who

had swarmed over the original Prince de Galles or Prince of Wales, the future Edward VII. Elvis, wearing for the first time his elegant dress blues and looking like a latter-day version of the Student Prince, instinctively fell into the pattern of his renowned and royal predecessor. Every night he ate dinner at the club; then, after the first show, he swept up the entire chorus line and carried it back to his hotel, where they partied extravagantly, until the phone would ring and the manager of the club would beg Elvis to return the girls so that the supper show could commence. Elvis would witness that show as well and afterward return to his suite with the girls, with whom he toyed till dawn.

When Elvis returned to Hollywood, he showed no sign at first of adopting this orgiastic pattern so close to home. He was still a little inhibited, still exhibiting traces of his mother's morality. Then, one night, a random occurrence initiated a chain of events that concluded with Elvis finding himself once again in a position to indulge his appetite for orgiastic parties. The decisive event was being asked to leave the Beverly Wilshire Hotel for precisely the same reasons that had led to Elvis's expulsions from hotels in Germany: extreme rowdiness.

On this particular night Elvis and the Guys were involved in one of those childish games in which he spent so much of his spare time in the early years: a water battle with squirt guns. What made the battle characteristic of Elvis was the violence with which he drove it, that innate violence that always made him take everything to the limits and beyond, never feeling that he had had enough of any game until limbs broke and blood flowed and screams of pain accompanied the pleasure.

First, one of the boys had slipped on the wet kitchen floor and gashed himself deeply on a broken bottle. Then, Red, Joe and Sonny grabbed Elvis and threw him on the floor. As Sonny held Elvis's legs and Joe his midriff, Red rubbed his palm back and forth over Elvis's nose, driving him completely crazy. When he had brought Elvis to the ultimate peak of rage, Red shouted, "Let go!" At that moment, Red and Sonny leaped up and ran for their lives. Joe, seeking to do the same, slipped and fell on the floor. Instantly, Elvis was on top of him, kicking him like a log as he rolled across the floor. Then, Elvis seized a guitar and, swinging it like an axe, hit Joe a stunning blow on the elbow. Joe screamed in pain and lay there watching his arm inflate like a balloon. Red and Sonny, who had circled back, realized now that the fight had gotten out of hand. They made a dash through a fire escape door and took off down the hall with Elvis in hot pursuit. When Elvis saw he couldn't catch up, he threw the guitar with all his might after the fleeing figures.

At that moment, an elderly lady who lived on the floor opened her door. Just as she was about to step out into the hall—whoosh!—a guitar flew by her nose, almost hitting her. Jumping back, she slammed the door and picked up the phone to call the manager. A few minutes later this worthy was upstairs demanding to know what was going on and inspecting with a horror-struck countenance the damage to the rooms. Next day, Elvis and his boys were asked to leave.

The Colonel decided at this point that it didn't make sense to confine these rambunctious boys to a hotel. They needed more space to stretch out—and they needed to be kept away from the little old ladies of this world. The solution to the problem was obviously a good-sized private house in some secluded spot. A short search turned up a unique residence in Bel Air that had formerly belonged to the Shah of Iran. It was a doughnut-shaped structure, ringed around a fifty-foot patio edged with shrubbery. Situated on the side of a winding hillside road called Perugia Way, the house overlooks the greens of the Bel Air Country Club. Carpeted with thick white shag, filled with expensive California-style furnishings and staffed by a black cook and houseman, this flying saucer was the perfect playpen for a wealthy young playboy. Soon it became legendary as the headquarters of the Memphis Mafia, the most intently partying group of bachelors in the history of Hollywood.

The Presley parties are invariably depicted as tedious get-togethers whose only singularity lay in the disproportion of men to women. Though literally thousands of young women were guests at these parties over the years, those who got beyond the formalities would not have been eager to recount their adventures for the benefit of the press. Nor would any reporter or editor who valued his job in Hollywood have been willing to publish such scandalous tales. Though one hears a great deal about the outrageous violations of privacy suffered by the stars, if we are to judge by the example of Elvis Presley, in his day one of Hollywood's greatest stars—and one about whose private life curiosity reached unprecedented proportions—there are no limits to what a celebrity can do and escape exposure in the film colony.

The parties, which swiftly became the focal point of Elvis's life, would commence every night after supper, at about ten. The basic idea was to fill the house with attractive young women who had been especially selected to conform to Elvis's exacting criteria. Elvis's tastes in women were just as fixed and unvarying as his tastes in food. It was only natural that a man who could subsist for six months at a time on a steady diet of burnt bacon, mashed potatoes, sauerkraut and sliced tomatoes would want one and only one kind of girl. The interesting question is: What is the female equivalent of the aforesaid diet?

Elvis liked small, kittenish girls who were built to his ideal proportions. They were to be no higher than five feet two and weigh no more than one hundred ten pounds. The prime areas of erotic interest were the ass and legs. Hair coloring, complexion, facial features were not important, though beauty was, naturally, desirable. What was critical was that the girls be as young as possible, certainly no older than eighteen, and that they be not too far removed from the condition of virginity. Married women were out of the question and a woman who had borne a child was a complete turn-off for Elvis Presley. As for clothing, Elvis liked to see a pretty girl dressed all in white. When she undressed, he was hoping to see that she wore white underpants. White panties were Elvis's erotic fetish.

All the Guys became at Elvis's urging quite accomplished procurers. Their readiest source of supply was the studios where Elvis worked. Most Presley pictures had party scenes that called for as many as a score of pretty young girls. The moment the first call for such extras went out, the Guys were busy among the applicants, like cooks in the morning market, making their selections for the Boss. After the studios, there were many other sources for Presley chicks: talent agencies, nightclubs, theaters, stores—Hollywood is full of pretty young girls, many of whom will do anything to advance their careers. All one of the boys had to do was mention that Elvis Presley was having a party that night at his home in Bel Air and the prey was winging toward the net.

Once the parties became an institution in Hollywood, a lot of girls started trying to crash the gate. On a typical evening, the whole street and the parking area before the house would be swarming with scores of young women who behaved very much like the crowd seeking admission to a popular discotheque. Like the patrons of a disco, they came in all sorts of costumes from simple cotton dresses to sweater and pants outfits to stylish frocks topped with fur jackets. Parking their cars along this once-quiet street, they would stand, lean or sit all over the property, chattering and gossiping and looking each other over carefully. The focus of everyone's attention was the heavy brown door to the house, which was opened from time to time by one of the boys, who would admit the girls he knew and tell the others to "try later." As at Studio 54, the decision as to how many and which girls to admit depended entirely on the demands of the party going on inside the house. Some of the more determined girls would remain standing in front of the door until two in the morning.

Once a girl was admitted to the house, she would be ushered about with great politeness by one of Elvis's man mountains. Her first impression was invariably one of great luxury and style. As you entered the house, for example, you could look straight through the foyer to the patio, which was romantically illuminated at night and filled with the plashing of a fountain at its center, where a statue emptied endless jugs from its shoulder. Sinking into the deep-pile carpet and following her guide as he turned to the left, she would enter first the living room, which was dominated by a fireplace above which hung a painting, actually a painted photograph, of Elvis, Gladys and Vernon in front of Graceland. The next room around the circle was the den; here the parties were always held. Loud rock music would be playing from an illuminated jukebox filled with Elvis's favorite records; a wet bar at the far side of the room would be piled high with refreshments suitable for a Sweet Sixteen party—soft drinks, potato chips, pretzels, cookies—and in the middle of the room a TV set, whose back was concealed by a folding mirrored-glass screen, would be playing with its sound turned off.

Facing the television, on a huge built-in sofa, the King would be enthroned with his feet up on a cocktail table. Flanked by a couple of his men and surrounded by a bevy of young women, he would be watching TV. No matter who arrived, even if she were the most famous or beautiful star in Hollywood, Elvis would not rise to greet her. "Get her coat . . . find out what she wants to drink." With such bossman orders, Elvis would beckon Tuesday Weld, Joan Blackman or Connie Stevens into the circle around him.

Elvis had a very sarcastic and vulgar sense of humor that would emerge when he settled down at ease and removed the phony mask of southern gentlemanliness that he wore in public. From years of listening to the local wits in his hometown—that type of southern joker who responds to every situation with a proverbial line and a snap of his extended fore- and midfinger—Elvis had developed quite a patter of Memphis jive. As the aspiring young extras and starlets sitting at his feet constantly looked back and forth from the silent video screen to the immaculately groomed and carefully dressed star, they would be treated to an endless stream of witticisms.

Watching Jerry Lewis caper on the screen, Elvis would sneer and drawl: "That's about as funny as a turd in a punch bowl." Or perhaps he'd say "as funny as a Smitty on a hearse." (A Smitty was the Memphis name for a device designed to make a teenager's motor roar.) Every time Elvis got off one of these gags, the Guys would roar with laughter. Their response would encourage Elvis to continue his bizarre commentary, which soon blurred into what must have sounded to the girls like a code:

"He's stronger than Tarzan's armpits. . . . He's been there since Hitler was a corporal. . . . He's wilder than a peach orchard boar. . . . Tell 'em where the cow et the cabbage! . . . That cat's lower than a whale. . . . Cute as a bug's ear. . . . So uptight you couldn't drive a straw up his ass with a ten-pound sledge!" Watching two guys back off from each other in a western, Elvis might crack: "He's scared and the other's *glad* of it!" Or if someone said, "If only so and so were to happen, then . . ." Elvis might retort scornfully, "If my aunt had nuts, she'd be my uncle!" The moment the laugh died, the whole party would fall silent and return to the basic activity, which was watching Elvis watch TV.

As there were perhaps forty or fifty girls in the house and only eight men, it would have been natural for the Guys to start hitting on some of these chicks. This was a practice that was sternly forbidden. Elvis considered any such advances highly improper, an act of *lèse majesté*, until he had exercised his prerogative to make the first choice. Allowing Elvis what was called "the pick of the litter" was an obligatory act of deference. To behave differently would be to invite some terrible explosion.

Elvis's temper and his overbearing manner had gotten much worse during his years in the army. The boys who had known Elvis for long said that the army had made him "mean." His ugly traits were greatly exaggerated by the presence of women. When girls were around, Elvis felt obliged to play the big shot, the boss. He would put one of his little cigars in his mouth, his Hav-a-Tampa Jewels or Rum Crooks, and hold it there a moment. If one of the boys didn't jump up and give him a light, Elvis would explode. "Goddamn it to hell! Am I gonna sit here all night like this, or is one of you lardasses gonna gimme a light?" That sort of behavior was supposed to impress the girls. Elvis didn't stop at just being overbearing. Sometimes he would humiliate his men so grossly that even these faithful flunkies were compelled to rebel.

Sonny West recalls a night when Tuesday Weld came to visit Elvis, bringing along a very attractive friend named Kay. As Elvis and Tuesday got deep into conversation, Sonny started promoting Kay, while preparing a drink at the bar. In the middle of Sonny's pitch, Elvis pops up suddenly between them, stares provocatively at the girl and says admiringly, "You're really pretty!" Then, he flits off to continue talking to Tuesday. Sonny resumes his efforts to woo the young woman and is starting to make progress when Elvis appears again, gives the girl one of his patented heavy-lidded stares and murmurs, "My man!" Just as Sonny is recovering from this fresh intrusion, Elvis swings back for a third pass at the target. This time, he gives the girl a little peck. When she doesn't object, he kisses her firmly on the mouth. She kisses him back. Sonny gives up in disgust and retreats to the other side of the room, where Alan Fortas and Gene Smith are watching the scene.

"He's smooth as silk," rumbles the admiring Fortas. "Yeah, he shot me right outta the saddle," concedes Sonny. Gene leans in confidingly at this point and, nodding his head toward the two women, he says: "Sonny, if you had your pick, which would you take?" Sonny replies without hesitating, "Tuesday—she's got some body on her!"

Elvis, who is always scanning the room, spots Gene and Sonny with their heads together. Instantly, he assumes that they're bad-mouthing him. Jumping up and walking over to the boys, he says, "What the hell are you two whispering about?" Sonny is dumbfounded. He's too embarrassed to repeat the conversation. His confusion confirms Elvis in his conviction that he was the topic of conversation. "If you don't tell me," he warns Sonny, "you're in big trouble." Sonny, exasperated, hurt, angry, looks at Elvis and exclaims: "Man, you have *changed!* I *quit!*"

In a flash, Elvis grabs a Coke bottle. Sonny barks, "You're not gonna hit me with no goddamn bottle!" Elvis backs down and relinquishes the bottle, but he can't control his anger. The moment Sonny starts walking out of the room, Elvis plants himself in the big boy's path. "You're not quittin'," snarls Elvis, " 'cause you're *fired!*" "Call it anything you want!" shouts Sonny. "I'm gettin' outta here!" Nobody could talk back to Elvis and get away with it. Flashing red, Elvis swings from the floor and hits Sonny squarely on the jaw.

If Elvis had been on a movie set, where he was always punching guys out, Sonny would have flown halfway across the room, smashed into a wall and come sliding down onto the floor like a stiff. Instead, he simply twisted his head with the blow and then turned back to stare at Elvis in shock and pain. As the tears started coming to his eyes, Sonny gasped: "I never thought you would hit me, Elvis!" Then, he turned and left the room.

It was the only time in Sonny's life that he didn't return a punch. If he had struck back, he would have knocked Elvis into the middle of next week. It never crossed Sonny's mind, though, to defend himself. Nobody ever hit Elvis. Though he abused them, humiliated them, hit them with his hands or kicked them with his feet or even drew weapons and threatened their lives, *nobody ever struck back at Elvis Presley.*

Sonny went to his room and packed. He called his girl and told her that he had quit his job. When he came to the front door, he found Elvis standing there alone. "You got any money, Sonny?" he asked. Sonny said he was okay. Elvis handed him a check, which he had had one of the boys draw. "Can one of the Guys take you someplace?" asked Elvis. "No, I called a cab," replied Sonny. When he pulled away from the house in the cab, Sonny saw Elvis standing in the doorway.

The other disaster that could ruin a party was a girl who dared to talk back or challenge the "Boss." Elvis had strict rules for feminine behavior. As long as women deferred to him, he was gallant to them. If, though, they "got down on his level," as the Guys put it, then Elvis was freed of the obligation to play the gentleman's role and was allowed to teach the girl her "lesson." One night, for example, the sophisticated daughter of a famous movie star came up to the house. Appalled, most likely, by the court of the Hillbilly King, she made the mistake of getting into an argument with Elvis. Galvanized by a terrible flash of rage, he leaped to his feet, seized the young woman by the hair, dragged her stumbling head over heels across a marble coffee table and into the next room, where he planted a very vigorous kick in her ass and ordered one of the boys to throw her out in the street.

Another night, while he was entertaining a young actress, Elvis got so enraged at something she said that he picked up a watermelon and threw it at her, hitting her a mighty thump on the ass. Throwing things like a hysterical woman was one of Elvis's more dangerous habits. One night, many years later, when he was having supper, Joanie Esposito, Joe Esposito's wife, said something that infuriated Elvis. Instinctively, he hurled the knife that was in his hand straight at her face. If Sonny West hadn't flung up his hand to block the knife, Elvis might have knocked out one of Joanie's eyes.

In 1963, Elvis did inflict a disfiguring injury on a young woman in this manner. She had demanded that one of the boys playing pool with Elvis move his car so that she could leave the party. Elvis was so enraged by the woman's insistence that he hurled his pool cue at her, striking her on the breast. The cue paralyzed a nerve in the breast, causing it to sag permanently. The most interesting fact about the story is that no compensation was offered the woman and none was sought. As always, Elvis walked away from his misdeed without any apology or desire to make amends. As far as he was concerned, the fault was all the woman's who had provoked him.

Assuming the party was not spoiled by some "fool" or some "bitch," the final phase, about 2:00 A.M., after the late movie, would consist of the "slipaway." Elvis would finally rise and make his way past the bar to the adjoining room, which was the master bedroom. This was the signal for all the Guys to take off the wraps. Like beggars at a royal feast, they were free now to enjoy the scraps. All the girls who had been passed over by the boss were fair game. If the boys could score, they carried their girls off to the other bedrooms. If they were failures, as was poor Lamar so often, they were delegated "night duty," which meant they lay down fully clothed in the living room to snatch some sleep before they were roused before dawn to carry home Elvis's girls.

"Girls" is the word because Elvis almost invariably retreated to his bedroom with two or three young women in tow. His preference for groups rather than for one-to-one encounters had hardened now into a habit. Most young men with such tastes are assumed to be prodigiously virile studs whose sexual appetites are so enormous that they cannot be satisfied by a single woman. This was certainly not the case with Elvis Presley. Generally speaking, he never had normal sexual relations with these girls. The reason? Elvis was a pervert, a voyeur.

What he sought as his erotic goal was a group of girls who would agree to strip down to their panties and wrestle with each other while Elvis stared out his eyes with a rocklike hard-on pressing up against his underwear. He accounted for this obsession by recalling an incident from his childhood: a moment when he had seen two little girls tumbling together on the ground with their dresses rising to show their crotches. In fact, with the fine focus characteristic of his kind, what Elvis described as his ultimate fulfillment was not the sight of the girls or even the crotch but the vision of black pubic hairs protruding around the edges of white panties. Out of all the sexual excitements in the world, this one teasing image represented the ultimate in arousal to Elvis Presley.

The panties were not just a tease, like the fan dancer's fan or the bubble-dancer's bubble. They were also a protective shield. Elvis could not tolerate the sight of a completely naked woman. If one of the gorgeous showgirls or actresses who filled his bed night after night were to disrobe completely in his presence, he would protest: "You have a beautiful body but I would feel better if you put something on." Elvis was just as loath to show his own body. As a rule no woman ever saw him undressed. His shyness focused on his penis, which he called "Little Elvis" and went to great lengths to hide. Instead of pissing in a urinal, for example, he would always go inside a stall, like a woman. He was not modest but ashamed. Like most country boys of his time, he was uncircumcised. A sensitive adolescent at heart, he saw his beauty disfigured by an ugly hillbilly pecker.

He complained also that when he engaged in intercourse, the foreskin, pulled back and forth in the grip of the vulva, would fray and tear, sometimes emerging bloody. There was an obvious solution to this vexing problem, but Elvis could not bear the thought of a knife cutting into Little Elvis. (Vernon was much braver. In his last years, when he became involved with a young woman, he submitted to the dread operation in the hopes of reviving his deadened dick. Perhaps that was what he meant when he once told Elvis: "You'll never be half the man your father was.")

In addition to being an orgiast and a voyeur, Elvis was also a lifelong masturbator. Every month one of the boys would be dispatched to those extended newsstands off Hollywood Boulevard to buy the boss all the latest "fuck books." The man might spend as much as forty dollars obtaining enough material to satisfy his master's appetites. Elvis would take a different magazine to bed with him every night and jerk off looking at the pictures.

If Elvis became sufficiently aroused by the spectacle of the girls wrestling, he might go down on a girl or dry hump her. Gene Smith recalls Elvis changing clothes after a date and looking like he sprayed his Jockey briefs full of whipped cream. If Elvis were feeling particularly daring, he might allow a girl to jack him off. One of the familiar tales of the Presley circle concerns the night Elvis went to bed with a famous Hollywood sex kitten. When this aggressive young woman—who had slept with half the men in the movie industry in the effort to advance her career and who had learned through that ordeal as much about men as any old hooker—divined where Elvis was at, she not only jerked him off with great skill but, when he ejaculated, she caught the semen in her hand and rubbed it all over her face like cold cream. Those two moves put Elvis completely in her hands.

If Elvis did have intercourse with an unfamiliar woman, he would never allow himself to ejaculate inside her. He was terrified of an unwanted pregnancy or a paternity suit—or so he averred. The Guys interpreted his anxiety as the product of some episode in his early years, when Elvis had gotten a girl pregnant. An exaggerated fear of knocking a girl up, however, is also characteristic of young men, especially adolescents, who suffer from sexual anxiety and are afflicted with other sexual problems, like premature ejaculation. Though Elvis Presley was always girl-crazy, this obsession can sort very well in a young man with a deep underlying fear of women, of marriage and of begetting children: all signs of masculine maturity.

These sexual predilections explain also how it was possible to go through so many women without ever once contracting venereal disease, the universal fate of the swinger. That Elvis escaped all the dangers of the game was owing not to good luck but to the most extraordinary self-control: a lock-hold on his sexual behavior that must have been powered by uncontrollable sexual phobias.

Looking at half-naked girls grappling with each other or jerking off while ogling the centerfold of *Playboy* or *Penthouse* were by no means the full extent of Elvis's voyeurism. As soon as he moved into the house on Perugia Way, he made provision for indulging this letch on the sly. He observed that the closet of his bedroom had a common wall with an adjacent bedroom. In the neighboring room, the wall was lined with floor-to-ceiling bookcases. Elvis and the boys removed a portion of the wall between the shelves and installed in the space a two-way mirror. Now, they were in a position to view everything that happened in the bedroom from a secure location in the closet. The only problem was that normally nothing was happening in this room. Elvis quickly solved this problem by ordering a couple of the boys to get girls into the room and have intercourse with them while he watched with the other Guys.

This sport had only one danger: With so many guys crowded in the closet chortling and whispering about the "action" they were watching, there was the distinct possibility that the sound would carry through the wall and alarm one of the girls who was being exploited. Again, Elvis came up with the answer: Whenever one of the boys was about to get down with a girl, he must make a point of turning on the radio in the room. He could say that it was more romantic that way or there was such beautiful music on such and such a station. Girls would go for crap like that and the sound of music would mask the mumbling behind the wall. Eventually, however, it was agreed by all hands that the little window they had opened was not adequate for the proper enjoyment of the show. In the next house the boys occupied, they installed a mirror that was as big as a suburban picture window.

Elvis's second house in Bel Air offered a total change in atmosphere from his first. Instead of an architectural whimsy, redolent of a sheik's tent, the new mansion on Bellagio Road was a classic 1920s movie star's mansion. Modelled upon an Italian villa of the Renaissance, the exterior boasted statues in niches, a steeply landscaped terrace and an old-fashioned swimming pool off to one side. The decor was baronial: a grand entrance foyer paved with marble and adorned with a sculptured fountain, an imposing open staircase to the second floor, an ornamented fireplace rivaling that at Pickfair.

People who have special appetites are very quick to spot novel ways of fulfilling them. No sooner had Elvis moved into this old mansion than he noticed a peculiarity in the dressing room that adjoined the swimming pool. Rather than waste time describing the vision that inspired this latest and grandest peephole, let's examine the finished product.

First, you have to imagine the King and his lusty men bidding a momentary good-bye to a covey of beautiful young women whom they have urged to change into bathing suits so they can all enjoy a dip in the pool. The moment the girls go clattering down the steps beside the pool to the dressing room cut into the sloping hillside, Elvis and the Guys dash around to the side of the building where there is a little louvered door at ground level that looks like a utility hatch. Opening this door, they crawl into a dark low space which they have laboriously excavated by hand from the foundation of the building. The dirt floor is covered with blankets because there is no room to stand. One wall of the room is a huge plate-glass window that looks directly into the women's side of the locker room. To the women, of course, this huge window appears as a mirror.

Lying on their sides and trying to breathe as shallowly as possible—heavy breathing fogs up the glass and spoils the view—Elvis and the Guys fall to studying the girls as they undress. Though it is often said that voyeurism is a scaredy-cat perversion, this new four-by-eight-foot window was, as the boys discovered, a great test of nerve. As long as the girls removed their clothes or made their toilettes from a distance, the peek effect was perfect. When a girl walked up close to the mirror and stared directly into it—while holding up, perhaps, one breast and then the other for examination—the more timid guys, like Lamar, would be terrified. It was hard to believe that this girl, just inches from your face, couldn't see you lurking there in the darkness.

Eventually, Elvis got anxious about this king-sized window and ordered it removed for transport to Graceland. There the boys sought high and low for a suitable place to install it, but the old house was very ill-suited to such contrivances. Finally, the mirror was stored in the attic, along with many other abandoned toys and devices for recreation. Meantime, the house on Bellagio Road received a new inhabitant who was destined to compensate Elvis for the loss of his old toy by sending the girls screaming around the house every night in a manner that was positively provoking.

Scatter was the ideal frat house mascot. A forty-pound, three-foot-tall chimpanzee, he had been trained by his first owner, a Memphis cartoonist who used him on his local TV show, to wear clothes, drink whiskey and raise hell with women. When Elvis first brought the beast out to Hollywood, he was enthralled with his antics. Elvis would treat him like a baby, carrying him around on his shoulders, showing him off for company and even changing his diapers. What tickled the Guys most about Scatter was the fact that he was so damn horny. Just let a girl step in the house and old Scatter would be hot on her tail. He would lift up her skirt and stick his head up toward her crotch. He would follow women to the bathroom or try to get inside while they were on the toilet. He would also chug-a-lug a few drinks at the bar, and then turn around on his stool and start whacking off in some girl's face.

Elvis was always thinking of fresh ways to use Scatter as a device for driving people crazy. He would have the chimp dressed up in his cute little middy suit and tennis sneakers. Then Scatter would be enthroned in the back seat of the Rolls-Royce Silver Phantom and driven about by one of the Guys wearing a chauffeur's cap. That night Elvis would scream with laughter as the chauffeur, generally Alan Fortas (who has a somewhat simian build), would recount the stories of how this motorist almost ran off the road staring at the chimp or how that old lady looked shocked or a cop on a corner did a triple-take as the car went by. What really bugged Elvis was that they could never find one of those trick cars, like they have in the circus, that can be driven from the rear by a hidden operator, while the ape sits up front turning the driving wheel. To roll down Hollywood Boulevard of an afternoon with Scatter at the wheel of a big costly Cad, casting Ubangi-lipped looks to right and left with a driver's cap on his head and his long funky fingers wrapped around the wheel—oh, God! Wouldn't that be heaven!

Short of the ultimate thrill, however, there were lots of other tricks you could play with the chimp. One of his most celebrated exploits was the time he got loose at the Goldwyn Studio and climbed up the drainpipe to the second-floor office of the boss, Sam Goldwyn. When

Scatter came swinging through the window, Goldwyn's secretary screamed in horror and fled from the room. Scatter kept on going until he was in the Big Man's private office. Before the astonished movie mogul could utter a word, the ape had leaped on his desk and was cavorting among his contracts, pub shots and pictures of his grandchildren. Fortunately, the animal was well diapered so he couldn't do anything totally outrageous.

The best fun Elvis had with Scatter was always some stunt involving sex. It was as if Elvis were using the beast as his proxy, as the perpetrator of all those crazy sex pranks that he would have liked to have played but didn't dare. There was a little stripper, for example, who was a regular at the Presley parties. Elvis would entice this girl to come up to the house; then he would persuade her to get down on the floor and wrestle with Scatter. She wasn't much bigger than the chimp. If you didn't look too carefully, you would swear that the horny ape and the hot little chick were getting it on. That killed Elvis.

Another time when one of the Guys went upstairs with a young woman who was an aspiring songwriter, Elvis got Alan and Sonny to slip Scatter into the bedroom after the couple had started balling. Scatter outdid himself on this occasion, eliciting from the girl some of the loudest and most piercing screams of his entire career. Sad to say, the Guy was so outraged that he picked up the beast and hurled it about ten feet down the hall.

Poor Scatter! He soon suffered the fate of all Master Elvis's other toys. He lost his charm and was shipped back to Graceland, where he was installed at the back of the house in an air-conditioned cage. Neglected after all the attention he had received for years, he pined and drooped and turned vicious. Late in the sixties, he bit a maid who was feeding him. Two days later, he was found dead in his cage.

About the time Scatter died, the steady advance of electronic technology provided Elvis at last with the perfect toy for a man who was an orgiast, a voyeur and a masturbator. It was the first Sony videotape machine for "home use." Once Elvis got this machine, he was enabled to seek relief from the monotonous routine of acting in films by getting behind the camera and functioning as a director. He soon found some cooperative young women and set to work turning out an endless series of bedroom follies. What he was after in these films was what he had been after all his life in sexual encounters: a chance to watch while beautiful young women grappled with each other and simulated lesbian sex. Naturally, no one but Elvis was permitted to view these hot reels.

Once, however, one of the Guys found the opportunity while Elvis was away from home to view some of the forbidden footage. What he saw shocked him profoundly. The two girls, naked save for white panties, who flashed on the screen were intimates of the Presley circle. They were giggling and wrestling and taking turns diving into each other's crotches. At the end of the film, Elvis suddenly popped up before the camera with a full erection and a very smooth jack-off motion.

Eventually, Elvis made a great auto-da-fé of his private videotapes. Yet some of the tapes escaped destruction. They are allegedly being peddled in Los Angeles at high but not exorbitant prices: five hundred dollars for a five-minute quickie and fifteen hundred dollars for a long-playing orgy. In that great black market that consists of bootleg Elvis records, TV out-takes and other scraps from the cutting room floor, these home movies must be the most sought-after items. As biographical documents, their value is also enormous. What could be more basic to the study of a great sex hero than a filmed record of his sex life? Perhaps that is what Elvis meant when he said that some day he wanted to write an autobiography entitled *Through My Eyes*.

Eventually, Elvis discovered a curious genre of soft-core pornography that appealed to him even more than his private videotapes or the hard-core Danish stuff that came on the American market in the late sixties. As this type of pornography pleased him more than any other, we are justified in regarding it as the clue to his basic sexual fantasies. Interestingly, these were of a highly hostile yet not conventionally sadistic variety. The films Elvis relished are called in the trade "cat films." Their subject is women fighting. The typical film opens up on a shot of a couple of tough, coarse-looking broads sitting on a sofa and having a violent quarrel about a man. Suddenly, one of the women reaches over and slaps the other's face. The second woman retaliates by grabbing her opponent's hair. Then, they really get into it like a couple of cats, screaming and clawing. Inevitably, their legs go up and the viewer gets a flash of their panties, which was the part that most excited Elvis. By the end of the film, the women have reduced each other to wrecks.

As it's impossible to watch two people fighting without identifying with one or the other, these films offered Elvis Presley the opportunity to experience vicariously the pleasure of beating up a woman while at the same time protecting himself psychologically from the shame or guilt that would have been entailed if it were a man with whom he was identifying, a man who would obviously be a stand-in for himself. That Elvis's basic relations with women took the form of push and shove is clear from his behavior during his teenage pajama parties. That there was an angry hard-on behind these little games we should not have known but for the cat films. His excitement in viewing these films suggests not just his fundamental hostility toward women, which is pretty clear from his stage act, but also the source of that hostility.

The typical woman in a cat film is a hefty, older woman of a type that Elvis could easily have associated unconsciously with Gladys. If this sounds improbable, bear in mind that nothing is more basic to a mama's boy than deeply buried hatred for the woman who has enslaved him and frustrated him and imprisoned him psychologically for a lifetime, including all the years after her death. To take a celebrated example of this phenomenon, the literary world's most famous mama's boy is Marcel Proust. After his beloved mother's death, Proust donated the furniture of her house to a male brothel he patronized, and he arranged to have rats, animals that he associated with his mother, trapped, caged and then impaled on long needles while the illustrious author watched their death agonies with fascination. It would be a very naive observer of the relations between Elvis and his mother who did not suspect that beneath the surface of obsessive love there did not lurk, as a kind of psychic counterpoise, an opposite and no less powerful emotion, which finding no outlet in relation to its proper object had necessarily to be worked off on some substitute target.

One cannot relinquish the subject of Elvis Presley's sex life without considering the widespread suspicion that he was latently or actively homosexual. Perhaps the most perceptive way of viewing this issue is to stress the fact that Elvis was above all an adolescent sex hero. Adolescence is a period of imperfect sexual differentiation, a fact that was once proclaimed by our very language: the word "girl," meaning in the vocabulary of Chaucer a young person of either sex. What Elvis projected through his epoch-making act was not just the enormous sexual excitement of puberty but its androgynous quality. Much of Elvis's power over young girls came not just from the fact that he embodied their erotic fantasies but that he likewise projected frankly feminine traits with which they could identify. This AC/DC quality became in time characteristic of rock stars in general, commencing with Mick Jagger and the Beatles (who had such ravishingly girlish falsettos) and going on to include Jim Morrison, David Bowie, Elton John and many figures of the Punk Pantheon. It's also worth noting that "punk" in its original meaning, as prison jargon, signifies the passive homosexual lover of a tough, typically older convict. (The subliminal meaning of Elvis's role in *Jailhouse Rock* is that he is Hunk Houghton's punk.) Indeed, it has always been a tradition of the rock world that the young studs who are the stars should have managers who are homosexuals and who "style" their boys in accordance with their own ideas of what is cute and kissy. Such was Brian Epstein with his punk, John Lennon.

When you dig down to the sexual roots of an Elvis Presley, you sense a profound sexual ambivalence. Elvis plays the strutting, overbearing macho in public; but in private he loves nothing better than to roughhouse with teenage girls with whom he exchanges beauty secrets. His basic erotic image is a crotch covered with white panties and showing a bit of pubic hair—an image no different essentially from male to female. Eventually, as we shall see, he staged orgies in which the star was an aggressive lesbian who not only wrestled with other girls but dominated them sexually, just as an aggressive man might dominate a submissive woman—while Elvis got his kicks by watching. The inference is irresistible, therefore, that at bottom Elvis identified with a strong, aggressive woman rather than a strong, aggressive man. As his mother was precisely such a woman, threatening to bash in his father's head with a heavy skillet while calling him "steercotted," it makes sense to conclude that Elvis was his mother's son in sex as in everything else.

The flourishing of Elvis's perverse sex appetites in the sixties is paralleled by the sudden escalation in his consumption of drugs during this period. Prior to 1960, there is no evidence that Elvis was habituated to any sort of drug but benzedrine or amphetamine compounds. These pep pills had been part of his life since his first days on the road, and his use of them had continued straight through the period of his service in the army. Once he got back to Hollywood, however, he suddenly began consuming a whole range of drugs that produce narcotic and hypnotic as well as stimulant effects. How he first discovered and familiarized himself with these drugs is unknown; but, considering his later practices, it is very likely that he owed his introduction to these dangerous pills to the doctors to whom he complained of his inability to sleep.

Elvis was always an insomniac; now, under the stress of making movies and overstimulated by the constant use of Dexies to get him going after nights with little or no sleep, he must have quickly approached that manic, round-the-clock sleeplessness that is typical of the speed freak. To one who believed that the solution to any problem of mind or body was a drug, nothing would appear more logical as an antidote to uppers than the use of downers. So, it is not surprising to learn that as soon as he became established at the Beverly Wilshire, he came to an understanding with a druggist at the Chrysler Pharmacy in the hotel lobby. This man began to supply Elvis with unlimited quantities of drugs without prescriptions at the price of one dollar a pill.

Soon Elvis was buying seven or eight thousand dollars' worth of pills at a time and paying for them by check. No less great than the volume was the variety of drugs that Elvis and the Guys began to experiment with at this time. They were into Dexamil, Quaalude, Percodan, Demerol, Seconal, Tuinal, Valium, Nembutal and Placidyl. One of the reasons there were so many different drugs is that Elvis discovered in this period what was to be, along with the Bible, his favorite book for the rest of his life: *The Physician's Desk Reference.* This bulky volume, with its exhaustive enumeration of every pill in the pharmacopoeia, accompanied by a full clinical description and a very tantalizing picture, became Elvis's favorite study. With his prodigious appetite for pleasure and his quick, retentive memory, he had both the motive and the means to explore all the resources of the legal drug world. So obsessed did he become with this theme that he even made a sly public confession. In an interview in *Parade* in November 1962, he is quoted as saying, "I've got very simple pleasures. I like to read medical books. One time in high school I thought I'd become a doctor." How sweet! How goody-goody! How sick!

Elvis's way of playing doctor soon produced near-fatal results. Gene Smith recalls driving back to Memphis at this time in a Dodge mobile home that Elvis used instead of taking the train. Smith was so overstimulated from being awake for three days and two nights on speed that he could not fall asleep. He complained to Elvis, who quickly upped with the cure: a 500-milligram dose of Demerol, a synthetic opiate. Smith popped the tiny white pill and waited for the anticipated relief. For another forty-five minutes he stared at the highway with his mind still racing the van. Finally, good ole Doc Presley gave the insomniac another 500-milligram pill. Smith retired to the back of the van and lay down on one of the beds.

An hour later, Billy Smith, who was riding up front with Elvis, who was driving, went to the rear to check on his cousin. He found Gene laid out cold, barely breathing and with a heartbeat so slow and faint that it seemed he must be near death. Billy had only recently been the one who discovered Junior Smith dead in his bed, probably the victim of an overdose. Now he realized that he was witnessing the same thing happening all over again. He rushed into the front of the van and warned Elvis. "Pull off!" he shouted, "I think there's something the matter with Gene!" "What do you mean?" demanded Elvis, steering the bulky vehicle off the road. "I shouted as loud as I could in his ear, and he didn't move a muscle," cried Billy. "I think he's dead!"

Bringing the van to a lumbering, lunging halt, Elvis scrambled into the back compartment, followed by Billy and Joe Esposito. After trying everything they knew to rouse the comatose drug victim, they hauled him out onto the highway. It was a freezing cold night. The unconscious man was clad only in jeans and a T-shirt. For three hours, the boys took turns dragging the limp body back and forth along the road. Finally, the drugged boy began to come out of his stupor. If Gene Smith had been allowed to lie in his bunk a couple of hours more, Elvis and the Guys would have brought him home dead.

This was by no means the only time when Elvis's reckless dispensing of drugs nearly caused a death among his friends and lovers. Like all heavy drug users, Elvis was keen on having everyone around him doing what he was doing. This pattern of imposing his addictions on his entourage is readily explainable by two of his basic character traits. On the one hand, he loved to wield authority, to be the boss and force others to do his bidding. On the other hand, like most drug abusers, he suffered from a vague sense of guilt that he sought to dissipate by telling himself that everyone was doing just what he was doing. Polypharmacy loves company.

It needs no saying that in forcing all this junk down other people's throats, Elvis was imposing on their trust and naivete. Ultimately, what he was doing was exploiting their attachment to him to gather them into the embrace of his own profoundly self-destructive life-style. Though Elvis figures in the Myth as a refulgent Lifegiver, a priestly figure dressed in white and dispensing love and vitality to the world gathered at his feet, in his private aspect he was precisely the opposite figure to that projected by the Myth. No less glamorous, possibly even more beautiful and seductive than the Lifegiver, in his private world he was that ancient figure of Hebrew legend, the *Maloch HaMovet*—the Angel of Death.

It is worth remarking in this connection that though Elvis turned square in his public image after the army years, he never altered in the direction of his private development, which carried him swiftly down the well-worn grooves of the drug underworld. Though he made his peace with the establishment and danced to the Colonel's tune on the day shift, at night he was still the same old cat, perpetually on the prowl, sniffing his way along the trail that led to ever more bizarre sexual perversions, drug addictions and spiritual and mental delusions and hallucinations.

Elvis Presley is therefore that classic American figure: the totally bifurcated personality. Always professing his undying love and loyalty to Ma, Country, and Corn Pone, always an unregenerate southern redneck who stopped just short of the Klan and the John Birch Society, he was also the first great figure in that devolution of American society that has led to the narcissistic, anarchistic, junked-up heroes of the world of rock and punk. A Faustian figure, like most of our American mythmen, he registers both poles of the American schiz with perfect clarity. What makes him so appalling and alarming—but, again, so *echt Amerikan*—is his incredible innocence and self-righteousness, his stunning incapacity to recognize or even sense subliminally the total contradiction that informs his being. Accustomed to living in two worlds simultaneously, the day world of the squares and the night world of the cats, he embraces disjunction as the natural and inevitable condition of human existence. It is this Janus-like existential stance that makes him appear so often an enigma. Yet, though he lacks a middle term that could unite the opposite and opposing halves of his soul, he makes perfect sense as a totally responsive being who found himself alive at a time when the national values pointed in divergent directions and who reacted by rushing off in both directions at once.

Chapter 24

Three Sisters

ELVIS prolonged his unconsummated relationship with Anita Wood until late in the year 1961. Then, one day, Anita came downstairs at Graceland and walked into the dining room, where Elvis and Vernon were engrossed in conversation. Out of the blue, she announced: "I've just decided that I'm going to leave." Before either man could respond, she looked intently at Elvis and delivered her curtain speech.

"We've been together for four and a half years," she said firmly, "and we just aren't going anywhere. I understand that Colonel Parker doesn't want you to get married, that it would be detrimental to your career and all that—but I'm getting older. I want a family and children. So I've made my decision."

No sooner were the words out of her mouth than Vernon started pouring soothing oil on the seething waters. "Anita," he said, "maybe you all will get back together. People . . . a lot of times, they'll go through bad passages and a few years later they'll be together and it'll be great!" Anita was not to be deflected by this nonsense from the main issue. "I've got to make a life for myself," she persisted. "I don't want to live this way for the rest of my years." Elvis had been sitting at the table during this unexpected outburst, saying nothing. Now, at last, he spoke.

"Little," he said solemnly, "are you sure? Are you *sure,* Little?"
"Yes," affirmed Anita, without a moment's hesitation. "I've got to go."
"Well," intoned Elvis, getting very churchy, "I pray to God that I'm
not making the wrong decision by letting you go." That remark almost
knocked Anita off her feet. Fuming, she thought to herself, "Well, you
can't do anything about it—I'm going!"

She would have been even angrier if she could have heard Elvis
discussing her with Sonny about this same time; in fact she would have
been furious. For while Elvis was pretending that Anita's departure was
a grave matter that demanded prayers for guidance, he had long since
set his heart on another girl and was just waiting for Anita to blow
away. When Sonny asked Elvis if he thought he might marry Anita,
Elvis replied with the air of a man who has considered a matter carefully
and come to a settled decision: "She's sweet, she's cute as hell," he
smiled; then, with a significant look, he concluded, "but, I can do better!"

Undoubtedly, he was thinking of Priscilla. He had talked to Priscilla
on the overseas phone many times since his return to America. He had
shown her picture proudly to all the Guys, who marveled at how mature
she looked for her age. He had even received some letters from her,
which Anita had discovered in the house in Bel Air, stuck in the pages
of a book. Though Priscilla might look mature, her letters proved that
she was still a child. That was, of course, a great part of her charm
for Elvis. Indeed, he had begun to think that if he could get her into
his hands while she was still so young and pliable, he could mold and
shape her into the woman of his dreams. This Pygmalion fantasy was
not just an idle whim. It sprang from the depths of his egocentric character. What's more, having experienced love first and most strongly as
the child of a totally controlling parent, it was only natural that he
should express his own love in precisely the same manner.

So, the moment Anita was safely out of the house, Elvis called Wiesbaden and begged Captain Beaulieu to allow Priscilla to fly to Memphis
for a Christmas visit. After giving lengthy assurances that she would
not be living under the same roof with him but would stay with his
father and stepmother in their home, Elvis got his way. Priscilla was
dispatched to him as a marvelous Christmas gift.

The visit proved a great success. It confirmed Elvis in his determination to gain possession of Priscilla. Persuading her to come live with
him was no problem. The real difficulty lay in persuading the Beaulieus
to agree to such a highly unconventional arrangement. To anyone but
Elvis Presley, it would have appeared an utter impossibility. What respect-

able middle-class American family would send its beautiful fifteen-year-old daughter to live with the world's most notorious sex symbol? How could a man who was a professional officer even entertain such a shocking proposal? How could any mother stomach it? Even if the parents could be prevailed upon to agree, how would they answer to their friends, to the press, to the world at large, so insatiably curious about every little detail of the famous star's life?

Elvis had always enjoyed great success in conning the parents of his local groupies; yet, what he had wanted in the past was nothing in comparison with this outrageous fantasy. We know most of the things he promised Priscilla's parents: That he would see to it Priscilla was well educated in a Catholic school. (As her education was virtually complete by this time, this promise wasn't worth much.) That she would be treated like a young woman of means, given her own car, fine clothes, etc. (Buying the girl outright, like the bride of some Arab sheik, was not, one presumes, a proposal that either party could entertain.) Finally, that he would marry Priscilla at some unspecified future date.

Priscilla's arrival at Graceland, in May of 1962, was kept as quiet as possible. Though everyone was told that Priscilla was living with her "guardians," Vernon and Dee, the staff at Graceland knew different because they saw the girl running around in the morning, wearing shorty pajamas. Though this story would have made a juicy item for the scandal sheets, virtually nothing appeared in print. It was yet another striking instance of how successful Elvis was at keeping his private life concealed from the press and the public. Indeed, it was a matter of critical importance that the truth about his relations with Priscilla be kept secret, for only recently two of the greatest heroes of rock 'n' roll had been crucified publicly—and one of them locked up in prison—for doing precisely what Elvis was doing now: cohabiting with a teenage girl.

Elvis's closest rival in the rockabilly world, Jerry Lee Lewis, had been the first to suffer. The irrepressible Jerry Lee had arrived in England in 1958, riding high on a tremendous wave of popularity generated by such legendary hits as "Whole Lotta Shakin' Goin' On" and "Great Balls of Fire." Received with tremendous enthusiasm by the British public, Jerry Lee was making a triumphal tour of the country when the news broke that he had married his fourteen-year-old cousin, Myra Brown. Instead of evading the issue, Jerry Lee brought his child bride onstage to greet the fans. The resulting explosion of public outrage blew Jerry Lee out of show business for the next ten years. After his English tour was canceled, his latest record blacklisted and his concert dates wiped out, he found himself right back where he started from down in Loosiana. The fact that he had *married* his teen queen did not mitigate the crime one bit in the eyes of the public. Imagine what the reaction would have been if this same public had discovered the rock star and his little girl were living together in sin!

An even worse fate befell Chuck Berry, who at this time was also at the peak of his career both as rock's greatest songwriter and one of its most popular performers. In 1961 Berry was convicted in St. Louis of transporting a fourteen-year-old girl across a state line, a violation of the Mann Act, and sentenced to three years imprisonment and a $5000 fine. On February 15, 1962, he was incarcerated in the United States Medical Center for Federal Prisoners at Springfield, Missouri. He was released on parole on October 18, 1963.

In cohabiting with a minor, even in arranging to transport her across state lines, Elvis was playing with dynamite. What's more, Elvis hardly knew Priscilla at this time and had no way of assessing what his success would be in his mad scheme to shape her into the perfect woman. Clearly, in this, his first major decision since his mother's death, he had run completely off the rails. The whole undertaking was crazy from the start. In time, it produced the disaster that finally broke Elvis Presley.

Though virtually every feature of Elvis's relationship with Priscilla was dubious, the public transformed this foredoomed affair into a fairy-tale romance. Priscilla was seen as Cinderella and Elvis as Prince Charming. Though Elvis's homes resembled Hugh Hefner's playboy pad a lot more than they did the enchanted castle, the infatuated fans insisted on viewing the pair as ideal lovers. Priscilla was perceived as a delicately budding flower which Elvis was guarding jealously for his very own. Not since Edward left the throne for "the woman he loved" has any such relationship been more totally misconstrued.

Once Priscilla had settled down at Graceland, she began to receive her training from Master Elvis. The first lessons were in makeup and hairstyling. Elvis liked his women to wear the heaviest kind of theatrical makeup: black mascara, batwing eyelashes, lots of color laid on in pancake appliers. Always obsessed with hairstyles, he insisted that Priscilla tease her hair up about twelve inches in a towering, heavily lacquered beehive. Marty Lacker recalls that the first time he met Priscilla, "she looked like she had about eight people living in her hair." Though Priscilla had an exquisite, doll-like kind of beauty, when Elvis got through with her, she looked like a tart.

Another feature of her appearance that changed immediately was the color of her hair. She dyed her towering, teased-up coif the same jet-black color that was Elvis's trademark. In fact, some people began to insist that Elvis and Priscilla were coming to look alike, that they were becoming twins. An extreme narcissist like Elvis might well have wanted his mate to be a female copy of himself. She was certainly his shadow or reflection at first: studying his tastes, conforming to his wishes, copying his style and personality. In making such a profound identification with Elvis, Priscilla might well have been motivated by a very deep desire to *be* Elvis. Envy so often passes for love.

In October, after Elvis left for Hollywood to start work on *Kid Galahad,* Vernon Presley enrolled Priscilla at Immaculate Conception Cathedral High School. The school is located in midtown Memphis on Central Avenue at Belvedere Boulevard. Considered one of the better Roman Catholic schools in the city, it was an obvious choice because of its convenient location. School had already begun when Vernon had his meeting with Sister Adrienne, the principal. She recalls that the enrollment was preceded by an extensive correspondence between her and the Presley attorney. Transcripts of Priscilla's academic records arrived, indicating that she should be placed in the senior class. In fact, Priscilla had so many credits already that it was decided that she should attend only half a day, leaving at lunchtime. At first, Sister Adrienne assumed that Priscilla was a member of the Presley family; but when the nun saw the transcripts from schools in Germany, she put two and two together and concluded that this was the girl Elvis had been dating in Germany.

Once Sister Adrienne realized that she was being asked to enroll in a Catholic girls' school a young woman who might be living with Elvis Presley in questionable circumstances, she sought the advice of her close friend on the faculty, Sister Loyola, who recollects the conversation clearly.

We were working on the school paper that day—I taught journalism—and the girls said to me, all excited: "Sister, Elvis's father is in the office talking to Sister Adrienne." Then they confessed that they had all been down on the floor looking through the keyhole to see Mr. Presley. I said, "Get back to work, girls; we're not concerned with Elvis's father: We're working on the paper." I was curious myself, but I didn't let them know it. When everyone left, I went into the office and Sister Adrienne said: "You'll never believe this, but Elvis has a protégé who wants to go here to school." I said: "Do you think he's in love with this girl? Do you think it's a girlfriend? It seems very strange." We discussed it at length and Sister Adrienne said, "This girl is supposed to be Catholic and her parents have agreed to let her come to Memphis from Germany and she will live in Mr. Presley's home—not at Graceland—and she will be properly chaperoned." Then she said, because we were very close, "Sister, do you think it's all right for me to take this girl?" I said, "If he assured you that she will be properly chaperoned and if she's living with Mr. Presley and not with Elvis, it seems to me that it will be all right."

The next day Priscilla arrived and was assigned to my class. I tried to prepare the girls because in a girls' school, they're much more given to emotional outbursts about boys than they are in a coed school. I explained the circumstances and said, "She's probably Elvis's girlfriend." They were very excited. Then this lovely little girl arrived. I remember she was very shy. She had very little to say. She came in and I assigned her a place and gave her the book list. Her face was packed with makeup and her hair was in a beehive. She had on so much makeup that you could not really tell what kind of girl was underneath all that stuff. Sister Adrienne told her, "Now, we don't say the girls can't wear makeup, Priscilla, but we like for it to be inobvious. Also we wear uniforms, and we will see that you have one. When you get the uniform, take all that makeup off. I think you will fit in better with the girls." It took a couple of days to get the uniforms and I noticed that she was coming to school overly dressed. Then one day she walked in wearing her uniform. It was a lovely uniform the girls wore: white blouse, plaid skirt and a little waistcoat. She looked darling. Her real beauty was showing.

The only thing I taught her was religion. I've often wondered since if she was really Catholic because when she was married to Elvis, they were not married by a priest and their little girl was not baptized as a Catholic. Sister Adrienne and I have discussed whether Elvis's father just wanted her to have the cloak of security that a Catholic school would provide. Maybe she wasn't Catholic at all. She didn't know the most basic things about our religion.

I had the top students in English. She was not a top student.

Her grades were average or below. She rarely committed herself a whole lot to anything. We have a lot of activities in sports, drama, school paper and yearbook. She didn't participate in any of the activities. The minute school was over, she was whisked away or she drove off in her Corvair. She told me that she was exhausted every day because she would stay up at night for parties and movies.

I asked her about her parents in Germany: if she missed them very much, if she wrote to them, if she heard from them. She would respond but not as most girls do, telling you all about their parents. She gave very short answers. She was never very close to her teachers, but she was very friendly and nice to the other girls. The girls would say to me: "Sister, Priscilla is a cute girl. She's neat." They used that word when they liked someone. "She doesn't brag, she doesn't put on, she doesn't mention Elvis." The girls were impressed at first by the fact that Elvis's father brought her to school in a big car. "Sister, she rides in that Cadillac with the television in it!" they said. But after about ten days, she came to school in a little red Corvair, and the girls were delighted with that. We had a custom here that once a week the girls could go out to lunch. She'd fill her Corvair full of girls and they'd go out to lunch. They were all excited to get a ride with Priscilla. They learned soon that she was the sort of girl who never did say a whole lot.

When graduation time came, we wondered whether Elvis would come and disrupt the ceremony. Graduation was held in the cathedral. That night I passed through the yard and I saw that Cadillac and I said to myself: "Oh, there he is!" I went over to get the girls lined up, to see that their robes were on right and everything. Two or three other young sisters went over to the car and spoke to Elvis and got his autograph. They asked him if he were coming in. He said: "No, Sister, I'm not going in. This is Priscilla's night. If I went in, it would disturb the graduation. I'll wait out here in the car until it's all over."

As soon as Priscilla was graduated from high school, she enrolled in a school that taught modeling and dancing. Her basic inclination was toward the world of style and fashion. Though Memphis was the worst place imaginable for a girl with such interests, she made the best of the situation, anticipating the time when she would spend more time in the much trendier milieu of Los Angeles. The West Coast was doubly certain to figure in her future because not only did Elvis spend a great part of every year in the area making movies but Priscilla's family was living now near Sacramento as a result of Captain Beaulieu's transfer to Travis Air Force Base.

It was while she was visiting her family in the summer of 1963 that Priscilla first became a target for the news media as a result of Elvis's love affair with Ann-Margret. The actress, who was now being called "the female Elvis Presley," had been thrown together with Elvis that August in Las Vegas, where most of the shooting was being done for *Viva Las Vegas*. At first relations between the stars were strained because Elvis swore that the picture's director, George Sidney, was sweet on Ann-Margret and was lavishing on her the best camera angles, the greatest number of close-ups and the other advantages that Elvis was accustomed to claiming. Naturally, he raised hell about this favoritism to Colonel Parker, who swooped down on the picture's producer, Jack Cummings. The Colonel was already very annoyed with Cummings because he had refused to allow Colonel his customary "side action."

Colonel had suggested, for example, that all the resort shots be done at the Sahara, which was owned by the Colonel's friend, Milton Prell. Cummings had pointed out that the Sahara was highly unsuitable and had cut a deal with the Flamingo. Colonel had offered next to contract a security force for the entire company. Cummings had told Colonel to worry about his own boy, while Cummings took care of his workers. Now the two men were ready to square off for the final round.

Cummings was a tough, acid-tongued veteran of twenty years in Hollywood. He also had the enormous advantage of being the son-in-law of Louis B. Mayer. The Colonel's attack took a typically childish form. He waited until a major sequence had been completed, entailing the title song of the picture. Then, he demanded that the whole costly take be shot again because the camera had not caught Elvis's feet. Cummings said that Elvis wasn't a dancer and his feet could be safely omitted. Colonel insisted on taking the matter to the top studio executives. Normally, in such a situation, the executives would have given in to the Colonel's demands just to placate the old man. This time, however, they were caught between the Colonel and the boss's son-in-law. The sequence was not reshot. Colonel was so enraged that when the movie was completed, he tried to sell Elvis's fifty-percent interest just so they could disassociate themselves with the project. *Viva Las Vegas* grossed $5.5 million, which is considerably better than most of the Presley pictures.

The principal reason for the success of the film was the remarkable Ann-Margret, who proved to be just what Elvis should have been in the movies: a talented, vivacious and erotically enticing performer who balanced nimbly on the line between the sexy and the lewd—the lifeline of every Presley formula movie. Even without the assistance of the director she was dating, she would have upstaged Elvis and outperformed him consistently. It is to Elvis's credit that he recognized her ability and did not allow their professional problems to stop him from paying his customary court to his costar. By the time the shooting on the picture had ended, Elvis and Ann-Margret were clearly involved in what was the only authentic romance in Elvis's long career of dating Hollywood actresses.

A sign of how infatuated Elvis became with Ann-Margret is the fact that for the first time in his life he began to disappear from his house for a day or two at a time, spending the stolen hours at Ann-Margret's place up in the Hollywood Hills. This violation of the rule that women had to come to him was just one of several signs that the Guys interpreted as indications of real passion. For her part, Ann-Margret announced that she and Elvis were going steady and she told one reporter that her huge round pink bed was a gift from Elvis. (Elvis gave fancy beds to more than one woman.) Some people interpreted the actress's remarks as just another publicity ploy. The truth would appear to be that there was a brief but intense affair, conducted right under Priscilla's nose.

Ann-Margret later became completely mute on the subject of her romance with Elvis. Evidently, the affair was broken off abruptly on Elvis's initiative and without any clarifying explanations. Not long after the two had ceased seeing each other, a couple of the Guys spotted Ann-Margret riding through Hollywood. Pulling up beside her, they struck up a fast conversation. "I thought you were in love," said one of them. "I thought we were, too," replied the actress. "Well, what happened?" said her questioner. "Ask your boss," the lady replied. "I haven't the faintest idea."

The explanation is probably quite simple. Ann-Margret was dedicated to her career; therefore, she was not a suitable mate for Elvis. His record of noninvolvement was virtually unblemished; it probably cost him no great effort to keep it perfect. Elvis's life was designed to allow him an endless series of one-night stands and short affairs, his commitment to marry Priscilla providing a perfect rationalization for his reluctance to become emotionally involved with any women.

By late 1963, however, Priscilla was out of school and beginning to show signs of restlessness. Life in Bluebeard's Castle was pretty dull. It was about this time that Priscilla began to display an interest in other men. At a gospel concert at the Auditorium (one of the very few public events that Elvis ever attended), she had seen a good-looking, blond, nineteen-year-old singer with the Stamps Quartet named Milan Lefevre. Though it was taking a great chance to reach out to another man in Elvis's hometown, filled with gossips and spies, Priscilla managed to get in touch with this young man and meet him several times either at the Auditorium or at the Whitehaven Shopping Center. Lefevre thought Priscilla was a real "fox." He felt she was pursuing him. Yet, nothing came of their meetings. The fox was not yet ready to pounce.

While Priscilla was flirting in Memphis, Elvis was grinding through three movies a year and thirty parties a month in Los Angeles. This schedule had gotten him so depressed that he was becoming quietly desperate. His consumption of downers was escalating steadily. His irritability was growing more marked every month. He was also starting to buck under the Colonel's yoke.

According to the Presley Myth, Elvis and the Colonel were deeply devoted to each other. Their stock exchange consisted of Elvis saying, "I love you, Colonel," and the old man replying, "You're all I live for, Elvis." The truth is that from the earliest years of the relationship there was a deep and ever-widening conflict between this famous pair. Elvis disliked the Colonel instinctively and dreaded those occasions when he had to confront his master. It's generally assumed that the total control that Parker exercised over Elvis's business was entirely owing to Elvis's distaste for business. It might have been Elvis's distaste for the Colonel that made him willing to do anything or sign anything just to get the old man out of his life again.

Once Elvis had concluded that the Colonel had conned him into going into the army, a development that led shortly to Gladys's death, Elvis's sufferings and Vernon's remarriage, Elvis must have viewed the Colonel with feelings of hatred. Yet he couldn't break with the old man because he was totally dependent upon him to revive his career. Once Elvis felt confident again, however, he started to give the Colonel the freeze. It was noted that the two would walk past each other on a movie lot without even saying hello. Colonel Parker soon demanded that every day he receive a report on Elvis from his foreman, Joe Esposito. Elvis resented this so much that he found a pretext for firing Joe in the fall of 1963. At that point he gave the job to Marty Lacker.

Fat, balding, Jewish, married with two children, Lacker, who had joined Elvis in 1961, was a one-time local announcer and DJ. Under his veneer of good ole boy conformity he was a rather different type from the rest of the Guys. (Elvis's predilection for Jews—George Klein, Alan Fortas, Marty Lacker, Larry Geller—is remarkable considering his background. Vernon was outspokenly anti-Semitic, always complaining that "Elvis is bein' screwed blind by them Jews out in Hollywood." The Colonel used to warn the Guys: "Watch what you say about Jews and homosexuals out here in Hollywood because you never know when you're talkin' to one of 'em." By entrusting Jews with important positions in his organization, Elvis was rebelling against the prejudices of his little world and especially against his father.) Lacker was completely devoted to Elvis and unresponsive to pressure from Colonel Parker. He could have performed a very valuable service for Elvis by jealously guarding his employer's privacy. Instead, he evinced a passive and acquiescent temperament, which led him eventually to second Joe Esposito's efforts to get back into Elvis's good graces. During the year 1964, however, Elvis was in the unique position of not having as his foreman a man who reported every day to Colonel Parker.

The rebellious attitude that Elvis evinced during this period toward the Colonel soon embraced every feature of his life. The rebellion was fueled by all the pressures, frustrations and disappointments of the post-army years. Above all, it was incited by the disgust with which Elvis viewed his once enthralling life and career. Elvis had always interpreted his success as a sign that he had been singled out by providence to accomplish some great mission here on earth. The problem was that as the years wore on, instead of the goal becoming clearer, it became ever more difficult to perceive. When he was younger, Elvis had enjoyed the reassuring effects of progress: He had seen one landmark after another race past him as he pursued his giddy career. With everything happening so swiftly, he could tell himself that if he just kept going, he was bound to reach his destination. Now, he had lost that simple faith. He had begun to suffer from the thought that he wasn't going anywhere. What *was* he doing? Just standing still, grinding out one crappy movie, one mediocre soundtrack album after another. Then, as reward for all his labors, he was always throwing foolish parties with foolish girls, parties that pleased the guests a lot more than they did the host. In fact, in his more depressed moments, Elvis began to think that he was actually worse off than he used to be because now, instead of exalting him, his life was beginning to degrade him. Elvis the Bad had been glutted, while Elvis the Good had been starved.

The self-hate of a narcissist is one of the most deadly of all emotions. It is the sadism of the self toward the self. Carried far enough, it can lead to a nervous breakdown or to suicide. During the spring of 1964, Elvis began to experience a crisis of self-loathing. He abandoned his customary life-style and instead of rushing maniacally from one sport or prank to another—denying his innate depression by the mindless pursuit of fun—he locked himself up in his bedroom at Graceland for days at a time, refusing to speak with anyone. The gloom that closed over Elvis alarmed all the Guys. Some of them said that if Elvis didn't find something fresh to live for, some new inspiration, he might crack up. Such was the situation on April 30, 1964, when word was received at the house on Perugia Way that Elvis's hairdresser, Sal Orifice, would not be able to pay his accustomed call. He suggested that a barber be summoned from Jay Sebring's fashionable salon. The appointment was booked and that afternoon, when the doorbell rang, one of the boys answered—and in walked the Swami.

Chapter 25

The Swami

LARRY GELLER was a young man slightly ahead
of his time. A tall, slender, good-looking New York Jew, he was
an early example of a type that swiftly became common: the low-
pressure, low-profile West-Coast hippie spiritualist and health food
faddist, who, as he labors every day at his manual craft, babbles
endlessly about meditation, vitamin E and the Third Eye. Elvis
sometimes referred jokingly to Geller as his "guru"; but you
wouldn't get far imagining their relationship in the terms suggested
by that appellation because Geller was no master and Elvis could
never maintain for more than a few moments the posture of the
disciple. The truth is that far from being Elvis's mentor, Geller
was just the match that touched off the emotional tinder that was
Elvis Presley.

Imagine in the first place how exotic Larry Geller must have
appeared in the dumb jocko-schloko Memphis-in-Bel-Air milieu
in which Elvis was imprisoned. In contrast to the beefy, blowsy
look of the Guys, Geller is thin, dark, *spirituelle;* his thoughtful
face with its dark soulful eyes is crowned by a great turban of
black hair. Everything about him proclaims the swami. Then, as
the skinny scissors snip and the spray nozzle hisses and the precious
jet-black dyed locks fall to the floor, words are spoken and looks

exchanged and heavy etheric vibrations registered that soon have Elvis hanging on every word, oscillating moment by moment from surliness to sincerity, from suspicion to faith, from despair to joy. One of the most telling exchanges occurred when the breezy, arrogant, spoiled-rotten Elvis said, "Don't worry about the hair on the floor—the maid will clean it up!" Instead of responding like any ordinary mortal and saying, "Okay," Swami Geller, the servant of servants, the beggar's bowl of barbers, the humble picker-up of learning's crumbs, murmured in his spooky spiritual voice: "I like to do my own cleaning."

Once Geller had hooked Elvis, his task became that of a spiritualist "connection." Every few days he was expected to deliver a new load of occult literature and engage in prolonged discussions of the books Elvis had already consumed. Elvis fell on these strange books with an appetite equal to that of the keenest Ph.D. candidate sitting buried in the stacks of some great library. In fact, you'd have to have the stomach of a bookworm to read the stuff that Elvis gobbled up in this period. He said his favorite subject in high school was English? You can believe it! Suppose you enrolled for a course in spiritualism and the professor handed you this list of required readings:

Vera Stanley Adler: *The Initiation of the World*
David Anrias: *Through the Eyes of the Masters*
Alice A. Bailey: *Esoteric Healing*
McDonald McBain: *Beyond the Himalayas*
Anne Besant: *The Masters*
H. L. Blavatsky: *The Secret Doctrine; The Voice of Silence*
Paul Brunton: *The Wisdom of the Overself*
Richard Maurice Bucke: *Cosmic Consciousness*
Cheiro's Book of Numbers
Joel Goldsmith: *The Infinite Way*
Manley Palmer Hall: *The Mystical Christ;*
                    The Secret Teachings of All Ages
Corrine Heline: *Sacred Science of Numbers*
Max Heindel: *The Rosicrucian Cosmo-Conception*
Krishnamurti: *The First and Last Freedom*
C. W. Leadbetter: *The Inner Life*
The Leaves of Morya's Garden
Nicholas Roerich: *Flame in Chalice*
Dane Rudhyar: *New Mansions for New Men*
Baird Spaulding: *The Life and Teachings of the Masters of*
                    the Far East

Tibetan Book of the Dead
Paramahansa Yogananda: *Autobiography of a Yogi*
The Urantia Book.

Heavy! Right? The real hard-core, mystogogical, table-rapping, apparition-looming, spirit-voices mumbo jumbo. The stuff you find in those dim little bookshops down at the bottom of Fourth Avenue or along Hollywood Boulevard with "OCCULT" lettered across their windows. Old these books are, many of them dating back to the days just before and after World War I, when this kind of rubbish enjoyed such a tremendous vogue that T. S. Eliot used it in *The Wasteland* as a symbol of the degradation of myth and ritual in the modern world.

Actually, it never makes any difference when these books are written because they are always composed of the same banal or preposterous ideas in the same familiar code phrases. Each successive author or age gives this stuff another stir in the pot and then pours out the familiar stew. Sometimes these authors go on pouring through a score of volumes. Getting the spirits to speak is as nothing compared with the difficulty in making them shut up. Or make sense. The reader is always being hailed, or better, *haled,* by pseudo-biblical prophet voices that cry out with the urgency of a great revelation. Then, as they maunder on for page after page of empty prose or kooky verse or abandon language in favor of diagrams, paradigms and arrangements of lotus blossoms, you realize that you've been had again by the spiritual hucksters, the heavenly con men, the charlatans of the soul.

What would make a young man like Elvis Presley spend years and years in the perusal of these queasy writings? What sort of compulsion could propel him through all this bad prose and quack verse? Just reading two or three of these books is a test of one's powers of self-discipline. Imagine what it takes to read hundreds of such volumes and then reread many of them and ponder their unreal substance! That he did read these books with great care is evident even from the appearance of his copies, dog-eared, travel-stained, heavily underscored on almost every page. Elvis committed many of the key passages to memory and would recite them aloud while Larry Geller held the book like a stage prompter.

The customary explanation of this mania is that Elvis was "profoundly religious." The difficulty with that answer is that none of these books deal with religion either in the strict theological or the common everyday meaning of the word. Spiritualism is not religion. It may be a substitute for religion or it may mask itself as an ancillary to religion in order to lull the fears of the pious and win for its dubious doctrines a wider following. At bottom, however, spiritualism is antagonistic to orthodox religion because so much of its substance is derived from heresies, superstitions and magical beliefs and practices that the great Western religions long since proscribed.

The particular tradition of spiritualism from which stem most of the writings to which Elvis Presley devoted himself for the balance of his life was established in the 1870s in New York City by the notorious and fascinating Madame Blavatsky. Elvis always had on hand copies of Madame Blavatsky's writings and those of her disciples, like Anne Besant and C. W. Leadbetter. In fact, one little volume purporting to be translations by Blavatsky of the most ancient runes of Tibet, *The Voice of Silence,* was such a favorite of Elvis's that he sometimes read from it onstage and was inspired by it to name his own gospel group, Voice. Though Elvis was so well acquainted with the Blavatsky school, who called themselves "Theosophists," he does not appear ever to have understood who Madame Blavatsky was or even what was the true purport of her writings.

Like Immanuel Velikovsky in our day, Madame Blavatsky argued that the world was once occupied by a master race, the Aryans, who possessed a special language and a vast store of knowledge that was so superior to anything the human race has created since that everything that is really profound in our modern philosophies and religions is just a broken and often miscomprehended fragment of the "Ancient Wisdom." The goal of Madame Blavatsky's labors in her two immense books, *Isis Unveiled* (1877) and *The Secret Doctrine* (1889), is to restore the Ancient Wisdom to something resembling its original character by a gigantic labor of synthesis, collecting bits and pieces of the shattered system of the Aryans in every civilization and culture on earth, ranging from the Indians and Tibetans, to the ancient Greeks and Egyptians, to the early Mexican and American Indian civilizations. All of this sounds pretty impressive until you start reading one of these books; then, you recognize that you are in the presence of a mind that is either very disordered or completely untutored or fundamentally fraudulent. For instead of a synthesis, these books produce about the same impression as would the pages of *The Golden Bough* if they were torn out in fascicles of two, three or four pages and then rearranged by being blown in a heap by a powerful fan. Mesmerism, vampires, mediums, the Vedas, spirit materialization, charming serpents by music, witchcraft, the resuscitation of buried fakirs, levitation, Atlantis—the whole range of the occult is crammed into these volumes without the slightest semblance of order or reason.

experienced most keenly, however, was not that of visionary or cloud shifter but that of healer of the sick. He had always wanted to be a doctor, and he had been reared in a culture that believed in faith healing. It's even possible that he may have witnessed ministers laying hands on sick people and literally tearing the illness out of their diseased bodies. Now he undertook to do the same thing himself, explaining to his friends that these efforts cost him a great deal because he had to take the pain of the afflicted one up into his own body. Like all healers, he experienced both failure and success. Consider a case that occurred in 1973, when Elvis sought to heal Sonny and Judy West's little boy, Brian, who was suffering from a burning fever.

By this time Elvis had had quite a bit of experience in his role as spiritual doctor; consequently, when he arrived at the Wests' home he had with him the tools of the trade. He produced a large green scarf, explaining that green was the healing color. He set upon his head a massive turban with a big glittering stone in its center. Laying the child on the green cloth, Elvis assumed the lotus position and went into deep meditation. Then he began to address the child, exhorting him to relinquish the fever and let it pass into Elvis. As Elvis bent lower to place his hands on the critical points of the child's body, little Brian became fascinated with the big stone flashing from Elvis's turban. The child reached up and tried to snatch the bauble. "Don't do that, Brian!" Elvis warned. Sonny and Judy sought to suppress their laughter. The kid was screwing up Elvis's act! Finally, having laid his hands on both sides of the child's head and on his solar plexus, Elvis turned to the parents and said: "I think the fever's breaking." Sonny touched his son but he discerned no difference. He humored Elvis by saying, "Yeah, I think it is." Meantime, he made a mental note to give Brian two more aspirins. Next day, however, Brian's fever broke. When Elvis called and got the report, he said: "Good, that pleases me. If you notice any change, let me know."

By the summer of 1966, when Elvis started filming *Spinout,* he had gotten so far into his role as Master that the performance he gave off the set surpassed by far his work before the cameras. No sooner did he arrive on location at Nagoura, just outside Los Angeles, than he began what the film magazines would have called a "whirlwind romance" with his costar, Debra Walley. Every moment the pair were not before the camera, they shared together, from breakfast in Elvis's trailer to lunch in the same luxuriously appointed vehicle to the hours-long phone calls that filled the evening after the rushes. It looked like one of those hot and heavy affairs that are supposed to boil up spontaneously on film locations. Actually, it was something much crazier and fraught with more serious consequences. Elvis had decided to blow Miss Walley's mind as only a great Master can affect a hungry and adoring disciple.

What made Debra Walley so hungry was precisely what had made Elvis so frustrated before he discovered spiritualism. This young actress, who was always playing silly little ingenues like Gidget or, in this picture, the kookie-pookie girl drummer in an all-guy rock band, this perennial teenie-weeny jumping bean with the bangs and the pop eyes was in fact a highly skilled and highly professional actress who had been born into show business and had been working in the theater since she was twelve. She had been on the verge of becoming a star of the Off-Broadway theater of her day (appearing in Chekov's *Three Sisters* at the age of sixteen), when she got sucked into the movie business and became an overnight sensation. Picked up like a toy train and put down again on a new set of tracks leading in precisely the opposite direction to that on which she had set her heart, she had allowed herself to be conned into playing the whole Hollywood game to the hilt. She had done the dumb beach-party pictures, appeared on the covers of the movie mags and the women's mags, and, finally, she had even made the ultimate commitment by marrying a very handsome and successful young actor with whom she had a child. Oh, she was a fabulous success! Didn't everyone around her on the location address her as "Miss Walley"? The only hang-up was that she missed the life she should have had and the people she should have known.

Comes now the Master. She had no big thing about Elvis Presley. She was never a fan. She didn't even regard Elvis as an actor. At the most, she observed that his physical appearance reminded her a little of her husband, John Ashley, who was then in the Philippines making a picture. Suddenly, Elvis was coming on to her: not in a sexual manner but in some strange new way that she had never before experienced. He was very intense, very earnest. At the same time, he was very warm and physical, always putting his arms around her and even kissing her. Yet he wasn't being seductive in any ordinary sense. It was more as though he was trying to communicate with her in a language she didn't yet understand.

No sooner do they commence their conversations than he lays on her a copy of *The Impersonal Life*. She's very bright, eager, the perfect pupil. That very night she goes through the whole book. Next morning in the trailer, he starts to give her a quiz. She makes an A + . Elvis is took himself, but probably expressing the same urgencies only in a far more confident and liberated spirit.

The world into which Debra Walley went spinning after her mind-blowing encounter with Elvis Presley was the brave new world of Rock. Commencing in 1963, when the first Beatles records made their way to America (on an obscure Chicago label named Vee-Jay that specialized in black R & B) and mounting to a sensational crescendo in 1964 with the arrival of the Fab Four in America, where they played to no less than seventy million people on the *Ed Sullivan Show,* the new rock—so called to distinguish it from the corny old rock 'n' roll of the fifties—had by the year 1967 reached a level of messianic fervor that impelled many observers to compare it to the Great Awakening or even the Crusades. Never before in the history of the world had any mass cultural phenomenon developed such power, authority and pervasiveness. One moment, there was this new fad among the teenagers for British boys in pipe-stem suits and soup-bowl haircuts; the next, there was this awesome human tide, this *Völkerwanderung,* that gathered up tens of thousands of young men and women, as in *The Invasion of the Body Snatchers,* and transformed them overnight into blissed-out Flower Children traipsing around like whacked-out Ophelias speaking in riddles and dancing like Isadora Duncan and gathering at immense encampments in unlikely places like Monterey or Woodstock, from which they had to be extricated by prodigious feats of paramedical ingenuity.

To anyone who was even semiconscious in this period, it was obvious that something big was happening. You couldn't switch on a radio or TV, pick up a newspaper or news magazine, without getting Rock right up the kazoo. Yet to that original Magical Minstrel, Elvis Presley, locked up in his luxurious bath-study in Bel Air like a Jacuzzi Faustus, there was nothing to Rock save a few cute tunes by the Beatles and the dread spectre of Commie drug-inspired youth revolt and youth degeneracy. On those rare occasions when Elvis came down from the mountain and surveyed the Cities of the Plain, the modern Sodom and Gommorah, strung out on Sunset Strip; or, when he listened with dark, angry brows to the obscenities of Mick Jagger and the horrible caterwauling of acid-rock bands—imagine! naming a kind of music after a *drug!*—Elvis would hurl down thunderous bolts of Jehovahan rage and righteous indignation.

No wonder, then, that when the Beatles first came to America—welcomed on the *Ed Sullivan Show* by a telegram wishing them every success and signed by Elvis Presley (though dispatched without his knowledge by Colonel Parker)—Elvis refused point-blank to meet these dubious encouraged to go much further. He takes her home in his big Rolls-Royce. He takes her into his bedroom. There, he lifts up the lid on a trunk and starts going through all the books it contains. He's like some little kid showing off his toys. Debra starts to get the bug. After all, Elvis Presley is one helluva salesman. A great "communicator," as they say on Madison Avenue. She's a born enthusiast. Mental touchwood. Poof! Up in smoke she goes as she burns through the books, the long swami raps, the silent sessions of unvoiced rapture as they hold each other tight in the trailer and strain for the still, small voice of Him!

Soon they're on that exhilaratingly naked plane of interaction where two people confront each other with a clearly declared purpose and nothing else to distract them. He tells her: "Look, we've only got this moment together: so let's have it completely. No holding back. No wasting time on trivialities. I've got the word. I want to give it to you. I'm not a man. I'm not a woman. I'm a soul, a spirit, a force. I have no interest in anything of this world. I want to live in another dimension entirely." Debra, a lapsed Roman Catholic, was thrilled. "I ate it right up," she says today, "like it was chicken soup. He treated me like an angel. I couldn't have had any more with him because I hated that macho life-style of his. In that world, I wouldn't have lasted ten minutes." Debra Walley's marriage didn't last any longer than it took to have one final session with her husband after he got back to Los Angeles.

In the movie with Elvis she played a rock drummer. Now she began an affair with a real rock drummer. She became a "cosmic flower child." She started dropping acid. She became the guru to her drummer, persuading him to get high with her. By the time of the Monterey Pop Festival the following summer, Debra is the perfect freak. She's sitting in the front row gonged to the gills, her hair out like Struwelpeter, bells around her neck and the world's biggest grin. Next, she's into photography, painting, songwriting. Finally, she gets so far out on acid that she has this final trip that takes her from being atop a mountain way down into a narrow corridor, where she meets a guy who says to her (like Elvis): "You're about to receive the word; but, when you get it, you won't be able to remain any longer on earth." At that point, she becomes alarmed. She realizes that not only has she thrown her career away but she is risking her sanity. A nervous breakdown follows and a period of hospitalization. Eventually, she pulls herself up and out of the breakdown and resumes her life, forming fresh relationships, having another child and eventually winding up today as a writer. It's quite a trip on which Elvis launched her, rather more dramatic than that which he young men who aspired to the hand of his daughter, the American youth audience. "Hell, I don't wanna meet them sons o' bitches!" exploded Elvis when the Colonel ran the proposition by him for the first time during the Beatles' initial tour in 1964. Even if Elvis hadn't entertained deep doubts about where these dudes were coming from, he wouldn't have been eager to meet them. Had he ever been keen to meet the stars?

The Colonel was not a man to take no for an answer, especially when the refusal came from his puppet, Elvis. Continuing his campaign to create the illusion of good feelings between his famous client and the Beatles, the Colonel sent next to the English boys a gift he knew would blow their minds: four fabulous suits of cowboy clothes, with ten-gallon hats and fancy boots and real six-shooters in leather holsters. It was the national equivalent of the key to the city. When the Beatles returned in 1965, they wore the outfits for one of their prodigiously successful dates. That was the signal to the Colonel to bear down hard on Elvis and make him receive his natural foes the next time they came around, as they were scheduled to do in the third week of August when Elvis was in Los Angeles working on one of his schmuckiest travelogues, *Paradise, Hawaiian Style*. "Okay, okay," sighed Elvis, conceding, once again, that he had been defeated. "But," he warned, "they're going to have to come up here to the house!" That was good enough for the Colonel. Now, he would be able to sit down face to face with Brian Epstein and tell him: "Elvis is dying to meet the Beatles."

At this time, Elvis was back in the circular house on Perugia Way, after living for a couple of years on Bellagio Road. During his absence, the circular patio in the center of the house had been roofed with glass and the space turned into a large game room with a pool table and various other adult toys. Elvis was still holding court, however, in the den, the scene of all those parties in the early sixties.

On the great night, Elvis took his accustomed seat on the long sofa against the wall, flanked by all his men: Marty Lacker, foreman at the time; Joe Esposito; Billy Smith, Elvis's little cousin; Jerry Schilling, a good-looking young man from Memphis; Alan Fortas; Sonny West; and a couple of new men: Mike Keaton and Ray Sitton, a 280-pound hanger-on from the Music Gate, whom everybody called "Chief." Soon this group was joined by the Colonel and Tom Diskin. The wives and children were sequestered in another room until the men should have finished their business.

Around nine in the evening, the Beatles arrived in a black limousine with a couple of bodyguards, a British pop journalist and Brian Epstein.

Virtually the entire Bel Air security force was on hand plus a contingent from the LAPD to prevent the fans from mobbing the stars or breaking through the gate into the parking area. On the way to the house, the Beatles had speculated on how they would find Elvis. "I expect we'll find he's just like one of us," remarked John Lennon. George Harrison was less confident. "I hope so," he said doubtfully, "some people are a let-down." Now as the new princes of rock were ushered across the thick white carpet and into the den, they could hear their records blasting from the jukebox.

When the Beatles entered, Elvis rose to greet them. Tanned by the Hawaiian sun, dressed casually in a red shirt, black windbreaker and skin-tight grey trousers, he looked healthy and relaxed. As Elvis smiled in recognition, John, affecting comical nonchalance, quipped, "Oh, there you are!" Formal introductions were made all round. Then, Elvis resumed his seat, with John and Paul on his right hand, Ringo and George on his left. As the jukebox continued to blare, alternating hits by the Beatles with hits by Elvis, nobody said a word.

The Beatles stared at Elvis. Elvis stared at the Beatles. None of the Guys felt it was his place to speak. Even the Colonel was oddly silent. Finally, when something like five minutes had elapsed, Elvis could bear the silence no longer. "Well, look," he protested, "if you damn guys are gonna sit here and stare at me all night, I'm gonna go to bed! Let's call it a night! I didn't mean for this to be like a thing—the subjects call on the king—or something like that! I just thought we'd sit and talk. We can talk about some music and maybe play a little, jam a little." The instant he said, "jam," all the Beatles cried, "What! God, we'd love to play with you!" The ice had been broken.

Soon the group had broken into separate circles. Elvis, John and Paul drifted into a quiet spot. "How many hits have you written now," asked Elvis, preoccupied as always by numbers and the sheer weight of the Beatles' triumph. John and Paul began earnestly reckoning, as if the figure had some special importance. When it was John's turn to ask a question, however, he wanted to know something crucial. "Why don't you go back to your old style of record," he asked. Elvis, who hadn't cut a rock single in years, offered his usual cop-out. "It's my film schedule," he explained. "It's so tight . . . but," he smiled, "I might do just one more for kicks." Lennon's comeback, "Then we'll buy it," was intended as a joke, but it signified clearly what the Beatles thought of Elvis's current work.

As Elvis chatted with John and Paul, Ringo started shooting pool on the table in the patio, surrounded by all the children of the entourage. Meantime, Colonel Parker and Joe Esposito laid hands on a cocktail table that opened up to become a roulette table. Appointing Joe croupier and himself pit boss, the Colonel called out in a formal tone: "The casino is open!" Immediately, he was joined by Brian Epstein, who had been as eager to meet the Colonel as the Beatles had been to meet Elvis.

After shooting some pool, Elvis broke out a bass guitar, which he was just learning to play. Ordering that the Beatles be equipped with guitars, he started to lead the jam session. The high point of the rave-up was Elvis picking out the bass bit on "I Feel Fine." "Coming along quite promising on bass, Elvis," said Paul encouragingly.

Then, it was time for one final chat on the long sofa about the fans and how it feels to face such immense and intimidating crowds as the Beatles had recently confronted at Shea Stadium. The once unimaginable range of experience that Elvis had been the first to traverse had now been scaled at an even higher altitude by the Beatles. The evening ended with the five young men comparing notes like astronauts discussing their trips to the moon.

The meeting was adjudged by all a success, except for George Harrison, who withheld himself from the conversation and behaved all night as if he were suffering from a fit of the pip. When it was time to leave, the Beatles said, "We'd like for all of you to come up to the place where we're staying tomorrow night." Elvis replied, "Well, I'll see. I don't know whether I can make it or not." Then, the Beatles turned to the Guys and said, "You're welcome with or without him." Several of the Guys said, "Fine!" The cagey ones, like Joe, held back because they didn't want Elvis to think they were too eager to hang out with his principal rivals. That sort of thing could make Elvis rage with jealousy.

The next night Marty Lacker, Jerry Schilling, Richard Davis and Sonny West went to see the Beatles in the house on Mulholland Drive which they were occupying for their week in Los Angeles. It was a big house with a spectacular and commanding view of the city. Once the Guys had settled into conversation with their hosts, John Lennon spoke up and in that marvelously candid style of his clarified the Beatles' intentions with regard to American celebrities. "Let me tell you guys something," he said: "There's only one person in the United States of America that we have ever wanted to meet—*not that he wanted to meet us!* And we met him last night. We can't tell you how we felt. We just idolized him so much. When we first came to town, these guys like Dean Martin and Frank Sinatra and all these people wanted to come over and hang around with us at night simply because we had all the women, all the chicks. We don't want to meet those people. They don't really like us. We don't really admire or like them. The only person that we wanted to meet in the United States of America was Elvis Presley. We can't tell you what a thrill that was last night!" There is John Lennon for you, telling it, as always, just like it is.

At this point, Paul offered to show the Guys around the house. As they are proceeding through the wing with the bedrooms, Paul opens a door, proclaiming, "This is George's room." As the Guys troop inside dutifully, they're startled to see that the room is not empty. George Harrison is in the room with Joan Baez. When the Guys appear at the door, she says "Hi!" Jerry Schilling is a great fan of Joan Baez; bumping into her in this manner renders him speechless. Paul continues on the tour breezily, as if nothing had happened. The moment Schilling can recover his breath, however, he's at Paul begging him to use his influence so that Schilling can get Joan Baez's autograph.

By this time, the tour has led outside the house to the pool, which sits atop a cliff that falls away from the house on the side overlooking the city. As the Beatles and the Guys emerge from the house earnestly discussing how they are going to obtain Joan Baez's autograph, a great racket reaches their ears. It turns out that two desperately determined teenage girls have risked their lives by climbing straight up the cliff face to reach the Beatles' house—and get their autographs!

The Guys had left Elvis sound asleep at the house on Perugia Way. Now they were eager to get back before the master arose and found them missing. The Beatles urged them to stick around and go out that night to the Hollywood Bowl and see the show. There was nothing in this world that the Guys would sooner have done—but the very thought of Elvis waking up and asking for them and then learning that they were off with the Beatles sent tremors of terror through their hearts. They declined the invitation and when they saw the Beatles again the following year on their third tour of America, the Guys had to decline again. A man may not serve, or even visit overlong, two masters.

In the spring of 1966, Elvis resolved, after an absence of two years from the recording studio, on making a major effort at reviving his moribund recording career. The Colonel's insistence on producing nothing but movie soundtrack albums had by this time made Elvis the laughingstock of the record business. For years his records had been mediocre, but at least they sold. Now they were so dreadful that even the fanatical Presley fans wouldn't buy them. Clearly, if Elvis were going to continue making records, he would have to take a new tack. Such a change was facilitated by the fact that Elvis's long-time producer, Steve Sholes, had retired for reasons of health and been replaced by a new man, Felton Jervis, who was very eager to refurbish Elvis's reputation. RCA, prohibited from cashing in on the new rock, must have been desperate to get something out of its once great pop star. Vast sums were being made again by rock stars: far more money even than had been made by Elvis in his greatest years. Bob Dylan, the Beatles, the Rolling Stones were not only piling up hit singles but selling albums in unprecedented numbers. The age of the "45" was over; now when people talked about a record they meant an album.

Having spent the past two years intensely involved with spiritualism, it was only natural that Elvis should have been inspired at this moment to record a great gospel album. Gospel had always been his favorite form of music; gospel was a music he had never stopped performing for his own pleasure; gospel would give him a chance to unite his deepest personal preoccupations with his musical talent to create for once a work that expressed his total being. It seemed like a very promising idea, and everything Elvis did by way of preparation increased the likelihood that he would produce a uniquely expressive album.

He decided, for example, to hire Jake Hess and his new quartet, the Imperials. Not just Hess but the old arrangements of the Statesmen were to be used in the album. A group of four female singers was also added so that the sound would have the fullness of a mixed choir. The band was recruited from among the best studio musicians in Nashville. The session was prolonged for three whole days so that every song could be brought to perfection. If ever in his career Elvis went all the way to achieve a work of art, this was the occasion.

How Great Thou Art was certified for a gold record. It also won a Grammy as the best gospel album of the year. (Colonel Parker got quite active in the Grammy organization and for the first time in years RCA began to receive some awards.) Commercially, therefore, the album bore at least the appearance of success. Artistically, however, it is one of the most disappointing performances in the Presley canon. Ever since "Crying in the Chapel," recorded in 1960 (though not released until 1965), Elvis had been singing gospel songs with a sugary and artificial voice that harkened back to the days of the first crooners. Now he orchestrated this phony religioso tone to create a new idiom that could best be described as religious easy-listening or Nashville Soul.

The essential ingredient in this musical pap is Elvis himself, whose holy crooning suggests the mock piety of a spooky funeral director. Swelling the concoction and giving it a specious fullness is the vocal chorus, which harmonizes everything in the tritest barbershop chords embellished with a high, other-worldly soprano. Through the entire first side of the album, every song is extruded from these vocal nozzles at the same slow puling tempo and with the same frozen attitude of spurious devoutness. The image that best fits this sacred snow job is of one of those gaseous, gelatinous, synthetic confections called Smoothies.

If spiritualism couldn't revive Elvis's talents, it was of no greater avail in the even more difficult struggle in which Elvis engaged in this period to change his head. One of the great principles of yogic literature, Elvis discovered, was the notion that to hear and feel the "high vibrations" through which the Masters communicate with the Adepts on earth, you have to be very quiet, very still, a human sssssh! Now this was an ideal diametrically opposed to the temperament of the world's greatest rock star. Elvis was as tightly strung as a violin, as manic as speed, as quick-tempered as a wildcat and perpetually onstage. How are you going to make a guy like this into a cigar-store Indian? One of his principal propaedeutics was a book titled *Autobiography of a Yogi* by Paramahansa Yogananda.

This book reads like a fairy tale. The young Adept is forever meeting great gurus who perform the most astonishing feats of mental telepathy, levitation, materialization and dematerialization. One of them even enables the future yogi to pass his college exams by putting all the right answers in his brain with a telepathic crib book. As for Yogananda himself, he's the original flower child. Nothing in his entire life ever sours for an instant the essential sweetness of his disposition. He's Yogi Bear.

Nor did anything become the Yogi in this life so much as the leaving of it. According to the report of the morticians at Forest Lawn (reprinted as a testimonial in all the brochures of Yogananda's Self-Realization Fellowship), "No physical disintegration was visible in his body even twenty days after death. . . . No indication of mold was visible on his skin. . . . No odor of decay emanated from his body. . . . This state of perfect preservation of the body is, so far as we know from mortuary annals, an unparalleled one." When Elvis was confronted by Doubting Thomases and men of little faith, he would throw this testimony in their teeth. How could you argue against incorruptibility?

Though this great guru died in 1952, long before Elvis discovered the Way, he left behind him a fully developed spiritualist academy with its main campus atop a mountain overlooking Pasadena. To this Laputan ashram Elvis loved to go because it fulfilled so perfectly all his ideas of how the higher life should appear. First, there was the winding journey up to the top of the mountain, commencing in the wicked valley and ending after countless hairpin turns on the heights. Your arrival in Shangri-La was signaled by two golden lotus buds atop the gate posts. The retreat was a perfect Raymond Chandler setting: a turn-of-the-century vacation hotel, with verdurous lawns constantly crossed and recrossed by mysterious women swathed in pale green, orange, blue and champagne-colored saris. There was a meditation garden, which Elvis duplicated immediately at Graceland. Down where the hill sloped toward the sinful city, the paths were barricaded because this portion of the grounds contained the quarters of the brothers and sisters who lived in celibate serenity, spending their lives in spiritual exercises, good works and meditation. When Elvis was told that this area was closed to him, it was all he could do to restrain the impulse to declare himself a celibate and plunge into the mysteries beyond.

The resident djin was a sweet, cooing pouter pigeon of a woman who called herself Daya Mata. Years before she had been Fay Wright of Salt Lake City. Then she had been drawn into the ineffable presence of the yogi, who, like most of his kind, had a great fondness for female disciples. (Remember the scandal when the Beatles, meditating on the banks of the Ganges, discovered the Maharashi making a pass at Mia Farrow!) Elvis was very taken by the soothing aura that emanated from Daya Mata. He called her fondly, "Ma."

When Elvis first met Ma, he asked her to authorize him to learn the secrets of Kriya Yoga, which is the ultimate notch on the scale of self-realization: the power to materialize and dematerialize at will, like a Homeric god. Ma laughed at this brash and naive proposal. She counseled patience, humility, perseverance—all the virtues in which Elvis was most lacking. He, in turn, offered money, which she gratefully accepted on behalf of the Foundation. (Giving money to these heathen so infuriated Vernon that he ordered the office staff at Graceland not to forward any letters from the SRF to Elvis.)

No matter how spiritual Elvis became, he could never attain the slightest degree of control over his terrible temper. Even when he was fresh from a soothing session with Ma, conducted in her top-floor retreat atop the mountain, the moment he got back on the level, he was prone to acts of irrational violence. Once as he was heading home from his

Shangri-La, he drove past a Gulf station at the foot of the hill where a couple of attendants were shadowboxing. Elvis ordered his big limousine to pull into the station. Rolling down the window, he made some sort of remark to the boxers, admonishing them to embrace love, not hostility. As his car pulled away, one of the dudes thrust up his finger in a fuck-you sign. That did it!

Instantly the car screeched to a stop and Elvis came charging out of the rear door. Advancing on the foremost attendant, Elvis threw a high karate kick that missed the man's body but sent his tire pressure gauge flying up in the air. Then Elvis whipped out a .38 from his shoulder holster and was just about to lower it when Hamburger James came rushing up from behind and shouted, "Gimme the gun!" Automatically, Elvis turned around and handed the astonished valet the weapon. In a second, they were back in the car and running for their lives, terrified that the evening paper would arrive with the headline: ELVIS PRESLEY THREATENS TO SHOOT GAS STATION ATTENDANT.

Whenever Elvis sinned against the great god Cool, whenever he tore up his living room with a barrage of karate kicks or drove through the closed gates of Graceland because they weren't opened swiftly enough or whipped out a gun and shot up some offending car (that wouldn't start) or some enraging TV set (that wouldn't hold the picture), he would experience pangs of guilt. If the pangs were keen enough, he would make amends. Interestingly, this atonement took the form of the penalty for murder in ancient civilizations: what the Anglo-Saxons called *wergild,* or man-money. Each time Elvis went crazy with rage, he would buy all the Guys extravagant and undeserved gifts. They might all receive Harley-Davidson motorcycles or Cadillac convertibles or even more expensive Mercedeses. Elvis didn't care whether the men kept the cars or sold them the next day. The important thing was that he bought his freedom from guilt.

Once this practice became common, it alarmed both Vernon Presley and the Colonel. Vernon was unable to do anything but beg his son to desist. His powers of moral suasion were limited by the fact that he was on the payroll for $72,800 a year and owed everything he had to Elvis. The Colonel was in a different position. When he saw that Elvis was likely in the future to literally throw his money away, the Colonel may have decided it was much better that he get the money instead of a lot of yes-men and girlfriends.

Precisely how the old man went about persuading Elvis to alter drastically their long-standing agreement by which the Colonel received twenty-five percent of Elvis's income after necessary expenses is a mystery. All that can be reported with certainty is that on January 2, 1967, Colonel Parker dictated a letter of agreement addressed to Elvis Presley that commenced: "As per our understanding on the telephone a few weeks ago, here is the amended agreement to our existing management agreement. As of this date all existing contracts change. The renewals will be 50% to Elvis Presley and 50% to All Star Shows [Colonel Parker]. All overages and profits, all expense payments will be 50% to Elvis Presley and 50% to All Star Shows." The letter goes on to stipulate that a like fifty-fifty split would be made of all income deriving from merchandising agreements and that the term of this new agreement would be January 22, 1976.

Fifty-fifty splits are rare in the modern entertainment business; but in the bad old days when unscrupulous white managers exploited black artists to the limits of rapacity, such outrageous spoliations were quite common. Duke Ellington surrendered fifty percent of everything he earned throughout most of his career to Irving Mills, as did Louis Armstrong to Joe Glaser. In defense of the old agents, it could be said that they were unique in even deigning to represent black artists and that the sums involved were never great. Colonel Parker, on the other hand, was representing the most famous entertainer in the world in deals that entailed millions of dollars. His only excuse for taking an exorbitant commission was that Elvis Presley was his only client.

Whatever leverage Colonel employed to get Elvis to start surrendering another twenty-five percent of his income, the fact speaks volumes for the character of the Parker-Presley relationship.

riage. As we have seen already, he had the sort of temperament that was highly susceptible to intense, love-at-first-sight affairs. All he needed to fall madly in love was just a glimpse of the right face. The very first time he laid eyes on Priscilla Beaulieu, for example, he experienced such an infatuation. He saw her as a teen angel, and no sooner did he feel the rush of romantic love than he associated it with the thought of marriage. This is precisely what he had done some years before with Debra Paget. Though the actress regarded him at first with scorn, he was willing after just a few weeks to make her his wife. Prior to Debra Paget, Elvis had sought to marry Dixie Locke, packing his bag and making as if to leave his parents' house. Marriage to Elvis was like orgasm to sex: It was the climax of his most passionate encounters. Yet, like orgasm, the urge to marry was not an enduring condition: It was just a feverish spasm of desire. If the offer was not soon consummated by the act, the impulse to make it soon subsided.

Once Elvis was past his first romantic infatuation with a woman, the character of his relationship with the woman began to change radically. The erotically charged emotion of the initial phase would vanish, and in its place would arise a totally different kind of connection. Instead of passion, the theme would now become play. Instead of heavy macho wooing, the roles would reverse and the woman would be expected to take the initiative. Soon, even this playful kind of love would evaporate, and Elvis would slip into his basic role, which was that of the child being babied by his adoring mother. It used to astonish the Guys, how swiftly this transformation could occur: how a girl whom Elvis had dated just a few times would suddenly start mothering him and pampering him and speaking to him in baby talk. He struck a chord in women, alright: the umbilical cord.

Once Elvis had brought a relationship around to this baby-mommy level, the promise of marriage was totally forgotten. After all, one doesn't marry one's mother. Quite the contrary: He enjoys the warmth of the maternal embrace while looking about for some nice little girl with whom, once again, to fall in love. This pattern explains every relationship Elvis ever had with a woman—except one: Priscilla. Elvis got himself in so deep with Priscilla he couldn't get out. Though Elvis prolonged his relationships with other women—Anita Wood before his marriage and Linda Thompson after the marriage—for just as long as he kept Priscilla dangling (five years seems to have been his proper limit), he did not make the mistake of committing himself in advance to these women as he did to Priscilla. By demanding and obtaining a mere child, by pledging his honor to a stern military figure like Major Beaulieu, Elvis created conditions of compulsion that would have made many men buckle under. Elvis was not, after all, a strong or rebellious personality. Elvis the Obedient was always stronger than Elvis the Rebel. Elvis the Angry was quickly smothered by Elvis the Guilty. Though Elvis was capable of cruel and ruthless behavior when he was operating behind a blind, he was extremely sensitive to any threat of public dishonor.

Having conceded this much to his character and his predicament, one must add that Elvis was perfectly capable of reneging on a promise or breaking a contract or backing out of any deal that he felt posed a deep threat to his own best interests. If the only pressures that had been brought to bear upon him in this case were the pangs of conscience or the distant rumbles of Major Beaulieu, it is very doubtful that Elvis would have married Priscilla and thereby placed in jeopardy both his career and his future happiness. No, the process by which Elvis was brought to marriage is far more bizarre than anything that would have befallen a more rational person.

The reason for the last-minute postponement of the marriage, after everyone had agreed that the ceremony should take place during or immediately after the Christmas holidays, is unknown and probably insignificant. What is important is Elvis's behavior during this time. Unlike the traditional bachelor who enjoys one last fling before he settles down to become a husband, Elvis, absorbed in spiritual pursuits, was not the least disposed to his customary dissipations. Nothing is more characteristic of the man who cannot face some grave problem than the development of a saving distraction. This is precisely what happened to Elvis Presley on the eve of his marriage.

Late one afternoon in February, while out riding in the country south of Memphis in Mississippi, Elvis steered his big Harley-Davidson motorcycle down a narrow blacktop road in the vicinity of the little town of Walls. Snow was on the ground and the light was already failing, when suddenly out the gloaming appeared to him the signal he had been so desperately seeking. There in a lonely pasture not far ahead arose before his astonished gaze an immense cross, standing over fifty feet high, illuminated eerily against the dun sky. What could such a portent mean? Elvis pulled off the road and scrutinized the scene carefully.

The cross was a massive object made of cast concrete and weighing many tons. At its foot was a small lake over which arched a distinctively oriental bridge. Nothing else was visible on the property except a charming little house set beside a gate in the chain-link fence that surrounded the acreage. Off in the distance there were some cattle barns and behind them, barely visible, a stand of trees. These physical properties were of no account. What mattered was the atmosphere of the place, which was fraught with strong religious overtones.

When Elvis got back to Graceland, he immediately put in motion an inquiry that soon revealed the property belonged to a man whom Elvis knew: Jack Adams, an airplane salesman. Back in the fifties, Adams had tried to sell the star a plane for his tours. Nothing had come of the effort because Gladys had told Adams that she was very alarmed at the thought of Elvis flying. Since that time, the men had never met again. Adams was still in the same business; he had an office not far from the farm Elvis had seen at a little local flying field called Twinkletown Airport. Just two days after Elvis first saw the great white cross looming from the pasture of Adams's farm, he and his boys pulled up outside the salesman's office in two big black Cadillac limousines.

Adams, an extremely polite and diffident sort of man who could easily compete with Elvis for the number of times he says "Yes, sir" or "No, sir" in an ordinary conversation, was startled when he looked out his window and saw the big cars disgorge their loads of heavyset men wearing western clothes. (The Guys had been doing a lot of horseback riding recently at Graceland and, at Elvis's urging, they had all adopted the western look.) The first men to confront Adams were Marty Lacker and Alan Fortas. They demanded to know whether his farm was for sale. Learning that it could be purchased for $530,000, they said that it was vastly overpriced. Just as the haggling began, Elvis walked into the room, having paused in the foyer to provide himself with a Coke from the machine. He asked if they could inspect the property. Adams immediately arranged for a guided tour. The visit wound up at the little house at the corner of the property. There Elvis and Vernon went into the sitting room alone and discussed the deal for fifteen minutes. When they were finished, Vernon asked Adams if Elvis could spend a night in the house. Adams pulled the key off his ring and told his prospective customer: "Delighted to have you."

A couple days later Elvis and Vernon turned up at Adams's office again. They told him that they liked the place and wanted to buy it just as it stood: with the cattle, the equipment, the furnishings in the house, everything on the property right down to the last roll of toilet paper. The moment the property was securely in Elvis's grasp, he started improvising what turned out to be a whole new design for his future life at home.

Dubbing his new place the Circle G Ranch, Elvis declared that it was time he and the Guys exchanged their old life-style at Graceland for a new way of life at the new Graceland, which would be constructed on the ranch. When they were just a bunch of young bachelors, nothing more was needed than a big house with a few servants to do the cooking and cleaning. For a group of solidly married mature men, the accommodations would have to take another form. Instead of one house, they would all require houses. Elvis would have the big house and each Guy would have a small house. It would be like a castle surrounded by cottages. Or, as a couple of the boys pointed out, it would be like that new phenomenon they were hearing so much about out on the West Coast—the commune!

Yes, that was the idea. Elvis Presley was going to establish the first commune in Mississippi. What's more, he was going to do it quickly. In fact, he wanted it done overnight. So whipping out the magic wand inscribed all over with dollar signs, Elvis began summoning up on this quiet and remote tract of land, not far from the crossroads called Bull Frog Center, a whole new plantation.

The first thing was to get all the Guys properly mounted. Elvis had bought some horses for Graceland—a beautiful golden Palomino for himself called Rising Sun, a little horse for Priscilla called Domino, and some other animals for the Guys. Now everyone had to get in the saddle and play cowboy. That meant even the enormously obese Lamar, whose horse reared up one day and threw him violently to the ground— to everyone's vast delight. Mounting the commune on horseback, however, wouldn't help them get around the rough back-country roads or trails on the ranch. So Elvis decreed that everyone must now be equipped with a pickup truck.

In no time a score of Rancheros, Camaros and El Caminos had been delivered to the ranch. Buying trucks, though, tickled some nerve in the one-time truck driver that responded so delightfully that he couldn't stop with just outfitting the family and the Guys—he had to go right on with his truck buying until he had equipped everyone in sight. Eventually, plumbers, carpenters, surveyors, anybody who showed up on the property were subject to an off-the-wall offer of a shiny new truck. Elvis got so carried away in the course of this binge that he started offering trucks to people to whom he had already given a truck. When they balked, he ordered them to find somebody else to whom to give the truck. In this manner, in a couple of weeks, Elvis bought enough trucks to outfit a company of motorized infantry. Marty Lacker recalls standing in front of the ranch office one night at two in the morning, watching Elvis operate a tractor, and suddenly finding Vernon Presley beside him looking distraught and holding out in the cold night air an enormously long strip of adding machine ribbon. "Marty, what am I gonna do?" cried out Vernon. "He done bought ninety-seven thousand dollars worth o' trucks!"

Once the rancheros had been equipped with Rancheros, the next problem was how to house them. By this time word of Elvis's spending binge had spread like wildfire over the whole area. Salesmen for every conceivable item made a beeline to the ranch and laid siege to the gate. Every time Elvis went in or out of the place, these hustlers would jump the Big Spender and start describing or demonstrating their wares. One dude was a salesman for mobile homes. He provided Elvis with the solution to his housing problem. If Elvis were in such a big hurry, why should he bother constructing buildings? All he had to do was buy a flock of mobile homes and park them on concrete pads. Elvis agreed and gave the necessary orders, but then a hitch developed because it turned out there were zoning rules even out here in the country. You couldn't just slap down a colony of mobile homes. This demanded an all-out effort to obtain variances from the zoning regulations. When the variances were obtained, the wand waved again and in a few days no less than six huge mobile homes were trucked onto the property and lined up in a row on their concrete pads.

Naturally, once the fans got wind of their hero's change of venue, they came flocking down to the ranch in great numbers and made a nuisance of themselves by standing around the gate or even climbing over the five-foot fence to check out the action at close quarters. Elvis had hoped to have more, not less privacy on his commune. Instantly, he waved the wand again and overnight fifteen-foot walls of cypress were erected along the borders of the property to shut off the view of the goings-on inside the ranch. These wooden walls didn't stop the curious. People who owned houses overlooking the ranch began to construct observation platforms on their rooftops, which would enable them and their guests to enjoy the forbidden spectacle. Soon Elvis was dismayed to discover that every move he made was subject to scrutiny from observers with field glasses, telescopes and photographers with telescopic lenses.

When Elvis bought the ranch, it was stocked with 150 head of prize cattle: Santa Gertrudises developed by Winthrop Rockefeller on the King Ranch in Texas. That was a good start, but it wasn't much fun simply owning the cattle: The real thrill was in adding to the herd or even in finding some new kind of livestock that would be more distinctively Elfin. Not far away, at Colliersville, Tennessee, Elvis learned there was a ranch that bred prize Tennessee walking horses. Elvis went immediately to the GLL Farms and met the owner, George L. Lenox, Jr. Though there were three hundred horses at the ranch, the only one that interested Elvis was the prize of the lot: a famous stud named Carbon Copy. The asking price for this one animal was $100,000. What restrained Elvis from buying it is unknown; but after repeated visits and discussions, he finally relinquished his plan to purchase the horse and establish the Presley stud.

Perhaps Elvis was dissuaded by the need to spend a lot of money on other things at the ranch. After all, he wanted to build a fine house there for himself and Priscilla. He had decided also that he needed a cattle barn with a capacity of a hundred animals. Meantime, his infatuation with every conceivable kind of vehicle had him now into buying three-stall horse trailers and tractors and all sorts of odd-looking farm machinery. There is no knowing how far Elvis might have carried this crazy binge, if the Colonel had not succeeded in heading him off by negotiating a fast movie deal that demanded Elvis's presence in Hollywood by late March. Vernon was on the phone constantly at this time begging the Colonel to find some way to avert the financial ruin that was threatened by Elvis's mad prodigality. Vernon's own efforts to put the brakes on by presenting Elvis with itemized lists of his expenses had met with no results at all. Elvis wouldn't even stop to look at the tabulations. The only hope was to employ the tactics used to curb bulls or tantrum-throwing infants—distraction.

By the time Elvis left to make *Clambake,* he had blown more than a million dollars in cash. He had also increased his already heavy payroll by engaging new men to run the ranch, and he was about to blow another large sum of money by purchasing and decorating a new $425,000 house in the Trousdale Estates, adjacent to Beverly Hills. Though the finances of the Presley organization have always been guarded like the gold at Fort Knox, there are a couple of very clear signs that indicate how close this binge came to breaking the Elvis bank. One is the fact that for the first and only time in his life, Elvis had to make some of his purchases on credit. The other is that later in the same year, he was forced to sell portions of his two publishing firms—Elvis Music and Gladys Music—to Hill and Range. Putting it all together, it is clear that this spending spree was not just a prank or eccentric fling. It was a statement, inspired by extreme psychological stress.

Apart from his effort to hold the Guys together by providing them with new homes and new toys in his immediate vicinity, one can see the spree as a desperate and reckless effort to indemnify himself for the enormous sacrifice he was about to make by getting married, as an effort to assert once again his complete control over his life, as an act of defiance against all the old fogeys who worshipped money—like the Colonel and Vernon—and simply as an exhibition of power and a manic outburst of that curious kind of euphoria that some people experience from throwing their money around.

Once the binge was over, however, Elvis woke up back in Hollywood, set to begin another of those horrible pictures that he had now come to loathe from the bottom of his heart. He was also suffering from the worst burden of excess weight he had ever acquired. For this is another and highly significant feature of his behavior at this time: He had indulged himself not just in a shopping spree but in an eating binge. Bringing one of his black cooks down to the house on the property, he gave her orders to bake him every day pan after pan of corn pone. Then, at mealtimes, he would take a glass that held a pint of buttermilk and soak inside it great chunks of the rich, heavy pone. Stuffing himself with this soggy, infantile food, he started putting on weight. As if this were not bad enough, he also indulged himself at this time with huge bowls of mashed potatoes and gravy as well as platters of sausage and home-baked biscuits. One month on this diet and Elvis weighed 210 pounds. When he stepped off the plane at L.A., the Guys who had remained on the Coast couldn't believe their eyes. Elvis was big as a hog.

Before Elvis could rid himself of the weight by his usual combination of powerful drugs and crash dieting, the director of the picture or one of the studio officials got sight of him. He communicated his alarm to Colonel Parker, who was quick to pass the message along to Elvis. Guilty as hell about having bloated up like a balloon, galled by the necessity of having to make another "travelogue" and disturbed most of all by the irrevocability of his commitment to marry Priscilla, Elvis fell into a profound state of depression.

On the night before the first day of shooting, he rose from bed—drugged, doubtless, with sleeping pills—and made his way to the bathroom of his latest Bel Air house, on Rocca Place. A TV set had been placed next to the tub, with its wire running across the floor. Elvis tripped over the cord and went head foremost into the tub. He lost consciousness and lay there for an indeterminate period of time. Then, gradually recovering consciousness, he hauled himself out of the tub and went back to the bedroom, where he fell sound asleep. The next morning, when he emerged from his room, he complained of a severe headache. Describing vaguely the fall he had taken during the night, he showed the Guys a large bump on his head. When Joe Esposito examined the swelling, as large as a golf ball, he notified Colonel Parker and summoned Elvis's doctor.

The doctor and a medical team arrived at the house almost at the same moment as the Colonel appeared with several film company officials in tow. The Colonel went into Elvis's bedroom alone and conferred there with the doctor. When the old man came out, he explained to all present that Elvis had suffered a severe brain concussion. He would be laid up in bed for some time and would require round-the-clock nursing. Work on the film would have to be postponed for at least several weeks. Then the Colonel turned on Larry Geller and told him to clean out all the books he had brought to the house. Geller was shocked, but he would have been far more shocked if he had known what Colonel Parker had in store for him.

The Colonel had been watching his chance to get rid of the Swami for a long time. He had smiled at Geller and complimented Geller, telling him that he would have made a marvelous magician because he knew so well how to control people and promote illusions. These little jokes were deadly signs, if Geller had known how to read them right. They signaled the Colonel's real view of Geller and portended an all-out effort to discredit the Swami in Elvis's eyes and then banish him forever. The moment Elvis took his fall, the Colonel saw the long-awaited opportunity. He represented to Elvis that all his problems were produced by the Swami and his books. If Elvis would just give up this spiritualist nonsense and go back to being the good boy that he had been in the old days, insisted the Colonel, everything would be fine again. The Guys would be happier, the Colonel would be happier, Elvis himself would be happier. They would be one big happy family again.

Though Elvis knew very well what the Colonel was about, he was in no condition to resist. He always shrank from any sort of confrontation with the Colonel and now was hardly the moment to make a stand. Elvis was weak, frightened, confused. He was like a sick little boy. The Colonel got everything he wanted. Elvis agreed that the books had damaged his mind. He did not object when the Colonel insisted that one of the Guys be present when Geller cut Elvis's hair so that there would be no temptation to go back to discussing the books. (This rule assured

that Geller would soon throw up his job and quit, which is exactly
what he did.) Finally, Elvis agreed to allow all his books to be taken
out and burned.

After a couple of weeks of close confinement to bed and severe restric-
tion of visitors, the patient was finally allowed to get up and dress. On
that day the Colonel called an important meeting of the entire group.
The meeting commenced with the Colonel and Joe Esposito going into
Elvis's bedroom for a private conference. Then, all three came down
to the living room where the Guys had assembled. Elvis looked pale,
listless, out of it. Colonel sat four-square, cigar fuming in the side of
his mouth, hands crisscrossed on the head of his cane. As Larry Geller
recalls the scene in the book he wrote with Jess Stearn, *The Truth About
Elvis,* the Colonel minced no words.

> "Things are going to change around here," he said. "First
> of all, the payroll is going to be cut back. Elvis has been spending
> too much money lately, and has gone beyond what he can afford."
>
> Larry looked at Elvis, half expecting a protest. But Elvis's
> eyes were on the floor. At no time did he look any of the group
> in the eye.
>
> "And don't," continued the Colonel, "bring your financial
> burdens and other problems to Elvis. If you have any problems,
> mention them to Joe Esposito. He will get in touch with me.
>
> "Leave Elvis alone. Don't expect him to be your counselor."
> His eyes fell on Larry for a moment. "What do you think he
> should do, walk down the street in robes like Jesus Christ, and
> save people? No, this boy has had a bad fall. He's not well. He's
> not in a position to help anybody. He's going back to the studio
> to start a picture. There's a lot of people depending on him to
> fulfill his obligations." His eyes moved around the group. "And
> I'm depending on you to help us."
>
> As he took in the attentive faces, his head nodded in satisfac-
> tion.
>
> "Elvis is an entertainer," he stressed. "He shouldn't fill his
> head with anything distracting him from what he is supposed
> to do." Again, his gaze fell on Larry. "You're all lucky to be
> here. If any of you don't like the way things are, you can leave.
> The door is open."
>
> Everybody nodded. Nobody was leaving.
>
> The Colonel leaned on his cane, and said, more amiably,

"When things get back to normal, the pay cuts will be restored." He turned to the silent Elvis. "We're more than fair. Aren't we, Elvis?"

Elvis nodded, his face devoid of expression.

Finally, the Colonel announced: "From now on, there is going to be a new foreman—Mr. Esposito." Then, turning to Marty Lacker, who was taken completely by surprise by this announcement, the Colonel added: "Mr. Lacker, you will be in charge of special projects. The first project is preparing for the *wedding*."

The Colonel had decided that Elvis should marry.

Chapter 27

The Colonel's Wedding

THOUGH Marty Lacker was ostensibly in charge of Project Wedding, it was all the Colonel's show. The Colonel contrived the event not to please Elvis or Priscilla, but to fulfill his own notions of what was appropriate. Indeed, it would be no exaggeration to say that Elvis's wedding was really the Colonel's wedding. The Colonel ordered the wedding, arranged the wedding, determined who should or should not be invited to the wedding and probably found a way to pay for the wedding by sticking someone else with the bill. This sucker was the Colonel's neighbor in Palm Springs, Milton Prell, who had recently purchased the Alladin Hotel in Las Vegas.

Sin City was a very unnatural place for a man to marry who lived in Memphis and had spent years defining himself not as a flashy showbiz type but as the All-American Boy. Vegas was the perfect place, however, for Colonel Parker. Not only could he free-load the wedding, but he could play hide and seek with the press much more easily here than in Memphis and he could use the distance of the event from Elvis's home as a convenient excuse for failing to invite all those people he was intent on humiliating.

Rewarding and punishing the Guys according to their desserts was one of the Colonel's major obsessions at this time. He had always detested the Guys as wasteful parasites and feared that the brighter ones like Red and Marty might find some way of gathering power into their own hands. He had put them in their place after Elvis's accident; now he decided to give them another dose of the same medicine just to make doubly sure that they didn't repeat their former indiscretions, like advising Elvis what songs he should sing. The Colonel's plan was to keep the wedding a deep dark secret from everyone but the principals until the very last minute. Then he would clap his hands and make all his puppets dance.

On April 29, 1967, the Colonel gave the signal. Elvis, Priscilla, the favored Guys and some of the other important guests were gathered together in a house in Palm Springs. Despite the Colonel's precautions, word of the impending marriage had leaked out and the press was all over the little town. On the night of April 30, Elvis and Priscilla flew into Vegas and went to the city clerk's office at four in the morning to obtain the wedding license. The following morning, May 1, was the time that had been appointed for the ceremony. The Colonel made it appear, however, that the wedding was to be held that afternoon. He told reporters that if they gathered at the Alladin Hotel at 1:00 P.M., he would have an important announcement to give them. They assumed the announcement would be that Elvis was about to get married, not that the event had already occurred.

That morning Marty Lacker—who had been asked at the last moment to share the honor of being best man with Joe Esposito—learned for the first time that none of the Guys save Joe and he would be allowed to witness the ceremony. This shocked him profoundly. He knew what such a slight would mean to the men who had shared Elvis's life for years. When he entered the suite where Elvis was to be married, he recognized that the excuse he had been given—that there wouldn't be space for the Guys—was just a lie. Red West, puzzled at not getting any word about the ceremony, went to Joe Esposito's room to find out what was happening. When he saw Joe dressed in a tuxedo and learned from his lips that the Guys were not to be present at the ceremony, Red went wild with rage. He charged down the hall and banged on the Colonel's door. When the old man opened up, Red denounced him and threatened to seize his cane and beat him up. Then, having vented his spleen, Red went back to his room, where his wife was in tears, and announced that they were not going to attend the reception. They were going to boycott the whole event.

With these sweet vibes filling the air, Elvis prepared himself for the great moment. He was extremely agitated and told Marty that this was the "showdown." His appearance and Priscilla's that day have been preserved in a lot of photographs. Both of them look comically vulgar. Elvis had his hair piled up in a huge conk like that worn by such black singers as Bobby "Blue" Bland. His tuxedo was so short in the jacket and so jivey in the cut that it might have graced some salesman getting married in the Bronx. Priscilla wore the traditional white gown, veil and train. She ruined the effect of bridal beauty and virginity by giving her face the full Cleopatra treatment with the heaviest kind of kohl-black eye makeup and a mane of dyed black hair that would better have suited a witch than a bride.

Despite Elvis's lifelong involvement in Christianity, his marriage was no different from that of any free-thinking, atheistic entertainer from Broadway or Hollywood. The service was not performed by a minister but by a Jewish judge, David Zenoff, who was—naturally!—an old friend of the Colonel. Priscilla had tinkered with the then traditional vows so that "love, honor and obey" now read "love, honor and comfort." Elvis completely missed the implications of this modification.

Present at the ceremony in Milton Prell's private suite were Vernon and Dee; Major and Mrs. Beaulieu with their two oldest remaining children, Donny (seventeen) and Michelle (thirteen); Colonel and Marie; Billy and Jo Smith; Patsy and Gee Gee Gambill; George Klein; and the two best men, Joe Esposito and Marty Lacker, with their wives, Joanie and Patsy. Grandma Presley could not attend because she was not up to the journey.

Once the ceremony had been completed, the Colonel ushered the newlyweds into a press conference. Answering a lot of stupid and embarrassing questions about his private life must have been the last thing in the world that Elvis Presley wanted to do at this moment; but the Colonel, operating according to his customary policy, was intent on getting some mileage out of the wedding now that it was a fait accompli. When the old man felt the reporters had had enough time, he signaled the end of the conference and led the way to the reception.

The guests included the Colonel's staff and many of his business colleagues. They did not include such Presley stalwarts as Lamar Fike and Sonny West, both of whom learned about the marriage through the media. The whole affair was right out of the top drawer of a hotel caterer. The food was rich and varied but it offered nothing that would appeal to Elvis's palate. The music was that strolling violin and accordion stuff that would have set Elvis's teeth on edge. Devoid of appropriateness, originality or taste, it was a perfect expression of Colonel Thomas Andrew Parker.

The least that Elvis might have salvaged from his wedding was a nice restful honeymoon in some lovely setting. Not even this was he allowed. Rushing back to Palm Springs that night, he was installed with his bride in a rented house. For the next couple of days, he was obliged to return to Hollywood to put the finishing touches on *Clambake*. One wonders why, after stalling so long, it was necessary that he suddenly marry at such an inopportune moment. When he was finally released from work, the best he and Priscilla could do by way of having a honeymoon was to go back to the ranch, where they holed up for a week or so with Lamar. Both of them were eager to go to Europe; but the Colonel told Elvis that Europe was off limits because his appearance there would produce complaints from fans that he never played in their countries. Instead of Europe, the Presleys wound up going to the Bahamas, which Elvis imagined would be similar to Hawaii. When he realized what a dull, stodgy place he'd chosen—and got a few days of rain—he made a quick retreat to Memphis.

On May 28 the couple held a reception for all the people in Memphis who should have been at the wedding reception. Events of this sort were always torture to Elvis. He wandered around that afternoon with a fixed smile on his face. His only consolation lay in the thought that this celebration marked the end of all the obligatory festivities attendant on the wedding. Not long afterward, he learned that Priscilla was pregnant. It's said that she was very unhappy about becoming pregnant so quickly. As she had lived on the most intimate terms with Elvis for four years, it's hard to believe that this sudden pregnancy was an accident.

During the winter following the marriage, Elvis made *Speedway* with Nancy Sinatra, who had always been an adoring fan and who, now that she was divorced from Tommy Sands, was feeling even more vulnerable to the attractions of her hero. Elvis, for his part, was inspired to indulge himself with Nancy in an orgy of the sort of pajama-party roughhouse that he always enjoyed with his teenage groupies in Memphis. Every day at lunchtime, Elvis and Nancy would go back to her dressing room trailer and play their games. Elvis would start by messing Nancy's hair or disarranging her clothes so that it would appear that they had been intimate. Or if he got really inspired, he might get her down on the floor of the trailer and dry hump her. As they tossed and turned, he would gasp in mock passion: "Did you come yet?" She would laugh hysterically, but at the same time she could feel his penis getting hard. He could feel it, too. He'd lean down close to her ear and whisper:

"Do you feel Little Elvis?" When they walked out of the trailer to begin the afternoon's shooting, they'd get off on the fact that people were staring at them or whispering behind their backs.

One day Priscilla turned up on the set to have lunch. She told Nancy that she was pregnant and was expecting the baby around the first of February, which was just a couple of months distant. Nancy Sinatra could not believe that Priscilla was at such an advanced state of pregnancy because it was virtually impossible to see any signs of the baby. "How do you keep looking so slim?" she demanded. "When I get hungry," Priscilla replied, "I eat an apple." "Good for you," said Nancy, thinking: "She's got her hands full trying to hold onto this man."

As the filming drew to a close, Elvis's pranks in the dressing room got more and more out of hand. One afternoon, Nancy's maid helped her undress and then left for the day. Nancy, clad only in jeans and brassiere, went over to her closet to remove the brassiere and put on a shirt. Just as she reaches in for the shirt, out of the closet pops Elvis! Feeling very vulnerable in her half-naked condition, she gives Elvis a startled look. Then she laughs and he grabs her and holds her close. "He just got very quiet," she recalls. "He just held me. He held me very quietly, very closely to him, and he lifted up my face and he kissed me and I started to melt. I really thought I was going to die. Then he pulled away and looked at me and said: 'I'm sorry. . . . I'm sorry.' And he went out."

Nancy Sinatra was determined not to have an affair with Elvis now that he was married. At the same time, it was impossible not to be tempted. On the last day of shooting, they were having lunch in the trailer out on location and the time came to do the final shots. "Well, Silly," sighed Nancy, "see you around." Then she rose to leave. "Wait a minute," he said, "come back." Then he pulled her down on a sofa at the back of the trailer. Putting her head on his shoulder, he held her for a while. Finally she said: "I really have to leave. I don't want to. I really have to." He responded by kissing her. "I kissed him back," she remembers. "I really kissed him back. With all my heart. Not sensually. No French kissing. It was a warm, sincere, I-love-you kiss. He looked at me and said, 'That's the first time you've ever kissed me, isn't it?' 'That's right,' I said. 'Why?' he wanted to know. I said, 'Cause I'm saying good-bye.' He gave me a big, brotherly hug and off I went. That was the last romantic moment. I treasure it dearly."

When Elvis got back to Graceland around Christmas time, everybody's mind was on the impending birth of his first child. Priscilla had gotten a book of names; from it, she and Elvis chose two pairs of names, one suitable for a boy, the other for a girl. Priscilla was convinced that she was going to give birth to a boy. She and Elvis determined his name should be John Baron. To Priscilla these names denoted "great strength and masculinity." If the child were a girl, they decided to call her Lisa Marie.

Elaborate preparations were made for the birth of the baby. Elvis summoned all the Guys to stand by him during this critical period. Though they didn't count for enough to be present at his marriage, they were expected to support him during the birth of his child. Actually, of course, there was nothing for these big dudes to do except drive Elvis and Priscilla to the hospital and sit around there waiting for the child to be born. Even so they managed to invest this simple action with a great deal of cloak and dagger persiflage.

Two cars were to be used: A blue Cadillac, which Charlie Hodge would drive, would carry Elvis and Priscilla to Baptist Memorial Hospital, not fifteen minutes from Graceland. Another car, a big black Cadillac gangstermobile, would carry the Guys, who would act as decoys, drawing off the fans who were apt to give chase once they saw one of Elvis's cars leaving Graceland. Arrangements had also been made to alert Vernon and Dee the moment everyone else headed for the hospital; and, of course, the other relatives who lived at Graceland would be expected to come along. To accommodate this mob an extra room adjacent to Priscilla's room had been engaged just as a lounge for the family. A couple of off-duty Memphis cops had also been hired to guard the mother and baby.

Shortly after eight on the morning of February 1, 1968, Priscilla felt herself going into labor and warned Elvis that it was time to leave. Elvis alerted the boys and the long-perfected plan was put into operation. The moment the two cars got outside the gates of Graceland, however, there was a mix-up and the decoy car went off to the wrong hospital, while Elvis's car was chased all the way to the hospital driveway. Having gotten Priscilla to the hospital, there was nothing for Elvis and the boys to do the rest of the day but sit around in the doctors' lounge on the second floor and make idle conversation. Elvis finally decided that he didn't look well enough for such an important event and went home to change his clothes. When he got back in the early afternoon, he was wearing a powder blue suit with a dark blue turtleneck. Now he was prepared to face the cameras.

As an only child who had been for his entire life the center of his world's attention, Elvis could not but have felt highly ambivalent about the birth of a child. As a man who had lived always in the midst of adoring women, he must have preferred instinctively the idea of a daughter. Yet as a highly conventional male, he would have been pleased with the notion of a son who would bear his name. As a perpetual adolescent, the idea of becoming a father, that is an adult, must have also produced very mixed emotions. As we shall see, Elvis never allowed parenthood to alter his behavior in the slightest or to cause him to add even one millimeter to his growth or maturation as a human being. Even so, no matter how keenly a person clings to his youth, no matter how resolutely he blocks out all signs of age, certain events signal the passage of years and the inevitable change of roles. The extreme nervousness and the signs of intense withdrawal which the Guys observed in Elvis that afternoon were not simply evidence of the customary and comical anxiety of the expectant father. They were the signs of a very rare crisis in the life of Elvis Presley: a moment of mortality that could not be ignored.

At 5:10 in the afternoon, Priscilla's obstetrician, Dr. Turman, walked into the lounge smiling. Addressing Elvis, he said: "It's a girl! Born nine minutes ago. A perfect, beautiful little girl. Priscilla is fine. It was a perfectly normal birth." "Thank God!" gasped Elvis. Then as the congratulations of the Guys rose around him, he exclaimed: "A telephone!" Rushing out into the hall accompanied by Vernon, Elvis called Minnie Mae while Vernon tried to reach the Beaulieus in California. A few minutes later, he's back in the lounge smiling. "You know what Grandma said?" he asks with a big grin on his face. "She said, 'I know she's a beautiful baby—always take care of her.'" Vernon returned at that moment to announce that he couldn't get through to the Beaulieus because their phone was continually busy. By this point the news of the birth has spread outside the hospital and the reporters and photographers and TV crews who have been standing by all day are clamoring for an announcement.

"You go, Dad," Elvis begged his father. "Tell them I'm a happy but shaky man." Vernon and Dee promptly left for the lobby of the hospital, where they confronted the press. Looking at some notes in his hand, Vernon announced: "It's a baby girl. She was born 5:01, February 1, 1968. She weighs six pounds, fifteen ounces and is twenty inches long. Her name is Lisa Marie. No special reason for that. They picked it out of a baby book. Both mother and baby are doing fine. The father is still shaky but very happy."

"How are you doing?" shouted a reporter. "How does it feel to be a grandfather?" Vernon smiled and drawled: "I can't tell yet. I haven't had time. It's been a long time since I've been a father. But my hair's turning gray. . . . I guess it should now that I'm a grandfather."

By this point Elvis was on his way behind a nurse to the fifth-floor nursery to see Lisa Marie. Gazing through the glass window, he sees the raw little infant held aloft by another nurse. The baby has dark hair and blue eyes. Her hair has been brushed back, tied in a knot and bound with a pink ribbon. The nurse offers to allow Elvis to hold the baby, explaining that usually this privilege is reserved for the mother but that Priscilla is still too groggy to take the baby. (She had been given Demerol and gas and awoke later with no recollection of having given birth.) Elvis stammered and said: "No, ma'am, Priscilla—Mrs. Presley—should be the first."

That night Elvis was wired for speed. No matter how many sleeping pills he took, he couldn't knock himself out. Finally, he called up Nancy Sinatra, who took his call in her kitchen. After it had gone on for an hour she slowly sank down onto the floor for the balance of the conversation. Elvis was in a highly characteristic frame of mind that night: brooding on how fortunate he had been and how fortunate his child would be. "I just don't know how I got to be so lucky," he exclaimed at one point. Still, such good fortune always put him in mind of those who weren't so fortunate. "I am so lucky and my little girl is so lucky. But what about all the babies born who don't have anything? Who don't have food!" As he explored this line of thought, he gradually drifted into his spiritual mood. Finally, he confessed to his unseen listener: "I should have been a preacher. I should have stayed with the church." This thought was always at the back of his mind now, and it would remain fixed there to the very end of his life. Like so many should-have-beens, it was just a sentimental fancy that was not supposed to bear any real weight. Naively, Nancy Sinatra remarked: "You probably wouldn't have this awareness now if you hadn't done what you did. You could go back into the church—Little Richard did it. You can do it." At that point, Elvis changed the subject.

Four days later, Priscilla was released from the hospital. She appeared before a throng of admiring spectators on the pavement before the main entrance riding in a wheelchair pushed by Elvis. She had teased her hair up into a towering Cleopatra mane and put on her batwing eyelashes and heavy makeup. She wore a suit with a miniskirt that rode up her thighs. Holding the baby in a big blanket like pharaoh's daughter with the infant Moses, she made a bizarre madonna.

Chapter 28

The Singer Special

As 1967 drew to a close, the fortunes of the Presley organization continued their long decline. The British Invasion of 1965 had now been echoed by a tremendous upsurge of pop music right under Elvis's nose on the West Coast. Jim Morrison and the Doors, Grace Slick and the Jefferson Airplane, Janis Joplin with Big Brother and the Holding Company, the Byrds, the Beach Boys, the Grateful Dead, the first concerts and light shows at the Fillmore West—all signaled the onset of the most feverishly creative period in American pop music since the midfifties. As the music industry rushed forward to exploit this frothing new wave of trend and talent, Elvis Presley, that fifties figure all alone in the sixties, was washed away by the tide and beached like a shipwrecked sailor marooned on a desert island. His record sales sank to an all-time low. No major studio would ante up the million dollars to make another of his silly beach-party, racing-car exploitation movies. Even the loyal Presley fans began to go whoring after strange gods. Judged by all the relevant standards, Elvis Presley was now just another famous has-been. His theme song could have been "I'm All Washed Up!"

At this moment of tight money, Elvis was still in the midst of his greatest spending spree. He blew $425,000 on a trashy new house atop a Beverly hill. It looked as though it had been designed by an architect from Hallmark Cards. A cardboard villa bedecked with a couple of ornamental features intended to suggest the French Riviera, the house was not even functionally adequate for Elvis's needs. It wasn't big enough to house his new family and his old entourage. It was also much too exposed to the incursions of the fans, to say nothing of the new race of crazy killers and kidnappers and assassins, about whom Elvis had been obsessed ever since the murder of Jack Kennedy. Soon, the new house would have to be abandoned. As for the ranch into which Elvis had poured so much money—without even counting the hundred thousand dollars worth of trailers and trucks he had bought for the use of his boys in the country—that dinky home on the range had lost its charm just as rapidly as any other toy. Meantime, it continued to eat up more money. As if all this weren't bad enough, Vernon, who didn't have enough business sense to run a corner grocery, had decided at this moment to do some speculating in the Texas cattle market. He soon lost his shirt: only it wasn't his shirt he lost—it was Elvis's.

As the ole Colonel sat in his carnival cookhouse office at the front of the MGM lot, the atmosphere was thick with foreboding. Was it possible that the game was up? Could the master player be running out of tricks? Though the endless round of busywork continued as always, there was a feeling in the air that if the Colonel didn't soon pull a rabbit out of the hat, they might all be looking for jobs elsewhere. It was at this crucial moment that the Colonel began to send out signals to NBC through his connections at RCA that he might be willing to do something he had always said was out of the question: star Elvis Presley in a TV special.

When this surprising news was passed along to NBC's vice-president in charge of operations on the West Coast, Tom Sarnoff, youngest son of that other famous showbiz commander, General David Sarnoff, a meeting was arranged to explore the idea. The Colonel, like any hustler eying a fresh mark, at first affected indifference to the proposal, treating it as if it were entirely NBC's idea and nothing in which he was eager to get involved. What he appeared most interested in talking about was his very own "special." Pulling out a radio press release headed "Elvis Presley Christmas Program," the Colonel proceeded to lecture Sarnoff on the beauty of this radio syndication that was being gobbled up by local stations all over the country. The Colonel had spliced together out of Elvis's old Christmas records a little program into which he had stuck, like the raisins in a plum pudding, several inane "greetings" from his boy. Especially in the South and Southwest, the sale of this piece of trash was going pretty well. As the show cost nothing to produce, it was turning a profit. In fact, the Colonel urged, training his canniest look on Sarnoff, if NBC wanted to do an Elvis special on TV, they might just want to follow the Colonel's lead and make it a Christmas show. Call it *Elvis and the Wonderful World of Christmas.*

Sarnoff expressed his appreciation of the Colonel's "creative input." Then, he reverted to the business that had brought him here to the kitchen: the terms on which the Colonel would allow Elvis to appear as the star of a one-hour special on NBC. He suggested that the Colonel bear in mind that one successful appearance by Elvis on the tube would lead naturally to further appearances in subsequent specials, perhaps three or four in as many years.

The Colonel replied that more was involved in a show like this than just a simple appearance on the air. For one thing, there would be reruns. What's more, the show was certain—like Elvis's movies—to generate a very valuable soundtrack album. RCA would appreciate that feature of the deal. As RCA and NBC were members of the same family, they could have a nice little thing going there. Then, of course, there was the matter of *prestige.* This would be the first time that Elvis had appeared on television since 1960—that was a long time ago! They couldn't complain that Elvis Presley had been overexposed. No, sir! Even more important was the fact that Elvis had never done a special. This would be a *first* for NBC. That, too, was a consideration. Oh, the more you looked into a deal like this, the more you saw in it.

The deal the Colonel cut didn't show any shakiness in his hand. From the demands he made, you'd never know his client was flat on the balls of his ass. Colonel Parker sold Elvis Presley to NBC as if he were offering them the first appearance in America of the Beatles. What was he asking? Here, basically, were his terms:

1. Elvis is to get his normal movie salary: $500,000. This is predicated on a fixed schedule of work: so many weeks at so many hours per day. If they go five minutes over the schedule, they will have to pay for the overtime on a pro-rata basis calculated on the boy's per diem salary.
2. NBC will have the right to screen the program twice. After that, ownership of the property reverts to the Presley organization. This will be in lieu of the percentage of the profits Elvis normally receives on his movie contracts.

3. The soundtrack album: This will be owned outright by the Presley organization, which will market it through RCA, according to the usual arrangement. This is a customary clause in all Elvis Presley contracts. Music is the Colonel's game. He has never given anyone a piece of an Elvis record.

4. Future shows: The Colonel would like to wait and see. One thought comes to mind. He would like to tie the show to a commitment from NBC to finance Elvis's next movie, which could be produced by Universal, which is now in bed with NBC. This proviso is subject to negotiation.

Tom Sarnoff denies that any tie-in with a future movie was involved in the contract for the special; on the other hand, Elvis's next movie, *Charro,* was made by Universal, which was in bed with NBC. Everything else was agreeable to the network, which appears to have been very eager to do a Presley special.

Once the terms of the deal had been set, Sarnoff receded from the picture and a new man came to the fore: Bob Finkel. The son of a pioneer motion picture exhibitor in Pittsburgh, Finkel had grown up in show business. He operated a so-called "in-house" TV production company called Teram, which put together programs for NBC-TV. Finkel had never worked with the Colonel or Elvis, but he knew them very well by reputation. He realized that he was stepping into a potentially explosive situation as the middleman in this first collaboration between the star with the world's most demanding manager and the giant network that was his boss. It was vitally important to the success of the project that a creative producer be found who had the special talents necessary to make this show an unqualified success. If Elvis Presley was going to make his first TV appearance since 1960 and do his first special ever, the eyes of the entire entertainment world were going to be keenly focused on the show—and on Bob Finkel.

Finkel made a decision at this point that was to have far-reaching consequences. Instead of calling in one of the make-no-waves hacks who were abundantly available to him, he got in touch with the most imaginative—but also the most independent, incorruptible and controversial—variety producer in the history of TV, the young Steve Binder. Even today, after twenty years in the business, Binder impresses one on first-hand acquaintance as being the type of earnest and idealistic young college instructor who is forever embarrassing the administration by his demands that students sit on the faculty council or that avowed enemies of the state be permitted to speak in chapel.

In 1967 he was still enveloped in the scandal produced by his latest show, which had violated one of the business's oldest taboos. In the finale of this program Binder had ordered his black male star, Harry Belafonte, to touch—yes, physically touch with his big copper-palmed hand!—his white female star, Petula Clark. Imagine! Here are these millions of conventional-minded Americans sitting comfortably in their living rooms being given this wonderful opportunity by Plymouth to relax and forget about the problems of their crazy country, when all of a sudden they're looking at the thing that disgusts them the most: a big buck nigger putting his hands on a pretty little white girl!

The hullabaloo raised by that idealistically inspired little embrace nearly blew Binder right out of the business. When the network's southern affiliates refused to air the show, Plymouth began to raise hell with the network. Soon, even the show's stars, who had reacted enthusiastically to the suggestion that they get "close" on camera, were recoiling in horror from their terrible sin. Petula Clark fled back to England and Harry Belafonte got so indignant that it looked like he might go on the *Tonight Show* and tell the public *not* to buy Plymouth. Now, in view of this subversive history, what would induce a showbiz veteran, a born survivor like Bob Finkel, to start in with a troublemaker like Steve Binder?

The answer lay in another Binder production, this one dating from 1965: *The T.A.M.I. Show*. As everyone in television knew, this program was not only the first but the finest full-scale treatment of rock and soul music ever put on the tube. From its opening shots—Jan and Dean skate-boarding across L.A. jump-cut to Diana Ross applying lip gloss at a distance of about six inches—*The T.A.M.I. Show* had squeezed into one dazzling synopticon nearly everything important that was happening in the music world at that glorious moment. From Diana Ross and the Supremes to Gerry and the Pacemakers, from Chuck Berry to Marvin Gaye, from the Rolling Stones to the Barbarians (a Boston group that featured a drummer with a hook for a hand), the program had blown the viewer's mind as no live music show has done before or since in the entire history of TV.

The climax of the show was provided by the most dramatic demonstration ever witnessed of the superiority of the traditional black R & B style over the newfangled English-oriented white rock 'n' roll. Like a professor illustrating a course in popular culture, Steve Binder had put on the screen back-to-back James Brown and Mick Jagger, each at the peak of his performing career. For ten electrifying minutes, Brown had jigged on one leg like an African witch doctor, while his fellow celebrants in this strange black rite had struggled to draw him off the dancing ground and lay him to rest under a series of ever more gaudy cloaks. Each time they appeared to have captured this madly possessed creature straight out of a voodoo hongan, he had erupted again in even more violent paroxysms of song and chorybantic ecstasy. When Brown finished his act and jivey Jagger came sashaying out to do his London School of Economics version of the "real" Negro rhythm and blues, you could practically see the flop sweat streaking his pale fleering face. Not even the sight of James Meredith being knifed to death under his nose at Altamont made Mick so sick as the thought of having to follow Soul Brother Number One. If Steve Binder had set out deliberately to illustrate Elvis's dictum—"Black musicians have more talent in their little finger than whites in their whole body"—he couldn't have found a more convincing illustration. One thing star and producer would share from the outset would be a common enthusiasm for the power of black culture.

What troubled Binder initially was simply the thought that Elvis Presley might have reached a point in his career where he was so locked into the pattern established by his movies that all he would want to do on a TV show was just standard stuff that every long-established entertainer runs through every time he is wound up and set ticking. Binder was an ambitious young Turk in his medium: He wasn't interested in "showcasing" once-exciting stars who had become showbiz automatons. What he had to know before he took even the first step toward producing an Elvis Presley special was whether Elvis Presley was willing to do something *special* or whether it was too late for him to make a fresh departure.

The first meeting commenced with the usual platoon arrival of Elvis, the Colonel and the Memphis Mafia. Binder had spent many years watching stars play games with their entourages. Elvis's Al Capone entrance struck him as par for the course. He suggested that the supernumeraries be allowed to rest their feet in the outer office while the principals withdrew to the conference table. Once Binder and his producing partner, Bones Howe (the same man who had once been a gaffer at Radio Recorders), had settled into their seats and confronted Elvis and the Colonel, the game of chess commenced. The Colonel made the opening move. It was a carefully considered gambit.

Colonel Parker told Binder/Howe that the historic show they were about to produce should be conceived in the first place as a costly "gift" to the American public from Elvis and the Colonel. The image summoned up by the Colonel was that of a mink stole or a gold watch, beautifully wrapped and lovingly placed beneath every American family's Christmas tree. As the card that accompanied the gift would bear also the signature of that eminently respectable American institution, the Singer Sewing Machine Company, it was essential that the producers maintain the proper moral tone for such an occasion.

They were fortunate, the Colonel continued, in being able to showcase a star who was synonymous with everything that was fine and wholesome in American life. Elvis was the dream of every little old lady in every Singer sewing machine center in the country. These women knew how good Elvis had always been to his mother. They also knew how deeply religious he was. As the success of Colonel Parker's recent radio syndication proved, everybody loved to hear Elvis sing Christmas songs. So, the obvious way to produce the show was to have Elvis sing about twenty Christmas tunes—carols, ballads, novelty numbers, nicely mixed, like a bouquet of pretty flowers (or a bag of freshly roasted nuts). Then, at the end of the show, he would give the little old ladies and their families one of his famous smiles, say "Merry Christmas everyone!"—and fade! Now, how's that for a prime-time winner?

When Steve Binder heard the Colonel's proposal, he was so appalled at the idea that he was struck dumb. For a long time, he could say nothing. Grimly, he realized that he was now face-to-face with the principal cause of Elvis's precipitate decline from the great fame he had once enjoyed. Here, sitting opposite him, was the real architect of all those horrible movies that were Elvis's celluloid tomb. Finally, Binder recovered his voice and began, like a shrink feeling out a new patient, to ask a few questions aimed at establishing where Elvis's head was at. Getting into a rap about a recent experience he had had with a group he was producing called the Association, Binder told Elvis that these singers had been offered the first crack at "McArthur Park" but had turned the tune down because it didn't fit their image. Coming now to the kicker of the story, Steve looked earnestly at Elvis and said: "What would you do if someone had brought you that song? Would you have recorded it?" Elvis didn't hesitate for a moment: "Sure, I'd record it!" he snapped. "I love that piece of music." Steve said nothing in reply, but he was impressed. If Elvis Presley could picture himself stepping that far out of character, perhaps he might go even further.

"What is your feeling about facing the public again on TV?" continued Dr. Binder. "Sheer terror!" confessed Elvis, never one to bullshit when he spoke of his fears. As the discussion continued, Elvis made his real feelings perfectly clear to his new producer. "You know," he explained, "for nearly ten years I have been kept away from the public. And the one thing that I always loved doing was performing in front of the public. But I'm not sure they're gonna like me now. I may be past that point in time." That was the whole issue as far as Elvis was concerned: "Will they still like me?" It was just what he had wondered at the very start of his career. Now, after all these years, he was right back where he had started—thanks to the skillful management of Colonel Tom Parker.

The meeting ended with an agreement. Elvis would go off to Hawaii to lose weight and get into shape for the big comeback bout. Binder and Howe would huddle with their production people and rough out the program for the show. Binder would be given a free hand save for one job: that of musical arranger. The Colonel made it clear that his slot must be filled by Elvis's own arranger, Billy Strange. Who is Billy Strange? Binder knew him well. Everybody in the business knew him. He had a little tag that some producer once stuck on him. It read: "You wind him up and he shows up." That was his rep. He was just one of those nothings who attach themselves to names. The first name he had latched onto was Nancy Sinatra, at the moment when she made her recording debut.

Binder was not happy having to put the music, such a vital part of the show, in the hands of a guy who was always turning up at sessions and saying: "There must be a mixup—I didn't get a call!" "Yeah," the producers would say, "I guess we goofed, Billy. But sit down, there's your chair and you got your guitar, and, no sweat, man, you're on the date!" But what could Binder do? Elvis was one of those stars who gave every twerp who shines their shoes a lifetime annuity.

Now Binder began to address himself to the great problem faced by every creative TV producer: "How do I get a good idea and, after I've got it, how do I get it past all the people who want to shoot it down?" The most important thing was to restore Elvis to the milieu in which he had attained his true fame, as a hot-as-a-pistol rock star shooting his wad right down the throats of hundreds of screaming teenies ga-gaing over him from ringside. That was the important thing: to put Elvis back in the ring.

The ring! Why, sure. Why not present him in the boxing arena? The great thing about the ring is that it cuts off the performer's retreat and compels him to work in every direction at once like a modern dancer. What's more, by surrounding the stage with cameras, including one directly overhead, Elvis could be literally gobbled up on the screen. Just to make sure that not one morsel of man-meat would be lost, Binder conned NBC sports into letting him have a hand-held camera and a special operator who could duck around the ring and catch Elvis at all the odd angles that are inaccessible to the clumsy floor and crane cameras.

In a couple of weeks, Binder and his staff of unknown but highly talented production people had hammered out the basic formula for the show. They all agreed that this rare occasion should be used as much as possible to illuminate the real Elvis. Though many people thought that at the age of twenty-one Elvis had sprung full-blown out of Colonel Parker's head, the truth was that he had his roots, his sources, in the culture of his own world. So they would do numbers on the gospel scene, on the rhythm and blues world, even on karate, which translates so naturally into choreography. At some point, Elvis would have to do a medley of his old hits, but this needn't be a mere rehash of old favorites or an exercise in nostalgia: they could make the old music and style come back to life again.

The most important thing in Binder's mind was to get Elvis out from behind his mask, to make him step forth and declare himself as a man, not just a living legend. Some way would have to be found to interview Elvis, to draw forth his ideas. Then, when the show reached its conclusion, Elvis ought to offer something more than just the usual kiss-off to the audience. He ought to make a statement: come right out and say that he knew what was happening these days and that he cared which way the world was heading. It was a big demand to make of a performer who was so swallowed up in such a dumb image; but what were they here for if not to do something original? That was Binder's goal. Now, could he sell it to Elvis Presley?

When Elvis got back from Hawaii, the big meeting was held: the meeting at which the producer pitches his idea of the show to the star. Binder didn't stop with just outlining the show. He told Elvis that this program was his Rubicon. If he chose to do the conventional show, like Bing Crosby or Perry Como going through their mindless routines, Elvis would condemn himself to following those older singers into that twilight zone where once-vital but now exhausted talents always end: enthroned in a dozing court surrounded by their faithful followers dreaming of the past. If, on the other hand, he rose to the challenge and took the risk of doing something fresh and different, he could be reborn! Millions of people would see the show. They would sit there like a jury.

Then, they would deliver an instant verdict. If it were favorable, Elvis could take off again with the excitement of a new discovery.

Binder saw immediately that he would have no problem selling this dream to Elvis Presley. Elvis was willing to take the dare. The problems lay with the network executives and with Colonel Parker. The network people were really scared at the idea of making the whole program an examination of Elvis. Though they were eager to exploit his fame, they didn't want to commit themselves to a one-man show. What they wanted was some "insurance": maybe a couple of guest stars to enlarge the attraction. Say . . . Milton Berle! Now, there was a good idea! Get a few laughs into the show. Or Sammy Davis, Jr.! Elvis dug Sammy. Sammy dug Elvis. Wouldn't hurt to have a black dude on the program: might do a lot for the ratings in cities like New York, Chicago, Detroit and Philadelphia. Binder had to do some fancy talking to get this idea out of the VPs' heads; he had to tell them how important Elvis really was as an American culture hero and how absurd it would be to dilute the impact of his first TV appearance since 1960 with acts you could see on any other show. Finally, he won the argument. Then, he had to deal with the Colonel.

Colonel Parker had made it clear from the first day they met that if this show didn't meet with his approval, it would never go on the air. He wasn't telling them what to put on the air, but if they tried to do something that was bad for his "boy"—well, they wouldn't have a show. So, with this ominous guillotine hanging above his neck, Steve Binder began his pitch to the ole Colonel.

Binder soon perceived that the Colonel was not going to insist that Elvis do twenty Christmas songs and split. One thing the Colonel would not allow, however: that was any effort to make Elvis come out on the tube and deliver a statement that could be given a social or political interpretation. Elvis was an entertainer, pure and simple. He wasn't running for office or saving souls or doing an editorial for *The New York Times*. Binder could forget about social consciousness. The show would end just where it was supposed to end, with Elvis saying, "Good night and Merry Christmas."

Having prevailed on all the basic issues but one, Binder felt he had the green light to go into production. Bones Howe had told Binder how Elvis used to run his sessions at Radio Recorders: so it was decided that they should make every effort to get Elvis once again to produce himself. They established a pattern of daily meetings at three o'clock every afternoon in the Binder/Howe offices in the glass-tower building it will be time for the woolly mammoth!" That was the attitude among the hipper people in the entertainment business. What Binder and his boys were doing was not just resuscitating Elvis but putting him back in touch with the contemporary world. Instead of presenting a carefully embalmed mummy from the fifties, they were striving to present a living, breathing, and hitherto unrecognized human being. And all the Colonel could say was: "Where's my Christmas music?"

Another advantage of the deal, as it turned out, was the fact that NBC was heavily committed to making this show one of the best specials ever produced on the network. The money the network got from the Singer Corporation didn't begin to pay for the cost of producing the show. As the scuttlebutt about this production spread through the industry, all sorts of sponsors began to call up Binder, asking to be cut in on the show or even given the full sponsor's role, which they said Singer had gotten for a song. They were right: The show was a monument to deficit financing. Every day, some fresh demand came from the production staff that spelled heavy bucks. Like this thing about the hundred guitarists for the opening sequence.

Steve Binder had decided that the show should have a really socko logo. He had had constructed for the purpose a set of enormous three-dimensional letters that spelled out in lights the magic word: ELVIS. Then, he got another flash. Instead of just lighting up the letters or having the dancers and singers cavort around them, why not reach deep into the old Busby Berkeley bag and do a whole production number right on top of the letters? The Elvis image—what was it? Young man with a guitar—right? Okay. They would make the logo and the image into one gigantic visual knockout punch. Animate the sign. Have it crawling with Elvises. That's it! Have a hundred black-clad, guitar-slingin', rock 'n' rollin' Elvises up there on those letters sockin' it to the people in stark silhouette. Normally, that kind of thinking is just a pipe dream. On this show, all it took was a phone call.

"Hello, Bob? This is Steve. Listen, for the opening number, I've just decided what we really need is a hundred guitar players. Yeah, I said a hundred." Oi! Imagine taking that one to the top! Still, Finkel did it. And he got Steve his hundred guitar players—for about one and a half minutes on camera! It made a pretty heavy one and a half minutes, though. Most important, it set the scale for the show as THE MOST.

As Binder got tighter with Elvis, he discovered that what his star needed to feel comfortable was to be surrounded at every moment by his special environmental bubble. Elvis always had to have his boys and his toys and his little world. That was the way to keep him happy and productive. Not one to mess around, Binder gave orders that the largest dressing rooms at the Burbank studios be converted at once into a hotel suite and furnished with every contrivance that could please Elvis Presley. As time neared for the actual filming of the show, Elvis moved into his dressing rooms and lived there just as he would at a hotel. Why, it was just like the good old days when he and the boys were at the Beverly Wilshire!

Once Elvis had been installed in his new quarters, Binder noticed another interesting feature of his star's life-style. Instead of knocking off at the end of the day's work and going out or falling asleep, Elvis loved to get the boys around him and have spontaneous sings that would last all night. Sometimes, when the crew would arrive at the studio in the morning, they would find the Guys still sitting in their rooms playing guitars and singing and having a ball with their boss. This recreation gave Binder his final inspiration for the show.

If the challenge of the program was to bring Elvis Presley out of the closet and into the open world of the TV camera, what better way could they do it than by simply borrowing the techniques of cinema verité filmmakers and rolling the cameras straight into Elvis's dressing rooms while he was playing and singing and joking with his famous Memphis Mafia? This idea got to be such an obsession with Binder that he decided finally that all the elaborate and costly production numbers didn't mean a damn in comparison to these behind-the-scenes scenes. Now, he had to go to work all over again to persuade Elvis and the Colonel that the very best footage they could shoot would be a private party in a dressing room.

This latest brainstorm produced the greatest resistance to date. Even Elvis, who had gone along with everything up to now, began to shake his head and raise objections. Sure, he loved to sit around in the privacy of his rooms and have a ball—but putting it all on camera for a zillion people to watch! Hey! That was going pretty far, wasn't it? When the Colonel heard the idea, he not only balked: His mind went into paranoid overdrive. He didn't just want to know how the idea would work or even whether it would work. He wanted to know why Binder would want to do such a thing. What was he up to?

At the inevitable meeting, Steve Binder found himself obsessively conscious of the Colonel's steely blue eyes focused in a look that he still can't forget. Binder knew all about the Colonel's prowess as a hypnotist. How could he not? So many times when he came out of his office after a long sit-down with Elvis, Binder found his staff running around on all fours acting like cats and dogs while the old Colonel sat in his chair with a big grin wrapped around his cigar watching his victims disport themselves on the carpet.

Now, Binder found himself getting the same treatment. "The Colonel," he recalls, "used to sit at a meeting with those cold steel-blue eyes staring at me like he was trying to get a subliminal message into my brain. I'd stare back, knowing that there was nothing he could do. Yet, he did convince me that there is such a thing as *mind control.* That strange hypnotic way he had of exercising total control and power over Elvis. That kind of hold is totally unexplainable in terms either of deals or loyalties between people."

The highly suggestible mind that surrenders so swiftly and so completely to one master, however, is capable of surrendering just as swiftly and completely to another. What Steve Binder didn't know was that he was beginning to exercise a very considerable power of his own over Elvis Presley. He was coming into focus in Elvis's mind precisely as had Larry Geller just a few years before.

Larry had popped up in Elvis's life just at the moment when Elvis was feeling total dissatisfaction with both his career and his life-style. Without even intending to do so, Larry had presented Elvis with a sudden revelation: There was another way to live that would get him out of this horrible bind. In a flash, Elvis had been converted to spiritualism. In no time, he was up to his eyeballs in occult literature and self-abnegation and having visions and even threatening to give up his career and become a monk in a monastery. The Colonel had nearly lost Elvis that time. If it hadn't been for the opportunity presented by that brain concussion, that timely blow to the head that knocked the stuffing out of Elvis, God knows what might have happened! Now, here was the same pattern, the same danger, asserting itself all over again.

One thing the old Colonel knew: You never get anywhere trying to lead a high-kicking bronc by the nose. No, you have to be shrewd, canny. You watch and wait. You let the horse knock himself out. Then, when he gets tired, you walk in and lead him away. Colonel was smart enough to see that this damn Binder wasn't completely wrong. He would produce one helluva show, and it would earn the Colonel a lot of money. After one more showing, they would own the show. What's more, the success of the show would make Elvis's price go way up for the next show. To cap it all off, the Colonel would parlay this show into a movie deal with Universal. The Colonel's strategy, therefore, was not to block the show or cause it to fail in any way. The trick was to make Binder work his tail off handing the Colonel a winner; then, when they had gotten their mileage out of Binder, toss him into the junk pile. Meantime, though, the best policy was to fight this dude every inch of the way and psych him out fore and aft just to make sure that he wasn't getting his hooks any deeper into Elvis than was absolutely necessary.

As for this crazy scheme of filming Elvis fooling around in his dressing room—why stop it? Let them do it; *but,* demand a veto on showing it if it did even the slightest damage to Elvis's image, that lovingly fondled and carefully gilded image that the Colonel had spent his life shining and polishing and peddling to millions of suckers and marks the world around.

After many sessions designed to suss out Steve Binder's secret designs, Colonel Parker gave his conditional approval to the plan to shoot Elvis at play. Steve, meantime, had decided to bring back Elvis's original band, Scotty Moore and D. J. Fontana. (Bill Black had died in 1965.) He was so keen on the impromptu jam-session atmosphere that he wouldn't even let D.J. touch his drum kit. He was going to sit in front of an empty guitar case or a newspaper and whack out the time with a pair of soft brushes. Wasn't that how they did it in those old thirties movies about jazz bands out on the road and doing a little home cooking in their berths on the Pullman trains?

Never in his entire career did Elvis ever look better than he did for the Singer Special. At thirty-three, he was at his peak. The years had taken the baby fat out of his cheeks and given him a more masculine appearance. Maturity had also made him seem less like the callow youth and more like the youthful man. Having paid some dues to life, he had a much more soulful expression in his face than he did when he was a smart-alecky punk teasing the girls at ringside. As the cameras, poring over him from every angle, would reveal, his classic features were even more finely molded than before and less encumbered than ever by the vulgarity of his youthful personality.

Another reason why Elvis looked so great that night is that he was wearing the best costume he ever donned. Bill Bellew, who after this show became Elvis's clothes designer for life, had decided that the most dramatic way of snapping Elvis into focus for the reminiscent segments of the show was to suit him up from head to toe in wickedly glinting black leather. He designed a fabulous black leather motorcycle jacket with a stand-up collar, heavy welts along the seams and a broad, double-buckled strap around each wrist. Leather likewise were the trousers, whose crease was a long, mean-looking leather welt. No shiny metal studs or ornaments of any kind were allowed to trivialize the effect of the costume. Elvis was a human truck tire.

(It has often been pointed out that this costume is inauthentic. Elvis never wore leather in his mythic period: that was Brando [or, later, Gene Vincent] whose crude jacket and ugly farmer jeans would make any self-respecting S/M freak gag because it was so baggy and gauche. The real model for Elvis's costume was Jim Morrison, who had just emerged as the surf-born Dionysius of West Coast rock, clad from head to toe in shiny black vinyl. What Belew did was bring Elvis back not as a waxworks replica but as an echo of a past that existed only in the imagination of the current generation, which was the best way to bring him back with a bang.)

Just before Elvis stepped out on the stage, the Colonel appeared for their final huddle. Everyone was ordered out of the dressing room. Binder used to wonder what these last-minute encounters comprised. Did the Colonel fix his steely-cold gaze on Elvis and tell him he was the hottest act in history? Or did he actually hypnotize him? It was apparent that whatever happened, it made a startling difference in Elvis. One moment he would be his usual quiet, diffident self: the bashful boy from Memphis town. The moment the Colonel finished with his protégé, the boy was another person. Now his theme was "I'm All Psyched Up!"

When Elvis climbed into the ring that night, he found his old sidemen, Scotty and D.J., waiting for him, looking remarkably the same as in the early days. Charlie Hodge was also on hand with his guitar, which made three musicians and one clown: Alan Fortas, who had been given a tambourine to bang and jiggle. Alan had been chosen for the role of henchman because Steve thought he corresponded best to the image of the Memphis Mafia: those big, gross, good-natured shlubs who were Elvis's abundant human ectoplasm.

According to the Elvis Myth, what happened next was one of the greatest moments in the history of rock, if not of show business in general. Elvis Presley, barred from the stage for years, cut off from his true love, the live audience, a refugee from a celluloid nightmare, armed with nothing but his trusty guitar and backed with nothing stronger than a couple of good ole boys, suddenly broke the symbolic silence of eight long years by raising his voice in the greatest shout since Achilles roared before the walls of Troy. As always, the Myth is totally false. As it happens, we can now go back and examine that moment in the most minute detail, thanks to a remarkable bootleg album issued by an underground outfit in Germany called audifön. No microphone up the sleeve, tape recorder in the briefcase job, this album was ripped off the original soundtrack by someone at RCA. It offers not only the first show but the second show as well, recorded before a fresh audience a couple of hours later on the same evening.

The first thing it tells us is that Elvis was quite right in describing his emotion on confronting a live audience for the first time in eight years as "sheer terror." The only way to excuse the performance he gave on this momentous occasion is to say that he was just too uptight to give a good account of himself. Though nothing was expected of him but the same songs and the same patter that he had been delivering all his life, he practically collapsed under the impact of the occasion. He couldn't think. He couldn't talk. He couldn't remember either the lines of his script or the lines of his songs. Everytime he made a remark, he turned on his last word with decimating self-consciousness and started putting himself on.

At first, he hardly speaks at all: He thumbs his guitar and jumps into a song, "That's All Right Mama." The scripters and producers had decided that his first recording was the natural point from which he should take off. The only problem with the plan was one that evidently never crossed the minds of those who conceived it: the vocal register, the tessitura, of the song was too high for the Elvis Presley of 1968. Elvis's voice had dropped perceptibly since he was a kid (he used to say that on his early records he sounded like a "chicken"), but he still thought of the song in the same key. The result is a very hoarse and painful effort to vocally get it up. It sets the tone for what follows.

Most great performers put into this same situation would not have behaved as Elvis did. They might have floundered, fumffered, fucked up; they might have found themselves tongue-tied and hoarse and short of breath: all classic symptoms of panic. As they felt themselves bombing, however, they would have rallied. They would have jumped to their feet, taken command, thrown away the script and, if necessary, dropped their pants. Not Elvis. He sits there with the water running out of the bath and makes feeble jokes about how much he'd like to get up and leave. He reaches for the script and starts to read it out loud—without really getting a laugh by doing the impermissible. Eventually, he does struggle to his feet; but he's ready to sit down again when he finds that the mike doesn't rise to meet him. Charlie Hodge, a natural-born performer, who worked his ass off during this session to keep up the infield chatter and cue Elvis into his lines and try to make the debacle a success, picks up the mike and holds it up to Elvis. Then Elvis starts complaining that there is no strap for his guitar. So Charlie starts singing the words, "no strap at all," to the tune of "One Night." Finally he gets Elvis functioning well enough so that this little bit could be cut out of the hour-long tape and exhibited in the final show as an example of Elvis's marvelous "spontaneity."

If this home-cooking session fails as a performance, does it succeed any better as a document, as a revelation of Elvis, which, after all, was the primary intention? The spectacle of a famous performer dissolving in self-consciousness and stage fright does have, it's true, a clammy, clinical kind of fascination. Though it makes one as uneasy as the sight of an open incision, you do get some startling glimpses of the patient's guts. What comes through is deeply ingrained self-doubt and self-derision: a great longing to have done with this terribly embarrassing subject of Me. Nobody who listens attentively to this recording is going to conclude that Elvis Presley was fond of himself. Quite the contrary: What one infers is that all of Elvis's fabulous success simply piled up on the surface of his being without ever seeping through to his resolutely self-hating and self-castigating core.

It's very interesting, in this connection, to observe what happens in the other "live" segment of the show, which was a stand-up solo performance of Elvis's early hits sung before an audience with the orchestral accompaniment prerecorded and piped onto the stage through shotgun speakers. Once Elvis gets up on his feet and frees himself of the encumbrance of his mind, his body starts to function, projecting forcefully and with growing conviction those deep erotic images that turned on audiences at every point in his career. It can't be said too often that the source of Elvis's onstage power was not his vocal performance but his erotic pantomime. The actual rebirth of Elvis on the Singer Special occurs at those moments, when, holding the mike in his fist and sinking down on his knees, he bends back in the phallic posture of the Limbo dancer, with his pubis thrust toward the audience, and scrunching up his face like a man coming to orgasm, he hollers from the bottom of his soul. That is the essential Elvis.

The aspect of the Singer Special that was to have the greatest influence on Elvis's future career was, interestingly enough, not the self-revelatory breakthroughs for which Steve Binder fought so hard, but the new musical horizons that were revealed to Elvis through the work of Billy Goldenberg and Bones Howe. It is no exaggeration to say that Goldenberg and Howe reeducated Elvis in contemporary commercial music and set him down in the groove in which he was destined to ride until the day he died. The reason they were able to exercise this profound influence on such a willful and self-repetitive performer is because they caught Elvis at just the moment when he had opened himself for once to far-reaching changes in his professional outlook.

Prior to the Singer Special Elvis had been trying, with the aide of his new A & R man, Felton Jervis, to climb back up out of the terrible hole into which he had fallen during the period of his mass-production moviemaking. Having allowed Colonel Parker to persuade him that there was no need to go into the studio and work with other musicians, Elvis had done no studio work at all during the years 1964–1966. Matters might have gone on like this even longer, if RCA had not started competing with the Colonel by releasing old Elvis recordings which invariably outsold the movie soundtracks. When the hapless Steve Sholes, a man whom Elvis despised, retired and Jervis took over, the Colonel agreed that Elvis could go back into the studio at Nashville and resume his recording career. By this point, however, Elvis's career was so shot that it was very hard to say how it should be resumed. Elvis's position on the musical *mapa mundi* was Nowhere. Until he did the Singer Special.

This show put him into a tight working relationship with a brilliant arranger and a hotshot engineer who was hip to the revolution in recording methods that had occurred during the sixties. Ironically, the essence of the whole recording revolution lay in an idea that Elvis Presley had helped to pioneer: the use of electronic devices not only to record but *create* fresh sounds. It was an electronically produced echo that had given Elvis's first and best records on Sun their distinctive acoustic aura. It was another electronic echo device that had made Scotty Moore's guitar sound with such a weird and haunting plangency. The young and inspired Elvis Presley had been packaged with all sorts of primitive electronic gimmickry and had ridden to fame with those tricks up his sleeve. Instead of remaining alive and open to all the new sounds that were pouring in on listeners during the sixties, however, Elvis stopped his ears and fell asleep. Pretty soon the Hillbilly Cat was swooning to corny Hawaiian beach lullabies, singing back-beat versions of Neapolitan love songs, doing the Mambo, the Cha-cha-cha and coming on like the last of the middle-aged crooners. From being one of the most sharply etched profiles in the history of pop music, Elvis had become a faceless hack who stood for nothing musically: or at least nothing that belonged to the modern world.

As far as learning to make full use of the modern recording studio, Elvis never caught up with his day. That challenge was beyond him. Though Bones Howe put him into the best studio on the West Coast, Western United, there was no way Elvis could work except to put on a show for the band with a hand-held mike in his fist. Still, he did get an idea of what modern recording techniques could do and began to look at sixteen-track boards as something more than engineers' toys. The really big breakthrough came, however, in the area of his instrumental sound, which, for the first time in his entire career, was produced by a full-scale studio orchestra. Here, he profited enormously from the vision of Billy Goldenberg.

The arranger's problem was essentially the same as the costumer's— only on a vastly greater scale. What Goldenberg was expected to do was to take the traditional Presley repertoire and whatever current music was used on the program and give it all a thrillingly contemporary treatment. Instead of the stale old sound of Sun or Nashville, these new arrangements had to pop, crack and sizzle with the extravagant new energies of the sixties. His solution to the problem was both brilliant and highly ironic; for, what he decided to do was to voice the music of Memphis's most famous singer in the marvelous new idiom of the Memphis Sound: the style created by Stax/Volt records, a black-oriented record company in Memphis that was now giving Motown a run for its money. You wouldn't think that you would need a Broadway showbiz arranger who didn't even dig the Presley idiom to show Elvis Presley how to renew his music by dipping it in the strong dark colors of his own hometown; but that is precisely what Goldenberg did—and what Elvis loved so much that he canceled his next recording session at Nashville and for the first time since his days at Sun employed a Memphis studio (Chip Moman's American Studios) and a backing comprised of many of the same musicians who are heard on the Stax/Volt records. (These Memphis sessions proved to be the most successful since 1960, yielding two gold albums, three singles that sold in the millions and several minor hits. Binder, Howe and Goldenberg had restored Elvis to himself just as successfully and in exactly the same way as Jerry Wexler did at this time with Aretha Franklin, who had also drifted far away from her roots in the gospel-toned world of soul. The only difference was that Wexler was acclaimed a genius but nobody outside the business recognized what had brought Elvis back to life musically.)

When Goldenberg pulled the wraps off his dazzling new translation of Elvis's favorite gospel, R & B and rock standards, the effect was startling. No Elvis Presley album either before or since has ever delivered so much musical energy, excitement or imaginative stimulation. Sure, the tempos are fast, the transitions abrupt, the atmosphere crepitating with heat lightning. This is show music, designed to propel dancing bodies and stand up to glaring scenery and reach out through that tiny, tinny, two-bit little speaker in the TV set and set the somnolent viewer's feet tapping and blood pressure rising. Sometimes the band blares like Saturday night on Beale Street; sometimes the sound hushes to the lonely soulful wail of a harmonica or the cat litter-matchbox scratch of pick on guitar frets. Sometimes the violins fill the atmosphere with a thick blue haze; then, the page turns and the trumpets screech like those big fat mamas shoutin' at the East Trigg Baptist.

The score was a feast for the ear and a revelation for Elvis. At four o'clock in the morning, he was up in the booth with Bones demanding to have the tapes spun again and again! Never again was he to walk out onstage without thirty pieces behind him. He had been weaned at last from the tuppenny sound of rock 'n' roll.

As the last numbers were put in the can, the filming and recording of the show was declared complete save for the finale. This was the last loose screw, the last unsettled issue. Steve Binder was still, after all these months, holding out for his original idea: Elvis should walk out on camera and say: "I care!" Colonel Parker was just as set as ever on having Elvis wind up the show in the customary noncommittal manner of all the big entertainers. After having listened to so many arguments and pleas against the good-night-and-Merry-Christmas bit, the Colonel was willing to make a concession. He said that Elvis could end with a song like "I Believe." Binder and Howe were nauseated at the idea of their original vision of Elvis Presley gurgling down the drain with something as phony and fraudulent as "I Believe." Even in Las Vegas, the idea would have been offensive.

Finally, Steve Binder thought of a possible solution. What if they were to write a piece of special material for Elvis? A song with an affirmative tone, an air of social awareness—not anything that would make the Colonel say no automatically but something that caught the tone of the message without spelling it out in so many words? It was a pretty vague and abstract set of specs that he delivered to Billy Goldenberg and the songwriter, Earl Brown; but they agreed to go off that night and give it a try. That was how the real pros worked, wasn't it? After six weeks in rehearsal and an exhausting five-hour tryout at the Nixon Theater in Pittsburgh, the old dudes who wrote the Follies and the

Scandals and all that jive would sit down on the stage apron at four in the morning with a bottle of bootleg booze and hack out the song that would be the big hit of the show when it reached Broadway.

Next morning, the pair showed up in Steve Binder's office. It was the tensest moment of the entire production. Now that they were almost finished with everything but the final edit, all the parties to the enterprise had closed in on Binder. In the very next office was Colonel Parker laying down the law to Bob Finkel and Tom Sarnoff and anybody else who would listen. He was explaining in no uncertain terms why Elvis could not, would not and should not go out and make some sort of incriminating lefto-pinko statement to millions of conservative-minded Americans just fresh from their Singer sewing machines. In Binder's office, Billy Goldenberg was seating himself at the piano while Earl Brown got set to plug the song they had written the night before: "If I Can Dream."

The song, which became Elvis's first big hit in years, was a typical piece of white soul concocted out of reminiscences of Ray Charles and lifts from the new Memphis Sound. It was frankly stagy and even a little hokey. But it struck the note of social aspiration without preaching, and it gave Elvis a chance to wind up the long show with a big powerful theatrical roundhouse punch. Elvis listened to it carefully; then, he demanded to hear it again and again. Finally, he turned to Binder and said: "I'll do it!"

Stepping into the adjacent office, where the Colonel was still holding forth on the impossibility of doing anything heavier than "I Believe," Steve announced: "We've got a new finale. It's called 'If I Can Dream.'" The Colonel turned white with rage. The people from NBC and RCA rushed into his adjoining room to hear Elvis sing the song. No sooner were the last notes out of his mouth than everybody was jumping on the bandwagon, congratulating Elvis, clamoring for the publishing rights and telling the Colonel that it was already a smash hit. The Colonel said nothing.

"If I Can Dream" was recorded by Elvis as a voice-over. After the band had left the studio, Elvis asked that all the lights be turned out. Taking the hand-held mike, he lay down flat on the floor of the blacked-out studio with the "cans" on his ears. Then, as the recorded orchestra finished its Burt Bacharachish intro, Elvis started singing and gradually worked his way up to the hoarse, shouting finale so reminiscent of the blind Ray Charles crying out in anguish from his darkness.

The last scene in the long saga of the Singer Special must be titled

"The Colonel's Revenge." When RCA was preparing to release the single of "If I Can Dream" and the soundtrack album of the Special, Steve Binder and Bones Howe demanded of the Colonel that they be cut into the royalties of the records they had produced and recorded. This was the moment the ole Colonel had been awaiting for a long, long time. He told the producers to read their contracts—and weep! He not only refused to give them more than a tiny token payment—which they rejected—he even refused to put their names on the single. (They finally did get credits—but no bread—on the album.) It was the old story of the music business all over again, the same story that once featured Arthur Crudup being screwed by Hill and Range, that once featured Elvis's name as author on songs of which he didn't write a word or a note, the story of crass commercial exploitation of creative talent that is the national anthem of American pop music.

The moment Elvis came charging offstage after his triumphant bout with the ghost of the past, he appeared a different person. "They still like me!" he blithered as he rushed into the dressing room. Then, confronting the Colonel, he swore: "I've got to get back in front of the public. We've got to go out on the road again!" Whatever Colonel Parker might have said or thought of this command, he realized soon that it had to be carried out. To the ole Colonel's credit be it said that no more than a year after Elvis came to his senses, he was opening in the greatest showroom in the world at the International Hotel in Las Vegas. Like a successful "analysis," the Singer Special had cured Elvis of his illness and pointed the way to his new happiness.

Chapter 29

Revival at Las Vegas

ONE of the greatest moments of the Presley Myth is Elvis's famous comeback at Las Vegas in 1969. If you read the story in the rock press or in one of the innumerable Presley fan books, it assumes the proportions of a showbiz legend. Elvis is portrayed as down and out, lost and rejected, the object of scorn to all but the faithful few. Then, through a combination of Colonel Parker's magical management skills and Elvis's wondrous talent, in one night the whole picture is reversed. Elvis is once again the darling of the American people, the greatest entertainer in the world and the king of rock 'n' roll. The refusal of even the best informed writers to present this episode in its correct colors is yet another example of the peculiar status of Elvis Presley as a figure of popular idolatry, a folk hero whose exploits must always conform to the pattern of a fairy tale.

Great comebacks are, of course, the stuff of showbiz legend. The miraculous resurgence of Al Jolson in *The Jolson Story,* the poignant recoveries of Judy Garland in her later years, these are tales that attest to the capacity of the great performer to rise to the most difficult challenges and reimpose his mystique on even the most indifferent or unsympathetic audiences. Such stories do not sort well, however, with the story of Elvis at Vegas. For one thing, Elvis's professional history was radically different from that of just about any entertainer in the history of the business. He was not a flash in the pan who suddenly died, only to be reborn many years later. He was not, on the other hand, like Jolson and Garland, a performer who had enjoyed great success for many years and then either through a change of public taste or a series of private misfortunes been reduced to the status of the has-been. Elvis was an entertainer who walked off the stage after just two years of unexampled popularity to devote himself to another medium, which made him rich but dimmed the luster of his original fame. There is absolutely no poignance in this history, no sense of defeat or rejection. Elvis wanted the money and the opportunity that Hollywood offered, and he got both to an unprecedented degree.

Elvis was only twenty-two years old when he left the stage; when he returned twelve years later, he was still a young man at the height of his powers. He was better looking than in youth; his voice was richer and stronger; his command of performance technique was greater. What's more, the timing of his return, though not deliberately chosen, was highly favorable. Nineteen sixty-nine marked the first year of rock 'n' roll revival, the irresistible longing to loop back, as in a time machine, to the magic moment in 1956 when it all began and experience once again—or for the first time ever!—the incomparable pleasure of being a screaming teeny submitting to that first musical rape. Not only is this a phenomenon that far transcends what has been traditionally understood as nostalgia: It is a mania that has persisted ever since, giving rise to wave after wave of rock 'n' roll revival, so that even today there is nothing more trendy than turned-up collars and gooey hair and the raucous sound of rockabilly. As students of contemporary culture have been remarking since the sixties, we are no longer a civilization that is capable of creative innovation; instead, we have become a civilization that survives through the incessant recycling of cultural waste products: cast-off clothes, old comic strips, rerun (or remade) movies, and, above all, that monotonously revolving kaleidoscope loaded with bits of shrewdly selected, skillfully cut and electronically enhanced gospel, blues, rock, jazz, pop, folk, pop, blues, rock, and so on, in endlessly shifting combinations of this week's, last season's, tomorrow's "sound."

Elvis Presley didn't launch rock 'n' roll revival nor even give it a distinctive image, as he did the original rock. The great downbeat for this regressive symphony, the first clear signal that it was time to play rock da capo, came from rock's greatest innovators and creative geniuses, the Beatles. It was in the winter of 1967–68, the fateful winter that blighted the brief spring and summer of the hippies, that the world's greatest trendsetters decided to do an about-face and retreat (with hip finesse) to their earlier manner or even to the styles of the old masters who had preceded them, like Buddy Holly, Chuck Berry, Little Richard and, of course, Elvis Presley. Their example was quickly copied by such enormously popular groups as Credence Clearwater, who demonstrated that even without the mystique of the Beatles, a band that could recover and concentrate the essence of the old rockabilly sound could achieve consistent top-of-the-chart success. At that point, the cells of memory burst open and out poured all those ancient rockers who had been Elvis's contemporaries. By the summer of 1969, you could see back on the boards every survivor of the fifties: Fats Domino, Little Richard, Bo Diddley, Chuck Berry, the Everly Brothers, Jerry Lee Lewis and the indomitable Bill Haley. Small wonder that by this time Elvis was beginning to drop hints that he would like to go back on the road.

Even so, his manager was very reluctant to make the move. Which brings us to the other part of this mythically distorted episode: the role of Colonel Parker. According to the Presley chroniclers, Elvis's reemergence at Las Vegas was a masterpiece of managerial manipulation. The Colonel, after shrewdly withdrawing Elvis from public performance at the height of his drawing power, now, no less astutely, decided to launch him again after nurturing the appetite for his reappearance by burying him for thirteen years in the unreal world of Hollywood exploitation flicks. Las Vegas was chosen as the launching site because it would offer Elvis the ideal audience—a couple thousand middle-aged people sated with food and drink—and because it would offer vast amounts of money.

The truth is that when Elvis began to have thoughts about returning to live performance, he gave no consideration to Las Vegas because he saw the resort as a most unsuitable place for his style of entertainment. How else, in fact, could he have seen it? Rock music had never attained any popularity in Las Vegas. All attempts to introduce the style had failed miserably. Las Vegas was, in fact, the one totally secure bastion of the traditional entertainment idioms, deriving from the Broadway theater, the New York nightclub and the Parisian follies. The heroes of Vegas were sophisticated old pros like Frank Sinatra, Dean Martin, Tony Bennett, Sammy Davis, Jr., Don Rickles, Buddy Hackett and Shecky Greene: performers with whom Elvis had no identification. Everything in Vegas was oriented to the "over thirties," a euphemism for the middle-aged and the elderly. Putting it all together, any sensible person would have said that Las Vegas was the worst place in America for Elvis Presley to attempt a comeback. As if all this were not bad enough, Las Vegas also had the distinction in Elvis's mind of being the only town in America where he had ever bombed.

Back in the spring of 1956, as he was making his spectacular take-off into national celebrity, Colonel had booked him into the New Frontier for two weeks. He was the star of a show that featured the silky string arrangements of the Freddie Martin Orchestra and the booze and gambling jokes of Shecky Greene. Elvis cut such an incongruous figure in that company that *Newsweek* likened his appearance to "a jug of corn liquor at a champagne party." The Las Vegas audience was described as sitting through Elvis's act "as if he were a clinical experiment." After two weeks of getting the cold shoulder from the old folks—as well as suffering the humiliation of seeing his name go from the top to the bottom of the marquee—Elvis exploded, telling the press: "I don't want no more nightclubs." For any other entertainer the recollection of this early mishap would have become a joke after the passage of thirteen years, especially if the performer had been as incredibly successful as Elvis and had reoriented his image and his career to middle-of-the-road conformity with popular taste. This was not, however, the way Elvis Presley's mind worked. He had forgotten nothing and forgiven nothing. At thirty-three he felt about Las Vegas precisely as he had felt at twenty-one; namely, that it was a good place to party but a bad place to play.

What Elvis thought, felt or wanted, was rarely a decisive factor in any decision concerning his career. The important consideration was what the Colonel thought. The joke is that even the Colonel, who spent half his life at Vegas gambling, had never considered booking his boy back into the resort until he received an offer that put the once unthinkable notion of Elvis in a showroom into a new and enticing perspective. To appreciate the significance of this offer, especially from the Colonel's standpoint, one has to recover for a moment a little of the curiosity and excitement that was aroused by the much-publicized announcement by Kirk Kerkorian in 1968 that he was going to lead America's most popular resort into the golden decade of the seventies by providing it with the world's largest and most lavishly equipped hotel.

As the news stories and prospectuses depicted the International Hotel, it sounded like one of those "world of the future" conceptions that used to tease the imaginations of Americans back in the thirties. Every feature of the hotel was colossal: a capacity of 1,500 rooms (two and a half times the size of the reigning favorite, Caesar's Palace); a height of thirty stories ("the tallest building in the State of Nevada"); the pool, a reservoir of 350,000 gallons ("The second largest man-made body of water in Nevada, second only to nearby Lake Mead"); the shopping concourse, with a score of boutiques, offering everything you could buy in a fair-sized town; the dining facilities, half a dozen American and ethnic restaurants—Mexican, German, Italian and Benihana Japanese; the casino, the largest in the world—natch!—with over a thousand slot machines. As for entertainment, the International would have not one but three major facilities—a lounge, a legitimate theater and a showroom—each offering a production that would rival or surpass anything that could be found in the entire resort. Clearly, therefore, the International was the ultimate resort hotel. In fact, it was not so much a resort hotel as it was a resort *in* a hotel: a totally self-contained, round-the-clock pleasure dome, where one could check in for a weekend or a week and never once feel the need to step out the door.

The Barnumesque grandeur of this conception was certain to have impressed itself on Barnum's foremost living descendant, Colonel Tom. The canny Colonel saw at once the great advantage he could reap by launching the publicity for Elvis's return atop the enormous wave of ballyhoo that would be generated by the hotel's first season. He recognized that the scale of this undertaking corresponded to his favorite billing of Elvis as "The World's Greatest Entertainer." What's more, as a deeply addicted gambler, the Colonel was attracted by the possibility of combining profit with pleasure.

Booking Elvis into the International for two weeks, however, wouldn't solve his career problems. If he were going to match the millions he earned in the movies with income from personal appearances, sooner or later he would have to go where the real money was—out on the road. What this gig would offer was a chance to break in his new act and get back into the rhythm of regular performing. So just when Elvis was starting to kick against the traces of his old routine, the Colonel was readying a new harness and surveying a new track at Las Vegas.

The man with whom the Colonel was dealing was the general manager of the hotel, Alex Shoofey. A tough little Lebanese whose nickname is "The Cleaver," Shoofey had a well-deserved reputation for being one of the shrewdest operators on the Strip. He had come to the Keno Kingdom back in 1948 in the same random manner that characterized the arrival of so many of the greatest figures of this Topsy-grown town. Having become a CPA in New York after the war, he had gone out to California to make his fortune running a gas station. When the business failed, he packed up his gear and started driving home. Going through Vegas, his old car broke down in front of a joint called the Club Bingo. Shoofey strolled inside and—Bingo!—he had a job working for the owner, Milton Prell. When Prell bought the Sahara, he made Shoofey its manager. It was at this time that the astute CPA first met Colonel Parker, the man who was fond of saying, "Fuck capital gains!"

When Kirk Kerkorian decided to build the International, he wooed Shoofey and his whole staff away from the Sahara and established them at the Flamingo, where their job was to recruit and train the staff for the International. Shoofey made such a good thing of the Flamingo that Kerkorian decided he would operate two Las Vegas hotels. Now, Shoofey was looking for big names to lend prestige to the International's first and most critical season.

Colonel and Shoofey couldn't agree on a price. Colonel took the position that his man was vital to the showroom's success; Shoofey argued that Elvis had been out of the game for a long time and was an unknown quantity in Las Vegas. When the Singer Special played, Shoofey was disappointed. "The show was not the big, big success they expected," he recalls. "In fact, it didn't come off. Elvis came on wearing his old leather jacket. It was a throw-back. It was unacceptable for Las Vegas."

When Shoofey did not call the Colonel with the anticipated offer, the Colonel called Shoofey. Once more they negotiated, and this time they made a deal. Shoofey had several acts in mind to open the room. He asked the Colonel if Elvis would like to have the honor. "Absolutely not," snapped the old man. "We will not open under any conditions. It's much too risky. Let somebody else stick his neck out." The Colonel was shrewd in making this stipulation, as events were to prove.

The showroom of the International is comparable in scale to every other feature of the building. Similar in plan to a huge municipal auditorium, one of those dreadful houses that are all spread and no height— the sort of stage that is perfect for only one famous act, the Rockettes— the Showroom Internationale is a solo performer's nightmare. Don Rickles, whom Shoofey had been very eager to engage, took one look at the looming balcony and said there was no possibility that he could do his act in such a vast and impersonal space. Finally, it was decided that the room should be opened by the hottest entertainer of the day, Barbra Streisand.

Elvis was very unhappy about the Vegas booking. Once again, the Colonel had thrown him into the lion's den. Now, it was his job to find a way to lick the beast. The Colonel's decision to keep him off the stage all these years had destroyed Elvis's confidence. No longer a cocksure kid who had but to walk out onstage to have the audience at his feet, he was now a young old pro, smart enough to recognize all the pitfalls that lay before him. One big problem was that he had no act. What was he supposed to do—go onstage with a five-piece rock band and start singing "Heartbreak Hotel"? That's what the Colonel wanted him to do. Now, how could Elvis do something as dumb as that? It would risk typing him as a relic of the past, a campy character out of a rock 'n' roll cartoon. What was even worse was the fact that he didn't dig the old rock any more; he had gone on to other things and so had the world. Why should he put himself in a rock strait jacket when he preferred so many other kinds of music?

What was the alternative? Put on a tux and play Dean Martin? That was just as ridiculous. Elvis had an image that was bigger than life. Whatever he thought about rock, people still loved it and he was its king. He couldn't disappoint the public and risk his neck by suddenly assuming a totally new identity. Then, there were all the problems that related to the Vegas audience. Elvis had spent his great years driving little girls to tears. Now he would be looking at bouffant hairdos and evening gowns and cleavage. He'd have men out there who were old enough to be his father and women old enough to be his mother. He sure as hell couldn't come on to these people the way he had to the teenyboppers.

He began to haunt the hotels. One night he walked into the lounge at the Flamingo and found the solution to his problem. The performer was a young, virtually unknown Welsh singer named Tom Jones. He was a good-looking, well-built stud dressed in a sharp tux with a vest and wearing a tight, groovy Afro. His voice was powerful, though his held notes sometimes wavered unpleasantly. His stance was commanding. As he would hit the long high notes, he would bend way back from the waist, giving the women at ringside a good long look at his crotch. His pants were so tight that they appeared to have been sprayed on. In the strong stage lights, you could see clearly the outline of his dick and his balls. In fact, the best word for his act was "ballsy."

The most astonishing thing about this young man was the effect he had on the women in his audience. As the show reached its peaks, stylishly dressed, carefully soignéed young matrons, many of them seated beside their husbands, would scream and throw their room keys at the singer. (Afterward the poor husbands would have to go onstage and retrieve the keys.) Some of them even got so nutsy, they took off their panties and tossed them into the lights. As Elvis looked on in astonishment, he realized that these women were feeling just what the little girls had felt at his shows back in the fifties.

When Elvis checked out Jones, he discovered that he was hot as a murder weapon. His records were going gold, he had a great new TV show in the works, his price was shooting up. The Flamingo was so eager to push him that they had launched a whole promotion keyed to the theme of "Tom Jones Fever." When you sat down at the table, you found a little bottle filled with pink "fever pills." When you turned on your radio, you got the latest report from the "fever clinics." The whole hype. The amazing thing was that it worked! Night after night, Tom Jones packed the room. It was said that the pit bosses and stickmen were complaining because their wives were pestering them constantly for tickets to the show.

Elvis got very friendly with Tom Jones. He even told the Guys, "Tom is the only man who has ever come anywhere close to the way I sing. He has that ballsy feeling, that 'I'm gonna shove it up your ass attitude.'" The only fault Elvis found in Jones's act was its blatant sex appeal. "I think that's very lewd," Elvis would frown, "showing his cock and his balls." "Hell, Elvis," Lamar Fike would carol, "you did the same shit in your time!" "No," Elvis would demur, "I was never vulgar."

All the same, the two men soon became fast friends. Elvis would hang out in Jones's dressing room, even walk out onstage while Jones was working. After the gig, they would go out together and get drunk. Jones drank champagne, Elvis vodka with orange juice to disguise the taste. Then, when they were mellow, Elvis would talk to the young singer, only five years his junior, like a father to a son. At the same time, this father was getting a lot of good ideas from this son.

When Elvis opened in Vegas, the professional show people who worked with both Elvis and with Tom Jones were astonished at how much the famous star had taken from the man he treated as his protégé. Nick Naff, director of publicity at the Flamingo and then at the International, summed up the borrowings neatly:

> What Elvis got from Tom was the trick of working the Vegas show stage. Tom showed him that you have to be dynamic and sensual in a way that gets through to the over-thirties. You gotta hit 'em right in the cunt. Tom gave Elvis those head shakes, the vocal accents on the bridges, the freeze poses at the end of the songs, the trick of wiping the sweat with a cloth and then

throwing it out in the house—all those things. The big difference
was that Tom did all this stuff instinctively. He just didn't know
any other way to work. Elvis was much smarter. He wasn't so
spontaneous, but he knew a good thing when he saw it. He took
Tom's stuff, translated it into his own style, rehearsed his ass
off and went over big with it. Elvis was much the brighter of
the two.

Tom had given Elvis the key to the house. The rest, for a performer
of Elvis's talent and resources, was relatively simple. The whole trick
was the image, the attitude. Once Elvis got that straight, he knew just
what to do. He wasn't going to stand there in a fancy tux flashing his
pecker. He had a better gimmick. For years he had been studying karate.
He was a second-degree black belt. Now what was ballsier than karate?
Those studs paced around on the mats like big cats. When they attacked,
they screamed like jaguars. They had dozens of great moves that were
as beautiful as any choreography. They also had that great look in their
eyes: that killer look, where the soul, the *ki,* comes flashing out of the
eye. Finally, there was the karate uniform, the *gi.* If you were going to
do karate moves, you couldn't have a better costume.

Calling up Bill Bellew, the costume designer whom he had met on
the Singer Special, Elvis ordered a number of specially designed *gis* in
black mohair. Some were in the traditional two-piece pattern; some were
all-in-ones to keep the jacket from flying up and exposing his midriff.
For the sash, Bellew suggested that he have a macrame belt made by a
Hawaiian-Japanese who was into the martial arts and would weave into
the belt all the appropriate karate symbols. This idea thrilled Elvis. It
was as if he were receiving a magic talisman that would protect him
on the stage.

Sartor resartus. When Elvis put on the new *gi,* he assumed instantly
his new image. He didn't jiggle and jerk any more. He took his stand
and held it, firm as a statue. He didn't walk in that old butchy style.
He padded back and forth like a cat-footed karate killer. When he got
into a hard-hitting tune, like "Suspicious Minds," instead of throwing
his body into some awkward rendition of the Shimmy or the Camel
Walk, he started throwing karate punches: kicks and chops that projected
powerfully the force of the music. In no time, he had his new act together.

Now it was time to attend to the music. Elvis started rehearsing a
full month before his opening. For the first time in his career, he assembled
a band of first-rate Los Angeles studio musicians: no more Nashville

cornballs or boyhood pals, like Scotty and D.J. Las Vegas was a big challenge and Elvis was determined to meet the challenge with all the power he could marshal.

Two weeks before opening, Elvis brought all his forces together at the International Hotel for a series of full-scale rehearsals. One of the things that had impressed him about Tom Jones's act, especially when he saw him work in Hawaii in May 1969, was the way the Welsh singer matched his powerful voice with the sonority of a full orchestra, producing those smashing showbiz climaxes that give you goose pimples. Though Elvis had only recently been carping at Steve Binder and Bones Howe about the dangers of "over-producing" his songs with a big studio orchestra, he now became passionately convinced of the importance of working with the largest possible backing. In addition to his five-piece virtuoso rock band, he engaged: the Imperials (a pop gospel quartet); the Sweet Inspirations (a black female soul trio); a harmonizing soprano with an extremely high "angelic" voice; and a thirty-five-piece orchestra with a conductor. With Charlie Hodge standing at his side with his acoustic guitar, Elvis mustered onstage *fifty* musicians and singers.

Naturally, the Colonel was furious at this extravagance. In a flash, he saw that Elvis's anxiety would wipe out their joint profits. In fact, he may have suspected that this was Elvis's true intention: an act of revenge inspired by the Colonel's callousness toward Elvis's feelings about Las Vegas. Elvis was heard to say at the time: "I don't care if I don't make any money so long as I give a good show." This was the kind of speech calculated to give the Colonel another heart attack. Colonel, for his part, went about puffing his cigar to a hot glow and demanding of no one in particular: "What the hell does he want all these people for? He doesn't need them! He's just *insecure!*" Ah, a line like that was designed to ricochet back off the Guys to Elvis, where it would hit him square in the balls. Elvis would send back his answer through the same set of human bounce boards. "I've got to have my *power!* I've got to have *dynamics!*" he thundered to the Guys. "You saw that stage, you saw what I've got to cover! What the fuck does that old bald-headed bastard think this is all about!"

By the time Elvis arrived in Las Vegas, Barbra Streisand had been working the showroom for two weeks. At this moment, she was at the peak of her career. She had just won an Oscar for *Funny Girl.* Her talents as a singer, an actress, a comedienne and an analyst of public taste promised that her Las Vegas debut would be one of the greatest events in the history of the resort. It was confidently expected that her engagement would establish attendance records, set benchmarks for musical and theatrical excellence and push the whole level of local entertainment onto a higher plateau. Then, the unthinkable happened. Streisand, ignorant of Vegas, puffed up with success, not really at her best before a live audience, came to town with an audaciously simple show. It was essentially a rehash of a program which she had given the previous summer at New York in Central Park. There were no warm-up acts, no jokes, no choreography or sets: just Barbra standing there under the lights with a fantastic hairdo, a splendid gown and the longest fingernails since the Manchu dynasty, singing her heart out into a jeweled hand mike. It was a stunning exhibition of vocal and stylistic virtuosity by the Heifetz of pop song. In New York, it would have killed the audience. In Las Vegas, after the stellar opening night, it produced shrinking houses and even snores.

Elvis slipped into the back of the balcony one night to watch his rival work. He pointed mutely to all the empty seats around him. Then, he settled down to listen to the program. He gave no signs of pleasure. He made sour faces when Barbra got into her Jewish obsessions. When it was all over, he turned to Lamar Fike and said two words: "She sucks!" Then, he went downstairs to the dressing room to tell Barbra how much he had enjoyed the performance. When he was admitted to the dressing room, he was astonished to find the great star alone. Elvis had never been alone for one moment in his entire life. Two or three men always accompanied him even to the bathroom. Streisand made no bones about her disgust with the audience and the hotel. "This place isn't even built yet!" she fumed. "I wouldn't be surprised if some night while I'm out there working some schmuck doesn't walk by with a ladder on his shoulder!" Then, vowing that she would never play Las Vegas again and wishing Elvis well on his engagement (doubtless with the same degree of sincerity as he had evinced with his phony congratulations), the two parted company.

As Elvis was straining every fibre of his being during the final days of rehearsal, even going so far as to strap weights on his legs as he worked to build up the muscles, Colonel Parker was having a field day blitzing the town and the nation with his publicity. Setting up his headquarters in a three-room suite at the end of the hall on the fourth floor, the old boy and his team—Tom Diskin, George Parkhill and Jim O'Brien—swiftly seized control of the hotel's public relations apparatus and readjusted it for their style of pitch. The hotel, for example, had wanted the radio spot announcements to be low-keyed and tasteful, with Elvis's voice in the background as the announcer extended an invitation. Colonel Parker would not hear of such a thing.

Soon the airwaves were filled with raucously echoing pitches: "EL-VIS!))) ELVIS!))) ELVIS!))) NOW!))) NOW!))) NOW!))) INTERNATIONAL HO-TEL!)))" The roads were lined all the way in from Los Angeles with socko billboard sheets. Every store in town was offered a window placard or a poster. Every unguarded wall was plastered with a quarter sheet. The newspaper ads were not just ads: They were two- and three-page sections devoted entirely to Elvis. You couldn't watch TV for an hour without getting an urgent spiel. All this round-the-clock activity, however, was just the buildup to the circus-hits-town bit the Colonel did the moment Barbra Streisand's engagement ended.

That night, the Colonel was standing in the hotel lobby with a huge crew, equipped with ladders, staple guns, lumber and vast quantities of posters and placards printed up by his old buddy Clyde Rinaldi, in Tampa. Abiding by the rules of professional etiquette, the old man did not permit one banner to be hung announcing Elvis's appearance until the contractual time of the Streisand engagement had run out. Then, at the stroke of midnight, he shouted at his crew: "Hit it!" Instantly, the men went into action. In a matter of hours, they had papered every public room in the hotel with Elvis's name and picture. They had constructed a booth next to the hotel entrance that sold souvenir programs, styrofoam straw hats, teddy bears. They hung banners from the ceiling, they supplied the maids with stand-up announcements to be placed conspicuously in every room on top of the TV set or the dresser. Next morning, when the hotel executives came to work, they were appalled to discover their immaculate new lobby buried under this junk blizzard. What could they do? As the marquee announced, in the largest lettering available and with a silhouette figure of the star, Las Vegas was now under the rule of ELVIS!

Opening night, July 26, 1969, the hotel offered a free dinner show to a specially invited audience. Naturally, the Colonel got control of the guest list and invited all his cronies from Tampa, Nashville and Hollywood, his doctor from Palm Springs, his wife's relatives and other such important figures. Oh, it was a star-studded assembly. The Colonel knew George Hamilton quite well. Minnie Pearl and Earl Scruggs were invited. Fats Domino attracted quite a bit of attention because he was virtually the only man of color among the two thousand guests.

The decor of the Showroom Internationale was just as preposterous as everything else in Las Vegas. Grander than the "Fountainblue," grosser than Grossinger's, it was adorned with three-dimensional putti stringing yards of swagging chiffon between plastic classic columns. The maitre d' and the captains wore frilly blue shirts under their elaborate tuxedos, and seated each guest according to a vast, astrological-looking chart. The New York rock press had been flown in en masse on Kirk Kerkorian's private DC-9, a stunning two-bedroom aerial yacht. Accustomed to nothing better than a paper plate laden with "soul food" and a plastic cup filled with sour wine, they were overwhelmed by the largesse that characterized the Presley opening. Small wonder that their notices of the event were so rhapsodic.

The two warm-up acts, the Sweet Inspirations and the comic Sammy Shore, can be passed over without comment as they were observed without interest by the audience. Then, the giant gold curtain fell. When it rose again, it revealed the philharmonic-sized forces of Elvis's accompaniment belting out a hot show-time rhythm. Suddenly, without a word of announcement, a figure dressed in black emerged from the wings at stage left. There was a gasp of recognition, then a mounting roar of applause that instantly became a standing ovation. Elvis, meantime, had strode to center stage, received his guitar from Charlie Hodge and assumed the classic spraddle-legged stance to kick off his first number. The uproar in the house was so great that he was stopped in his tracks. Smiling foolishly but unwilling to break the spell by saying anything, he held the band in check for a few moments. Then, he cried: "One for the money!" The band shouted back, *"Ba-dum boom!"* "Two for the show!" *Ba-dum boom!* "Three to get ready and *go, cat, go!*" He was off and running on fast "Blue Suede Shoes."

What followed was a case of old Cokes served up in shiny new cans. Elvis's special arrangements, which could not match the rock poetry of Billy Goldenberg's, had the effect at fast tempos of seizing the singer, as if in one of those old vibrating belts, and shaking him violently on what sounded like one note until he was breathless. Then, panting, gasping, apologizing—at one point he said, "You all just look at me a couple minutes while I get my breath back!"—he would swig down a cup of Gatorade, like a spent athlete, and return to his musical exercise machine. On the first slow tune, "Love Me Tender," he strolled around the stage apron, kneeling down to kiss one woman after another. He was determined to make contact with the "over thirties." His first medley—"Jailhouse Rock," "Don't Be Cruel," "Heartbreak Hotel" and "All Shook Up"—betrayed a sarcastic and spoofing attitude, as if he were saying: "I'm not twenty-one any more and neither are you, so we won't take these old toys too seriously." All the best material appeared in the latter part of the show, where he got into his recent hits, "In the Ghetto" and a six-minute take-out on "Suspicious Minds," which built up to a bacchanalian climax, the trumpets screaming, the drums roaring, the choral voices shouting out their lungs. All in all, it was a show that offered a lot more to the eye than to the ear and a lot more to the viscera than to the mind. Elvis was blowing it out, belting his songs, producing broad, coarse effects that were appropriate to all the broad, coarse sensibilities in his audience. When he walked off that night, the flacks, the fans, the rock critics and the music businessmen hailed the performance as a triumph. As such it was reported the following week from coast to coast.

Next day at noon, Colonel Parker met with Alex Shoofey in the deserted and eerily lit showroom. Originally, they had agreed to get together just to talk over the opening and make any little readjustments that might be necessary. Shoofey arrived, however, with something drastically different in mind. He had been enormously impressed by Elvis's new show. He hadn't attended the rehearsals and didn't know what to expect. After his experience with Barbra Streisand, he was very worried. Then he had seen something that he hadn't even dared to hope for: a real honest-to-god Las Vegas stage show. Instantly, his mind had started spinning like a computer. He saw the chance of a lifetime. Now, he was going to grab it.

Seating himself at a table about the size of a roulette wheel, the small but tough-looking CPA confronted the obese man with the long cigar drooping from his lips. The two of them looked exactly like what they were: the dealer and the dumper. Now, they were going to play a little game. The stakes? Elvis Presley's future. Shoofey knew exactly how to deal with the Colonel. The best approach was always to lay it on the line, which is just what Shoofey proceeded to do.

"Colonel," he said in his raspy New York voice, "I'd like to draw up a new agreement with you—for five years." "No!" snapped the Colonel, astonished at this development. "It's too big a risk. I know what you're thinking. You were impressed by the show last night; but, remember, that was only *one show!* You don't know what will happen next." Shoofey's mouth drew back in a sharklike grin. "Colonel," he said, "I'm a gambler. I'm willing to go right now, take a five-year contract. Two appearances a year, four weeks each appearance." Colonel was still shaking his head. This wasn't good business. "Alex," he said, getting personal, putting on his I'm-old-enough-to-be-your-father air: "I wouldn't do it this way. I would go on the basis of the right of first refusal." Shoofey was not dissuaded in the least. Leaning across the table and fixing the Colonel with a hard, unwavering look, he reached for his sinker. Speaking the language of the professional gambler, he croaked: "I'll take the cut!"

As Shoofey spoke, the Colonel started scribbling figures on the table-cloth. It was an old dodge of his, a device to give him more time to think—without looking the other man in the eye. The more he scribbled, the more the proposition appealed to him. What was it that appealed to him so much? Money? A giant figure that would eclipse any price ever paid in Las Vegas? That's what everybody thought at the time, and that's what most people believe to this day. Every article, every book says it. Elvis Presley made a million a month in Vegas. Or was it even more? With all the expenses and freeloading and stock options, the smartest operators in Vegas figured Elvis was good for $400,000 a week. The truth was far otherwise.

Elvis had come into Vegas with a four-week contract calling for a salary of $100,000 per week. Now, Shoofey upped the offer to $125,000 a week for two months per year, with the price to hold for the next *five years.* Believe it or not, the Colonel bought it. He gave Elvis away for a price that would soon be surpassed by attractions of far less drawing power. Shoofey himself was staggered by his own success. He calls it "the best deal ever made in this town." That is probably an understatement. Consider what he got that day.

The International's showroom was rated at a capacity of 1,500. By squeezing (and paying off the fire inspectors), the room could actually accommodate two thousand. With a fifteen-dollar minimum, that comes to a minimum of $30,000 a show for the house. Figure two shows a night for twenty-eight consecutive nights, and you get a bottom figure of $1,680,000. Naturally, the room took in much more because half of these shows were dinner shows with big tabs. The gross for the month, therefore, far exceeded two million dollars—and this happened twice a year for five years. The punch line to this golden yarn is that the showroom was budgeted, as are all Las Vegas hotel entertainment facilities, to oper-ate at a *loss,* entertainment being in Vegas just one of the baits that are offered the suckers to get them to the gambling tables. You always hear about the records that Elvis established at Vegas. The record that most impressed hotel men was that Elvis Presley was the first act in the history of the resort to earn a hotel a profit on its show.

When the Colonel and Shoofey finished negotiating the big issues, they came around to the fringe benefits. Kirk Kerkorian had lured men like Shoofey to his side by offering them options on the new hotel's stock. He had instructed his manager to offer options to all the big acts that played the hotel. It was a way of binding the entertainers to the establishment, making them feel that they were working for themselves. Shoofey offered the Colonel options on twenty thousand shares of hotel stock at five dollars a share. Barbra Streisand had snapped up the stock without a moment's hesitation. Shoofey expected the Colonel to follow suit. Instead, the old man said: "Keep your stock. I don't believe in stocks." The stock soon rose to $70 a share.

The Colonel said that he would expect a bonus if they continued to do good business. Shoofey was perfectly agreeable. He was also very clever about the bonuses. Instead of setting a limit on what he would offer, he used to ask the Colonel at the end of each engagement what *he* wanted. Shoofey was counting on a modest demand. If the demand were too great, he could always try to cut it down; but if it were an appropriate sum, it would make both him and the Colonel look good if they played it like gentlemen. Shoofey was not disappointed in his reckoning. The Colonel's demands were very modest. Though Elvis made millions for the International Hotel, he never got more than $50,000 over his contract price. As for his personal expenses, they amounted to very little. The same, however, could not be said about Colonel Parker's expenses. Here, we come to the other side of the Colonel's most peculiar deal.

In selling Elvis short—and never obtaining more than $150,000 after four years of fantastic success—Colonel Parker appears to have made a colossal error of judgment. What's more, he appears to have acted completely out of character. After all, what is the Colonel's essence? Making demands! Asking for unheard-of sums of money. Squeezing the suckers for every last dime. In a word, getting *his!* Now, here we see him suddenly going for a long-term deal that he doesn't believe in on principle and which, in practice, turns out to be a bad deal, which he doesn't even seek to renegotiate. How does one explain such a thing? If the Colonel had been a ten-percenter or even a quarter-sharer, it would have been bad for him. As a fifty-fifty partner in every deal Elvis made, it looks as if he screwed himself out of a pile of money. Appearances are deceiving, however, especially when you are considering the activities of a man as devious as Tom Parker. Consider the deal from his angle.

Colonel saw from the jump that Elvis was always going to blow an enormous amount on these Las Vegas shows. He knew that the nut would never get any smaller; in fact, it was bound to get bigger and bigger as the supporting acts and the musicians increased their demands. As the Colonel's share was of the net, not of the gross earnings, no matter how hard he bargained to raise Elvis's price, his own income was never going to be anything extraordinary in Las Vegas. What he needed, therefore, was some way of getting *his*. Now, as an inveterate gambler, as, in fact, one of the highest rollers in the history of Las Vegas, the Colonel had an interest in the resort that had nothing to do with the showroom. What he really needed was a break at the casino.

Once Elvis was established at Vegas, the Colonel began to gamble on a scale that astonished everyone. The old man would drop every night between $50,000 and $75,000 on the roulette wheel and the crap table. One night Lamar Fike saw the Colonel gamble steadily for five hours. Soon, according to Alex Shoofey, the Colonel's losses amounted to at least a million dollars a year. Elvis's gross annual income never exceeded seven million dollars. Deducting expenses and taxes from this sum, the Colonel's share could never have exceeded by much what he dropped at Vegas. The question arises, therefore, how did the old man sustain this level of expenditure?

The answer is that the Colonel had mastered the art of living on nothing a year. Just consider what he got out of the International Hotel alone. The hotel provided the Colonel with a year-round three-room suite, all of his food and drink, much of his transportation costs, the food and dining paraphernalia for his Palm Springs home and—virtually unlimited credit at the casino. In turn, the Colonel kept Elvis working until the end of his life for a salary that never exceeded $150,000 per week, the figure he negotiated on the expiration of the first five-year contract. Though Elvis's contract was not an exclusive arrangement and every hotel in Las Vegas was bidding for his services after he finished his semiannual appearance at the International, Colonel never entertained such an offer for a moment. He offered his hotel a monopoly on the greatest attraction in the history of the resort in exchange for various arrangements by means of which he got *his*.

Elvis was destined to return to Las Vegas again and again in the next seven years, falling into one of those treadmill patterns that characterized his entire career. Every August and February, like clockwork, Colonel Parker would throw a switch and the machine would spring into action. At first Elvis got some pleasure from his new success. He tinkered with his image and his repertoire. When he opened for the second time, in February 1970, he had a totally new look.

Not since Marlene Dietrich stunned the ringsiders with the sight of her celebrated legs encased from hip to ankle in a transparent gown had any performer so electrified Las Vegas with his mere physical appearance. Bill Bellew, who had been very cautious up to this point about designing any costume that would make Elvis look effeminate, decided finally to kick out the jams. Now Elvis faced the house encased in a smashing white jumpsuit, slashed to the sternum and lovingly fitted around his broad shoulders, flat belly, narrow hips and tightly packed crotch. And then there were his pearls—loads of lustrous pearls, not sewn on the costume but worn unabashedly as body ornaments. Pearls coiled in thick bunches around his neck, pearls girdled his tapered waist in a fabulous karate belt, rope of pearl alternating with rope of gold, the whole sash tied over one hip with the ends dangling down to brush one knee. With his massive diamonds flashing pinks and purples from his fingers and his boyish smile flashing sheepishly through his huge shag of shiny black hair, Elvis looked like a heaping portion of male cheesecake ripe for the eyeteeth of the hundreds of women ogling him through opera glasses or lunging at the stage like gravid salmon hurtling a cataract.

Elvis also relaxed and regained his old confidence. He would kick off the show now James Brown style by collaring the mike and shaking it to the beat of "I'm All Shook Up," the kettle-drumming orchestra shaking its elephantine body behind him. Coming to the guitar break, Elvis would strum the acoustic instrument slung on a white band about his neck with the carelessness of a practiced faker. Then the number would end abruptly with the martial artist snapping into profile and thrusting his guitar bayonet-wise at the chorus.

The rest of the evening would pass smoothly as he glided through medleys of old tunes or lounged in elaborately upholstered versions of his new anthems. Every number would end with a classically struck profile, the white-clad figure with the Grecian features suggesting a space-age version of the Discus Hurler or the Laocoön. Between numbers he would offer glimpses of his wry humor: "My mouth's so dry, feels like Bob Dylan slept in it all night." Finally, the performance would come to its conclusion with the Vegas equivalent of one of those sunset-in-the-Rockies numbers from the old *Ziegfeld Follies.*

Silhouetted against a cerulian blue cyclorama, the Las Vegas Philharmonic, the front rank of black-clad, guitar-slingin' Memphis Mafiosi and the integrated chorus of the Imperials and the Sweet Inspirations would be transfigured by a flood of rich amber light pouring in from the Valley of Loose Gold. As the massed players and singers sustained a mighty cathedral chord, the Sun King would fall on one knee in the classic Jolson-gladiator pose, flinging wide his arms in a grand salute to his assembled court, which he seemed destined to reign over forever in eternal youth and jollity and jamboree.

Chapter 30

The President
Will See Mr. Presley

ELVIS was just winding up his first appearance at
Las Vegas in August of 1969 when the Sharon Tate murders burst
like a bomb in his brain. He saw in these murders a prophecy of
his own doom. As he pored over the newspaper accounts and talked
on the phone with law enforcement officials in Los Angeles, he
became obsessed with the idea that he, Priscilla and little Lisa Marie
might be the next victims of the crazy killers. Wasn't he an object
of envy and hatred? Didn't he and his family live in a cul-de-sac
up in the hills of Los Angeles, where it would be easy to enter in
the middle of the night and kill, kill, kill?

Instantly, Elvis ordered the house on Hillcrest Drive guarded
by uniformed security men night and day. He vowed to spend as
little time as possible in Los Angeles, whose inhabitants he had
said always were the biggest bunch of freaks in America. Still, the
more he thought about his danger, the less these protective measures
reassured him. Putting rent-a-cops around his Trousdale house was
not sufficient. What Elvis required was absolute security, the kind
of security that was enjoyed by the president of the United States.
The president had his uniformed guards, alarm systems and all
the mechanical protection that human ingenuity could devise. Ultimately, though, what really secured him from harm? The Secret

Service. Those neat, efficient-looking dudes in dark suits, who were sworn to put their body between the president's body and the onslaught of any assassin. That was the sort of protection that Elvis craved: a wall of human flesh. A group of men who were tough, well-trained, well-armed, totally dedicated and willing to take the bullet that was meant for him. Now, where could he find such men? It must have been with a great sense of relief that he recognized that he had them already. Sure, they were the Guys!

Some of the Guys were worthless as bodyguards. Charlie was just a little mascot. Joe was strictly for business. Lamar, if he fell on you like a Secret Service man, would kill you with his weight. Still, Elvis had some boys who were real bad-asses, like Red and Sonny West. Ole Red had been working since leaving Elvis with Bob Conrad on the TV series *Wild, Wild West.* Now that the show had gone off the air, Red had returned to Memphis where he had gotten involved with Chips Moman at the American Recording Studio. Elvis was sure he could bring Red back into the fold. Meanwhile, he had already put Sonny on the payroll. With the proper training, Sonny could become a real gunslinger. He was huge, fearless, naturally loyal and aggressive. Elvis would soon have that big boy leading his security forces with a snub-nosed Colt Python stuck up his armpit, barrel foremost, in a quick-release holster. Still, he needed a lot more hired guns.

Guns, Elvis reasoned, were really the whole secret of security. If everybody had a gun and knew how to use it, who would dare to mess with them? Elvis himself always owned guns, carried guns, shot guns and believed in guns. Now, he decided to get everybody guns. In the course of the next four years, he must have bought at least 250 guns. All the Guys carried guns. There were guns in all of Elvis's homes, in Elvis's cars, on Elvis's own person at all times. He started putting a gun next to his bed when he slept and next to his plate when he ate. There were so many guns that after a while, they lost track of them all. (Becky Yancey, one of Elvis's secretaries, remembers her husband sitting down on a sofa at Graceland one day and feeling something hard under the cushion. It was a gun.)

Elvis purchased most of these weapons himself, his favorite store being Kerr's Sporting Goods, a couple of blocks from the Beverly Wilshire Hotel, in the heart of Beverly Hills's swank shopping district. Kerr's is one of those fancy, snobbish, super-WASPy establishments, like Abercrombie & Fitch was in New York, whose clerks develop as they get older a very icy and condescending manner that virtually challenges each new customer to prove that he's good enough to deserve the store's merchandise. As these prim and alum-mouthed gentlemen of the counter saw it, to buy costly, finely crafted guns, you ought to be either an authentic sportsman, a marksman or a gun collector. It's easy to imagine the disgust the salesmen felt when Elvis would blow in, wearing his latest street costume: an all-black outfit with a high Napoleonic collar, a white four-in-hand tie, numerous gold chains and perhaps a cape and a gold-tipped ebony walking stick. Instead of examining a few weapons carefully and asking a lot of technical questions—or recalling the time when he was out in the bush and this big rhino came charging through the zanzenoobie bushes—Elvis would say, "Lemme see that one and that one and that one . . ." until he had bought every fancy engraved, inlaid, chased and gilt pistol in the case at prices that went as high as $3,500 a pop. What's more, instead of acquiring these weapons as esteemed artifacts with the intention of mounting them in special cases under glass, Elvis would heft them, sight them, load them with live ammunition and stick them under his belt. Then, he'd walk out the door, jump behind the wheel of this yellow Didamasa Pantera 265 or his black Dino Ferrari and try to beat the light!

Eventually, Elvis's collection of weapons constituted a veritable reliquary of pop culture heroes. Just by fondling these guns or strapping them on his body or, best of all, firing them, Elvis could experience the thrill of identification with his favorite military, law-enforcement or gangster types. His gilded, pearl-handled nine-millimeter Beretta automatic, for example, was the same weapon that James Bond carried, only the snobbish 007 would have turned up his nose at Elvis's gaudy model, preferring the hi-tech chic of a steel-blue barrel and a skeleton grip. Elvis's Walther PPK/S double-action automatic, so square, compact and sinister looking, with its blue-black finish and snub nose, is, like the Beretta, a favorite weapon of undercover agents, particularly the CIA. The graceful Mauser Luger, on the other hand, summons up the world of the *Wehrmacht* in the Great War: a German officer in a tight field-grey tunic with the Iron Cross dangling at his neck and his machine-pistol strapped high above his hip in an elegant enclosed holster, like a camera case. The Colt .45, of which Elvis owned many copies, likewise evokes World War I; in fact, the replicas that Elvis purchased were stamped with the dates 1917–1967, indicating that they had been manufactured to commemorate the fiftieth anniversary of this classic and klutzy weapon. Drastically different associations hallowed the nickel-plated, long-barreled Colt .44 magnum revolver. This hand cannon had been made famous by its use by Clint Eastwood in *Dirty Harry*. As soon as Elvis saw this movie, which made an enormous impression on him, he went out and bought this enormously powerful weapon, which can penetrate an engine block or even shoot down an airplane. Like Clint Eastwood, Elvis wore his .44 in a bulging shoulder holster.

Some of Elvis's weapons had very dubious associations. His antique Carl Hauptmann-Ferlach double-barreled hunting rifle was the prize weapon of Hermann Goering. A magnificent specimen of the nineteenth-century gunsmith's art, the rifle has a stock of Circassian walnut, hand-carved and inlaid in ivory carved with deer and elk; the barrel is chased in gold. Goering was a prodigious hunter who would butcher hundreds of animals in a single day, shooting from blinds past which his beaters drove whole herds of beasts. Elvis scorned hunting because it was a sport that demanded quiet, patience and cunning. The only hunting Elvis ever did was shooting snakes along a mudbank. He owned enough shot-guns and rifles, however, to have furnished the armament for an old-fashioned African safari.

Most of Elvis's weapons possessed a distinctly lethal character. They did not suggest sport, marksmanship or gun collecting so much as they did an obsession with killing human beings. He owned, for example, a .300 magnum assassination rifle that broke down to fit inside an attaché case. Naturally, it was equipped with a telescopic sight. Elvis owned also some very intimidating machine guns. He possessed an early model of a .22 caliber machine gun with a horizontal drum, the design of a famous gunsmith, Dick Casule of Salt Lake City. With this weapon, now widely used by the police, a lone man could lay down a tremendous barrage, all of it quite deadly at short range. Elvis's prize automatic weapon was his classic 1927 Thompson submachine gun, the original Tommy Gun, with the perpendicular drum and the slotted muzzle brake to reduce the bucking recoil from the big .45 caliber shells. This gun was obtained for Elvis by his friends in the Chicago Mob.

In some periods of his life, Elvis was a pretty good shot with a handgun. It all depended on how much he practiced. Here he experienced a certain difficulty, for as the district around Graceland became thickly settled, Elvis's middle-class neighbors began to complain every time he and the Guys would indulge in an orgy of shoot-'em-up target practice. The shooting was done, to be sure, under rather unsafe conditions. Adjoining the low building in the backyard of Graceland that was used for an office was an old smokehouse. Elvis had installed inside the door of this wooden structure two rows of sawed-off telephone poles that sustained targets shaped like human silhouettes. The idea was that all the spent or ricocheting bullets would be caught inside the shed and not fly loose so that they could cause injury. The problem was that the power of the weapons that Elvis was firing was so great that sometimes the bullets would drill through the walls and carry many yards before they fell to the ground. These red-hot slugs also had incendiary properties. Once Elvis set the building afire with a prolonged burst from an M16.

When the neighbors' complaints about the constant gunfire at Graceland had brought the police to his door a score of times, Elvis reacted as he did always in such situations: He vowed that he would make himself proof against complaint even if he took it into his head to fire his guns all night long. A contractor was summoned and plans were drawn for a four-stall firing range that would be sunk nine feet below ground in the backyard. When it came time to begin the excavation, Elvis lost interest in the project. It joined the circular movie theater, the recording studio, the helicopter pad and all the other dream projects that were designed at one time or another for this same backyard.

Shooting at targets, no matter how you did it, could never rival the pleasure of shooting at human beings: the most dangerous game. So Elvis introduced a new sport at Graceland that deserved the title War far more than his old collision combats at the Rainbow Rollerdome. The new version of War was fought by teams armed with explosive fireworks. First, the Guys would drive over to West Memphis in Arkansas, where fireworks were legal, and buy two or three thousand dollars' worth of Roman candles, skyrockets, baby giants, firecrackers and "nigger chasers"—jet-propelled snakes that took fast, unpredictable turns along the ground until they exploded. Then, they would don air force jumpsuits, with gloves, helmets and goggles. Dividing themselves into Red and Blue teams, they would face off at point-blank range with as many as twelve Roman candles in each hand and engage in two- or three-hour shootouts.

Invariably, there were painful and sometimes serious injuries. Richard Davis almost lost an eye once when a ball of flaming phosphorus struck him in the face. Elvis had a big scar on his neck from a hot shot that slipped down his collar and burnt him fearfully. As with so many of Elvis's games—the skate battles, the daredeviltry on the roller coaster, the midnight racing in cars and on motorcycles—the fun was edged with terror. Elvis seems never to have enjoyed himself fully unless he was tempting fate to roll him a seven.

Once Elvis got on his gun kick, guns became, after cars, his favorite gift item. He gave guns not only to the Guys but to the men he most admired, like President Nixon, to whom Elvis presented one of his commemorative Colt .45s, and Spiro Agnew, for whom Elvis selected a Colt .357 snub-nosed magnum.[1] Though you might expect that a heavy macho type like Elvis Presley would think that guns were exclusively a man's prerogative, you would be completely wrong. Elvis gave many guns to women, insisting that they ran no risk from the law in carrying weapons concealed in their purses because any real he-man lawman would respect a lady's desire to protect herself from injury or dishonor. This passing out of guns to girls became so habitual with Elvis that every time he dismissed a young woman with whom he had spent the night, he would give her with his farewell kiss a sinister looking .38 Python. As Elvis saw it, guns are a girl's best friend.

When Chemical Mace was made available for civilian use, Elvis bought dozens of canisters and distributed them among the women in the group, as well as to his female employees. Unfortunately, the little gold-finished canisters got mixed up sometimes with other items in the ladies' purses. When Elvis opened at the Sahara Tahoe in July 1971, he arranged to have Priscilla, Norah Fike, Joanie Esposito and Judy West flown up from Los Angeles aboard a Lear jet. As the plane was preparing to land, Priscilla asked Judy: "Do you have your breath spray?" Judy reached inside her bag and pulled out the dispenser. Opening her own mouth wide, she pushed down on the release—and gave herself a searing and asphyxiating blast of Chemical Mace! As she screamed and gasped for breath, the vapor from the dispenser spread through the cabin, causing all the other women to start coughing and crying. Drifting further, through the open door to the pilot's cabin, the irritating mist produced the same symptoms in the crew, which was now in the midst of its landing maneuvers. Taking the ship aloft again, the pilots circled the airport until the air cleared.

When Judy came staggering off the plane, everyone was shocked by her appearance. She looked like a purple-snouted mandrill. The Mace contained an indelible dye designed to mark fugitive "perpetrators" so they could be easily identified and captured. The injury to her vanity was transitory; the painful chemical burn she suffered in her mouth produced permanent scarring. When Elvis heard the story, he laughed. What the hell! He didn't tell her to shoot herself in the mouth, did

---

[1] Agnew declined his gun, explaining that a public official could not accept gifts from a citizen.

he? Nonetheless, he changed his policy with regard to issuing dispensers of Chemical Mace. Now he insisted that the canisters be finished in black.

Elvis's security mania soon stirred up one of his oldest and deepest fantasies: his longing to be a highway patrolman. After he got out of high school, his ambition was to qualify for the force when he reached his twenty-first birthday. Now that he was nearing his thirty-fifth birthday, he finally realized his long-deferred aspiration. First, he had himself appointed a special deputy to the sheriff of Shelby County, the politically ambitious William N. "Bill" Morris. When a new sheriff, Roy C. Nixon, took office in October 1970, Elvis had himself reappointed as chief special deputy. Subsequently, he persuaded Nixon, who was destined soon to become mayor of Memphis, to deputize all the Guys, including Vernon and Dr. Nichopolous. These appointments entitled them to receive official identification cards, wear a badge and carry a concealed weapon. The presentation of badges didn't end there, however. At Christmas, Sheriff Nixon and Elvis's friends presented Shelby County's most famous deputy with a gold belt buckle that bore a replica of his sheriff's star engraved with his number, six, and encrusted with diamonds. Elvis presented the sheriff, in turn, with a pistol.

Having made such a good start at becoming at last a shield-wearing peace officer, Elvis was inspired now to acquire comparable badges and credentials from all parts of the country. Soon he had obtained through Colonel Parker's influence the badge of the Palm Springs police department. With the aid of his powerful attorney, Ed Hookstratten, Elvis became a member of the Beverly Hills police department. Eventually, he would carry about with him a leather attaché case into whose lining had been fixed no less than thirty different badges, representing as many communities or law enforcement agencies, including even the Canadian Mounted Police. Elvis treated his badges exactly like a kid who collects bubble gum cards or postage stamps: He would give an expensive gift to a captain in Denver so that he could "trade up" from lieutenant to captain in that town, with the ultimate goal being to cop the chief's badge. Though the badges were treated like pop bottle caps, they were potent symbols of authority. They offered Elvis a marvelous opportunity to misrepresent himself as an authentic law enforcement official, an advantage he employed on numerous occasions, stopping airliners at the point of take-off, countermanding the orders of local police officers and threatening with arrest anybody who got in his way.

Once he had his deputy's star, Elvis began hankering after another important symbol of office: the blue identification lamp that is used in Tennessee by the police when they are working out of an unmarked car. After pulling a few strings, Elvis obtained Sheriff Nixon's very own blue flasher. Now, fully equipped at last, patrolman Presley embarked on his long-deferred career.

Picture the scene. You are driving along a road on the outskirts of Memphis and exceeding the speed limit by ten or fifteen miles an hour. You glance in the rearview mirror and are startled to see rapidly overtaking you a mysterious midnight-blue Mercedes sedan with a blue light flashing imperatively from its dashboard. Without a moment's hesitation, you apply the brakes and pull over on the shoulder of the road. The Mercedes pulls to a stop beside you. Out the window on the driver's side appears the head of Elvis Presley. "Sir," says the world-famous superstar, "do you realize how fast you were travelin'? We got a law in this town, and we aim to see that it's kept." Then, holding up his sheriff's badge to make the proper impression of authority, Elvis continues: "I'm putting you on warning now. If you are caught speeding again, you will be subject to arrest and fine. Blah, blah, blah." Then, having laid down the law to the astounded motorist, Elvis cranks up his powerful car and speeds off in search of more lawbreakers.

It's not likely that anyone stopped by Elvis in Memphis would fail to recognize the city's most famous native son; this same instant identifiability didn't always hold in other parts of the country. Elvis's stepbrother, Rick Stanley, recalls driving along the freeway in Los Angeles with Elvis in his Dino Ferrari and coming upon a wreck at the side of the road. Elvis stopped his car immediately, got out and approached the policeman who had taken charge of the situation. Introducing himself and offering to be of assistance, Elvis was anticipating a warm welcome. Instead, the cop rounded on him and snarled: "Man, I don't care *who* you are—just get in your car and get out of here!" Actually, you can't blame the cop. Here he is hard at work, when out of the blue comes some fat freak in a Prince Valiant costume claiming to be Elvis Presley! Now, what the hell would anybody do but tell this Hollywood weirdo to get back in his Batmobile and split? Elvis was so shocked by the cop's command that he jumped back in the car and roared off. As he drove away, though, he mumbled angrily, "Tell *me* what to do! *Me,* a federal agent!"

Yes, Elvis's career in law enforcement had carried him to the top of the profession in a rise almost as spectacular as that of his early years in the music business. In just one year, Elvis rose from the lowly position of deputy sheriff of a county in western Tennessee to that of agent in one of the federal government's most exciting and glamorous anticrime forces: the Bureau of Narcotics and Dangerous Drugs. Even more impressive is the fact that having received his first appointment from a local sheriff, he received his last from the president of the United States: Richard Milhous Nixon. As this story has never been told before in all its bizarre detail, we have to begin early in 1970, when Elvis got very friendly with a former sergeant-in-charge of the Los Angeles police department's narcotics squad, John O'Grady.

O'Grady came into Elvis's life when Ed Hookstratten recommended that Elvis hire the ex-cop, now a private eye, to investigate a North Hollywood waitress named Pat Parker who had brought a paternity suit against the star. The suit was based on false and preposterous accusations, but it entailed a lot of pretrial preparations: lie detector and blood tests, background investigations, depositions, etc. During this time Elvis got tight with his new private investigator, a man with a very colorful background and a talent for spinning tales, as his entertaining book, *O'Grady,* testifies.

During the fifties, when he was "The Big O," the terror of Sunset Strip, the most gung-ho narc on the West Coast, O'Grady racked up an incredible total of 2,500 busts of drug dealers and drug users. His specialty was busting jazz musicians, whom he detested especially because as youth heroes they set a bad example for the younger generation. O'Grady felt exactly the same way about drug-using rock stars, but he made an exception for Elvis Presley.

To the veteran narc, it was obvious from the first that Elvis was a "hype." In the course of their initial meeting at O'Grady's office on the Sunset Strip, Elvis rose to go to the men's room and walked straight into a wall. Yet, it was just as clear that Elvis was a passionate believer in law enforcement, especially the rigorous enforcement of the drug laws. O'Grady decided to resolve this ambivalence by involving Elvis at every opportunity in police work. He imagined that the more Elvis learned about drugs, the greater his fear or his shame would become, until eventually he would renounce the stuff. What O'Grady could not imagine was that Elvis was perfectly comfortable leading a double life in which at one moment he was going out to bust a bunch of dope-smoking hippies and the next he was using all his wiles to con some druggist or doctor into giving him an illegal prescription for some dangerous and strictly controlled drug.

O'Grady did succeed, even beyond his wildest dreams, in making

Elvis a dedicated champion of drug-law enforcement. Night after night, he would sit with his client recounting an endless series of fascinating stories about raids and busts, undercover work out on the street and famous entertainers who were really hypes. Elvis, who reacted to this sudden opening of a new and mysterious world in much the same way that he did to the appearance of the Swami, would sit spellbound, urging O'Grady on to further revelations of secret police techniques. Soon, Elvis had become so infatuated with his new friend that after every story, he would sigh wistfully and say, "Man, I wish I could be an undercover narcotics detective!" O'Grady, giving his glass of Jack Daniels a swish, would reply with his customary deadpan sarcasm: "I wish I could be Elvis Presley."

Though the tough ex-cop made light of Elvis's dreams of joining the LAPD as an undercover man, Elvis's hankering for this new role, this new thrill, became obsessive. One night Elvis was seated in an upstairs room at the La Scala Restaurant on Santa Monica Boulevard with Priscilla, Joe, Charlie, Sonny and O'Grady. The maitre d' came to the table and told Elvis that Paul Newman's kids would like to meet him. "Fuck Paul Newman and his kids!" burst out Elvis, who had run into the actor recently at Kerr's and become convinced that Newman, preoccupied with his shopping, was snubbing him. With that sort of reaction fresh in his mind, you wouldn't expect that O'Grady would have reacted positively when, a little later, a waiter came to the table and whispered in the eye's ear that Paul Frees was downstairs and was eager to come up and meet Elvis.

Frees is a man both known and unknown to every TV watcher and radio listener in America. He is the voice of the Pillsbury Doughboy, the Pittsburgh Paint Peacock, Kellogg's Toucan Sam, Walt Disney's Ludwig Von Drake, Captain Crunch, Boris Badenov, Inspector Fenwick and so on through a thousand and one commercials, animations and narratives for the past thirty-five years. If this had been all that Frees had to recommend him, however, he would not have gained an audience that night with the King. What made O'Grady turn around and start talking up this old acquaintance to Elvis was the little known fact that Frees was America's foremost police buff.

For years the invisible man with the ubiquitous voice had been performing at police benefits, contributing to police charities and cutting into cops like O'Grady, who would reciprocate by taking Frees out on drug raids. As Frees earned a million dollars a year and the narcs were often reduced to scrounging for wheels, O'Grady would sometimes throw his surplus prisoners into Frees's Rolls-Royce for conveyance to the station house. O'Grady estimates that in drug-saturated Marin County, Frees must have participated in at least two hundred raids. In fact, it wasn't long before his meeting with Elvis that Frees had become the recipient of a remarkable honor bestowed upon him by the Bureau of Narcotics and Dangerous Drugs at the behest of its special counsel, John Dean. With all this background at his fingertips, O'Grady didn't have much trouble in getting Elvis to agree to meet this remarkably interesting but oddly mysterious character.

The man who appeared next was short, stocky, middle-aged and flashily dressed with a massive gold chain swagged across his vest. His head was leonine, the hair brushed forward across the bald brows, the eyes masked with big shades and the golden mouth covered by a thick, brushy RAF mustache. If you didn't know who he was, you might have mistaken him for a South American don. Elvis was intrigued by him immediately, and soon the two flamboyantly attired vocal virtuosos were engrossed in conversation.

They found common ground in their mutual hatred for rock groups like the Beatles, who sang about drugs and used drugs and by their example encouraged millions of kids to become heads. Elvis explained that this was all part of a Communist conspiracy to weaken America by undermining the morals and health of the youth. He then went on to attack stars like Jane Fonda, who in his opinion were "Communist sympathizers," or stars who exhibited a profound scorn for lawfully constituted authority, like the Smothers Brothers.

Once the similarity of their opinions had brought the men into an amiable intimacy, Elvis asked Frees if he could demonstrate some of his famous voices. Frees, a born performer and master of a hundred shticks, obliged instantly. As the table roared with delight, like children at a birthday party, the vocal magician segued effortlessly from his March of Time Stentor to his kooky Nutty Peanuts to his bemused ole Cap'n Crunch to his slyly humorous Inspector Fenwick to all the twerpy little villagers in the Green Giant commercials, until he got down finally to the voice of a disgruntled ant, who sounded exactly like the late Ned Sparks.

Once the show was over, O'Grady suggested that Frees do an encore. As everyone present was united in a common loathing for junkies, pushers and drug smugglers, what would be the harm if Frees were to show Elvis and his family his "credential"? At that point, Frees reached inside his jacket and produced a flat leather case like a passport wallet. Flipping

it open, he laid under Elvis's nose a remarkable document. It was emblazoned with the official seal of the Department of Justice and the insignia
of the Bureau of Narcotics and Dangerous Drugs. It displayed an identification photo of Frees, along with his fingerprints and vital statistics. It
was signed by John E. Ingersoll, the director of the drug agency. The
most impressive feature of this credential was the title it bestowed on
its bearer. It informed the reader that Paul Frees was an "agent at large"
of the Department of Justice. In other words, this fifty-five-year-old radio-
TV entertainer, this million-dollar-a-year residuals tycoon, was a full-
fledged federal narc with ambassadorial privileges and immunities.

O'Grady, who practically drooled with envy every time he ogled
this "beautiful credential," explained its full purport to Elvis. At that
moment, Elvis realized that instead of having to sate his cop lust by
collecting dinky shields, like those of a deputy sheriff of Shelby County
or a member of the Palm Springs police department, he could have
the boss badge. He could go after the magic emblem of a federal narc!
Gazing raptly at the document, as if he were beholding the Holy Grail
or the Shroud of Turin, Elvis murmured: "There isn't much that I've
got that I wouldn't give to have one of those!"

The Saturday before Christmas, 1970, Elvis gave the folks at Graceland a stunning exhibition of how a narc goes underground. On that
day, Elvis got into a big fight with Vernon and Priscilla over the issue
of his Christmas shopping. Vernon had just received some shocking
bills from Los Angeles. At Kerr's, Elvis had bought thirty-two handguns,
including a gold-inlaid .357 Colt Python ($1,950) and a gold-plated .44
Ruger Blackhawk ($1,850). The other weapons had ranged in price from
a thousand dollars down to sixty-six dollars for a tiny, two-shot over-
and-under Derringer. The total bill for handguns was $19,792. This was
nothing, however, compared to the bills from the car dealers. Elvis had
purchased *ten* Mercedes sedans, which he planned to give away like
three-speed bikes. This tab added up to $85,000!

Elvis could never bear to be challenged about anything and especially
could he not tolerate criticism of his spending sprees. Vernon and Priscilla, on the other hand, were both as tight with a buck as Elvis was
prodigal. Elvis's spending alarmed and horrified them in precisely the
same degree that it made him feel happy and fulfilled. They were always
at war about money. This day would have been no different from many
others if Elvis had not seized the opportunity to punish both his father
and his wife while at the same time giving himself a rare thrill.

Rushing up to his room, he dressed himself in one of his most extravagant and swashbuckling costumes. He donned a purple crushed-velvet suit and cape, with the immense gold-buckled belt bestowed on him by the International Hotel for breaking all attendance records. Slipping a massive Colt .45 into his shoulder holster and a Derringer in his boot, he topped off the outfit with a jeweled white cane. Stalking out of the house, he jumped in a car and drove to the airport alone. Walking up to the American Airlines counter, he asked when the next plane was leaving. Informed that a Washington flight would soon depart, Elvis bought a ticket with his gold star American Express Card and allowed himself to be ushered into the VIP lounge.

At this point, Elvis must have felt like he was flying around in outer space. Never before had he left the city alone. Only the heady game of Undercover Narc could ever have inspired such derring-do. Merely being *alone* must nearly have given him the bends.

Once he settled into his room at the Washington Hotel, a drab old establishment near the White House, his mood began to change. Sure, it had been fun, riding in a cab. Fun when he ordered the driver to stop at the doughnut joint, where some dumb "nigger" recognized him and screamed about the diamonds on his hands. Elvis had told that black boy that he aimed to keep all his diamonds—then he gave him an eyeful of the .45 under his arm. The best fun was when he registered at the hotel desk. He had used the name Colonel Jon Burrows, which was a variation of the name Colonel Parker always used when he didn't want to reveal his identity.

When Elvis settled down in front of that hotel room TV, the manic phase of the high began to wear off. Here he was, the most popular man in the world, and he didn't know a soul. Finally, he got an inspiration. Why not fly out to L.A.? Picking up the phone, he put through a call to London Towne Livery Service in Beverly Hills. This was a limousine service that Elvis used often. It was operated by a British actor, Gerald Peters, who has appeared in scores of movies and TV shows playing immaculately groomed and utterly imperturbable English butlers. Elvis, who had a nickname for everyone, called Peters "Sir Gerald." It was late Saturday night when Peters received a call from a Mr. Jones in Washington, D.C. The first thing that Mr. Jones wanted to know was whether Peters was alone. When Peters confirmed that he was alone, the voice on the other end of the line said, "Do you know who this is?" "Why, you're Mr. Jones, sir," replied Peters instinctively. The voice, suddenly shrinking to a whisper, responded: "Sir Gerald, it's *me!* Are you sure you're alone?" Recognizing his caller now as Elvis Presley,

Peters assured him that he was alone, though now he suddenly realized why he had been receiving calls all evening from Elvis's men in Memphis and Los Angeles pretending to be motivated entirely by sociability but asking a lot of pointed questions about the whereabouts of the Mercedes limousine which Peters rented from Elvis when the star was out of town.

"I'm flying into L.A. tonight, arriving at three in the morning," continued Elvis. "Will you meet me?" Peters, concerned by his client's strange manner, replied by asking him if anything were wrong. Elvis reassured him, but he ordered Peters to say, if he received any inquiring calls, that he had not heard from Elvis. "Very good, sir!" sang out Sir Gerald to the King.

Elvis could not long survive without the supportive presence of the Guys. He decided now to call Jerry Schilling, who was not currently on the payroll but working as a film editor in Hollywood. Jerry agreed to meet Elvis at the airport that morning. When Elvis disembarked from the plane, he was accompanied by two TWA stewardesses, one on either arm. He was not feeling well: one eye was infected and his face seemed slightly swollen. As soon as they arrived at the house on Hillcrest Road, a doctor appeared and gave Elvis a shot that knocked him out till the next afternoon. That day when Gerald Peters reported for work, Elvis told him the story of his quarrel with Vernon and Priscilla. Peters recalls that Elvis sounded just like a bewildered little boy as he said: "I can't understand it, Sir Gerald. Why were they so mad at me? It was *my* money. I earned it."

Now that Elvis had recovered from his journey, he decided it was time to turn around and fly back to Washington. He wanted Jerry to accompany him. Jerry said that he was due to report for work on a new job Monday morning and that if he didn't show up, he might be fired. Elvis acted hurt. Jerry felt guilty. As always Elvis's selfish whim took precedence. At ten that night when he took off for Washington, Elvis had his baby-sitter in the next seat.

On the same Red-eye Special was Senator George Murphy. Soon the famous singer and the old hoofer were deep in conversation. Elvis explained that he was bound for the nation's capital to offer his services to the government in the war against drugs. He planned to pay a call at the Bureau of Narcotics and Dangerous Drugs and then seek a meeting with J. Edgar Hoover. Could Murphy give him a hand? The Senator replied that he would make an appointment for Elvis the following morning with the director of BNDD, John E. Ingersoll, and also call the offices of the F.B.I. Encouraged by this unlooked-for support, Elvis now got a real inspiration. He decided that while he was in Washington, he would make an effort to see President Nixon. As there was no time to arrange this meeting through intermediaries, Elvis would request an appointment himself.

He set to work at once and wrote a letter to Nixon. He explained the dangers the country faced from entertainers like the Beatles and Jane Fonda. He offered to throw his own weight onto the other side of the scale. Then he rounded off the note with a request for an immediate appointment, stating that he could be reached at the Washington Hotel, where he was registered as Colonel Jon Burrows. As soon as Elvis and Schilling got off the plane, they drove to the gates of the White House where Elvis, dressed still in his bizarre costume, got out of the car and introduced himself to the guard. Handing the smiling but perplexed sentry the letter, Elvis got back in his car and drove on to the hotel.

At this point, Jerry Schilling demanded that Elvis allow him to call Graceland to assure the people there that Elvis was safe and also to summon Sonny West, Elvis's bodyguard, to Washington so that Schilling could fly back to Los Angeles and salvage his job. While these arrangements were being made, Elvis went off to the Justice Building for his keenly anticipated meeting with the top narc. As it turned out, he had to make do with the deputy director of the drug agency, John Finlator.

One can picture Elvis sitting beside Finlator's desk, like a naive but idealistic pupil explaining to the school principal why all the students should be organized at once into companies, platoons and squads so that they could drill every day and prepare to defend their country. When Elvis wound up his pitch by requesting that he be given a BNDD badge to facilitate the good work he intended to do with the youth of America, the official replied that such a request ran directly counter to government regulations. Only bona fide agents of the Bureau could be issued the Bureau's badges. Finlator was also obliged to decline the offer of a cash donation from Elvis: $5,000—to an agency whose annual budget was about fifty million dollars. When the meeting ended, Elvis was just where he should have been: standing in the office of the drug agency with egg on his face.

When Elvis phoned Schilling at the hotel to report the failure of his mission, he received electrifying news. Schilling had just put down the phone after receiving a call from the White House. He had just been speaking with the President's secretary. "The President will see Mr. Presley." That's what the woman had said! Can you dig it! Nixon had cleared time on his schedule just so he could see Elvis that day. The letter had turned the trick!

Why was Nixon so eager to see Elvis? Clearly, it is to the advantage of any politician, even the president, to press the palm of a great celebrity. But to drop the business of state on the spur of the moment and give his undivided attention to a rock 'n' roll singer—that goes a bit beyond the usual behavior of even the most celebrity-conscious president. No, the reason Elvis got such a royal welcome that day at the White House was quite specific. As always, Elvis's unconscious timing was perfect.

Richard Nixon was poised to launch at that very moment a mighty new crusade against drugs. He planned to label drug abuse "America's Number One Problem." Not content with just denouncing drugs or beefing up the federal drug budget, Nixon was already planning to set up a drug superagency, modeled along the lines of the F.B.I. and the C.I.A., called the Drug Enforcement Agency. The cost of this new secret police force would be staggering. By Fiscal Year 1974, Nixon would have raised the drug law enforcement budget 1,100 percent above what it was when he took office in 1968. From $69 million in FY 1969, the crusade against drugs would inflate this cost by FY 1974 to an astounding $719 million. Now, just as he is about to sound the clarion call to the nation—which kept insisting foolishly that there were bigger problems than drugs, like the war in Vietnam—along comes one of the greatest heroes of American youth, Elvis Presley, America's Number One Entertainer, proposing to talk to the Number One American about America's Number One Problem! No wonder Nixon cleared some time in his crowded schedule. This was an opportunity for a real summit!

Nixon's right-hand man in the new drug crusade was a young zealot with an oddly ornithological name: Egil Krogh. When Elvis, Jerry and Sonny (who arrived in the nick of time) were ushered into the Oval Office, they were met outside the door by Krogh. He told the Guys that they would have to wait in the adjoining Federal Building because if more than one visitor joined the President at a time, special security measures were required. The Guys were disappointed because Elvis had promised them that they would meet the President; but they marched off behind an aide, Jeff Donfeld, to await the outcome of the historic confrontation.

When Elvis walked into the Oval Office, he was high as a kite. He had cranked up on speed for this great moment. He was also exhibiting the signs of another drug problem in the red and itchy rash which had developed in the past twenty-four hours over his face and neck. Eager to look cool and in command, Elvis had topped off his cape and cane outfit with a pair of amber-tinted shades. When Nixon got a load of Elvis's fancy threads, he said, "You dress pretty wild, don't you?"

Without dropping a beat, Elvis answered: "Mr. President, you got your show to run and I got mine!" That took care of that issue. Actually, as Elvis looked over Nixon, with his bent back, neck-brace posture and long, jowly face, he must have felt he was back on the Ed Sullivan show.[1]

Elvis's rap began with the advocacy of himself as "living proof that America is the land of opportunity." Overnight, he had gone from truck driver to superstar, proving the reality of the American dream. Now, he explained, his greatest concern was with the youth of America, who had been seduced into drugs and immorality by the "filthy, unkempt appearance and suggestive music of the Beatles." Likewise, he inveighed against the Smothers Brothers, Jane Fonda and others of their ilk, who had "poisoned young minds by disparaging the United States in their public statements and unsavory activities." Now, Elvis claimed, he was devoting much of his free time to meeting with small groups of young people, including "anti-establishment" college students, and using his authority to change their ways and solve their problems. (He neglected to say that these little groups were invariably composed of good-looking girls and their greatest problem was that they were not permitted to remove their white panties.) Elvis, was, therefore, ideally suited to become the President's ambassador to troubled youth.

As Elvis delivered this inspiring speech, marred only by his incessant scratching and rubbing of his drug-inflamed face and neck, Richard Nixon must have been profoundly gratified. He not only agreed that Elvis had the power to work miracles with youth, he told Elvis that any time he desired he could exchange his career in show business for an equally successful career in politics. Already former entertainers like Senator George Murphy and Governor Ronald Reagan had demonstrated the power of showbiz in the political arena. What was their power in comparison to Elvis's power, the power of the "King"? There was just one rule that he must never forget, warned Nixon, raising a minatory finger: "Never lose your credibility."

Oh, it was a marvelous meeting, a great coming together of matching

---

[1] Future generations will howl with laughter when the tape-recorded interview of Nixon and Presley is finally released as the comedy album of the year. Meantime, we have to make do with a rough reconstruction of this historic event. Fortunately, just ten days after Elvis visited the White House, on December 21, he paid a visit to F.B.I. headquarters and a memorandum of his interview with the Bureau's Assistant Director, Thomas E. Bishop, was prepared for the benefit of his chief, J. Edgar Hoover. As Elvis invariably made everything he did into a routine, we are justified in assuming that the tone and substance of his remarks to the F.B.I. director echoed his line with the President.

minds. Why, they were like two politicians with the same constituency—
what Nixon had so poetically characterized as "the Silent Majority."
Now Nixon realized that the Silent Majority had found its voice in
Elvis Presley.

Finally, the moment came when Elvis turned to the President and
told him that if he were to accomplish the greatest amount of good in
this new crusade to free the nation's youth of the curse of drugs, he
should be able to carry the badge of a full-fledged federal narcotics agent.
Nixon smiled and said wistfully, "I don't have much power around here,
you know. I'm really just a figurehead. Getting you a badge, though,
is one thing I can do!" With that, he switched on his intercom and
gave the order to have a BNDD badge and a complete set of credentials
prepared immediately for Elvis Presley.

Elvis thanked the President and then made one more modest request.
Would the nation's leader agree to take another minute to meet Elvis's
personal bodyguards, the men who watched over him night and day?
Nixon agreed and his receptionist was ordered to summon Jerry Schilling
and Sonny West. While the boys were on their way to the Oval Office,
Nixon excused himself for a moment so that he might sign a stack of
documents that had just been laid on his desk. As Elvis wandered around
the Oval Office, taking in the chintz-covered furniture, the pictures of
Nixon and Ike on the wall, the fire in the grate and the impressive
stand of flags flanking the President's desk, he kept watching Nixon
out of the corner of his eye. Imagine his astonishment when, after signing
the papers on his desk, the President turned to the aide waiting to remove
the documents and said: "What was this I just signed?" Elvis would
repeat that story till the day he died.

Over in the Federal Building, meantime, the call from the Oval Office
had been received by Jeff Donfeld. As Jerry and Sonny sat there watching,
they saw their guide pick up the instrument and say: "Yes . . . yes
. . . well, I'll be damned!" Then, he announced, "Fellas—you're goin'
to see the President!"

See him is exactly what they did. When the doors of the Oval Office
were opened, the President was standing at his desk reading a document,
just as if this were a scene in a movie. Jerry and Sonny were so awestruck
that they didn't dare to move. Elvis had to go to them and practically
haul them into the room. As soon as the introductions were made, Nixon
balled up his fist and gave Sonny a friendly shot in the shoulder, remarking
to Elvis, "Boy, you've got a couple of big ones here! I'll bet they take
good care of you." "Yes, sir!" echoed Elvis.

Pictures of everyone standing together were snapped now by the White House photographer. Then, Nixon presented the boys with pairs of cufflinks stamped with the presidential seal. The historic meeting was over—only Elvis wasn't quite satisfied. "Sir," he confided, leaning in toward the President—"they have wives, too." "Oh, of course!" bumbled Nixon, repairing to his desk, from which he extracted a pair of pins with the presidential seal. Now, all smiles, the King of Rock 'n' Roll concluded his audience by presenting the President of the United States of America with a deadly-looking Colt .45.

Ten days later, Elvis was back in Washington with his entire entourage for another visit to the Justice Building, this time to the headquarters of the F.B.I. Elvis and the Memphis Mafia were scheduled to receive what the F.B.I. described as a "very special" tour of the Bureau's facilities and Elvis was to have a private meeting with the Assistant Director, Thomas E. Bishop. Hours were consumed in visiting the various laboratories, record-keeping facilities, firing range, etc. Like visitors to a distillery, who are offered from time to time samples of the product, VIPs at the F.B.I. get to examine a Manlicher Carcano of the type that was used to assassinate President Kennedy and, as a special treat, they are invited to don ear protectors and fire the G-man's trademark weapon, the Tommy Gun. Naturally, it is an iron-bound rule that visitors must surrender on entering the building any weapons they may be carrying. Elvis decided to see if he could get away with violating this rule. He had nearly completed the inspection tour when his concealed weapon was revealed in a most embarrassing manner. Leaning over a water cooler, his two-shot Derringer slipped out of his breast pocket and landed squarely in the wet basin. The escorting agents were blasé about the infraction. In fact, they claimed they knew all along that Elvis was "packin' heat" because of the way he carried his left shoulder.

All this rubbernecking was interesting, but the real payoff for the visit was Elvis's appointment with Hoover's assistant director. What Elvis had in mind for the F.B.I. was something a little heavier than just his customary denunciations of Commies and junkies. As he got deep into his rap, he offered to help the Bureau in its work. Speaking of the people in show business "whose motives and goals he is convinced are not in the best interests of this country," Elvis volunteered, according to an F.B.I. memo, "to make such information available to the Bureau on a confidential basis whenever it came to his attention." Slashing through the bureaucratic gobblydegook you could sum it all up in one line: Elvis offered to work as an *informer.*

The interview concluded with Elvis paying fervent tribute to J. Edgar Hoover. "Presley noted," according to the memo prepared after the occasion for the Director, "that in his opinion no one has ever done as much for his country as has Mr. Hoover, and that he, Presley, considers the Director the 'greatest living American.' " This paean led up to an urgent request for a face-to-face interview with the "greatest living American," Elvis giving as his contact "Col. Jon Burrows, 3764 Highway 51 South [the address of Graceland], Memphis, Tenn., telephone EX7-4427."

Elvis left F.B.I. headquarters confident that he would soon meet the legendary Director. If he had been able to read what the Assistant Director reported to his boss, Elvis would have been highly indignant. "Presley's sincerity and good intentions notwithstanding," wrote Bishop, "he is certainly not the type of individual whom the Director would wish to meet. It is noted at present that he is wearing his hair down to his shoulders and indulges in the wearing of all sorts of exotic dress." *Sartor resartus.*

Just one year after the Tate-LoBianca murders, Elvis was suddenly faced with the deadly threat for which he had so long been steeling himself. On August 26, 1970, the chief of security at the International Hotel in Las Vegas (where Elvis had opened two weeks before) received a call from a man who identified himself as "Jim Reeds." He said that he had information that Elvis was to be kidnapped that night by two men who had attended a party with Elvis prior to his departure from Los Angeles. The next afternoon, Colonel Parker received a call from a man with a southern accent who said that Elvis would be kidnapped that weekend. The following night, this series of threats reached its climax with a call of a more disturbing character. Joe Esposito's wife, Joanie, who was at home in Los Angeles, received an anonymous call, actually two calls, in the course of which a whole extortion scheme was presented. The unknown voice said that a madman who felt that Elvis had "done him wrong about a year ago" was on his way at that moment to Las Vegas, armed with a gun that had a silencer and bent on murdering Elvis. The caller demanded $50,000 in small bills in exchange for the killer's name and license number.

Nothing was said to Elvis about these threats for fear that he would not be able to perform. Colonel Parker and Joe Esposito got in touch with the local F.B.I. agent, as did Ed Hookstratten, who believed that the threats were associated with the paternity suit against Elvis that was still in progress. The F.B.I. man was impressed by the fact that the anonymous caller had been able to learn Joe Esposito's unlisted number in Los Angeles; otherwise, he saw no cause for alarm.

A few days later, one of the Guys went down to the lobby to collect the group's mail, which was kept in a special box behind the registration desk. In the mail, he discovered a showroom menu bearing Elvis's picture on which had been drawn a gun pointing at Elvis's head. Some sort of message was printed beside the gun, but it could not be deciphered until it was recognized as mirror writing. Putting the menu up against a looking glass, the words became legible. They read: "Guess who, and where?" This time the F.B.I. man said, "We have to take this one seriously."

Seriously is exactly how Elvis had been taking the possibility of assassination for a long time. So serious had he been that he had armed everyone in his entourage, drilled himself and them at the firing range, sent Sonny West to school at the sheriff's office in Memphis and worked out the most elaborate security arrangements with the International Hotel that human ingenuity could suggest or money could buy. Now that the threat that had inspired all these precautions had materialized, you might suppose that Elvis would derive some comfort from the fact that he was so well prepared. Nothing of the kind!

Elvis reacted as if he were standing naked before the killer's gun. He panicked. He broke down, sobbing uncontrollably and crying, "Why would anyone want to kill me?" He called to his aid every tough guy he could recruit. Karate coach Ed Parker was flown in from Los Angeles. Red West was brought in from Memphis. When Red walked into the Imperial Suite, Elvis threw himself into his old protector's arms. John O'Grady recommended that Elvis hire the former bodyguard of the mayor of Los Angeles, a steely-eyed human panther who walked on the balls of his feet and was a fast-draw expert and a dead shot with his nine-millimeter, fourteen-shot automatic. Six to eight F.B.I. agents were rushed to Las Vegas and even a couple of Secret Service men. Elvis Presley was now guarded even better than the president of the United States.

The hotel, which looked on all these preparations with dismay, urged Elvis to cancel his engagement. Elvis, after prolonged consideration, decided that he must take the risk. If word got out that he could be intimidated so easily, blackmailers all over the country might try to shake him down. Even so, he was not going to step onstage until every conceivable precaution had been taken. Two doctors and a complete medical emergency team, with resuscitation equipment and a supply of the right type of blood, were stationed backstage. Two ambulances were parked at the stage door. Lamar Fike was put in charge of the showroom lights,

with orders to keep the room half lit at all times, while being prepared
to raise the lighting to the maximum at the first sign of trouble. Everyone
was given orders that if he saw anything that looked suspicious, he was
to shout the code word "Floor!" At that signal, Elvis would throw himself
to the floor, while Sonny or Red, whoever was closest, would hurl himself
across Elvis's body as a human shield.

By the next night Elvis's panic had turned into a snarling sadistic
rage. He called a meeting of the Guys. For once, he let them see what
was in his mind. He told them that the thing he hated even more than
the thought of being wounded or killed was the image of his assassin,
some idiot like Sirhan Sirhan, sitting there after the murder with a grin
on his face and not a mark on his body, exulting in the fact that he
had brought down the King! As he flashed on this image, Elvis went
livid with rage. He turned to Red and, leveling his voice like a gun, he
spelled out slowly and malevolently the punishment that was to be administered to his attacker. "I don't want the man to just die! I want you
to gouge out his eyes. I want you to kick in his nuts. I want you to
put your foot in his face! Do anything you can to waste him."

That night the agents and the Guys felt like the garrison of a fort
anticipating attack. Armed men were posted at the entrance to the showroom, where they subjected the arriving guests to close scrutiny. Other
men were stationed in strategic positions in the house and backstage.
The nine-millimeter killer planted himself squarely before the stage, where
he could scan the entire room. Before Elvis went onstage for what he
feared might be his final performance, he called Priscilla and Lisa Marie.
In a strangely solemn voice, he said that he loved them. Neither his
wife nor the musicians knew that his life had been threatened.

All through the show that night Elvis's mind was running like films
on a split screen. With one part of his consciousness, he was concentrating
on giving a tight, clean, professional performance. On the other side of
his head were flashing images of shadowy killers. Every few minutes
Elvis would ask himself: "Is that sonovabitch really out there?" At one
point in the performance, when he sang "You've Lost That Lovin' Feeling," the blocking called for Elvis to turn his back to the house as the
stage lights were all extinguished save for a pin spot on the back of
his head. Elvis flashed: "This is it! Now, you're a perfect target." Then,
as he stared at his drummer, Ronnie Tutt, who was positioned directly
behind the singer, Elvis thought: "You poor bastard—if he misses me,
you're a dead man!" The lights went up again and the show went on
without incident, until, suddenly, a voice rang out from the back of
the room.

"Elvis!" cried a man's voice. As the house lights shot up, Elvis dropped to one knee, ready to pull his gun, ready to take his dive, ready for anything, as he struggled to see through the glare of the stage lights to the rear of the room. As every guard in the house felt his scrotum tighten and his heart start to race, the mysterious voice spoke again, saying: "Can you sing 'Don't Be Cruel?'" It was an iron-bound rule that Elvis Presley never took requests. Elvis leaped to his feet and shouted, "I'll sing anything you want!"

The next few nights were still very tense, but when nothing more was heard of the madman or the extortion plot, the anxiety ebbed away. Elvis had faced his worst fear. After a terrible ordeal, he had been spared. Now he knew exactly how it felt to have your life threatened by a dangerous lunatic. That experience was soon followed by his own deterioration into homicidal madness.

Chapter 31

Death Threats

LESS THAN four months after becoming a mother, Priscilla began the ardent pursuit of the lover for whom eventually she broke up her marriage. Ironically, the occasion that inspired this fateful affair was one that had been contrived by Elvis. It was a grand karate tournament held on May 28, 1968, at Honolulu. Elvis had gone to Hawaii that week to vacation at the Ilikai Hotel. When he arrived, the media were blaring forth announcements of the event, which pitted the famous fighters of the islands against the champions from the mainland. The sponsor of this dramatic contest was a Hawaiian-born Los Angeles karate instructor whom Elvis had met years before at the Beverly Wilshire, Ed Parker.

Though it was totally out of character for Elvis Presley to appear at any public event, the prospect of seeing so many great fighters in a single night overcame his customary caution. Summoning Parker to the hotel, Elvis arranged to slip into the Honolulu International Center after the house lights were extinguished so that he could enjoy the matches under conditions of comfort and safety. Among the karate stars who appeared that night was Mike Stone.

Stone, a native Hawaiian with a Caucasian father, resembles those Afro-headed, fist-saluting black athletes who were typical of the sixties. A cocky-looking dude with a killer glint in his eye,

Stone is your classic martial artist. Born on the island of Oahu, he got into karate while serving a hitch in the army. Discharged in 1963, he started training intensely for competition. Within six months he was appearing in local matches. By 1965, he was Western U.S. karate champion. By 1966, he was International Grand Champion. At that point, he married and opened a school in southern California. Though officially in retirement, the prospect of a free trip to Hawaii was enough to lure him back into the ring.

Stone struck a nerve in Priscilla Presley that was set to vibrate. As she sat there in the dark watching the swarthy, crudely featured athlete in the white *gi* chopping and kicking his opponents into submission, she decided impulsively that this was the man she really wanted. Stone himself was later to express the most profound astonishment that any woman would wish to exchange the great Elvis Presley for an impoverished, married and not very handsome karate instructor. If he could have seen himself that night through Priscilla's eyes, he might not have been so surprised. The man she saw bore a certain resemblance to Elvis— he wore a similar costume, was applauded as enthusiastically and was a recognized star. The difference was that Mike Stone was the reality of which Elvis Presley was simply the semblance: Stone was an authentically virile man.

Virility had become the basic issue in the Presley marriage as far as Priscilla was concerned. The moment she had announced that she was pregnant, Elvis had stopped having sexual relations with her. Now that the baby was born and Priscilla was looking as lovely as ever, Elvis gave no sign of resuming sexual relations with her—ever! This was not so surprising, in view of the fact that Elvis had always been averse to sex with married women and abhorred the thought of having intercourse with a mother. In fact, with every woman with whom he became seriously involved, Elvis would display the same pattern. First he would demand that she treat him as if she were his mother by petting, pampering and baby-talking him. Then, when he had gotten his heart's desire, he would begin to exhibit the symptoms of what might be called the Sword in the Bed Complex.

The archetype for this behavior pattern is the scene, famous from medieval legend, in which the knight-lover, like Sir Lancelot or Sir Tristram, goes off into the forest with his queen-mistress and beds with her in a romantic woodsman's cabin. Honorable, even in the midst of Oedipally tainted adultery, the knight lays his sword, edge up, between the queen and himself. Thus is it is that they are discovered by her husband, his master, the king. Thus it is, too, that mama's boys must lie abed with their mistresses or wives, whom they are prone to call "Mommy" and toward whom they suffer soon a mysterious loss of "affect."

As a naive young woman, Priscilla could not possibly have foreseen what was in store for her when she insisted on Elvis marrying her and then immediately became pregnant. These developments destroyed whatever remained of her original relationship with Elvis, which was based entirely on the fact that she embodied not womanly maturity or maternity—God forbid!—but an angelic girlish innocence, so inviting to the hand of the Lolita lover and the eye of the sly voyeur. The celerity with which Priscilla found a new mate once she became a mother suggests that she recognized that Elvis's sexual withdrawal was permanent. It also indicates that she did not want to go on living indefinitely without romance, passion, masculine strength and authority—all the fundamental affections that had been denied her during her eight-year pajama party with Elvis.

Now Priscilla enrolled herself in Chuck Norris's karate school, knowing that sooner or later her involvement in the tight little world of karate would bring her into contact with Stone. It did. At the Long Beach International Competition, Priscilla informed the surprised Stone that she would much prefer to have him as her instructor. He pointed out that his school, at Westminster, was eighty miles from Los Angeles. Priscilla made light of the problem. The following week she appeared in the company of her close friend, Joanie Esposito, who had offered to do the driving.

Priscilla proved an adroit pupil. She was also very charming. When Stone invited her home to meet his wife and family, she snapped at the invitation. She became friendly with Stone's wife and spent the evening turning over the pages of the family's photo album. Stone was no happier with his marriage than was Priscilla with hers. He was ready for an affair. Priscilla, however, having brought matters to a head, was overwhelmed now with anxiety. She didn't trust herself to go off alone with the man she had been pursuing. She persuaded the compliant Joanie to join her on a double date, Joanie riding in the front of the car with Chuck Norris, while Priscilla and Mike snuggled in the back seat.

The first time the lovers stepped out in public, Priscilla insisted they employ all the precautions of secret agents. Though her anxiety proved to be highly exaggerated, it was perfectly normal. Not only was she surrounded by a network of domestic spies, she lived in a world in

which, she assumed, she could be easily recognized as the wife of Elvis
Presley. This latter fear was dissipated in an amusing manner on that
first day.

Boarding a tourist boat bound for Catalina, Stone walked twenty
paces behind Priscilla, acting as if he didn't know her. When they got
aboard, he sat five rows behind her. Even so separated, Priscilla acted
as nervous as a jackrabbit. Every time a tourist pointed his camera out
the window, she would cringe and pull down the long bill of her cap
over her face, which was heavily masked by oversized sunglasses. Ironically, though no one recognized her, many people recognized *him!* Soon
Stone detected a certain chagrin in his mistress, who found herself again
the unnoted companion of an acclaimed man.

Once the affair had become a settled relationship, Priscilla put it
on a well-organized and secure basis. Whether taking dancing or karate
lessons, studying to be the ideal wife or the ideal mistress, Priscilla Presley
was efficient and disciplined. As soon as she saw that she and Stone
were destined to spend a lot of time together on the sly, she found the
perfect love nest. It was a little beach apartment in the obscure community
of Belmont Shores, thirty miles south of Los Angeles.

Having found a place where no one was likely to recognize her,
Priscilla set to work to decorate the hideaway in accordance with her
romantic fantasies. It was the day of the hippies, the earth people. Like
her counterpart, Margaret Trudeau, Priscilla was a very stylish hippie.
She did up this little pad in earthen colors and rich natural textures
and lit it at night with numerous multicolored candles. Beside the murmuring sea, she contrived a cave of love.

Many nights, as Priscilla and Mickey lay in each other's arms, he
would paint for her even more romantic scenes from his homeland in
Hawaii. (It was one of the ironies of this affair that the cuckolding of
the star of *Blue Hawaii* and *Paradise Hawaiian Style* should have been
done by a Hawaiian.) With Stone, Priscilla experienced the reality that
Elvis could at most feign on the screen. "We made love very often,"
recollects Mike Stone. "It wasn't just a desire for sex—it was love. Priscilla was starved for affection. She was warm and loose and funny. She
was born again."

What a contrast, this intensely erotic and exotic life with her dark
virile lover (whom some of the Guys claimed later was "half nigger")
with all those years of watching Elvis nod out at dawn after a long
night of Clint Eastwood and cheeseburgers at the Memphian. What a
difference to be spending so much time with a real man instead of a

human myth. How thrilling to have a life of her own instead of one assigned to her by her keeper. To feel the powerful naked body of a superbly conditioned athlete next to her instead of the alternately obese or diet-starved body, all bundled up in pajamas, of a man who hated to bathe. Sometimes Stone would ask her: "If anything ever went wrong with us, would you go back to Elvis?" Priscilla would invariably reply: "No, I could never go back. I've finally come out in the world and started living."

Priscilla concealed her affair for three and a half years. The great length of this subterfuge tells a lot about the Presley marriage. Clearly, the marriage entailed so little intimacy or even cohabitation that Priscilla was at liberty to make what was in effect a second marriage, establish a second home and lead another, far more engrossing life, without disturbing the façade of her relationship with her husband. If this seems hard to believe, consider for a moment the character of this so-called marriage.

Elvis was almost invariably absent. It drove him crazy to spend more than a week or two with Priscilla so he contrived always to have some excuse to be away from home. Once he resumed touring, he made it a rule: "Wives don't go on tours." The purpose of this prohibition was well understood by all involved. When Elvis spent a month at Las Vegas, for example, he would preside every night over a party that all his courtiers anticipated with pleasure. All afternoon and evening, the Guys would cruise the lobby of the hotel lining up girls for the evening. This practice became so familiar that the girls who wished to be invited adopted the practice of seating themselves on a particular sofa where they were sure of being noticed and summoned to the royal presence. It was well understood among the girls that if they wanted to be invited back to subsequent parties and enjoy such privileges as free admission to the shows, they would have to accommodate the Guys. Naturally, many of them aspired higher.

Elvis's parties at Las Vegas were no different essentially from his parties in the old days in Bel Air. Always there was the sense of attending a court function, where the primary attraction lay in feasting your eyes on the King and gaining the opportunity to catch his eye and perhaps win his favor. Elvis would be pretty wired up after his second show; it would take him the rest of the night to calm down. His favorite way of spending this time was holding court with a circle of admiring young women.

If he were particularly inspired, he might order a karate demonstration. Working with Red or Sonny or someone else willing to play "dummy," Elvis might demonstrate how he could go up against a man carrying a pistol and disarm him with his bare hands. Nobody in his right mind would attempt such a feat, not even the greatest karate champion, but Elvis rehearsed the routine endlessly like an obsessed ballet master. Sometimes, Elvis's coordination would be so impaired by drugs that he would strike out with uncontrolled violence. On quite a few occasions he contrived to kick his dummies in the balls, and once, demonstrating with a young woman, he fractured her ankle. These little mishaps apart, Elvis's karate exhibitions were generally the high points of an evening spent in his company.

As dawn neared, Elvis would signal Joe Esposito or Hamburger James that he was ready to retire. Immediately an order would go down to the kitchen for the final meal of the day, usually a couple of cheeseburgers. At the same time, Elvis, who had made his selection among the ladies present, would suggest to the girl that she follow Joe into the bedroom and make herself comfortable. It was a fixed protocol of the court that King Elvis never retired publicly with any woman save his consort. The girls would be led into the bedroom by the majordomo, who would show them which bathroom they could use and instruct them how to prepare themselves for receiving the King. It was very important that the girls be scrupulously clean: So it might be suggested, very tactfully, of course, that they might want to brush their teeth or use the other hygienic facilities. As Elvis abhorred the sight of a naked woman, unless he was wildly aroused, pajamas and lounging robes were provided for the overnight guests. The most critical thing in any encounter with the King was, of course, that his dignity be maintained. Joe would always take pains to explain to the girls how they were expected to behave. He would make it clear how intolerable any vulgarity or unladylike behavior was to Elvis. Then, wishing them a cheery good night and a pleasant time, the majordomo would withdraw.

The next person who would appear in the royal bedchamber would be a waiter rolling a cart with Elvis's food. The waiter would place a cloth on the bed and stand by to serve Elvis when he entered the room. Elvis would don his pajamas in his bathroom and slide under the covers to eat, propped up on pillows behind his head. Then, signing to the waiter to remove the silver covers, he would gobble up his cheeseburgers. The chances of any sex act occurring before Elvis went off to sleep were small. To become aroused, Elvis would have to watch other people having intercourse in one of the other bedrooms of the suite. Then he would leave on the run to ram his charge home into his own companion. Normally, at some point after dawn, the King would abruptly nod. If the girl were wise, she would take her cue and nestle peacefully under the covers, a human teddy bear.

When Elvis was not enjoying himself with the women he encountered at his parties, he was accompanied by one of his steady girlfriends. During the same engagement in the fall of 1970 which had produced a threat to his life, he made a conquest of which he and his boys were particularly proud: nothing less than the girlfriend of the powerful media executive, Jim Aubrey. At that time, Aubrey was president of MGM, which was preparing to make a documentary about Elvis. Appearing in Elvis's dressing room after opening night to meet the star and congratulate him on the show, Aubrey brought with him a dark, sultry and faintly Indian-looking girl. Though it was a grave violation of the code of macho ethics to attempt to seduce another player's woman in the man's very presence, Elvis was feeling so sure of himself that night that he began to flirt with this beautiful girl in a manner that was obvious to everyone in the room. When he asked her for her telephone number, she reacted with great embarrassment; but he insisted so strongly that finally she scribbled on the piece of paper he held surreptitiously beneath the table: "Barbara Leigh, 213 487–9344."

When Barbara got home the next day, she found her phone ringing. It was Elvis, begging her to turn around and rush back to Las Vegas. She countered that she had a date with Aubrey that weekend to go sailing on his yacht. Elvis was so insistent that finally she agreed to break her date and come back to the International. When she got into the hotel, she was met by a couple of the Guys, who rushed her to a special apartment with a big round bed which Elvis maintained for guests who could not stay in his suite. When Barbara asked if arrangements had been made for her to see the show that night, the Guys acted very alarmed and said that she would have to stay put until they brought her to Elvis. Late that night, she was finally admitted into the presence. Elvis explained with much laughter that the reason he had kept her away from the showroom was that Jim Aubrey had also returned— with Joanne Pflug (of M.A.S.H.).

Barbara, a model and movie actress, a southern girl from a very poor family, became a great favorite of Elvis's. During the next year, she traveled extensively with him on tour, stayed with him at his homes in Memphis and Los Angeles, slept with him in the marital beds. When, in March 1971, Elvis was suddenly hospitalized with secondary glaucoma

that could have resulted in partial blindness, instead of calling Priscilla
to his side, he called Barbara, who flew across the country. She held
his hand at the most critical moment, when Dr. David Meyer of Memphis
inserted a hypodermic needle directly into Elvis's eyeball. Elvis squeezed
Barbara's hand so hard he almost broke it. Eventually, the affair faded
away because Barbara believed that Elvis would never leave Priscilla.
As events were to prove, she was both right and wrong.

Even when Elvis would return to Priscilla's company, he would hardly
have his feet up on the table before he announced that he needed to
"unwind." That was the code word for "orgy." Immediately, Joe Esposito
would be on the phone lining up the showgirls from Las Vegas and
Los Angeles. Frank Sinatra's private jet would be chartered to fly the
girls down to Palm Springs, where Elvis maintained a house with high
walls. The King and his men always had enough pills to supply a dispensary. For a big party, somebody would go out and score four or five
lids of grass. The food would be brought into the house precooked,
eliminating the need for tattletale servants. The only time a maid ever
set foot inside one of Elvis's Palm Springs homes was when the freakout
was over and it was time to clean up the mess.

The routine was an obscene and decadent parody of the good old
days in Bel Air. Around six in the evening, everybody would turn on.
Then the whole gang would get naked and jump in the pool. The usual
water games would soon have the Guys and girls well aroused. Then
the chasing and screaming phase would commence. Soon the satyrs would
seize their prey and drag them off to the numerous bedrooms ranged
around the pool like the rooms of a motel. Elvis himself never participated
in these games, which were too threatening to his shallowly rooted masculinity. While the orgy whirled around him, he would be locked up in
his bedroom like a pornographic filmmaker shooting his latest triple
X-rated product. His cast would be three, four or five splendid bodies
from the best chorus lines in Vegas. These girls were not permitted to
play with the Guys. They were "on exclusive" with Elvis. If Elvis was
lucky, he would have the star of his orgies present: a beautiful lesbian
from the Sahara Tahoe, who was very adroit at arousing the other girls
and getting them to abandon all their inhibitions. Sometimes this woman
would generate so much steam that the girls would forget all about
Elvis, writhing ecstatically on his big bed with no thought but of their
own pleasure.

For a voyeur, this state of being present yet invisible at the orgy
represents the ultimate in excitement. One night, having watched this

inciting spectacle with pounding heart for nearly two hours, Elvis got so carried away that he did something that was totally out of character. He opened the big French windows of his bedroom and stepped out on the patio, where he exhibited himself to the gang around the pool. He was totally naked and had hooked one of the Colonel's canes over his erect penis. What an image! But what does it mean? Does it shout, "Fuck you, Colonel Lardass!" Or is it an unconscious confession that Elvis has lived his whole adult life with the Colonel's hook deep in Elvis's dick?

Priscilla must have had more than an inkling of how Elvis "unwound." She was of a highly suspicious turn of mind; but even if she had been as innocent as a child, she would have been wised up by the incriminating evidence she discovered at the house during her own visits there. In 1970, for example, after watching Elvis open at Vegas, Priscilla and Joanie Esposito decided to spend a few days sunning themselves in the desert. When they arrived at the house, they checked the mailbox. Inside, they discovered a couple of thank-you notes that had been sent by the girls who had enjoyed the last party at the house. One little missive on colored paper was signed, "Miss Lizard Tongue." When Priscilla found this shocking confirmation of what she had long suspected, she flew into a rage. Seizing the phone, she called Elvis at the hotel. The moment he answered, she started denouncing him for his cheating ways. Mingled with her rage was a feverish curiosity. All through the conversation, she kept demanding, "Who is Miss Lizard Tongue?"

Elvis was a firm believer in the maxim: "The best defense is a good offense." Instead of backing up under the fury of Priscilla's attack, he brazenly informed her that the letters were just crank mail from fans whom he had never met. He hadn't the faintest idea who was Miss Lizard Tongue. She must be some crazy girl with hot pants. He then swung around to counterattack, demanding to know what right she had to upset him just before he went onstage. Didn't she realize that she might make him so nervous that he would blow the show? How did she think he earned the living that kept her in fancy clothes and cars and mansions she spent fortunes decorating? When Elvis got through with Priscilla, he had her beaten so badly that she wound up making apologies for even calling him. There you have, in miniature, the Presley marriage.

In February 1972, after years of leading a double life, Priscilla finally decided to tell Elvis the truth. She announced to the astonished Mike Stone: "I'm going to fly up to Las Vegas this week and tell him the truth. It's time we stopped hiding like this. I want everyone to know how much I love you and that I am going to live with you." This was a brave decision, a brave speech; there is no reason to assume, however, that when Priscilla walked into Elvis's dressing room that night—taking care not to arrive until the second show was over—she had any intention of confessing she had a lover. All that was necessary at first, she knew, was to say that the marriage had failed and she wanted her freedom. Or, perhaps she could just say that she felt the need to be alone for a certain time in order to come to terms with herself—or some such tripe. Alas, there was no way to exit gracefully.

No sooner did Priscilla start reciting her carefully rehearsed lines, standing alone with Elvis, now, in the bedroom of the penthouse, than he shocked her by tearing off her clothes and practically raping her. When this act of manly possession failed to weaken her resolve, he changed his tactics abruptly and swore that he would make any sacrifice to maintain the marriage. He would give up his tours and remain at home. He would become the perfect husband and father. They would start all over again and have a new life together. Priscilla countered that he had promised all these things many times before and nothing had ever come of his vows. Now, it was too late. He could not change, but she had changed. She had grown, developed, matured. She was a different person now from the little Cilla he had reared in Graceland. As far as she was concerned, he was free to do as he had always done. She, however, had the right to lead her own life. Elvis had no choice but to let her go.

A day later, Mike Stone witnessed Priscilla's arrival at their little pad in Belmont Shores. She drove up in an old station wagon stuffed with luggage and personal belongings. Lisa Marie was also in the car. Priscilla was ecstatically happy. With a triumphant cry, she announced that she had left Elvis and come to live with Stone. From the overflowing store of things at Monovale Road, she had taken just what was most essential to her needs and abandoned the rest. Stone was astonished. It was hard for him to believe that this woman who had everything, including the most desired man in the world, had given it all up for him, a poor karate instructor still burdened with a wife and child. Priscilla was the greatest romantic since the Duke of Windsor.

Obviously, they couldn't continue to live in their little hideaway. It was time, once again, for Priscilla, that instinctive nest builder, to find and furnish yet another home. This time her fancies led her to the soaring futuristic apartment complex at Marina Del Rey, the home of the swing-he extended an invitation to spend the weekend at his house in Palm Springs. He assured the girls that they would be put up in their own rooms at a local hotel and that they would be treated with the greatest respect and courtesy. They agreed to join him and added to their original number one girl more—Kit.

She was a very proper young lady. A Roman Catholic, reared in accordance with very strict principles, she never swore, smoked, drank or did anything naughty. Though she was twenty-four years old, she was still a virgin. Oddly, though, she did have a steady boyfriend whom all the other girls called King Kong. This dude was a slick-haired macho who ran a beauty supply business. It was incomprehensible how such a goody-goody as Kit could be involved with such an ape. As it happened, however, just at the moment of Kit's meeting with the King, she was starting to break up with Kong.

The moment Elvis laid eyes on Kit, he was smitten. As always it was love at first sight, the perfect girl, where have you been all my life and when are we getting married? Naturally, Elvis was inspired to great heights of southern gentlemanliness, hovering attentively over Kit's every dainty gesture. When the weekend party had ended, Elvis and Kit were stuck on each other. No sooner was Kit back in her apartment in Los Angeles than the wires were burning up with calls from Elvis. Soon he was down to get her in his forty-five-thousand-dollar custom-built Stutz Blackhawk, which blew Kit's mind. Not long afterward, while motoring home one afternoon, Kit pointed at a "darling" little sports car driving past them in traffic. Elvis said nothing; but a couple hours later, Kit's roommate got a call from Elvis. "Get her out in the street," he demanded. "Tell her the dog needs walking or something—I'm bringing her a new car!" When the great moment arrived, Kit was out on the pavement playing her part according to the script. Elvis drove up, shadowed by the boys, of course, in the brand new car. Hopping nimbly out the door, he approached his beloved with the car keys in one hand and in the other the title to the vehicle. As Kit came gurgling and gasping to his side, Elvis bowed and said: "Your wish is my command!"

No sooner did Kit begin to enjoy the good things in life than out of nowhere appeared the threatening Kong. Raging with jealousy, the beast pounced on Kit and began to lash her with the thongs of a Savonarola, falsely accusing her of being a fallen woman, a concubine, a receiver of harlot's gifts. As if this weren't bad enough, the monster went to the press and told the reporters all about Elvis's "latest affair," even providing the hungry journalists with pictures of Kit. Instantly, the press was all over the little apartment house where Kit lived. This was hot stuff. Elvis Presley, separated from his wife, dating a gorgeous dancer! Hey! How often did you get a story like this about the King!

One afternoon, matters got so out of hand that poor Kit picked up the phone and called Elvis. She told him that reporters and photographers were all over the building and that she was afraid to go out the door. One guy in particular was so aggressive that she feared he was going to break into her apartment, boo hoo! A call from a maiden in distress has always been the ultimate summons for a southern gentleman—or a comic strip hero! Elvis barked: "Hold on! I'll be there in a minute!" Then, before you could say—"It's a bird! It's a plane!"—it was a *Presley!* roaring up to the door in his powerful black Stutz Blackhawk and dressed to the nines in a black Napoleonic suit with a white tie and a case full of police badges and a load of expensive weapons. Hard at his heels followed the Guys. Elvis rushed into the apartment as if he were a fire chief and started shouting orders. "Joe, you take the stairs! Sonny, out back! Jerry, check the roof!" In no time Elvis's private SWAT team was swarming all over the building. Meantime, Elvis was holding poor quaking Kit in his arms and swearing that so long as he was alive no one would ever harm her.

Finding a new mate for the Minotaur made the Guys feel good. Just hip enough to be really dumb, these boys assumed that they could placate Elvis like a baby by sticking a new doll in his hand after the first one had been snatched away. This was a complete delusion as events soon proved. For while Elvis was out on tour or back home in Los Angeles or Memphis, he called Priscilla every day. The boys assumed that this was a sign that he still missed her and was sweet-talking her into returning. Actually, the calls were of a very different nature. First, Elvis would get a heavy load on and sink down into that black hole where deeply self-pitying junkies always fall. Then, he would start to lacerate himself with humiliating or enraging thoughts. He would see himself, the King, reduced to a ridiculous figure, a mere cuckold, a man who couldn't hold his own wife. Then, he would think of her seducer, a goddamned nigger bastard with an attitude on him that made you want to cut his nuts off. Then, he would veer back from rage to self-pity, thinking of how sad it was that a man who had everything couldn't look forward to coming home and finding his wife and baby waiting for his return. Back and forth he would crawl in his mental cave, until he had worked himself into a murderous rage. Then, he would call Priscilla and tell her that he was coming down to the Marina that night.

He was going to be carrying his M-16 automatic rifle and he would have all the Guys with him armed to the teeth. She would see what a piece of shit she had picked to fall in love with. She would see Mike Stone down on his knees vomiting with fear, begging for his life. She would see what a white man does to a wife-stealing nigger!

These threats terrified Priscilla. At first she kept them to herself. Stone would come home and find her white with fear. He'd ask her what was wrong, and she would make some implausible excuse. Then, one night, when Stone was in the apartment, the phone rang. As Priscilla talked, she began to get hysterical. "What's wrong, honey?" asked Stone. "It's Elvis," she said. "He says he's flying down here from Las Vegas with the Guys, and he's going to make me watch while he makes you get down and crawl." Stone shouted across the room so that Elvis would hear him distinctly, "You tell that sonovabitch that I'm not hiding anywhere. He knows where to find me when he wants me. I'm not afraid of him *or* his bodyguards." When Priscilla hung up, she was shaking with fear. "You don't understand how dangerous he can be when he gets into these black moods," she gasped. "If he says he's going to kill you, he might try it." Stone laughed off her fears but agreed to be careful. Later, in Hawaii, karate friends told him that Elvis was gunning for him. They offered to hit Elvis. Stone rejected the idea as "ridiculous."

The death threats from Elvis did not stop. He continued to call week after week, month after month. Sometimes he would tell Priscilla what a fool she was to run off with a pauper when she had a man who could give her anything in the world. Sometimes he would pour abuse on Mike Stone, calling him obscene names and suggesting that he was just a pimp living off Priscilla's money. Eventually, he would always work around to the thought that obsessed him: the threat to kill or maim Mike Stone while Priscilla was forced to stand by helplessly watching the hideous scene.

As these threats continued for nearly a year and a half and as they came very close to fulfillment on one occasion, they cannot be discounted as a momentary aberration. They were profoundly revealing expressions of Elvis Presley's psyche. The first thing they show is that Elvis's aim is way off the mark. Why should he be focusing all his rage on Mike Stone when it was Priscilla with whom he should be angry? The obvious answer is that according to the macho code which Elvis embraced, women are possessions that can be stolen by other men. Elvis was furious at Stone because he was a thief. Yet it is just as apparent that Elvis cared nothing for Priscilla as a woman or a wife. So why should he go out of his mind when someone else laid claim to her? Knowing the Oedipal character of Elvis's personality, it appears much more probable that his rage was triggered by a deeper disturbance. As a mama's boy nothing could threaten him more or inspire greater rage than the thought of his "little mama" being taken away from him by another, especially by a more virile man. Surely the prolonged, profound and murderous malevolence of his reaction had to be grounded in some such serious threat to his essential well-being.

As for Stone, it's perfectly clear that he was just the "other man," the inviting blank that can be scribbled over with all the most hateful and paranoid delusions that a highly disturbed mind is capable of forming. Stone was like one of those silhouette targets that Elvis used to riddle with machine-gun rounds in the smokehouse behind Graceland. A blank "assailant," "nigger," "wife stealer," whatever Elvis's imagination carica- tured him as being at any particular moment. Even so, he was not the only target at which Elvis was shooting when he made his death threats. Though the shots were aimed entirely at Stone, their greatest effect was registered by Priscilla. Elvis knew this perfectly well; in fact, it was part of his intention to punish her severely in the very act of wooing her back by scaring her out of her wits.

Though Elvis never stopped making threats, he never made good on any of his promises of retribution. This, too, is a most revealing feature of his behavior. Elvis was a man who ruled by fear and intimida- tion. Everyone around him was always motivated by the thought that if they crossed Elvis, he might go crazy and do something violent. He was like that anarchist in Conrad's *The Secret Agent,* who walks around with a bomb always in his pocket. At the slightest threat, he is prepared to blow up both his adversary and himself. Yet, like so many men who rule by fear, Elvis was basically chicken. He wouldn't hesitate to hit a woman or one of his henchmen because he knew there was no danger they would hit back. He was always quick to whip out a gun and threaten anybody who displeased him because he was confident that his victim wouldn't retaliate by drawing a weapon himself. When it came down to scratch, however, Elvis was terrified at the thought of answering for his violent impulses and destructive instincts. Though as Red West said, "Elvis had a need to kill," Elvis could not kill or even work off his rage in a fist fight in his later years. His only outlet for the profound anger that filled his soul was to make death threats.

By July 1972, Priscilla could bear the nightmare of her life no longer.

that for the only time in his adult life, he went for about a year without seeing any other women. Eventually, though, he found fidelity confining. He began to invent excuses to go off by himself so that he could enjoy his former pleasures. Linda recognized this demand for what it was and rose to the challenge. She told Elvis she didn't want their relationship to deteriorate into the hypocritical pretences that had characterized his marriage and, for that matter, all his relationships with women. She wanted everything to be out front. They came to an understanding that allowed him considerable freedom. They even got so chummy on this issue that Elvis would sometimes introduce his latest discovery to Linda, and all of them would go out together as a threesome. When the date was over, Elvis might discuss his new chick with Linda, soliciting her opinion of the girl's appropriateness to his needs. This was not only having your cake and eating it: It was the first and only time in Elvis's entire life that he had experienced sexual freedom without suffering from guilt. It was a startling contrast with his marriage.

In addition to being a very free and harmonious relationship, Elvis's involvement with Linda Thompson fulfilled completely his lifelong yearning to reconstitute the total trust and intimacy he had once enjoyed with his mother. Nor was it simply his relationship as an adult with his mother that he revived at this time but the even more satisfying relationship he had had with her as a little child. Nothing in Elvis's history is more astonishing than the degree to which he regressed to infancy in this period, unless it be the fact that this relapse was attended by so little shame. It's true, of course, that Elvis had always demanded that women mother him, wait on him and coddle him, conversing with him in that special baby talk he had used with Gladys. Now, however, he wasn't content to play at being a baby: He wanted to experience again the relationship of mother and child in the most literal manner.

He called Linda "Mommy" and she called him "Baby Buntin'," which comes from an old southern nursery rhyme, "Hush, Baby Buntin', Daddy's gone ahuntin'." "Buntin' " is, of course, the familiar word "bunting," which is used in the South for the wrappings around an infant, its swaddling clothes. So Elvis was a baby in swaddling clothes and even, sometimes, in diapers. Lying for days on end in bed, comfortably swaddled and blissfully stoned, Elvis would have Linda read to him from his favorite books or simply watch over him as he gazed bemusedly at the television screen. When it was time to eat, she would feed him by hand. When it was time for his sleeping medication, she would administer the dose. Soon they had reconstructed the atmosphere and regimen of the nursery.

Clearly, this whole pattern of behavior was a reaction to the trauma of discovering Priscilla's infidelity. Unmanned by sexual betrayal, Elvis reacted by regressing to an infantile state of being. It was also the counterpoise to that other and fearful reaction which had transformed him into the nightmare persona of the midnight caller threatening horrible violence and even murder. As always with Elvis, we see the contrasting extremes between which he was condemned perpetually to oscillate. One minute he is the gun-wielding bad-ass; the next a mewling infant lisping to his mommy in baby talk.

These extremes had a profoundly deleterious effect on Elvis both psychologically and physically. This was the period when he finally became a hopelessly addicted junkie, a delusional paranoid and a bloated, dysfunctional and frequently sick man with a vast range of symptoms, all of which could be ascribed to one basic disease: total incapacity to deal with reality. The only effective remedy for this condition, interestingly, was a rare challenge posed to Elvis's talents as an entertainer.

The Satellite Show, *Aloha From Hawaii,* was announced by Colonel Parker and NBC at the conclusion of Elvis's engagement at Las Vegas in the fall of 1972. At first glance, it appeared to be the most awesome application of modern technology to show business since the astronauts' vaudeville act on the moon. Elvis Presley was to stand on the stage of an auditorium in Honolulu and be televised by equipment whose signal would be bounced off an orbiting telecommunications satellite and showered down over half the world. For one night Marshall McLuhan's "global village" would become a literal reality. Staring into their domestic hearths, all the villagers would see the same shapes in the electronic fire and hear the music of the spheres.

To make the program pay its enormous cost of about two and a half million dollars, however, it was necessary that it play everywhere in prime time, which necessitated in turn that the global village be divided into marketing areas and the program peddled country by country, a rather less sublime image. Eventually, instead of one awesome broadcast, anticipating the world of the future, economics dictated a live show aimed at Japan, followed two days later by a taped replay in Europe, followed a couple of months later by a second rebroadcast in the States: an arrangement that points backward to the early days of network TV when programs like *Your Show of Shows* were broadcast live from New York and then relayed across the country one and two hours later by kinescope. What the great global telecast reduced to in real terms was something far less thrilling than the hype with which it was packaged.

For a hustler, however, illusion is reality. As a hustle, the Satellite Show was worthy of Barnum.[1]

What most appealed to the Colonel about the satellite deal was the opportunity it provided to showcase Elvis's stock Las Vegas showroom act as a stupendous feat of performing by the World's Greatest Entertainer. Though nothing out of the ordinary was demanded, except that Elvis lose weight, though not even Elvis's schedule was disrupted because the dates for the broadcast and taping were dead time before the winter opening at the International Hotel, Colonel felt quite secure demanding his price: one million dollars plus reversion of the show to Elvis and himself after two repeats. As for NBC, which had to pay the cost of rigging the auditorium in Honolulu, leasing the satellite, hiring an independent producer (Marty Pasetta, who does the annual Oscar awards show) and clearing the air time, it was motivated in large part by the desire to aid its satellite company, RCA Victor, which was being strongly pressured by its foreign companies to present its greatest star abroad, especially in Japan. So enormous was the demand for Elvis in Japan that the broadcast was parlayed into an Elvis Presley Week, which reached its climax at seven-thirty Saturday night, January 12, 1973, when Elvis's share of the viewing audience was a staggering *ninety-eight percent.*

RCA also decided to record the show and issue it as a two-record album. Though most of the songs had been recorded by Elvis time and again, particularly on his wretchedly produced live concert albums, the great ballyhoo given this recording made it appear to be both a historic document and an extraordinary performance. Another sales feature was the use of the brand new quadraphonic process. This was a ludicrous idea because conditions in the field were highly unfavorable for making such an experiment and because virtually none of its purchasers would ever be able to play it on a four-channel system. As it turned out, last-minute engineering problems rendered this "state of the art" recording distinctly inferior to even a mediocre stereo disc, with startling fluctuations in the volume levels and bad mike balances distorting the sound. Considerations of quality, however, had never counted for anything where the Elvis public was concerned. For years Elvis's albums, which were packaged and even mixed under the Colonel's supervision, were among

[1] Though Colonel Parker has always been credited with conceiving this show, the idea was actually suggested by the President of RCA Victor, Rocco Laginestra, who concedes (with a smile) that Colonel had never so much as heard of a telecommunications satellite.

the shlockiest products produced by any major record company. Elvis would explode in rage when he heard the finished disc and discovered that the Colonel had ordered the engineers to raise the level of Elvis's voice far above that of his accompaniment. As for the album jackets, they were about as sophisticated as an old-fashioned billboard. So it is not surprising that the people who bought all those styrofoam boaters and pink teddy bears bought this bad album. The "package" sold an impressive two million "units."

Everyone who recalls Elvis's appearance on the Satellite Show remembers how well he looked. He was exceptionally slender, deeply tanned, dazzlingly costumed and utterly charming in manner. Never at any time in his entire career had he made a better physical appearance. Even allowing for all the arts of media illusion, the choice of the right camera angles, lights, colors, makeup and costume, Elvis could not have looked so well if he had not prepared himself carefully for this occasion. For three months he restricted himself to a diet of tiny, frozen-food packets that added up to only five hundred calories a day. This punishing diet he supplemented with daily injections of vitamins and a hormone extracted from the urine of pregnant women. As all of Elvis's subsequent life testifies to his tendency to let himself go until he became a grotesque-looking monstrosity, it is important to recognize how different his fate might have been if he had been stimulated from time to time by other such challenges as this program presented. Imagine the inspiration Elvis would have derived from a great tour of Europe or the Orient or a two-week stand in some vast hall in London or Tokyo or an around-the-world tour! How much greater his will to live and exercise his talents if instead of being worked like a mule at Las Vegas or toured through the sticks or shut up in paranoid seclusion at Graceland, he could have enjoyed a royal progress that would have taken the World's Greatest Entertainer all over the world! This raises the vital question: Why didn't Elvis Presley ever tour abroad?

Elvis was always eager to play in foreign countries. From as early as 1957, he was telling the press that he would soon be going to England, Australia or continental Europe because demand for his appearance in those countries was so great. At the press conference after his initial opening at Las Vegas in 1969, he spoke of going soon to Europe. Time and again, European, Australian and Japanese promoters offered fabulous sums to persuade the Colonel to allow Elvis to leave the United States. One English promoter was so eager to book Elvis that he offered a million dollars for a single night's work plus transportation across the

Atlantic and back on a plane with a capacity of one hundred and thirty-five passengers. Even more extravagant was the behavior of a Japanese promoter whom Alex Shoofey introduced to the Colonel.

The moment this man was ushered into the Colonel's fourth-floor suite at the International, Colonel snapped: "I want two million dollars on my desk tomorrow. I want you to make sure you cover this whole desk." The Japanese replied, "No problem." Shoofey jumped in at this point to assure the Colonel that the man, whom he knew well, had immense financial resources and the money was in American banks. His bluff called, Colonel grumbled, "Don't wanna go to Japan." Then he said: "Tell you what I would like to do. I'd like to do a picture. But you have to come up with a million dollars that's mine, for *me* alone! Understand me? I get a million right off the bat before I sign. You pay for the movie and everything, and then we'll split the distribution. Okay?" The imperturbable Japanese replied, "Okay." Exasperated, the Colonel barked, "Forget about it!" Shoofey was amazed and bewildered by this exchange because, as he puts it: "In Japan they would have paid a hundred dollars to see Elvis."

As money was the Colonel's raison d'etre, his behavior in cavalierly dismissing these golden offers seems absolutely inexplicable, until you associate it with certain other oddities in the man's conduct. Colonel Parker has always displayed a profound reluctance to cross any border where you have to show a passport. Though he was quite comfortable taking Elvis to Canada or Hawaii, he never once visited his "boy" during the fifteen months Elvis was in Germany. Jean Aberbach went to Europe, Hall Wallis went to Europe, Freddy Bienstock went to Europe but Colonel never came over for as much as a weekend. Why? At the time the Colonel told the wife of Dave Gardiner, the southern good ole boy comic, that he couldn't obtain a passport because he was a "foundling." This story is an obvious fabrication, but it does underscore the most likely reason why Tom Parker never took Elvis abroad: The Colonel does not have a passport and did not wish to apply for a passport.

Apart from sheer perversity, why would Colonel Parker sacrifice millions of dollars over an issue as trifling as a passport application? Did he fear that the application might raise questions whose answers the Colonel does not wish to give? One such question might have been: "Are you an American citizen?" Colonel Parker has always maintained that he is an American citizen, citing a number of ways in which he could have become a citizen: adoption by American parents, service in the American army and marriage to an American citizen. All of these avenues toward naturalization were dependent in the old days, however, on legitimate entry into the United States. Gabe Tucker, who has been one of the Colonel's cronies since the early forties, appears to be persuaded that the Colonel did not enter the country legally. In the book he produced with Houston gossip columnist Marge Crumbaker, Tucker quotes Elvis Presley as his authority. "I just feel in my bones that the Colonel is in this country illegally," Elvis remarks at one point in *Up and Down With Elvis.* "Hell, I think the Colonel was born in Holland or Sweden somewhere. He probably got here by jumping ship, finding a job in a carnival, and making up all that stuff about being born on the road heading south." At another point in the book, Tucker remarks: "Colonel had a personal fear of walking across that American boundary line," citing instances that go back to the days when Colonel was managing Eddy Arnold. In light of these disclosures, the many peculiarities in the Colonel's life-style noted before could be seen to have arisen from the need to invent and maintain a fictitious past that would mask the Colonel's real history.

It is a sign of how taboo the notion of a foreign tour was in Colonel Parker's mind that at the very moment when he was spurning offers for millions of dollars from European and Japanese promoters, he was busy concocting a deal whose only acceptable rationale is a desperate need for money. In March 1973, the Colonel sold outright to RCA for $5.4 million (and a seven-year guarantee of $500,000 a year against royalties) Elvis Presley's entire record catalogue. The value of these more than seven hundred chart records was literally inestimable. Though, on the one hand, the records were old merchandise that had been issued and reissued, packaged and repackaged a number of times, they were, on the other hand, of immense potential value. Particularly at this moment, with Elvis back in favor again, wowing them at Las Vegas and on tour, profiting from the rock 'n' roll revival and looming before millions of people as the King, the future earnings from his immense and unique catalogue could be seen as a virtual Golconda. It's significant of the vitality of this material that no sooner did RCA obtain complete possession of the masters than the company began releasing a series of retrospectives, titled *Elvis Presley—A Legendary Performer,* that proved highly successful. Considering, too, that Elvis was earning immense sums again, thanks to his recent movie, TV, showroom and concert profits, it seems very strange that his manager would want to close out all the future royalties on twenty years of record-making for even so large a sum as $5.4 million. When you add the further fact that Elvis had no means of sheltering this huge dollop of cash, which would simply be dumped atop his other income, already sufficient to put him in the highest tax bracket, the whole deal becomes preposterous as business and clearly contrary to the artist's best interests. As it turned out, after splitting the money with the Colonel fifty-fifty, Elvis netted only about $750,000.[2]

If you look at the deal not from Elvis's but the Colonel's point of view, the perspective changes radically. Elvis was only thirty-four years of age; with any sort of luck, he could profit from his old recordings for another twenty or thirty years and then pass on the property, enhanced immensely by his death, to his heirs. Colonel was sixty-four with a bad heart. His expectations were foreshortened by age, health and indifference to the future. The Colonel's view of the future is well expressed in a conversation he held with Lamar Fike in 1965, when Parker was fifty-six. "How much longer do I have to live?" asked the Colonel rhetorically. "Ten or fifteen years, if I'm lucky. I'm gonna live it like I wanna! I don't give a shit! I do like I want to, I spend like I want to. I take care o' my people. Fuck it! Talk about leave it to somebody—why should I leave it to somebody? Ain't nobody I wanna leave it to!" What concerned the Colonel was not the future but the present. In that present, however, he was spending his money at an alarming rate.

Colonel Parker's huge gambling losses at the International Hotel were secured both by his ability to pay and by the management's gratitude toward the Colonel for giving them Elvis Presley at a low figure and never demanding to renegotiate. This cozy arrangement was threatened, however, in February 1972, when Kirk Kerkorian sold the hotel to the Hilton chain. At that moment, a clean broom began to sweep through every room of the huge establishment, including the showroom and casino. Though Alex Shoofey remained for the time being as the general manager, he was threatened with a loss of the total control he had enjoyed under his former boss. Now he had to deal not with a great venture capitalist but with professional hotel managers who prided themselves on their ability to keep track of every last pat of butter going through the labyrinthine machinery of their biggest house. Yet for all their expertise in running conventional hotels, the Hiltons were not yet expert in

[2] Owing to the lucrative side agreements which he attached to the buy-out, Colonel Parker wound up with $1,550,000 *more* than Elvis plus ten percent of the net profits of RCA Record Tours, which was sponsoring Elvis's road shows. Elvis, for his part, got a royalty rate that was only half that being paid at the time to stars like the Beatles, the Rolling Stones, and Elton John. He was also stripped of the protection provided by the standard auditing clause, which was deleted from the agreement, leaving a conspicuous blank space on the face of the contract form.

managing gaming establishments. Soon the new owners and their general manager came into conflict on the issue of how to deal with Colonel Tom Parker.

As Shoofey recalls, Barron Hilton ordered his manager one day to get aboard the company plane and fly down to Palm Springs to lay down the law to the Colonel. Shoofey objected vehemently to what he regarded as a foolish order. "You don't go to Palm Springs and tell the Colonel anything!" he rasped. "Colonel Parker—*minus* Elvis Presley—is the best customer you ever had at this hotel. He's good for at least one million dollars a year. You know what you do with a million-dollar customer? You pick him up at night, carry him to bed and kiss his goddamn ass!" When this argument failed to persuade, Shoofey drew on his knowledge of gambling. "There are two types of gamblers," he explained to Barron Hilton, "dangerous and nondangerous. Colonel Parker is a nondangerous gambler. The longer he plays, the more money you get. He cannot win! Do you know what a hotel would pay for a guy that cannot win?" Shoofey finally carried his point; but not much later, he resigned. At this point, the Colonel found himself dealing with people who didn't share Alex Shoofey's policy for dealing with big-time gamblers.

Jean Aberbach, who had developed a close relationship with Tom Parker over the years, recalls this period vividly. He sees it as a watershed in the Colonel's life. "Some people," he says, "are split personalities at the same moment; others are split personalities at different moments. The latter explains Colonel Parker. Up to the time he discovered Las Vegas, he was a loyal, wonderful human being. But this Las Vegas thing changed his entire personality. His gambling . . . he lost enormous amounts! He was forced to deal with the people to whom he lost the money. So he might have lost control. He was forced to do many things that he otherwise might not have done. He was forced to go in directions in which he otherwise might not have gone. . . . The Colonel sold for a flat fee all the income that was to be made from the records. It certainly fit in with his need to come up with money because there are certain people to whom you cannot owe money."

The crisis in Colonel's affairs described by Jean Aberbach not only explains the shortsighted management policy implicit in the catalogue sale but also reveals on a deeper level the astonishing similarity in temperament between the Colonel and Elvis. Just as Elvis was accustomed to living for the moment, squandering his money with the excuse that "you don't come back for an encore," so we now see Colonel Parker acting on precisely the same principle. Both men appear bent on playing their parts, strutting across their stages, without concern for future consequences. Dominated and obsessed alike by their images, their exaggerated sense of self-importance, they resemble characters in comic strips rather than real human beings. Elvis thinks that if he buys a hundred pickup trucks or herds a hundred groupies through his hotel suite or psychs his men up to risking their lives for him, he has power. In truth his acts of acquisition, seduction and authority all bespeak the same emptiness, insatiability and paranoia. The Colonel, secure in the expectation of limitless credit, stands at the crap table betting "around the horn," laying every possible wager in a pattern that insures great losses. As the same audience that has applauded Elvis in the showroom marvels at Colonel's profligacy, the old man revels in his moment of glory. He, too, has "power."

Less than two weeks after the Satellite Show, Elvis opened again at Las Vegas. The first week went smoothly, though he complained of a heavy mucous discharge that forced him constantly to turn away from the audience and cough up a glob of phlegm between each number. Diseases and disorders of the upper respiratory system had begun to plague him during the past year. A local nose and throat specialist, Dr. Sidney Bower, could not account for this particular symptom. He prescribed a nasal douche, rest and avoidance of drugs. At the same time that Dr. Bower was treating Elvis's throat and warning against drug abuse, Dr. Thomas "Flash" Newman (so called because of the dispatch with which he made his calls) was whisking into Elvis's dressing room every night to give him an injection of "B 12" before he went onstage. Dr. Newman is a small, dapper, grey-haired man who dresses like a golfer and speaks in a high, light, whispery Irish voice, always punctuating his conversation by saying, "God bless you, Joe" or "God bless you, Lamar." In addition to giving Elvis his vitamin shots, Dr. Newman was responsible for seeing that Elvis got to sleep every morning around dawn.

Insomnia had been the bane of Elvis's existence since adolescence. Beginning in 1960, with his return to Hollywood, he had begun to rely on sleeping pills as a diabetic relies upon insulin. He had grown accustomed to taking heavy doses of Pacidyl, Valium, Percodan and Demerol every night. Such heavy downers often caused him to fall asleep in the middle of a sentence or even a meal. One moment he would be sitting at the table, piddling with his mashed potatoes. The next, he would be head down in the slop. Linda Thompson once left Elvis for a moment while he was eating a bowl of chicken and rice soup. When she returned, she discovered him with his face totally submerged in the dish. If she hadn't pulled his head back before it was too late, he would have earned the doubtful distinction of being the first man in history to drown in a soup bowl.

Drugs like Percodan and Demerol contain synthetic opiates that have all the dangerous properties of natural opiates. They are addictive and if used continuously must be taken in ever-increasing quantities to compensate for the tolerance that the body quickly develops. It is unclear when Elvis Presley first became addicted. Perhaps it was as far back as the early sixties, when he first began his study of the *Physicians' Desk Reference* and obtained access to a wide range of drugs. It was in the nature of things that eventually he would graduate from the lesser opiates to the most powerful of the lot, the notorious Dilaudid. There can be no question that Elvis was using Dilaudid by 1972 because a couple of the more astute Guys saw the name on the medicine bottles. What's more, we know that Dilaudid was Elvis Presley's favorite drug. Pat West, Red's wife, recalls Elvis listening to a family discussion of drugs one day and remarking, "I've tried them all and Dilaudid is the best."

Dilaudid has been called "drugstore heroin," the implication being that even though it is legal, Dilaudid is as powerful and dangerous as the proscribed drug. The truth is even more startling. Dilaudid is much stronger than heroin: 2.5 times as strong, to be exact; five times the strength of morphine. That's why it is prescribed for all the most excruciating kinds of pain: deep knife wounds, extensive burns and terminal cancer. As Dilaudid is always full strength and heroin is invariably cut, a small, cheap dose of the legal drug will produce the same effects as a couple of hundred dollars' worth of the diluted illegal drug. Why, then, it will be asked, do junkies spend immense sums of money and incur other serious risks scoring for heroin if all they need to get high is a pill sold in any big-city slum for about twenty dollars? One answer is that heroin "holds" much better than Dilaudid. Though Dilaudid is supposed to be effective for as long as six hours, it won't hold a hard addict much longer than two or three hours. As such addicts dissolve the pills in water and shoot the solution into the mainline, and as they soon begin to have a lot of trouble getting a "register" because their veins collapse from this abuse, it makes a great deal of difference whether they are using a drug that demands three or four injections each day or six or seven long sessions probing desperately for a hit.

Apart from these quantitative differences in holding power, there are qualitative differences between the effects of synthetic opiates and refined natural opiates. Junkies insist that the pleasure of the heroin high far surpasses, both in the initial flash and the subsequent head, the sensations they experience on Dilaudid. This being the case, it would seem natural for Elvis Presley—whose favorite motto was "Take it to the max!"—finally to exchange the legal for the illegal drug and become at last a regular old boot-and-shoot junkie.

Though it's very likely that at some time or other Elvis tried heroin, in the manner of today's Beautiful People, by snorting it like cocaine, he never appears to have been a heroin addict or to have developed the obscene habit of the mainlining addict who, not content with simply injecting himself with the drug, insists on jacking back the blood in the chamber of the syringe and reinjecting himself a number of times in a kind of venous masturbation. Though Elvis began in 1972 to take enormous quantities of both Demerol and Dilaudid through injections, he would never use the needle on himself and he always skin-popped instead of taking the drug in the veins.

Putting all these facts together, you get the picture of a man controlled by an easily comprehended psychological taboo. Though Elvis would concede that he was deeply dependent on drugs, he could not tolerate the image of himself as a "junkie." Junkies were loathsome creatures whom he would have liked to have seen rounded up by the police and put in prisons, along with their pushers. (In fact, on more than one occasion, Elvis hatched elaborate plots for personally assassinating the most notorious pushers in Memphis.) No one could ever stigmatize him with this hated label, he persuaded himself, because he did not conform to the three-part definition of a junkie. A junkie Elvis defined (and taught the Guys to define) as someone who (1) uses heroin; (2) injects himself; (3) mainlines. Elvis did none of these things: QED—Elvis was not a junkie. How did Elvis define himself in terms of drugs? He was a man martyred by his career and fame, who lived under enormous and unnatural pressures that interfered with his natural functioning and produced distressing medical problems, like insomnia, that demanded treatment with certain legal medications. *Medications:* That was the crucial code word for dope in Elvis's dialect of double-talk and his exercises in doublethink.

This sort of preposterous rationalizing was actually once very common in America: back in the days before the Harrison Act, when hundreds of thousands of neurasthenic ladies who suffered from undiagnosable but severely debilitating complaints took every day their measured doses of those patented "elixirs" and "tonics" that were in fact laudanum: or, in plain English, opium dissolved in alcohol. That someone living in the midtwentieth century, especially someone as bright and hip and well-versed in drug description as Elvis Presley, could have deluded himself with such transparent pretences would appear unbelievable if we had not had already such abundant evidence of Elvis's profound capacity for self-delusion and self-escape. Once you learn the rules of Elvis's mental game with drugs, they make perfect sense not only in terms of their purpose but in the larger terms supplied by his personality. Once again you confront the essence of his being: his profoundly divided self.

On February 1, 1973, Priscilla arrived at Las Vegas with Lisa Marie to celebrate the child's birthday. The dining room of the penthouse was decorated with balloons and streamers. A birthday cake with five pink candles was set on the table. Priscilla had come with Joanie Esposito and one of her little daughters. Both women stayed close together and said virtually nothing to Linda Thompson, who was now established as Elvis's regular companion. While the children and the other guests ate the birthday dinner, Elvis and Priscilla withdrew to another part of the suite to have a serious discussion. When it was over, they returned to the table.

As soon as they arrived, Lisa looked up brightly and said: "Didn't you make things all right, Daddy, so that we can be back together again?" Elvis practically strangled. Priscilla told the child that they would have to leave soon for the airport because she had to be in school the next day. Spoiled little Lisa flared up instantly: "But the party just started!" she protested. "Do what your momma says, Lisa," Elvis warned in a low, forced voice. He knew that he would be blamed if the child misbehaved at this moment. Then he embraced her impulsively and lifted her clear out of her chair. "Daddy, you made me drop the piece of cake on the floor," the child complained. Elvis put her back into her chair and said softly, "I'm sorry, honey, I'll buy you another cake tomorrow."

That night, Elvis had to cancel the late show. The next night, he canceled the midnight show again. He couldn't sleep. His eyes showed great black rings. Instead of holding court with the Guys, he secluded himself in his bedroom. A storm was brewing and the Guys could feel it. Then, one night in the dressing room down under the stage, as Elvis was putting on his costume, he recounted to Hamburger James a dream he had had the night before.

In the dream he was on trial for his life. The prosecuting attorney was Colonel Parker. The chief witnesses for the prosecution were Priscilla and Red. No one would defend Elvis. All the Guys had rejected him. Among the jury, the only two who were sympathetic to his case were his Jewish jewelers in Beverly Hills, Schwartz and Ableser. The judge wore a white robe and carried a black medical bag. "What does it mean, E?" asked Hamburger James. Elvis replied, "It means the end is near."

This dream, whatever its ulterior meaning, represents with cartoonlike clarity many of the most basic features of Elvis's life and psyche at this critical moment. The courtroom suggests the coming divorce proceedings. The Colonel appears as the arch accuser, the prosecutor. He is the man who told Elvis when they made their first deal—"If you ever do anything to make me ashamed of you, you're through!" Priscilla and Red, the two people closest to Elvis emotionally, are both depicted as aggrieved parties, as, indeed, they had every right to be. The notion that the Guys had rejected Elvis is a typical expression of his oft-repeated statement that none of them were really his friends but that all of them were simply seeking to exploit him. The Jewish jewelers, who had designed the TCB symbol, are a puzzle; but the "Chosen People" are always benign presences in Elvis's private mythos. The judge in the white robe suggests, of course, Elvis in his white stage costume. The medical bag belongs to the judge. Is he a doctor, like Flash Newman, condemning Elvis for his addiction? Or is he Elvis, condemning himself? Whatever meaning one infers from the dream, its ominous tone and the resigned and hopeless air with which Elvis read it prepare one for what happened next.[1]

[1] The foregoing account of Priscilla Presley and Mike Stone's relationship is based primarily on interviews with the latter.

Chapter 32

A New Kind of Hit

THE WEEKEND following the ominous dream, there was a violent incident on the stage of the Showroom Internationale. A group of flashily dressed men with swarthy complexions, accompanied by some of the local hookers, took places at the end of one of the long tables that run up to the edge of the stage apron. When the party had been seated, another member arrived, spectacularly costumed all in white, with a cape, hat and cane of the same color. As he greeted his friends, they applauded and received him as if he were their leader.

During the course of the performance, one of the men in this ringside party jumped up on the table and from the table hopped onto the stage. As he advanced toward Elvis with a jacket over one arm, Red West rushed up behind him. Grabbing the interloper's head in a hammerlock, Red ran him right off the stage and into the arms of a security guard who searched him immediately for concealed weapons. No sooner did this happen than another member of this same party leaped onstage to aid his comrade. He was stopped by the tall, dour-looking J. D. Sumner, who told him in his deep barrel-tone voice: "Pal, get off! You can't come up here onstage!" With that the man cocked his fist, which was covered by adhesive tape. Elvis came rushing over and assumed a karate fighting stance.

507

Before any blows were exchanged, Jerry Schilling seized the man and pushed him violently off the stage so that he fell back on his back atop a table. Now a third man came charging onto the stage, followed by a whole string of people who probably wanted to help Elvis. One by one, friend or foe, they were pushed back by Sonny West and Jerry Schilling, who were soon involved in a vigorous game of King of the Mountain.

During the height of the melee, Elvis kept flourishing his hands and legs karate-style, shouting, "Let 'em go! Let 'em go!" as if nothing would have pleased him better than to get a crack at these unknown assailants. When Sonny, who had been reinforced by this time by numerous security men and house detectives, looked around and saw how manic Elvis had become, he rushed over and seized Elvis in a bear hug, as would a parent trying to restrain and calm a hysterical child. "Elvis! Elvis! They're gone!" cried Sonny, trying to still the panic he saw in Elvis's face. Finally, Elvis recovered himself and resumed his position before the audience, to whom he apologized for the disturbance, complaining only that he hadn't been allowed a shot at the interlopers because he would have "kicked their asses." So far as the audience was concerned, the incident was over; but that wasn't the way Elvis felt.

The moment he came offstage, he started an investigation into the incident, which he swore was a plot against his life engineered by Mike Stone. He pointed to the fact that the men were foreign-looking and one of them had tape on his knuckles. They were Hawaiian karate killers, Elvis insisted, who had been foiled only because he and his men were so well prepared. Having recognized one of the call girls with the men, Elvis got her on the phone. (Elvis was very well acquainted with the local whores.) She told him that it was worth her life to talk about these men, who were definitely shady operators. This revelation fueled Elvis's paranoia even further. Now he was Dirty Harry, deeply involved in a dangerous case, pushing the local police to get the men's rap sheets and discover exactly who they were.

Far from being Hawaiian karate killers, they turned out to be South American porno and go-go girl hustlers from Lima, Peru, whose heaviest rap was toting an unlicensed weapon. They had not been armed. The bit of tape around the one dude's fist was explained by the fact that he had slammed his fist into a slot machine that didn't pay off at the Landmark. The more the incident was investigated, the more obvious it became that all the first man had wanted to do was shake Elvis's hand and present him with the jacket that he had carried onstage. Everything that followed was triggered by Red West's strongarm tactics.

Nothing could persuade Elvis that he had not missed death by a narrow margin as a result of Mike Stone's imagined machinations. Till the day he died, Elvis carried about with him the rap sheets he had obtained from the police. He told the story of the attack countless times, embellishing it, like Falstaff, so that the number of his attackers constantly increased and his own heroic exertions reached the point where he was standing off fifteen men single-handed. In fact, the incident had a vastly different conclusion from that over which Elvis crowed.

When he got back to the safety of his penthouse the night of the incident, he called up the security detail that had taken the four men in custody. He told the guards that when they released the men, they should tell these guys that if they didn't get out of town instantly, they wouldn't leave alive. The guards were so submissive to Elvis's orders that they did just what they were told. The South Americans, who came from a world where death threats are a serious matter, panicked and demanded an armed escort to the airport.

Elvis was now meeting Dr. Newman before and after every show. The moment Elvis would arrive in the dressing room, he would say, "Where's Flash?" Then, as soon as the nattily dressed, silver-haired doctor appeared, he and Elvis would disappear into the bathroom, where the Doctor stuck Elvis with a hypodermic syringe. As soon as Elvis returned to the dressing room after the show, Newman flashed on the scene again, closeting himself briefly with Elvis in the little bathroom. Two shows a night, four visits from the doctor. What is the logical surmise? Powerful stimulants to get Elvis up for the show. Powerful sedatives to get him off after the show. Then another tug on the human yo-yo before the next show. Finally, late at night, perhaps four or five in the morning, the indefatigable Flash—"the speediest sixty-year-old man in the world," as the Guys called him—would pop up again in the bedroom of the penthouse to give Elvis his sleeping potion by hypodermic.

Though Elvis was being medically "managed" twenty-four hours a day, he was still like a human bomb. All it took was one minor incident to trigger off the final explosion. The cause was that perpetual source of outrage, Elvis's exacerbated relationship with Priscilla.

Priscilla was quite content to cut the domestic ties that attached her to Elvis, but she was reluctant to abandon her excellent black maid, Henrietta. An arrangement was worked out that enabled Henrietta to retain her job with Elvis and at the same time do some work for Priscilla. Naturally, this opened a conduit of information between the two households. One day while Henrietta was talking with Hamburger James, she confided that Priscilla had Lisa Marie sleeping in a crib at the foot of the bed in which Priscilla slept with Stone. The implications of this false tale are as clean or nasty, as harmless or damaging, as the mind of the man who repeats it. Hamburger James blames himself today for ever repeating this bit of gossip, but repeat it he did, to Red West. West, who as the sequel will show, appears to have had a profound antagonism to Mike Stone, relayed the story to Elvis.

Elvis, it will be recalled, had slept for many years in the same bed with his mother and father. This might have disposed him to regard such arrangements as being quite harmless. Instead it disposed him to kill. On the night of February 19, after the second show, Sonny, Red and Lamar were sitting in the living room of the penthouse drinking beer when Elvis called for them from the master bedroom. What happened next has been sensationally but accurately described in the opening pages of the West-Hebler book, *Elvis—What Happened?*

When Sonny got into the bedroom, he found Elvis dressed in his pajamas and sitting on the bed yoga-style. Linda Thompson was beside him. Elvis, who had been looking worse every day for a week, was now a ghastly apparition. He was drenched with sweat, stoned blind and obviously plumbing the depths of one of his darkest, blackest moods, the sort of anihilatory rage into which he would work himself after days of brooding over some painful insult or injury. Elvis commanded Sonny to come near. Then he said, "Look into my eyes, Sonny, look into my eyes." Sonny recognized instantly what Elvis was about: He was trying to hypnotize Sonny just as Elvis had seen the Colonel hypnotize Sonny on a number of occasions. As soon as Elvis felt he had Sonny under control, he began to fill the mind of his bodyguard with posthypnotic suggestions and commands.

"The man has to die," rumbled Elvis, slurring his words and struggling to look hypnotic. "You know the man has to die. The sonovabitch has to go! You know it, Sonny, you know it. There is too much pain in me and he did it! Do you hear me? I am right. You know I am right. Mike Stone has to die. You will do it for me. Kill the sonovabitch! Sonny, I can count on you, I know I can!" Sonny had seen Elvis emotionally disturbed many times. He was also very much aware that Elvis was an actor and could feign emotions. This time there was no feigning. As Sonny looked at Elvis, he realized that his boss meant every word he said. This was a command.

Sonny started to reason with Elvis, to talk him out of this mad notion.

He told Elvis that though his pain was terrible, it was wrong to talk about killing a man. The man didn't intend to hurt Elvis, certainly not to kill him with rage and grief. Nothing Sonny said made the slightest impression on Elvis. He continued to sit there like a fat, sweating Buddha, with his eyes glaring hate instead of love, his mouth opening and repeating over and over like a man in a malarial delirium: "Mike Stone must die, he must die, he has no right to live."

Finally, Elvis could brook delay no longer. Rolling clumsily out of his enormous platform bed, he staggered to his clothes closet, rummaged inside and then turned to confront Sonny with an M-16 automatic rifle in his hands. At this point, Linda Thompson who had been watching this scene with slowly mounting terror, started screaming: "What's the matter with him? Won't somebody do something? Calm him down, for God's sake!" Elvis shoved the gun into Sonny's hands. Sonny started to retreat, walking backward toward the door, protesting at every step. Elvis, stung to fury, hurled himself onto the bed, screaming: "Doesn't anyone understand? Why can't you all understand *this man must die!*" Then, he started clawing the wall, trying to climb it. Sonny saw this as an act of insanity. He flung out of the room carrying the automatic rifle, which he hurled with disgust into a wastebasket. Now it was Red's turn to deal with Elvis.

Red was just as appalled at Elvis's madness as was Sonny. An angry man himself, he was at a loss to deal with this kind of crazed malevolence. Fortunately, Linda had her wits about her. She picked up the phone and called the house doctor, Elias Ghanem, who promised to come up immediately and give Elvis a calming shot. Meantime, Elvis continued to repeat the same demand that Mike Stone be killed. Not until the doctor's needle had squirted a powerful sedative into Elvis's veins did he stop raving. When at last he lapsed into sleep, Red consoled himself with the thought that next day everything would be different. Old E had simply blown his stack. He would be a different man in the morning.

When the next day came, however, Elvis had not relented one jot in his determination to have Mike Stone killed. Only now, he did not tell Sonny or Red to do the killing: He told Red to hire a hit man to do the dirty job. At first, Red did not take the order seriously; but when every day Elvis kept renewing the command, stressing that this was something that could be done and must be done and was Red's responsibility to do, Red began to feel that perhaps Elvis was right. Stone was a monster. He had destroyed a marriage. He had driven Elvis insane. Finally, Red succumbed to Elvis's demands. He got the number of a member of the Mob. Soon the Memphis Mafia was talking to the real Mafia. It took no time at all to cut the deal. The Mafia dudes said they would be honored to help out a man as great as Elvis Presley. They set a modest figure for their work: ten thousand dollars. A trifle! No more than the cost then of a new white Lincoln Mark V Continental. Finally, Red was able to go to his master and give him the word that the hit had been contracted.

The last night of the engagement, February 23, Red knocked on the door of Elvis's dressing room twenty minutes before show time. He was admitted and Hamburger James sent out into the lounge. Red told Elvis that one word from him would send Mike Stone to his grave. Elvis pondered the idea anew. Then, he said: "Aw, hell, let's just leave it for now. Maybe it's a bit heavy. Just let's leave it for now." Red felt enormously relieved. Looking back on the event later, he realized that he must have been acting like a mindless zombie, totally subservient to Elvis's mad will. To be more precise, one could say that he had been acting as if he were simply the embodiment of Elvis's anger, which is, in fact, what his role had been for many years in Elvis's life. Only never before had it been so clear. As Elvis used to say, "Red is anger." He should have said: "Red is *my* anger."

Though Red experienced a keen sense of relief when he was released from his dreadful mission, Elvis could not share this comfort. He experienced a profound sense of depression. Rage that cannot be released through action soaks back into the mind as deep, self-destructive gloom. The very night that Elvis renounced his plans for revenge, he nearly died.

It was shortly before dawn when Linda awoke, brought to consciousness by some intimation that her "baby" was ill. The first thing she noticed about Elvis was that he wasn't breathing normally. Indeed, he appeared to be having great difficulty in merely drawing breath. His breaths were long and strangled. They subsided for so long that it seemed each time as though he wouldn't breathe again. When Linda tried to shake Elvis awake, he did not respond. Now she noticed that he was ice cold. Greatly alarmed, she called Joe Esposito, who promised to get Dr. Newman up to the room as quickly as possible.

Newman recognized Elvis's condition instantly as a drug overdose. Normally, the medical response in such a situation would be to call an ambulance and rush the patient to an emergency room. This was not a normal situation. It was vital that Elvis not become the center of a scandalous incident that might seriously damage his career and the reputation of the whole resort. Even the Mob doesn't kill in Las Vegas. So the doctor applied the standard resuscitation procedure unaided. A Dilaudid overdose produces first a shortness of breath, a slowness of heartbeat, a lowering of blood pressure that signals a profound depression of the central nervous system. As this process continues, the patient slips into a deep coma until finally he reaches the terminal state: cardiac arrest and death.

The answer is a procedure with which Elvis himself must have been very familiar because it is printed on the endpapers of his favorite book, the *Physicians' Desk Reference*. First, the physician must facilitate breathing by sticking a pipe down the patient's throat. Then, he injects a chemical antagonist to the narcotic, like naloxene hydrochloride. Next, a catheter is inserted in the penis and the bladder is drained to determine the degree of dehydration, for the shutdown of the central nervous system results also in kidney failure. Fluids are then infused intravenously in accordance with the volume of urine. How long it took to bring Elvis around and what incidents occurred during this perilous process is information known only to the two or three people who were present. The next day the Guys were told only that Elvis had taken a bit too much of his medication and had to have the doctor in the middle of the night.

After this close call, Elvis lay low for a couple of months. In April he made a brief tour of the West Coast, thirty pounds overweight and clearly suffering from drug addiction. He wound up the tour with a stand at the Sahara Tahoe. Here again he got so wiped out on his medications that the final portion of the engagement had to be canceled. The public was given the excuse that Elvis was suffering from "throat congestion" or "pneumonia." The situation appeared so threatening to those around Elvis that the boldest and most resourceful of them, Ed Hookstratten (a friend of the Colonel, who must have seconded the lawyer) decided to take matters into his own hands and attempt to save Elvis's life by means of a stratagem.

Hookstratten realized that there was no point in trying to persuade Elvis to relinquish drugs voluntarily. What the shrewd and tough attorney had in mind was an attack on the doctors who supplied the drugs. Engaging John O'Grady and another private eye named Jack Riley, Hookstratten ordered the detectives to ferret out the principal prescription writers and discover their modus operandi.

At the end of a six-week investigation, O'Grady and Riley were able to identify positively three doctors and one dentist who were major sources. (Oddly, they failed to identify Dr. George Nichopolous, who was later exposed as the supplier of prodigious quantities of dangerous and addictive drugs.) Most of the prescriptions were made out to the Guys and their wives or even to Lisa Marie. They were filled in Las Vegas at the Landmark Pharmacy, directly in sight of the International Hotel, and delivered to Elvis's suite, where they all wound up in Elvis's hands.

When the two tough-talking detectives confronted the doctors with the evidence of their deeds, they made no effort to protect themselves through denials. The doctors simply said that if it were not for their work, both Elvis and the public would be much the poorer. Evidently the federal and state authorities concurred with this judgment, for when the results of the detectives' investigations were presented to the appropriate law-enforcement agencies, no action whatsoever was taken.

Elvis had so many doctors all over the country that it would have been a major undertaking to identify them all and determine what contribution each made or did not make to Elvis's constantly widening pattern of drug abuse. Like all junkies, Elvis was an adroit feigner of medical complaints. If all else failed, he would rip out a tooth filling and get a fix from a local dentist. Any doctor or dentist who appeared the least bit disposed to hero worship or financial opportunism was fair game for the insatiable Elvis. No sooner, for example, did the house doctor of the International Hotel, Elias Ghanem, display concern for the famous star, than Elvis began wooing the doctor in the most extravagant manner. Dr. Ghanem reciprocated with true Arab hospitality by providing Elvis with a haven in the doctor's home.

Slight, swarthy, with typical Lebanese features, Elias Ghanem is a very boyish-looking forty-three. Dressed like a swinger in tight hip-huggers and a clinging body shirt whose open collar reveals a massive gold medallion on a chain, he receives you in a low medical building adjacent to the hotel. His private office is decorated like a suburban parlor, but its walls are covered with photographs showing the little doctor in close, often affectionate contact with famous celebrities. As he speaks, in a low, intimate, earnest voice, he toys constantly with a lock of thick, black, slightly greying hair. Smiling, he confides that many of his celebrated patients have suffered from rather embarrassing complaints. One homosexual star had hideous herpes sores all around his anus. Another middle-aged swinger, recovering from open-heart surgery, had his stitches ruptured by an overactive playmate. The doctor, you learn, has two valuable specialties: He is expert at emergency room procedures and the treatment of "Vegas throat," a condition highly disturbing to singers, produced by the arid and particulate-laden air of the desert.

Dr. Ghanem has amassed an extraordinary amount of wealth in the short time he has been in practice. Seven years after his arrival at Las Vegas, a young, unknown and in no way remarkable practitioner, he owned his own one-story medical building and a luxurious house on the border of the country club, while holding a sizable interest in a bank, a travel agency and a charter air service, Jet Avia, that boasts one twelve-million-dollar four-engine jet, but is best known for the crash of two Lear jets in the same day, January 6, 1976, one of them carrying Frank Sinatra's mother to her son's opening at Caesar's Palace.

As for Dr. Ghanem's relationship with Elvis Presley, it was of such value that it inspired Elvis to shower the doctor with such costly gifts as a sixteen-thousand-dollar Mercedes and a forty-two-thousand-dollar Stutz Blackhawk; on the doctor's side, it inspired him to build an especially designed room on top of his house just to accommodate his favorite patient. One would expect this room to be luxurious, judging from the style of the rest of the house, which, though small, glitters with opulence and fulfills every fantasy of desert chic, down to a cocktail table in the conversation pit that rises and falls at the press of a button. What the Presley room suggests, however, is not just luxury but the sort of decor and paraphernalia with which a great magnate might furnish the boudoir of his movie star mistress.

The room is carpeted to the ankles in thick shag. The bed is raised on a dais and fitted with mirrors around the top and headboard. A few steps from the foot of the bed is an erotic-looking oval Jacuzzi lined with fake onyx veined with gold and controlled with gold faucets. Beside it is an elaborate dressing table. A humidifier sits on the floor. The windows, looking out on the greens of the golf course, are heavily shuttered. Beneath them is a bookcase filled still with Elvis's spiritualist books. Opening one at random, you see the familiar underscoring beneath the words: "Should I return, you would not recognize me." It is said that Elvis would enter this soothing environment to lose weight through a remarkable Sleeping Beauty diet that allows the patient simply to snore through the unpleasant days of self-denial. Dr. Ghanem scoffs at this notion. He says that Elvis used the room to retreat from the pressures of his life, and that he often conducted with Elvis long, probing conversations. "What were they about?" you ask. He replies, "Drugs."

Dr. Ghanem admits freely that he gave Elvis injections before and after his shows at Las Vegas. What he denies heatedly is that he ever gave Elvis dangerous or addictive drugs. In fact, he insists that he worked hard to wean Elvis from the addictions engendered by the practices of other doctors. When asked whether it was true that before the show he would stuff up Elvis's nose wads of cotton soaked in liquid cocaine— a preparation a number of the Guys also enjoyed—Dr. Ghanem explains patiently that this was a drug called Lidocaine. (Lidocaine is a local anesthetic widely used to cut cocaine.) When you ask Dr. Ghanem about the story told by a couple of the Guys that they intercepted a Mason jar filled with pills sent by Dr. Ghanem to Elvis in Memphis, he says he has no recollection of the incident. According to Dr. Ghanem, most of the drugs he administered to Elvis were harmless placebos.

Elvis's most important source of drugs in his later years was Dr. George Nichopolous of Memphis. Dr. Nick, as everyone calls him, is another instance of a young, unknown and unremarkable physician who established an extraordinarily close and compelling relationship with Elvis Presley. It was early in 1967, at the time when Elvis bought the ranch in Mississippi, that these two men were brought together by chance. Elvis was suffering from saddle sores. He couldn't get in touch with his regular doctor. George Klein's wife suggested her boss, Dr. Nick. Anyone who stepped inside the charmed circle of Elvis Presley's life wanted to remain there. What's more, Elvis was often willing to give them a chance if they proved faithful. What Elvis sought in everyone was not intelligence or skill or credentials but loyalty, dependability and submission. Dr. Nick was abundantly endowed with the virtues that meant the most to Elvis. Almost immediately the young doctor, who had only begun to practice medicine seven years earlier, became Elvis's regular physician.

No sooner did Elvis come out of the hospital in the spring of 1973 than he was hit by a legal action that had scandalous overtones. Priscilla Presley had discovered in the nine months since the signing of the marital termination agreement that the amounts of money stipulated in this agreement were wholly inadequate for her life-style. Her combined alimony and child support payments came to only fifteen hundred dollars a month. Now Priscilla claimed that the figure should be ten times as much. What's more, she had gone into the dress designing and manufacturing business in January 1973, with Olivia Echeverria, using the name Bis and Beau, and she required more money to capitalize this endeavor. Elvis had been generous to her, after his fashion, furnishing her new apartment in the Marina Del Rey at a cost of $50,000 and giving her an expensive new Jaguar. What Priscilla was seeking now was not more gifts or special allocations but an entirely different separation agreement based on a division of their community property.

As she had signed and lived with the old agreement for so long, accepting all the monies that Elvis had offered her, she had now to find some strong legal grounds for setting aside the previous settlement. Engaging a lawyer for the first time, she presented the Superior Court of the State of California in May 1973 with a motion to set aside the agreement on the grounds of "extrinsic fraud" (a civil not a criminal action).

The nature of the alleged fraud was set forth not only by her attorney, with his various points and authorities, but in a personal declaration that was soon to be exploited by the movie magazines with sensational effect. To imagine the impact of the following statement, one has to bear in mind that up to this moment hardly one word of a scandalous character had ever appeared in print concerning Elvis Presley and very little concerning the nature of his marriage, his wife or his decision to sue for divorce. Now after seventeen years of silence, the following remarks were put into the public record by Priscilla Presley and swiftly smeared all over the hitherto immaculate Presley image:

> Since I was sixteen years old I have been living with my husband's family and during that time I developed trust and confidence in my husband, his father and other persons associated with them. During our marriage I was never involved in my husband's business or financial affairs. I was never informed of my husband's income nor the nature and amount of property which we had accumulated. My expenses were paid through an unlimited checking account upon which I wrote checks. Although I signed federal income tax returns I never examined the returns and do not know what income was disclosed by him.
>
> In August, 1972, my husband told me that we should agree to a division of property. . . . I told him that I would accept $100,000 because I assumed it was fair. . . . A few days later I was called by Mr. Hookstratten and asked to come to his office to sign the papers. When I got to his office he had the papers prepared and he told me that it was necessary for a lawyer other than him to look at the papers for me. He told me he had made arrangements with Mr. Robert Brock whose offices were in the same building and that he would take me there. Mr. Hookstratten told me Mr. Brock might ask me about my husband's finances

and start to discuss money with me but he told me if this happened
I should not pay any attention to what Mr. Brock said regarding
money and to tell Mr. Brock that Mr. Hookstratten had fully
informed me about finances and that I did not need his help
concerning that subject.

Mr. Hookstratten took me to Mr. Brock's office and left me
there. Mr. Brock already had a copy of an agreement in his hand
which he had apparently obtained from Mr. Hookstratten. He
asked me if I knew what the paper meant. I told him that I
did. He then asked me if I knew how much money my husband
received as residuals, royalties, and other income. I told him that
Mr. Hookstratten had informed me about all these matters and
that I was fully aware of my husband's finances. Mr. Brock then
asked me to sign a letter to him stating that I had not employed
him for the purpose of advising me about my husband's assets
or income. I was in Mr. Brock's office for about fifteen minutes.
I then signed the Property Settlement Agreement believing that
I was getting my fair share of our property and believing that
in any event I would be taken care of by my husband in the
future as I had in the past.

A few days later I received a check for $50,000. I was told
by Mr. Hookstratten that I should put the money in the bank
and leave it there so that I could have it for my future needs.
After that I began receiving $750 twice a month. This money is
not enough for me to live on. . . . I signed the Property Settlement
Agreement because both my husband and Mr. Hookstratten told
me that it was fair and represented what I was entitled to. . . .
Had I known that I was entitled to one-half of the community
property and adequate spousal support based upon my husband's
income and our previous style of living and had I known that
the sum of $100,000 as my share of property and $1000 a month
was not fair, I would not have signed the Property Settlement
Agreement.

Both Elvis and Hookstratten responded to these charges independent
declarations denying Priscilla's allegations and offering their own, quite
different, versions of the story. They contended, plausibly, that Priscilla
had been informed that she could obtain a larger settlement but had
insisted that $100,000 was sufficient. Her story was "copy," however,
and theirs was not. Hookstratten dissociated himself from this undesirable

case and substituted another attorney. This new attorney, Harry M. Fain, took a deposition from Priscilla in which he forced her to admit that she knew very well the character of her husband's work, including the fact that he made a lot of money, and that she had actively participated in the purchase and furnishing of their three California houses. He could not get her to admit that once or twice in the years when she was signing Elvis's income tax she took a peek at the net income line. She insisted to the end that she had no idea of what the form in her hand said. Though the efforts of Fain weakened Priscilla's case, they did not by any means destroy it.

Now, Priscilla's lawyer began to demand Elvis Presley's financial records, a demand that drove both Elvis and Vernon to the limits of outrage but which could not be denied. At this point, the case started to get hectic. At issue were such questions as whether the California law, which demands a fifty-fifty split of community property, applies to a man whose domicile is in Tennessee, whose law has no such provision for the division of property in divorce. Also there were knotty questions concerning what part of Elvis's income was his as an unincorporated business and what part was his as a private person and so on ad infinitum.

It's not hard to imagine the effect of Priscilla's demands on Elvis. Now, in addition to the mortal wound he had suffered to his pride, he was facing the possibility of an enormously costly divorce settlement. Even apart from the financial threat, there was the enraging sensation of having his most private affairs, including his confidential financial records, ripped open and studied by lawyers seeking ways to strip him of his property. Coming after a prolonged period of emotional stress and drug abuse, this latest crisis undermined the last supports sustaining Elvis's sanity. Now, he began acting like a lunatic.

During his customary August-September engagement in Las Vegas, everyone noticed how ill he looked and how heavily he was leaning on his drug crutch. Suffering constantly from sleeplessness, though absorbing immense quantities of narcotics and hypnotics, Elvis soon became wildly erratic in behavior. One night the maitre d' of the Italian restaurant at the hotel told Elvis a long tale of woe. The man claimed that for no good reason, he was about to be fired by the Hiltons and thrown out in the street. Elvis, whose sense of injured innocence was a lot stronger than his sense of reality, responded by promising the Italian that the problem would be swiftly solved. That night when Elvis got onstage, he stopped the performance to announce to two thousand guests in the showroom that he had just discovered that Conrad and Barron Hilton were about to perpetrate a terrible act of injustice. Then, as everyone listened in astonishment, he recited the pathetic tale of the little maitre d' and wound up the yarn by denouncing the Hiltons and demanding that they reinstate the man immediately.

Colonel Parker had just finished negotiating a new arrangement on Elvis's behalf that would reduce his engagements at the hotel from four weeks at a stretch to two. The Hiltons could have made serious objections to this cutback, but they had been very sympathetic to Elvis's complaints about the punishing effect of such long runs. Now, no sooner do they conclude the deal that lets Elvis off the hook than Elvis turns around and gives them a black eye in front of their own guests.

As soon as the show ended, Colonel Parker—who had been sitting backstage during Elvis's rap and had groaned repeatedly, "No! oh, no!"— came storming into Elvis's dressing room intent on rebuking him for this outrageous and irrational act. Elvis was in no humor to suffer a tongue lashing. As soon as the Colonel launched into his speech, Elvis turned on the old man and told him off in the most insolent manner. When Colonel Parker renewed his charges, Elvis raised the issue of the Colonel's gambling, pointing out that the reason they could not entertain the lucrative offers that were being made by other hotels, like the soon-to-be-opened MGM Grand, the biggest hotel in town, was because the Colonel had to offer Elvis to the Hiltons as payment for his gambling debts. "You can't talk to me like that!" exploded Colonel Parker. "The hell I can't!" snapped Elvis. "Then I quit!" barked the Colonel, rising to leave. "You can't quit," sneered Elvis, "because you're fired!" "I have quit," countered the Colonel, "and I'm calling a press conference tomorrow to explain the whole situation." By the time the old man was out of the dressing room and heading up the hall, Elvis stuck his head out the door and shouted: "I'm calling a press conference tonight!"

No press conference was called by either man, but the Colonel sat up till dawn drawing up an enormous bill of charges, which he claimed was money that was owing him from past operations. Having completed this tally and seen to its delivery, the Colonel and his staff decamped.[1] For the next ten days, Elvis was on the rampage. Night and day he gave orders one minute and countermanded them the next. He insisted that no one leave him at any time, even to sleep. One morning, Red West had taken a sleeping pill and was just falling to sleep, when there

[1] Colonel always had a large sum owing him during Elvis's last years. Elvis's 1974 tax returns show that the Colonel took only twenty-five percent that year, though he was entitled to far more. When Elvis died, he owed Colonel Parker one and a half million dollars.

was a loud banging on his door and the voice of one of the Guys shouting: "Elvis is up and wants you to go to the dentist with him." The thought of getting back into his clothes and going on this nitwit mission was almost more than Red could bear. Grumbling, he got himself together and reported for duty in Elvis's suite, still grumbling. Elvis, alert always to the slightest sign of insubordination, came charging out of his bedroom and confronted Red. "If you're so goddamned sleepy," he thundered, "get your ass back downstairs and go back to bed!" "No," sighed Red. "I'm here to do my job." Again, the implication was clear that only duty motivated him. Elvis was so annoyed by this attitude that he ducked back in his room and came out a moment later with his M-16, which he pointed straight at Red's chest. Responding as Sonny had years before when Elvis socked him in the jaw, Red gasped, "Elvis, after all these years, I never would have believed that you would point a gun at me!" Then, recovering his nerve, he turned mean and threw the challenge back in Elvis's face: "Go on, you bastard, pull the trigger—kill me!" At that point, Elvis put up the gun; as he turned to put it in his room, he gave Sonny, who was standing nearby, a fast wink.

Elvis also had a violent falling out with Jerry Schilling during this engagement, which commenced with Schilling keeping to his room for a couple of days and came to its climax with the two men squaring off for a fight, each one egging on the other to make the first move. At this time, Elvis seemed intent on driving his closest intimates away. Most of the Guys were making excuses to escape. Lamar left for a funeral. Red went back to his family. As soon as the engagement concluded, Joe Esposito and Jerry Schilling took off for Europe. Finally, Elvis began to calm down.

One morning early, he told Sonny to get the Colonel on the phone. Sonny rang just as the old man was walking into his office in Hollywood. Elvis spoke with the Colonel briefly, and they made up their differences. This is precisely what most of the Guys had anticipated would happen, although Lamar had insisted that Ed Hookstratten was standing in the wings ready to make his entrance as Elvis's new manager. Hookstratten, who is one of the foremost managers of showbiz and athletic talent, with a roster of clients that had included Cary Grant, Glen Campbell, David Merrick, Joseph Levine, Jim Brown, and Rowan and Martin, had discussed the possibility of taking over as Elvis's manager back in 1970, when the Colonel was so ill that it appeared he might be forced to retire. Nothing had come of the suggestion then nor did it now. (It was not until the very end of Elvis's life that any serious effort was made to terminate this famous relationship; then the initiative came not from Elvis but from the Colonel.)

When "Hell Week" finally ended, Elvis decided that it was time that he and his remaining men have a little fun. Picking up some girls, they went down to Palm Springs for a week's rest and recreation at the house on Chino Road. Elvis's date was a pretty teenager who had been since childhood a devoted fan. One night they went to bed and drank a lot of Hycodan, a blood-red, cherry-flavored cough syrup with a narcotic base. When neither Elvis nor the girl made an appearance the following morning, Sonny West entered the bedroom.

The room was freezing cold. Both Elvis and the girl were unconscious. The empty bottle of Hycodan was on the bed table. Sonny suspected an overdose immediately. "C'mon. Wake up!" he shouted. When neither of them responded, his alarm mounted. Raising the girl's eyelids, he saw the eyes were as fixed and unwavering as marbles. Listening to her breath, he heard what sounded like a death rattle. Slapping her hard across the face, he was horrified to see that she didn't move a muscle. Elvis appeared just as inert. For one second, Sonny thought that both of them were dead.

Then he scrambled around to Elvis's side of the bed and slapped his face. The blow produced a low moan. Lifting Elvis's lids, Sonny saw the sightless eyes rolling from side to side. Elvis, at least, could be saved. Sonny picked up the house phone and called their local physician, Dr. Kaplan, who said that he would be at the house in a few minutes.

Now Sonny alerted the other guys, Charlie Hodge and Hamburger James. Immediately, they fell to plotting who would take the blame if the girl were found dead. As both Sonny and James were married, the obvious choice was Charlie. He agreed to say that the girl was his date and that he had offered her the deadly syrup. Next, they began to think of the other girls in the house. They mustn't be allowed to know what was going on, or they might talk and the whole outrageous story would get into the papers. James agreed to keep the girls occupied in a room at the rear of the house and prevent them from getting out until the crisis had passed. By this time the doctor was at the door.

Dr. Kaplan took one look at the girl, who by this time was turning blue, and picked up the phone to order an ambulance. Elvis was just getting his head up when he heard the doctor's call. "You don't have to do that," Elvis said. "Just give her a shot of Ritalin [a central nervous system stimulant] and she'll come around." The doctor explained that the girl was near death and would have a chance of recovery only if she were rushed to an intensive care unit. As the argument mounted, the ambulance, warned not to use its siren, arrived. The girl was put on a stretcher and borne out of the house. As soon as she was removed, Elvis got on the phone and called the Colonel, a man who had extensive influence in Palm Springs.

That night the girl began to come out of the coma. Sonny, who was deeply concerned about her condition, had gone to the hospital. The doctor told him that he was very worried about possible brain damage produced by prolonged deprivation of oxygen. Sonny sat down beside the bed and began to call the girl softly by name. Suddenly, her eyes popped open. She turned and glared at Sonny. Then, she sprang out of bed, hissing like a wildcat. Sonny was stunned. "What's the matter with her?" he gasped. "She doesn't know where she is," replied the doctor, leading the girl back to bed. "Will she be all right?" persisted Sonny. "We don't know how long her brain was deprived of oxygen. We'll just hope for the best," answered Dr. Kaplan.

Eventually, the girl recovered sufficiently to leave the hospital and return home. The Colonel had done his hush work well. Not a word about the incident leaked to the press. Another Presley skeleton had been neatly locked in its closet. Just to make doubly sure that there were no dangerous grievances, the Colonel offered the family money. The girl's mother—who was a great fan of Elvis's—refused to take even a penny. Elvis never visited the girl or called her, save for once when she was long out of danger. He told her, "Honey, when you're feeling better, I'm gonna take you on tour with me." He never took her anywhere nor did anything for her. He wiped her off his mental slate. Sonny saw the girl a year later at a show. She struck him as being a different person. Instead of an easy laugh and an open demeanor, she seemed unnaturally quiet and withdrawn. She told Sonny that she held no grudge against Elvis. She regarded the whole incident as entirely her own fault.

The long postponed divorce was granted on October 9, 1973. Elvis and Priscilla appeared at the court in Santa Monica: When they left the judge's chambers, they posed, smiling, for the photographers, giving the impression that, as always, they were the best of friends. Under the new settlement, Priscilla received far more money than she had under the original agreement. She obtained in cash $750,000, with a commitment to receive another $1,250,000 in monthly payments of $6,000. Her alimony was increased to $1,200 a month but reduced from five years to one. The child support figure was raised from five hundred dollars a month to four thousand. Priscilla was also granted half the proceeds from the sale of the house on Monovale Road, valued with its furnishings at half a million dollars, plus five percent of the stock in two of Elvis's publishing companies: Elvis Presley Music and Whitehaven Music. As before, Lisa Marie was to live with her mother but her custody was to be shared by Elvis and Priscilla. Considering the fact that during this period Elvis's annual income rose to seven million dollars, this settlement is not notable for its generosity. On the other hand, its cost to Elvis in mental turmoil and emotional anguish was incalculable.

All of Elvis's intimates agree that the fatal decline that ended in his death began during the period of his conflict with Priscilla over her affair with Mike Stone. Up to the day when he was forced to recognize that his wife had rejected him for another man, Elvis Presley was riding high. He may have betrayed his talent or developed a soul-shriveling life-style or planted the seeds of self-destruction with his dependency on drugs, but the man's basic strength was still intact and capable of revival. Once he suffered the castrating blow of Priscilla's infidelity, he was like Sampson, shorn of his locks by Delilah. He could rage and bellow and threaten to shake down the world, but in truth he was the broken column. It took a few years before this blow registered its full and fell effect. Meantime, he was still free to swagger and posture and lord it as the King of Rock. In truth, however, he was like Eliot's Fisher King: a man who has suffered a crippling wound and is presiding over an emotional wasteland. Never again could he convince himself that he was what he had once been: a man who had never known defeat.

Had Elvis Presley been made of better stuff than comic-book fantasy and Hollywood heroics, the disaster of his divorce might have straightened him out instead of reducing him to a helpless infant. The strengthening that suffering confers on men, however, is contingent on their learning the truth about themselves and the world. No narcissist can ever afford to learn the truth about himself. That is the meaning of the ancient myth, in which Eros goes to Tiresias to complain of his rejection by Narcissus and demand some appropriate punishment. Tiresias warns: "If he learns the truth about himself, he will die." Elvis Presley made sure that he would never have to face the truth about himself. He escaped into a cloud of unknowing called narcosis. Drifting back into a fetal Eden, he experienced that sensation of "oceanic" bliss that enables a man to imagine himself a god even as he is sinking into a condition more pitiful than that of any beast.

Elvis's decline into infantilism and drug invalidism had no effect on his popularity as an entertainer or his status as the King. One of the bizarre ironies of his career, always characterized by the incongruity between his limited talents and his limitless fame, was the way his myth imposed itself on the world in later years, mounting to ever greater peaks of popularity and power, while the man who was the object of all this adulation was steadily declining to the condition of a hapless wretch. Ultimately, the only way to account for this awesome disparity between cause and effect, between the moribund star and his immensely vital image, is to invoke concepts like royalty or divinity that explain how even a man so far gone that he can barely mount a stage can compel the admiration of millions of people the world around because they believe that in his grotesque body and deadened mind there lies some wondrous essence that gives life to their own humble existence.

Chapter 33

Easy Come, Easy Go!

BY THE AGE of forty, Elvis Presley had earned a hundred million dollars—and was broke! The explanation for this astounding state of affairs is found in the deadly combination of profligacy and stupidity. Elvis operated always on the principle that "you don't come back for an encore." This great truth inspired him to become the world's foremost impulse buyer. The tale of his spontaneous extravagances is as long as it is bizarre. The fourteen Cadillacs that he bought in one night at Memphis, winding up the performance by inviting an old Negro woman who happened to be passing by to pick out any machine she fancied; the sudden mania to acquire airplanes—after a lifetime of being afraid to fly—which made him soon the master of a fleet of four multiengine aircraft; the disposition to set his favorites up in new houses, an impulse that was extended in the case of Linda Thompson to include not only a house for her but a house for her parents and a house for her brother—this kind of spending, though suitable to a prince, could only reduce him in the end to a pauper.

Spending money was something that Elvis did in a progressively more reckless and self-destructive fashion as he grew older, exactly as he increased the number and potency of his drugs. When he was young, as we've seen, he was tight with a buck, like his father.

527

Then, when he got religion in the midsixties, he began to obsess about texts like, "It shall be harder for a rich man to enter heaven than for a camel to pass through the eye of the needle." At that point, he started to indulge himself both in fantastic spending sprees and in spontaneous gift offerings to the Guys. What characterized the final phase of his money madness was the act of throwing money away. Though Elvis never quite got to the final symptom of this disease, the flinging of bills into the street, he came pretty close. Consider two acts of extravagance from his final years. The first is of the old self-indulgent variety, but carried to insane lengths. The second is a perfect specimen of spending as a self-destructive stunt.

One evening late in the year 1975, Elvis was sitting with a couple of the boys at Graceland describing the marvelous peanut butter and jelly sandwiches that he had been served at a hotel in Denver. When somebody remarked reflexively, "Boy, I wish we had some now!" a bell rang in the drug-numbed mind of Elvis Presley. It was like the fairy tale of the three wishes: You couldn't want anything at the palace of the Rock King that you didn't instantly get no matter how trivial the wish or how costly the effort to fulfill it. Leveling a heavy-lidded look at the speaker, Elvis growled, "Let's go get 'em!" That was it! Next thing the boys knew, they were aboard the four-engine Jet Star heading out toward the Rockies. En route, they called the hotel by skyphone and placed their order with room service. When the plane landed, six cars from the hotel were standing out on the tarmac. From each car one great tray of carefully wrapped sandwiches was removed and loaded reverently aboard the transport. When the last tray had been carried like the boar's head to the cabin, the hatch was closed, the engines were fired and the big plane went thundering down the strip heading back to Memphis, nearly a thousand miles distant. That mess of peanut butter and jelly sandwiches cost the King sixteen thousand dollars.

During the same or the following year, Elvis found himself one night working a little town in North Carolina. He hated working such places, but as he deteriorated under the influence of drugs and began to draw a drumfire of savage criticism from the local press, his bloated appearance compelled Colonel Parker to carry his freak further and further away from the major population centers so as to expose him only to those people who wouldn't have cared if Elvis had come onstage trundling his belly in a wheelbarrow. The trouble with these good folk was that, though Elvis worked to them like a traveling evangelist, holding up his right hand as if "testifying" and bawling out spirituals, there were nights when they reacted much as had the very first audiences Elvis faced when he was just a lad touring the Bible Belt with Bob Neal. By this point Elvis was not like other entertainers, who must work harder when they encounter resistance in the audience. Elvis was the King. The King doesn't have to work to win an audience. Hell, it's the King's role to give audiences! So on this particular night, looking out into the house and seeing that he wasn't getting the proper adulatory reaction, Elvis suddenly called a halt to the show.

As everyone onstage looked on incredulously, the King waved in from the wings the royal goldsmith, a nondescript little jeweler from Memphis named Lowell Hays, who, like everyone else around Elvis, had gotten his foot in the door and found himself like a man with a winning lottery ticket. Elvis had commanded Hays to accompany his King on all tours, carrying with him at all times—on pain of banishment!—a box filled with gaudy but costly female jewelry. Whenever the spirit moved him, the King would beckon to his jeweler, survey the treasures in the box and make an appropriate selection for his favorite of the moment. In this manner in a few years, Hays sold Elvis $800,000 worth of jewelry.

Once the goldsmith had come out onstage with his box, an incongruous, almost invisible figure when standing next to his huge master, opulently attired like a great white carnival reveler from Rio, Elvis ordered the box opened, hovered over it a moment with his own richly jeweled hand and finally settled on a brilliant. "Lowell, whass' this I got heah in mah hand?" asks Elvis like a TV interviewer, tipping the royal mike toward the stage-frightened jeweler. "Elvis, that theah is a star sapphire with six baguettes in a white gold settin'." "What's it worth, Lowell?" asks the interviewer. "That one goes for thutty-five hundred dollahs, Elvis." With that Elvis turns around, a big grin on his huge egg-shaped face, and squinting into the stage lights, he pins a little old granny in gingham in the front row. Walking over, holding the ring before him like a butterfly, he leans down gallantly and, speaking into the mike, he offers the gem to the old woman: "Grandmah, I want you to have this now 'cause you remind me 'zactly of my own gran', Dodger, back theah in Memphis." With that, he hands the ring to the astonished woman—and the whole auditorium explodes in cheers, whistles, screams and applause. Now he's got 'em!

Another man would figure that he'd made his point. Not Elvis. The Monarch of Momentum, His Supremest Extremist, Elvis can't stop with just one spectacular gift. He has to go on and on, until he has emptied the jeweler's box—then, he has to give a royal command to fill the box again for further giving. At least $35,000 worth of jewelry was distributed that night to the first couple rows before Elvis would resume the show. Poor old Vernon, fresh out of the hospital because of a heart attack, had to be supported to the dressing room after witnessing his son's ultimate act of folly. It's easy to imagine what effect this story had on Colonel Parker; the old man must have chewed the tip off his cigar thinking what should be done before Elvis went completely crazy and gave away Graceland.

Though it probably wouldn't have made the slightest difference in the final reckoning if Elvis had earned ten times one hundred million dollars, the fact is that he earned far less than he would have if he had managed his money sensibly. If he had sheltered his income from the taxman and invested it intelligently, Elvis Presley could have become as wealthy as Bob Hope. That Elvis never had a tax shelter or an investment portfolio or even a pension plan can be laid squarely to the account of Colonel Parker, who dreaded the thought of some shrewd money manager sticking his nose into the Colonel's dealings with Elvis. So instead of making his money work for him, Elvis followed the advice and example of his manager and flung it all away. This infantile behavior he justified by insisting that any time he chose he could earn immense sums simply by stepping on a public stage. This was no idle boast, as Elvis demonstrated time and again during the seventies.

At the end of 1975, for example, the Presley finances were so depleted that the Colonel said their only hope lay in playing a long shot. Though never once in twenty years had they worked on New Year's Eve, this year they would do the unprecedented. The easiest shot would have been the Hilton at Las Vegas, which made them a handsome offer; but the Colonel was looking for megabucks. He found them way out in the sticks in Pontiac, Michigan, where there was a promoter eager to play Elvis in the arctic immensity of the 80,000-seat Silver Dome sports arena. Trying to fill such a house on New Year's Eve was an extremely dangerous maneuver: a bad break in the weather and the whole event would turn into an enormous fiasco. The ole Colonel was nothing if not a gambling man. He decided to take the chance. Gallantly, he led his forces into the far north, arriving in town early to direct personally the preliminary publicity barrage.

When the great night came and Elvis, fresh from buying everyone diamond jewelry for Christmas or giving himself some well-deserved gift, like a new four-engine plane, turned up in his Prince Valiant costume, the atmosphere was not exactly soulful. The Silver Dome is an immense color-coded, deep-freeze tank, with a flying saucer ceiling high enough to accommodate a fifteen-story building and acoustics comparable to the Carlsbad Caverns. When Elvis walked out onstage, he couldn't find his band. Casting frantic glances to right and left, he located the players finally, huddled a couple of stories below him on a platform so drafty that they were all wearing overcoats. As Elvis threw himself into his first numbers, standing all alone atop the towering stage, like an obese go-go girl, he experienced suddenly not that lovin' feelin' but the shame and terror of feeling a cold draft blow up his ass where his pants had split. Fighting gallantly to protect his endangered rear, he went on with the show, until the last volley of trumpets and drums. Then, he reeled offstage, practically screaming for his "medication." The following week, it was announced in all the trades that Elvis Presley had broken the record for "single date by single attraction" by grossing on New Year's Eve $800,000.

Such enormous earning power may appear to justify even the most reckless life-style. Its true effect was simply to draw Elvis ever deeper into debt. In 1974, for example, he played the staggering total of 152 shows. Two-thirds of these performances were one-night stands, which meant that for most of the year Elvis was cut off from the comforts of home and condemned to live in the hotels and motels found in towns like Monroe, Louisiana; Auburn, Alabama; Hampton Roads, Virginia; and Murfreesboro, Tennessee. Considering the condition of Elvis's mind and body, this was a heroic effort. Nor did it go unrewarded. Elvis earned in this one year the stupendous sum of seven million dollars. A king's ransom! Yet it was not enough to allow Elvis to break even. At year's end, he was forced to tap his bank account for $700,000, just to pay his bills.

Where did all the money go? Precisely where it always went. High operating costs, including $1.7 million for the services of Colonel Thomas Andrew Parker, gobbled up four million dollars. Of the remaining three million, fifty percent went for taxes. Elvis's net income was a paltry $1.5 million. Still, many men could scrape by on that sum. Not Elvis. In addition to his heavy nut, his basic living costs, he had incurred such extra expenses as his father's quarter-million-dollar divorce settlement, the cost of buying several multiengine airplanes and the sizable expense entailed in hiring a private gospel group (in addition to the one he used onstage) that would follow him around the country, adding its three voices to his in impromptu all-night sings. The bill for this extravagance was ten thousand dollars a month plus all expenses. Among the hidden costs of living like a king was an estimated half-million dollars poured out on the purchase of drugs and their transportation by an endless series of couriers from the Landmark Pharmacy in Las Vegas to wherever Elvis might be at the moment out on the road. Though Elvis bought his drugs dirt cheap at standard retail prices, his doctors were not so inexpensive.

All of Elvis's money problems reduced ultimately to his attitude: that stubborn and sometimes violent refusal to recognize that there were any limits to what he could spend. Elvis was confirmed in his contempt for reality by the Colonel. Like characters in an allegory, Elvis and the Colonel had become hypostatized ideas: Elvis the emblem of self-gratification, the infinitely indulged, endlessly spoiled child, who spends his life stuffing himself with goodies; the Colonel the grim, military per-sonification of worldly power, hard-fisted manipulation of money and relentless day-and-night work. So caricatured did these identities become over a period of twenty years that Elvis and Colonel became like charac-ters in an animated cartoon.

To the very end of the relationship, however, people in show business were saying that Elvis and the Colonel were the perfect combination. The Colonel had freed Elvis of all the time-consuming, bewildering and exasperating problems of business so that he could devote himself entirely to his art. Yet, when you're a commercial artist, as was Elvis, it's question-able whether there really is any difference between art and money because the art is done for the money and the money is the measure of the art. Though Colonel Parker insisted that he never interfered in any way with Elvis's art, the truth is that by managing Elvis's business as he did, the Colonel exercised a profound and decisive effect on Elvis as an artist. Though he didn't tell the singer what songs to sing, he set him up in the music business in such a way that Elvis could not sing any song that was not offered to him by his publishers, who, in turn, confined Elvis to the kinds of music that they could obtain on their terms and actively discouraged him from reaching out for better music from sources that the publishers could not control. Likewise, though the Colonel never told Elvis how to read even one line in all his movies, by working out the formula for the Presley picture and by confining Elvis to such pictures throughout his film career, the Colonel destroyed Elvis as a film star. The division between art and business proved in practice, therefore, an unreal distinction.

Allowing Colonel Parker to take complete control of his career was not only ruinous to Elvis as an artist: It was just as destructive to him financially. For though the Colonel was highly ingenious in his schemes for making money, in order to maintain the control on which his own wealth depended, the Colonel had to keep Elvis perpetually in the position of the donkey plodding after the carrot. An Elvis Presley who had learned to make his money work for him or an Elvis Presley who had learned to live within his means would not have been an Elvis Presley whose life was in the hands of Tom Parker. Ultimately, therefore, Colonel's management of Elvis was self-serving, for the enrichment of the Colonel and his grateful business partners.

Like all hustlers, the Colonel distrusted everyone instinctively and assumed that everyone was on the make. Yet when the question of his own dealings was raised, the Colonel would climb up in the pulpit and start sermonizing about the sacred value of trust and how impossible it is to do business on any other basis than one of absolute trust. He would insist that his word was his bond. His handshake was as good as any contract, blah, blah, blah. This line of malarkey never impressed, one can be sure, such shrewd operators as Hal Wallis, Jean and Julian Aberbach, Hank Saperstein, Abe Lastfogel or any of the successful businessmen with whom the Colonel traded. They recognized the Colonel for what he was and acted accordingly. The only person fool enough to swallow the Colonel's bunkum was Elvis.

Though he had every reason to be distrustful of a man like Tom Parker, especially in his later years when Colonel's addiction to gambling became obvious, never once in twenty-two years of professional association entailing hundreds of millions of dollars did Elvis Presley demand any general accounting from Colonel Parker. Undoubtedly, the mere suggestion of an audit would have produced a tremendous explosion of emotional fireworks by the Colonel, who would have retaliated by making all sorts of counterthreats, including the ultimate threat—and bluff—to quit. As Elvis was not the sort to suffer any sort of pain or embarrassment over a mere matter of money, he never made any such demands. Nor were his contracts, all of them personally authored by the Colonel, designed to provide for such a contingency. The first five-year contract with RCA had contained the standard clause stating that if no objection to the accounting were raised in one year, the matter could no longer be opened. The second contract, for seven years, executed after Elvis came out of the army, contained no audit provision whatsoever (though it did contain sizable payments to the Colonel for unspecified services). Ultimately, therefore, Elvis had to take everything on trust. Or to put it differently, Elvis got what Colonel gave him.

All that Elvis ever knew about his business was that every week or ten days a note would come from the Colonel's office reporting a sum or sums received from one or more of the great number of companies that sent remittances regularly to Elvis Presley. Numbers would appear, tagged with cryptic notations. Sums would be deducted for this or that reason. All Star Shows (Colonel Parker) would deduct its twenty-five percent or fifty percent—and that would be that! An accountant in Memphis would collect these statements every month, tote them up on an adding machine and use them to prepare tax returns. Oh, saintly simplicity!

After Elvis' death, the truth about the Colonel's management began to come to the surface, bit by bit. One day in Nashville, for example, Joe Mascheo, who had worked with Elvis for years as a singer in the imperials but who now held a desk job with BMI, took it into his head to punch out Elvis's account on the computer. He was curious to learn how many hundreds of thousands of dollars his former boss had earned over the years in performance royalties on the famous songs for which he had cut-in deals. Imagine Mascheo's astonishment when the computer returned a list of twenty-seven songs, for which Elvis was credited as coauthor, with the notation: "Not affiliated." Unable to believe his own eyes, Mascheo punched the data back into the computer again. Once more the startling line came sputtering out: "Not affiliated." Assuming that he had made a mistake, Mascheo now punched in the code for ASCAP, the other major royalty collecting agency. Once again the computer responded: "Not affiliated."

This was amazing! Here was a man who owned a one-third interest in many of the most popular songs of the twentieth century, who had his name on the sheet music and record labels of immense hits like "Heartbreak Hotel," "Don't Be Cruel," "Love Me Tender"—and he never received a nickel in broadcast composer royalties! Where had all this money gone?

When the Colonel saw that Elvis was starting to break down from heavy drug abuse, he determined to protect his interests in every way possible. After all, the old man hadn't spent a lifetime in show business without learning what happens to pig junkies. He must sometimes have been reminded of the fate of his old crony, Oscar Davis, who booked Hank Williams for a New Year's show and received delivery of a corpse. Oscar ended his days broke, after having earned and gambled away vast sums of money. For years before Davis died, Colonel used to put a little check for his fellow player in the mail every month. It was like a paper caput mortuum.

Two devices of self-protection lay in the Colonel's hands. First, he could demand a bigger share of Elvis's earnings; second, he could sell his interest in Elvis to another party. The principal source of Elvis's income in the seventies was his concert tours. In February 1972, Colonel had gotten Elvis to give him a one-third commission on the profits of these tours: "In consideration of the rendition of our complete organizing of tours, handling all transportation . . . tour supervision, etc." In fact, what Colonel did was put the tours in the hands of the well-known promoter, Jerry Weintraub, who engaged Concerts West to do the real work of running the tours. Colonel Parker's labors consisted in little more than checking out the locations in advance and increasing the number of radio spots if the concert was not a sellout. Now, on January 22, 1976, he demanded for these meager services a further increase in commission to a flat fifty percent of the net profits for all tours, TV specials, merchandising arrangements, etc. By this point, Colonel was close to the goal prophesied by the "overages" agreement of 1967: a down-the-middle division of everything Elvis earned. As for Elvis, he was now sustaining rank after rank of managers, agents, merchandisers and promoters, like one of those circus strongmen with a pyramid of other men piled on his shoulders.

Now that the end was near, all of Elvis's jockeys were maneuvering for a bigger share of the stakes. In 1974, Colonel Parker set up a corporation entitled Boxcar Productions, which appears to have been designed partly with the idea of giving his old guard a final bonus. To Boxcar were transferred all the merchandising rights in the name and image of Elvis Presley. The stock was divided as follows: Tom Parker, forty percent; Tom Diskin, fifteen percent; George Parkhill, fifteen percent; Freddy Bienstock, fifteen percent; Elvis Presley—fifteen percent! How's that for a deal? Not only did Colonel and his cronies take eighty-five percent of the stock, but they also took substantial annual salaries and bonuses. The Colonel's salary in 1976 was $36,000. Tom Diskin's salary as president was $46,448. Don't get the wrong idea, though—Elvis got a salary, too. He received $10,500.

Dumping Elvis proved a much more difficult and disturbing task than cutting deeper into his earnings. Inevitably, the Colonel's overtures leaked out, producing a rash of stories in the press. An item in the *Nashville Banner* was particularly disturbing because it quoted sources close to the Colonel as saying that the old man needed cash to pay his gambling debts (one million dollars in December 1976 alone), being no longer able to discharge these debts as he had in the past by trading off Elvis's services at the International. The Colonel threatened the paper's editor with a suit for defamation if he did not print a full retraction. The editor told the Colonel to go right ahead with his suit but to be prepared to see all his gambling records subpoenaed as evidence at the trial. That prospect silenced the Colonel. As matters turned out, Colonel discovered that his fears about Elvis's death depriving him of income were like the reports of Mark Twain's demise, "highly exaggerated." Elvis would die soon, but the event would only improve the Colonel's business.

Cutting into the dying King became the major preoccupation of every member of the royal court in the final years. One of the most successful petitioners for financial favors was the court physician, Dr. George Nichopolous. Elvis, it appears, could not deny his doctor any more than his doctor could deny Elvis. First, the doctor received the customary gift of a home, but it was a home on a much grander scale than was ever given to any other royal favorite, including Vernon. Three hundred fifty thousand dollars was the price of the doctor's new house, which in Memphis in the midseventies was a very expensive residence. Then, the doctor decided to join a medical group that built a $5.5 million medical center equipped with all the latest and most costly equipment. Again, it is likely he found support in his principal patient. The greatest boon the doctor craved, however, was something that had nothing to do with his personal comfort or professional practice. A skillful racquetball player, Dr. Nichopolous fancied himself as the man who would popularize this sport on a large scale in America and in the process reap the vast profits that belong to the owner of a successful franchise operation.

Presley Center Courts was conceived as a chain of fifty racquetball installations all across the country, with the pilot facilities being built in Memphis and Nashville. Associated with Dr. Nick in the project were a Memphis bond salesman named Jim McMahon, who was the only businessman in the deal, and Joe Esposito, who was cut in for a share of the business as a reward for his indispensable services to Elvis. The arrangement was that a contractor would build two courts for about a million dollars and rent them back to the corporation for $12,000 a month each. The basis of the whole undertaking was a commitment by Elvis to underwrite the project to the tune of $1.3 million in exchange for a twenty-five percent share of the stock.

was "one of the happiest moments of my life") was not only an act of
injustice but an act that invited retaliation. In short order, the men
made a deal with *The National Star* to expose Elvis in a paperback
book. They were promptly assigned a hotshot Rupert Murdoch reporter
named Steve Dunleavy, who concentrated on giving his exposé a sensational air. When Elvis got wind of this deal, he began to get uncomfortable. He offered to buy off the bodyguards for a hundred thousand dollars.
They stuck to their guns—in every sense of the word. They were so
concerned about the possibility that Elvis would order them killed that
they put in a safe deposit box a lengthy statement identifying their likely
assassins and some highly damaging photographs and other documents.
Instead of hiring a killer, Elvis worked himself into a murderous rage
one night in Los Angeles and tried to persuade David Stanley to go
out gunning for Red and Sonny. David, a tough, salty kid, ridiculed
Elvis's macho rhetoric and told him that Lisa Marie would be more
ashamed of a father who was a murderer than one who was exposed
as a drug addict. Elvis simmered down.

Elvis's prolonged relationship with Linda Thompson also concluded
in 1976. Linda had been everything to Elvis that a woman could be
for four and a half years: mistress, mother, wife, sister, daughter and
concubine. She had demonstrated an extraordinary capacity to adapt
herself to Elvis's bizarre way of living and his extremely demanding
and exasperating temperament. Inevitably, during this long and trying
relationship, her attitude toward Elvis had changed drastically.

Originally, Linda had been a stagestruck young woman in love with
a great star. She loved the touring, the elaborate and luxurious travel
arrangements, the trappings of the royal progress. Most of all, she loved
her proximity to the throne. Apropos of this period, she quotes the
phrase: "Power is the greatest aphrodisiac." If Elvis was like Jack Kennedy riding about in *Air Force One,* Linda was Jackie—and had the
mountain of luggage to prove it! She would come out in front of the
stage at a concert for the express purpose of signing autographs. She
was in showbiz heaven.

When, after the first year or eighteen months, Linda had lived through
her initial infatuation, she began to see Elvis in a different light. She
realized now that he was a drug addict, the most compulsive womanizer
imaginable, a supreme narcissist and a man who was profoundly averse
to marriage. She had also by this time established a friendly relationship
with David Briggs, a tall, ordinary-looking Nashville studio musician

who worked in Elvis's road band as a keyboard player. David offered Linda some of the attention that she was obliged to pour out day and night on Elvis. Gradually, Linda began to alter her relationship with Elvis to make it conform with the old formula: "romance equals finance."

Over the next few years, she acquired everything that she needed to make a fresh start. Elvis bought her an ugly new brick ranch house in a development near Graceland, and gave her $75,000 with which to furnish the place. She filled it with bright green shag carpeting and white garden furniture, including a white piano, giving the whole establishment the look of a California leisure house focused on a large outdoor pool. Linda accumulated a quarter of a million dollars in jewelry and had an extensive wardrobe of the kind of stagy clothes that Elvis loved, purchased at Giorgio's in Beverly Hills or Suzie Cream Cheese at Las Vegas. When Vernon beefed at her spending ten thousand dollars at a shot in a dress shop, she countered by protesting good-humoredly that she never had a chance to go shopping because of Elvis's schedule: The size of the bill reflected not her extravagance but the rarity of the occasion.

During her last year with Elvis, Linda obtained an apartment in Los Angeles and began to put out feelers for film and TV work. She was represented by Ed Hookstratten, and eventually, after the breakup of her relationship with Elvis, landed a steady job as a sexy comedienne on *Hee-Haw*. The best-educated person ever to survive in Elvis's company (Elvis once told a reporter: "I'm afraid of intellectuals—they bring dissension and envy and jealousy.") and one of the most cheerful, Linda won the good will of everybody in the Presley family and entourage. She saved Elvis's life on more than one occasion and made extraordinary efforts to accommodate herself to his needs. Ultimately, however, the only relationship that any woman could sustain with Elvis Presley was that of an infinitely loving young mother with her very sick and cranky child. Linda played this role to the hilt, entering the hospital with Elvis when he was drying out from drugs and lying by his side night after night as they watched the babies in the nursery on closed circuit TV. Even in the hospital, however, Elvis always had someone who would smuggle him in some drugs. Eventually, Linda realized that if she wanted to have a life of her own she would have to break free of Elvis's morbid grasp.

The termination of the relationship was not totally amicable. Elvis called up John O'Grady one night and told him to throw everybody out of the house on Monovale Road, including Linda. She, for her part, blew $25,000 in a final shopping spree and then held Elvis to a promise to send her on vacation to Europe. Taking along a girlfriend to keep her company, she went through another $25,000 abroad. Alluding with a laugh to her $50,000 kiss-off, she slaps one impressive hip and quips, "I hit him where it hurts the most—right here!"

Chapter 34

So Shall It Be in the End

WHEN AN interviewer asked Ginger Alden, the woman Elvis was engaged to marry at the time of his death, what she felt on meeting the great star for the first time, she exclaimed: "Well, you expected trumpets or something!" It was true. By the end of his life, Elvis Presley was hallowed by fame and ringed with the nimbus of the superstar. Though the man was moribund, the Myth was vibrantly alive. Elvis could have echoed that Caesar who murmured at his expiration, "I feel myself becoming a god!"

Especially was the King awesome to a twenty-year-old girl like Ginger, who had grown up in Memphis. Almost as soon as she could walk, her mother had taken her to Graceland, where they stood outside the fence waiting to catch a glimpse of Elvis riding his big Palomino down the hill to the Music Gate to sign autographs for the fans. When Ginger was five, her mother brought her to the Fairgrounds on one of those nights when Elvis had rented the whole park. Elvis patted little Ginger on the head and took her with him on the roller coaster. It's not hard to imagine how overwhelmed she felt the first time she was summoned to the King's palace. She went in the company of her two sisters, one of whom, Terry, was the new Miss Tennessee, and therefore a prime candidate to succeed the old Miss Tennessee, Linda Thompson.

At the time, Ginger looked rather like Rita Hayworth before she was transformed by the Hollywood image-makers: a voluptuous heart-shaped face with big sloe eyes, full lips, a slightly cleft chin and a widow's peak: a sensuous but slightly coarse beauty combined with a figure a trifle too ample for current taste. When the King exercised his right to the pick of the litter, he surprised everyone by choosing Ginger instead of Terry. Doubtless he was impelled by her obvious innocence and naivete, qualities that he prized above all in women. Having chosen such a young and simple sweetheart, he prepared now to enjoy the kind of pleasure that a rich, powerful and thoroughly jaded older man can have with a silly little girl. No, he wasn't thinking about taking her virginity or introducing her to anything kinky in the way of sex or drugs; he just wanted the thrill of "blowin' that child's ever-lovin' mind!"

On their first date, they took a spin out to the airport in the Stutz Blackhawk. When they arrived at the gate of Memphis Aero, Elvis inquired casually if Gingerbread, as he had dubbed her, would care to go for a little hop aboard his Jet Star. Naturally, she agreed. As they boarded the big plane, they met Elvis's favorite cousin, Patsy Gambill, Uncle Vester's daughter, and her husband, Elvis's former valet, Gee Gee, as well as some other guests. Just as they were about to take off, Elvis announced that their destination was Las Vegas. Ginger was startled. "I have to call my mother!" she gasped. "You can call your mother as soon as you get there," replied Elvis smoothly, while fastening his safety belt. Glancing anxiously about her, Ginger observed that everyone else was laughing and chattering as if they were about to go on one of the fun rides at the Fairgrounds. Meekly, she submitted to her fate.

Seated face to face with Elvis, Ginger noticed during the course of the long flight that Elvis was examining her on the sly. He'd sneak a peek, then turn to stare out the window with a little smile on his lips. Puffing on a skinny cigar, he seemed very much at ease. Sandwiches were served. The plane purred along. Finally, the King called for his makeup kit.

When he received the battered box, he rummaged in one of the drawers until he found a little plastic cross. Motioning for Ginger to bend forward, he looped it around her neck. It was a worthless trifle that he had picked up somewhere or perhaps been given by a well-wisher. Then, groping inside another drawer, he withdrew a solid gold bracelet and slipped it on Ginger's wrist. When she turned it around, she saw that on its surface, picked out in glittering little diamonds, was the word

"Elvis." Looking up, she found herself staring directly into Elvis's blue eyes. His sensuous lips opened, his famous voice murmured, "This will show everybody that you belong to me." Ginger was thunderstruck. She didn't dare to reply except to say in her clear, musical voice, "Thank you."

When they arrived at dawn at Hughes Air Terminal, they were met by a couple of limousines and rushed to the Hilton. The next thing Ginger knew, she was alone in a hotel room with Elvis, who gave every indication of being about to retire to bed. At this instant, all the doubts and fears that had been gathering for hours at the back of Ginger's mind suddenly burst forth in a flood of anxious questions and images. "Will he expect me to sleep with him? Did he bring me out here just for *that?* What will happen when I say, 'No'?" She postponed the confrontation briefly by picking up the phone and calling her mother. When she explained that instead of being in Memphis she was now in a hotel in Las Vegas with Elvis, she anticipated an outburst of anger at the other end of the line. Oddly, her mother, after registering surprise, made no outcry at all. When Ginger put down the phone, however, she was trembling.

Elvis offered her a pair of pajamas and suggested that she go in the ladies' bathroom and change. She noticed that it contained an odd-looking fixture, which she surmised must be a bidet. When she emerged, feeling very vulnerable and uncomfortable, she found Elvis already in bed wearing an identical pair of pajamas. He beckoned her to his side. She slipped under the covers and lay there rigidly. He extended his hand. She clasped it. She waited for his words, his touch. Finally, she heard an odd sound. Turning to gaze at him, she discovered that he had dozed off and was snoring, his hand still in hers.

That evening, they arose, dressed, ate a meal in the room and left again for the airport. Without going anywhere or doing anything or even popping a coin in a slot machine, they boarded the plane and flew back to Memphis. The next day, Elvis was scheduled to leave on tour. Ginger contemplated her strange experience as if it had been a dream. Now it was over, she thought. He had been "a perfect gentleman." She had been "honored by his presence and everything." She would never see him again. What else was she to think?

Just a week later, however, she received another call from Elvis. This time he was in San Francisco. He was dying to see her. She must come and see his show. He would send his plane to pick her up. Could she leave the next morning? Hastily assembling a few things and borrowing a "dressy" dress from Terry, Ginger suffered herself to be picked up in a big car, carried to the airport, put aboard the Jet Star and flown across country to Elvis. When she arrived at the hotel in San Francisco, she was shown to her room by one of the Guys. Unpacking was the work of a moment. She freshened up her makeup. Then, she didn't know what to do.

Through the entire afternoon and evening she sat in her room without so much as receiving a phone call. Finally, as the evening wore on, she began to get very hungry. She hadn't eaten anything since breakfast. Now she was starving. She knew she could order food from room service, but she was reluctant to incur the expense or charge anything to Elvis. She kept debating what to do until it got so late that she had to go to bed. Next morning, when she awoke, there was still no sign of Elvis. Now, she was starting to feel very uneasy. She wanted to go home. Where was she? What was going on?

Had Ginger known the answers to these questions, she would have been astonished. In fact, she might even have relinquished the idea that Elvis was "a perfect gentleman." What had happened was really quite embarrassing. It was one of those *Box and Cox* comedies in which every inveterate womanizer must some day play the foolish starring role. Though Elvis and Linda Thompson had concluded their relationship, Linda had turned up in San Francisco and spent a couple of days with Elvis. He knew she was leaving and was so certain of the day that he had arranged to have Ginger fly out on the same day in a revolving door arrangement that would protect him from even a moment's loneliness. When the time came for Linda to depart on the Jet Star, she insisted on spending another night in San Francisco. Elvis did not want to provoke a scene because he couldn't tolerate hassling. So there was nothing for it but to keep Ginger stashed below stairs in her holding pen until his penthouse suite was cleared of Linda. Someone should have been constantly checking on Ginger's condition, chatting her up, making sure she was fed, offering her excuses for the delay. Alas, there had been an outrageous failure to TCB. Hence, Ginger's weird welcome.

The morning after Ginger arrived, Linda took off with her baggage train. Her room, adjoining Elvis's, was given a fast but thorough going-over. Then, Jerry Shilling came knocking at the perplexed Ginger's door, telling her: "We're going to move you." She should have picked up the nearest heavy object and saluted him with a deadly blow. Being a nice obedient belle, about a hundred fathoms out of her depth, she followed her guide up to the floor where the group was quartered. Ushered at last into Elvis's room, she discovered him sitting at breakfast clad in a blue robe with a monk's hood and wearing sunglasses. He got up and greeted her warmly. He asked her about her flight, as if she had just stepped off the plane. Naturally, Ginger said nothing about the depersonalizing experience she had undergone during the past twenty-four hours, sitting alone in a hotel room without the faintest idea of what was happening. She must also have eyed Elvis's burnt bacon and Spanish omelette with greedy eyes.

That night Elvis was playing at Anaheim. He took Ginger with him in the limousine, but then he left her backstage while he put on his costume and makeup. As she wandered about, watching all the activity prior to the show, she felt again as though no one would come near her. No one would, in fact, until her status had been clearly defined. If she proved to be just a one-night stand, she would become fair game for the Guys. If, on the other hand, Elvis showed a real interest in the girl, she would become strictly taboo. When Elvis reappeared, he ordered a chair placed for Ginger at the edge of the stage, where she would have a perfect view of his performance. The Guy who brought the chair offered her a bit of advice: He told her that when Elvis went into "Can't Help Falling in Love," she should duck off and head for the limousine at the stage door.

Never once during the whole show did Ginger stop worrying about her cue. When Elvis finally went into his closing theme, she got down on hands and knees and started crawling offstage so as to present the lowest possible profile. As she was making her escape in this rather undignified posture, she was suddenly struck by the sound of Elvis's voice booming over the auditorium's sound system, commanding—"*Stay!*" Looking over her shoulder like a startled cat, she realized that he was hollering at *her!* It was another of those shocks that were now defining the rhythm of her existence. "I couldn't believe," she explains, still astonished, "that right in the middle of a big hit song he would say, real loud, 'Stay!' " The whole thing was so confusing to her that the moment Elvis turned his back, she slipped away and ran to the car. When Elvis joined her a little later, with a towel around his neck and his whole body steaming like a horse hot from a race, he was very annoyed. He chewed out the Guys, complaining that they hadn't kept Ginger onstage for the very last moments of the show when he did all his spectacular karate kicks and chops. Because they fucked up, she had missed the best part—and he had lost the chance of impressing her with his prowess!

There were other ways, of course, to "blow her ever-lovin' mind"; for example, the magic wand routine. A few days later, in Las Vegas, he decided to give Ginger the knockout blow. Picking up the phone at four in the morning, he called Gerald Peters. He told the imperturbable Englishman, long since accustomed to receiving bizarre and oddly timed commands, that he must go forth at once and procure for immediate delivery, that very day in fact, a white Mark V Lincoln Continental.

Peters discovered the moment he set out to purchase the car that the machine could not be purchased. Ford was six months behind in its delivery schedule. Every dealership on the West Coast had long since been cleaned out. As no true Elfan could ever abandon a mission on behalf of his King, Peters got in touch with Ford in Detroit. He threaded the office labyrinth and discovered the secretary who was conversant with the delivery schedule for the car. He begged her to tell him whether there were any dealers in California who had just received white Mark Vs. She told him that the information was confidential. He offered her fifty dollars. She still seemed reluctant. Finally, he pronounced the magic words—"Elvis Presley." Instantly, she revealed the whereabouts of the cars. Peters located quickly the last unsold car. Rushing to the showroom, he wrote out his own check for $17,000 and drove the big bomb off the floor and straight to the Hilton Hotel in Las Vegas. Thus is served a king!

The punch line of the story is that after Peters had driven the Mark V across country to Memphis the following week, he discovered that Elvis had already bought Ginger another car. She had complained the Lincoln was too big for her, so Elvis gave her instead a nifty little Cadillac Seville, his favorite lady's model. What had Ginger been driving prior to receiving these biggies? Giving you her blankest Candy look, she confides: "I had a three-speed bike."

Even in Las Vegas, after having known Ginger for less than two weeks, Elvis was hinting broadly at marriage. He would say that when he closed his eyes, he could envision Ginger in a white bridal gown. Ginger was startled by these remarks. At first she thought, "Wait a minute, this isn't right!" Once she got close to Elvis, her attitude changed. Now she thought, "Hey, I really care for this person!" Soon, she was studying ways to accommodate herself to Elvis's strange life-style and make him happy.

She would read him to sleep in the morning or watch closely while he made his preparations to go onstage. He was very keen on having her study him. He would insist that she be present while he had his hair washed or as he prepared his throat gargles. Once he said to her: "I want you to watch carefully the way I walk." Then, he paced back and forth across the room. "Do you see anything special?" he demanded. Ginger didn't see anything remarkable about the way Elvis walked, so, just as a joke, she answered: "One leg is shorter than the other." Elvis threw a fit. He was outraged. Finally, he calmed down and explained to her that his walk was *"catlike."* Poor thing, she would never have guessed the secret word in a hundred years. In fact, to this day she describes the whole experience of living with Elvis by repeating constantly the same phrase: "I was in a daze."

Nine weeks after meeting Ginger Alden, Elvis decided that he wanted to marry her. Consulting the indispensable *Cheiro's Book of Numbers,* he discovered that the ideal moment for the engagement would be that very day, January 26, 1977. Clearly, some fast action was necessary because an engagement means an engagement ring and the ring that a king offers his bride is no ordinary ring. Around one in the morning, the King called the royal goldsmith to give him the order. As was so often the case, the royal command could not be filled in the allotted time. Elvis wanted a ring the size of the one he wore, which was eleven and a half karats, delivered to his house that very night. When Lowell Hays told the King that it was impossible to get such a big stone out of a jeweler's safe in the middle of the night, Elvis took the objection as a stinging challenge. After hours spent in terse, urgent calls of the sort you would make if your mother were dying and there was just one chance left in the world to save her but it demanded a coast-to-coast flight in an Air Force fighter with the serum in a special box that had to be kept at all times at absolute zero—after playing this game of phony crisis and long-shot triumphing over enormous odds—Elvis agreed finally to the sensible (and amusing) suggestion that he surrender his own stone and have it set as an engagement ring. Early the next day, he had the precious ring, which the jeweler told him was now worth about $70,000.

Having taken such pains to obtain the ring, Elvis offered it now in the most romantic setting imaginable—his bathroom. (Bear in mind that for Elvis, as for any junkie, the bathroom was the seat of countless blissful fantasies, like this one of getting engaged.) When the great moment arrived, Elvis played his part to the hilt. He seated Ginger in his black leather and chrome reading chair next to the toilet. Then he sank down onto his knees on the thick red shag carpeting. His speech was more touching than any he had ever delivered in his many movies. Never, he said, had he thought he would find someone so beautiful in his own backyard. Now, for the first time in his entire life, he realized what it meant to be truly in love. Other times, when he had been in love, he had been forty percent happy or even sixty percent happy; but this time he was one hundred percent happy. As he spoke, Ginger started crying. When he said, "Will you marry me?" she said but one word, "Yes."

Elvis reached into his pocket and pulled out the ring. Carefully, he fitted it on her finger. When he rose to his feet, he took her by the hand and led her out of the bathroom into the bedroom. There she found Charlie Hodge with Rickey and David Stanley. They all knew about the engagement. They offered congratulations and embraced the happy pair. Elvis was ecstatic. Ginger found that every time she raised her hand to look at her ring, the hand trembled uncontrollably.

No date was set for the marriage, but many plans were made. Among the changes that were destined to take place was another total renovation of Graceland. Elvis had already made some significant changes. Ginger had noticed that when she first visited Elvis, everywhere she looked in his rooms, there were pictures of Linda. Then she discovered that there was a small bathroom off the upstairs office that had obviously been Linda's dressing room. After Ginger returned from Las Vegas, all the pictures were gone and the bathroom had been repainted in Ginger's favorite colors. When she remarked on the changes, Elvis told her that Linda had put up all the pictures of herself while he was off on tour. He spoke of Linda as one aggrieved, complaining especially of the fact that she had asked him repeatedly to marry her. "I thought the man was supposed to do the asking," he grumbled. Now that he had the right sort of woman, his sweet Gingerbread, he wanted to proclaim her presence by constructing an art studio behind the house (Ginger dabbled in painting), as well as a movie theater that would have a dais with two thrones: one for the King and one for his Queen.

Ginger, for her part, was well pleased to become Elvis's queen. She says: "I came to feel that maybe that's why I was put on earth. If I could make Elvis happy, I would have served my purpose. He wanted a son. He wanted me with him night and day." This last desire was a demand that Elvis had made always of everyone who was close to him. Now for the first time in his life, it began to create problems. When Elvis asked Ginger to leave home and move in with him, she flatly refused. She justified her refusal on both moral and practical grounds. To her moral objections, Elvis had no real rejoinders; after all, he was the "perfect gentleman." When she argued that her constant attendance on him was unnecessary because he was surrounded by other people who could attend to his needs, he flared up angrily and barked: "Ginger, those people are not my friends! Do you think that if it wasn't for their paychecks that they would be around?" This statement shocked Ginger, who assumed, as did everyone, that Elvis regarded his men as bosom buddies. She refused to alter her stance, however, insisting that she had to spend time with her family and continue living at home.

This resistance might not have angered Elvis if she had not enlarged it to include refusals to travel with him on his tours or to his record sessions. It was just after the happy time of their engagement that the first such disagreement occurred. Elvis was scheduled to go to Nashville to cut some records. It was an important date because RCA was clamoring for fresh material. Elvis made all the arrangements on the assumption that Ginger would accompany him. When she said that she hated Nashville and didn't want to go there, he left without her. By this point in his life, the prospect of recording disgusted him, which is why RCA could never get any new "product" out of its superstar. If Elvis couldn't sweeten the experience in some way, he couldn't bring himself to make the effort. He stalled the sessions for three days. Each day a large number of musicians and singers would gather and wait patiently for him, running up a good-sized bill for the company. Elvis remained sulking at his hotel, alternately pleading with Ginger to join him or getting so whacked out on drugs that he couldn't rise from his bed. Finally, at the end of three days, he turned around and went back to Ginger.

It was a pattern that repeated until Elvis's death. Time and again this simple, modest, conventional girl brought the King to his knees by refusing to do his bidding. At the age of forty-two, Elvis was getting rejections from a twenty-year-old girl who was his fiancée! The situation enraged him so much that one night when she left the house, he ran down the stairs after her brandishing a pistol, which he actually fired over her head as a warning of what would happen if she did not return. That night, he got her back. On another occasion, when he saw that she was getting ready to leave, he told David Stanley to let all the air out of her tires. When she came back into the house to demand an explanation, she found him hiding under the bed and shaking with laughter. Asked to sum up Elvis in one word, Ginger replies unhesitatingly: "Headstrong!"

Not only did Ginger refuse to oblige Elvis on numerous occasions—she even challenged his right to behave capriciously at other people's expense! Just a week before he died, in August 1977, Elvis announced that he was taking all the kids in the entourage to Libertyland, the renamed and refurbished Fairgrounds. When the great night arrived,

Lisa Marie was visiting her father and there were a number of other children present, including Ginger's niece, Amber. Ginger and the little girls had worked themselves up to quite a pitch of expectation, when suddenly it was announced that Elvis had canceled the plan. This was the sort of killjoy trick that Elvis had been playing all his life on the Guys. They had long since learned that if you showed too keen a relish for a certain project, you were courting a last-minute cop-out by Elvis. Anything the Guys were eager to get, they kept at a very low heat. Ginger, innocent of such wiles, couldn't understand what had happened. She marched into Elvis's bedroom and demanded an explanation. "Why aren't we going," she asked, quite reasonably. Elvis replied, "We can go another night." This was not a satisfactory answer—but when had the King been obliged to answer to anyone? Ginger, in an act of unprecedented *lèse majesté,* refused to take no for an answer. "Everyone's dying to go. . . . They're all ready. . . . Why can't we go tonight?" Now, Elvis was forced to offer an excuse. "Everyone out there has gone home already," he explained lamely. Ginger looked at Elvis in astonishment and said, "Elvis, I thought you once told me you could do *anything!*" After that challenge, there was nothing for Elvis to do but pick up the phone and order everyone rounded up again so that the canceled visit could be made that very night.

In July 1977, the first copies of the West-Hebler book, *Elvis—What Happened?,* started appearing in the jobbers' racks of drugstores, supermarkets and airports all over the country. For the first time in his long and carefully guarded career, Elvis was going to have his covers pulled. It was an ominous moment. Elvis was at his wits' end. One night he received a call from Frank Sinatra, who offered to use his "influence" to have the book quashed. Elvis had hated Sinatra all his life. Even in his moment of greatest need, he could not accept his rival's help. He declined the proffered aid. Meantime, he read the book in fits and starts, suffering agonies when he reached the parts about his reckless use of drugs. There had been rumors for the past few years that the federal drug authorities were going to investigate Elvis's doctors. In Denver, for example, some police officers with whom Elvis was hobnobbing picked up a prescription for Dilaudid in his hotel room and recognized that their honorary captain was a hardcore junkie. They offered to slip him into a sanitorium. Elvis left town like a bandit. Now, with this stuff coming out, how was he going to hold on to his connections? Night and day, he wracked his brain for some scam to take off the heat. Then, one night, he found the answer.

Chapter 35

One Last Night of Fun

ON AUGUST 15, 1977, Elvis Presley was scheduled to depart on a twelve-day tour that would begin at Portland, Maine, and take him to Utica, Syracuse, and Uniondale, New York; Hartford, Connecticut; Lexington, Kentucky; Roanoke, Virginia; Fayetteville and Asheville, North Carolina; and home to Memphis for two final shows. Elvis awoke about four in the afternoon and called for his extra-strong, almost syrupy coffee. He ate no solid food because he was fasting to reduce his weight. As always his awakening was a slow and difficult process, a laborious reversing of the physical and mental machinery slowed virtually to a stop by massive doses of barbiturates and opiates. Eventually, he got out of bed and went into the bathroom to make that long and elaborate toilet that was designed to restore him, like a man taking rejuvenation treatments, to the image of youthful beauty and vigor.

By early evening, he had gone so far as to step out of doors, a thing he did rarely in his last years, where he watched Lisa Marie riding merrily about the back of the house in the specially built electric golf cart that was her favorite toy. The child had been sent to Graceland for a long visit by Priscilla, who was eager to cheer up Elvis and distract him from his worries about the book. For this last night at home, Elvis had planned one of his favorite

555

treats: He had ordered that the Ridgeway Theater be reserved after the last show and that a print be obtained of his favorite recent movie, *MacArthur.* Doubtless he looked forward to the scene in which the great general, brought home in disgrace from Korea, stands up in the American Senate and delivers his eloquent farewell address, a speech that Elvis had memorized twenty years before and recited so many times since. Yes, Elvis was perfectly capable of seeing now a parallel between his own fate and that of his hero, MacArthur. They had both served their country with genius and devotion; they had both been acclaimed the greatest heroes of their time; and now Elvis, like MacArthur, was being humiliated unjustly by people who owed their lives to him. No wonder he was calling for this film again at this moment. It spoke to his condition.

As it turned out, Elvis was deprived of this last night at the movies. The projectionist said he could not work late, and no one else could be found to take his place. Casting about for something else to do, Elvis decided abruptly to see his dentist, Dr. Lester Hofman. Calling the dentist at his home after supper, Elvis explained that he was about to leave on tour and needed some last-minute treatment. Dr. Hofman, who had known Elvis for years and who drove a Cadillac that he had received from Elvis, made light of the inconvenience. He agreed to open his office for an appointment that night at ten-thirty.

Though Dr. Hofman did fill, according to his own account, an upper right first bicuspid and an upper left molar that evening, it is doubtful that Elvis's motive in suddenly seeing the dentist was purely medical. As the prescription records compiled after Elvis's death indicate, on this day Dr. George Nichopolous prescribed for his famous patient the following drugs:

Amytal: 100 three-gram capsules and 12 half-gram ampules. Amytal is a barbiturate which in high doses has a pronounced hypnotic effect. As it is not manufactured in ampules, the compiler of this record may have confused Amytal with Amytal Sodium, which *is* packaged in half-gram ampules and sold in boxes of six. Amytal Sodium is a very powerful drug whose proper medical application is in the treatment of grave disorders, such as convulsions, meningitis, tetanus or strychnine poisoning.

Quaalude: 150 300-milligram tablets. Ludes are one of the most widely abused drugs in the world. Called "wall bangers" by the kids, they produce the slurred speech and loss of muscular control that were such conspicuous features of Elvis Presley's behavior in later years.

Dexedrine: 100 five-milligram tablets. These little golden "hearts" are the most familiar form of speed.

Biphetamine: 100 twenty-milligram spansules. This is the familiar "Black Beauty," a powerful amphetamine that is surpassed in effect only by the injectable varieties of speed, like Methedrine.

Percodan: 100 tablets. Percodan is another drug that has been used by heads for many years. Unlike the other preparations on this list, Percodan is a compound of five different drugs that act in concert to relieve pain. The principal ingredient, oxycodone, is a narcotic with effects similar to morphine.

Dilaudid: Fifty four-milligram tablets and twenty ccs of two-milligram solution. Elvis was furnished with the drug in both oral and injectable form. The solution was provided in a multiple-dose vial rather than in a fixed-dose ampule, thus allowing him to inject far more than the normal dosage.

Stockpiling drugs in this manner on the eve of a tour was standard practice with Dr. Nichopolous. The reason was simply that doctors cannot write prescriptions in any state but the one in which they are licensed to practice medicine. As this tour was of less than two weeks duration, the list indicates clearly not only what drugs Elvis was taking but the rate at which he was consuming them under Dr. Nichopolous's supervision.[1] Actually, of course, Elvis had access to drugs from many other sources, as no junkie ever recognizes the concept, enough. Hence, the sudden inspiration to go to the dentist this night, otherwise a rather odd substitute for an evening at the movies.

Elvis left Graceland for his dental appointment about ten in the evening. He was wearing a blue jogging suit with the letters DEA (Drug Enforcement Administration) blazoned across the back. He was accompanied by Ginger, Charlie Hodge and Billy Smith. As he drove out of the Music Gate for the last time behind the wheel of his Stutz Blackhawk, he was hailed by a handful of fans. One of them snapped a picture that shows an obese and gross-looking Elvis wearing his trademark shades and with the hood of his suit pulled over his head.

Arriving at Dr. Hofman's office on Estate Drive in a prosperous neighborhood in East Memphis, Elvis appeared to be in high spirits.

---

[1] Dr. Nichopolous argued at a medical board hearing after Elvis's death that these drugs were intended for the whole touring group but were prescribed for Elvis so that he would receive the bill.

"Isn't this an ugly girl here?" he jested as he introduced the beautiful Ginger to Dr. Hofman. Then, as she sat in the waiting room and the two Guys trailed off somewhere, Elvis closeted himself with the dentist.

Dr. Hofman recalled later that Elvis inquired about the dentist's wife, Sterling, and boasted of his new Ferrari. When the session ended, Dr. Hofman made a request. "Listen," he said, "next time you're going out to California, I'd like to come. It would be a nice surprise if I could drop in on my daughter out there." "Sure," answered Elvis, "there's always room on the plane—you know that!"

When Elvis got back to Graceland, it was nearly twelve-thirty. A small crowd of fans was still hovering around the gate. One of them was Robert Call from Pierceton, Indiana, who had come to Memphis with his wife and four-year-old daughter, Abby, expressly for the purpose of taking pictures of the family against the backdrop of Graceland. As Elvis pulled up to the gate, Mrs. Call had the little girl in her arms. She raised the child to Elvis's car window. Automatically he grinned and waved his hand. At that instant, Robert Call, using a twenty-dollar Instamatic with a flash cube, snapped the last picture of all the millions of pictures that were taken of Elvis Presley.

Back at the house, Elvis showed unwonted energy in calling the men on duty up to his room and making inquiries about the arrangements for the tour. He was told that every concert was sold out. The Colonel was already at Portland, Maine, with the advance party. The musicians were leaving after dark from Los Angeles on the Jet Star, which would be captained by Milo High. Everything was in order, as always. Everybody was taking care of business. Elvis, for his part, had come up with a list of five or six new songs that he wanted to try out on this tour. He asked Dick Grob, the former Palm Springs cop who was now working the security detail, to see if he could find the lead sheets for the songs. As Elvis and Grob continued their conversation, the topic of the recent press reports concerning Elvis's health and the shocking revelations in *Elvis—What Happened?* came up.

Elvis was going to face the public for the first time on this tour knowing that many of them had read this book and were examining him for signs of drug addiction. He certainly didn't look very well. Though he had been fasting for the past two days, he weighed 255 pounds. His weight troubled him so much that he had even told Ginger that they should go to a fat farm, an idea that would never even have crossed his mind in the old days. Still, he was confident he could deal with the public. The trick was simply to give them the kind of show that would make all the ugly rumors look ridiculous. "Dick," Elvis said, winding up the conversation, "we'll just show them how wrong they are. We'll make this one the best one ever."

At two-thirty in the morning, Elvis called Tish Henley—Dr. Nichopolous's head nurse, who lived with her husband in a trailer behind Graceland—and told her that Ginger was suffering from menstrual pain. Nurse Henley testified at a hearing after Elvis's death that she dispensed one tablet of Dilaudid. Ginger recollects nothing about suffering menstrual cramps on this evening or receiving any medication. The little white pill went straight down the throat of Elvis Presley. It had such a good effect upon him that he was inspired once more to take up his favorite theme: his forthcoming wedding to Ginger.

Calling her into his office, where he had been watching TV, he started building chapels in the air. He said they should be married in a church of pyramidal design. (Charlie Hodge had gotten on a pyramid kick and persuaded Elvis that such spaces concentrated precious spiritual energies.) Though the wedding was going to be Elvis's production, he said that he wanted the occasion to reflect Ginger's tastes as well. For example, he wanted to know what color she preferred for the limousines. Before she could answer, he told her that he had some original ideas about organizing the security forces so that they wouldn't mar the appearance of the event. Then, at last, he came around to the theme that obsessed him most of all: Ginger's bridal gown.

Priscilla had offended Elvis with her gown. Impelled by her crazy pinch-penny attitude toward money, she had bought an inexpensive gown and fitted it with a train herself. Elvis wanted Ginger to have the most magnificent gown imaginable. There were certain features he described with such vividness that Ginger has never been able to forget them. He told her: "Your dress is already being made. I want you to have small rosebuds with gold sparkles that will shine in the light. I want you to wear glass slippers, like Cinderella. I . . . ." "But, Elvis!" broke in Ginger (who, as we have seen, was of a commonsensical turn of mind), "they don't even have my measurements!" Elvis smiled knowingly at this remark. "Well," he said, "they'll just have to come here and give you a fitting." Oh, he was high that night!

Finally, he disclosed the most thrilling idea of them all. He was considering announcing their engagement from the stage here in Memphis on August 27, the last night of the tour. Ginger was breathless when she heard these words. As she listened for further revelations, she was surprised to see Elvis leap up and pace excitedly back and forth in the room. Now he started explaining who was going to be present at the ceremony. There would be many famous people and public officials: mayors, governors, congressmen. Unlike the last time when he had been married by a judge of the Nevada State Supreme Court, this time he was determined to be married by a judge of the national Supreme Court. As that image flashed through his hopped-up brain, he exclaimed—"God! *It's gonna blow all this stuff sideways!*" Ginger couldn't imagine to what he was alluding, though he repeated the statement several times, like a man relishing a marvelous thought. Obviously what he had in mind was the ultimate riposte to the West-Hebler book.

Here these guys were saying that he's a junkie freak, an evil dude who lays around stoned out of his gourd blasting away at TV sets with pistols. *Then,* he steps out in front of his own people in his own hometown and tells them: "I'm getting married! Here's my fiancée!" Wow! Elvis Presley getting married! That announcement would blow any story in the world off the front page and set every woman in the country blithering and gossiping and crying like a baby. Then, as the capper to the whole scam, he would be surrounded at the wedding by public officials and police officials and all the straightest, strictest, law 'n' order ole daddies in the country, with a Supreme Court judge standing up there like Judge Stone pronouncing the vows. After a snow job like that one, who would ever believe that he was a junkie? Ha! Elvis hadn't spent a quarter of a century with Colonel Parker without learning a thing or two about manipulating public opinion.

As Elvis raved on that night, probably feeling the tongue-loosening effects of those big Black Beauties, he thrilled Ginger time and again with the sweet and sentimental things that he said. Just the other day, he told her, he had been talking with his father. Poor Vernon! He was so ill. Nowadays, the doctor didn't allow Vernon to walk more than fifty feet at a time. His health was very precarious. Yet, he was so happy with his new companion, a former nurse named Sandy Miller. Elvis and Vernon had been talking about Elvis's relationship with Ginger. "Does she do little things for you, son?" Vernon had asked. Elvis assured him that Ginger did. Then, they had drifted to the differences in age between Elvis and Ginger: Elvis was old enough to be his fiancée's father. Vernon had assured Elvis that this was no problem; in fact, if anything, the shoe was on the other foot. "What could a thirty-year-old woman do for you?" asked Vernon, adding before Elvis could reply, "What could a sixty-year-old woman do for me?" Gladys would have been sixty-three now, if she had lived; but Elvis let the remark pass. Then,

Valmid tablets and a "Placidyl placebo." Valmid is a nonbarbiturate hypnotic, and two of these elongated pale blue pulvules are a standard prescription for insomnia. Placidyl is another sleeping pill. Dr. Nichopolous dispensed this drug in staggering quantities to anyone in the Presley organization who complained of sleeplessness. (Marty Lacker has testified that between January 1971 and October 1976, he received from Dr. Nick 6,464 doses of Placidyl, plus numerous other drugs.) The drugs were given to Aunt Delta, who brought them up to the bedroom and handed them to Elvis. Receiving these pills was the last act anyone in the group witnessed Elvis perform, save for Ginger.

Groggy and nearly asleep, she saw Elvis pick up another book, this one on the interesting topic of the Shroud of Turin, and start to go into the bathroom. "Precious, I'm gonna go in the bathroom and read for a while," he explained. "Okay," she sighed, "but don't fall asleep." He smiled at her and answered, "I won't."

What happened during the next six hours is unknown. Before retiring Elvis had given strict orders that he was not to be disturbed. The only evidence of what occurred is in the analyses that were made of the internal organs removed at the autopsy. Regrettably, these documents have never been released and the information that has leaked out entails a number of contradictions. According to Dr. Bryan S. Finkle, director of the University of Utah Center for Human Toxicology, one of the three laboratories that analyzed the tissue samples, Elvis's body contained at death no less than eleven different drugs. The most plausible of the unauthorized accounts suggests that Elvis took either before retiring to the bathroom or during the time while he was still trying to fall asleep the following drugs:

Methaqualone—Quāālude
Diazepam—Valium
Ethinamate—Valmid
Chlorpheniramine—an antihistamine, such as Donatussin drops
Meperidine—Demerol
Codeine—Hycodan
Morphine—Dilaudid
Three kinds of barbiturates—Amytal, Carbital, Seconal
Ethchlorvynol—Placidyl

This list suggests a pretty busy night. If one didn't know a lot about Elvis's astonishing pattern of drug abuse, he might infer that the use of so many drugs at one time was the product of some great crisis or

a bad breakdown. Actually, this was probably no more than was customary for Elvis. The quantities found in his body after death offer no support
for an interpretation of suicide. As is clear from everything that occurred
during this last night, Elvis was in good spirits, high as a kite, enjoying
his life and imagining future pleasures and even triumphs. If the night
were any different from other nights of the period, the difference would
have to be ascribed to its greater happiness, activity and optimism.

Around two in the afternoon, Ginger awoke in the big bed, still
wearing her exercise suit. It didn't surprise her that Elvis was not at
her side. For all she knew, he had gone downstairs or even left the
house. The only thing that occupied her mind was the thought that
within a matter of hours she would be leaving to go on the tour. Suddenly,
it occurred to her to call up David Stanley's girlfriend, Cindy Mies,
and find out if she were going, too. The girls chatted briefly, and Ginger
learned that Cindy had been invited to make the trip. That pleased Ginger
because she would have another young woman to keep her company.
Then, she called her mother to say that she was coming home directly.
Only after she had been on the phone for a quarter of an hour did it
occur to her that Elvis might still be in the bathroom.

Getting out of bed she crossed the room and knocked on the door.
"Elvis?" she called. Getting no response, she knocked again and again.
Unlike Linda Thompson, who would have barged right in to check on
Elvis, Ginger was reluctant to violate his privacy. Finally, she opened
the door and peeped inside. What she saw was Elvis doubled up face
down on the floor, almost as if he were in a fetal position. Clearly, he
had been sitting in the black leather and chrome chair reading and had
toppled forward onto the floor. The book was still lying on the chair.
In falling, his head had struck a hair dryer that someone had left on
the floor. If it had been anyone else Ginger had found in this condition,
she might have been alarmed. With Elvis, this kind of thing was normal.
He was always dropping off abruptly from the effects of his sleeping
potions and landing head first in the most unlikely places. Ginger hated
to see him in these grotesque positions, but there wasn't any reason to
panic.

Walking over to him, Ginger called, "Elvis!" Then, suddenly, she
began to feel alarmed. The thought crossed her mind that he might
have struck his head in the fall and injured himself. She reached down
and touched him. He was as cold as ice. Again, this was typical. Sleeping
for hours without stirring in a room whose temperature had been forced
down twenty degrees by a powerful air conditioner, Elvis often felt icy

to the touch. Finally, Ginger knelt down and turned Elvis's head around so she could see his face. Now, for the first time, she was gripped by terror. Elvis's face had become a grotesque mask, purple with engorged blood, his teeth set in his lolling tongue. Trembling, she raised one of his closed eyelids. The eye was blood red and motionless. The thought that Elvis was dead never once entered Ginger's mind. She was certain that he had collapsed from the medication and struck his head on the floor. He had injured himself. But he was certainly still alive.

Standing up again, she reached for the phone next to the toilet. She pressed the button for the kitchen and heard the voice of the cook, Pauline. "Who's on duty?" Ginger asked anxiously. When she heard it was Al Strada, she said, "Would you tell Al to come up here really quick?" Then, she started out of the room to meet Al coming up the stairs.

Now she was convinced that something was terribly wrong, but the thought of death had still not forced itself into her mind. Al came running up the steps, where Ginger met him as she came down. "I think something's really wrong with Elvis!" she blurted out. "Come and look at him!" Al didn't speak a word. He took one look at Elvis; then he said, "Let me get Joe up here." Picking up the phone, he called downstairs. Joe had just arrived at the house to supervise the departure for the tour. He charged up the stairs and came hustling into the bathroom.

Having been through this business so many times before, Joe knew exactly what to do. First, he turned Elvis over on his back. As he did so, he heard a sighing sound that convinced him that Elvis was still breathing. Turning the body over, however, produced a grotesque sight. The legs remained rigidly flexed at the knees. It looked as though Elvis were trying to touch his chin with his kneecaps. Ginger had never heard of rigor mortis. She stood there marveling at the odd position of her lover's legs. Joe reacted very differently. He leaped up and grabbed the phone. Punching into an outside line, he tapped out the emergency number. Talking rapidly to the dispatcher, he explained that someone was having great difficulty breathing at 3764 Elvis Presley Boulevard. He told the dispatcher to tell the ambulance driver to come straight through the gates and drive up to the front door of the house. The name of the victim was never mentioned.

A minute later, Unit Six of the Memphis fire department emergency division got the call. Charles Crosby and Ulysses Jones started racing toward Graceland at 2:33 P.M. Though all they had was the address, they knew it was Graceland. In fact, they had an idea who it was they were supposed to succor. Once before they had been summoned to the house to rescue Vernon Presley, who was succumbing to a heart attack. They had rushed the old man to the hospital and saved his life. Trained paramedics, the men were prepared to find the same situation and apply the same remedy: CPR (cardiopulmonary resuscitation).

Meantime, at the house, Joe was down on his knees giving Elvis mouth to mouth resuscitation or, alternately, pounding on his chest, while Al Strada stood at the phone making call after call for help. The first person called was Dr. Nick, who was at Doctors' Hospital, five miles distant. The operator informed Strada that she would page the doctor by beeper. She advised him to keep a phone line open. Then Strada called Dr. Perry Holmes, a local physician in Whitehaven, whom they used sometimes for minor complaints. Learning that Dr. Holmes was also out of the office, Strada slammed down the phone. Moments later, Dr. Holmes's associate, Dr. James Campbell, was told of the call by his receptionist. He called Graceland and got Aunt Delta. She told him that her nephew was experiencing some difficulty breathing. She asked the doctor if he could come to the house immediately. He suggested that they bring Elvis to his office.

By this time, everyone at Graceland was crowding into the bathroom in a vain effort to save Elvis. Charlie Hodge arrived and started shouting, "Breathe, Elvis, breathe!" Aunt Delta fell on her knees to continue the mouth-to-mouth resuscitation. Then Vernon, desperately infirm and barely able to climb the stairs, came gasping into the room. At the first sight of Elvis, he started wailing: "Son, don't die! Son, don't leave!" Ginger was wandering around in a daze when she heard Lisa's voice, as the child climbed the stairs to the second floor. As Ginger rushed to the bedroom door to intercept her, Lisa yelled, "What's wrong?" "Nothing!" cried Ginger, reaching down to seize the child. "Something's wrong with Daddy and I'm going to find out!" shouted the little girl. Then she darted around the other end of the landing to enter the bathroom from the opposite side. "Al!" shouted Ginger, "Lisa's trying to get in!" Strada swiftly threw the lock on the bathroom door.

Suddenly, the two paramedics burst upon the scene, having dashed up the stairs unheard by the people in the bathroom. Pushing away the dozen people who had squeezed into the room, the firemen looked down and saw a man who was so disfigured that neither of them recognized the most famous man in Memphis. Ulysses Jones recalls that this totally unfamiliar-looking man was "clothed in pajamas—a yellow top and blue bottoms. From his shoulders up, his skin was dark blue. Around his neck, which seemed fat and bloated, was a very large gold medallion. His sideburns were grey. I knelt down and checked the pulse and shined a light in his eyes. There was no reaction. No pulse. No flicker from the eyes. He was cold, unusually cold. The people around me were weeping. 'Is there anything you can do?' they cried. I couldn't give them an answer. Suddenly a young man [David Stanley] blurted out, 'I think he ODed.' It was the second time that an overdose was mentioned. The first time was at the door of the house where a guard had said, 'He's upstairs and I think it's an OD.' I inserted an airway tube into his throat and gave the nearest man a squeeze bag for pumping air into his lungs." The other paramedic, Charles Crosby, recalls: "It took five of us to lift him onto a stretcher. He must have weighed two hundred fifty pounds. The pajama top was unbuttoned all the way down, and I could see the great big rolls of fat on his belly. It looked like he had been dead for at least an hour."

As the men jockeyed the stretcher around the corners and down the stairs, feeble, emaciated old Vernon tried to follow, crying and calling: "Son, I'm coming. . . . I'll be there. . . . I'll be meetin' you there!" Two of the Guys had to forcibly restrain Vernon, who could have dropped dead of a heart attack at any moment.

Just as the ambulance was preparing to roll down the driveway, Dr. Nick came racing up to the house. He had spoken to Joe just after the paramedics had arrived and been told that Elvis was still breathing. Now, he climbed into the ambulance and started massaging Elvis's heart. At 2:48 the ambulance cleared the gates of Graceland and took off at speeds that reached eighty m.p.h. for Baptist Memorial Hospital. All through the incredibly swift seven-minute trip, Nichopolous kept shouting: "Breathe, Elvis . . . come on, breathe for me!" Said Jones: "All the way to the hospital, the doctor had this look of sheer disbelief that this could have happened to Elvis."

At the hospital's communications center, a call was received now from the speeding ambulance: "Have a white male, approximately forty, under CPR, no response." Immediately, a summons sounded from every loudspeaker in the building: "Harvey Team report to E.R. [Emergency Room] . . . Harvey Team report to E.R. . . . Harvey Team report to E.R." Harvey Teams are groups of emergency specialists who literally come running the moment the arrival of a critically injured or dying patient is announced.

Elvis was borne into Trauma Room Number One, a small operating theater, and laid out naked on a surgical table. Instantly, his body was covered with monitoring electrodes, as the doctors and technicians struggled to revive him with oxygen, mechanical respiration and injections of powerful stimulants. For nearly half an hour they worked on him but all their labors were in vain. Finally, they abandoned the effort and classified the case as a DOA: dead on arrival.

All this while, Joe Esposito, David Stanley and Maurice Elliott, the vice president of the hospital and its principal public relations officer, waited for word in an adjoining emergency room. Finally, at three P.M., the door to Room Number One opened and out came Dr. Nick, with his head hanging. Looking up at Joe Esposito, the white-haired Nichopolous said, "There is nothing we can do . . . we tried." Then, as his eyes began to water, he herded everyone out of the room, turning to close it behind him as if he were sealing up a tomb. Ten minutes later a nurse emerged carrying a bag which contained Elvis's necklace, rings, bracelet and pajamas. She gave the bag to Nichopolous. Now, it was his painful duty to break the news to the family. This was not just a task that was hard to perform for emotional reasons: There was a distinct possibility that the news might kill Vernon Presley. Nichopolous persuaded the two paramedics who brought Elvis into the hospital to drive him back to Graceland and stand by until it was clear that Vernon would survive the shock of his son's death.

Once the ambulance had left Graceland, Vernon, Sandy, Aunt Delta, Aunt Nashville, and some members of the staff drifted into Minnie Mae's room where they began to pray for Elvis. Ginger had felt she should ride in the ambulance with Elvis to the hospital, but before she could gather up her resolution to go, the door slammed shut. Suddenly, she felt that she had been shut out of his life. "I never felt so alone in my life," she recalls. Then Aunt Nashville put her arms around Ginger and sought to comfort her. "He's going to be all right," she soothed. "He's got so much to live for." Ginger felt so much better at this moment that she was impelled to comfort someone else. She thought of Lisa and went upstairs to find the child. Entering the little girl's room, Ginger said, "Lisa, your daddy's gonna be okay." Lisa was easily persuaded that there was nothing to fear. Soon she was chasing merrily from room to room, playing with Amber.

Now Ginger went downstairs and while she was standing in the parlor, Dr. Nick walked into the house flanked by the two paramedics. He didn't say a thing. The moment Vernon, who was seated in a chair, caught sight of the bag in the doctor's hand, he fell backward, crying, "Oh, no, no! I know he's gone!" Nichopolous was virtually speechless. "I'm sorry," he murmured, but his words were drowned out by the wail that went up from everyone in the house. Screams, cries, moans and curses filled the air. Suddenly, people started running aimlessly in every direction. Little Lisa was beside herself, crying, "My daddy is gone! I can't believe my daddy is gone!" Before anyone could reach her, she dashed halfway up the stairs toward her room. Then she darted back down again and ran into the kitchen. A second later she came tearing back into the drawing room. Vernon was sobbing and shaking in every limb. Nichopolous got the old man to his feet and led him slowly into the kitchen. Ginger recalls staring out the back window toward the pasture. "It was like all the leaves were dying," she recalls. "It was weird . . . like everything died." She kept saying to herself, "No, no!" Finally, Dr. Nick came back into the parlor and signed to the paramedics that they could leave. Then, he picked up a phone and called Maurice Elliott. It was time that the announcement be made to the public.

By the time Maurice Elliott got the go-ahead from Dr. Nichopolous, the hospital had been laid under siege by the press corps. Word of the crisis had spread from the reporters who routinely monitor police and fire emergency calls. Then the rumors had begun to fly. Elliott had stalled the press, saying that Elvis was having difficulty breathing. Now, at last, he could disclose the truth. Joe Esposito, who had been closeted during this time in Elliott's office, making calls to the Colonel and Tom Huelett of Concerts West, was asked if he would like to make the announcement. He said he couldn't face the press. It now became Maurice Elliott's duty. He called in the reporters and told them that Elvis had been pronounced dead at three-thirty, apparently from heart failure. He stressed, however, that nothing official would be forthcoming until that evening, when a press conference would be called to release the results of an autopsy.

The autopsy is a traditional ritual of royalty. At the French court, whenever a member of the ruling family died, the other members would assemble in the bedchamber, just as they would for a birth, to witness the court physician dissect the body, each organ being plopped into a fine silver bowl. The reason for this practice lay in the fear of poisoning, which, strange to say, was precisely what Vernon Presley believed was the cause of Elvis's death. Actually, Vernon knew as well as anyone in the inner circle that his son was a confirmed drug addict. The staff of Baptist Memorial Hospital knew a great deal about Elvis's addiction because he had gone there several times to kick his habit, his most recent stay being in April. Their knowledge was shared undoubtedly by the Memphis Medical Examiner, Dr. Jerry Francisco, whose responsibility it was now to establish the cause of this sudden death in a relatively young man.

Within an hour of Elvis's death, his body was brought into the hospital morgue, where an unusually large number of people were present, including as many as eight pathologists. Though autopsies are usually conducted by one forensic pathologist and an assistant, in this case the combination of curiosity coupled with the desire to have every detail witnessed and verified as a protection against charges of carelessness or unprofessional conduct produced an extraordinary multiplication of medical men, as it did also of laboratory reports and independent analyses of the findings. It is one of the great ironies of Elvis Presley's life that his death, which was the subject of intense scientific scrutiny, should have been enveloped in the same cloud of mystery that long enshrouded his birth.

Elvis's body was laid out on a stainless steel table, equipped with a sink and drains, under a battery of powerful lights similar to those used in operating rooms. The autopsy was conducted by Dr. Eric Muirhead, chief of the department of pathology. Dressed in a gown with a plastic protective apron and flanked by his assistant, notebook in hand, the pathologist commenced the process by examining carefully the surface of the body, which he would have found pitted with countless needle marks. Under the skin he would have found traces of the hematomas produced by earlier injections. Once every detail of the surface had been noted, the internal examination commenced.

The procedure is to make a Y incision: two long cuts from the shoulders down to the belly button and then a single incision down the abdomen to the pubis. The skin is then lifted back and secured so that the pathologist can examine the underlying tissues and muscles. Next the rib cage is cut with a saw so that the chest plate can be removed, exposing the heart and lungs. Each major organ is examined, removed and weighed. Slices of the organs are taken and put into bottles filled with preservatives for microscopic examination and chemical analysis in the toxicology laboratory. Elvis's heart was found to be enlarged, his arteries somewhat clogged and his liver—the organ most affected by drug abuse—so diseased that it looked exactly like pâté de foie gras.

After opening the stomach and examining its contents, which would normally have included some half-dissolved pills,[2] and after tapping off samples of the body fluids—blood, bile, urine—the final task is the examination of the brain. The scalp is cut and pulled both backward over

---

[2] The gut-paralyzing effect of opiates greatly retards digestion, which is one of the reasons why drugs ingested by mouth are so slow to produce their effects in addicts.

the nape of the neck and forward over the face to expose the surface of the skull. The entire top of the head is then cut off with a power saw, which sends puffs of dust into the atmosphere, against which the operators protect themselves by donning face masks. When the top of the skull is lifted off like a bowl, the brain beneath is examined and then scooped out for sampling and sectioning.

When every part and organ of the body has been exhaustively examined and a great number of tissue samples taken, the three-hour procedure terminates with the remains of the brain being put back inside the skull and the internal organs gathered in a bag and stuffed back inside the body cavity, which is then stitched up. Encased in a paper shroud, the corpse of Elvis Presley was now ready for the embalmer and the cosmetician.

At the same time that Elvis was being cut up in Memphis, he was being repackaged in New York. Colonel Parker received Joe Esposito's announcement that Elvis was dead in his hotel suite at Portland, Maine. After a brief conversation, the Colonel slumped for a few moments in his chair. Then he called Vernon Presley at Graceland. Colonel told Vernon that it was vital they act immediately to protect their own and Lisa Marie's interests. What concerned the Colonel especially was the prospect of a wild exploitation of Elvis's name and image by a horde of unauthorized souvenir and paraphernalia manufacturers and merchants.

As soon as the Colonel received Vernon's permission to carry on, the canny old man put into effect a long-meditated plan. Getting in touch that very afternoon with Harry "The Bear" Geissler, president of Factors, Inc., a merchandising company whose hottest item was a Farah Fawcett-Majors T-shirt, the Colonel commenced the negotiations that concluded two weeks later with Factors obtaining exclusive rights to the Presley merchandising in exchange for a $150,000 guarantee and a sizable royalty on every item sold. Colonel chose Geissler, it has been said, because Factors had once been forced to pay one hundred thousand dollars in damages as a merchandising bootlegger. Operating on the principle that it takes one to know one, the Colonel reasoned that Geissler, whose contract obliged him to prosecute bootleggers, would be the ideal man to police the Presley market.[3]

It is highly significant that the contract with Factors was negotiated

[3] Two months after Colonel signed with Geissler, the FBI received a tip that Factors had defrauded three of its licensors of a substantial sum in royalties. The company pled guilty to three counts of mail fraud.

by Colonel Parker not on behalf of the Presley Estate but with his company, Boxcar, Inc. The deal Colonel made with Vernon Presley provided for two fifty-fifty splits: half of the income received by Boxcar would be paid to Colonel Parker as manager; the other half would be divided equally between Boxcar and the Estate. The upshot of this arrangement was that Colonel and his men obtained *eighty-two percent* of the merchandising income. Another oddity of the deal was the ten percent off-the-top commission given to William Morris, an immense sum of money that Colonel characterized later as a "finder's fee."

At eight o'clock the night of Elvis's death, the medical examiner and Dr. Nichopolous held a press conference to disclose the gross findings of the autopsy. Dr. Francisco said that the death appeared to have been caused by "cardiac arrythmia," or, in plain English, an erratic heartbeat. Asked to elaborate, the coroner averred: "There was severe cardiovascular disease present. He had a history of mild hypertension and some coronary artery disease. These two diseases may be responsible for cardiac arrhythmia, but the precise cause was not determined. Basically, it was a natural death. It may take several days, it may take several weeks to determine the cause of death. The precise cause of death may never be discovered." Strike "discovered" and substitute "disclosed," and this statement becomes a prophetic utterance.

Chapter 36

Sixteen Coaches Long

LESS THAN an hour after the announcement that Elvis was dead, a thousand people had gathered at the Music Gate. An hour later, the crowd had swollen to three thousand. By the following afternoon, when the gates were opened to allow mourners to view the body, twenty thousand souls had lined up along Elvis Presley Boulevard. The great stationary parade stretched back for nearly a mile. As it began to shuffle forward, fresh arrivals appeared at the end of the line. No matter how many people passed through the gates and mounted the driveway and entered the house, there were just as many who arrived at that moment a mile distant to take their places. When the gates were finally forced shut at six-thirty that evening, eighty thousand men, women and children had come to pay their respects to the King.

Many of these people came from afar. The newsmen arrived first, pouring off the planes at Memphis Aero, dressed in khakis and toting their gear like combat troops going into action. They were followed by waves of fans, who took off from all over the world in a wild lemming rush to Memphis. Some of the faithful were so distraught that they abandoned their most vital duties. One young mother from Illinois was charged with child neglect when it was discovered that she had left a two-, a four- and a five-year-old child in the care of a twelve-year-old baby-sitter so that she could fly to Graceland.

When the fans arrived, or even before they left home, they ordered flowers. The customary floral offerings did not suffice. They demanded the symbols of their cult. From all over the world, orders poured into the florists of Memphis for guitars, hound dogs, teddy bears, broken hearts, bibles and, above all, crowns. Hundreds of floral crowns had to be fashioned with inscriptions that read "The King," "To Our King," "The Only King." The symbolic and ritualistic mania that had always characterized the faithful now reached its final frenzy. Soon the supply of flowers in Memphis was exhausted. Orders were dispatched to other cities. Their supplies were also quickly depleted. Eventually, two great airlifts were organized, which brought in from California and Colorado an emergency supply of five tons of flowers.

One hundred vans were pressed into service to deliver the flowers on a round-the-clock basis. The first displays were brought to the house and set up in the drawing room, where the body was to be laid out. As more flowers were received, the music room, the dining room, the trophy room, the den were swiftly filled. Still the flood of flowers poured in, increasing rather than diminishing in volume, until there was no alternative but to start setting out the largest pieces before the house. Soon the entire length of Graceland was staked out in floral displays that threatened eventually to inundate the property. As the mourners began to form their great line during the night following Elvis's death, taking their positions in the dark like those first crowds twenty-one years before in Times Square, the sickly sweet odor of funeral flowers came wafting down the hill from the house.

Eventually, the floral flood overwhelmed the property. When the number of tributes had reached three thousand, orders were given for the flowers to be transported to Forest Hill Cemetery. If the period of mourning had been protracted for just two more days, Elvis's fans would have poured enough flowers into Memphis to line the highway to the cemetery. The funeral cortege would have resembled those oriental religious processions in which priests and potentates proceed to the shrines upon elephants that tread ponderously on carpets of blossoms.

At six minutes past noon on the second day, as the oppressive heat of August was made even more unbearable by a smoggy mist, the waiting crowds were electrified by the appearance of a motorcade advancing along the boulevard with flashing dome lights and the low moan of muted sirens. It was the hearse bearing the body to Graceland. The

Music Gate was swung wide by two details of police, six men to each wing. Then they were forced shut against the protesting fans, as the big white hearse ascended the curving driveway. Elvis came home for the last time encased in a nine-hundred-pound seamless copper casket. No undertaker in Memphis possessed such a costly casket. It had been flown in overnight from the manufacturer in Oklahoma City.

When the massive lid was raised, Elvis's intimates were horrified by his appearance. The embalmers had not succeeded in restoring the mutilated corpse. The fat face swollen with engorged blood had proven an insurmountable obstacle to the local morticians. Elvis appeared to have a swelled head. Larry Geller was on hand to style the hair for the last time. He did the best he could; but at one point in the afternoon, a sideburn came loose and had to be glued on afresh.

Elvis was costumed for his final appearance in a white suit that he had received from Vernon as a Christmas gift. He wore a light blue shirt and a dark blue tie. On his hand shone his gold and diamond TCB ring with its two lightning bolts. As he looked so deformed, a strict ban on pictures was imposed. Nonetheless, one of Elvis's poor relations, Bobby Mann, smuggled a Minox camera into the house and took the shot that was published in *The Enquirer*. The picture shows the face in profile buried deep in the satin lining of the coffin. The facial configuration and particularly the dark shadowing around the eyes made Elvis in death resemble Gladys.

As the day wore on, the late summer heat became ever more oppressive. The sufferings of the devoted reached alarming proportions. The local Red Cross had stationed its canteen in the midst of the mourners and had erected first-aid stations in tents on the lawns of Graceland. As one mourner after another fainted, cries of "Medic! Medic!" resounded up and down the line, as on a battlefield. At the same time, the mood of the crowd began to change.

When the first crowds had gathered at Graceland, their demeanor had been that of people who had just received some crushing blow, like a sentence to prison. They were limp, broken, glassy-eyed. They would slump down on the curb to bury their faces in their hands and cry. By the afternoon of the second day, the mood had shifted to one of seething hysteria. There were outcries and scuffles. Wild rumors ran up and down the lines. Frenzied speculations were exchanged. There was a feeling that now anything could happen. The police were apprehensive. At all times, two helicopters were overhead, searching the crowds for signs of incipient violence. On the ground, the detail assigned to

Graceland was never less than 150 uniformed men. As a special precaution, a National Guard unit was called out and military sentries posted before the house.

When the gates were thrown open at three in the afternoon to the mourners, the mood changed yet again, this time to an attitude of anxious anticipation. It was obvious to everyone that it would be impossible for all those who had lined up to enter and leave the house in the two hours allotted for this purpose. The question now became: Would they get in? After making such great efforts to see Elvis one last time, would they reach their goal? When the hour of five arrived, only a fraction of those who had come had been admitted to the house. Though they were rushed past the coffin with the greatest speed commensurate with dignity, there was no admitting them all. Vernon Presley, vulnerable as always to such appeals, authorized the extension of the viewing period another hour and a half, until six-thirty. By that time, about twenty thousand had filed before the casket. Finally, orders were given that no more were to be admitted.

Police officers, using bullhorns, announced that the gates were going to be closed. There was a tremendous uproar, as the people cried, "No! No!" or "Just a half hour more!" For one dreadful moment, it was feared there might be a riot. Would the fans stampede through the gates and dash up the driveway to the house, like a rock 'n' roll crowd charging the stage? The officials commanding the police and the troops massed all their men behind the gates. Prepared to call for immediate reinforcements, they gave the order to close the entrance. When the patrolmen started pushing the gates shut, the people gave ground. The point of danger was past. Soon the crowds were melting away. They would mass again the following afternoon, when they came to see the funeral procession.

On the morning of the third day, at four A.M., there were still many people standing outside the stone fence of Graceland under the yellow sodium vapor lights. Suddenly a white Ford racing up the boulevard swerved in and out of the crowd, knocking down several people and causing a frantic outcry. The driver was arrested just a block away: He was a nineteen-year-old lad named Treatise Wheeler. With him were a couple of teenaged girls and a number of cans of beer, some full, some empty. As the arrest was being made, the paramedics rushed to the aid of the people who had been hit. All three of them were teenaged girls. Two of them were dead. The third was critically injured. The moment the crowd realized what had happened, it came charging down the street to seize the driver. Cries of "Lynch him!" "String him up!" were heard. The police threw their man and his companions into a squad car and left the scene hurriedly.

This third day, August 18, was declared by the governor of Mississippi, Cliff Finch, a day of mourning. Governor Ray Blanton of Tennessee also ordered all flags in that state lowered to half mast. President Carter issued a statement at the White House, asserting that "Elvis Presley's death deprives our country of a part of itself," and concluding that "he was a symbol to the people the world over of the vitality, rebelliousness and good humor of this country." From countless other sources all around the world came tributes and recollections and statements of regret and loss.

On the day of the funeral, at nine o'clock in the morning, a fleet of vans began to pour in and out of the gates of Graceland, carting off the thousands of floral displays, which were being conveyed to the cemetery. The mood of the crowd, which had shifted so many times, suggested now the atmosphere before one of Elvis's out-of-town shows. Souvenir hawkers worked the long lines, peddling Elvis T-shirts or selling postcards of Graceland or serving soft drinks and ice cream. The fans were engrossed now in comparing their collections of memorabilia or boasting of how many years they went back with the King or how many miles they had traveled to this sacred spot. As the time for the funeral neared and the special guests began to arrive, including a couple of indubitable celebrities such as Ann-Margret and George Hamilton, speculation and rumors began to build about who else would appear or who had actually gained entrance unnoticed. It was widely rumored, for example, that Burt Reynolds had slipped into Graceland riding in the back of a bread truck.

Bread had been the primary thought in Colonel Parker's mind when he had arrived that morning, dressed in a loud aloha shirt and wearing an admiral's cap. He had spent the previous day in New York firming up his deal with Factors, Inc. Now it was vital that the Colonel get "Mr. Vernon's" signature on the dotted line. Sitting down at the dining room table, clearly within sight of Elvis in his casket, the Colonel explained his proposition to the doddering father and collected the desired endorsement.

The funeral service was a hopelessly inadequate ceremony. The arrangements were improvised by half a dozen competing people, all of whom were eager to assert their authority, but none of whom had the remotest idea of what was appropriate or how to achieve the goal. Elvis would have wanted a funeral comparable to the grandiose wedding ceremony that he had spent his last night imagining. He would have relished the thought of a grand ritual conducted in the Auditorium and witnessed by all the highest government officials and showbiz celebrities and carried by the media all over the country like the obsequies for Jack Kennedy. A believer that all religions were one, Elvis would have welcomed a service in which ministers and rabbis, priests and yogis, took turns at the altar. (In his last years Elvis wore habitually about his neck a cross and a Star of David, explaining, "I wouldn't want to be kept out of heaven on a technicality.") The King demanded the service of a king, but what he got was about right for some cornball country yodeler destined for the Hall of Fame in Nashville.

Colonel Parker invited Elvis's warm-up act, the comedian Jackie Kahane, to deliver the eulogy. The old Jewish joker did the best he could. As he stood before two hundred guests squeezed into the drawing and dining rooms, with the musicians behind a screen in the music room, he began: "When Colonel Parker hired me, he said, 'Keep it clean.' Elvis Presley always stood for clean entertainment." The next speaker was a local minister of no distinction, who was supposed to be Vernon's minister, although none of the Presleys ever went to church or had any dealings with ministers—a breed toward whom Elvis was always very sarcastic. This poor man delivered himself of an address that could have come off the back of one of Elvis's shlocky record albums: "Elvis never lost his desire to stay in close touch with humanity"—this of a man who was the most notorious recluse in the history of the entertainment business. The third and briefest speaker was the TV evangelist Rex Humbard, whose association with Elvis consisted of one brief backstage meeting, in the course of which Elvis had suggested that the Second Coming might be nigh. Had it not been for the efforts of the gospel singers behind the screen—Jake Hess, James Blackwood and J. D. Sumner with their groups and Kathy Westmoreland with her high "heavenly" voice—the ceremony would have been an utter fiasco.

Finally, the moment came for which everyone was longing. The enormously heavy casket was shouldered by Elvis's pallbearers: Lamar Fike, Charlie Hodge, Gene Smith, George Klein, Joe Esposito, Billy Smith, Jerry Schilling and Dr. Nichopolous. As they were carrying the coffin through the house door, there was a loud cracking overhead and a dead limb fell from one of the oak trees. Lamar recalled Elvis saying many times: "Wherever I am, if there is a way to communicate with you— I'll find it!"

Epilogue:
Always Elvis

WHEN THE WORD that Elvis Presley had died was received in Hollywood, one cynical showbiz kibitzer cracked: "Good career move!" He was right, of course. Elvis live was a problem. Elvis dead was a property. In fact, in the year after his death, he became the hottest property in the business. The explanation for this bizarre phenomenon lies in an ancient, seemingly remote theory about the connection between royalty and divinity.

During the Middle Ages, when everyone from the simplest peasant to the most sophisticated theologian believed, in Shakespeare's words, "There is a divinity that doth hedge a king," an elaborate doctrine and practice was developed for distinguishing between the king as man and the king as god. At royal funerals, for instance, the wasted or bloated corpse of the king was conveyed through the streets in a coffin surmounted by an exact replica of the king as he appeared in his prime, dressed in his coronation robes and bearing in his waxen hands the orb and scepter, symbols of his dominion over the world. The effigy signified the king's immortality, his "body politic": a body devoid of "Defects and Imbecilities," which, though man-made, was imperishable, as opposed to his natural body, which, though made by God, was corruptible. Now let us apply this theory to the death of the King.

581

The moment Elvis was pronounced dead, his immortal body, which we call today his "image," was released from the encumbrances of his mortal frame, with its all-too-obvious defects and imbecilities. The result was an instant resurrection. Overnight, the King sprang up again with all the force that belongs to an immortal. The first sign of his revitalization was the ubiquity of his image. Everywhere you turned you saw his face and heard his voice. RCA's pressing plant labored around the clock struggling to satisfy the overwhelming demand for his records; eventually the company was to announce that its total sales of Presley products had reached the awesome total of *one billion units.* At the same time, TV stations all around the world began to run Elvis festivals that put all his films back into circulation. The paraphernalia industry discovered in Elvis such a Golconda that soon whole stores or even, as across the highway from Graceland, an entire shopping center filled up with souvenirs—two hundred million dollars' worth in the first year alone! Sheer numbers, the awesome scale of his success, its unimaginable immensity, had always been a vital element in the Elvis mystique. Never during his life, however, had the King's visible presence ever swelled to such colossal proportions. Only by dying could Elvis live up to his Barnumesque ballyhoo, as "The World's Greatest Entertainer."

This final burgeoning of the King could be dismissed as simply an illusion, the product of the customary posthumous reprise of a great entertainer's works and days. To view Elvis Posthumous in this light, however, would be to miss the point entirely; for what was asserting itself after his death was not simply nostalgia or the compulsion to rerun his career. Quite the contrary, Elvis's death marked the beginning of a second life in which he both grew enormously as a man and asserted himself through important new dimensions as a performer.

Elvis had been so totally concealed and controlled during his lifetime that only after his death did the public begin to get even the most rudimentary idea of what sort of person he was. Commencing with the West-Hebler book, *Elvis—What Happened?,* which sold an astounding five million copies, every member of the Presley entourage, right down to his hospital nurse and his household cook, struggled to let the Cat out of the bag. Most of these people knew so little about Elvis and were so fearful of saying what they did know that the net effect of this vast outpouring of books was simply to heighten the curiosity and increase the perplexity that had always been the lot of the public. Nonetheless, some of the books offered solid information. Soon the vaporous outline of the mythic Elvis began to fill with jarring facts and shocking revelations.

At the same time that the King's literary image was undergoing a radical transformation, his physical image was likewise being altered by the appearance of hundreds of candid photos that offered a very different picture of Elvis from all those carefully posed shots that had poured for a quarter of a century from the Colonel's publicity mill. Especially revealing were the photographs by Alfred Wertheimer, who had dogged Elvis in the spring and summer of his most memorable year, 1956, catching him in the act of thrusting his fat tongue into the mouth of a backstage groupie or taking a fresh pair of Jockey briefs from the hand of his doting mother or hunkering on the globular, nubby-textured, dowel-legged furniture of the house on Audubon, listening to his own records, while showing a bare back spotted and pitted with acne and a sullen, sensual and self-absorbed face, like the face of a young George Wallace.

Even more penetrating were the photos snapped by a Munich nightclub photographer, Rudolf Paulini. What these pictures documented was the blank, listless, half-stoned yokel that Elvis became when he was separated from his showbiz persona. A big baby-faced boy with short unruly hair, dressed in ugly, ill-fitting civilian clothes, he allows himself to be taken with every ugly hussy in torn net stockings and sleazy sateen leotard. As the dancers and hookers of this upholstered sewer entwine themselves about him, flashing manic grins revealing those bad European teeth in those old-fashioned horse gums, Elvis offers himself up like a life-sized dummy.

Not just the man but the performer continued to emerge after his death. Though RCA had nothing better to offer than gleanings from its soon exhausted archives, the record bootleggers, those great friends of the fans, cut the legal knots that had long restrained the release of Elvis's most significant live sessions. The legendary Elvis of the *Louisiana Hayride,* the Dorsey Brothers shows and the Hawaiian benefits appeared. All the jams from the Singer Special were offered in two beautifully packaged albums from Germany that far surpassed both in interest and in appearance any legitimate offerings of Victor. In yet another illicit release came at last the most sought-after tape in the history of rock 'n' roll: the fabled "Million Dollar Quartet," an impromptu sing in the Sun Studio around Christmas 1956, by the three greatest heroes of rockabilly: Elvis, Jerry Lee Lewis and Carl Perkins (minus the anticipated fourth voice, Johnny Cash). Though in this instance the reality of the recording hardly matched the glamour of its legend, the value of the disc as a document was enormous. At last you were inside the Sun Studio listening attentively as Sam Phillips' greatest singers did what they most enjoyed doing: pickin' and singin' their favorite rock songs and hymns.

Death also made more visible the magical and religious powers of the King. The immense and inexhaustible appetite for Elvis souvenirs and memorabilia provided an awesome demonstration of *mana:* the supernatural force that is believed to lodge in certain beings and which can be transferred from their bodies to other bodies by means of physical contact. The Veronica, the replica of the cloth that St. Veronica pressed against the face of Jesus as he bore the cross, thereby capturing his likeness, is the classic example of mana in the West. Now a similar transfer was effected from the face of the star who so often identified himself with Jesus to the bodies of his fans through the medium of the celebrity T-shirt.

As for the notion of the King's divinity, it was exemplified in a manner that far surpassed the symbolism of the medieval monarchs. Instead of a mere wax dummy, Elvis had for his emblem of perpetuity a whole legion of living effigies: the Elvis impersonators. These strange figures sprang out of the soul of the Elvis cult, which had always entailed flagrant mimicry, as had the celebration of Elvis's only rival for the title "World's Greatest Entertainer," Charlie Chaplin. Like the Little Tramp, the Hillbilly Cat inspired his admirers, all those hungry souls desperate to participate in his being and exercise his magic, to make the most extravagant gestures of identification.

What one saw after Elvis's death, however, was not just emulation but replication: the rite according to St. Xerox. Like those mythical soldiers sprung from dragon's teeth, there appeared overnight a new class of entertainers who were not so much mimics, impersonators or impressionists as Elvis clones. Some of these human effigies were so fantastically dedicated to their assumed identity that, like transsexuals, they submitted their bodies to plastic surgery so that their natural resemblance might be heightened to virtual indistinguishability. Their only problem lay in the fact that Elvis's image had changed so much over the years, from the skinny Hillbilly Cat to the obese showroom stud, that what they really needed was not so much plastic surgery as some pneumatic device that would allow them to inflate and deflate at will like balloon dolls.

Even as the Elvis clones started to appear on the nightclub stage and the TV screen (some of them making as much as $15,000 a week at Las Vegas, where the real Elvis had bombed during his last engagement), the latest development in American popular culture became the New Wave–Punk phenomenon. One of the most striking features of the estate, which after Vernon's death in June 1979 devolved on Lisa Marie, received about half as much.

Then, just as everything was going so nicely, the good ship Hustler struck a submerged mine. On September 29, 1980, the probate court at Memphis received a fifty-two-page report on the management of the Elvis Presley Estate prepared by a court-appointed attorney, Blanchard E. Tual. The occasion for his appointment had been the presentation of a petition by the executors of the estate—Priscilla Presley, Joe A. Hanks (Elvis's former accountant) and the National Bank of Memphis (Elvis's former bank)—for approval of all the financial transactions they had made with Colonel Parker on behalf of the estate. Once this approval was granted, the executors intended to put the wealth of the estate into a trust fund, which might remove it from any further public scrutiny. When Judge Joseph W. Evans read the petition, he was troubled by the enormous commissions the Colonel was charging the estate. Instead of giving his approval, he appointed a guardian ad litem, or temporary guardian, for Lisa Marie, charging him with the duty of representing and defending the child's interests.

Blanchard E. Tual could have discharged his responsibility with a relatively narrow inquiry focusing simply on the final compensation agreement; instead, he chose to investigate the entire field of the Colonel's dealings with Elvis, which soon entailed an extensive and unprecedented inquiry into the hitherto carefully guarded network of relationships between Colonel Parker and RCA Victor, Hill and Range, William Morris, Factors, Inc., and a host of other major entertainment companies. Proceeding with skill and address, Tual was able in six months to report in impressive detail on what amounted to a quarter century of financial transactions entailing billions of dollars of gross earnings. What he discovered added up to a searing indictment of Colonel Parker's management of Elvis from first to last.

The report revealed the exorbitant commissions the Colonel had charged Elvis; the deals and arrangements that were contrary to the star's best interests; the failures of fiduciary responsibility; and, in a crowning irony, the extreme impropriety of the Colonel's continuing to act after Elvis's death precisely as he had when his client was alive. For the conviction that "nothing has changed" had passed out of Colonel Parker and into Vernon Presley and the trustees with such force that it had hypnotized them all into acting in a manner that was not only unjust to Lisa Marie but arguably illegal. For as the guardian ad litem demonstrated, the enabling agreements were simply updated versions

this new fad was the fashion look it inspired: punks togged out in the bop clothes and greasy hairstyles, as they struck the rough trade poses, that comprised the image of the original Elvis. The result was that not only the King's men but the King's people were transformed into Elvis clones. At a New Wave club in the late seventies, you could see a horde of Elvis lookalikes thrilling to the performance of an Elvis epigone, like Elvis Costello, whose music was directly inspired by Elvis's first rockabilly recordings. No more perfect illustration could be found of the idea of "coming together."

The customary interpretation of such surrealistic hall-of-mirrors scenes is that they are products of nostalgia, a much-abused term whose meaning has now been stretched beyond its tolerable limits in the effort to avoid recognizing how inadequate is this concept for explaining current sensibility. Nostalgia in its conventional sense means the longing for some treasured moment in one's past. This could hardly be the inspiration for the Punk Generation because its members were not yet born when Elvis the Pelvis was at the peak of his fame. Not recollection but infatuation is the key to Punk: infatuation with a pop myth, a hipper, harder version of *Happy Days,* an idealized epoch that the current generation did not experience but which it feels it should have experienced because it was the last moment that offered the bliss of unself-conscious adolescent joy. Punk, in fine, is pop culture's counterpart to the romantic's infatuation with the Middle Ages or the eighteenth-century cult of antiquity.

All the bizarre phenomena that followed upon Elvis's death can be interpreted as expressions of the fundamental conviction that the King was not dead but alive. It is not surprising, therefore, that the more fanatical Elfans should have labored to prove that he was not even dead, physically, or, at least, that he had not died of natural causes. Thus, it was often said among the fans that Elvis had staged his death. What was more interesting than this familiar fantasy was the reason given for the hoax. It was widely believed that Elvis had removed himself from the world in order to escape the fans![1] A more sophisticated version

---

[1] The most frequently cited cause for Elvis's death in the six hundred interviews conducted for this book was persecution by his fans. No one but his intimates realized that Elvis exulted in his public's extravagant behavior and often sought to provoke it. Elvis's real attitude toward the fans is neatly conveyed in an anecdote told by Gerald Peters, his limousine driver. On the first occasion Peters drove for Elvis, the fans started to chase the car. Peters executed a brilliant maneuver and eluded his pursuers. Instead of praise, however, he received a rebuke. Elvis warned him never again to flee the fans. The proper procedure, he explained, was to drive along as if they were unobserved; in other words, to offer themselves to their voyeuristic public with the unconcern of professional exhibitionists.

of this pipe dream had Elvis checking into some mysterious West Coast clinic the moment he learns he is dying so that from healthy cells removed from his diseased body he can be regenerated as a clone. *Official UFO* magazine offered a one-hundred-thousand-dollar reward for any information concerning this spooky creature.

Even if a fan couldn't swallow the crazy notion that Elvis was still alive, he didn't have to accept the fact that the King's death had been inevitable. After all, who was to say what—or *who*—had killed Elvis Presley? The idea that the King had not died a natural death was voiced on ABC's *20/20* by Geraldo Rivera. The aggressive TV reporter, a former cop, thrust the finger of accusation squarely at Dr. George Nichopolous, Dr. Elias Ghanem and Dr. Max Shapiro, a Los Angeles dentist with whom Elvis had been very friendly. Rivera's most impressive offering was a copy of the confidential report by Bioscience Laboratory analyzing the specimens obtained through the post-mortem. A battery of eminent forensic pathologists was shown the report, and they all agreed that the cause of Elvis's death was *polypharmacy,* the lethal interaction of a number of drugs taken concurrently.

Rivera also denounced Dr. Jerry Francisco for covering up the true cause of Elvis's death. The case against the coroner was built on uncontradicted assertions that the contents of Elvis's stomach had been destroyed before the autopsy; that the police had closed the case the night of the death, long before the full findings of the autopsy were available; and that the supervising pathologist and his assistant had not concurred with Dr. Francisco's final pronouncement, that there was "no evidence of drug abuse." Efforts by ABC to set the matter to rest once and for all by obtaining a copy of the autopsy were foiled when a Memphis court ruled that the autopsy, having been requested by the deceased's family, not the county, was protected by the privacy rule for fifty years.

The charge that the King had been " murdered " was lodged by John Lennon just before he was murdered. In an interview in *Newsweek,* Lennon drew on his closely parallel experience as a superstar and long-time drug user to locate the ultimate cause of Elvis's death in his life-style, which consisted in being surrounded by people who would do anything to satisfy their master in order to protect their own favored positions. As Lennon grimly quipped: "It's the courtiers that kill the king."

The man who knew best what killed Elvis was also the man most determined to act as if Elvis had never died. Not more than a few minutes after he received the news of Elvis's death, Colonel Parker told Lamar

Fike: "Nothing has changed. This won't change anything." Soon the old man demonstrated exactly what he meant. Shifting into high gear, the Colonel started cutting deals and laying out cards so fast that in the first year of his posthumous career Elvis Presley made far more money than he had during any year of his life. Colonel had always had the nerve to ask for the top price; now his bluff reached overweening proportions. When NBC wanted to use five minutes from an old Elvis special for the company's fiftieth anniversary program, Colonel demanded five hundred thousand dollars. When he started peddling the rights to an Elvis documentary that would employ all the stuff in Elvis's private film stash, the asking price was ten million dollars.

So carried away did the old man become with the idea that he was still representing "The World's Greatest Entertainer" that he tried to play Elvis one last time at Las Vegas. Taking a leaf from the great Barnum's book—the Barnum who rallied from the news that Jumbo the Elephant had been killed by ordering the huge beast stuffed and put on exhibit—Colonel Parker staged a festival titled "Always Elvis" at the Hilton International in September 1979, substituting for his 255-pound "boy" a 450-pound, $150,000 bronze statue that resembled an enormous souvenir paperweight. The suckers were inveigled into paying the customary admission price for an Elvis show, fifteen dollars, to be admitted to an exhibition room that contained, like a gyp show at the carnival, nothing better than a few old costumes on dummies that were too small for the sleeves and an endless array of paraphernalia displays presided over by peddlers who had paid the Colonel a good price for the privilege of displaying their wares in such a prime location.

Colonel's next brainstorm was bottling Elvis. He authorized the Frontenac Vineyards at Paw Paw, Michigan, to offer 120,000 bottles of a white wine with a picture of Elvis on the front of the bottle and on the back a commemorative poem by the Colonel. The poem earned the Colonel over $28,000 in royalties, making him, line for line, the best-paid poet in the world.

The first three years after Elvis's death were the Colonel's glorious Indian summer. Though the grosses tapered off after the incredible first year, the operating expenses were virtually nil. What's more, the Colonel was no longer troubled by the defects and imbecilities of an aging and drug-addicted star. He had finally found the perfect client: one who never talked back or made trouble, one who was forever young and sexy. Elvis earned twenty million dollars in this period. No living entertainer could match that figure. The Colonel took the lion's share, and of the same contracts that Colonel had drawn with Elvis when he was alive; therefore, they continued to rest on the basic assumption that both parties *were* alive! The Colonel's supreme creation, the Elvis Myth, now suddenly boomeranged and came back to strike the old man down in the act of exploiting his creature.

Even more ironic was what happened next. Not long after the report was filed, newspapers and magazines all over the country began running stories about how Colonel had taken fifty percent of Elvis. These stories threatened the Colonel's reputation nearly as much as the stories about drug addiction had damaged Elvis before his death. Naturally, they deeply disturbed the old man. One night while leaving his office in the RCA building in Hollywood, the Colonel slipped and fell on the threshold of an elevator. Stunned by the fall and burdened by his enormous weight, he found himself unable to rise. The elevator door, which had recoiled after the first impact, now rolled back again like a rubber-edged guillotine and struck the Colonel's recumbent body. Over and over again, the door buffeted the old man, until he was rescued. He could hardly have been beaten worse if he had been set upon by the King's immortal body, chopping and kicking his lifetime persecutor with the full power of a karate killer. His injuries included a permanent disability in his right shoulder.

The Colonel remained undaunted. When people would inquire about his arm, suspended in a sling like a wounded soldier's, he would reply: "Doctors say I may never get full use of it again, but . . ." here he would make a Fagin-like gesture, rubbing together thumb and forefinger—"I can still grab ahold on them big checks."

On July 31, 1981, the guardian ad litem filed a final report that was far more damaging than his original statement. This document revealed several private financial agreements between Colonel Parker and, respectively, RCA, the Hilton International, and Jerry Weintraub's Management III: an arrangement that the guardian stigmatized as a "textbook-type conflict of interest." When these agreements, of which Elvis had no knowledge, are added to all the side agreements Colonel contrived for his own benefit after Elvis's death, without the knowledge of the Estate, the picture of Parker and RCA that emerges is one of possible conspiracy and fraud. Parker appears a conman who enriches himself by selling his client short or allowing Elvis or his heirs to be cheated. Drawing his conclusion from a mountain of evidence, the guardian concluded his report by denouncing Colonel Parker and RCA for "collusion, conspiracy, fraud, misrepresentation, bad faith, and over-reaching."

Once the dirty little secret of Elvis's management was out of the bag, matters swiftly took their course. On August 14, the probate court ordered the Presley Estate to sue Colonel Parker within forty-five days. The Court requested further information concerning the deals with RCA Records within ninety days before ruling on the possibility of litigation. The Court also ordered audits of accountings from Factors, Inc., and Chappell Music, which manages Elvis's publishing companies. At the same moment, the news broke that IRS had raised its assessment of the Presley Estate in light of the guardian's disclosures to twenty-five million dollars. The resulting demand for fourteen million six hundred thousand dollars in additional taxes presented the Estate with the grave threat of bankruptcy. In short, after twenty-six years of uninterrupted success, the world's most celebrated artist-manager relationship had exploded in scandal. (As this book went to press, the legal imbroglio was becoming more complicated every day. Colonel Parker commenced his counterattack by denying any wrongdoing.)

Though Colonel may end his days enmired in exasperating litigation, while all his Presley income lies frozen in escrow, his final effort on behalf of his boy has been crowned with characteristic success. In April 1981, at Memphis, Colonel's long-heralded documentary on Elvis had its premiere. If the filmmakers, headed by David Wolper, had set out to sound simultaneously every note of the King's posthumous career in one profoundly ambiguous chord, they could not have succeeded better.

The notion that the King is still alive is proclaimed by the very title, *This Is Elvis,* which sounds like an urgent introduction to a hot new star, or, at least, one at the peak of his popularity. The basic form, a biography, narrated primarily by an Elvis impersonator, suggests you are getting the story straight from the King's own lips as he watches his life flash before him in his Howard Hughes hideout. His existential status is complicated even further by the constant intercutting of authentic documentary footage with episodes of "docudrama" (filmed with a slightly misted filter) that star Elvis clones playing opposite actors who represent friends and relations who may appear elsewhere in the documentary sections in their own persons. The grand effect is that of a spooky spectacle in the illusion tent at the carnival, or, better, a heart-tugging (and purse-emptying) séance conducted by Madame Blavatsky with her life-sized puppets.

The greatest puppet of all is Elvis, who is finally reduced to spouting all those ideas about his life which Colonel Parker put into the mind of the scriptwriter: an oblique but compelling form of ventriloquism.

Paradoxically, however, at the same time that Elvis is being reduced to the status of a dummy, he is released at last to give the greatest performance of his career by being permitted to play in scene after scene (extracted from old kines and TV outtakes) the only hero he could have ever impersonated successfully: himself. His greatest scene is a tour de force of histrionics.

You see Elvis at the end of his life standing onstage, looking like a great white clown. He is smiling but sweating so profusely that his face appears to be bathed in tears. Going up on a line in one of those talking bridges he always had trouble negotiating, he comes down in a kooky, free-associative monologue that summons up the image of the dope-crazed Lenny Bruce or the mind-fuguing Jonathan Winters. For thirty or forty seconds of mental free-fall, you are up in that padded cell atop Graceland watching Elvis blither with tightly shut eyes as he voices all the crazy ideas that come thronging into his dope-sprung mind.

The effect of this startling soliloquy, embarrassing at first, is ultimately exhilarating. The whited sepulchre of the World's Greatest Entertainer falls apart before your eyes and out of the plaster shards comes flaring the soul of the King, gibbering Monty Python nonsense patter and sneering hipster obscenities. Suddenly, you snap to the fact that Elvis ended his life not entirely defeated or demented but fighting to the last, with crack-brained audacity, to break free of his imprisoning image.

Index

this new fad was the fashion look it inspired: punks togged out in the bop clothes and greasy hairstyles, as they struck the rough trade poses, that comprised the image of the original Elvis. The result was that not only the King's men but the King's people were transformed into Elvis clones. At a New Wave club in the late seventies, you could see a horde of Elvis lookalikes thrilling to the performance of an Elvis epigone, like Elvis Costello, whose music was directly inspired by Elvis's first rockabilly recordings. No more perfect illustration could be found of the idea of "coming together."

The customary interpretation of such surrealistic hall-of-mirrors scenes is that they are products of nostalgia, a much-abused term whose meaning has now been stretched beyond its tolerable limits in the effort to avoid recognizing how inadequate is this concept for explaining current sensibility. Nostalgia in its conventional sense means the longing for some treasured moment in one's past. This could hardly be the inspiration for the Punk Generation because its members were not yet born when Elvis the Pelvis was at the peak of his fame. Not recollection but infatuation is the key to Punk: infatuation with a pop myth, a hipper, harder version of *Happy Days,* an idealized epoch that the current generation did not experience but which it feels it should have experienced because it was the last moment that offered the bliss of unself-conscious adolescent joy. Punk, in fine, is pop culture's counterpart to the romantic's infatuation with the Middle Ages or the eighteenth-century cult of antiquity.

All the bizarre phenomena that followed upon Elvis's death can be interpreted as expressions of the fundamental conviction that the King was not dead but alive. It is not surprising, therefore, that the more fanatical Elfans should have labored to prove that he was not even dead, physically, or, at least, that he had not died of natural causes. Thus, it was often said among the fans that Elvis had staged his death. What was more interesting than this familiar fantasy was the reason given for the hoax. It was widely believed that Elvis had removed himself from the world in order to escape the fans![1] A more sophisticated version,

---

[1] The most frequently cited cause for Elvis's death in the six hundred interviews conducted for this book was persecution by his fans. No one but his intimates realized that Elvis exulted in his public's extravagant behavior and often sought to provoke it. Elvis's real attitude toward the fans is neatly conveyed in an anecdote told by Gerald Peters, his limousine driver. On the first occasion Peters drove for Elvis, the fans started to chase the car. Peters executed a brilliant maneuver and eluded his pursuers. Instead of praise, however, he received a rebuke. Elvis warned him never again to flee the fans. The proper procedure, he explained, was to drive along as if they were unobserved; in other words, to offer themselves to their voyeuristic public with the unconcern of professional exhibitionists.

of this pipe dream had Elvis checking into some mysterious West Coast clinic the moment he learns he is dying so that from healthy cells removed from his diseased body he can be regenerated as a clone. *Official UFO* magazine offered a one-hundred-thousand-dollar reward for any information concerning this spooky creature.

Even if a fan couldn't swallow the crazy notion that Elvis was still alive, he didn't have to accept the fact that the King's death had been inevitable. After all, who was to say what—or *who*—had killed Elvis Presley? The idea that the King had not died a natural death was voiced on ABC's *20/20* by Geraldo Rivera. The aggressive TV reporter, a former cop, thrust the finger of accusation squarely at Dr. George Nichopolous, Dr. Elias Ghanem and Dr. Max Shapiro, a Los Angeles dentist with whom Elvis had been very friendly. Rivera's most impressive offering was a copy of the confidential report by Bioscience Laboratory analyzing the specimens obtained through the post-mortem. A battery of eminent forensic pathologists was shown the report, and they all agreed that the cause of Elvis's death was *polypharmacy,* the lethal interaction of a number of drugs taken concurrently.

Rivera also denounced Dr. Jerry Francisco for covering up the true cause of Elvis's death. The case against the coroner was built on uncontradicted assertions that the contents of Elvis's stomach had been destroyed before the autopsy; that the police had closed the case the night of the death, long before the full findings of the autopsy were available; and that the supervising pathologist and his assistant had not concurred with Dr. Francisco's final pronouncement, that there was "no evidence of drug abuse." Efforts by ABC to set the matter to rest once and for all by obtaining a copy of the autopsy were foiled when a Memphis court ruled that the autopsy, having been requested by the deceased's family, not the county, was protected by the privacy rule for fifty years.

The charge that the King had been "murdered" was lodged by John Lennon just before he was murdered. In an interview in *Newsweek,* Lennon drew on his closely parallel experience as a superstar and long-time drug user to locate the ultimate cause of Elvis's death in his life-style, which consisted in being surrounded by people who would do anything to satisfy their master in order to protect their own favored positions. As Lennon grimly quipped: "It's the courtiers that kill the king."

The man who knew best what killed Elvis was also the man most determined to act as if Elvis had never died. Not more than a few minutes after he received the news of Elvis's death, Colonel Parker told Lamar

Fike: "Nothing has changed. This won't change anything." Soon the old man demonstrated exactly what he meant. Shifting into high gear, the Colonel started cutting deals and laying out cards so fast that in the first year of his posthumous career Elvis Presley made far more money than he had during any year of his life. Colonel had always had the nerve to ask for the top price; now his bluff reached overweening proportions. When NBC wanted to use five minutes from an old Elvis special for the company's fiftieth anniversary program, Colonel demanded five hundred thousand dollars. When he started peddling the rights to an Elvis documentary that would employ all the stuff in Elvis's private film stash, the asking price was ten million dollars.

So carried away did the old man become with the idea that he was still representing "The World's Greatest Entertainer" that he tried to play Elvis one last time at Las Vegas. Taking a leaf from the great Barnum's book—the Barnum who rallied from the news that Jumbo the Elephant had been killed by ordering the huge beast stuffed and put on exhibit—Colonel Parker staged a festival titled "Always Elvis" at the Hilton International in September 1979, substituting for his 255-pound "boy" a 450-pound, $150,000 bronze statue that resembled an enormous souvenir paperweight. The suckers were inveigled into paying the customary admission price for an Elvis show, fifteen dollars, to be admitted to an exhibition room that contained, like a gyp show at the carnival, nothing better than a few old costumes on dummies that were too small for the sleeves and an endless array of paraphernalia displays presided over by peddlers who had paid the Colonel a good price for the privilege of displaying their wares in such a prime location.

Colonel's next brainstorm was bottling Elvis. He authorized the Frontenac Vineyards at Paw Paw, Michigan, to offer 120,000 bottles of a white wine with a picture of Elvis on the front of the bottle and on the back a commemorative poem by the Colonel. The poem earned the Colonel over $28,000 in royalties, making him, line for line, the best-paid poet in the world.

The first three years after Elvis's death were the Colonel's glorious Indian summer. Though the grosses tapered off after the incredible first year, the operating expenses were virtually nil. What's more, the Colonel was no longer troubled by the defects and imbecilities of an aging and drug-addicted star. He had finally found the perfect client: one who never talked back or made trouble, one who was forever young and sexy. Elvis earned twenty million dollars in this period. No living entertainer could match that figure. The Colonel took the lion's share, and the estate, which after Vernon's death in June 1979 devolved on Lisa Marie, received about half as much.

Then, just as everything was going so nicely, the good ship Hustler struck a submerged mine. On September 29, 1980, the probate court at Memphis received a fifty-two-page report on the management of the Elvis Presley Estate prepared by a court-appointed attorney, Blanchard E. Tual. The occasion for his appointment had been the presentation of a petition by the executors of the estate—Priscilla Presley, Joe A. Hanks (Elvis's former accountant) and the National Bank of Memphis (Elvis's former bank)—for approval of all the financial transactions they had made with Colonel Parker on behalf of the estate. Once this approval was granted, the executors intended to put the wealth of the estate into a trust fund, which might remove it from any further public scrutiny. When Judge Joseph W. Evans read the petition, he was troubled by the enormous commissions the Colonel was charging the estate. Instead of giving his approval, he appointed a guardian ad litem, or temporary guardian, for Lisa Marie, charging him with the duty of representing and defending the child's interests.

Blanchard E. Tual could have discharged his responsibility with a relatively narrow inquiry focusing simply on the final compensation agreement; instead, he chose to investigate the entire field of the Colonel's dealings with Elvis, which soon entailed an extensive and unprecedented inquiry into the hitherto carefully guarded network of relationships between Colonel Parker and RCA Victor, Hill and Range, William Morris, Factors, Inc., and a host of other major entertainment companies. Proceeding with skill and address, Tual was able in six months to report in impressive detail on what amounted to a quarter century of financial transactions entailing billions of dollars of gross earnings. What he discovered added up to a searing indictment of Colonel Parker's management of Elvis from first to last.

The report revealed the exorbitant commissions the Colonel had charged Elvis; the deals and arrangements that were contrary to the star's best interests; the failures of fiduciary responsibility; and, in a crowning irony, the extreme impropriety of the Colonel's continuing to act after Elvis's death precisely as he had when his client was alive. For the conviction that "nothing has changed" had passed out of Colonel Parker and into Vernon Presley and the trustees with such force that it had hypnotized them all into acting in a manner that was not only unjust to Lisa Marie but arguably illegal. For as the guardian ad litem demonstrated, the enabling agreements were simply updated versions of the same contracts that Colonel had drawn with Elvis when he was alive; therefore, they continued to rest on the basic assumption that both parties *were* alive! The Colonel's supreme creation, the Elvis Myth, now suddenly boomeranged and came back to strike the old man down in the act of exploiting his creature.

Even more ironic was what happened next. Not long after the report was filed, newspapers and magazines all over the country began running stories about how Colonel had taken fifty percent of Elvis. These stories threatened the Colonel's reputation nearly as much as the stories about drug addiction had damaged Elvis before his death. Naturally, they deeply disturbed the old man. One night while leaving his office in the RCA building in Hollywood, the Colonel slipped and fell on the threshold of an elevator. Stunned by the fall and burdened by his enormous weight, he found himself unable to rise. The elevator door, which had recoiled after the first impact, now rolled back again like a rubber-edged guillotine and struck the Colonel's recumbent body. Over and over again, the door buffeted the old man, until he was rescued. He could hardly have been beaten worse if he had been set upon by the King's immortal body, chopping and kicking his lifetime persecutor with the full power of a karate killer. His injuries included a permanent disability in his right shoulder.

The Colonel remained undaunted. When people would inquire about his arm, suspended in a sling like a wounded soldier's, he would reply: "Doctors say I may never get full use of it again, but . . ." here he would make a Fagin-like gesture, rubbing together thumb and forefinger—"I can still grab ahold on them big checks."

On July 31, 1981, the guardian ad litem filed a final report that was far more damaging than his original statement. This document revealed several private financial agreements between Colonel Parker and, respectively, RCA, the Hilton International, and Jerry Weintraub's Management III: an arrangement that the guardian stigmatized as a "textbook-type conflict of interest." When these agreements, of which Elvis had no knowledge, are added to all the side agreements Colonel contrived for his own benefit after Elvis's death, without the knowledge of the Estate, the picture of Parker and RCA that emerges is one of possible conspiracy and fraud. Parker appears a conman who enriches himself by selling his client short or allowing Elvis or his heirs to be cheated. Drawing his conclusion from a mountain of evidence, the guardian concluded his report by denouncing Colonel Parker and RCA for "collusion, conspiracy, fraud, misrepresentation, bad faith, and over-reaching."

Once the dirty little secret of Elvis's management was out of the bag, matters swiftly took their course. On August 14, the probate court ordered the Presley Estate to sue Colonel Parker within forty-five days. The Court requested further information concerning the deals with RCA Records within ninety days before ruling on the possibility of litigation. The Court also ordered audits of accountings from Factors, Inc., and Chappell Music, which manages Elvis's publishing companies. At the same moment, the news broke that IRS had raised its assessment of the Presley Estate in light of the guardian's disclosures to twenty-five million dollars. The resulting demand for fourteen million six hundred thousand dollars in additional taxes presented the Estate with the grave threat of bankruptcy. In short, after twenty-six years of uninterrupted success, the world's most celebrated artist-manager relationship had exploded in scandal. (As this book went to press, the legal imbroglio was becoming more complicated every day. Colonel Parker commenced his counterattack by denying any wrongdoing.)

Though Colonel may end his days enmired in exasperating litigation, while all his Presley income lies frozen in escrow, his final effort on behalf of his boy has been crowned with characteristic success. In April 1981, at Memphis, Colonel's long-heralded documentary on Elvis had its premiere. If the filmmakers, headed by David Wolper, had set out to sound simultaneously every note of the King's posthumous career in one profoundly ambiguous chord, they could not have succeeded better.

The notion that the King is still alive is proclaimed by the very title, *This Is Elvis,* which sounds like an urgent introduction to a hot new star, or, at least, one at the peak of his popularity. The basic form, a biography, narrated primarily by an Elvis impersonator, suggests you are getting the story straight from the King's own lips as he watches his life flash before him in his Howard Hughes hideout. His existential status is complicated even further by the constant intercutting of authentic documentary footage with episodes of "docudrama" (filmed with a slightly misted filter) that star Elvis clones playing opposite actors who represent friends and relations who may appear elsewhere in the documentary sections in their own persons. The grand effect is that of a spooky spectacle in the illusion tent at the carnival, or, better, a heart-tugging (and purse-emptying) séance conducted by Madame Blavatsky with her life-sized puppets.

The greatest puppet of all is Elvis, who is finally reduced to spouting all those ideas about his life which Colonel Parker put into the mind of the scriptwriter: an oblique but compelling form of ventriloquism.

Paradoxically, however, at the same time that Elvis is being reduced to the status of a dummy, he is released at last to give the greatest performance of his career by being permitted to play in scene after scene (extracted from old kines and TV outtakes) the only hero he could have ever impersonated successfully: himself. His greatest scene is a tour de force of histrionics.

You see Elvis at the end of his life standing onstage, looking like a great white clown. He is smiling but sweating so profusely that his face appears to be bathed in tears. Going up on a line in one of those talking bridges he always had trouble negotiating, he comes down in a kooky, free-associative monologue that summons up the image of the dope-crazed Lenny Bruce or the mind-fuguing Jonathan Winters. For thirty or forty seconds of mental free-fall, you are up in that padded cell atop Graceland watching Elvis blither with tightly shut eyes as he voices all the crazy ideas that come thronging into his dope-sprung mind.

The effect of this startling soliloquy, embarrassing at first, is ultimately exhilarating. The whited sepulchre of the World's Greatest Entertainer falls apart before your eyes and out of the plaster shards comes flaring the soul of the King, gibbering Monty Python nonsense patter and sneering hipster obscenities. Suddenly, you snap to the fact that Elvis ended his life not entirely defeated or demented but fighting to the last, with crack-brained audacity, to break free of his imprisoning image.

Index

ABOUT THE AUTHOR

Albert Goldman was born at Dormont and reared in Mount Lebanon, Pennsylvania, suburbs of Pittsburgh. He studied the theater arts for two years at Carnegie Tech's Drama School; then, after a brief stint in the wartime navy, he returned to study at the University of Chicago, from which he was graduated with an M.A. in English Literature and election to Phi Beta Kappa. While studying with Lionel Trilling and Jacques Barzun for his Ph.D. at Columbia, he fell in with the Lenny Bruce gang, from which experience emerged his best-selling account of the counter-culture's greatest comic and social satirist, *Ladies and Gentlemen—Lenny Bruce!!* Mr. Goldman has taught at practically every college in New York, commencing with Columbia and including Brooklyn, Hunter, Bernard Baruch, City, the New School, the School of Visual Arts, and Columbia General Studies, where he spent the last nine years of his twenty-three years of teaching, holding the rank of Adjunct Associate Professor of English and Comparative Literature.

Albert Goldman began his career as a cultural journalist and music critic with *The New Leader*. He has also written for *Commentary, The New Republic, The New York Review of Books, The Nation, Commonweal, LIFE, New York, The Sunday Times, Vogue, Cosmopolitan, Book World, Esquire, High Times,* and *Atlantic Monthly.* He founded and was chief editor of *Cultural Affairs*, the magazine of the Arts Councils of America.

Albert Goldman is also the author of *Carnival in Rio, Disco, Freakshow,* and *Grass Roots.*